D1008518

Locations of Federally Recognized Tribes, 1990

In a Barren Land

Also by Paula Mitchell Marks

Turn Your Eyes Toward Texas
And Die in the West
Precious Dust
Hands to the Spindle

IN A BARREN LAND

AMERICAN INDIAN DISPOSSESSION AND SURVIVAL

Paula Mitchell Marks

William Morrow and Company, Inc.
New York

E98
L3M375

Copyright © 1998 by Paula Mitchell Marks

All rights reserved. No part of this book may be reproduced or utilized in any form or by any means, electronic or mechanical, including photocopying, recording, or by any information storage or retrieval system, without permission in writing from the Publisher. Inquiries should be addressed to Permissions Department, William Morrow and Company, Inc., 1350 Avenue of the Americas, New York, N.Y. 10019.

It is the policy of William Morrow and Company, Inc., and its imprints and affiliates, recognizing the importance of preserving what has been written, to print the books we publish on acid-free paper, and we exert our best efforts to that end.

Library of Congress Cataloging-in-Publication Data

Marks, Paula Mitchell, 1951–
    In a barren land : American Indian dispossession and survival / by
Paula Mitchell Marks.
        p.   cm.
    Includes bibliographical references and index.
    ISBN 0-688-14143-9
    1. Indians of North America—Land tenure.   2. Indians of North
America—Removal.   3. Indians of North America—Government policy.
4. Indians, Treatment of—United States.   5. Land tenure—Government
policy—United States.   6. United States—Race relations.   7. United
States—Politics and government.   I. Title.
E98.L3M375   1998   97-28377
973'.0497—dc21   CIP

Printed in the United States of America

First Edition

1   2   3   4   5   6   7   8   9   10

BOOK DESIGN BY BERNARD KLEIN

www.williammorrow.com

For those who survived the barren lands,
and especially for those who didn't

Preface and Note on Use of Terms and Sources

In introducing the seventh printing of her landmark *A History of Indians of the United States,* noted historian Angie Debo wrote, "It is, of course, impossible to carry on original research for a book of this scope. It is based on general knowledge of the work of many historians."

The same is true of this narrative of Indian land loss and survival. In dealing with such a large and multifaceted subject, I did not have the luxury of working with many specific primary sources. I did, however, have the luxury of absorbing a range of exciting classic and contemporary scholarship in Indian history, works that refine and redefine our understanding of what has happened to American Indians in the last four centuries and what they have managed to do about it.

Thus, while what follows tells a story familiar in its broad outline to the most cursory student of American history, I hope that it will also significantly deepen and extend the reader's understanding of the challenges that the descendants of America's first peoples have faced, and the questions that all Americans need to face as Indian tribes reassert their rights to land and self-governance.

In relating this story, I have repeatedly encountered two problems. The first has to do with words attributed to Indians in historical accounts and records. When they first encountered European immigrants, natives belonged to "oral" cultures, everything remembered and shaped through a spoken tradition. As Anglos established control, Indians learned to read and write through instruction in the English language, and the Cherokees instituted a written form of their own language. Yet at each stage of Indian-white interaction, those tribes still struggling against dispossession generally had few members proficient in spoken English and fewer still—if any—who could decipher the Anglos' strange, scribbled form of communication.

This means that some of the Indian words passed down in official and unofficial records have no doubt been garbled or twisted—inadvertently or for political reasons—by the people who translated and recorded them. Some even have been fabricated. One brief mid-nineteenth-century speech by Chief Seattle has survived in the historical record, but it bears little resemblance to the stirring address to government officials long attributed to him and popularized—with editing and additions—in the 1970s. Both this address and his eloquent "letter" to President Franklin Pierce appear to have Anglo origins (one in 1887, the other in 1972) and "myriad mutations."

How accurate, then, are quotations attributed to Indians? The researcher can only take care to use reputable historical sources and to acknowledge when an account's veracity is questioned, as has been the case in recent years with the classic *Black Elk Speaks,* John Neihardt's first-person narrative of Lakota Sioux Black Elk's life.

Ultimately, the researcher must also rely upon a sense of how human beings can be expected to respond to given situations. As historian Daniel Richter notes of the Iroquois, "The critical edge that frequently appears in the written record suggests that much of what the Indian speakers intended found its way to paper." I think this is true of the recorded quotes in these pages.

The second problem involves what identifying terms are appropriate today. It has become politically correct to refer to the people who were in North America at the coming of the Europeans—and to their descendants—as Native Americans or indigenous peoples. I have generally limited the use of these terms in favor of the more succinct and familiar "Indian," basing my decision in large part on the fact that many of the people to whom the term refers, while recognizing its European origins and inaccuracy, continue to use it to define themselves. For example, members of the Minnesota Indian Affairs Council, representing eleven reservations, recently reiterated their 1978 request to news media and government agencies that the term "American Indian" be used. I have also used "native" in historical situations in which natives and newcomers were clearly distinguishable.

"Tribe" has proven another troublesome term. I use the word as the easiest way to signify a particular Indian group distinguished from other groups socially, politically, culturally, and—often—linguistically. Yet many of the tribal names familiar to us today represent the melding of different fluidly organized cultural communities as a result of Indian-white interaction. Historian Robert Utley explains, "Even as late as the middle of the nineteenth century, the peoples called Nez Perce or Paiute or Apache associated only loosely in tribes. The tribe of our modern understanding took shape under the pressures of white societies just then beginning the period of serious encroachment."

Many Indians today prefer the term "First Nations" for the power and unity it conveys. With its connotations of formal political structure and centralized power, the phrase does not fit well with our knowledge of the loose band-level organization of many of the precontact Indian groups. But the word "nations" is often appropriate because various tribes and various confederacies of tribes have clearly and historically had the political strength and status of independent nations.

As for the Europeans who became Americans and their descendants, I have avoided the practice of calling them simply "Americans," as such use implies that Indians are not. Instead, I have alternated the dated but usefully generic term "whites" with various related terms: "Anglos," "colonists," "European Americans," etc. I also use "non-Indians," a generic term that encompasses the other racial and ethnic groups involved in making American history. But in the contest for land and resources, European Americans, specifically Anglo-Americans, undeniably were the ones developing and exerting power.

The reader will find that I also occasionally use two somewhat loaded and divergent terms in regard to white immigrants: "invaders" and "settlers." Whether those of us who are Anglo-Americans like it or not, "invaders" is all too apt a term from the perspective of the people who were already here. It is not my intent to tarnish all the actions and motives of our immigrant forebears, who suffered and worked and persevered to create homes and communities in a land new to them, nor to denigrate their own genuine attachment to a particular American location or region over generations. I still find the more favorable (to Anglos) "settlers" useful because it clearly shows the immigrants' intent.

However, I think we must acknowledge that the story has too often been told from the viewpoint of the victors in the struggle for North

American empire. As David Weber has pointed out, "resettlers" has more accuracy, given that settlement by Indian families occurred long before the coming of Europeans.* And just as Indians were settlers, they were also immigrants, led by circumstance—in the case of this narrative, almost invariably by white pressure—to come into a country new to them. My occasional use of the term "immigrant" to refer to Indians as well as whites reflects this reality.

As an Anglo-American, I do not presume to speak "for" Indians—they are quite capable of doing that themselves, if others will only listen. However, I have tried to emulate some of the best modern historians by looking at events with the primary focus on the population being displaced—the ones who didn't write the history—and by acknowledging Indians as active, resilient, and varied *people* pursuing strategies for survival, not as passive and somehow less-than-human pawns.

I hope I have succeeded in this regard; to do otherwise would dishonor both the memory of those who fought for their lands and cultural survival and the resolve of those still fighting to be heard.

---

*This understanding of prior exclusive Indian occupancy was challenged in fall 1996 by the discovery in Washington State of "Richland Man," a skeleton of what appears to be a European male and one which has been carbon-dated to 7300 B.C. At the time of this writing, scientists and native Pacific Northwest groups are battling over the control of this find and its significance.

Acknowledgments

I am indebted to the many researchers, writers, and scholars who have preceded me in seeking to record and interpret American Indian experience; their work has stimulated, buttressed, and broadened this narrative, and many of their names can be found in the Notes and Bibliography.

I am particularly indebted to Dr. Joseph O'Neal, who as an anthropologist and professor of Native American studies thoughtfully critiqued the chapters in progress and forgave my use of the term "Sioux" (common in historical writing, but considered too imprecise in anthropological study).

Others who read all or part of the manuscript, shared valuable insights, and offered balanced perspectives are Native American studies scholar D. L. Birchfield of the Choctaw tribe, sociologist Dr. Michael Farrall of the Potawatomi tribe, and journalist David Pego of the Chippewa tribe. Their comments, along with Dr. O'Neal's, strengthened the narrative. In the few instances in which I did not take these readers' advice, I trust that the book did not suffer unduly for it, and any mistakes and weaknesses are my own.

Thanks are also due my editor, Harvey Ginsberg, and agent, Lois Wallace, whose encouragement and guidance made this effort possible and enhanced the result. The critical-inquiry students in my classes at St. Edward's University offered apt suggestions when I shared passages in need of editing. The St. Edward's library staff provided cheerful, timely, and expert assistance; Aimee Myers merits special mention in this regard, and Dianne Brownlee repeatedly produced information on even the most obscure references.

Ivan Marks and Jerry Weller knew how to get me through computer crises, and various other friends, colleagues, and family members—particularly Mark Mitchell and Janet Knight—served as sounding boards for ideas and interpretations. Joyce Gibson Roach was a treasured traveling companion in the Indian Southwest, Justin Coe helped in the process of mapping out Indian country, and Elaine Bargsley worked her usual magic in producing the maps in these pages. My thanks to all.

Finally, I remain deeply grateful for and to Alan and Carrie, who live with and love me through the challenges of this writing life.

Contents

Preface and Note on Use of Terms and Sources vii

Acknowledgments xi

Introduction xv

ONE
"An Uneasiness on Our Minds" (1607–1764) I

TWO
"Nothing Will Satisfy Them but the Whole of Our
Hunting Grounds" (1764–1816) 33

THREE
"Get a Little Farther" (1817–1843) 59

FOUR
"I Am Driven Away from Home" (1817–1843) 89

FIVE
"Take Away Your Paper" (1844–1860) 113

SIX
"Run Them About" (1861–1886) 146

SEVEN
"I Hope to God You Will Not Ask Me to Go to
Any Other Country" (1861–1875) 172

EIGHT
"Cornered in Little Spots of the Earth" (1875–1886) 192

NINE
"Gumbo with Greasewood on It" (1887–1910)   215

TEN
"Where Are We Now?" (1911–1930)   244

ELEVEN
"Who's Got the Button?" (1930–1950s)   270

TWELVE
"Our Land Is Everything to Us" (1950s–1964)   292

THIRTEEN
"Until We Have Regained Our Rightful Place"
(1964–1979)   316

FOURTEEN
"There Is No Place but Here" (1980–1996)   350

        Notes   381

        Selected Bibliography   427

        Index   435

Introduction

Clear the way
in a sacred manner
I come
the earth
is mine
—*"The Earth Is Mine," Sioux war song*

You are on Indian land.
—*1990s bumper sticker*

You could take any road, really, any road within what we now know as the United States, and pass through homelands lived in and loved long before the advent of European explorers, traders, and settlers. For example, take Interstate 40, heading west out of its starting point in Greensboro, North Carolina, and you are traveling the lowlands and uplands of what once was populous Catawba Indian country.

Follow I-40 into the southern Appalachian homelands of the Cherokees, bisected by the Tennessee state line (which has little meaning on this journey, but we modern travelers need our bearings), and enter the piney woods region of the Creeks, then the floodplains on which the Chickasaws sought out high forested sites to locate their pole-frame houses. These three groups, the history books tell us, were removed west of the Mississippi in the nineteenth century, and the history books are right, although "removed" is too convenient a euphemism and although a Cherokee reservation just a few miles from the roadway testifies to a persistent Indian presence.

Beyond the Creek and Chickasaw lands, I-40 advances through present-day Arkansas and Oklahoma, traversing the interior highlands, which the Quapaws called home, and the prairies native to the Wichitas, subsequently termed "Permanent Indian Territory" for a patchwork of more than sixty displaced Indian groups identified and acknowledged by the United States government as politically distinct tribes. With one exception, the areas reserved exclusively for each tribe have been wiped off the map, but a strong Indian identity remains, particularly in the form of the large and active Cherokee Nation, which regained federal recognition as a tribe in 1971.

Now I-40 ribbons the prairies and the Texas plains, which the Comanches knew as well as a skilled navigator knows open sea or air, and probes the high deserts in which Apaches survived and thrived generation upon generation. At Santa Rosa, New Mexico—Apache country—you can take the exit to Fort Sumner, about sixty miles south of the interstate artery. On the banks of the Pecos River the fort sits bleak and ghostly, symbol of the suffering of the Mescalero Apaches and Navajos jammed together here by the United States Army in 1864 under what can only be described as concentration camp conditions.

And here I will tell you that while you can indeed take any road to reach an Indian country, I-40 is a better choice than most. It's not just that the road runs through "Permanent Indian Territory," rich in native heritage, or passes near an Indian landmark of surpassing sorrow, but that it takes you to places that have been Indian country for generations beyond remembrance.

Pick the road up again, follow it into Albuquerque, and you are surrounded by the reservations containing the still vital pueblos of peoples sprung in ancient times from the harsh and beautiful lands of the Southwest. Pause at Acoma Pueblo, a 350-foot-high mesa village just a few miles off the road, and consider that indigenous peoples have been living here, up against the sky, for over a thousand years, the earth and air saturated with old souls.

Proceed on the road to Gallup, and you are on the southeastern edge of the largest Indian reservation in the United States today, that of the Navajos, extending over more than seventeen million acres. To most Americans, this dramatically sculpted expanse encompassing parts of New Mexico, Arizona, and Utah may seem alien, or at least exotic, the stuff of Tony Hillerman novels. To the close to 144,000 Navajos who live on the reservation and to many of their kin, descended from those who returned from Fort Sumner in 1868, it is home. And within its broad outlines, another boundary encircles more than a million and a half acres that comprise the Hopi reservation, the Hopi having an even longer, deeper claim to this area of the world. South of the Navajo and Hopi reservations, south of I-40, spread two reservations bigger than the Hopis': the Tohono O'odham (Papago), second largest in the United States, and Fort Apache (White Mountain Apache), sixth largest.

The sizes are deceiving, for much of the story that follows centers on the ways in which even sections of reservation land have passed out of Indian ownership, if not out of Indian jurisdiction. Further, we must remember that these reservations encompass only a part of each Indian group's former homelands—often, if we expand our vision to reservations nationwide, a very small part with little in the way of natural resources or with resources historically managed and controlled by non-Indians.

In addition, it is important to note that many have been forced far from their regions of origin, uprooted repeatedly, and thrown together with people representing different—and even hostile—native groups. On top of these jarring dislocations, generations of Indians on the reservations have led troubled and impoverished existences under the near-total control of representatives of United States government and culture.

Hemmed in as Native Americans have been, buffeted and often lost to hopelessness, they have fought to hold on to homelands, to adapt as traditional cultures to new lands and to changes in the land, to regain regions and sacred places lost.

The Europeans and Americans who dispossessed the Indians recognized their prior rights and their vigorous, abiding connection to the land, but rationalized away the former and sentimentalized the latter as characteristic of a vanishing race.

They did not vanish. From a low of 237,000 in the last decade of the nineteenth century, the enrolled membership of the 547 federally recognized Indian groups (including those in Alaska, outside the scope of this narrative) now stands at close to a million, while another million Americans who cannot or choose not to gain federal recognition also identify themselves as Indians.

The 1990 census showed about 685,000 Indians living on reservations, lands held in trust for them by the government, or other clearly identifiable native enclaves, such as native Alaskan villages. In the "conterminous" territory now divided into 48 states—the vast middle of North America which is our focus—there are 314 federally recognized tribes. Some 300 reservations, most administered by the federal government, are clustered and scattered through 33 states.

On or off the "rez," federally recognized or not, many Indians continue to be vitally concerned with land issues. For four hundred years, the struggle for the land has been the defining characteristic of Indian and European-American interaction. American Indians are neither the first nor the last to find themselves dispossessed by a technologically superior culture, but they have been remarkably persistent and consistent in speaking out for their own prior rights and for Indian ownership and control of land as the basis for their survival as individuals and as indigenous peoples.

The groups we have come to know as tribes did not inhabit a static world before the arrival of Europeans. The Indians whom nineteenth-century immigrants found established in Minnesota as the eastern Sioux had probably migrated from the American Southeast in the fourteenth century. Perhaps in the same period, Canadian bands immigrated to the American Southwest and adapted well to Pueblo cultures there, becoming known as the Navajos and Apaches. (Some Hopis still regard the Navajos as opportunistic latecomers after more than six centuries of coexistence.)

Precontact Indians shifted about in response to changing environmental conditions, including a bitter drought that drove people from the Great Plains in the thirteenth century. Bands wanting or needing new territory sparked confrontations over the land and its resources, especially good hunting areas, and occasionally earned the label "invaders," aggressively edging out or displacing those in their way. Indians also shifted between bands, formed fluid confederacies, and shared hunting grounds, river valleys, and bays, such arrangements smoothed by the natives' limited numbers and the abundance of land.

But by the time Europeans entered the "New World," most groups had inhabited particular regions for many generations. Each had a naturally defined area recognized by others as its own. A river or ridge might trace the edge of a territory, often with a "buffer zone" beyond.

For those Indian communities who invested time and energy cultivating the soil, boundaries and agreements were particularly important. Colonist and reformer Roger Williams would write of the New England agriculturalists, "The *Natives* are very exact and punctual in the bounds of their Lands, belonging to this or that Prince or People."

Within their home regions across the continent, Indians made seasonal moves, taking advantage of nature's changing bounty. They knew where and when to hunt and gather wild foods and medicines—acorns, bulbs, berries, nuts, roots, seeds. Families and bands marked certain sites—a berry patch, a trapping location—that were considered theirs on the basis of long-term use. They fished the streams, an early New England immigrant finding the natives "experienced in the knowledge of all baits, and diverse seasons . . . knowing when to fish in rivers, and when at rocks, when in bays, and when at seas."

Many—far more than Anglo culture would acknowledge—cultivated crops near village sites in the warmer months, leaders sometimes designating agricultural tracts for family use. Indians periodically moved their village sites and altered the land to their purposes—in forested areas, for example, by burning off undergrowth to create a more enticing habitat for deer or elk, to make travel easier, and to kill off troublesome insects.

Most Indians were able to live well by their own standards in this way. The land provided, as they often pointed out in response to the blandishments of white officials bearing treaties, gifts, and promises of continuing supplies. "My people do not want anything from the 'Great Father' you tell me about," a Miwok Indian of California would declare. "The Great Spirit is our father, and he has always supplied us with all we need."

Indians took deep satisfaction in what the land offered. "The Crow country is a good country," a Crow named Arapooish would proclaim. "The [Creator] put it in exactly the right place; while you are in it you fare well; whenever you are out of it, whichever way you travel, you fare worse. . . . The Crow country is exactly the right place." It contained, he explained, "good things for every season."

Among these "good things" were healing plants and the nourishing earth itself—"If we are wounded, we go to our mother [earth] and seek to lay the wounded part against her, to be healed," explained Bedagi, or Big Thunder, of the New England Penobscots.

Many Indian groups believed that in a previous age "humans and animals had lived and talked together," that all creatures were related and all creatures mattered. Some Indian languages had no word equivalent to "pest" in English. "Everything on this earth has a purpose," Lakota Sioux Madonna Swan's grandmother explained, "the ants, badger, deer, even the flies!" As a result, she cautioned, "you should treat animals kindly and don't kill them for no good reasons."

Indian groups could be wasteful, as were the Potawatomis who in the late 1670s were reported slaughtering more than five hundred bears as retaliation for a bear's dismembering of a Potawatomi youth. The Delawares by the 1780s were notorious among other Indians for their extravagant killing of game animals, although by this time, European trade factored into their actions.

The most cited example of precontact Indian wastefulness has been the Plains Indian practice of running buffalo over a cliff and using only a small portion of the kill. The waste, while real, was a result more of circumstance than of recklessness. Hunters could not control the number of stampeding buffalo. Often "the number of workers who could butcher was small compared to the kill," and the kill site's distance from the main camp made it difficult to haul much back.

Whether Indians killed many buffalo or few, it stands to reason that any human group eventually has an impact upon the land it inhabits. For example, native hunters often depleted the wildlife surrounding a village. However, as the band followed its cycle to other locations within the homeland, the local animal population again grew and flourished.

And when resources were limited, Indians cultivated them with care. A traveler in 1811 in a region that would later become part of Nebraska found the Pawnees "carefully husband[ing] and preserv[ing] from injury" the few trees and wild plum bushes growing there. They also apparently took care "not to overcollect" the wild onions and Indian potatoes. Natives along the Columbia River in the Pacific Northwest caught what fish they needed, then removed their weir barriers from streams so that other fish "could go upstream and lay their eggs," thereby ensuring a good catch in years to come.

Such examples make it hard to refute the idea that Native American cultures, when able to operate as they wish, have shown themselves skilled at using the land and its resources without using them up. This has been in part a practical response to scarcity, in part an acknowledgment of the centrality of the natural world to Indian lives. For the Navajos, for example, nature was "an all-inclusive organizing device" around which their culture revolved, from which they sought to draw order and harmony.

In particular, Indians found sacredness in places. Every group had these places, has them still. Mountains, caves, lakes, mesas, springs—all are imbued with a sense of the holy, as evidenced by a Taos woman's comment on Blue Lake in the Sangre de Cristo Mountains of New Mexico, a sacred location returned to the Taos Indians in 1970: "I think of it as an altar." To some Indians, every familiar area has something of the sacred about it.

Locations are steeped in tribal myth and ritual, in the group's sense of its identity and its understanding of the world. In western Abenaki tradition, the Champlain Valley now forming the western border of Vermont is the place where their legendary heroes performed their deeds and brought into being the world as the Abenakis knew it. The Hupas of northern California centered creation in their Hoopa Valley and called themselves Natinook-wa, "the people of Natinook, the place by the river to which the trails lead back."

On the Great Plains, after the Sioux Sun Dance had ended, the pole was left standing, and those who later had occasion to pass by would, as Luther Standing Bear relates, "stand for a long time in reverent attitude because it was a sacred place to us." Perhaps similarly significant ceremonies were being recalled by occasional Indians observed during the nineteenth century quietly visiting mounds in their old Virginia homelands.

Perhaps, too, the locations were burial sites, among the strongest of sacred places to many, a reality underlying the Native American Grave Protection and Repatriation Act of 1990. As Chief Joseph of the Nez Perces explained after his desperate attempt to reach Canada and avoid being forced onto a reservation in Idaho, his dying father had told him of their Pacific Northwest homeland, "This country holds your father's body. Never sell the bones of your father and your mother.'' In 1879, in exile, Joseph said, ''I love that land more than all the rest of the world. A man who would not love his father's grave is worse than a wild animal.''

Implicit in Joseph's words is a deep and natural longing for home, a sense of being torn from one's place in the world. This sense of identity tied to place fed the horror with which Indians greeted attempts to dispossess them. ''Our lands are our life and breath,'' declared a Creek chief. ''The earth is part of my body and I never gave up the earth,'' the Nez Perces chief Toohoolhoolzote would proclaim to whites who wanted it.

In their early encounters with whites desiring their lands, Indians expressed two interrelated beliefs: that land was not simply property to be bought and sold, and that God in indisputable wisdom had placed the Indians in their homelands and the whites in their own places far distant.

The Kickapoo prophet Kennekuk in 1827 asserted that the earth belonged only to the ''Great Spirit,'' that ''no people owns the land.'' Joseph argued that territory was ''too sacred to be valued by or sold for silver and gold,'' in 1879 asserting, ''I never said the land was mine to do with it as I chose. The one who has the right to dispose of it is the one who has created it.''

This conviction reflects an Indian distinction between individual or group ownership of land, as understood by Europeans and European Americans, and the right simply to use its resources by hunting, gathering, and planting using nonintrusive methods. At the same time, it reflects a belief that Indians could claim a powerful form of ownership, one directly from God. ''I claim a right to live on my land,'' said Joseph, ''and accord you the privilege to live on yours.'' An earlier resistance leader, Tecumseh, had struck a more emphatic note in explaining pointedly that the Great Spirit ''gave the white people a home beyond the great waters,'' the Indians the game-filled American expanses, ''and he gave them strength and courage to defend them.''

As Indian defenses crumbled, natives also argued for their land rights on the basis of long-term commitment. ''We fought and bled and died to keep other Indians from taking [Crow country],'' an Absaroka Crow identified only as ''Curly'' would insist. ''You will have to dig down through the surface before you can find nature's earth, as the upper portion is Crow. The land, as it is, is my blood and my dead; it is consecrated, and I do not want to give up any portion of it.''

Indian arguments carried no weight at a bargaining table with representatives of an Anglo culture bent on expansion and the imposition of marketplace values. To Toohoolhoolzote's arguments that the sacred earth ''should not be disturbed by hoe or plow'' or the natives wrenched from it, General O. O. Howard in 1877 responded, ''We do not wish to interfere with your religion, but you must talk about practicable things. Twenty times over you repeat that the earth is your mother. . . . Let us hear it no more, but come to business at once.''

Indians could and did reason more persuasively that their claims lay in the recognized sovereignty of each group in its particular area and in their long-term use of its natural resources, including some visible changes in the landscape. But the newcomers recognized Indian sovereignty only when it was convenient or they were compelled to, and they refused to see significant evidence of Indian occupancy, adopting the rhetoric of *vacuum domicilium* (''vacant'' lands can be made our homelands). They also used ''lawful war'' (if the Indians resist, we are justified in going to war and taking the spoils), ''civil'' versus ''natural'' rights (the Indians as ''savages'' have a natural claim but not a full legal one), and Manifest Destiny (God created the land for the westering immigrants, people who really knew how to use it).

As a result, at different times and in different places, each group of Indians felt what Satank of the Kiowas expressed in 1867: at first the world had ''seemed large enough for both'' native and non-Indian, but its ''broad plains seem[ed] now to contract'' for the former.

Natives saw in this shrinking their own dismal ends. Of the Apaches, Geronimo said, ''When they are taken from [their] homes they sicken and die.'' Satanta of the Kiowas, faced with reservation living, announced, ''I don't want to settle. I love to roam over the prairies. There I feel free and happy, but when I settle down I feel pale and die.''

Geronimo's people, taken from their beloved southwestern fastnesses to the inhospitable climate of Alabama and Florida, wasted away in droves. Satanta died a suicide, jumping off a balcony of the Texas penitentiary where he had been incarcerated indefinitely.

Such wrenching dislocations and untimely deaths fed apocalyptic visions. Kicking Bird of the Kiowas, witnessing the bloodshed in the South Plains War of 1874–1875, predicted that all the Indians would soon be killed and their absence would cause the earth itself to "turn to water, or burn up," as "It is our mother and cannot live when the Indians are all dead."

Yet the Native Americans' story is at least as much one of creative survival as it is of death and destruction. From east coast to west, they fought for the land by every means available, recognizing its central importance to their cultural identity. Stripped of their homes anyway, stripped of some two billion acres of the New World, they were pushed onto territory often literally and figuratively barren and placed under the debilitating control of white bureaucrats.

Indians adapted to their changing circumstances, but they never lost their sense of the centrality of place. "Everything is tied to our homeland," the Flathead anthropologist D'Arcy McNickle would explain in 1961. "Our language, religion, songs, beliefs—everything. Without our homeland, we are nothing." Jimmie Durham, a western Cherokee, would tell a congressional hearing in 1978 that "Eloheh," the Cherokee word for land, "also means history, culture, and re We cannot separate our place on earth from our lives on th nor from our vision nor our meaning as a people."

Further, Indians never accepted the injustice of their di sion. Although John Neihardt's classic account of Sioux hol Black Elk's life is now under attack for its degree of veracity, t mmed incredulity he attributes to Black Elk regarding the Sio o conflicts of the late nineteenth century rings true: "Wher went, the soldiers came to kill us, and it was all our own co

What follows, then, is an account of how Native ns have struggled for the right to hold on to or reclaim land refore to hold on to or reclaim a knowledge of who they wei they are, and who they can and will be.

You shall live in square grey houses
　　in a barren land.
　—Lakota holy man Drinks Water's prophecy to his people

To the edge of the earth,
　to the edge of the earth,
　　to the edge of the earth.
Snap all the people! Snap all the people!
To the edge of the earth,
　to the edge of the earth.

　　　　　　　　　　　—Wintu shaman's song

IN A BARREN
LAND

Locations of various eastern tribes at the onset of Anglo expansion

←———————→

Chapter One

"An Uneasiness on Our Minds"
(1607–1764)

> We told you a little while ago that we had an uneasiness on our minds, and we shall now tell you what it is: it is concerning our lands.
>
> —*Mohawk speaker, Albany Congress, 1754*

They were strange and rather pitiful, the voyagers who sailed into the bay and up the river and began scratching out an odd sort of village on a swampy peninsula. They showed little ability at gathering or growing things to eat, at fishing or hunting. They did not adapt well to the climate and grew sick. They fought among themselves and failed to make proper seasonal provisions. Surely they would tire of such an existence and go back to their own lands. At one point, the whole group did sail away. But soon they returned.

The natives of the bay area at first found this incursion only mildly disturbing. They had repeatedly come in contact with crews of ships from across the ocean. The natives no doubt knew of the short-lived village of voyagers on an island to the south some three decades earlier, and they easily recalled that in the same period one of their own number, a young man who had been kidnapped by a ship's crew, had returned in a vessel accompanied by eight men in long robes.

These men had constructed a lone wooden "mission" on a river feeding into the bay. A group of natives, perhaps angered by the missionaries' attitude toward their own religion, perhaps eager to avenge the kidnapping of natives by ship crews, had killed the eight after only a few months' coexistence.

Now the natives killed a few of the newcomers forging into their

hunting grounds. Others they helped, sharing food supplies and showing them how to plant corn and tobacco, squash and beans, how to
dam part of a stream to trap fish, how to hunt deer and otter, opossum
and turkey.

Meanwhile, more people from across the ocean came—not just
men, but women and children. Their fields and dwellings spread outward from the initial village, which they called Jamestown, all along
the river, which they called the James, completely unconcerned with
what the natives called it. The wild game fled into the oak and pine
forests. The newcomers' livestock trampled the fields on which the
natives, now often ill with strange and terrible maladies, grew their
crops. The newcomers talked and acted as if the whole region belonged to them, even alleged that some distant authority told them
they could have it.

And sooner or later each native awoke to the chilling realization
that the strangers were "a people come from under the world, to take
their world from them."

We understand the struggle for New World empire in varied and complex ways as we near the twentieth century's end, but the story of
American Indian land loss and survival rightly begins where the old
American history books began: in 1607 with Jamestown, the first permanent English settlement in what would become the United States.
At the time the English ships sailed into Chesapeake Bay, and for
many generations thereafter, Great Britain was only one of various
European powers contending for portions of the North American continent, claiming lands on behalf of their rulers and their God. But the
use to which the British wished to put the new lands distinguished
their efforts from those of the other two major rivals, France and
Spain.

The French had less interest in settling immigrants in North America than in swelling the coffers at home. They established Quebec the
year after Jamestown's founding, using it as a base from which to
glide down the St. Lawrence River and develop a generally friendly
and mutually beneficial fur trade with the natives of the Great Lakes,
the Ohio River Valley, and beyond—the prairies and plains west of
the Mississippi River. The French also would plant themselves at the
mouth of the Mississippi on the Gulf Coast, founding New Orleans

and following the river into the interior from the south, setting up such trading posts as St. Louis.

Indians and Frenchmen did not always live harmoniously, and the French were not above callously manipulating Indian against Indian. But the close and open interaction of native and Frenchman made them to some observers "almost one people."

The Spanish had penetrated from the Caribbean into the Southeast almost a century before the arrival of Jamestown's colonists, even attempting a settlement—San Miguel de Gualdape—on the Atlantic coast in 1526 in present-day Georgia. (St. Augustine, their oldest permanent settlement, would begin taking shape in Florida some forty years later.)

Like the French, the Spanish were primarily interested in exploiting the land to increase their riches in Europe, but they did so through often brutal subjugation of the natives. Typical was the edict carried by Francisco Vasquez Coronado on his 1540 North American expedition: natives were to submit to the Spanish crown and become Christians or face slavery, exile, or death. Submission often brought a form of slavery anyway, as the Spanish frontier forces of soldiers and friars conscripted Indian labor and restricted Indian lives from Florida to the Far West.

Yet as the Spaniards cut a path of violence and coercion, many natives remained free and in possession of their homelands. In part, this was because Spain could never manage to draw enough colonists to dominate a region. In part, it was because Spain actually would prove "more zealous than any other European power" in acknowledging the legal rights of natives. Frontier Spaniards also, like the French, tended to be accepting of racial intermixing, not given to rigid segregation of "red" and "white." Most important, like the French, the Spanish "had a place [for native groups] in the overall imperial scheme of empire," even attempting unsuccessfully to make them the colonists in frontier mission chains.

The British, when they came as traders, valued the natives as the French did: as suppliers of furs and as markets for European goods. British colonizers and settlers were different. Arriving on the eastern coastline of what is now the United States, the "Anglos" and other northern Europeans wished, like the Spanish, to subjugate the natives. Unlike the Spanish, after an initial period in which the Indians might prove helpful to a settlement's survival, the newcomers deemed them not necessary, mere "cumberers of the ground." While the Spanish—and later the Mexicans—sought to "integrate" Indians, Anglos "sought to segregate them."

In the colonial period—as in subsequent eras—colonists with these aims pressed in upon the Indians, who were already experiencing a variety of stresses caused by contact with European traders and European viruses. The immigrants further upset the rhythms of Indian life. They reluctantly recognized some form of Indian land rights at some point in the dispossession process, then sought to extinguish those rights, the "elimination of Indians from settled areas" quickly becoming "a distinguishing characteristic of the Anglo frontier."

Natives, no strangers to shifting environmental and social conditions and alliances, found themselves struggling with massive, fundamental changes. The settlers and officials with whom they came in contact were often the most grasping, insensitive, and ruthless members of the encroaching culture. Natives were forced to compete with the newcomers and with each other for land and resources, and they remained or became divided—often deeply and irrevocably—over how to meet the threat of land and cultural loss.

But they developed strategies to hold on to their homelands for as long as they could, then devised ways simply to survive as groups and as individuals in an increasingly bounded and alien environment. In doing so, they shaped a remarkable record of resistance, adaptation, and renewal, one that cannot and should not be ignored as the American nation hurtles into the twenty-first century with its relationship to Indian America—and the concept of Indian identity itself—being more complex and problematic than ever.

At the coming of the Jamestown colonists, Chesapeake Bay area natives, like most other natives living within the contours of the future United States, tended to identify with a particular village or band rather than to give allegiance to a fixed, centralized political and social authority. In other words, they did not think of themselves as members of a single "tribe," despite commonalities in culture and language.

Nonetheless, a man named Wahunsonacock had emerged as military leader of approximately thirty Tidewater groups in some two hundred villages. To the colonists, who picked up the name "Powhatan''—the group to which Wahunsonacock belonged—he became Powhatan and the natives of the area became the Powhatan tribe, or—more accurately—the Powhatan Confederacy.

This confederacy could easily have devastated the fledgling settlement. Yet with the newcomers Wahunsonacock observed an oft-troubled peace, lulled perhaps by the colony's small and rocky start, its slow growth in the early years, and his daughter Pocahontas's 1614 marriage to Jamestown tobacco planter John Rolfe.

Besides, it was apparent that the colonists needed the natives more than the natives needed the colonists, as one young Indian reminded Jamestown leader John Smith. The people of the settlement, he pointed out, could not survive without partaking of the Indian harvest and would ''have the worst by our absence'' should the cultivators ''abandon the Countrie.''

The settlers at Jamestown could also be seen as a potentially valuable addition to the trading and cultural mix in the region and as potentially valuable allies in native warfare. In this sense, they could with the Powhatans create a ''middle ground'' of the type historian Richard White has found operating between the French and the native groups of the Ohio Valley and Great Lakes before 1763, a place in which different cultures through accommodation to each other created mutually satisfying alliances.

At the least, even if the newcomers did not prove to be useful traders or allies, the natives at first could easily avoid them—there was world enough.

Yet warning signs abounded. Both the Powhatans and the immigrants early took captives as negotiating tools; Pocahontas had first been brought to Jamestown a prisoner. Colonial leaders in particular were quick to use coercion and subjugation. In 1608, stymied in his efforts to trade for corn with the Pamunkeys of the Powhatan Confederacy, Jamestown's John Smith pulled a pistol and held it to the chest of Powhatan's brother Opechancanough in front of the gathered Indians, forcing a promise of foodstuffs. The colonists, under orders from England to make Powhatan a ''subject king'' to James I, guided the reluctant leader through a farcical ceremony—''a fowle trouble there was to make him kneele to receave his crown,'' as it required ''so many persuasions, examples, and instructions as tired them all.''

Language differences were usually quickly, if imperfectly, addressed by Indian and white traders and other middlemen experienced in a multilingual world. In a common early frontier development, Indian women who entered into relationships with white men provided a significant language bridge. Still, miscommunication was common, and it was used to the whites' advantage in the making of uneven "agreements." As a Penobscot Indian would note, "I know not what I am made to say in another language, but I know well what I say in my own."

Cultural differences proved daunting. Both natives and newcomers possessed a sense of ethnic superiority, but the latter had greater unity and superior technology, especially when it came to weapons of war—gunpowder, firearms, steel swords. They also shared with other Europeans a conviction that Indian societies were simply primitive (and base) approximations of European communities rather than distinctive non-European cultures with their own complex structures. Despite the colonists' own often bitter struggle to survive through the first decade—and the pronouncements of concern for Indian souls—the newcomers could and did act with ruthless and concerted force against anything they perceived as an Indian transgression. They killed and dismembered captives and marched into villages, burning houses and—as the British had done in Ireland—destroying crops.

The natives could be aggressive and brutal, too. What our popular history overlooked until fairly recently is that they usually acted this way in a desperate response to white encroachment—in the words of the Seneca Cornplanter "rather than submit to . . . unjust demands which seemed to have no bounds."

By the time Powhatan died in 1618, the British settlers were pushing deeper inland toward the mountain range that would become known as the Appalachians, occupying Indian lands on the upper James and Chickahominy rivers. In 1622, the Tidewater Indians exploded by mounting a war against the invaders. Led by Opechancanough—identified in some accounts as the kidnap victim who had accompanied the ill-fated Jesuit missionaries decades earlier—they killed almost a third of the twelve hundred Virginia colonists before the settlers mounted a successful counterattack.

The victors, "abandoning whatever notions they had about converting the aborigines," followed with a decade-long period of harassment, including repeated burning of native corn crops, until the

Powhatans were pushed inland, beyond the fall line. One colonist exulted that "by right of Warre" the English could now "enjoy [the natives'] cultivated places," adding, "Now their cleared grounds . . . shall be inhabited by us."

The way for such victories was paved by the viruses that Europeans—and the small but growing number of Africans—brought with them, having built up immunities after prior epidemics in their homelands. Precontact Indians did not inhabit a disease-free Eden, but neither is there evidence that they suffered the "contagious 'crowd' diseases endemic to Europe."

From Columbus's voyage onward, travelers introduced to the Americas a Pandora's box of diseases: smallpox, measles, cholera, diphtheria, plague, typhoid fever, and certain influenzas. The newcomers also may have brought the first New World instances of such scourges as malaria.

By the time the Jamestown settlers arrived, Indian numbers had already fallen through intermittent contact with virus-carrying Europeans, and deadly maladies were spreading far beyond the point of contact, ravaging even interior Indian groups that had not yet seen a stranger from across the sea. The arrival of colonists of course intensified the spread of sickness, in part because the children among them were "prone to carry viruses to which most surviving European adults had developed immunity." And the colonists' cows, horses, and pigs all carried diseases to which previously unexposed humans were susceptible. The people at Jamestown the year after it was established reported a devastating epidemic among the Chesapeake Bay Indians. By 1700, the population of the Powhatan Confederacy would shrink to one twelfth of its estimated 1607 size, primarily due to disease.

Natives sought spiritual and practical ways to halt the nightmarish losses, but neither prayer and ritual nor other traditional remedies seemed to have an effect. In fact, standard Indian treatments—purging, sweating, and fasting—only exacerbated diseases such as smallpox, for sufferers needed to be kept "dry and well-nourished."

The catastrophic declines lead to speculation whether the natives' homelands could have been taken from them without the help of microbes, despite the Europeans' superior weaponry. While Indians tended to group in small units at the village and band level, scholars keep revising upward the number of Indians in the New World before

Columbus. For many decades, the accepted total for all of the New World in 1492 was one million; five million is now a conservative estimate for those in the conterminous United States only—east coast to west, Canadian to Mexican borders. Some researchers argue for triple this number or more.

Clearly, the large number of Indian deaths from epidemics prior to white settlement—and the resulting weakening in the fabric of Indian life—greatly enhanced the colonists' chances of gaining land and power. Nowhere is this more obvious than in New England, where the second successful British colonization effort began with the arrival of the Pilgrims in 1620.

William Bradford would write of the Pilgrims' first glimpse of the northeastern shoreline, "What could they see but a hideous and desolate wilderness, full of wild beasts and wild men—and what multitudes there might be of them they knew not." Bradford's words contain unintended irony. New England groups with whom the Pilgrims—and, in 1628, the Puritans—might have come into immediate conflict already had overwhelmingly succumbed to smallpox and other infectious diseases transmitted by European traders and sailors, primarily the French.

For example, the Pawtuxets, who lived in this "vast disaster zone" in which the Pilgrims would settle, were devastated by disease between 1615 and 1619. Tribal member Tisquantum, or Squanto, who would prove an invaluable friend to the Cape Cod settlement, returned home after his kidnapping by a British sea captain, slavery in Spain, and a sojourn in London to find his approximately two thousand tribesmen, women, and children had vanished. Some survivors may have fled to other native groups, but most had simply died.

A further irony in Bradford's statement is his reference to "wilderness," for much of the coast bore evidence of human clearing and cultivation. The Narragansetts of Massachusetts had, according to early European observers, cleared the forest "for a distance of eight to ten miles from the coast—no small feat." Southern New England groups maintained hunting parks by periodically burning off brush and, like the Chesapeake Bay Indians, they combined hunting and fishing with farming, giving the lie to the colonial insistence that natives did not cultivate the land.

Those northeastern groups that survived the epidemics remained to be reckoned with, but that was easy enough at first. Some initially welcomed the newcomers as allies against stronger Indian groups, allowing the English to establish towns "without acknowledging the existence of native sovereignty or title." Some of the natives on whose lands the English were already establishing their fields and farms were paid off with trade items and wampum, the shell beads they valued as a medium of exchange, when they claimed title. The disease-weakened Wampanoags entered into a "mutual assistance pact" with the Puritans, letting them occupy unused land.

Such agreements clearly meant different things to native and immigrant. Early colonial governments treated native land claims the way a lawyer would a nuisance suit, in the spirit of a 1629 Massachusetts Bay Company directive to pay when "any of the salvages [sic] *pretend* right of inheritance to all or any part of the lands graunted in our pattent." The English chose to interpret the resulting agreements as "deed[s] of cession legitimizing their seizure of unspecified acreage."

The Wampanoags and other natives certainly did not do so. Operating from their own quite different understanding of land ownership, natives granted "usufruct rights" only, limited permission to "use an area for planting or hunting or gathering," as they themselves did.

Yet microbes continued to undercut native resistance to immigrant settlement and to English definitions of land ownership. Puritan minister Increase Mather would note that three years after the arrival of the first Puritans at Massachusetts Bay, the Indians "began to be quarrelsome" over land matters, but "God ended the Controversy by sending the Smallpox" among them. (Mather's comment echoes that of a Spaniard in the conquest of Mexico a century earlier: "When the Christians were exhausted from war, God saw fit to send the Indians smallpox.") Two years later, another smallpox outbreak among New England natives led to an estimated mortality rate of 95 percent in some areas.

If Mather viewed epidemics as God's protecting the interests of his "elect," the natives found their own understanding of the world shattered, their familiar cultural, spiritual, and economic moorings stripped away. Among other serious consequences, they could not follow their old subsistence patterns—planting, hunting, gathering—at crucial times in the seasonal cycle. Those who survived epidemics were still weak, hungry, and susceptible to other maladies; women not only faced fewer marriage prospects but were less likely to conceive, or to bear healthy children. Spiritual, medical, and political leaders died— "All those . . . who had sense are dead," complained Mohawks negotiating with Kahawake Iroquois—or simply seemed bereft of power. People forgot rituals and traditions or simply gave them up.

Adding to the sense of disorientation, of a world strangely and disturbingly altered, the most afflicted tribes continued to be pressed by their native neighbors who had escaped the worst ravages, the coastal Pokanokets, for example, being forced to give way to the Narragansetts at a site favored by both on Narragansett Bay.

Even more disturbing were the escalating attempts at control by the immigrants establishing colonies all up and down the eastern seaboard. In 1635, the British governor of Maryland told Indians of the region that they must submit to English law any of their number who killed a colonist. A native leader tried to explain how the Indians settled such a matter, pointing out that "since that you are heare strangers, and come into our Countrey, you should rather conform yourselves to the Customes of our Countrey, than impose yours upon us . . ."

In fact, as Indians already had governance structures, however loose or unfathomable by European standards, much Indian warfare against whites can be seen as attempts by the natives to "enforce their [own] legal norms on a disorderly frontier" filled with lawless newcomers.

Yet further disquiet stemmed from the ways in which warfare intensified with the coming of the Europeans. Eastern Indians were no strangers to violent conflict; they repeatedly mounted what they considered "justified reprisals" against other individuals or communities. Further, groups such as the Pequots forced less aggressive bands from choice lands. But wholesale killing of noncombatants and "the total war that involved systematic destruction of food and property" were generally outside the experience of the coastal Indians before the development of frictions with the European immigrants.

New England's Pequot War of 1636–1637—the culmination of tensions between Pequots inhabiting the fertile, game-filled Connecticut Valley and encroaching colonists looking to claim more land—included the massacre of as many as seven hundred Pequots, mostly women, children, and old men, at "Mystic Fort," their palisade on the Mystic River. A British participant in the attack recalled that even when he and his companions set fire to the fort, some of the men refused to come out, flames consuming the "very bowstrings" they were attempting to use in defense. Others—men, women, and children—fled the fire to be "entertained with the point of the sword."

The Pequots had tried to enlist the neighboring Narragansetts in a military alliance. William Bradford reported the Pequot perception and argument: that "the English were strangers and began to overspread [Indian] country, and would deprive them thereof in time, if they were suffered to grow and increase." But alliances would prove hard to establish or sustain; political consensus *within* an Indian community was a hard enough feat, and logistical problems in establishing and maintaining Indian unity would abound at the same time that whites practiced divide-and-conquer techniques. In this case, the Narragansetts and the Mohegans held old grudges against the Pequots and, under pressure, chose a more immediately advantageous alliance with the British.

The Narragansetts balked at the slaughter at Mystic Fort and at what followed: most of the remaining Pequots were gradually rounded up and killed or sold into slavery, shipped as far away as the West Indies. As a people, they were officially erased from existence. No one in New England was even allowed to call himself or herself a Pequot, not that many would be brave or foolish enough to do so in the wake of Mystic Fort. Meanwhile, the Pequot lands of southern New England were thrown open to white settlement, and the smaller tribes who had "relied upon the Pequot for protection" became subjugated to the colonial powers, relinquishing "some of their choicest land."

In Virginia, Opechancanough mounted a final unsuccessful series of raids to repel British colonization there. Thirty-seven years after the strange settlers had sailed into the Tidewater region, the elderly Powhatan leader was captured, carried into Jamestown on a litter, and shot to death by a guard.

The fate of both the Pequots and the Powhatan Confederacy under Opechancanough sent a chilling message to other Indians whose lands extended to the eastern coast. But through the mid-seventeenth century, most managed to coexist with the British settlers while retaining some autonomy, their relationship to the newcomers at worst "interdependent" rather than "dependent," although the degree of a tribe's autonomy usually corresponded to its distance from the nearest immigrant settlements.

Early in each colony's development, the colonial government outlawed individual land deals with natives. Tribes retained power through British recognition, however grudging, of their land rights and sovereign nation status and through their desirability as allies. British settlers and officials could be only so blind to the fact that a land was already inhabited, even cultivated. Besides, as the contest for empire among the various European nations intensified, one European power would find itself forced by another equally covetous European power to deal officially with the natives on land issues.

The British, French, and Spanish continued to compete for native trade and political allegiances. So did the Dutch, who had purchased Manhattan Island, site of their New Amsterdam, from the Manhattan Indians for a pittance in trade goods in 1626. So, too, did the various British colonial governments; both the struggling Virginia colony and the struggling Carolina colony sought alliances with the same native tribes in hopes of bettering their own position in relation to the other and in relation to the Spaniards to the south.

Thus, natives held on to a place within the changing order. They retained large tracts of land, allowed settlers use rights on certain portions, dealt as middlemen in the fur trade with the natives to the west, provided their labor services to the colonies, and served as a market for European goods.

Like European viruses, however, European trade—for such diverse items as guns and sugar, iron cooking pots and metal knives—greatly altered and ultimately devastated native worlds. In responding to the European demand for furs, Indians moved their villages to be close to European trading operations. Within the villages, old communal patterns of sharing and social leveling began to give way to new economic and political distinctions—or, conversely, old status roles crumbled, as when wampum, a sign of status, "became an item of mass consumption" through trade with the Europeans.

As a result of trading opportunities, natives also widened their hunting patterns and came into direct competition with each other. The balance was upset between those having access to European goods and those who did not. In the mid-1600s, members of the Iroquois Confederacy—Cayugas, Mohawks, Oneidas, Onondagas, Senecas—

pummeled and pushed their Algonquian neighbors westward, while the Crees displaced the Sioux in northern Minnesota, in each case in large part because their contact with European commercial interests gave the aggressors superior weaponry and clout.

Trade also undermined native life through the availability of alcohol. It was all too easy for many of the people, disoriented by disease and wrenching change, to drink to excess, adding significantly to their own miseries and those of their communities. "I am going to lose my head," declared a Cayuga in the 1660s, "I am going to drink of the water that takes away one's wits."

Whether or not natives used European weaponry to best their neighbors or became addicted to strong drink, they did become dependent on the flow of European goods. As early as the 1660s, southern New England Indians, accustomed to trading for such items as cloth, guns, and kettles, had lost much of their old self-sufficiency. The Creeks in the South, who by the turn of the century had aligned with Carolina colonists against the Spanish in Florida, were judged to "have forgotten the chief part of their ancient mechanical skill, because Anglos "suppl[ied] them so cheap with every sort of goods." The result, as one colonist explained, was that they would not "be well able now, at least for some years, to live independently of us."

As long as the natives had something to trade for European goods, they were not completely ensnared. But when the immigrants no longer needed their aid or assistance, and when game and fur-bearing animals became scarce, native bargaining power evaporated. What else did the indigenous people have that immigrants wanted?

The answer, of course, was land. The natives knew that its ownership was crucial to autonomous survival, so much so that "to maintain their land base, Indians made major cultural adaptations, short of national suicide, to the presence of European powers." Yet as early as 1633, land had replaced furs as the principal commodity for exchange in the Massachusetts Bay area. By the mid-seventeenth century, some tribes were caught so firmly in the line of British settlement that they were rapidly losing their home territory and with it their freedoms—political, economic, social.

Colonial governments judged, conveniently for their purposes, that Indians could lay claim only to acreage that showed "improvements" by European standards. This meant fencing, plowed fields, evidence of domestic livestock raising—all of which ran counter to Indian husbandry practices. Absent from the definition were not only the clamshell-dug fields of the Indian groups who depended partially on agriculture, but the "clam banks, fishing ponds, berry-picking areas, [and] hunting lands" from which they and nonagricultural groups drew sustenance.

Throughout the decades and centuries of Anglo expansion, there were those among the newcomers who rejected and challenged such self-serving perspectives. One of the first in this minority chorus, New England firebrand Roger Williams, decried the settlers' failure to recognize and respect Indian land claims based on seasonal usage, and he asserted that even kings had no right "to take and give away the Lands and Countries of other men."

The West India Company had instructed the Dutch to obtain voluntary land cessions, not ones gained "by craft, or fraud, lest we call down the wrath of God upon our unrighteous beginnings." And many early New England cessions were voluntary. But "voluntary" obscures the fact that natives—quickly outnumbered by the immigrants in some locations—had few options, given the lack of a military or political alliance and continuing power struggles among tribes. Indians simply were unused to forming a political identity with other natives across cultural and kinship lines.

The first reservation in the United States—twelve hundred acres carved in late 1638 out of the Quinnipiacs' Connecticut homelands for their residence—resulted from the vastly outnumbered tribe's decision to trade the domination of more powerful tribes "for the comforts afforded by the proximity of English settlers."

The basic intent of a "reservation" has always been to segregate natives within defined geographical boundaries, but the motives behind this action have varied. Clearly, representatives of the advancing Anglo frontier were anxious simply to get Indians out of the way. They also, at various times, saw the reservation—often called "plantation" or "colony" in these early years—as a place of relative safety for beleaguered natives. Here Indians could either, according to two divergent lines of thought, live out their days as a "vanishing" race or, separated from the more degrading aspects of white culture, become "civilized" and attain a foothold in American life.

Indians found the whites' map and survey lines incompatible with their own understanding of the land's contours, uses, and meanings; they almost uniformly resisted moving to or staying on reservations unless they perceived no other options. But American history of the seventeenth, eighteenth, and nineteenth centuries is a story of natives running out of options; some tribes would feel that the advantages outweighed the drawbacks, especially if they could stay on part of their original homelands.

So it was with the Quinnipiacs. Reservation status allowed them to continue to live in familiar territory and to obtain such items as warm clothing and cooking utensils from the British. They retained some freedoms, but were clearly restricted and dominated: by the presence of a Puritan agent, by laws requiring them to get authorization from the colonial government before letting any outsiders reside among them, by a disturbing policy that allowed the English "exclusive and unlimited access to [reservation] meadow and timber."

About six years after the Connecticut reservation's inception, the leaders of tribes within Massachusetts's boundaries were induced to give up jurisdiction over their lands, and thus possession itself, as far as New England authorities were concerned, and committed themselves and their subjects to live under the colony's "just lawes and orders." Such "just lawes and orders" passed in the years immediately following included fines for not wearing hair cut "comely, as the English do," and the death penalty for denying "the true God."

Beginning in 1646, a Puritan named John Eliot even established "praying towns" for Christianized Indians. These were precursors of the highly controlled Indian reservations of the mid- to late-nineteenth-century West, although not as poverty-stricken, isolated, and isolating. At the price of their freedom and cultures—at the price, in other words, of their very identity—Indians gained a somewhat protected and secure place within the new order, where they would be "civilized" with missions and schools.

New England Indian leaders protested the creation of praying towns, but colonial administrators—and their successors—saw nothing wrong with this coercive combination of church and state. Like the Spanish friars establishing their missions on the Florida and New Mexico frontiers, on the New England religious reservation, the missionary controlled (as much as he could) various aspects of native life. Under his direction, the residents of a praying town laid out English-

style villages and engaged in English-style farming as their chief occupation, abandoning the old mixed-subsistence patterns that Anglos
considered at best a "transitional stage" in civilization's development
rather than "stable systems in their own right."

The Indians in the planned towns also adopted an English-style
form of government in which they might or might not be allowed to
select their own representatives. Either way, the representatives had
little real power. Everywhere they turned, natives met with strange
laws forbidding the practice of native religion—which colonial officials derogatorily termed "powwowing"—and outlawing other traditional customs, such as women "living apart so many dayes" during
their menstrual periods. The laws set forth by missionaries and colonial governments stipulated that natives had to behave in certain ways,
dress in certain ways, live in certain ways that were foreign to them
and not required of members of the new dominant culture. In other
words, white authorities tried to exert a measure of social control not
found in even the most straitlaced Puritan towns.

"Praying Indians" maintained some autonomy by resisting certain
of the strictures placed upon them—for example, by remaining in their
traditional wigwams, portable, cool in summer, warm in winter, rather
than taking up residence in the frame dwellings favored by agents and
missionaries. They also, both by choice and by necessity, worked
within the new culture in old ways that allowed them some freedom—
making and vending baskets, harvesting and selling game for food.

Many simply fled the English-style towns. As one official mourned,
"They can live with less labour, and more pleasure and plenty, as
Indians, than they can with us." His comment echoed the query of a
Micmac Indian to a Frenchman: "Which of these two is the wisest
and happiest—he who labors without ceasing and only obtains, and
that with great trouble, enough to live on, or he who rests in comfort
and finds all that he needs in the pleasure of hunting and fishing?"

An estimated eleven hundred "praying Indians" remained in Massachusetts in 1674. If it is easy to dismiss these people as weak ac-
commodationists, some of the conversions were genuine and
long-lasting. If others were less so, as historian David Weber has
pointed out regarding European conversion efforts in general, natives
"cooperated only when they believed they had something to gain from

the new religion and the material benefits that accompanied it, or too much to lose from resisting it."

Meanwhile, eastern tribes independently maintaining land claims struggled with English definitions of property rights as they experienced increasing pressure to sell them or simply to give them up. Their options: removal to a small "reserved" portion, like the Quinnipiacs, or migration westward, beyond the lands immediately desired by the British but occupied by other Indians.

The pressures took various forms. Not only did colonial governments attempt to deny Indian title to lands or to offer a pittance for them, but individual European immigrants got around or ignored restrictions on land deals with Indians.

Many used the English courts to their advantage. An Indian who killed a settler's livestock ravaging the Indian's cornfield found himself in court, as did many a native charged with some odd infraction of English law. Faced with a substantial fine, the Indian would be "rescued" by an Englishman who paid the amount in exchange for a short-term land mortgage on which the Englishman could foreclose. In more direct land grabs, traders and immigrants would use liquor to win land concessions from inebriated natives who might or might not actually represent peoples holding rights to a territory. Or they would simply force Indians from desired property with "threat of violence."

With such tactics and tensions, a major war had the inevitability of a summer storm. It came in New England in summer 1675, a blood-smeared tempest. The Wampanoags, the Narragansetts, the Nipmucs, and members of other tribes from across the region ravaged frontier settlements under the leadership of Metacom, a Wampanoag known to the colonists as King Philip. "King Philip's War" raged through most of the next year, Metacom declaring, "[We] have let them have a hundred times more land, than now . . . [I] have for my own people."

Despite this evidence of a strong Indian alliance under Metacom, other Indians entered the fray on the side of the settlers (now more numerous than the natives), and the powerful Iroquois to the west did not allow the "hostiles" to fall back to their territory to rest and recoup. Metacom was betrayed by a fellow Indian and cut to pieces, as were any hopes of an independent or even "interdependent" Indian presence in southern New England.

*   *   *

By the end of the seventeenth century, the Indian groups who had greeted the settlers of Jamestown and southern New England had declined and dispersed, pushed to the periphery of their lands and of colonial culture by English farm and artisan families who were escaping dwindling landholdings and uncertain livelihoods in their own homelands. In Virginia the government allowed squatters to locate legally on riverbanks across from Indian towns, even though a treaty of 1677 had assured the natives control over a three-mile radius from these towns.

Indian treaties were from their earliest use the means by which the English—and later, the Anglo-Americans—legitimized their encroachment on lands occupied by the natives. As the often uncomprehending and already outnumbered natives were compelled to give up their shrinking holdings, those who remained worked for prominent settlers or "flit[ted] about the edges of colonial settlement, camping here and there for a few months before moving on" and thus making use of what resources they could find without calling too much attention to themselves.

In New England, Massachusetts Indians could be bound over for three months of indentured servitude if they were discovered outside the county in which they officially resided. Many New England natives fled beyond the reach of the English, farther into the New England hills and valleys, many to the French mission villages of Canada.

The natives' deep and intricate relationship with their homelands had been hopelessly compromised, their old survival patterns rendered futile, thanks to a host of changes created by the arrival of the Europeans. As early as the 1640s, the once bountiful deer were becoming scarce in southern New England, leading the Narragansett Miantonomo to call upon other natives to kill the European settlers but not their cows, which "should be used for food 'till our deer be increased again."

The natives participated in commercial overhunting for hides while it helped them maintain a balance of economic power, but they ultimately paid a high price. As the wild-animal population dwindled, native hunters had to fix carefully the boundaries of each group's hunting grounds; as the animals disappeared, the Indians lost both trading power and an essential aspect of their diet and culture.

Environmental havoc did not stop there. "Since these Englishmen have seized our country," Miantonomo charged, "they have cut down the grass with scythes, and the trees with axes. Their cows and horses eat up the grass, and their hogs spoil our bed of clams; and finally we shall all starve to death."

Everywhere, the English altered the landscape, "taming" a "wilderness" that the natives considered no wilderness at all. Unlike the Europeans involved in the fur trade, these English were interested in "exploiting resources such as fish and sassafras that did not require native cooperation." They cut down the trees for the timber market in England. They also cut them for their own uses. Indians did, too, of course, but a New England household "probably consumed as much as thirty or forty cords of firewood," or "more than an acre of forest," in a year, and the households were multiplying.

The settlers simply burned the forests as well—not in the measured Indian way, but in an attempt to clear as much land as possible as quickly as possible. This naturally led to environmental changes. For example, wild animals fled now inhospitable habitats. Water did not seep as easily into the soil, so there were new runoff patterns, increased flooding, and erratic shifts—"stream levels came to vary so greatly that some dried up altogether for extended periods of the year."

The settlers' free-ranging livestock, too, altered the natural balance. Natives were used to a single tame four-legged animal: the dog. Now hogs and cattle not only destroyed Indian crops, but "competed with the native wild-animal population for food resources," overgrazing, contributing to the spread of weeds, and compacting the soil in a pattern similar to one occurring in Spanish America. "Your hogs & Cattle injure Us You Come too near Us to live & Drive Us from place to place," a Maryland Indian called Mattagund charged in 1666. "We can fly no farther let us know where to live & how to be secured for the future from the Hogs & Cattle."

The settlers' plows ripped into the earth, destroying native plants in favor of cultivated ones. Farmers quickly wore out the soil by planting a single crop—instead of the Indians' nutrient-rich mixing of corn and beans—and by "letting their livestock eat cornstalks and other unharvested material which could have been plowed back into the soil" to enrich it.

In addition, the newcomers altered the waterways and the fish population by constructing dams and millponds and clearing rivers and creeks of debris. They blazed their own trails and established "new seasonal routines," such as livestock roundups for branding.

Unlike the natives, the Europeans oriented their seasonal routines around one permanent location, "English fixity" supplanting at least some degree of "Indian mobility." The changes in the land, and the increasing English political, social, and economic dominance, as early as the 1630s led Indians to adopt this fixity as well. In southern New England, natives "took to occupying coastal sites year-round in order to stockpile shellfish so that they could make wampum on an extended scale." They also found it increasingly prudent to stay together in larger numbers in "permanently fortified sites."

All of this meant that Indian lives and lifeways were being constricted, whatever eastern lands they occupied. Yet even as the natives on the front line of English settlement dealt with this bitter truth, other eastern tribes were developing their own paths of resistance and accommodation.

In the period between the aftermath of King Philip's War and the 1763 Treaty of Paris, the English solidified their control in the eastern regions they had initially occupied from Virginia to southern New England. The Connecticut court in 1717 judged that "all lands in this government are holden of the King of Great Britain" and that "no title to any lands in this Colony can accrue by any purchase made of Indians on pretence of their being native proprietors thereof." Again, the Indians were denied legitimate claim to the land.

Some were moved about like chess pieces by the ascendant colonies. Virginia's government about 1715 convinced three hundred people, remnants of the Saponi, Occaneechee, and Tutelo tribes, to relocate to a frontier reservation, where they were to serve as "border guards," although certainly not roving ones, as they had to obtain permission to travel off their six-mile-square parcel. The governor of New York tried to resettle the Schaghticoke Indians at the mouth of the Mohawk River "to strengthen Albany's defenses [against the

French] and, no doubt, keep an eye on Indians who might be wavering in their loyalties.'' But the Schaghticokes quietly trickled away.

Some natives sought to return to their old homes under any conditions, their efforts "hint[ing] at a profound sense of loss and testify[ing] to the powerful hold of ancient sites.'' But the old problems had only been compounded, as Saponis and Cheraws, members of the Catawba Nation, found in 1732 when they received Virginia's permission to resettle on a river in their homeland. They were soon scattered by the hostilities visited on them by both colonists and raiding Nottoway and Iroquois warriors.

In the midst of English America, the remaining Indians lived precariously. The Ockehocking Lenape Indians of Pennsylvania retained liberty of movement on the five-hundred-acre remnant of a previous grant, but without holding a clear land title, they justifiably voiced "great uneasiness at the uncertainty of their Settlem'ts.'' The resurrected Pequots of Connecticut, allowed a seventeen-hundred-acre rock-filled reservation, labored mightily in the manner advocated by colonists, clearing the land, planting crops and fruit trees, and stringing fences across the hills.

Their labor earned the covetousness of their farming neighbors and a nightmare of harassment. The colonists "Removed a great part of our Gennerrell field fence to arrect their own fense,'' the Pequots complained to Connecticut's governor in the 1730s. Immigrants' livestock trampled Indian corn; immigrants' hogs had the run of Indian orchards. If the Pequots protested, the owners "Thretten us . . . to beat our Brains out'' and "cut our Stoaks [stalks] some time when Corn is in the milk.'' When the neighboring farmers started building houses on Pequot land and planting crops, it became all too apparent that "there Chiefest desire is to Deprive us of the Priviledg of our Land and drive us off to our utter ruin.''

The Nanticokes of Maryland faced similar problems, as interlopers burned down their seasonal hunting cabins, claiming that the land "appeared . . . deserted and abandoned'' and therefore should revert to the colony. Most of the Nanticokes joined a gradual and reluctant migration to Canada, while the remnants of various Maryland Indian groups stayed put and petitioned the governor for action to correct their "Pitiful Situation and Condition.''

Those holding on to small tracts of eastern lands split over whether to rent land and timber rights to outsiders. Such deals were fraught with uncertainties—would the natives receive only a pittance for valuable resources, or perhaps nothing at all, the renter simply refusing to pay? Colonial governments sought to safeguard Indians in their jurisdictions, but also to control them. "Discreet persons" were appointed from among the whites "to have the inspection and more particular care and government of the Indians in their respective plantations," as the reserved lands were often called. These "discreet persons"—the forerunners of nineteenth-century Indian agents—varied in their abilities, their sympathies, their ethics, and their influence.

Meanwhile, land conflicts between native and immigrant continued to flare along the moving English frontier. Representatives of British colonization followed the rivers inland along the southern Atlantic coast, penetrating the pine-forested homelands of the Tuscaroras, Catawbas, and Yamasees, moving along the river bottoms shaded by red gum and cypress trees. The colonizers pressed onward into the southern woodlands, into the regions inhabited by Cherokees, Creeks, and Chickasaws.

The English also spread outward from the mid-Atlantic coast to the Appalachians. In New England, they thrust into the lands of the Iroquois Confederacy among the mountains, forests, and streams of present-day upstate New York, and entered the fir and spruce fastnesses of northern New England where the northern Abenakis and their neighbors lived.

Like the "subdued" tribes, these natives already had experienced some of the changes wrought by European incursions: disease, trade, and shifting power alliances. They reacted with dismay and determination to the English advances. Abenakis vowed to "not cede one single inch of the lands we inhabit beyond what has been decided formerly by our fathers" and forbade transgressors "to kill a single beaver, or to take a single stick of timber on the lands we inhabit."

The hard-pressed groups had absorbed—and continued to absorb—a variety of captives and refugees from the conflicts among the English, the French, and the Indian nations. Adopting members from other native groups was an ancient practice—again, precontact Indian communities had a fluidity that the word "tribe" does not convey. But now Indian groups were reconfiguring in response to new pressures.

The Iroquois, buttressed by European weapons, had created refugees among Indian peoples farther to the west, having forced a variety of Algonquians, among them the Fox, Sauks, Potawatomis, and Ottawas, into Winnebago and Menominee lands. Now, struggling to hold on to trade and political advantages in their strategic crossroads location between the Genesee and Mohawk river valleys, the Iroquois sought captives and refugees among the vanquished and among the Indians and Europeans to the east. The Senecas of the Iroquois Confederacy "adopted whole villages of Hurons after the breakup of the Huron 'nation' under Iroquois attack," while Iroquois Confederacy members contested for the Susquehannocks, driven westward by the British in Maryland and Virginia.

Populations thinned by disease and rendered politically and economically vulnerable needed to claim as many members as possible. While this strained a tribe's shrinking resources, it was fairly easily accomplished when a western or northern branch of a tribe took in cousins from another location. For instance, Abenakis temporarily beyond the path of New England settlement sheltered their southern countrymen and women, thereby recouping losses incurred through disease and war.

The grafting was more of a problem when refugees or captives came from a different cultural, political, and social environment. The Iroquois used ritual humiliation and torture, followed by lavish generosity and affection, to break down and replace their captives' old identities, but—just as with subsequent white efforts to "assimilate" the Indian—the eradication was never complete. People compelled to change by force remained distinctive individuals or subgroups within the "host" culture.

Still, by taking in other natives—and English captives, some of whom chose to remain among the Indians—extended and interrelated Indian groups were showing creative adaptability and building their identity as tribes, as political and cultural units to be recognized by the invaders. In many cases, remnants of various distinct groups coalesced to form a new identity, as did various Virginia and Carolina natives who became the Catawbas. In all such cases of intermingling, people struggled to draw strength from diversity, while loyalties within the new tribal unit shifted along with changing political, economic, and social conditions.

Meanwhile, trade continued to alter and undermine native life. By the 1700s, some trans-Appalachian bands were relocating to be close to European traders. From the southern homelands of the Creeks to the French forts dotting the trans-Appalachian northwest, Indian dependence on European trade goods grew as the one clear and uncontested native role in the developing economy—hunting—declined. Natives had less with which to bargain for goods, and while they might be able to do without European fabric or cooking pots, they often had to have European weaponry in order to keep from being overrun by other, well-armed tribes.

The traders—British, French, and Spanish—all sought to bind the natives to them, encouraging them to forget the old ways of subsisting, to look to the traders for repair or replacement of often shoddy merchandise, even to develop a taste for the liquor that sapped strength and resources from Indian communities.

These communities often fought back against the liquor trade. For example, Shawnees in Pennsylvania in the 1730s tried to limit the number of rum kegs that traders could bring into their community, then "staved and spilled all the liquor in their town . . . about forty gallons thrown into the streets" and vowed "to leave off drinking for four years."

Epidemics could not be combated so directly. In 1759, a smallpox outbreak swept the Catawba Nation of Carolina, killing as many as six out of ten. There were understandable suspicions among afflicted Indians that the invaders used disease as a weapon against them. In some cases, at least, these suspicions were justified. In possibly the most notorious case, the arrogant British general Jeffrey Amherst hatched a plan in 1763 with a willing subordinate to spread smallpox among resistant Pennsylvania Indians by distributing disease-infected blankets.

The extent to which Anglos purposely infected or tried to infect Indians is still a matter of some debate. It should be noted that as smallpox vaccines became increasingly available after their discovery in 1796, white officials responded by initiating inoculation efforts among the native population.

Others would undoubtedly have been only too happy to infect the Indians they encountered—an 1852 San Francisco resident would tell an official that "it would be a good thing to introduce the smallpox" among California Indians. But such an effort would have been a hit-or-miss proposition. Europeans had no great knowledge of the intricacies of disease transmission. Still, they could hardly have mounted a more effective viral warfare than that which occurred.

Wars, too, continued to batter and scatter Indian peoples. Tribes used European weaponry to best each other, either in an escalation of previous rivalries or as a means of gaining and maintaining power in a sea of shifting alliances, tribal and European. Many tribal clashes were brutal, the Iroquois practicing such cruelties as impaling captive Indian children on stakes for their pursuing relatives and community members to find. Increasingly, however, extreme violence erupted as a result of tensions between natives and settlers unable or unwilling to see Indian hostility as anything more than "some ingrained cultural belligerence."

The Tuscaroras, abysmally treated by North Carolina traders and settlers, ignited into violence against settlers when a Swedish immigrant group seized a land tract from them in 1711. The Tuscaroras fought back and forth with North and South Carolina militias, who were aided by Yamasees and other Indians, until Tuscarora power was broken in 1713. Colonists sold most of the Tuscaroras into slavery; some escaped to Iroquois territory, where they became the Sixth Nation of the confederacy.

The colonists' allies, the Yamasees, meanwhile became increasingly embittered by their own exploitation. Immigrants raped Indian women while their men were pressed into colonial service; they also killed the Yamasees' hogs and chickens and helped themselves to Indian corn, watermelon, and peas. The Yamasees retaliated with raids in 1715, forcing much of South Carolina's colonial population into Charleston. South Carolina's militia almost annihilated the Yamasees. Survivors found refuge in Spanish Florida, where the Spanish mission effort had foundered and where native groups—the Timucuans, the Apalachees, the Calusas, the Tocobagas—had virtually died out or been dispersed.

The results of these two wars were already numbingly predictable: "practically all the territory in the Carolinas east of the Appalachians was open to white settlement."

Yet other Indian groups—and new tribal combinations—just beyond the English frontier held fiercely to their land bases and to their political independence. A Jesuit missionary explained, "There is not one savage Tribe that will patiently endure to be regarded as under subjugation to any power whatsoever; it will perhaps call itself an ally, but nothing more." The governor of Canada, accused of inciting the Abenakis of Vermont against the English, would protest that the Abenakis had informed him they would make war upon the British whether he was involved or not, as they were doing it "not for him . . . but for themselves."

As long as various powers contended for control of American territory, native nations could pick their friends and foes and could survive by balancing contending groups against each other. The Creeks, for example, "by 1700 . . . were in direct and frequent contact [and trade] with the Spanish in Florida, the French in Louisiana, and the British in Carolina." Over the next six decades, despite the advent of English colonists, they managed to maintain a careful neutrality, which "[kept] their European neighbors at arm's length" while solidifying their own power over other southeastern tribal nations. Of the Algonquian groups of the Ohio River Valley and Great Lakes, one Frenchman wrote in 1750 that it was clearly to their advantage that "the strength of the British and the French remain nearly equal, so that through the jealousy of these two nations, those tribes may live independent of, and draw presents from, both."

Yet behind every interaction with the English, their settler population burgeoning with aggressively independent Scotch-Irish frontier families, was the threat of loss of land and sovereignty. When Ohio River Indians in a 1750s dispute with the French looked to aid from British Virginia, they found "the Virginians were more interested in obtaining title to the Ohio country than in helping [them] defend it against the French."

In particular, the Indians to the west of British settlement loudly protested the appearance of English forts in native territory. The Indians rightly surmised that the forts presaged an English occupation; even the Oneidas who had embraced Christianity "demanded that these forts be pull'd down, & kick'd out of the way." The Abenakis of Vermont in midcentury warned the British against trying to establish a presence in a portion of Abenaki territory not then in use, and backed up the successful warning with the reminder that they were allied with other tribes and with the French. At the same time, they refused the French permission to erect a trading post in their hunting grounds. Later, when the British and Americans tried to claim Indian lands, natives would remind them that they had acknowledged these lands as Indian by their requests to place forts upon them.

Increasingly, British officials and colonists claimed that lands had been ceded to them because they had obtained the agreement of one native or group of natives. Indians argued that these people had no power to speak or bargain for them, and indeed, often the bargainers had little or no connection with the natives affected. Particularly galling to the Algonquian tribes of the Ohio River Valley was the apparent Iroquois cession of their lands to the British in 1744 and 1754, the Iroquois claiming to have won the lands through conquest.

Even if an Indian ceding land was from the group that occupied it, of course it did not follow that he could or did act on behalf of that group; as Mohawk leaders would protest of a land cession, the signers "had as good a right to sell as they have to come and dispose of the city of New York." Whites early learned to find a male native willing to bargain, whatever his status or lack thereof, and then press their claims by insisting on his imaginary authority.

In a situation aggravating to or beyond the comprehension of the impatient newcomers, even a genuine Indian leader usually had little more bargaining power than the average tribal member, since native tribal structures seldom centered on one strong political figure able to command the populace. "Brethren, you know that we have no forcing rules or laws among us," one Mohawk had explained in the late 1600s.

In land negotiations, the warriors often stepped to the forefront. "Now, Brother," the Iroquois Scarooyady warned Virginians in 1753, "I let you know that our Kings hav[e] nothing to do with our Lands; for We, the Warriors, fought for the Lands & so the right belongs to us, & we will take C   of them."

Some tribes, ca   e middle of complex competing interests, were able to   their usefulness to the British as a buffer between th   s and a hostile French or Indian presence; unlike th   d Virginia groups and the Schaghticokes, they w   position of land ownership and independence.

          tered their subsistence strategies to maintain as much free-   possible, despite diminishing land bases. The western Abenakis continued their old lifeways by shifting their movements and periodically returning to their old home areas. The Catawbas, pressed westward by colonists, continued to range freely through their western territory and successfully adjusted their hunting patterns to changes and reductions in their territory.

Still, the influx of settlers required a larger adaptation. For one thing, the newcomers continued to sabotage native lifeways by their very presence. The Iroquois Cannesatego showed how tenuous their survival on homelands had become by telling British treaty makers that he could give them very few skins in token of an agreement reached: "We are ashamed to offer our Brethren so few, but your Horses and Cows have eaten the Grass our Deer used to feed on . . . we are really poor."

Strategies for survival necessarily changed over time. "Almost surrounded" by colonists by 1755, the Catawbas demanded and got a measurement of their remaining lands and used it both to keep squatters out and to make rental arrangements with settlers. Although the Catawbas would have preferred to keep the land to themselves, they carved out a niche as "landlords upon whom hundreds of men and women depended."

They maintained their own law and order on the reservation, and asked for training and schooling for their children—not to adopt European lifeways so much as to have the skills to remain independent. They altered their lifestyle in some ways but not in others, living in log cabins but arranging them as they had their bark homes, continuing to wear nose rings, continuing—despite the cabins—to move about seasonally. They were confident enough of having their rights protected that when an Indian agent attempted to foist poor beef upon them, the Catawba chief Nopkehe "tuck [a sample] tide to his Sadle all the way to Salsbury [North Carolina] Cort, and tould the Cort [the agent] gave him nothing but Stallion Cows and Charged the Contery a great price."

Colonial governments, at various times and in various places, did try to respond fairly to Indian concerns. Sometimes this was out of political necessity, as when the British government, embroiled with the French in the struggle for empire, decided to take a more conciliatory approach to the Ohio Valley tribes, and in 1756 induced Pennsylvania officials to stop pressing questionable land claims wrung from the Iroquois. By the same token, Georgia colonial leader James Oglethorpe probably argued for Creek rights to lands not then being used by them in order to keep the Creeks from allying with the Spanish.

In other cases, officials simply sought to do an increasingly difficult job in safeguarding Indian land rights. This included safeguarding those rights from other Indians, as shown by a 1746 appeal to the Rhode Island General Assembly. The Narragansetts had been placed on a reservation in 1709; now some of the tribal members were renting fertile croplands to colonists, "without the knowledge and consent of the sachem's [chief's] widow and the tribal council." The General Assembly stopped the practice and also heeded native appeals to halt individual sale of tribal land.

There was always the danger that one or more tribal members would undermine the security of all the rest. Alcohol in particular continued to contribute a frightening uncertainty and decay to Indian cultures. The British government could not halt its sale, and traders and frontier settlers alike used it to further disorient and dishearten Indians who might be induced to do anything for the temporary escape the liquor provided.

The Catawbas complained mightily about the effects of alcohol on their young men; knowledge both of its effects and of other coercive measures of the English probably fed the Catawbas' attempt to get laws passed prohibiting the sale of reservation land "even with their own consent."

The biggest threat to the security of Indian lands in the mid-1700s, however, was not corn whiskey or even the designs of the British government. Instead, the escalation of what are known as the French and Indian wars was altering the balance of European power in North America, with devastating consequences for the natives, and British colonists were ignoring their own government's edicts in their quest for land.

The French and Indian wars, the long struggle between the British and French in North America, culminated as part of the Seven Years' War (1756–1763) raging in Europe. The two powers clashed along the St. Lawrence River, in the western New York lands of the Iroquois, and across the Alleghenies in western Pennsylvania, the British advancing into the Ohio River country, long a stronghold for French trade interests.

Between 1760 and 1763, as the British established their own forts west of the Appalachians and Alleghenies, the Algonquian tribes of the Ohio River Valley and the Great Lakes sought to deal with the troublesome intrusion in various ways. They could not muster an allied resistance, or even refrain from bitter intertribal fighting—Miami against Shawnee, Sauk against Illinois. Many did fight as independent allies on the side of the French, either because they preferred the French presence or because they wanted both the French and British off their lands and considered the latter the more potent threat. The Delawares had already been pushed westward by the English; one named Ackowanothic observed that the French could be "drive[n] away . . . when we please," unlike the English, who were "such a numerous people."

Some negotiated with the British in hopes that an alliance would garner a British promise to "draw back over the mountain" after the war. The tribes were uneasy about the outcome: "Why don't you and the French fight in the old Country, and on the Sea? Why do you come to fight on our Land?" the Delawares asked the British representatives, concluding, "This makes every Body believe you want to take the Land from us, by force and settle it."

Christian missionaries had been active among the Algonquians; like Indians elsewhere, the besieged natives had sought to add Christian teachings to or incorporate them with their own understandings of the spirit world. Delaware prophet Neolin, infusing his traditional message with the Christian influence of Quaker and Moravian missionaries, had been preaching a return to the "Good Road," arguing that God intended natives to follow a different path from that of the invaders. He offered a picture of a God offended at the Indians' overhunting, drinking, and other European-influenced departures from the Good Road.

The Ottawa leader Pontiac picked up this generalized call for moral reform and directed its message against the British. In "Pontiac's Rebellion" of 1763, Algonquians from a dozen or more tribes attacked British forts and settlers, trying to eradicate this unwelcome presence. They extracted a bloody toll, but failed to stop the occupation.

Actually, the British government itself was seeking to draw a vertical western border of settlement from the Great Lakes, down the Appalachians, and southward to the Gulf of Mexico, in large part as a means of gaining some control over the colonists in their contacts with the natives. Meanwhile, the English and other immigrants along the East Coast now numbered close to 1,300,000; immigrants were probing ever deeper into the eastern forests and over the crest of the Appalachians. In Georgia, colonists had ignored Governor Oglethorpe's defense of Indian land rights and were busily appropriating Creek lands, despite the fact that the Creeks had carefully granted them only the use of certain areas. At Fort Pitt, where the Ohio, Monongahela, and Allegheny rivers came together, Colonel Henry Boquet in 1761 had issued an edict against immigrant squatters west of the Alleghenies, then found the edict challenged by the lieutenant governor of Virginia. Perplexed, Boquet worried that "he did not know which he was supposed to 'oppress,' the settlers or the Indians."

As Boquet struggled to fulfill his role, England, France, and Spain lurched toward diplomatic decisions that would eventually affect all inhabitants of North America.

In the early 1700s, Spain's power in the Southeast and Southwest was fading. Spain had built a southwestern empire on the *encomienda* system, in which favored Spanish subjects received the right to tribute from Indian laborers, although not outright possession of their land. The excessive and unjust labor demands, however, whether from friars or from *encomienda* holders as government-sanctioned officials, had led to Indian revolts, including the stunning Pueblo Revolt of 1680 that drove the Spanish out of much of the Southwest for thirteen years. After the Spanish returned, some Pueblo Indians chose to leave their ancestral homes "rather than continue to submit to Spanish rule."

Meanwhile, the French began making serious inroads on Spain's northern frontier, establishing themselves on the Gulf Coast at the mouth of the Mississippi River, founding New Orleans, and claiming as "Louisiana" an inland empire surrounding the great river. Further, they outdid the Spanish in trade with the Indians west of their southern Mississippi River base, cultivating trading lines that stretched onto the Great Plains. At the same time, the English in Carolina were encroaching into the Southeast, building a trading alliance with the southern Indians.

Hamstrung by its own shortsighted trade policies and an "eroding economic status," Spain couldn't compete with the British and French traders. Then the French found themselves harried in their Seven Years' War with England. In 1762, they ceded to Spain, their ally in the war, all of Louisiana west of the Mississippi River.

When France, Spain, and England finally met at the bargaining table in Paris in 1763, Indian claims to North America were ignored. Spain passed to England its claims to Florida in exchange for the return of Havana (seized by the British in 1762) but held on to the French-ceded New Orleans and western "Louisiana," the great swath of forests, prairies, and plains stretching from the Mississippi to the Rocky Mountains. France signed away to England all of Canada as well as the vast region west of the Appalachians and east of the Mississippi River.

Eyeing its new western lands, the British government wanted to keep its trans-Appalachian military posts but prevent uncontrolled settlement from spilling over the mountains. The Proclamation of 1763 drew a tentative boundary line along the Appalachians' crests: immigrant settlements to the east, native communities and lands to the west. Yet the Shawnees and other natives already had come upon enough clearings and cabins and aggressive immigrants to know, probably better than the government itself, that no imaginary line would protect them from invasion.

Chapter Two

←———→

"Nothing Will Satisfy Them but the Whole of Our Hunting Grounds"
(1764–1816)

> At first, [the white men] only asked for land sufficient for a wigwam; now, nothing will satisfy them but the whole of our hunting grounds, from the rising to the setting sun.
> —*Shawnee leader Tecumseh, 1810 or 1811*

> The United States sought expansion with honor. But above all it sought expansion.
> —*Historian Peter Iverson*

In 1793, with officials of the new American republic pressuring them to take money for lands already overrun by white immigrants, Algonquian-speaking native groups of the Ohio River Valley countered with an alternative. Their people, they noted, found money worthless and would not sell their homes for any price. On the other hand, the settlers obviously were poor "or they would never have ventured to live in a country which has been in continual trouble ever since they crossed the Ohio."

Couldn't the government, then, bestow the money earmarked for the Indians upon the settlers as inducement to leave? Native leaders suggested that the government add to the amount the annual payments it had promised to them. "If you add also, the great sums you must spend in raising and paying armies with a view to force us to yield our country," they reasoned, "you will certainly have more [than]

MAINE
(CLAIMED BY MASS.)

NEW HAMPSHIRE
MASSACHUSETTS

NEW
YORK

RHODE ISLAND
CONNECTICUT

PENNSYLVANIA
NEW JERSEY
DELAWARE
MARYLAND

VIRGINIA

Atlantic

NORTH
CAROLINA

Ocean

SOUTH
CAROLINA

INDIAN COUNTRY

LOUISIANA

GEORGIA

WEST FLORIDA

BRITISH TERRITORY

INDIAN TERRITORY

SPANISH TERRITORY

PROCLAMATION LINE
OF 1763

Gulf of Mexico

EAST
FLORIDA

The Proclamation Line of 1763

sufficient for the purpose of repaying these settlers for all their labor and improvements.''

As far as most whites were concerned, the Indians might as well have asked the government to reverse the sun's course through the heavens. The population of the nascent United States would swell by a third between 1790 and 1800 alone. During the period 1764–1817, first the British, then the American government achieved very little control over the burgeoning stream of immigrants.

Further, whatever the government did do became increasingly tied to the interests of immigrants and land speculators. In the space of fifty years, virtually every Indian tribe remaining east of the Mississippi would confront the threat of dispossession, while the tribes beyond would find their world eroding as well.

In the wake of the Proclamation of 1763, the British government tried to maintain an Appalachian boundary line. Northern and southern superintendents of Indian affairs were appointed to regulate land and other issues. Troops were dispatched into Indian country to evict squatters and burn their cabins. But in a typical incident involving the destruction of two illegal settlements, an observer reported that within months the cabins had been rebuilt, with ''double the Number of Inhabitants . . . that ever was before.''

Besides, government officials had their own long-term plans to maintain and extend military outposts beyond the mountains, even to create settlements at the outposts. Natives recognized that, whatever white officials said, forts meant Anglo expansion. ''When a fort appears,'' declared the Shawnee Cornstalk, ''you may depend upon it there will soon be towns and settlements of white men.''

Within the thirteen colonies, the makers and enforcers of laws tended to ignore or encourage the immigrants' seizure of Indian land. Even when colonial officials tried to safeguard boundaries, the trespassers came, and natives found them ''a lawless sett'' who had clearly slipped the restraints of ''their wise People.'' If the immigrants refused to recognize British law, they were certainly unlikely to recognize or respect Indian land claims and sovereignty.

Westering immigrants were not insensible to the grievances behind the Indian hostilities. James Harrod, leader of the first colonization into Kentucky in 1774, shot and stabbed an Indian to death in a melee between natives and woodcutting settlers. His wife reported Harrod "distressed . . . wish[ing] never to kill another of the poor natives, who were defending their fatherland." But the incident did not sway Harrod from his own frontier endeavors, and many of his fellow immigrants demonstrated a callous and often violent contempt for the natives, regarding them indiscriminately as "barbarians" and "savages."

Adding to the enmity, immigrant and native clearly were competing for the same resources. In the Ohio Valley, for example, both groups combined farming, grazing practices, and hunting in order to survive. As the settlers extended and adapted their hunting routines, the Delawares, who had already been pushed westward, responded defiantly: "The Elks are our horses, the buffaloes are our cows, the deer are our sheep, & the whites shan't have them."

The Delawares and other tribes reacted with consternation as the English extended their occupation of the "middle ground," long amicably shared with the French, between the Ohio and Mississippi rivers. Natives now regularly came upon and had to detour around burgeoning settlements and heavily garrisoned forts where they had lately camped, hunted, and moved freely.

Shawnee war leader Charlot Kaske complained, "The English come and say that the land is theirs and that the French have sold it to them. You know well our fathers have always told us that the land was ours." Even beyond the Mississippi, a British military and trading presence was growing, leading the Osages to announce, "We only want to have the French among us." The lands belonged to the Osages, they declared, by virtue of inheritance from ancestors. "Leave, depart, depart, depart," they instructed the British, "and tell your chief that all the red men do not want any English here . . . leave and do not come back anymore."

One particularly troubling development for the tribes was the unrestrained flow of liquor that accompanied British expansion. "Rum will kill us," the Shawnees and Onondagas told a visitor, "and leave the land clear for the Europeans without strife or purchase."

Young Indian men stole to support their drinking habit. They gave up the hunt—or hunted indiscriminately in order to exchange hides for alcohol. They ignored the counsel of their elders. Some became liquor traders themselves, as ruinously grasping to their people as the Anglo rum dealers. Young women entered the trade by selling their sexual favors for rum, then "carr[ying] it to Indian men to whom they sold it at high prices."

As the Algonquian groups in the Ohio River Valley and surrounding the Great Lakes tried to deal with such disruptive developments, they were trapped in the bargaining between the British and the fading Iroquois Confederacy. British authorities remained all too eager to accept Iroquois claims of having conquered and appropriated the lands of tribes to the west; the Iroquois were all too ready to seize what bargaining power they could.

In 1768, various Algonquian and Iroquoian representatives met at Fort Stanwix with British officials in order to sort out land matters and to follow up on the Proclamation of 1763 by setting a new "permanent" boundary west of the original line. British authorities afforded the Iroquois a central negotiating role, and the Iroquois spokesmen gave up not only what the negotiators had first sought, but a vast portion of Shawnee and Cherokee territories desired by speculators, although the latter had never by any measure been a part of the Iroquois empire.

Even the Iroquois were aghast at the concessions. "When our chiefs returned from the treaty at Fort Stanwix," the Seneca Cornplanter noted to British officials, "our nation was surprised to hear how great a country you had compelled them to give up to you, without your paying to us any thing for it. . . . We asked each other, 'What have we done to deserve such chastisement?' "

Settlers and speculators, government-sanctioned and unsanctioned, quickly erased even the boundaries outlined in the Treaty of Fort Stanwix. The natives of two massive regions, the one that became known as the "Old Northwest"—Ohio, Indiana, Illinois, Michigan, Wisconsin, and northeastern Minnesota—and the one we know today as the American South, found their position in relation to the invaders increasingly tenuous. As American colonists struggled to win independence from the "mother country," these native Americans, from the Potawatomis of the Great Lakes to the Choctaws whose villages stretched to the Gulf of Mexico, struggled to maintain their own political independence and to hold on to their own "mother country."

*   *   *

Resistance in the period between the Treaty of Paris and the American Revolution came primarily from the Shawnees and Cherokees, adjoining tribes in the immediate path of colonial expansion from Virginia, the Carolinas, and Georgia. The Shawnees protested Iroquois claims to their lands, but they found the Pennsylvania colonial government, the British government, and the encroaching settlers all turning a deaf ear. Many natives decided to remove westward rather than become "hemmed in on all sides by the White people, and then be at their mercy."

The era of forced removal had not arrived; westering Shawnees chose the survival strategy that seemed best to them. Yet obviously such a partial migration fragmented tribes, and weakened any political and economic strength the remaining members might have. Soon Virginia Governor Lord Dunmore started parceling out Shawnee land as bonuses to men who had fought under him in the French and Indian wars. The Shawnees who had remained responded by attacking immigrants and by besting a volunteer force sent to subdue them. But the resistance faltered when the Iroquois rejected a plea for assistance, and Virginian colonists in 1774 forced the Shawnees to move northward, relinquishing what would become Kentucky.

Meanwhile, the Cherokees, who inhabited the southern Appalachian mountain region, were entangled in "almost constant warfare with the colonists on their lands." Cherokee leader Old Tassel told South Carolina's governor, "We have no place to hunt on. Your people have built houses within one day's walk of our towns." He—or the interpreter or scribe—outlined the situation by mixing pained pleading to "our elder brother" (the form of address reflecting the immigrants' growing dominance) with unquenched assertiveness: "We don't want to quarrel . . . we therefore hope our elder brother will not take our lands from us, that the Great Man above gave us. . . . We are the first people that ever lived on this land; it is ours."

With the tensions between the colonists and the British government mounting, the Cherokees and the other threatened tribes again gained some bargaining power as potential allies or neutral military powers. Yet the extended American Revolution (1775–1783) would further undermine the lives and fortunes of the native peoples in the path of settlement.

*   *   *

In the Revolution most Indians sided with the British, first because the British government seemed to offer more stability and recognition of native claims than did the expansion-minded and often hostile colonists, second because the British did woo Indian allies while the colonists generally were content to press for Indian neutrality.

In the Northeast, the Old Northwest, and the South, the British developed Indian fighting forces. Members of the Iroquois Confederacy—Cayugas, Mohawks, Onondagas, and Senecas—bloodied the New York and Pennsylvania frontiers to the point that George Washington had to move a large force westward. In the Old Northwest, the British deployed Indian armies from their Detroit headquarters. Shawnees, Delawares, and other Algonquian tribes effectively harried Kentucky and western Pennsylvania, sparking a counteroffensive by George Rogers Clark. In the South, the Cherokees, Chickasaws, and Creeks—many formerly trade and military allies of the Carolinians— forced southern militias into action by harassing the western reaches of Virginia, the Carolinas, and Georgia using arms provided by British agents in Florida.

There has been speculation that the British could have won the war if they had "take[n] full advantage of their numerous and powerful Indian allies," better organizing and equipping them and giving greater support and authority to effective Indian military leaders. Instead, they involved Indian fighting forces and then, "with more warriors engaged in the British cause than ever before and with those warriors inflicting costly defeats on the Americans," the British capitulated, leaving their allies high and dry. Suddenly, the redcoats were relinquishing land claims to the American rebels, leading one Wea Indian to offer a sad assessment recorded in elegant English diction: "In endeavouring to assist you it seems we have wrought our own ruin."

During the war, Indian groups had demonstrated that they could live without American trade goods; the Piankashaws returned to bows and arrows for hunting, Wabash villagers clothed themselves in buffalo skins. But both during and after the Revolution, Indians paid a high price for their involvement. Some tribes and confederacies had split in their allegiances, chief among them the Iroquois. While the other four nations within the confederacy had taken up the British cause, the Oneidas and Tuscaroras had sided with the colonists. In a grim scenario that would be repeated by other tribes later, during the American Civil War, Iroquois fought Iroquois, razing neighbors' villages.

More unified groups faced devastation as well, as colonial troops invaded Indian communities, killing residents, burning or tearing down houses, and ruining crops waiting to be harvested. Colonists used the war as an excuse to take more Indian land. For example, Cherokee engagement in the Revolution had waned by 1780, but Carolina militiamen continued to invade and destroy native villages, trying to force further land cessions. George Rogers Clark, responding to Indian raids in Kentucky, mounted a campaign against the Shawnees of Illinois, even though their participation in the raiding has been judged minimal. By forcing these Shawnees into Indiana, Clark simply took advantage of "an opportunity to detach a huge chunk of territory and people from the British empire and open up the way to Detroit." Individual immigrants and groups also used escape from the war as an excuse to move westward and appropriate Indian lands.

Some Indians fared well at war's end. The British provided limited land grants in Canada for Iroquois allies. The Stockbridge Indians of Massachusetts as colonial allies were rewarded with New England land grants, although not the ones they requested. South Carolinians acknowledged the sacrifice of the Catawbas, who had paid for their allegiance to the revolutionary cause by losing their homes to British soldiers' torches. This acknowledgment could take indirect forms; when the governor in 1785 began talking about having the state rent the Catawba reservation and using the money to "civilize" them, the legislature, "noting that the Indians had not requested any such favors, refused to go along."

Nonetheless, the framers and citizens of the new republic had little interest in recognizing Indian wartime allegiance or in affording them a place in the republic. The fledgling American government had during the war established an Indian Department with northern, middle, and southern branches. It also followed the lead of the British and colonial governments by outlawing land deals between Indians and colonists, and began making treaties with tribes, the first an agreement with the already uprooted Delawares to allow troops to pass through the Ohio Valley region in which they now lived.

However, as historian White has aptly noted, immigrant hatred of Indians "controlled backcountry attitudes and eventually American policy during and immediately after the Revolution." This meant that Indian land claims were often ignored or peremptorily dismissed, and some natives now found themselves caught in the consequences of a previous removal. The Savannah River Chickasaws had moved to their river location when Charleston officials wanted to use them as a frontier buffer. They stayed for more than half a century, but when immigrants wanted the land, the Chickasaws couldn't claim it as ancestral homeland. After they backed the British in the Revolution, the South Carolina legislature judged "there was no evidence that they had ever been anything more than tenants at will of the colony."

The western Abenakis of northern Vermont, who had split in their allegiances during the Revolution, had strong ancestral claims to the land, but now "often had to sit by" while the Iroquois insisted to American officials that the Vermont homelands belonged to them. The Iroquois did not succeed, but at least they were recognized and heard; the Abenakis had no political standing whatsoever. Many followed friends and relatives to Canada. Those who stayed in Vermont "found themselves . . . relegated to the status of unwelcome wanderers in their own country."

The "unwelcome wanderers" across the eastern regions survived by retreating to isolated areas—"a swamp, a hollow, an inaccessible ridge . . . the backcountry of a sandy flatwoods." Their contemporaries who had held on to identifiable eastern reservations remained more visible and more exposed; those who had enjoyed some autonomy became increasingly vulnerable to and dependent upon the dominant culture as represented by traders, settlers, government officials, and missionaries.

In response to the proselytizing missionaries, the Seneca Red Jacket noted in 1792, "We have scarcely a place left to spread our blankets. You have got our country, but you are not satisfied. You want to force your religion upon us." He suggested that his people be allowed to wait and see what impact recently arrived preachers would have on the natives' white neighbors: "If we find it does them good and makes them honest and less disposed to cheat Indians, we will then consider again what you have said."

The rapacious among their neighbors were so far from demonstrating Christian virtues that some natives actively sought the appointment of Indian agents as a form of protection. The Seneca Cornplanter in 1790 asked Pennsylvania officials that his interpreter, Joseph Nicholson, be designated "to take care of me and my people" in the light of "repeated robberies . . . murders and depredations committed by the whites against us."

But with Indian agents "be[coming] an institutionalized part of the federal bureaucracy in the 1790s," the potential was increasing for ignorant or grasping bureaucratic appointees to take power over native lives. The Catawbas of South Carolina lost to the state governor their right to select their own agent, and soon had one who cheated them out of their rights to a valuable fishing site.

For an honest and conscientious man, the job of Indian agent was one of the most difficult the government had to offer. Natives regarded him with suspicion and wariness—or with great and desperate expectation—while anything he did in their defense, or simply out of a sense of responsibility or solicitude, raised the ire of neighboring whites and failed to combat government bungling and indifference.

Whatever the agent's efforts, both the government and the surrounding culture, with its celebration of individualism and economic gain, put tremendous pressure on eastern reservation Indians to give up their communal identity, foreshadowing the allotment policies of a century later. Nowhere is this reflected more poignantly than in a 1789 petition by the Mohegan Indians to the Assembly of Connecticut: with "Hearts full of Sorrow and Grief," they noted that "one Dish and One Fire will not do any longer for us—Some few there are Stronger than others and they will keep off the poor, weake, the halt and the Blind. And Will take the Dish to themselves." Therefore, they asked "That our Dish of Suckuttush may be equally divided amongst us, that every one may have his own little dish by himself, that he may eat Quietly and do With his Dish as he pleases; and let every one have his own Fire."

The tribes of the Old Northwest and the South continued to struggle against such a fate. In 1783, the fledgling United States claimed all the land east of the Mississippi River—847,000 square miles. With colonial charters stretching all the way to the great river—for example, making Kentucky and the land to the west part of Virginia—the federal government in the 1780s was obtaining cessions of western lands from the states and setting up a process for bringing these lands into the union as territories and, eventually, as states.

Despite the new nation's claims and plans, federal and state officials remained under some pressure to acknowledge Indian land rights, with Europeans and American citizens vocally challenging the rationalizations used to take native lands. Besides, the republic did not yet have the military power to force the breakup or removal of many of the trans-Appalachian tribes, and Indian warriors were using the obvious American designs on native territory to spur their more peaceable fellows into resistance.

American officials countered with a "new stance as seekers of peace and reconciliation rather than as conquerors." The Indians of the trans-Appalachians received various assurances, including one in the policy-establishing Northwest Ordinance of 1787: "their lands and property shall never be taken from them without their consent."

Officials confidently anticipated winning such consent, little recognizing or understanding that most Indians would never voluntarily relinquish their homelands. As the government bumped repeatedly against this truth, its policy became based on dividing and conquering and on asking for land until it could demand acreage. Meanwhile, settlers would continue to ignore boundary lines, occupying native ground and altering the environment in ways that rendered it unfit for traditional native life.

After the Revolution, the Old Northwest remained in a state of flux. Pushed westward, remnants of tribes that had once occupied the northeastern frontier of European America—groups such as the Iroquois and the Delawares—mixed with natives of the Great Lakes and Ohio River Valley as settlers continued pouring into the valley. Two years after the war, an estimated 2,200 immigrant families had disregarded posted warnings and had located in groups of a few dozen north of the Ohio River on acreage acknowledged by the government as Indian property.

For many of the Indians of the region, the war had never ended, especially since Britain continued to provide intermittent support for raids against the former colonists in hopes that the new republic would founder. Indeed, a large part of the young United States' federal budget went into attempts to overcome Indian resistance.

Yet, confusion and dissension sapped native villages of their strengths. Old patterns had broken down. In those groups maintaining a distinction between war leaders and peace leaders, the former had seized much of the latter's power (a common response to invasion). Neither "could restore political order . . . nor assert uncontested leadership." As Indians gave in to the continuing temptation to overhunt for trade purposes, and as immigrants extended their hunting, the game disappeared, forcing natives into livestock raising for subsistence. With the United States pressing for land cessions to legitimize and extend settler incursions, natives were divided over who could speak for them, what they should say, and how they should say it. To further complicate matters, as Indian bargaining power shrank, the potential grew for "puppet" leaders selected and controlled by white officials, who designated the whole region "Northwest Territory" in 1787.

Men known as "treaty chiefs" tried to walk the treacherously thin line between conciliation and submission. In 1788, Huron and Iroquois treaty chiefs met with United States officials at Fort Harmar at the mouth of the Muskingum River in present-day Ohio. They signed away more land and acknowledged previously disputed land cessions, but insisted that this was the final concession of Algonquian acreage.

The treaty chiefs satisfied neither the whites, who wanted more, nor many of their fellow Algonquians, who wanted to drive the invaders back rather than part with another foot of land. Resistance leadership now centered in the villages of the Delawares, Miamis, and Shawnees.

Together, Algonquian warriors from across the Northwest Territory deployed against settlers, surveyors, land speculators, volunteer militias, and the United States military. Under the Miami chief Little Turtle, in 1790 they trounced Brigadier General Josiah Harmer's combined militia and regular army force. The next year they achieved one of the most dramatic Indian victories in American history by defeating Revolutionary War veteran and Northwest Territory Governor Arthur St. Clair in a battle along the upper Wabash River. Twenty-one Indians were killed, while six hundred of St. Clair's fourteen-thousand-man force lost their lives, some after capture. The victors "stuffed the mouths of the [enemy] dead with soil—satisfying in death their lust for Indian land."

For a brief time after the Wabash victory, the Indians of the Old

Northwest felt that they had regained some of their bargaining power, and they drew support and hope from the British forts situated south of the Great Lakes, in defiance of England's end-of-Revolution treaty with the United States. American officials wearied them with treaties and talk of treaties, but the war leaders in ascendancy refused to countenance any boundaries besides those established in the 1768 Treaty of Fort Stanwix, in which all the lands west of the Ohio River remained in their possession.

The United States government sent General "Mad" Anthony Wayne, another Revolutionary War veteran, into the field against these "hostiles." They met in August 1794 near the present border of Ohio and Michigan at Fallen Timbers, a spot where a storm had uprooted trees and scattered debris. In the battle that ensued, Wayne surrounded and routed the Indians, who tried to flee to nearby Fort Miami, a British post. The garrison barricaded its doors against its Indian allies, fearing that the fort, too, would fall to the canny Wayne.

Few Indian defeats have been as searing as the one at Fallen Timbers. For more than three decades, the tribes of the Northwest Territory had been fighting first the British, then the U.S. invasion, and had endured the accompanying loss of their land and way of life. Shawnees and Delawares, Ottawas and Chippewas, Potawatomis and Kickapoos, Hurons and Miamis, greatly weakened and divided, now came to a treaty session with Wayne at Greenville, Ohio.

Leaders still argued against the government's movement of boundary lines, Little Turtle explaining that the U.S. line "cuts off from the Indians a large portion of country, which has been enjoyed by my forefathers [since] time immemorial," as evidenced by "the print of my ancesters' houses . . . everywhere to be seen in this portion." He and others also pointed out that they had been defending their lands from invasion and contested the idea that these lands had passed from the king of England to the United States.

But natives squabbled among themselves over who owned which portion of the territory and who might represent all. So demoralized were they that the Hurons, Delawares, and Shawnees "even asked Wayne to supervise the division of the lands among them."

The Treaty of Greenville stripped Indians of 25,000 square miles between the Ohio River and Lake Erie. Some of the native leaders who signed the document died mysteriously soon thereafter, leading to rumors that either the Americans or resistant Indians had poisoned them. If the latter, it would not be the last time a treaty chief was executed for relinquishing Indian land.

In the wake of the Treaty of Greenville, traders pumped thousands of gallons of liquor into the Indian communities closest to Anglo settlement; the result in the villages was alcoholic near-anarchy, with drunken despair and violence—often directed against the chiefs—spreading as inexorably as the most infectious virus.

Meanwhile, United States officials continued to lay plans for expansion, in 1800 splitting the Northwest Territory in two and calling the vast western block—homeland of the Piankashaws, Potawatomis, Weas, Sauks and Fox—"Indiana Territory." President John Adams appointed as governor of the new political region William Henry Harrison, a veteran of the battle of Fallen Timbers and former Northwest Territory delegate to the United States Congress.

Holding out the promise of "annuities"—annual payments of money and goods—Harrison effectively coerced the remaining treaty chiefs into land cessions totaling thirty-three million acres during a seven-year period. These dizzying losses culminated in the Treaty of Fort Wayne in 1809, more than two and half million acres passing hands for "less than two cents per acre" and a promise of small annuities.

Why did the Indian leaders assent to these land cessions at Greenville and Fort Wayne? For one thing, the power imbalance was already all too apparent, the whites possessing both more effective weapons of war and greater political unity. Many Indians had to conclude, as had the western Seneca war-chief-turned-treaty-chief Cornplanter, that "If we do not sell the land, the whites will take it anyway." Land claims among Indian groups themselves had become more confused and complex, and the natives knew whites would not examine too closely a willing seller's assertion of ownership. If a group refused to deal, it might find the land it claimed sold out from under it. This way, they could at least hold on to a small portion of their native country.

They did so because the land was important to them, but also because there seemed no place to go. As one Ohio Valley band had concluded, "We can retreat no further, because the country behind hardly affords food for its present inhabitants, and we have therefore resolved to leave our bones in this small space to which we are now confined."

Reflecting this relative powerlessness and lack of options, "treaty chiefs" had become "annuity chiefs," dependent upon treaty money, goods, and services to provide for the needs of their people.

These needs were becoming greater with the further influx of settlers. An old Indian, bemoaning the lost days of French and Indian sharing of woodland resources, complained to Harrison, "Now if a poor Indian attempts to take a little bark from a tree to cover him from the rain, up comes a white man and threatens to shoot him, claiming the tree as his own." Algonquians responded with dismay to settler restrictions against controlled burning of the woodlands to create deer forage: "If we are not permitted to set fire we cannot live . . . if we set fire to the weeds or grass, it is to live on the game, we have no other means to subsist."

The annuity chiefs at least assured another means of subsistence. If the old ways were being irrevocably lost, the land made insupportable, a good annuity chief would get for his people what he could by whatever means he could. The former warrior Little Turtle grabbed annuities for his Miamis "at almost every cession of land, often by challenging the claims made by other peoples," then handled the annuity payments in a generally fair and magnanimous manner.

But the stance of Little Turtle and other annuity chiefs angered and disgusted natives who would rather fight than give up another meadow or elm grove, another hill or brook, and with it another degree of independence. In Tenskawatawa, the Shawnee prophet, and his brother Tecumseh, these Indians found new leaders.

Tenskawatawa believed, as did many others, both Indian and immigrant, that God had not meant for the two races to live together. In Tenskawatawa's view, the newcomers "poison'd the land." The game had disappeared "half a tree's length under the ground," and Indians needed to listen to and obey the Great Spirit in order to call the animals back. Like the Delaware prophet Neolin before him, Tenskawatama preached a mixture of native and Christianized beliefs in order to get the Indians back on the right moral and spiritual road.

He also made the most marked attempt yet at "pan-Indianism"— not simply a military alliance between varied Indian groups, but the forging of a shared cultural and political identity. In 1806, he defied the Treaty of Greenville by establishing right at Greenville a town in which members of different tribes could come together. Two years later, calling for a halt to Indian land cessions, he started a second pan-Indian community, Prophetstown on the Tippecanoe River.

Tecumseh spent little time in his brother's towns, for he was busy with his own alliance efforts, traveling as far south as Creek country to deliver a vehement call for Indian unity. "Where today is the Pequod [Pequot]?" he asked the Choctaws and Chickasaws. "Where is the Narragansetts, the Mohawks, Pocanokets, and many other once powerful tribes? . . . They have vanished before the avarice and oppression of the white men. . . . So it will be with you. . . . Soon your mighty forest trees will be cut down to fence in the land which the white intruders dare to call their own."

Tecumseh advanced the idea that the land belonged to all Indians in common, that "no tribe has a right to sell, even to each other, much less to strangers, who demand all and will take no less." Envisioning a great, stalwart confederacy stretching from north of the Great Lakes to the Gulf of Mexico, he urged, "Any sale not made by all is not good. . . . It requires all to make a bargain for all."

So adamant were the brothers regarding Indian lands that they reportedly offered to submit to execution if William Henry Harrison would pledge on behalf of the United States to "neither buy nor take any more land from the Indians."

It was not a pledge that Harrison was disposed or empowered to make. Ohio had become a state in 1803, Michigan a territory in 1805. In 1809, the government split Indiana Territory in two, the great region from the junction of the Ohio and the Mississippi rivers northward to the banks of Lake Superior, and from the shore of Lake Michigan westward to the Mississippi being designated "Illinois Territory."

Tecumseh drew supporters from Florida to the Canadian border, but most of his backing came from the natives of this westernmost territory—Chippewas, Kickapoos, Menominees, western Potawatomis, Sauks and Fox, Winnebagos—who were threatened but not yet overwhelmed by white land hunger and were not tied to the United States by the Treaty of Greenville or by subsequent annuity agreements.

In order to challenge the growing United States hegemony, however, Tecumseh needed more support, preferably from an ally with access to European fighting power. Reluctantly, Indian memory still fresh of the British treachery at Fort Miami, he negotiated with English officials. When the War of 1812 erupted between England and its former colonies, Tecumseh and his Indian army quickly aligned with the British. They fought long and hard, only to watch British troops begin pulling back into Canada as United States troops thrust toward victory. Tecumseh pleaded with the British commander at least to leave arms and ammunition, as "We are determined to defend our lands" to the point of "leav[ing] our bones upon them."

Almost twenty years had passed since Indian hopes of fending off invasion had splintered among the debris and carnage at the battle of Fallen Timbers. Tecumseh had provided a new reason to hope, but in 1813, gamely covering the British retreat, he fell on the battlefield. The consequences of the withdrawal of their last European allies would be felt both among the northwestern tribes and the natives locked into their own struggles in the South.

In the space between the Revolutionary War and the War of 1812, the southern tribes west of the Appalachians and east of the Mississippi also faced the increasing encroachment of white settlements on their lands and insistent United States government officials armed with treaties of dubious value and meaning to the Indians. The fortunes of two of the major southern tribes, the Cherokees and the Creeks, demonstrate the puzzles and pain, the changes and constants of the era.

The Cherokees lived in farming and hunting villages scattered through the southern Appalachians, a region encompassing western North Carolina, Virginia, South Carolina, northern Georgia, and northeastern Alabama. They also inhabited the Great Valley of eastern Tennessee. In the early 1760s, the Cherokees had briefly fought the British and lost some of their eastern lands as a result. Nonetheless, they had sided with the British in the Revolution, many Cherokees continuing to fight the American presence after the war.

At the same time, the boundaries of eastern Cherokee land were becoming increasingly porous. The Revolution had brought into Cherokee country army deserters from both sides as well as British Loyalists. At war's end, there arrived European-American traders and other workmen—blacksmiths, coopers—some "too incompetent to find employment in white communities.'' Many of these intermarried with the natives.

Other immigrants continued their quest to claim native lands, and the American government came bearing treaty after treaty. The game was growing scarce and being taken by white hunters, undercutting both one feature of the Cherokees' subsistence lifestyle and commercial opportunity. The old communal living patterns and ceremonies were disappearing as Cherokees living closest to the spreading settlements began to adapt to the forms of white culture.

Others resisted by moving to the western edge of their home territory. Those who could tear themselves from their kin and homelands even picked up and moved beyond Cherokee country, several hundred crossing the Mississippi to Arkansas, beginning in 1782. "We had hoped the white men would not be willing to travel beyond the mountains,'' resistance leader Dragging Canoe explained. "Now that hope is gone.''

In 1785, government agent Bennett Ballew reported more than three thousand intruder families living within the boundaries of the Cherokee Nation. When young warriors killed one family—"after receiving reiterated insults and injuries,'' Ballew reported—settlers "laid waste their cornfields and fired houses with Cherokee women and children inside.''

Again, government officials came bearing treaties to get the Indians out of the way of settlement. Cherokee desperation at the inexorable advance is amply illustrated in the words of Tickagiska King: "We are neither birds nor fish; we can neither fly in the air, nor live under water.''

Cherokee leader Corn Tassel eloquently and rationally rejected treaty overtures. "Under what kind of authority, by what law, or on what pretence,'' he asked, did the newcomers require "nearly all the lands we hold between your settlements and our towns, as the cement and consideration of our peace?'' If the invaders were basing their claim on "a bare march, or reconnoitering,'' then the Cherokees could demand that the invaders move their settlements back a hundred miles to the east, "whither some of our warriors advanced against you in the course of [one] campaign.''

Corn Tassel argued that both "the law of nature and the law of nations'' of which the officials talked belied their demands. "You say:

Why do not the Indians till the ground and live as we do?" he said. "May we not, with equal propriety, ask, Why the white people do not hunt and live as we do?"

Other Cherokee leaders challenged the creeping paternalism of white officials, one noting that the now common practice of calling whites "the older brother . . . should have been reversed, for the red people dwelt here first." He nonetheless reluctantly acquiesced to the language of subjugation.

Most Cherokees in the "Upper Towns," those closest to immigrant settlements, adapted to Anglo-American ways. They asked for those gendered symbols of "civilization" so dear to missionaries and other civilizers—plows and looms—and showed an eagerness to use them born in part of adaptability and in part of dire necessity. In 1792, the Cherokee chief Bloody Fellow cited the loss of game and of cheap trade goods, and called for the government to follow through on a 1791 treaty promising "ploughs, horses, cattle and other things for a farm," for "this is what we want. . . . We must plant corn and raise cattle." Although Indians of the Southwest, influenced by the Spanish, had already developed sheep, horse, cattle, and goat herds, this Cherokee willingness to raise cattle reflected a shift among eastern Indians, who had tended to view livestock "as [nothing] other than problematic."

Many of the Cherokee treaty chiefs asked not only for livestock and farming implements, but for "government-built gristmills, sawmills, and cotton gins," for roads, for tollgate and ferry franchises. They showed a readiness to lease "the tribe's timberlands, salines, saltpeter caves, iron ore deposits, and other resources" if they could control and make money from them.

The treaty chiefs did not act strictly from self-interest. They included other tribal members in their plans for economic advancement, and they hoped to strengthen tribal land ownership in general by building a strong economic base. They also retained by treaty the right to deal with intruders on Cherokee land as they saw fit.

But every treaty diminished the tribe's sovereignty, its status as a separate, independent nation. For example, the agreement of 1791, in addition to promising "implements of husbandry," restricted the Cherokees' self-government; they could no longer "declare war or . . . make treaties of trade and alliance with European nations."

In the Tennessee Valley, the Cherokees of the "Lower Towns"—many of them refugees from the Upper Towns—continued to resist accommodation and loss. By the early 1790s, the Cherokees had become "virtually subjugated" to European-American culture. They did not inhabit controlled reservations, but their lands and liberties had been effectively restricted. At about the time of the battle of Fallen Timbers to the north, when the war power of the Old Northwest tribes was broken, the Cherokees of the Lower Towns ceased to mount armed resistance as well.

They were divided over which course to take—to unite and try to hold out against further land cessions, to split into separate bargaining entities, or to follow other tribal members to the new lands across the Mississippi.

The Ozark highlands of northern Arkansas and southern Missouri resembled the Appalachian highlands and proved a powerful lure. Those who stayed shifted within the old shrinking homelands; by 1799, "the tribe's demographic center was now one hundred miles southwest of where it had been in 1776," with new towns in northwestern Georgia and southeastern Tennessee replacing the lost town sites to the east.

Within their homeland, Cherokees still possessed certain rights. They allowed Moravian missionaries to live among them and educate their children, but they could evict the missionaries if they wished. In this, and in other efforts to retain some independence on a reduced land base, they were supported by the administration of Thomas Jefferson, who succeeded John Adams as president in 1802.

Then France, who had regained from Spain a claim to the regions between the Mississippi River and the Rockies, sold the claim to the United States in Jefferson's Louisiana Purchase of 1803. Spain, already forced out of most of the Southeast as well, clinging to its southwestern claims, and building what empire it could in California, protested the extent of United States claims based on the Louisiana Purchase. But Jefferson had obtained for the new republic 822,000 square miles, encompassing all or most of the present states of Louisiana, Arkansas, Missouri, Iowa, Minnesota, North and South Dakota, Nebraska, Kansas, Oklahoma, Colorado, Wyoming, and Montana.

The United States had been putting enough pressure on the Cherokees and other southern Indians that some had "removed" to the southern portion of this great territory of their own accord. Now Jefferson began to envision mass removals to the new western territory—still voluntary, but encouraged by the United States government. He found enough takers that by 1810 an estimated two thousand Cherokees had become the "western" Cherokees of Arkansas.

This division naturally hurt any Cherokee chances for a show of political unity, a fact not lost on the eastern Cherokees, who "condemned [the] emigrants as traitors . . . for moving west without the consent of the Cherokee nation."

The eastern Cherokees had made rapid progress by white standards, an 1810 inventory finding among them "19,500 cattle; 6,100 horses; 19,600 swine; 1,037 sheep; 467 looms; 1,600 spinning wheels; 30 waggons; 500 ploughs; 3 saw-mills, 13 grist-mills &c." But they were feeling intense pressure and, like the Indians rallying around Tenskawatawa to the north, responded with a religious and spiritual revival, one in a series of Native American "revitalization" movements in response to crushing threat and loss.

In January 1811, three Cherokees had a vision of the nation being forsaken by its spiritual Mother, who would come back "if you put the white people out of the land and return to your former manner of life." The vision had a pacific element to it—"You may keep good neighborly relations with [the white people]"—but the ache of land loss was palpable—"just see to it that you get back from them your old Beloved Towns."

For two years, the Cherokees entered into a revival of the old customs and ceremonies, but they did not have the military or political power to reclaim their "old Beloved Towns." They did not fight the invaders. Instead, they wound up joining with them and with one faction of their southern neighbors, the Creeks, in order to fight another Creek faction.

The term "Creek" covered a confederacy of native groups linked throughout Georgia and Alabama and extending into southern Tennessee and northern Florida. Within the southern portion of this region, myriad riverways and a band of rich black soil veined the coastal plains. In the thickly forested northern portion, rolling uplands alternated with steep mountain ridges and beautiful, fertile river valleys. Such variety and abundance whetted the land hunger of stridently aggressive Georgia immigrants.

After the Revolution, a series of "unauthorized and fraudulent treaties" allowed Georgia to lay "spurious claim" to a big part of Creek hunting territory. In 1790, the Creeks legitimized Georgia's claim to part of the territory, already overhunted by immigrants, in exchange for a clear-cut recognition of remaining boundaries.

Still, the Georgians and the United States government pressed, both to take the remaining lands and to place their own "agents of civilization" among the natives. In 1796, tribal leaders agreed to take two blacksmiths, but spurned an offer of Anglo schooling for their children. Regarding land cessions, they were adamant: "The land belongs to the Indians and they wish to keep it . . . and hope the white people . . . will . . . keep their goods for other purposes."

But like the Cherokees, the Creeks were splitting internally. Some chose to remove westward, the Alabamas and Coushattas migrating all the way to Spanish Texas. Among the remaining Creeks, the people of the Lower Towns, the more peaceful "White Sticks," were closest to settlement, more rapidly losing their hunting grounds, and more rapidly adapting to the immigrant culture. In annuities, they accepted "hoes, axes, plows, and spinning wheels," while the natives of the Upper Towns, the "Red Sticks," were more interested in "guns and ammunition."

As time passed and the leadership of the Upper Towns began to resemble that of the subjugated Lower Towns, the anger of frustrated Red Stick warriors detonated. With the United States distracted with the War of 1812, the warriors, partially supplied by the Spanish in Florida, began attacking settlers. In August 1813, they killed about four hundred who had "forted up" for protection on the Alabama River. This incident led the Tennessee legislature to call in military commander Andrew Jackson. With army regulars, with militiamen from Tennessee, Georgia, and Mississippi Territory, and with regiments of White Stick Creeks, Cherokees, Chickasaws, and Choctaws, Jackson crushed the Red Stick resistance.

Whatever his record elsewhere, Andrew Jackson stands as one of the premier villains in American Indian history. At this point in his rise to national prominence, he forced both his White Stick allies and the Red Sticks to cede more than twenty million acres in Georgia and Alabama—two thirds of their territory—as payment for the cost of the "Creek War." Some Creeks migrated to Spanish Florida and joined the Seminoles, or "runaways," the remnants of various southern tribes. Others clung to their diminished territory, determined to remain.

But the governments and citizens of Tennessee, Alabama, and especially Georgia were demanding of the federal government that the southern Indians all be removed to the west. Georgia officials vociferously cited an 1802 agreement requiring the federal government "to remove the Indians from [the state] 'peaceably' and 'on reasonable terms.'"

The hostility the Creeks faced is evident in Georgia Governor David Mitchell's 1813 demand for restitution from the Creeks "for every piece of property allegedly lost, destroyed, or stolen in the state since 1775." When the appointed Indian agent resisted, Mitchell accused him of "over-zealousness . . . in the interest of the Indians."

If conditions were becoming increasingly worse for the southern Indians, where were they to go? The United States government did not yet have a coherent plan for removal to the west. Furthermore, contrary to Anglo perceptions and wishes, the trans-Mississippi region was not one great *tabula rasa*. Other Indians, other tribes were already rooted there, many of them veterans of trade with the French and the British.

Back when the Powhatans and the Wampanoags and other coastal Indians were first dealing with the strange settlers from across the sea, Siouan peoples were being pushed from their Ohio woodlands by neighboring tribes. They crossed the Mississippi and split into five groups along a north-to-south continuum. The Poncas and Omahas inhabited the eastern Plains of present-day South Dakota and Nebraska. The Kansas moved onto the Plains of southern Nebraska and the northern portion of the region that would later carry their name. The Osages ranged the area where Arkansas, Kansas, and Oklahoma now meet, and the Quapaws located to the south of them, in present-day Arkansas.

By the beginning of the eighteenth century, life on the Plains portions of these new homelands—and on the Plains to the west—was changing dramatically. The Spanish had brought horses across the Rio Grande, the southerly Plains tribes acquiring them in the early 1600s. Firearms were filtering into the region from various European powers.

Among the Indians, more mobile and more aggressive buffalo-hunting cultures were aborning.

Of the seventeenth-century Indian immigrant groups, the Osages developed the strongest presence. They adapted well to their "edge habitat" of prairie, plains, and woodlands, combining their old forest forms of agriculture with plains buffalo-hunting and annual sojourns on the prairies. With three significant river arteries in their region—the Arkansas, the Mississippi, and the Missouri—they quickly established a congenial trading relationship with the French similar to that of the Algonquians still in the Ohio River Valley. The weapons the Osages obtained from European traders, and their prominence in the eighteenth-century fur trade, enabled them to cow less well-armed neighboring tribes, including their cousins the Quapaws and Kansas, and to limit incursions by equally well-armed tribes east of the Mississippi. They harried and narrowed the borders of the declining Caddo Nation, which had occupied lands extending outward from the convergence of present-day Oklahoma, Arkansas, Texas, and Louisiana for an estimated thousand years.

Thanks in part to this military superiority, for a few generations, the Osages managed "to control the rate of change so that they could incorporate new elements and graft new features onto their older and more familiar cultural framework." By the late 1700s, however, their efforts in this regard were being undermined by the long-term effects of European trade and by the removal of first the French and then the British presence.

The Spanish and French markets for skins and pelts led the Osages not only to range more widely, to clash more often with neighboring tribes, and to locate closer to the European trade in the Arkansas River Valley, but also to abandon old economic and political village structures, and—ironically, given white insistence on Indian farming as a "civilizing" process—to trade old farming patterns for a "seminomadic plains hunting" life.

Not quickly, but gradually and surely, they became dependent on European goods. Meanwhile, the French pulled out, and the British put pressure on the Indians of the Old Northwest and the South, who looked to the Osage country and saw that it was good, still blessed with game and other natural resources. The Shawnees and the Delawares, the Cherokees and the Choctaws began raiding across the Mississippi River. Then with the end of the Revolution, the British check on American expansionism was lost. Experiencing increased pressure from citizens and officials of the new republic, small groups from among the eastern tribes began moving across the Mississippi onto Osage lands.

When after the turn of the century United States policy makers began to talk about removing all eastern Indians to the west, Osage territory appeared a prime location. Thomas Jefferson wanted to "consolidate" the Osages and use part of their territory to relocate southeastern Indians.

The Osages could not give up the flow of European arms and other supplies now provided largely by American traders. The Pawnees, whom they had pushed northward, and the Caddos, whom they had pushed to the south, constantly stood poised to challenge them. The eastern tribes pressed in, and the Osages were beginning to lose their arms advantage in relation to the western tribes.

This situation explains in large part the disastrous treaty by which the Osages in 1808 relinquished more than "50,000 Squar[e] Miles of excellent country," including most of the richly forested Ozark hills. The agreement provoked such an outcry among those Osages who had not participated in its signing—and among those who insisted that the agreement was simply for the sharing of hunting lands—that Louisiana Governor Meriwether Lewis modified the document to include Osage hunting rights. The bottom line, however, remained the same. The Osages were threatened with loss of United States trade and with identification as enemies of the republic if they refused to sign.

In signing the document, the natives also committed, whether many realized it or not, to locating near the government's Fort Osage and to accepting basic aspects of white life: "a blacksmith, grain mill, plows, two log houses, and a trading post." Many of the northern Osages did come to live briefly near the post, some planting corn crops. But the fort provided no protection in this exposed site from attacks by other Indians, and besides, a spot fixed and controlled to a degree by American officials held little appeal for a people used to moving freely through a region familiar to them. By summer of 1812, when the United States government was busy officially declaring war on England, the Osage encampment had been abandoned.

Unlike many eastern groups, the Osages did not ally with the British in the War of 1812. They remained tied to the new nation through the trade that was so necessary to their continued survival. But the American victory in the war would have serious repercussions for the Osages, and indeed for all Indians.

The British presence as a potential check on American expansionism disappeared for good, and the republic was growing in power, into a sense of what would soon be called its "Manifest Destiny." Although the Senate Committee on the Public Lands in 1817 affirmed natives' "right to remain in possession of the lands they occupy" and to remove only voluntarily, prominent American leaders felt otherwise. In the same year, President James Monroe made a one-sided argument cloaked as a universal ethic: "no tribe or people have a right to withhold from the wants of others more than is necessary for their own support and comfort."

Both Andrew Jackson and Secretary of War John C. Calhoun advocated Indian removal, with Calhoun completely denying native rights and native sovereignty: "Our views of their interest, and not their own, ought to govern them." Calhoun's words clearly boded ill for the future of independent Indian bands and nations on the lands that had nurtured and sustained them.

Chapter Three

"Get a Little Farther"
(1817–1843)

I have listened to a great many talks from our Great Father. But they always began and ended in this—Get a little farther; you are too near me.

—Creek chief Speckled Snake, 1829

We have a Country which others covet. This is the only offense we have ever yet been charged with.

—Cherokee chief John Ross

The Rock River courses through the northwestern corner of Illinois, meeting the Mississippi River's broad expanse at a point called Rock Island. Here in spring 1828 sat the village of Saukenuk, to which the Algonquian Sauks, or "Sacs," returned every year after a winter of hunting on the prairies. Here they lived in bark-covered lodges and tended their summer fields of corn, pumpkin, and squash.

The Illinois land ownership of the Sacs had been under dispute since 1804, when some Sacs and members of an allied group, the Fox, all apparently plied with liquor, had signed a treaty in St. Louis. In essence, they had agreed to vacate all tribal holdings east of the Mississippi once settlement reached these lands. Their payment: two thousand dollars and goods worth a thousand.

Because their region remained the far western frontier for European Americans, the Rock Island Sacs had continued for a quarter-century virtually unchallenged by white settlement. When periodically reminded of the 1804 treaty, they would argue that they had not signed away their land and had no intention of doing so, that the treaty signers had had no authority to give away Sac holdings and had been duped in the bargain.

Meanwhile, the population of the United States continued to burgeon, each of the first three decades of the nineteenth century, like the 1790s, marked by a growth rate of almost one third. Immigrants kept pressing westward to the Mississippi, with occasional conflict and violence between them and natives.

A Rock Island Sac named Ma-ka-tai-me-she-kia-kiak, or Black Hawk, had fought in Tecumseh's resistance, but had since signed a truce with United States officials, unaware that the truce contained a provision confirming the hated Treaty of 1804. Now in 1828, as the Sacs began preparing the soil for planting, an agent came from the United States government to tell them that they must move within a year across the Mississippi, the new "permanent" dividing line between white and Indian land.

Black Hawk couldn't believe it: "I was of [the] opinion that the white people had plenty of land, and would never take our village from us." When another Illinois Sac leader, Keokuk, agreed to remove to the hunting grounds across the river in the present state of Iowa, Black Hawk extracted from him a promise to attempt a deal with United States officials whereby the Rock Island village at least would remain secure. Black Hawk's band went into hunting camps in the winter of 1828–1829, planning to return as usual to their home ground.

Word came, however, that settlers had moved into the village, claiming to have acquired the land from Quash-qua-me, chief signer of the 1804 treaty. Black Hawk made the ten-day return journey to discover the Sac cornfields being divided and fenced and a family occupying his lodge. Unable to communicate with them, he obtained an interpreter to write a message: "Not to settle on our land—nor trouble our lodges or fences—that there was plenty of land in the country for them to settle upon—and they must leave our village, as we were coming back to it in the spring."

Black Hawk delivered the paper. Unable to gauge the response but later insisting that he "expected . . . they would remove" after receiving it, he crossed back over the ice-choked Mississippi and sought the advice of the Winnebago prophet White Cloud. The prophet "agreed that I was right, and advised me never to give up our village, for the whites to plough up the bones of our people." The prophet also suggested that Keokuk be persuaded to return to Illinois as well.

Black Hawk made his way back to his people's hunting camp, and they returned to Rock Island, to find that more invaders had arrived and that the cornfields had been completely fenced. Keokuk appeared, but only to urge the other Sacs to remove. They did not do so, instead spending the summer of 1829 uneasily trying to share the village with the newcomers, who quickly undermined any attempt at coexistence. They made the natives drunk on whiskey, "cheat[ing] them out of their horses, guns, and traps" and making the sober Indians anxious "for fear some of the whites might be killed by [the Sacs] when drunk." This fear was fed by the beatings the newcomers visited on the Indians for even the smallest infractions—eating an ear of corn from a cornfield, opening a fence thrown across an Indian road in order to guide a horse through.

Striking most closely at the natives' ability to survive was the immigrants' appropriation of the best cornfields. One Sac felt secure when he planted his crop on a small island, but a newcomer, seeing the shoots coming up strong and healthy, "took his team over, ploughed up the corn, and replanted it for himself," leaving the Indian in tears at the thought of "the distress his family would be in if they raised no corn." Other Sacs were "permitted" a small plot for planting by the whites.

Through all of this, Black Hawk sought to protect his people and their rights, at one point taking a group of young men to destroy the whiskey cache of a man who had ignored repeated entreaties to stop his liquor sales to natives. Black Hawk also repeatedly called upon the Indian agent and other officials, arguing that Quash-qua-me and his band "*denied,* positively, having ever sold my village; and that, as I had never known them to *lie,* I was determined to keep it in possession." Nonetheless, the trader informed him in the fall, the village land was to be broken up and sold to individuals; if the Sacs returned in the spring, they would be forcibly removed.

In their hunting camp that winter of 1829–1830, Black Hawk's band, for the first time in his memory running short of provisions, determined to follow their usual pattern by returning to Rock Island and to resist any attempt at removal. They convinced some of Keokuk's people, no doubt homesick and disappointed with the difficulty of farming the prairie, to accompany them, and in the spring all set about yet again to repair Rock Island lodges and find places where they could plant their corn crops.

Black Hawk's own account of this wearing resistance shows that he repeatedly restrained his people in the face of provocation and sought to find and believe white promises of justice. But it was unthinkable to him to relinquish the "ancient village where all of us were born, raised, lived, hunted, fished and loved, and near which are our corn lands, which have yielded abundant harvests for an hundred winters, and where sleep the bones of our sacred dead, and around which cluster our fondest recollections of heroism and noble deeds of charity done by our fathers." Furthermore, he remained convinced "that land cannot be sold," that "the Great Spirit gave it to his children to live upon, and cultivate, as far as is necessary for their subsistence." Thus, he became the leader of the last significant effort of the Indians of the Old Northwest to retain their lands.

In the period 1817–1843, virtually all the remaining tribes holding land east of the Mississippi came under siege by settlers and government officials, who adopted increasingly coercive measures for their subjugation and removal. Tribes were seldom now regarded or treated as sovereign nations. States clamored to take control over natives and to force them off desirable lands—often broadly defined as any lands within state boundaries. The federal government in 1824 shifted responsibility for Indian affairs from the secretary of war to a Bureau of Indian Affairs within the War Department. The creation of this agency—which also became known over the years as the Office of Indian Affairs, the Indian Office, and the Indian Bureau—did not reduce government vacillation in its relations with tribal members determined to stay put. The government ultimately denied their rights by allowing self-interested politicians and other Anglo expansionists to become Indian agents, and by failing to uphold a host of clear treaty promises, instead forcing new treaties upon the natives and joining the clamor for wholesale removal.

This period, then, assumed critical importance for three broad Indian populations: the inhabitants of the Old Northwest, the groups just west of the Mississippi, whom the government wanted moved in order to make room for eastern tribes, and the major tribes of the South, whose fortunes in this era comprise one of the bleakest stories in Native American history.

*　　*　　*

The years 1818 and 1819 saw a flurry of land-cession treaties by members of such Old Northwest tribes as the Shawnees, the Delawares, the Kickapoos, the Miamis, the Weas, and the Potawatomis. The end of the War of 1812 had greatly weakened their powers of resistance and encouraged further white immigration into the Ohio River Valley and the western Great Lakes region. Many of the Northwest Indians had already been pushed to the edge of their homelands and beyond; many chose to migrate on their own across the Mississippi River, to lands on which they had previously hunted. Even here, however, government officials pursued them with treaties; in 1825, officials convinced Shawnees living in southeastern Missouri to "get a little farther" by crossing the Missouri River into what would become Kansas. Again, Kansas was familiar territory to many of the hunters of the Old Northwest, and there was much good soil there for agriculture, so a voluntary movement to the wood- and prairielands of both Kansas and present-day Oklahoma continued among members of the northwestern tribes.

As the example of Black Hawk suggests, many members of the more westerly tribes in the old homelands held on through the 1820s: Sacs and Fox, Potawatomis, Kickapoos, Winnebagos. Sometimes the natives simply agreed to depart, then didn't. Sometimes they actively resisted, as in a short-lived Winnebago uprising born of government efforts to remove them from country containing valuable lead deposits. Indians charged they had been promised a continued supply of lead for their bullets used in hunting. But, explained a Winnebago named Spoon Decorah, "We never saw any of our lead again, except what we paid dearly for; and we never will have any given to us, unless it be fired out of white men's guns, to kill us off."

In 1825, President James Monroe offered to the U.S. Congress the idea of the wholesale removal of Indians across the Mississippi. The area between the Missouri and Red rivers began to be conceived of as a designated Indian country. In 1828, with Andrew Jackson's election, the American nation took a giant step toward such a policy. Then, in 1830, Congress passed Jackson's Indian Removal Bill, which gave the president authority to "transfer any eastern tribe to trans-Mississippi River areas."

The bill did not pass without vehement opposition. Representative Edward Everett asserted, "The evil, Sir, is enormous; the inevitable suffering incalculable . . . we ourselves, Sir, when the interests and passions of the day are past, shall look back upon it, I fear, with self-reproach, and a regret as bitter as unavailing.''

Everett's words are prescient, but, especially in the case of the southern Indians, humanitarians and officials sympathetic to the natives thought removal was the only solution in light of their worsening treatment by immigrants and by the states. Whether a cruel land-grabbing device or an attempt to aid the native population, the bill was directed more at the populous, still entrenched southern Indian nations than at the northwestern groups. But its intent was clear: remove across the Mississippi all Indians belonging to identifiable eastern tribes that lived in the path of frontier settlement. As a result, in 1832, many of the remaining Indians in Indiana, Illinois, and Michigan Territory came together to fight under Black Hawk's leadership.

Despite his resolve, Black Hawk had been driven across the Mississippi by the appearance, in June 1831, of a combined force of Illinois militia and federal troops; this show of force had led him to agree to abandon Saukenuk for good. But as frictions continued between the natives of the region and the immigrants, he proceeded to draw to him across the river the disaffected and determined among the Winnebagos, Potawatomis, and Kickapoos. In 1832, with a force of six hundred, he returned to Saukenuk and traveled to the Winnebago and Potawatomi villages along the Rock River, seeking further support.

The response among the potential allies was disappointing, and Black Hawk twice tried to send truce representatives to the militiamen and federal troops again massed to stop him. Both times, the soldiers fired upon the flag bearers.

Indians and whites alike floundered into a confused war; many of the natives whose allegiance Black Hawk had counted on turned to aid the soldiers instead. The Sac leader determined to rejoin Keokuk across the Mississippi, then veered toward Chippewa country. Most of his band chose to continue toward Keokuk's village, only to be attacked by troops who caught up with them just as they forded the river. The survivors had barely rallied for escape when they were attacked by Sioux.

Disheartened at the lack of Indian unity and at the cruel fate of his people in the waters of the Mississippi and on its western banks, Black

Hawk stopped in the Winnebago villages and turned himself in to their agent. Taken downriver to a military jail where he would be shackled, he "surveyed the country that had cost us so much trouble, anxiety, and blood," viewed the immigrants' "fine houses, rich harvests, and every thing desirable around them," and mused "that all this land had been ours, for which me and my people had never received a dollar, and that the whites were not satisfied until they took our village and our grave-yards from us. . . ."

The Black Hawk War aroused white fears in Indiana, Illinois, Michigan, and Missouri, and was used as a rationale for stepping up the removal of Old Northwest tribes, including those who had joined the United States soldiers in the recent struggle. A new round of land cessions resulted in late 1832, Superintendent of Indian Affairs William Clark ominously warning the Kickapoos of Missouri and Illinois "not to 'neglect this opportunity of leaving a country where you have long been looked upon with suspicion, and where you will surely be treated as enemies.' "

In 1833, as the Kickapoos began departing for Kansas, a large number of Potawatomis balked at their own removal, holding out for an inspection tour of the five-million-acre Platte River region promised them. Eventually, worn down, they agreed to give up "an immense territory in Wisconsin, Michigan, and Illinois" for the new country, sight unseen. A major problem throughout this era, however, was that when the government told the Indians to "get a little farther," it wasn't far enough for the settlers. Before the Potawatomis could even get moved, Missouri had annexed the promised Platte acreage and the government was substituting land for the Indians in the present state of Iowa.

Among the holdouts were Winnebagos, who complained bitterly of an 1837 treaty as being fraudulently presented, its Indian signatures then obtained under duress. The remaining Indiana Potawatomis, too, found themselves bound by a questionable 1837 treaty. Potawatomi chief Menominee, vowing never to leave his home and his ancestors' graves and looking to President Martin Van Buren for justice, blasted the treaty officials: "The President does not know the truth. He does not know that your treaty is a lie. He does not know that you made my chiefs drunk, got their consent, and pretended to get mine."

Soldiers came to force Menominee and his people westward in August 1838. In the same year, Black Hawk died in Iowa, having been allowed to return to his people after acknowledging Keokuk as head chief. The grave of the man who had wanted to stay at his birthplace of Saukenuk and protect the bones of the sacred dead was vandalized in 1839, his skull featured in a traveling tent show.

By the time Black Hawk had mounted his resistance campaign, the Osages and other natives in the heartlands immediately to the west of the Mississippi were being squeezed almost to the point of disintegration. To the west and north ranged formidable Great Plains enemy tribes—Comanches and Kiowas, Wichitas and Pawnees. On the other side pressed the United States government, looking for a place to remove eastern tribes to, and aggressive migrating eastern Indians themselves, elated at finding good hunting grounds once again.

In 1818, the Osages were compelled by United States treaty to give up many of their remaining hunting grounds to their bitter enemies, the westering Cherokees; in 1825, with eastern Indians overrunning their home region, they were pressed into giving up all but a fifty-mile wedge. In seventeen years they had relinquished "nearly 100,000,000 acres," receiving in return "$166,300 in livestock, horses, farming equipment, cash, and annuities—one penny for each six acres."

As with the earlier failed attempt to fix the Osages around Fort Osage, few actually moved onto the fifty-mile tract. Those who did proved desultory farmers, in part because tending crops continued to expose them to raids by other Indians. Outside the designated acreage, the Osages dug in, repeatedly refusing to move from their old homes even as it grew increasingly difficult to sustain life in them. Many were reduced in the game-scarce winter of 1830–1831 to butchering the hogs and cattle of Cherokee and Creek migrants, sparking further enmity from these parties and from white settlers, who saw the most desperate measures as naked and willful aggression.

Influenza hit the Osages in the years 1829–1831, cholera ravaged them for the next few years, and smallpox and other epidemic diseases also arrived in inundating waves. Again, the viruses undermined the firmest determination among an embattled people. In 1838, Cherokee agent Montfort Stokes reported the Osages starving, their attempts at crops a failure, the game gone, and their promised annuities nearly at an end. The sympathetic Stokes was irate. He reported that the annuity ''was never sufficient to buy a blanket for each family,'' after recipients paid the cost of the necessary thrice-yearly prairie hunting expeditions; further, ''every principle of Justice and Equity demands from the Government of the United States, that this people should not be abandoned and driven to the condition of robbers and perhaps shortly annihilated.'' Stokes had himself participated in making a ''good treaty'' with the Osages in 1833, but President Jackson had rejected it, promising ''that something shall shortly be done for 'them.' '' Nothing had been done. The year after Stokes argued on their behalf, the remaining Osages were forced into a strip of present-day southern Kansas.

The story was similar to the south, along the river valleys of Louisiana and Arkansas, where the Caddos were pressed to remove to smaller and smaller portions of their homelands to make room for both eastern Indians and the white settlers who would spill over any boundary. The latter soon predominated. ''Our last two agents . . . have driven a great many bad white people off from our lands,'' Louisiana Caddos along the Red River explained to President Jackson in 1835, but the current agent ''says he does not know what will be done with us or for us.'' Of course, this was Jackson's own stratagem, a fact the Indians probably knew, for they concluded with a ''sorrowful solution'': ''offering all our lands to you which lie within the boundary of the United States, for sale, at such price as we can agree upon in council one with the other.''

The government offered $30,000 in goods and horses, plus a cash annuity of $10,000 annually for five years. To those reluctant to sign away a million acres of ancestral homeland, one chief, Tarshar, offered a sad challenge.

> Are you not starving in the midst of this land? And do you not travel far from it in quest of food? The game we live on is going further off, and the white man is coming nearer to us; and is not our condition getting worse daily? Then why lament for the loss of that which yields us nothing but misery? Let us be wise, then, and get all we can for it, and not wait till the white man steals it away, little by little, and then gives us nothing.

The Caddos relinquished their remaining lands in the United States. The first annuity payment arrived in ten boxes marked as valued at $1,000 each. The agent would not allow the Indians to open the boxes until they signed a paid-in-full receipt. They resisted but were told "if they did not take what was offered, they would have nothing." The items in the boxes, including trinkets and cheap rifles, might generously have been valued at $1,500 total.

Some Caddos removed to Choctaw country, some to Mexico, most to their cousins in Mexican Texas. With Texas winning independence from Mexico in 1836, Texans began trying to push the Caddos out of this region as well.

With the exception of the Black Hawk War, the dramas and defeats being played out in the Old Northwest and across the Mississippi in the early nineteenth century were dwarfed by events in the South, where the five major tribes—Cherokee, Chickasaw, Choctaw, Creek, and Seminole—mounted substantial holding actions against the tide of settlement and governmental pressure. These attempts to remain in possession of native soil were hard enough to mount and sustain before the Indian Removal Bill; afterward, they would prove impossible.

While the goal of staying on homelands was the same, the means now varied sharply. For the Cherokees and Creeks, eastern survival seemed to hinge on a strong and hitherto unknown political unity, supplemented in the case of the Cherokees by major adaptations to white ways. For the Seminoles, survival seemed to hinge on warfare.

Many of the Cherokees, of course, had already proven highly adaptable to "civilization," the men becoming European-style farmers, the women cultivating household skills that the new dominant culture valued in "goodwives." Between 1817 and 1830, many Cherokees removed voluntarily to Arkansas Territory. Most of those who remained continued major adaptations, showing a strong entrepreneurial spirit in keeping with that of their white neighbors, using tribal member Sequoyah's creation of a Cherokee syllabary to become literate and even to support a Cherokee newspaper, and setting up at their capital of New Echota in Georgia a democratic government modeled after the United States' own.

The Cherokees' well-tended plowed-and-fenced fields, their increasingly educated population, and their vigorous New Echota government clearly demonstrated their ability to remake their nation along European-American lines without losing its distinctiveness and self-sufficiency. Yet many settlers and state and federal officials, including the president of the United States, would actively cling to the "wandering savage" stereotype more advantageous to their own ends.

In 1823, when President Monroe urged the eastern Cherokees to remove to Arkansas, they responded with a spirited reminder:

> . . . we beg leave to observe and to remind you that the Cherokee are not foreigners but original inhabitants of America, and that they now inhabit and stand on the soil of their own territory and that the limits of this territory are defined by the treaties which they have made with the government of the United States, and that the states by which they are now surrounded have been created out of land which was once theirs, and that they cannot recognize the sovereignty of any state within the limits of their territory.

On such matters, the eastern Cherokees were agreed. But increasingly they split along a fault line that runs deeply and inexorably through both historical and contemporary Indian country. To what extent should Indians adapt to white culture? Generally speaking, those with mixed lineage adapt most readily, forming a "progressive" block, while traditionalists, usually those with the strongest tribal bloodlines, remain resistant in order to preserve their indigenous identity as fully as possible. Tensions between these two groups grew during the late 1820s as the mixed-blood Cherokees adapted and prospered.

Despite the differences, however, the pointed reaction of mixed-blood Cherokee newspaper editor Elias Boudinot to Anglo plans for Cherokee removal resonated for all: "Where have we an example in the whole history of man, of a Nation or tribe, removing in a body, from a land of civil and religious means, to a perfect wilderness, *in order to be civilized.*" And the Cherokees still managed to show a political unity surprising among American natives unused to centralized political power. This unity was generally strengthened by the ascension of John Ross to principal chief in 1828. Ross, with his white trader father and mixed-blood mother, had more Anglo than Indian blood and moved easily through the forms of white culture; at the same time, he stood forcefully for a continued distinct Cherokee nation in the East.

This was the last thing that Georgia's government and citizenry wanted, especially when valuable gold deposits were discovered on Cherokee land in 1829, shortly after Andrew Jackson's election to the presidency. Soon the state of Georgia enacted laws not only forbidding the Cherokees to mine the gold on their own lands, but seeking to strip the tribe of any recognition as a separate nation or any protection under the law. The draconian edicts included one forbidding the Cherokee national council to hold session—except "for the purpose of ceding land"—and another outlawing Indian testimony against whites in court, thereby stripping the Cherokees of important legal rights in land claim disputes. In fact, the state laws now specified that the 6,000 square miles of Cherokee land were to be divided by lottery into 160-acre land lots and 40-acre gold lots for settlers, goldhunters, and speculators. Any tribal member "who sought to influence another not to emigrate to the West" could be imprisoned.

As if this were not enough, the federal government under Jackson, armed with the Indian Removal Bill, was also mounting a campaign to force the Cherokees out. Nonetheless, the tribe took Georgia to federal court. In the 1831 *Cherokee Nation* v. *Georgia,* Chief Justice John Marshall gave the natives some hope, but also further muddied their status by concluding that the nation was "a political entity capable of managing its affairs," but also a "domestic dependent nation"—a distinction "not known before in international law"—rather than a separate "foreign state" able to challenge Georgia's extended jurisdiction. The United States Supreme Court said that the Cherokees had rights, but it did not afford them the political status to protect those rights.

Meanwhile, powerful whites persisted in looking at the Cherokees and their native neighbors as stereotypical Indians, the U.S. House Committee on Indian Affairs noting that with game disappearing rapidly from the South, the natives' decline in their homelands was assured. "Whoever really believes that the Cherokees subsist on game, is most wretchedly deceived," raged Elias Boudinot in the columns of the *Cherokee Phoenix. "The Cherokees do not live upon the chase, but upon the fruits of the earth produced by their labor,"* their game hunting limited to "about as much as white people do in new counties."

Cherokee leaders were faced with a growing sentiment for removal among the beleaguered people themselves. The fact remained, however, that every Cherokee who went west weakened the future of the nation in the East, especially since Georgia settlers streamed onto the vacated lands, ignoring their continued status as part of the Cherokee Nation's holdings. Federal "removal agents" were circulating through the country, offering the Indians fifty cents apiece to enroll with them, a first step toward removal to "Indian Territory," where the western Cherokees now resided, having agreed in 1828 to give up their briefly held Arkansas homes. Native leaders threatened whippings to any of the eastern Cherokees who accepted, but such coercion did not sit well with an increasingly vocal removal faction.

Then events took one promising turn. It started when the state of Georgia seized, convicted, and jailed two white missionaries living among the Cherokees without registering with the state and taking its loyalty oath. The case of the imprisoned missionaries went to the Supreme Court in 1832 as *Worcester* v. *Georgia*. In this instance, Chief Justice Marshall and his colleagues resoundingly affirmed the Cherokee Nation's independence from the state:

> The Cherokee Nation, then, is a distinct community, occupying its own
> territory, with boundaries accurately described, and which the citizens
> of Georgia have no right to enter, but with the assent of the Cherokees
> themselves, or in conformity with treaties and with the acts of congress.

The decision had an electric effect among the Cherokees, who saw it as assurance that they would not be removed, that they would finally be left in peaceful possession. There was great celebration, and those who had signed up for immigration to Indian Territory tried to vacate the removal camps in which they were living. A Cherokee leader named John Ridge jubilantly wrote his nephew Stand Watie, "Since the decision of the Supreme Court, I have felt greatly revived—a new man and I feel independent."

Seven years later, Ridge would be dead, assassinated—along with editor Boudinot—for his part in the ultimate relinquishing of eastern

Cherokee lands. The dismal spiral of dispossession had not been arrested with the Worcester decision, had not even really been slowed. President Andrew Jackson himself reportedly remarked, "John Marshall has rendered his decision; now let him enforce it." Both the federal and state governments—and marauding whites who burned cabins and fields and cheated and roughed up families—continued to grind away at the Cherokees.

Over and over, the natives asked the federal government simply to secure to them the rights already agreed upon in various treaties. Over and over, Jackson's officials told the Cherokees that they could not do so while the tribe remained in Georgia (some also remained in North Carolina, where a white merchant named William Holland Thomas helped them resist involuntary removal). The truth was that, with few exceptions, officials would not bring the power of the federal government to bear against the southern states in Indian matters.

Jackson's administration couched its obdurate stance in humanitarian terms—they wanted the Indians removed for their own welfare. In response, John Ross in early 1833 pointedly asked the president "how, if he could not protect them in their rights in Georgia, he could protect them against similar evils in the West."

Ross and other Cherokee leaders through the early 1830s traveled to Washington in hopes of gaining support for their continued identity as a nation in Georgia. A New York *Observer* correspondent noted of a party of delegates, which included John Ridge, that they were "well-dressed gentlemen of good manners—themselves good society for any sensible man—sitting at the publick tables throughout the City—undistinguished from the common mass except it be in superior delicacy of feeling." He also judged even the younger members of the group more knowledgeable of "the institutions, laws, and government of the United States than a larger fraction of those, who occupy a seat in the House of Representatives."

However, the governor of Georgia deemed the Cherokee emissaries unwilling to cede land "wholly undeserving the courtesy and marked attention of the official authorities at Washington," and those authorities adopted a similar attitude. Jackson did offer the Cherokees $3 million for their homelands, if they would depart for Indian Territory. But Ross maintained that the gold mines alone had more value. Besides, the Indians had not traveled to Washington to agree to remove.

Predictably, the government was having a hard time finding a place to remove them to. The western Cherokees, most of them now separated from their eastern kinsmen and women for a number of years, insisted that the treaty they had made with the government in 1828 entitled them to all the Cherokee lands in Indian Territory, although they showed some willingness to accept refugees on terms. Meanwhile, the poorer eastern Cherokees—mostly full-blooded tribal members—were finding it increasingly difficult to survive on their home ground. In part, this condition stemmed from the inevitable changes and dangers posed by the encroaching settlers, in part from an attendant feeling of insecurity and hopelessness—why plant crops or plan for winter?—as other Cherokees continued to trickle away and as the state continued to tighten its stranglehold. Many were reduced to digging roots in the forests for food.

Others clung to comfortable homes, the "average Cherokee family" in the mid-1830s living in "a modest log cabin on their own farmstead," where they had "about eleven acres" in cultivation—corn, other vegetables, cotton—and raised hogs and cattle. But many of this group were affected, too, for Georgia flagrantly proceeded with its lottery of occupied, treaty-held Indian lands. Even the prosperous John Ross was evicted from his farmhouse and ferry business, although the lottery winner for his property temporarily "allowed" the ill Mrs. Ross to remain in the home.

Under such pressures, it is no wonder that more and more Cherokees chose to take their chances in the West, gathering in removal parties and departing on their own or under a federal removal agent. One such agent found himself affected by the leave-taking spectacle of strong men crying, parents "turning with sick hearts" from their departing children and brothers and sisters "with . . . brimful eyes . . . wringing each others hands for the last time."

Up until this point of departure, many changed their minds, such was the pull of home and of the Cherokee leadership. In an 1834 incident, leaders succeeded in winning back almost eight hundred people from the removal camps.

The fault line, however, was deepening. Tired of the struggle to remain and convinced that taking their chances in the West would be preferable to a spiral of degradation in the East, a "Treaty Party" led by John Ridge, his father, Major, and his cousins the editor Boudinot and Stand Watie emerged among the eastern Cherokees. This group journeyed to Washington in early 1835 and signed a document in which they agreed to sell the eastern lands for $4.5 million and move to the West, if the tribe as a whole would ratify the agreement.

The Georgians and Jackson's government almost had the Cherokee lands in their grasp, but there was that pesky matter of tribal ratification. Seventeen thousand Cherokees remained in the East, most of them still vehemently opposed to removal. The government nonetheless called a treaty meeting. Three hundred to five hundred Indians— men, women, and children—attended. Out of this conference came the 1835 Treaty of New Echota, and the government claimed to have secured tribal agreement for land cession and removal.

"Sir, that paper . . . called a treaty, is no treaty at all," wrote removal agent Major W. M. Davis to President Jackson. "[It was] not sanctioned by the great body of the Cherokee. . . . I solemnly declare to you that upon its reference to the Cherokee people it would be instantly rejected by nine-tenths of them, and I believe by nineteen-twentieths. . . ." General Ellis Wool, charged with removing tribal members en masse in 1837, would write, "It is . . . vain to talk to a people almost universally opposed to the treaty and who maintain that they never made such a treaty."

President Jackson flatly dismissed such objections, in September 1836 pronouncing that native arguments were "entitled to no respect or consideration whatever," as "nineteen-twentieths of the Cherokees are too ignorant and depraved to entitle their opinions to any weight or consideration in such matters."

John Ridge reportedly said, "I know that in signing this treaty I have signed my own death warrant." He would be dragged from his bed and stabbed to death, but not without first seeing and living the consequences of the treaty.

Whites used the disputed treaty—and the money promised the Indians—to seize more land and to bring suit against the natives, even, Major Ridge mourned, charges "for back rents for our own farms." In 1837, General Wool found many of the Cherokees "living upon the roots and sap of trees" and refusing to take food or clothing from the government, "lest they might compromise themselves in regard to the treaty." He reported, "Many have said they will die before they will leave the country."

John Ross brought to Washington a petition protesting the Treaty of New Echota, a document signed by close to sixteen thousand Cherokees, but the government held fast to a May 1838 forced-removal date. Martin Van Buren, who succeeded Jackson as president, had been inclined to allow the Cherokees more time to wrap up their lives and businesses in the East and make preparations, but the governor of Georgia railed at any delay. On the appointed day in May, Cherokee families found troopers on their doorsteps, ready to force them upon what would become known as the "Trail of Tears."

Although the Cherokees' final major struggle to remain in the East is better known, the Creeks' experience resembled and in some ways surpassed it in terms of drama, frustration, and suffering. Having been forced into a huge land cession after the Creek War in 1814, the Creek Nation still held by treaty extensive lands in Georgia and Alabama. As they sought to maintain possession, they encountered increasingly self-serving Indian agents and other officials. Up until the Creek War, the agents sent among the Creeks had been generally hardworking and principled men, but the federal government made a number of singularly wrongheaded moves in its subsequent appointments. For example, it damaged its own plans for both Creek and Cherokee removal by granting removal-agent status to some of the very men who had done the most to drive the Indians from their homes. And it allowed other truly appalling political appointments. In 1817, Georgia Governor David Mitchell, one of the most rabid opponents of Indian rights, became the Creek agent.

Mitchell "brought hard-core corruption to the Nation." As disburser of government funds that were promised in previous treaties— funds increasingly needed by the Lower Town Creeks, especially as old subsistence patterns failed—he refused to follow the government's directive to pass the money to the Creek headmen, instead pocketing the cash and doling out provisions from a store he had established. To enhance his own schemes and to promote removal, he actively worked to destroy any Creek political unity, employing bribery and threats.

The National Creek Council, however, continued to solidify in its resistance to further land loss. In the past, Creek government had operated loosely at the national level, regional leaders being able "to dispose of surplus lands independently.'' Now the council, in an attempt to hold on to the remaining land base, took upon itself all power and responsibility for land agreements; anyone who attempted to make a separate deal with whites faced the death penalty.

In charting its course, the council faced a maddening refusal by many immigrants to consider it a legitimate sovereign body with whom they had to deal on anything resembling equal terms. It also faced a patronizing United States government, which couched its offers in brazenly insulting terms by any but the most myopic standards, pledging ''to promote [the Creeks'] domestic manufactures, and extend their agricultural pursuits. . . . In short, to make them useful to themselves and to mankind.''

The council and the nation also had to face the selfish and ultimately catastrophic actions of a Lower Town headman, one William McIntosh, or White Warrior.

McIntosh was Mitchell's partner in the general store. More important, he led a group of Lower Town residents who, in 1821, gathered at a tavern to sign the Treaty of Washington, sacrificing a large expanse of Creek land. The council reluctantly accepted this treaty because it would help erase debts and because the cession left the Creek heartland intact. However, what remained was ''the irreducible minimum needed to maintain life in the East,'' and the council reiterated its law regarding land sales. Backed by the majority of the Creek Nation, the council declared, ''On no account whatever will we consent to sell one foot of our land, neither by exchange or otherwise,'' and it ''*positively decline*[d]'' any program of removal across the Mississippi.

In 1825, William McIntosh and some of his confederates negotiated deals for themselves with United States government officials—cash for land cessions. Reminded by the council of its edict but promised protection by the officials, they signed away all the Creek lands in Georgia—a few million acres—and ''the northern two-thirds of the national domain in Alabama . . . Upper Creek country, heavily used, occupied by many towns and several thousand people, and quite beyond the most elastic interpretation of McIntosh's pretended power to sell any Creek land.''

McIntosh's was one of the most breathtaking betrayals in all of Indian history. And it was perpetrated with the aid of United States officials, who also disregarded their own authorities, for President Monroe had told them that Creek Council approval would be required.

Nonetheless, the United States Congress quickly ratified the "Treaty of Indian Springs." The Creeks, who had protested through David Mitchell's successor, agent John Crowell, were stunned, unbelieving. Faced with a *fait accompli,* they asked pointedly "if property sold by an unauthorized person can't be recovered by its owner."

A Creek squad dispatched by the council executed McIntosh and his confederates, the nation seeking to reassure its Georgia neighbors "that this was a legal execution (as indeed it was)." But whites determined to drive the Creeks out made McIntosh the martyred hero; the council were bloodthirsty savages operating in defiance of the peaceful goals of a great Indian statesman.

As in the Cherokees' situation, Georgia state officials openly defied the federal government in any of its attempts to grant the Creeks a fair hearing or even a well-planned removal. Georgians wanted the Indians out immediately; survey crews were dispatched to begin apportioning the land. Under President John Quincy Adams's orders, federal troops marshaled to halt the precipitous rush, but the state militia assembled in defiance, and the federal government backed down, cajoling and coercing the Creeks in Georgia to hurry and remove—if not to the West, at least across the Chattahoochee River to Alabama.

The Creeks peacefully and repeatedly insisted that the 1825 treaty was fraudulent. They rejected the treaty payments and won the sympathies of federal officials sent to deal with them, one military commander becoming convinced that they would "readily lay down their lives upon the land in which the bones of their ancestors are deposited . . . and die without resistance, that the world shall know, that the Muscogee Nation so loved their country, they were willing to die rather than sell or leave it." He concluded, "I trust and hope their appeal will not be unavailing."

The Creeks' adamant and peaceful resistance won for them a victory rare in the annals of Indian history, as President Adams overrode the ratified treaty and agreed to renegotiate. But in the face of Georgia's intransigence, Adams saw no solution but removal. He met with Creek delegates in Washington, finding their "appearance . . . remarkable for its 'dark and settled gloom.' " Negotiations dragged on, the government insisting on cession of all of present-day Georgia, the Creeks arguing to retain about one third of the territory. "You know that we have no land to spare," argued Creek leader Little Prince. "You know that we have been selling our land to our father the president until we have but little left. . . . You know that we are very thickly settled. . . . We cannot comply with the talk of our father because we have no land to spare."

One despairing chief, Opothleyaholo, tried to commit suicide in his hotel room. Soon thereafter, President Adams had a treaty drawn up to reflect the Creeks' stance, but Georgia bucked and bellowed and the Senate wouldn't ratify it. Finally, the delegates had no choice but to sign away all their extensive Georgia lands for "$27,491 plus $15,000 in goods, school tuition money, and improvements."

In the late 1820s, Georgia Creeks streamed onto the lands of their Alabama kin, some seven thousand arriving in 1827 alone, "many of them Skeletons and their bones almost worn through the skin." Alabama Governor Israel Pickens refused to follow Georgia's tawdry strategy of insisting on the validity of the Treaty of Indian Springs, but he did want the Creeks removed from the three-million-acre Alabama remnant of their homelands as well.

The Creek Nation began to fray. Like the Cherokee Council, the Creek Council held firm against removal, but many individuals and families determined that leaving was the only survival strategy worth pursuing, for the United States government was making promises to assist migrants, and Alabama began extending its jurisdiction over the natives. Georgia placed patrols at the line between the two states to keep Creeks from returning to hunt and forage, while the Alabama legislature passed a bill outlawing Creek hunting, trapping, and fishing outside Creek holdings. At the same time, the Georgia Creeks were straining the resources of their Alabama kin, who numbered about fourteen thousand.

As the Georgia patrols attest, Creek movement to Alabama did not lessen tensions with Georgia; border disputes continued to the point that the federal government had to intervene.

President Adams did so in a stunning blow to Indian sovereignty: by moving federal troops onto Creek lands. The move flouted previous policy, in which native permission was always—except under conditions of war—sought to cross boundaries. It also ignored explicit treaty provisions and "set a dangerous precedent for using the threat of force in time of peace to win concessions from Indian nations."

All of this happened *before* the most powerful and purposeful opponent of tribal identity in the East took office. With Andrew Jackson's election, the Creeks' ability to be heard virtually vanished. Like the Cherokee delegations to Washington, the Creeks were met by officials who refused to deal with them on any terms other than removal. Unceasingly, the Jackson administration told the delegates that it would not protect them against state governments' extension of power. "It is idle to console yourselves with the hope that Congress will interpose in your behalf," Secretary of War John Eaton told them. "Congress has no power over the subject. Your Great Father has none. It belongs to the State in which your lands are situated, to regulate and to direct all affairs within her limits, and nothing can prevent it." Eaton even indicated that Jackson would close down the federal Creek agency in a bow to state jurisdiction.

The Creeks still refused to cave in, their delegates tenaciously arguing for their established treaty rights. Back in the Creek Nation, in February 1830, an old leader named Tuskeneah halted a United States mail coach crossing Creek lands. He had, Tuskeneah said, been a friend to the whites through various treaties. But the soldiers were allowing whites to stream into and "spoil" the country.

Tuskeneah reported that Creeks who dared to cross back into Georgia in diminishing hopes of finding game for survival—admittedly sometimes killing settlers' livestock—were slaughtered as if "they had been so many wild hogs," while whites with impunity were "spoil[ing] our Range, they kill our hogs & cattle they kill your white children['s] stock running in my country and lay it to my red children to have to bear the blame."

To all of this, the Jackson administration had only one answer: accept removal.

The Creek Council began pushing for a compromise. They agreed to divide up the nation's holdings if they could reserve portions of the region, including their own "Beloved Towns." In March 1832, the United States government approved this plan, granting a section of land to each headman, a half section to each head of the family. In a move resembling subsequent "allotment" policies, the government pledged to provide some protection by overseeing these sections as "trust" property for five years, during which individual "grantees could not sell their reserves . . . without federal supervision and approval." Each Indian owner would then receive a fee-simple patent, granting unrestricted title to the parcel.

Despite this arrangement, the United States government, the governments of Georgia and Alabama, and the citizens of Georgia and Alabama still pressured the Creeks to migrate to the West. The government promised to pay for removal, to provide support in the first year, and to deny "any State or Territory [the] right to pass laws" for the transplanted Creeks, who "shall be allowed to govern themselves, so far as may be compatible with the general jurisdiction which Congress may think proper to exercise over them."

There seemed, then, to be only two courses: remain on the Alabama homelands and make major adaptations to white culture in hopes of being allowed to remain in peace, or remove to the West. Most Creeks chose the former. But now they faced their bitterest onslaught yet. The unscrupulous among the residents of Georgia and Alabama mounted a reign of terror. In September the Creeks petitioned the secretary of war: "Instead of our situation being relieved as was anticipated, we are distressed in a ten fold manner—we are surrounded by the whites with their fields and fences, our lives are in jeopardy, we are daily threatened. . . . We are prevented from building new houses, or clearing new fields."

Even though the Indians' landholdings had supposedly been secured for five years, whites simply moved in, challenging the natives for ownership, destroying their crops and food stores. The natives attempted to fight back with whatever means at their disposal; one group of full-blood Creeks, their houses burned, placed a mixed-blood claimant upon their desirable property in hopes of staving off further invasions.

The invaders, however, also continued to circumvent land trust provisions, buying or leasing Indian acreage in uneven and often fraudulent exchanges. Individuals and speculating land companies would bribe or intimidate another native to stand in for the true owner in land transactions. Or they would lease the land, then build up a fraudulent account against the owner and demand the deed. Or they would simply rely on false claims in county courts. The natives could not testify on their own behalf and often found themselves in jail signing away land and property.

All of this did not happen without concerned protest by other whites, one writing, "I have never seen corruption carried on to such proportions in all of my life before. A number of the land purchasers think it rather an honor than a dishonor to defraud the Indian out of his land." A treaty official, noting white encroachment and intimidation, wrote the secretary of war in 1833, "You cannot have an adequate idea of the deterioration which these Indians have undergone during the last two or three years, from a general state of comparative plenty to that of unqualified wretchedness and want."

Although the Creek Council continued to exist, the nation had virtually disintegrated; the Creeks were now leading dangerously exposed and impoverished lives in Alabama, many of them succumbing to the lure of the liquor bottle. "They linger, however, about their homes with great fondness," a treaty commissioner reported in November 1833, "and arrest any disposition to move on the slightest evidence of adequate protection where they are."

The "slightest evidence" was provided by the federal government, which did make a few attempts to remove squatters from Creek lands. How feeble were such efforts is reflected in the remarks of a group of Creeks to one of the agents charged with certifying land transfers. They had, they explained, "borne with oppression until further forbearance has ceased to be a virtue." While they struggled at home for a subsistence, "other Indians" sold these homes, "our all, the only means for our support." When the owners protested their loss, the agent simply repeated that he would "enquire into it."

> You place the burden of proof upon us . . . but worse than all this, and more to be regretted, is the fact, through fear of the merciless hordes who surround your office, our people cannot speak to you in defense of their just rights without subjecting themselves to punishment.

In April 1835, importuned both by the Creeks and by citizens shocked by the blatant corruption being played out, the federal government halted Indian land sales and ordered an investigation of the ones already certified. But by this point, the Creeks were wholly demoralized and easily duped by speculators, who warned that answering a federal government summons to Columbus to address the land problems would allow the government to seize them and force them westward.

In that same year, the Creek Council finally announced their intention to remove—"the white man has taken possession, and has every advantage over us; it is impossible for the red and white man to live together." Still they delayed, for "it was with the utmost reluctance that they consented to give the land away; it was like pulling out their hearts, and throwing them away." They may have hoped for a last-minute reprieve from the federal government. Its best response was simply to try to assist them in settling up affairs prior to moving. Yet more and more Creeks roamed about homeless and unable to provide for themselves, having lost their livelihood through fraud or having sold whatever they had left, only to see the pittance received for it quickly vanish.

The situation ground along until what has been called the Creek War of 1836, in which Creek warriors clashed with Georgia and Alabama militiamen. This was by no means a concerted Creek resistance; other Creeks tried to quell the hostilities to the point of putting warriors in irons. But it was just what the invaders needed.

In fact, many observers at the time found the "war" a too convenient excuse to deflect attention from some of the more brazen corruption. The Montgomery *Advertiser* stated flatly, "The war with the Creeks is all a humbug. It is a base and diabolical scheme, devised by interested men, to keep an ignorant race of people from maintaining their just rights, and to deprive them of the small remaining pittance placed under their control."

The humbug worked. Pressure mounted for removal. Peaceful Creeks, even those under a federal removal agent, were forced by aggressive whites to hurry from their homes, while leg irons for the march westward were prepared for those Creeks who had dared to defy the dispossession the treaty-bound federal government had failed to stop.

Long before the final "war," even before the loss of Georgia lands, some Creeks had disappeared into the swamps along the rivers of Spanish Florida, where a less politically unified but ultimately more effective resistance to domination and removal had begun. Here, in the late 1700s, remnants of various tribes, such as the Yamasees and Yuchis, had come together with Creeks and with runaway African-American slaves to become the Seminoles. The intermixed bands built thatched-roof open-walled homes and poled along the waterways in dugout canoes. They planted crops, raised livestock, hunted, and gathered, digging the coontie root from which they ground flour for bread.

Florida's status as Spanish territory, and as a region generally unsuitable for the kind of agricultural immigration that was occurring to the north, at first provided some protection for the Seminoles. But by the second decade of the nineteenth century, white immigrants and troops were crossing the Georgia-Florida boundary to capture slaves slipping into the swamplands. This and the troops' incursions into native hunting grounds sparked the First Seminole War, 1817–1818.

In a foretaste of events to come, the Seminoles repeatedly melted into the swamps as Andrew Jackson, fresh from his victory against the Creek Red Stick faction, pursued them with federal troops, Georgia militia, and White Stick Creeks. Jackson's force destroyed Seminole communities and supplies when they found them, making the natives wary of staying in one place and planting crops. The troops also launched an offensive against the Spanish, besieging one of their forts and precipitating an ultimatum from President Adams that the Spanish either bring the Seminoles in line or relinquish the territory.

In 1819, Spain gave up Florida, which in 1822 became a United States territory with Jackson himself as governor. Of course, he set out to push the natives off the better lands being eyed by settlers. In treaty negotiations in 1823, one prominent Seminole leader, Eneah Amathla, noted, ''We rely on your justice and humanity; we hope that you will not send us south to a country where neither the hickorynut, the acorn, or the persimmon grows; we depend much upon these productions of the forest for food; in the south they are not to be found.''

Nonetheless, by promising to leave certain chiefs in possession of better tracts, Jackson won an agreement—the Treaty of Camp Moultrie—whereby many Seminoles were to move from the rich soil areas of northern Florida to the poorer lands around Tampa Bay.

But they didn't. Over the next few years, they simply tried to avoid the settlers and slave catchers filtering across the Georgia line. Clashes escalated, not only over the land and its resources, but over slaves.

Both the whites and the Creeks from whom some of the Seminoles had separated saw the black people among the Seminoles as escaped slaves or potential slaves. Among the Seminoles themselves, some blacks had the status of slaves, but it was a mild form of bondage in which they pledged loyalty and a small tribute from their labors.

The territorial and United States governments began encouraging the Seminoles to remove to the West, but the tribespeople were both uninterested and rightly suspicious that they would be forced to live among the Creeks, who had often tried to seize the slaves among them. The Seminoles wanted to live under Creek domination no more than they wished to live under Anglo-American domination.

With Jackson's ascent to the presidency and with the enactment of the Indian Removal Bill, the government at first busied itself dealing with other tribes. In 1832, however, a federal agent was sent to press the Seminoles for removal to the West. He found many of them starving, drought having taken their crops and the wild game becoming more difficult to find.

But they resisted talk of removal. Although this was not their ancestral homeland, it *was* their homeland, and most simply didn't want to leave the environment that had nurtured them for many years.

They advanced other arguments as well, still rejecting the government's plans to place them among the Creeks and worrying over moving to a cold climate when they had been reduced almost to nakedness. The agent's promise of blankets and clothing upon arrival in the West probably did little to assuage their concerns regarding the journey.

The government coerced some of the Seminoles into an 1832 treaty in part by threatening that the annuity due them under the treaty of 1823 would forthwith be paid to the Creeks. It also appeared to offer an important concession, allowing an exploring party to visit the new country set aside for Creeks and Seminoles and to report back to their kinspeople in Florida, who could then accept or reject the tract.

The exploring party responded positively to the prairie lands carved from territory reserved for the Creeks but judged them dangerous, with the proficient Plains horsemen and raiders among the Pawnees posing a threat to the immigrant tribes. The United States government took this qualified approval on the part of the delegates as the acceptance which by treaty was the prerogative of the whole tribe.

The Seminoles stayed where they were, and again both sides came to the treaty table. This time, however, a growing Seminole faction was speaking out in disgust at the previous treaties. "My Brothers! The white people got some of our chiefs to sign a paper to give our lands to them," declared resistance leader Osceola, "but our chiefs did not do as we told them to do; they done wrong; we must do right." Osceola argued that the Great Spirit had not directed the Seminoles to leave their homes and that they should mount an armed resistance and treat any tribal members willing to go as enemies. "When the agent tells me to go from my home," he related, "I hate him, because I love my home, and will not go from it."

The military now began coercive measures, jailing Osceola, whom the painter George Catlin would judge "a fine and gentlemanly look-ing man with a pleasant smile," until he agreed to sign another re-moval treaty. Osceola did so, but then promptly killed one of the proremoval leaders, throwing to the winds the money the unfortunate man had received for his livestock in preparation for removal.

The government gave January 1836 as the date at which removal would proceed—forcibly, if necessary. But when troops arrived in December 1835 to carry out the edict, a Seminole war party nearly wiped them out, and the Second Seminole War erupted, with Osceola vowing to fight "till the last drop of the Seminole's blood has mois-tened the dust of his hunting ground."

Thus began one of the longest, costliest conflicts in American his-tory, a war closely resembling the United States' subsequent draining and ambiguous combat in Viet Nam. Seminole warriors would strike and fade into the swamps, where their families were sequestered and even the corn fields were carefully hidden. The government would expend an amount estimated as high as $40 million and 1,500 soldiers' lives in an unsuccessful attempt to extricate approximately 1,500 peo-ple from Florida.

Osceola won some daring victories before being tricked into cap-tivity at a peace conference. "I shall never forget that day, nor the sad, disappointed face of Chief Osceola and the other Indians," army Captain John Masters would relate. "I thought it too unjust for any-thing." Osceola would die in jail in 1838 of a reported throat afflic-tion, but other leaders carried on the battles. Meanwhile, soldiers proceeded with a scorch-and-burn policy, torching Indian homes, when they could find them, seizing cattle, and destroying stored provisions.

The troops' partial success in this regard—and the constant necessity to be on the alert and on the move—led various Seminole groups to consider removal, but they remained understandably skittish. In one instance, a faction met with white officials to sell their cattle and prepare for removal, but were scared off by slave hunters moving among them looking for escapees.

By 1838, both the Seminoles and the army fighting force were heartily sick of the war. One young Seminole, Hallec Hadjo, told army commanders that the Seminoles "would thankfully receive" from them "any part of [the Florida country], however small." The general then in charge of the offensive, Thomas Jesup, was more than happy to let them have it, writing the secretary of war that "we have committed the error of attempting to remove them when their lands were not required for agricultural purposes; when they were not in the way of the white inhabitants; and when the greater portion of their country was an unexplored wilderness, of the interior of which we were as ignorant as of the interior of China."

Jesup's arguments against further attempts at removal were answered with orders to continue fighting, and the military gradually pushed the Indians southward. In 1839, some of the Seminoles struck an agreement with the military to "retire to the country near Lake Okechobee with guarantee of protection from the whites if they would remain in the country designated," but both white encroachment and the refusal of other Seminoles to locate in this area doomed the plan.

By 1840, many of the Seminoles were so exhausted and emaciated that they could not maintain the fight. Yet they still insisted the country was theirs, and held out hope of being allowed to remain. An army officer on the scene, Ethan Allen Hitchcock, mused over the situation in a letter to his brother, reasoning that "if the Indians had no right to the country before the treaty (which has been alleged) they had an undoubted right after it." In fact, five years after eagerly volunteering to "punish" the Indians, he concluded, "I now come, with the persuasion that the Indians have been wronged and I enter upon one of the most hopeless tasks that was ever given to man to perform."

The Second Seminole War never reached a clear end, but three years later as a colonel, Hitchcock would direct the surrender of one of the prominent war chiefs, delivering the chief and his band to federal authorities at Port Leon. As they approached the port, Hitchcock allowed the Indians to send a war yell over the waters, then watched as a sense of doom seemed to envelop the group, the men falling silent, the women crying. Hitchcock tried to buoy their spirits with promises of kind treatment, and in particular took time to console a woman with a baby in her arms, "to tell her that she would soon be happier than she had been &c., reminded her of their having lived more like wild animals than like human creatures, but that now they would begin to have houses and make gardens etc., and could bring up their children to something besides war." She responded with a gale of tears.

A few hundred Seminoles remained in Florida, living autonomously in the swamps. After Choctaw removal, an estimated 7,000 Choctaws still clung to the pine-covered hills of their Mississippi homeland. About 1,400 Cherokees—roughly 1,100 in North Carolina, 300 "in nearby parts of Georgia, Alabama, and Tennessee"—still refused to depart. But most members of vital early-nineteenth-century eastern tribes had left their homes forever for the new lands promised to them forever, the lands across the Mississippi.

In 1826, the Chickasaws had argued, "If we should exchange our lands for any other . . . the consequences may be similar to transplanting an old tree, which would wither and die away, and we are fearful we would come to the same. . . . If we should consent [to removal] we should be likened unto young corn growing and met with a drought that would kill it." Indian experiences on the trails and upon arrival in the new lands would demonstrate both the truth in these words and—paradoxically—a people's ability to survive uprooting and drought conditions.

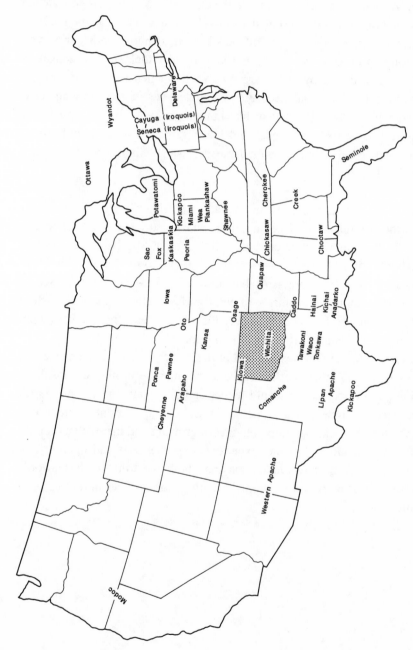

Previous locations of Indian Territory tribes (Indian Territory shaded)

Chapter Four

←——————→

"I Am Driven Away from Home"
(1817–1843)

Last evening I saw the sun set for the last time, and its light shone
upon the tree tops, and the land, and the water, that I am never to
look upon again.

—*Menewa, Creek*

I have no more land,
I am driven away from home,
driven up the red waters,
let us all go,
let us all die together
—*Creek removal song*

Forced suddenly from their farmsteads by United States troops carrying out the federal government's removal edict, the Cherokee group
had camped for three months in a hodgepodge of bark-covered shelters under military supervision. Now the time had come for them to
join other Cherokees on the reluctant march westward—the "Trail of
Tears." With "sadness of the heart" the people lingered over good-
byes to the sick who were unable to make the journey, then took up
their places in a growing line of wagons.

An old chief led them mutely on horseback, followed by a number
of solemn mounted young men. Behind the procession, the temporary
shelters blazed and curled into ashes. Ahead, the sun shone bright, but
an ominous cloud rose on the western horizon, accompanied by a
ripple of thunder. Silently, the exiles moved on under a brilliant but
troubled sky.

"Long time we travel on way to new land," an anonymous Cherokee would recall. "People feel bad. . . . Women cry and make sad wails. Children cry and many men cry, and all look sad like when friends die, but they say nothing and keep on go toward west."

Through the decades of intense struggle in the eastern heartlands, from the 1810s to midcentury, more than a hundred thousand natives, members of nearly thirty tribes, were removed, or removed themselves, across the Mississippi in response to white pressure. In the 1830s and 1840s, they relinquished 100 million acres in the East in exchange for "32 million western acres and 68 million dollars in annuity pledges."

The exodus peaked in the 1830s with the forced removal of the five southern tribes—Choctaw, Creek, Cherokee, Chickasaw, and Seminole—who made up the bulk of the migration. At one point in late 1836, some thirteen thousand men, women, and children of the southern tribes waited at Memphis under government-sanctioned removal agents for the steamboat transportation that would form one stage of their journey to Indian Territory.

Up until 1830, most emigrating eastern Indians were making a voluntary if reluctant shift to western hunting lands, where tribal members could escape Anglo encroachment and domination. After the Indian Removal Bill of 1830, as migration increasingly appeared the only way to survive, some bands continued to travel westward on their own. Others traveled under government agents; some, deemed hostile for their continuing resistance, traveled in chains.

For all, the trails were hard. And they would lead the survivors to new stresses in the West as factionalism continued to sabotage tribal unity, as the United States failed to follow up on its promises even as it sought to extend its control, and as new difficulties developed with kin who had preceded them across the Mississippi and Missouri and with other natives for whom the new territories remained ancestral homelands.

As keen as the Jackson administration had been to uproot the large southern tribes, government officials in 1830 had given little thought to the particulars of moving many thousands of peoples, from babies to infirm elderly, across the swamps and rivers and forests and hills of the Deep South and of Tennessee, Kentucky, Missouri, and Arkansas. In December Jackson directed that the Department of the Army coordinate the removal, but the following spring, government officials remained unsure as to whether they were responsible for the Indians' whole journey or simply for the portion beyond the Mississippi. (The latter still involved for most traveling parties a long trek across Arkansas.)

The appointment of removal agents to collect the natives in their homelands and oversee the exodus soon gave the government the illusion of a controlled and orderly migration. Various overland and water routes were plotted, the latter using both steamboats and flatboats. But the government-sponsored removals were ill-planned, underfunded, and generally inhumane affairs from start to finish. If some of the travelers did fare better than others, it was only because they managed to hold on to some of their possessions and autonomy, had a humane and resourceful native leader or removal agent, or were simply lucky enough to escape some of the major pitfalls of the journey.

Of the major southern tribes, the Choctaws began removing under government direction and control first, some four thousand assembling at Vicksburg, Mississippi, in November 1831 as the first step toward departure. By February 1833, the government had removed an estimated six thousand Choctaws, with a thousand more traveling on their own.

The Creeks finally faced massive removal after the Creek War of 1836: almost fifteen thousand were deported in that year, with five thousand following in the next. Both the Chickasaw and Cherokee peak migrations began in 1837, although most of the close to seventeen thousand eastern Cherokees would have to be driven from their homes the next year before turning to the West. One Georgia volunteer would later state flatly that although he subsequently fought in the Civil War of 1861–1865, seeing ''men shot to pieces and slaughtered by thousands,'' the Cherokee removal ''was the cruelest work I ever knew.''

The forced removal of Seminoles began with a party of about twelve hundred in 1838 and continued—whenever Seminole fighters could be coaxed or tricked into government hands—through the early 1840s.

Most Indians showed a strong preference for traveling on their own.

And because the government would just as soon not bother with the logistics, it acceded to this, for years allowing those natives who removed themselves a payment of $10, often collectible only at journey's end. Other groups accepted government assistance, but managed to maintain some autonomy. For example, the Chickasaws, with funds from land sales financing their migration, were able to take an active and decisive role in their own emigration, requiring government agents to assist in the movement of extensive baggage and numerous ponies.

But most natives who held out against removal until the bitter end found themselves so impoverished, so dependent upon the government for protection of their very lives, that traveling independently seemed an impossibility.

For many, whatever homes and possessions they had once had were gone before they consented to removal or were forced into it. Some had had little to begin with and had long since begun eating roots and bark to stay alive; others had gradually gone from plenty to need as whites cheated them out of land and goods. In some cases, such as that of the first westering party of Seminoles, other natives had long before driven them from their cabins and livelihood, incensed at their willingness to deal with the invaders.

The natives who still held a number of possessions were often forced to abandon even the most basic. With the Cherokee removal of 1838, General Winfield Scott wrote regretfully of "the loss of their property consequent upon the hurry of capture and removal," leaving his charges without "bedding, cooking utensils, clothes, and ponies" that would make the trip bearable.

Many found themselves suddenly stripped and nearly defenseless. When two thousand much-harassed nonhostile Creeks were being forced out of Alabama in 1836, the removal agent wrote that charlatans "preyed upon them without mercy," carrying out "fraudulent demands" until "they were robbed of their horses and even clothing." Of the Cherokees who were forced into precipitous removal in 1838, another agent wrote, "The property of many has been taken, and sold before their eyes for almost nothing—the sellers and buyers, in many cases having combined to cheat the poor Indians" just as they found themselves harried from their homes.

The trauma of these forced removals was compounded by white

men who appeared and openly helped themselves to the Indians' stock and household items and even dug up graves searching for silver jewelry and other valuables.

The United States government lured many desperate emigrants with promises to provide for their needs, but it failed to produce anything resembling adequate necessities for the journey, despite the efforts of hardworking removal agents. Natives arrived at the gathering points for departure without shoes and with only the thinnest summer clothes. An agent at one such Choctaw rendezvous, in snowbound Vicksburg in December 1831, noted, "They are generally very naked and few moccasins are seen among them. . . . If I could have done it with propriety, I would have given them shoes."

Removal accounts abound with references to ill-clad people suffering from cold, as the government continued to push the departures through the snow and freezing spells of the winter months. Some emigrants did possess warmer clothing, but the contractors failed to transport it. Some were promised blankets only upon their arrival in the new country. Others received one blanket per family, a cruel allotment for parents and children buffeted by winter storms and bone-chilling temperatures. One sympathetic military removal agent, Captain John Page, taking a party of Creeks westward in December 1833, paused "6 or 7 times a day" to warm the wailing children riding atop the wet, cold tents in the wagons. He had fires built and bundled the little ones in "anything I can get hold of to keep them from freezing." Page noted sadly, "I used to encourage them by saying the weather would moderate in a few days and it would be warm, but it never happened during the whole trip."

Cold—or hot—and weary, emigrants who depended upon Uncle Sam also had to adjust to a strange and paltry diet based on flour and salt pork, when available. Agents had difficulty getting the full monies appropriated by the government to feed the emigrants. Suppliers often failed them at a critical provisioning point in the journey, or the provisions sat and spoiled at one place when they were needed at another.

Animals, too, suffered from the lack of proper planning and funding. One Choctaw agent was given only $100 to pay for food for his numerous charges and any necessary feed for their four or five hundred horses. Almost half the horses died, starved and worn out, while traversing a swamp. The government ignored its agents' suggestions that money to feed horses and livestock would be well spent in speeding the emigration.

Delays were caused by stray cattle searching for forage, but also by a variety of other troubles. Wagons broke down. Roads gave out in swamps and bogs. Rivers rose and impeded progress. One Choctaw group spent a full week averaging only six miles a day through a swamp, most of this wading knee- to waist-deep. A Seminole agent reported "the earth covered with water . . . our Waggons mired at every step."

White immigrants had endured such trail hardships and would continue to do so, but they were moving forward of their own free will, eager to embrace the possibilities ahead. By contrast, many of the Indians had departed only with the greatest reluctance. In one leave-taking, Choctaw women had moved among the oaks and elms surrounding their cabins, "stroking the leaves . . . in silent farewell." A Choctaw agent noted, "The feeling which many of them evince in separating, never to return again, from their own long cherished hills . . . is truly painful to witness; and would be more so to me, but for the conviction that the removal is absolutely necessary for their welfare."

It was only natural that the emigrants would continue to show a reluctance to move on, exasperating many of their agents. A Cherokee agent more sensitive than most recognized why "the people are very loth to go on, and unusually slow in preparing for starting each morning": they were moving "not from choice to an unknown region not desired by them."

Some of the exiles also delayed in the early stages of the journey because just getting out of the bitterly contested and thickly settled areas felt liberating, especially when an abundance of game along the routes renewed their sense of self-sufficiency. A Chickasaw agent wrote in frustration at one point that his charges "have refused to proceed; they throw their baggage out of the Teams which have been provided for their transportation, say they will have their own time and manner to get to their country, and seem to take great satisfaction in disregarding all directions and orders they receive from us." He reported them hunting and "loitering" around frontier homes, concluding, "They have not shown the least disposition to be hostile, but there is behind their actions some thing I cannot account for."

That "something," of course, was a resurgent spirit of independence and resistance to Anglo domination. It was evidenced as well in the actions of a large group of Chickasaws whom a removal agent found encamped near Helena, Arkansas; they "refused to be enrolled and refused to have any whites with them," instead paying their own way and setting their own pace, with a long pause for a winter hunt.

Most of the Creeks, the Cherokees, and the Seminoles, however, had been reduced to the status of prisoners and pawns before embarking on the journey; the ways in which they delayed along the route reflected their defeated and coerced status.

For example, there were frequent delays due to heavy drinking. Although agents struggled to keep liquor out of their charges' hands, wily Anglo men delivered it to the most out-of-the-way locations, to people who had watched their homes torched, who had been robbed and separated from loved ones, who had set out on the trail without a pot to cook in or an overshirt to ward off the chill. In some cases, the women upbraided husbands, fathers, brothers, and sons for allowing such horrors to happen. The gods seemed cruel or absent, any tribal or individual spiritual power lost forever. The world had been wrenched terribly, irrevocably out of kilter, and the people drank.

"Nocowee has given himself up to the bane of death [whiskey] and I have altogether lost his services," wrote one agent of a Cherokee leader. "Our police has to drive him along the road sometimes fettered." If these lines portray Nocowee's personal humiliation and tragedy, they also hint at the tremendous humiliation and despair his companions must have felt at the downfall of one of their own just when group strength was most needed. A Creek removal agent reported his sober charges being incensed at all the whites with whom they came in contact because of the free flow of liquor on the trail, accompanied by "the most brutal scenes of intoxication" among their fellows.

Widespread illness on the trails both contributed to and resulted from drunkenness and despair. Dysentery and "bilious fevers" struck repeatedly, especially on the Mississippi steamboats, where the exiles experienced crowded and unsanitary conditions on a diet of unfamiliar salt rations and brown river water. Cholera was the greatest scourge of the weary and vulnerable emigrants, whether on water or land. "Death was hourly among us, and the road lined with the sick," wrote one Choctaw agent. "The extra wagons hired to haul the sick are about five to the 1,000; fortunately they are a people that will walk to the last, or I do not know how we could get on." At least this agent was able to procure extra wagons; in many parties, the emigrants were compelled to discard their few remaining possessions by the side of the road in order to make room in the wagons for the sick.

Demoralized and debilitated parties of natives with press-on-at-all-costs agents left bodies by the side of the trail, barely covered with brush and certain to lure wolves and other wild animals. Sometimes, even the dying were left behind; the granddaughter of a survivor would relate, "A crude bed was quickly prepared. . . . Only a bowl of water was left within the reach." How painful this abandonment of both the dead and living loved ones was to people who stressed kinship ties, who revered their ancestors and their grave sites, can only be imagined. It is significant that natives objected to steamboat transportation in large part because of the fear of dying on board and being cast into the water.

Exiles did press agents for delays to nurse the sick, to allow a loved one to die as peacefully as possible, and to bury the dead with some ceremony. One removal agent, witnessing a solemn and orderly Cherokee trail burial, was moved to write, "There is a dignity in their grief which is sublime; and which, poor and destitute, ignorant and unbefriended as they were, made me respect them."

Even in the midst of the worst suffering on the trail, Indians maintained some autonomy, unity, and hope. When in the summer of 1838 forced marches of Cherokees proved disastrous because of heat, drought, and illness, Cherokee leaders convinced General Scott to allow the people to remove themselves in the fall, with Chief Ross directing the operation. In one Creek traveling party, men "carrying reeds with eagle feathers attached to the end . . . continually circled around the wagon trains or during the night around the camps . . . to encourage the Indians not to be heavy hearted nor to think of the homes that had been left." In some bands, leaders allotted seeds for members to carry, symbols of hope for a new home. One Creek party, assessing their own bitter experience, wrote, "Tell our people behind not to be driven like dogs."

The travelers were sometimes buoyed by kindnesses from whites along the trails. Louisiana and Kentucky residents tried to provide aid, and citizen protests of the Indians' treatment made their way to Washington. A man who had encountered a ragged, burdened, shoeless, and frozen Cherokee party traversing Kentucky in January 1839 wrote pointedly, ''When I read in the President's Message that he was happy to inform the Senate that the Cherokees were peaceably and without reluctance removed—and remember that it was on the third day of December when not one of the detachments had reached their destination; and that a large majority had not made even half their journey when he made that declaration, I thought I wished the President could have been there that very day in Kentucky with myself, and have seen the comfort and the willingness with which the Cherokees were making their journey.''

When the Creeks who were judged hostiles were brought into Montgomery, Alabama, in 1836, many of them manacled and their despair palpable, the Montgomery *Advertiser* editorialized on the tragedy of ''the remnant of a once mighty people fettered and chained together forced to depart from the land of their fathers into a country unknown to them.'' If this smacks of the elegiac—''lo the poor Indian is passing, but we don't have to feel any responsibility about it''—it at least acknowledged past Indian power and homelands.

In contrast, the Arkansas *Gazette* characterized a party of Seminoles as ''the most dirty, naked, and squalid'' of the migrating Indians yet seen, reinforcing a primitive stereotype without taking into account the fact that these people had been forced westward without adequate provisions after a wearing guerrilla warfare.

Removal agents, too, could prove grossly insensitive. A Seminole agent acknowledged that as many as 150 of his charges were ill and that travel conditions were poor, but he responded to a plea from the Indians to allow the sick a day of rest, thereby delaying the journey, by complaining about ''the degree to which those people seem to have been humored, petted, and pampered.'' An agent who was moving Choctaws by steamboat would not allow them to go ashore to relieve themselves, even posting a man keep them from alighting when the boat did stop for wood. He also judged a previous agent had ''spoiled'' the Choctaws by allowing them such ''indulgences'' as the continued possession of their hominy mortars, familiar food-preparation tools which would seem crucial to people hoping to survive in a new land.

Many thousands did not survive the trip. The eastern Cherokees lost an estimated one fourth of their population—some four thousand men, women, and children. The Creeks and Seminoles had even greater losses—as much as one half the tribes when deaths during an initial adjustment period in the West are included. Epidemics and accidents contributed harrowingly to the losses; five or six hundred Choctaws died of smallpox in the journey across Arkansas, and more than three hundred Creeks drowned in the sinking of the steamboat *Monmouth*. (This incident provoked some public outcry against contractor cupidity in jamming the unwilling emigrants on unseaworthy vessels.)

As the eastern emigrants struggled to survive to reach Indian Territory, other Indian emigrants, who had preceded them across the Mississippi and Missouri, were fighting for survival, too. The world the exiles were entering was as complicated and unstable as the one they had left.

While some United States policy makers had determined that all or most of the lands across the Mississippi River in the Louisiana Purchase would be Permanent Indian Territory—and had wooed Indians with this idea—earlier European claims and Anglo expansion in the early nineteenth century undercut any such agreement. The Mississippi and much of the country west of it already had been claimed, explored, and developed for trade by both France and Spain.

While France had relinquished its claims to the interior United States, Spain still claimed a big portion of what would become the American West. In the eighteenth century, as Anglos had pushed westward, the Spanish had vigorously pushed northward, establishing missions, *presidios,* and small colonies in Texas and California. They had reestablished their presence in New Mexico and Arizona after the daunting 1680 Pueblo Revolt. They had also explored into Utah and Colorado.

The United States insisted that the Louisiana Purchase included Texas; Spain insisted that it did not. The Adams-Onis Treaty of 1819 supposedly settled the matter by affirming United States claims to Florida and Spanish claims to Texas.

Yet Texas was becoming increasingly enticing to a burgeoning trans-Mississippi Anglo population. Louisiana became a state in 1812.

In 1819, Anglo migration across the Mississippi River led to the creation of Arkansas Territory. Even more activity was occurring just to the north, where settlement along the western bank of the Mississippi and along the Missouri River led to Missouri statehood in 1821.

In another significant shift, Mexico won its independence from Spain in 1821 and inherited the European power's land claims. Mexico and the United States began a long dispute over boundaries.

All of this obviously affected those Indians who had already uprooted and reestablished themselves in hopes of escaping Anglo settlement and control. Representative are the Cherokees who began moving into Texas in 1819. They had first separated from the eastern nation by attempting to locate in Arkansas, but the Osages, who had inhabited the region for generations, treated them as a threat. Members of various other immigrant tribes, too, sought refuge and a new home in the same good hunting and farming areas. So did the Anglos spilling into the Louisiana Purchase.

Many of the Cherokees had held on amid the disorder and competing interests in Arkansas until 1828, when they signed the agreement to remove to Indian Territory. Those who moved to Texas did so in hopes of securing a new homeland under the Spanish, and then under the Mexicans.

At first, such an outcome seemed possible. In the early 1820s, the Cherokees and members of other displaced tribes—notably the Shawnees and Delawares—received official Mexican sanction to locate in Texas. The Cherokees hoped to convince Mexico of their usefulness by acting as "a pacifying and unifying element" among Indians in Texas and serving as a "buffer" against the Anglo-immigrant culture to the east.

However, the Mexican government, eager to buttress its northern frontier in whatever way possible, in the early 1820s began allowing Anglo settlement in Texas as well. True to the pattern of European powers, it granted two Anglo-American colonizers the promising East Texas lands on which the Cherokees had settled.

The Cherokees remained on the lands they hoped to own, while Anglo colonizers faced a host of problems in carrying out their grand designs. These *empresarios* solicited Cherokee allegiance. In 1826, the first and most effective of them, Stephen F. Austin, asked the Cherokees for help against the Comanches to the west and other hostile tribes, promising that if they would participate in a punitive expedition "it will be the means of securing your land in the country for as many of your nation as wish to remove here."

Feeling slighted by the Mexican government, the Cherokees in Texas cooperated with the incoming Anglos in hopes of achieving just that, even joining the 1826 Fredonian Rebellion, when a Texas colonizer tried to set up a separate republic in East Texas. They survived this debacle, and by 1828 were a few hundred strong, spread among a few towns and along an agricultural frontier. Furthermore, they were thriving, selling their farm products, livestock, skins from hunting, and homespun cotton cloth in the Spanish-founded town of Nacogdoches.

The Mexican government contemplated moving the Cherokees and other "friendly" Indians westward as a means of insulating Mexican Texas from the Comanches. But under the dictator Antonio López de Santa Anna the fledgling nation soon had its hands full with a rebellion of Anglo immigrants and republic-minded Mexican Texans.

In 1836, as their eastern kin fought to overturn the Treaty of New Echota, the Cherokees living west of the Sabine River found themselves residents of the Republic of Texas, governed for the most part by immigrants from the southern states. This government moved swiftly to restrict the Cherokees to a reservation, which would have a government agency upon it. Cherokees agreed to the plan "because [it] promised to give them a permanent home in Texas."

Instead of security, however, the group experienced greater uncertainty. The reservation lines remained undrawn. More Anglo-American immigrants poured into East Texas. Mexico threatened to retake the territory it had lost, and attempted to draw the Indians in as allies. The shaky republic courted them as well. But both the Mexican and Texan governments suspected the immigrant Indians of aligning with the other—or with hostile Indians.

By 1838, the Texas Cherokees were under tremendous pressure from other settlers and speculators to vacate the lands they had already spent many years improving in the style of white farmers. Sam Houston, president of the Texas republic, had lived among the Cherokees and championed their rights, but read the situation all too well.

The Indian lands are forbidden fruit in the midst of the garden; their blooming peach trees, their snug cabins, their well-cultivated fields, and their lowing herds excite the speculators, whose cupidity, reckless of the consequences which would ensue to the country, by goading the Indians to desperation, are willing to hazard everything that is connected to the safety, prosperity, and honor of the country.

Surveyors finally came to mark the boundaries of the reservation in 1838, but in that year Mirabeau Lamar replaced Houston as Texas president. A former Georgian, Lamar demonstrated all too well the attitudes that had led the Texas Cherokees to flee their southern homelands in the first place. In his inaugural address, he announced, "The white man and the red man cannot dwell in harmony together. Nature forbids it." Instead, clinging to a "savage" stereotype of Indians in general, he proposed "push[ing] a rigorous war . . . without mitigation or compassion, until they shall be made to feel that flight from our borders without hope of return, is preferable to the scourges of 'war.' "

The Lamar administration embarked on a plan to remove all Indians who had immigrated into Texas. It did offer to cover some of the Cherokees' losses—"improvements, crops, and property"—and to provide a military escort through "wild Indian" country. These promises were not tested, for the harassed Cherokees balked at a stipulation that they give up their gunlocks. They began an independent exodus, along with various Delawares, Shawnees, and Kickapoos. When the Texas military followed, a massacre ensued, some Indian survivors trying unsuccessfully to return to their Texas homes, others crossing the Red River into Indian Territory.

Through the decade of the 1830s, eastern Indians had been coming into the western territory reserved by the United States government for them—present-day Iowa, eastern Kansas and Oklahoma, southern Nebraska—and pitching tents or building log cabins on the prairies and in the woodlands. Each of the exiled tribes had a designated region. For example, the lands of the Indians from the South spread across present-day eastern and central Oklahoma, Choctaw in the southeastern corner and Chickasaw to the immediate west, both in the country between the Red and Canadian rivers. Creek land lay above that region, chiefly between the North Canadian and the Cimarron rivers. (The Creeks and the Seminoles were to share this territory, although the Seminoles would finally be granted their own separate region along the north bank of the Canadian in 1856.) North of the Cimarron, the Arkansas River stretched into the new Cherokee country.

These lands, promised to the tribes forever, offered significant advantages. For one thing, they were far from barren. Although the Seminoles in particular would have trouble adjusting to a climate more extreme than that of their beloved Florida, the soil promised a bounty of both wild and cultivated plants, the creeks and rivers flowed brightly, the timber grew tall and varied.

In theory, at least, tribal members could locate wherever they wished in relation to these resources. They were to be free to reestablish their own governments and cultural traditions along lines that seemed suitable to them. They could choose whether to welcome missionaries or not. They could travel and trade at will. They could make use of the promised assistance of the federal government in getting established without being forced to make major land concessions or jettison all traditional living. In all these ways, this Indian country little resembled the restricted reservations that were soon to become a prominent and dismal feature of the trans-Mississippi West.

At the same time, there was no escaping the fact that most of the eastern Indians had been forced into the prairie regions under debilitating circumstances, were pressured to adapt to white modes of living, and remained at least partially dependent on the promises of a United States government that gave evidence of poor and inadequate planning at almost every turn. The cards were stacked in favor of those Indian immigrants who had already shown some adaptability and accommodationist tendencies, had stayed healthy on the trails, and had arrived with funds in hand from sales of land and possessions in the East—various Chickasaws and members of the Cherokee Treaty Party, for example. But struggle characterized the early years in Indian Territory for all, as it had during the final years in the East.

First, throughout the 1830s, and well into the 1840s, most of the exiles were straggling into Indian country worn out, traumatized, impoverished, and homesick. "People sometimes say I look like I never smile . . ." one Cherokee would note, "but no man has laugh left after he's marched over long trail . . . most of time I am keep thinking of Old Nation and wonder how big mountain now looks in springtime, and how the boys and young men used to swim in big river."

In the early months and years, many went about malnourished and too depressed and distracted about their uncertain situations to plant crops, even if tools and seeds could be had. Even those who threw themselves gamely into the battle for survival were struck down by fever, cholera, smallpox, influenza, and a host of other diseases.

More than one fourth of the Creek Nation—some 3,500—expired in the year following the tribe's forced migration. They did not have the health, the tools, or the provisions to establish an independent presence; many stayed close initially to the forts the United States government had erected as Indian country gateways and supply points.

Occupying these forts were officers and enlisted men who held the cultural prejudices of the era, but did not generally have a political stake in Indian-white relations and were not seeking Indian lands or Indian trade. In this sense, contrary to the stereotype of army aggression, the military in Indian Territory "usually represented the interests of the Indian more conscientiously than any other frontier institution." Officers worked to supply the immigrants with food and tools, to help them organize and settle, to provide protection against unscrupulous whites and hostile western Indians, and to promote peace among different immigrant tribes and different tribal factions.

Conscientious Indian agents and other officials with the fledgling Bureau of Indian Affairs did the same; in fact, the timely aid of Thomas Hartley Crawford, commissioner of Indian Affairs in 1838, has been credited with keeping the western Seminoles from extinction. However, the bureaucracy in general moved with painful slowness and inefficiency.

Most immigrants desperately needed anything and everything— felling axes to cut the timber and construct cabins, yard goods to make clothes, guns and ammunition to hunt game, seeds to grow crops. Yet the government for whom the officers and agents worked failed to send appropriate or adequate goods, or entered into contracts with corrupt middlemen.

A small band of Minnesota Chippewas who removed under treaty chief Eshtonoquot in 1839 found no promised government provisions in their new Kansas location, leading Eshtonoquot to ask, "How are we to live? We have no guns [and] no shoes to keep our feet from freezing. . . . These things make me sick in my Heart. We have nothing left to sustain life.''

Eshtonoquot and his band would survive and establish good farms, but the early months and even years were encircled with want and worry. A substantial group of Creeks who agreed to government terms and moved to Indian Territory in 1829 lived for years without the supplies that had been promised to help them get established. The country offered rich hunting and farming possibilities, but guns, ammunition, and farm tools remained scarce, procured from independent traders to whom the Creeks had to promise their annuity payments.

Even more serious was the situation of the western Seminoles, who received only the scantiest and most intermittent annuity payments, in part due to their recent hostile status, in part to an irresponsible disbursing agent. They had been loath to give up their rifles, cooking pots, and other necessities in the East, but were persuaded to do so by promises of receiving replacements in the West. Four years after their arrival, they were still waiting for these items.

The government did provide large, mixed amounts of goods for various groups at various times—rifles, powder, iron, steel, axes, hoes, blankets, cloth and clothing, plows—but supply seldom met demand. Blankets arrived in the spring, after they were most needed. Sometimes the items provided revealed a deplorable lack of concern or understanding, as when the Creeks, experienced farmers with a long history of adaptation to white ways, received such "wild" Indian goods as beads and "squaw axes."

One of the more bitter and persistent supply problems involved food. All but the most demoralized Indians were ready to grow crops, to hunt and raise livestock. But in addition to the problem of provisioning for farming, hunting, and livestock raising, months of toil could yield nothing. The first group of Choctaws from the government-induced migrations planted and tended corn along the Arkansas River in 1833, only to see it washed away in a tremendous flood, along with corn cribs, livestock, houses, and other structures.

Both in the beginning of their new lives and periodically thereafter, the immigrant Indians had to rely on the government and its contractors for such staples as beef, flour, and salt. It was some help to stay as near to the supply points as possible, but even then, contractors often failed to appear. "I am here starving with the Chickasaws by gross mismanagement on the part of the contractors, and when our situation will be bettered is hard for me to tell, for it is one failure after another without end," wrote an official at a supply depot in 1838. "I begin to think that we will have to starve to death or abandon the Country."

Contractors repeatedly offered beef and other foodstuffs at inflated weights. In fact, one official was fired for attempting to give the immigrants their full, government-specified amounts. Even worse, inferior or rotten foodstuffs were routinely foisted upon the Indians, who complained—as did some of the officers and agents responsible for supplying them—but to no avail. No longer could an Indian confidently take the offending goods directly to a high government official, as the Catawba chief Nopkehe had. Sometimes the officers and agents contributed to the problem, as when Fort Gibson personnel sent the Choctaws beef "spoiled and unfit for consumption by the soldiers." When the Indians rejected it, an officer had it "scraped and re-brined" and "issued some barrels of it."

The Indian immigrants were made to feel like beggars, many compelled to return again and again to supply areas in hopes of rations, only to finally accept a pittance. One Creek man, who had traveled a great distance to claim a cattle ration for his family and others, made the mistake of requesting that the livestock be delivered to him early so that he could herd the animals home before nightfall. He was punished for his temerity by being the last to obtain the ration; the wild cattle escaped from him in the dark, leaving his family and his neighbors meatless for some time.

In such circumstances, each tribe had greater need than ever of presenting a unified front to make itself heard. But with the influxes of immigrants growing in the 1830s, many tensions surfaced. Those who had migrated before the forced marches had already adapted and developed in different ways from their cousins following the trails across the Missouri, the Red, and the Arkansas. The newcomers themselves often arrived deeply factionalized. And different groups responded in different ways to the political, economic, and cultural challenges confronting them in the new country.

The Cherokees provide the most obvious example of a nation profoundly divided. The Arkansas Cherokees who had removed to Indian country in 1828 had developed their own governance system, had chosen which traditions to retain, and had developed methods of living off the new land, primarily through adaptive farming. In the late 1830s, they were confronted with a flood of people with whom their kinship ties had considerably weakened, and they were expected to absorb this multitude into their domain.

First to come were various members of the eastern Treaty Party, many of whom had managed to avoid the destitution that would characterize the forced removal of the eastern Cherokees. The Arkansas Cherokees—the "Old Settlers"—looked with suspicion upon this group, convinced that the newcomers might be plotting another treaty, one to annex Indian Territory to Arkansas.

Then came the thousands of Cherokees who had held out against removal. They arrived impoverished and physically and emotionally drained, but, under the leadership of John Ross, still possessing a strong political and cultural identity. And they far outnumbered both the Old Settlers and the Treaty Party; in 1841, there would be approximately twelve thousand Cherokees under Ross, four thousand Treaty Party members, and only two thousand Old Settlers.

In addition, a fourth group—the Texas Cherokees—followed on the heels of the easterners. This group, having been further removed from Anglo-American influence for most of its existence, remained more traditional in its governance structures and social life than did the others. It was also, however, a small and marginal addition to the new Cherokee Nation. The infighting that took place was spurred by continuing tensions among the other three groups.

The reunited Cherokee Nation had a mandate from the United States government to reorganize its own government and produce a new constitution. Mandate or no, the Cherokees were quite aware that they needed to unite politically as quickly as possible, in part to fight for clear title to their portion of Indian Territory, in part to demand reparations for their losses in the East.

Yet the Old Settlers, despite their suspicions, were initially led into an alliance with the Treaty Party through a common fear of the large and politically unified Ross party. Treaty Party leaders—John and Major Ridge, Elias Boudinot, Stand Watie—have been painted in historical texts as both villains and tragic heroes. The latter view is more fitting, in that they were genuinely concerned with the survival of their people. However, Treaty Party leaders did enjoy benefits for cooperating with the United States government, and they retarded reunification by refusing to accept most of the Cherokee Nation's support of longtime principal chief John Ross.

This resistance, along with continuing bitter resentments over the Treaty of New Echota, led to the assassination of both Ridges and of Boudinot in three different locations on the same day in 1839. Stand Watie picked up the standard and opposed Ross at every turn, charging him with a hand in the murders. Ross nonetheless managed to forge an agreement whereby the eastern and western Cherokees could be reunited under one government. Four fifths of the Cherokees, including many Old Settlers, approved a new constitution and selected Ross as principal chief.

Stand Watie and the Treaty Party fought against any recognition of the Ross government in Washington, D.C. And Washington listened to these primarily mixed-blood, white-educated leaders who, unlike their fellow mixed-blood, Ross, had proven cooperative in the past. The United States government withheld money due the Cherokees, and questioned the validity of Ross's tribal reorganization even as he tried to marshal his political forces to fight for title to the western Cherokee lands.

Not surprisingly, all the political infighting and instability—along with the large influx of needy Indian immigrants—led to continuing unrest and violence in Cherokee country in the late 1830s and early 1840s. In the wake of the murders of the Ridges and Boudinot, revenge killings and destructive raids occurred to the point that "near civil war existed."

Still, the Cherokees struggled to become one people again. Other tribes simply continued to develop deep divisions between the traditionalists and progressives. In the early 1830s, the Vermillion Kickapoos and the Prairie Kickapoos in Kansas "quarreled constantly over moral, financial, and legal matters." The Vermillion band adapted quickly to Anglo-style farming while maintaining a strong Indian identity. The Prairie band, resistant to adopting Anglo lifeways but lacking other viable options, proved more susceptible to alcohol and gambling. Putting down few roots and remaining dissatisfied, many of them would migrate to Texas, Mexico, and Indian Territory.

The Creeks split into numerous Lower and Upper Creek villages, "more political than geographical divisions." Most of the Lower Creeks recognized Roley McIntosh, brother of the infamous William, as their chief; the Upper Creeks continued to rally around Opothleyaholo, who had led a final resistance in the East. The Lower Creeks continued to adapt and acculturate to white ways, while the Upper Creeks sought to guard their culture, often through coercive measures such as fining people for not attending the traditional Green Corn Dance and prescribing lashes for those who adopted Anglo dress or practiced the Anglo-Christian religion.

The Creeks resisted their federally appointed agent's urgings to create an Anglo-style government, instead continuing to rely on occasional policy-setting meetings among chiefs. It would be many years before they would establish a constitutional government with a single set of leaders, and even then, the move would be over the objection of many of the Upper Creeks.

If member of the same tribe had trouble living as one people, attempts by both the United States government and the Indians to unite members of different tribes created even greater difficulties.

For example, upon arriving in Indian Territory, the Seminoles discovered that their fear of being forced to live among the Creeks was valid. They refused to move onto land with the Creeks, instead camping around Fort Gibson "for several years in a state of unrest, confusion, and discontent . . . arresting all efforts to reestablish themselves." The Creeks exacerbated the situation by behaving just as the Seminoles had predicted they would, grasping at control over the black members of the Seminole population. Tensions were somewhat eased when government officials arranged for many of the Seminoles to move to a section of unused Creek territory.

A more agreeable relationship was reached between the Choctaws and the Chickasaws when the latter found themselves blocked from their own section by hostile Indians. The two southern tribes had intermarriage and language ties, and their treaty with each other gave the Chickasaws political identity as members of a Choctaw district and most privileges of Choctaw citizenship.

Yet the Chickasaws clearly lived on Choctaw sufferance, unable to develop their own institutions. The arrangement ultimately "caus[ed] irreparable harm and delay to the progress of both tribes" in the new country.

Most tribal land-sharing arrangements were forced or at least encouraged and coordinated by the United States government. Some were a result of tribes taking in refugees on their own. Either way, the influx of relatively destitute people created a strain. Creek chiefs appealed to the government for provisions on behalf of a group of Apalachicola Indians placed on Creek lands; the newcomers were "in a deplorable situation; a good many of them are naked and have no means by which they can obtain subsistence."

Opothleyaholo reported to a government agent an apparently independent unification agreement between the Upper Town Creeks and a Shawnee chief in 1840. The Shawnees, Opothleyaholo reported, had never received any of the $2,000 annual annuity promised to them in a treaty of 1817; Opothleyaholo requested that this money be forwarded with the Creek annuity in anticipation of the merging of the needy Shawnees into the Creek Nation.

Congress did occasionally provide extra funds to help the relocated Indians get on their feet or improve their situation. Soldiers and federally appointed agents worked to obtain for the Indians the provisions, money, and skilled help they had been promised upon removal. Government-appointed craftsmen (some of them Indian or part-Indian) worked as blacksmiths and wheelwrights to provide the tools for survival and growth in a new country. Missionaries provided necessary education for young Indians who would need to know how to live in an altered world.

Of course, most of these representatives, even the most honest, industrious, and sympathetic, also chipped or pounded away at Indian independence and identity. The missionaries in particular provided problematic assistance. Sincere in their desire to help the Indians, they often failed to provide the kind of practical knowledge natives realized they needed to have. Choctaw chief Mushulatubbe, who would establish a traditionalist enclave on the Arkansas River, complained in 1830, "We have employed and payed Yankee Missionaries for twelve years; for which we have Recd. no compensation; we hav never recd. a Scholar out of their Schools that was able to keep a grog shop book."

Instead, missionaries often sought to impose on the Indians rigid cultural standards. A missionary who worked among the Choctaws would recall as evidence of his spiritual charges' savagery that they traditionally planted corn "not secured by any fence." And the land was not plowed, but "dug up with hoes, and planted without rows, or in any order." Further, and most disturbing in light of Anglo gender roles, *this labor was performed by the women.*

Indians retained the right to refuse to accept missionaries onto their lands, and the Creeks did so. In 1842, the Lower Creeks relented and agreed to have a missionary start a school, but even Roley McIntosh, who represented the relatively acculturated half of the tribe, noted forcefully, "We don't want any preaching; for we find that preaching breaks up all our old customs—our feasts, ball plays, and dances— which we want to keep up."

Indians naturally attempted to use the missionaries' knowledge and skills to their own advantage. The Choctaws certainly did so, placing missionaries in schools set up with monies gained from the sale of their western lands to the Chickasaws. As young Choctaws went through the schools, and through Indian academies in the East, the tribe was able to turn fairly quickly to the hiring of Choctaw teachers. If these teachers had been inculcated in Anglo values, they were none-theless Indians, providing a bridge between the two worlds.

In fact, when one looks at the historical record, prosperity began to come to Indian Territory primarily through the Indians' own resil-ience, adaptability, and effort. With a little climatic luck, they were soon raising bounteous crops. Choctaw farmers supplied army garri-sons with corn by contract, while the Creeks became known as good cattle and hog raisers. They also worked both independently and com-munally in raising surplus crops of corn and rice.

Selling the surplus could prove difficult. Distance was often the problem—the Chickasaws could not get their bumper corn crop to market in 1843. The Indians also found themselves discriminated against, as when a military edict stopped their sales at Fort Gibson. "Both the Creeks and Cherokees think it hard and unfriendly that here in their own Country they are denied the benefit of a convenient market," wrote Cherokee agent Montfort Stokes, noting that Arkansas settlers were coming to the fort and trading at will: "If there is any good cause for these restrictions, I confess it has escaped my notice."

Despite such setbacks, an Indian economy continued to grow, and many immigrants settled down to comfortable if simple living. The Creeks, for example, were reported inhabiting sturdy log homes and grinding their corn in hollowed-out log mortars, as they had in the past. While there were few prosperous Cherokees—and those inevitably mixed-bloods—most tribal members "enjoyed a standard of living as high as, if not higher than" that of nearby white settlers.

Further, despite divisions and enmities, Indians worked together to address mutual problems and concerns. One way in which they did this was by temperance measures and temperance work. Alcohol had continued to be a scourge in Indian country, especially for those closest to the Anglo settlements. The Cherokees started a temperance society in 1836, its ranks soon swollen by veterans of the Trail of Tears who had been disgusted by the scenes of drunkenness and debilitation that heightened the horrors of the journey. The Creeks soon outlawed the sale or use of liquor in their country, leading travelers to comment favorably on the peace and sobriety they found among the people.

The exiled southern nations also led in gathering Indians of different tribes to exchange views and counsel. One of the largest such events in the immigrants' early years in Indian Territory began on a summer day in 1843. People from eighteen immigrant and native tribes—among them Seminoles and Creeks, Wichitas and Osages, Delawares and Shawnees—came together in the new Cherokee capital of Talequah to talk about the challenges they still faced and the ways in which they could support each other. They spent four weeks visiting, comparing, consulting, and reaching various agreements, one that no tribe would "sell, cede, or in any manner alienate to the United States any part of their present territory" without gaining the approval of other tribes. They had not been withered by drought, but were growing stronger and surer.

Meanwhile, to the north, settler wagons had begun rolling along the banks of the Platte River, bound for the fertile Willamette Valley, in a far western region claimed by both the United States and Great Britain. The people rebuilding their lives in Indian Territory would be relatively safe for a time, but every turn of the wagon wheels signaled a challenge to the land tenure of every native and immigrant Indian in the West.

Locations of various western tribes at the onset of Anglo expansion

Chapter Five

← →

"Take Away Your Paper"
(1844–1860)

Why do you ask me to sign away my country. . . . I have no other home than this. . . . Take away your paper. I will not touch it with my hand.

—*Chief Joseph of the Nez Perces, about 1855*

You have pulled all my wings off.
—*Moses of the Flatheads, 1855*

In the autumn, as the goldenrods and asters flowered and faded on the tall-grass prairies, Omaha men always left their earthlodge villages in present-day Nebraska to hunt game. In 1853, some crossed the Missouri River to their traditional hunting territory—part of what whites now considered the state of Iowa—and found the game still plentiful.

The Omahas had not ceded this region. However, the farms and towns of white immigrants—primarily from the Old Northwest but also from the South, the East, and Europe—were spreading along the pleasant forested river stretches, their own rough roads snaking across the grasslands. They did not want the Indians ranging over the land.

At a meeting between the Indian hunters and these new occupants, an Omaha named White-Buffalo-in-the-Distance tried to explain that while the immigrants kept their livestock close to them, the Indians depended upon "wild animals, which are beyond our dwelling place, though they are on our land." White Buffalo and a farmer then fell to arguing over who did own the land, the Indian asking, "Why do you consider me a fool? You are now dwelling a little beyond the bounds of the land belonging to the president."

To the farmer's insistence that the Omahas accept the immigrants' boundaries or face a fight, White Buffalo responded, "I will go beyond. You may fight me. As the land is mine, I shall go." The Omahas proceeded with their seasonal routine, at one point successfully fighting off a large contingent of whites bent on forcing them out of the country.

The next year, at the treaty table, the Omahas would lose the Iowa hunting grounds.

Much was happening in the American nation of the mid-nineteenth century to alter drastically the lives of Indians in the West. As on previous frontiers, white settlers were moving westward in advance of official government sanction and support. In the 1840s, they were bound for the agricultural frontier of Oregon. With two momentous and near-simultaneous events in 1848—the discovery of gold in California and Mexico's cession of California and southwestern land claims in the Treaty of Guadalupe Hidalgo after the Mexican War— the string of wagons became an armada. By the 1850s, immigrants were spilling onto the prairies across the Missouri and fanning through the Far West; by the end of this decade they were also scattering settlements through the plains and mountains in between.

The bulk of the immigrants, Americans of northern European extraction, carried with them an assumption of their own innate superiority as "civilized" people and that corresponding sense of Manifest Destiny, which reassured them that in representing Western civilization and progress, they were meant to come into the land and claim it. The United States government—made up of European Americans of the same mind-set—began carving territories across the western landscape.

Numbers tell much of the story. At midcentury, the population of Indians beyond the Mississippi has been estimated at some 360,000, including the northern and southern Plains tribes, the eastern Indians who had been pushed into the southern Plains tribes' territory, Texas natives and immigrants, natives within the "Mexican Cession" (California, New Mexico, and most of Arizona), and indigenous peoples of the Pacific Northwest (Oregon, Idaho, and Washington). At this same point, "the United States . . . boasted a population of more than 20 million," and by 1860, "1.4 million would live in the West."

During the period 1844–1860, then, the "Permanent Indian Frontier" evaporated, and with it the government policy of simply pushing natives westward. At the same time, treaties to remove western natives proliferated; between 1853 and 1856 "more Indian acreage was alienated than in any other period."

Where were the natives to go? In 1848, William Medill, commissioner of Indian Affairs, proposed the creation of Indian "colonies," areas in which to collect the native population as "the whites filled up the country around them." The idea of controlled Indian enclaves could be traced all the way back to New England's praying towns, as could the accompanying emphasis on "civilizing" the natives, who were to be "taught to support themselves by farming, insulated from white vices, and uplifted by white virtues." But for the first time, the federal government began developing concerted policies to achieve these ends, policies that would greatly curtail or obliterate remaining Indian freedoms.

Four distinct types of Indian country could be identified in the mid-nineteenth century. Indians still occupied—officially or unofficially—scattered tracts in the East. Tribes from the East lived on western lands granted them "as long as the grass shall grow," where they were "expected to govern and support themselves," the latter through voluntary farming, hunting and gathering, government-controlled trading, and handling of annuities. Natives of the West still inhabited and at least partially controlled the resources of their regions, along with westering Indians independently seeking a renewed land base. And then there was the Indian country that was haltingly but inexorably being devised for natives as an instrument of government control: the western reservation. In each environment, Indians continued to develop survival strategies.

Along the eastern seaboard, those remnants of native tribes who had managed to maintain an Indian identity and a small land base for generations had to remain ever-vigilant. In New York, the Ogden Land Company, which had bought Iroquois land from another land company in 1810, endlessly harassed the Senecas, but also, ironically, kept the land-ownership picture so clouded that it forestalled other plots to take the Senecas' reservations. In Virginia the combined Pamunkey and Mattaponi bands in 1843 and 1844 found their claim to a small reservation challenged by white neighbors, who argued that racial intermixing over the years had undercut any ownership based on a distinct Indian identity. The Pamunkeys and Mattaponis responded by instituting strict laws against intermarriage.

The most effective—and most complex—strategy for survival was to make major adaptations to white cultural and economic realities without sacrificing Indian identity. Even this strategy had not worked for the "Civilized Tribes" in the South, but the Narragansetts of Rhode Island managed such a balancing act in this period. They had accepted "several English lifeways and values," including "the male's surname for the family, private individual land ownership, inheritance of land through either the father or mother." They worshiped as Christians and sent their children to state-subsidized schools. They participated in the local economy, some of the men working as stonemasons, and families raising sheep and selling the wool to nearby textile mills.

At the same time, the Narragansetts maintained separate institutions (the church and schools were Indian) and safeguarded their common land rights. Their 1850 constitution specified that a cedar-tree swamp could only be cut for use by tribal members and further stipulated that "All Lands Belonging to the Tribe that is Leased Let or Rented by the Committee [the tribal council] to any Person or Persons Shall be Let With a View to improve Them as well as for the Profit—The Committee Shall see that the Young wood is not cut to Waste for Hudge Hopps nor Poles."

Such evidence of economic and cultural autonomy did not obscure a generally dismal picture in the East. A state commissioner's report of 1861 outlined health conditions on Massachusetts reservations between 1849 and 1861, conditions that would become all too familiar on western reservations as well: "alarming rates of mortality of up to 33 percent or more," due primarily to "consumption, smallpox, a variety of infantile diseases, [and] drowning," along with old age. And liquor, its sale banned on the reservations, still flowed unrestrainedly, devastating individuals and communities.

Whether a tribe was faring well or poorly, the pressure to remove continued. In 1840, the government of South Carolina, pursuing the old get-a-little-farther policy, had pushed the Catawbas into an agreement whereby the state would purchase for them a remote mountain tract, possibly near the remaining North Carolina Cherokees, and pay them $2,500, plus $1,500 a year for nine years. Should a site not be found, the Catawbas would receive $5,000, plus the $1,500 annuity.

The Catawbas had divided as to what to do and where to go, most preferring to remain on their homeland or nearby. Some had moved in with the Carolina Cherokees, but disliked the pressure to conform to Cherokee language and lifeways. Others relocated to a new—and of course smaller—reservation that was finally provided for them on former Catawba lands in North Carolina. However an authoritarian Indian agent and the lack of a fall harvest caused most Catawbas to flee, which left the reservation for years virtually deserted, its population at one point a Catawba woman and six children.

The Catawbas wound up "living everywhere and nowhere, without lands and without homes." Some made their way to Indian Territory and were taken in by the Choctaws. Others drifted back to the old reservation, where South Carolina officials relented and allowed them to remain.

In the South, however, the federal government, state governments, and private citizens all continued to squeeze Indian enclaves relentlessly. Through the 1840s, the Choctaws remaining in Alabama and Mississippi fought off continuing federal and state-government attempts to remove them. Their situation is portrayed vividly in a complaint they made to a white official in 1849 regarding "the acts of those persons who profess to be agents of the Government to procure our removal":

We have had our habitations torn down and burned; our fences destroyed, cattle turned into our fences & we ourselves have been scourged, manacled, fettered and otherwise personally abused, until by such treatment some of our best men have died.

Many Choctaws were willing to leave if they could obtain payment for their eastern land, take their livestock and possessions with them, and travel under a humane agent. Unfortunately, government attention to such basic considerations appeared no more likely in the 1840s than it had in the previous decade.

The one remnant of an eastern tribe that did gain important removal concessions from the government still refused to depart. After the

Second Seminole War ended inconclusively in the early 1840s, the federal government, spurred by whites within and along Florida borders, tried repeatedly to entice the remaining Seminoles to depart for Indian Territory, in 1849 offering payment for "all cattle, hogs, crops, and other property abandoned or left behind," provisions and the services of a physician on the journey, a year's subsistence in their new home, and cash payments to every emigrant. Sums of as much as $10,000 were offered individual leaders.

Still, the four to five hundred remaining Seminoles said no. "We did not expect this talk," announced a leader named Assunwha, who had turned over Seminole killers of a white man in an attempt to maintain peace. "When you began this new [removal] matter I felt as if you had shot me. I would rather be shot." Assunwha left no doubt where he stood: "I will not go, nor will our people. I want no time to think or talk about it, for my mind is made up. . . . I did not expect this talk, and had I done so I would not have helped to deliver up these men to you."

Even the Florida legislature's banning of any trade with the Seminoles did not succeed in moving them, although it rendered them unable to buy food or to get ammunition to hunt food. Seminoles even freely assisted military explorers and surveyors in the hope that when the visitors "saw how poor and worthless the country was" they would leave it to the natives.

In 1857, most of the remaining Indians in the Everglades were finally forced or cajoled from their homes by army officers and agents, aided by western Creeks and Seminoles. The resistance leader Coacoochee, or Wild Cat, reluctantly surrendered, although, he contended, he would "rather be killed by a white man in Florida, than die in Arkansas.

. . . I asked for but a small piece of this land, enough to plant and live on far to the south—a spot where I could place the ashes of my kindred—a place where my wife and child could live. This was not granted me. I am about to leave Florida forever and have done nothing to disgrace it. It was my home; I loved it, and to leave it is like burying my wife and child. I have thrown away my rifle and have taken the hand of the white man, and now I say take care of me!

Like so many before him, Wild Cat found that taking the hand of the white man did not lead to a change in fortunes. Instead, he later reported, his party was "transported to a cold climate, naked, without game to hunt, or fields to plant, or huts," the children "crying like wolves, hungry, cold, and destitute." Yet the territory carved out in the West remained the eastern tribes' last best hope—if they could hold on to it.

By the mid-1840s, holding on to the new land was proving impossible for many of the Old Northwest tribes. At federal-government urging, they had relocated across the Mississippi from their Illinois and Wisconsin Territory homelands, to lands between the Mississippi and the Missouri rivers. This good farming region had become part of Iowa Territory in 1838 and the state of Iowa in 1846, forcing some of these tribes into a dizzying set of moves.

The Winnebagos were again pushed to a western reservation, in the area that would soon become Minnesota Territory. In 1855, they were pressured into exchanging this land for another reservation in the territory, yet they adapted readily to the new location. One Winnebago chief, Little Hill, would recall of the Minnesota days, "We used to live in good houses, and always take our Great Father's advice and do whatever he told us to do. We used to farm and raise a crop of all we wanted every year . . . we had teams of our own. Each family had a span of horses or oxen to work, and had plenty of ponies."

But the Winnebagos' tenure here was to be short-lived as well. Meanwhile, the eastern Sioux, natives of Minnesota, were pressed in the 1850s into ceding 28 million acres "in exchange for annual annuities" and a Minnesota River reservation. The state of Minnesota was carved from the territory of the same name in 1858.

The Potawatomis and the Mississippi River Sacs could reasonably expect greater stability in their new location: present-day Kansas, across the Missouri River from the state of Missouri. Here by 1850, residing on various reservations, were "thousands of Indian immigrants," including Missouri Sacs, Iowas, Kickapoos, Shawnees, Delawares, Chippewas, Munsees, Ottawas, Peorias, Kaskaskias, Weas, and Piankashaws.

The immigrant Indians living in Kansas continued to follow their traditional ways in many respects. Missionaries found them resistant to conversion attempts, one writing in 1842, "The poor Indians seem wonderfully contented with their old way of living. Their prejudices [are] strong and hard to overcome." Even the most accommodationist of them often rejected the missionaries' desire to preach in Indian communities, instead cultivating them as legal advisers and advocates in Indian business dealings with the government and white citizens.

The displaced groups also sometimes welcomed missionary schools, but such a welcome was by no means assured; "the Iowas consented to send only orphans of mixed Indian and white parentage" to a Presbyterian school established with funds from their removal treaty, and the Sacs "refused to allow any of their children to attend."

In addition, the new Kansas tribes tended to reject the village sites and the unfamiliar log cabins provided for them by the U.S. government, and continued their warrior traditions, so troubling to agents and missionaries, in clashes with the Sioux and Pawnees to the west.

Many recognized that unity was imperative for survival, "that their own ways helped them to remain unified," and that they had a better chance of becoming rooted if they adapted at least in part to white ways.

The Vermillion Kickapoo had been pushed from Illinois to Wisconsin to Kansas. Most of them continued to wear native dress and to live in traditional homes. They continued to own and manage land in common, even though it was divided into family plots. The men continued to hunt buffalo on the plains. At the same time, the prophet Kenekuk, who had passively resisted removal to the West for many years, led this band in avoiding the liquor bottle, seeking peaceful relations with Indian and white neighbors, and marshaling their resources and skills to create Anglo-style farms. Anglo neighbors acknowledged the group's "Protestant-like work ethic" and their clear contribution to the local economy through sales of corn, potato, pumpkin, and livestock.

The Kickapoos' efforts were ultimately of limited usefulness against Anglo expansion. No sooner had most of the Old Northwest tribes become established in Kansas and southern Nebraska than white settlers began pushing across the Missouri toward them. The Kickapoos found white trespassers harvesting the limited timber on their prairie reservation, even setting up a sawmill. The federal government did send troops to remove the trespassers but also—in an already time-honored pattern—began to accommodate the invaders by reducing the Indians' land base.

The result: in 1853 and 1854, the commissioner of Indian Affairs, warning the Indians that they would do well to hold on to what they could, "obtained land cessions from eleven tribes in Kansas and three in southeastern Nebraska cutting their holdings from eighteen million to one and one-third million acres." The Shawnees lost seven of every eight acres originally granted them. The Kickapoos "signed away all but 152,417 acres of their 1,200-square-mile Kansas reservation." Some took as an ominous sign the tremendous storm that followed the signing, just as an earthquake had followed the signing of their first removal treaty in Illinois.

One group of Sacs refused to move within the reduced boundaries of their Kansas reservation. The agent cut off their annuities, and the Sacs survived without them for two years before reluctantly shifting onto the designated land.

Most groups, including the Vermillion Kickapoos—now combined with Potawatomi allies—quietly set about reestablishing themselves. They still occupied fertile lands; they still enjoyed some autonomy. But two troubling and interrelated problems continued to develop. First, some of the tribes, whether they knew and understood it or not, had signed treaties containing allotment provisions. This meant that they had agreed to abandon the communal land base in favor of small individual or family tracts, the remaining reservation land to be opened to white settlement and speculation. And those who had not signed such agreements were under increasing pressure to do so.

Second, Kansas and Nebraska were about to be made United States territories by act of Congress, further undermining tribal possession and tribal presence. Aware of the danger, delegates from various immigrant tribes traveled to Washington to try to make their voices heard.

The delegates had barely crossed the Missouri when white settlers and speculators crossed the other way and began staking out acreage on the reservation, contending that the land was theirs for the taking. The federal government had restricted appropriation of lands that were identified as part of the public domain, but the invaders argued that such restrictions did not apply to Indian-occupied tracts. A trader wrote that they were marking where to place their cabins and writing their names on tree trunks, until "there is not a grease spot left unclaimed within my knowledge; and still claim hunters are passing daily."

Passage of the Kansas-Nebraska Act of 1854 gave sanction to the attempts to get the remaining Indian land in Kansas, through seizure, fraud, or purchase of tracts held in common or individually. Railroad speculators added to the atmosphere of confusion and exploitation by snapping up "surplus lands" on the allotted reservations. They also bought rights-of-way across Indian lands from the Delawares and other tribes who hoped to obtain something approximating their worth, a belief in which they were "sadly mistaken."

In the late 1850s, the situation worsened with the development of "Indian rings"—shifting alliances of "Washington bureaucrats, congressmen, businessmen, army officers, Indian agents, and even tribal 'chiefs,' " the last group seeming to legitimize the rings' frauds in the face of humanitarian protests by other whites.

It seemed as if Kansas Indians seeking to hold on to acreage could trust no one. In 1860, Baptist missionaries and the agent to the Ottawas "arranged a deal with Ottawa leaders willing to accept bribes in exchange for tribal property." The conspirators appropriated one fourth of the Ottawas' lands—some twenty thousand acres. They claimed it would be used for an Indian university; instead, the acreage was quickly thrown open to white speculation.

Some of the tribes, such as the Shawnees and Delawares, splintered and drifted under such an onslaught, unable to overcome their own factionalism and endemic drunkenness born of bitterness, instability, and despair. Others, such as the Vermillion Kickapoos and the Chippewas and Munsees (the latter two bands combining in 1859), continued to buttress their Kansas presence and claims through peaceful and industrious farming. Still others, such as the Wyandots, sought refuge to the south, among the immigrant tribes already in present-day Oklahoma. Here, along with the major southern tribes and a host of smaller ones, they bought time.

In eastern and central Oklahoma, still unorganized Indian country ostensibly off-limits to whites, members of the immigrant tribes in the 1840s and 1850s worked toward greater stability and even prosperity.

The Cherokees and Choctaws led the way, continuing to show a strong ability to adapt to Anglo culture without giving up their distinctive tribal identities. By the end of the 1840s, the Cherokees had "far surpassed the provincial life of their closest white neighbors in frontier Arkansas." The John Ross party had staved off an attempt to split their political opponents into a separate government, and the democratic government at Talequah was proving as vigorous and effective as the old one at New Echota. Churches and "improvement societies" flourished, as did schools and seminaries, the Cherokees' public schools "[becoming] the first free, compulsory, coeducational system west of the Mississippi."

The Choctaws, too, continued their emphasis on education, by 1850 boasting numerous schools staffed by Choctaw teachers using the native language. Both they and the Cherokees also continued to show that they were adept at Anglo-style farming. An 1856 observer in Choctaw country found well-fenced farms on which sat "good cabins with plank floors, stone chimneys, and glass windows," while the farmyards were filled with "horses, cattle, cows, working oxen, hogs, sheep, geese, turkeys, guinea fowls and chickens." In the fields grew cotton and an abundance of grains and vegetables, while apples, plums, peaches, and pears ripened in nearby orchards. Wagon roads veined the countryside and led to "horse mills, cotton gins, grist- and sawmills, blacksmith shops and ferry boats."

Members of other tribes established themselves more slowly. The Chickasaws showed tremendous industry, "mak[ing] more corn than will subsist them," but in the late 1840s they remained shut off from markets because of their remote locations. Then a market came to them—gold rushers crossing the territory in 1849—and in the early 1850s both the Chickasaws and the Choctaws were able to profit from trade.

The Creeks, too, proved industrious. By the late 1840s they were exporting large shipments of corn and enjoying a flourishing livestock trade with buyers from Illinois, Indiana, and Missouri. Yet they continued to decline in numbers, from a total of 24,000 "enumerated by name and town before their forced removal in 1836" to "only 13,537 by the census of 1859." The commissioner of Indian Affairs reported in 1859: "All that can statistically be said of the Creek people is, that they are not increasing in population, and that in property and improvements of schools and farms, they are only slowly advancing, but, perhaps, quite as much as could be expected of a people in their circumstances and condition.''

Of the five tribes recognized as "civilized" by the whites, the Creeks and Seminoles had suffered more fully as groups for their resistance to removal and had more trouble adjusting in the West, where the United States government persisted in trying to push them together. Like the Creeks, the Seminoles continued to lose population through their long removal period, dropping by almost 40 percent in three decades. They remained scattered and lacking in annuities, both unable and unwilling to develop educational initiatives. Some—led by the disappointed and intractable Wild Cat—had sought a new home in Mexico.

Even after the 1856 agreement by which they received their own territory—based in part on their promise to prevail upon the remaining eastern Seminoles to migrate—the Seminoles stayed in Creek country and both groups fared relatively poorly. Over the years government officials did attempt to secure some funds and other assistance for them, but those Seminoles arriving from the extended war in the East were exhausted, embittered, and—even had the government followed through as it should have on its promises of agricultural assistance— uninterested in taking up uncertain and difficult farming on the prairies after life in their old country of "summer, game, fish, clear waters, and orange groves.''

The continuing arrival of members of various tribes kept much of Indian Territory in a state of flux. For example, the Choctaws and Chickasaws were induced to lease land in 1859 to Indians who had been driven from North Texas—mostly Caddos and southern Comanches. These natives had lived—at first, peacefully—on the Brazos and Clear Fork reservations, suffering along with white immigrants from raids by white outlaws and nonreservation Indians.

The men of the reservations had even served as "active guardians of frontier whites,'' recovering stolen stock for the settlers and participating with Texas Rangers in expeditions against raiders. However, the continuing association of some reservation residents with "uncontrolled'' nonreservation kin and friends—and the white propensity to class all Indians as hostile—had led to increasingly virulent white resistance to the reservations, even to calls for the extermination of their residents.

The situation had escalated to the point that the reservation Indians had been compelled to abandon their crops and schools in order to fortify reservation boundaries against attack from organized settlers. (The story of Indians constructing breastworks—with the aid of federal troops—against an Anglo onslaught provides an interesting counterpoint to accounts of pioneer Texans "forting up" against Comanche and other raiders.)

Finally, Texas followed the lead of Georgia and Alabama decades before, even those citizens who were sympathetic to the Indians concluding, in the words of Governor Hardin Runnels, that whether or not reservation Indians were guilty of raiding, "there is to be no more peace as long as they remain on [Texas] soil."

The Comanches, Caddos, and related bands agreed to move across the Red River to Indian Territory on Texas Indian agent Robert Simpson Neighbors's apparently honest but overly optimistic promise of an extensive land refuge of their own. "I have this day crossed all the Indians out of the heathen land of Texas and am now out of the land of the Philistines," the beleaguered Neighbors wrote to his wife in September. Neighbors was soon murdered by an irate Texan who resented his efforts on behalf of the dispossessed, and the Texas Indians found themselves just one of a number of groups being thrust onto leased Indian Territory lands.

Government-promised annuities should have cushioned the transition for most immigrants, as well as aided the more established residents of Indian Territory. But the annuity system continued to lurch along ineffectively, with frequent delays. In 1857, the commissioner of Indian Affairs reported that the Creeks suffered annually from pneumonia outbreaks, "and this has been greatly increased by the delay in their annual payments into very late in the fall or commencement of winter when they have frequently to assemble to receive their money without any shelter or protection against the most inclement weather."

In some cases, the money continued to be paid to chiefs for disbursement—a good idea if the man was careful and judicious, a bad one if he had made himself a "chief" only in the eyes of Anglo authorities, if he lacked ability as a manager, if he played favorites, and if he exhibited strong self-interest. In 1854, some Chickasaws were accused of trying to return to a traditional hereditary chieftain-ship system in order to get their hands on tribal annuities.

Direct payment had its drawbacks as well. "For some days I have been in a busy crowd . . . " wrote an observer in Creek country in 1848. "The tribe gathers here from every corner of the land, and with them every white to whom they are owing five dollars. . . . At the close of the payment the Indian will not have a dollar." This questionable practice would become systemized in the West, with "politically well-connected traders" occupying spots at disbursing tables "to collect real or fictional debts run up . . . by the Indians."

The traders also used their supplies of liquor to part Indians quickly from cash. The borders of Indian Territory tribal lands teemed with liquor traders, the Red River with steamboats dispensing whiskey. The pervasiveness of heavy drinking—along with factionalism, lawless-ness, uncertain economic fortunes, hostile western Indians, and pres-sure from whites wanting Indian lands—led different groups in Indian Territory to seek a way out of its borders even as new Indian immi-grants sought refuge within them. Some drifted back to their old homelands, where they predictably led meager and uncertain lives on the periphery of white culture. Others explored the possibility of setting up independent communities in Mexico.

The tribes also sought—often successfully—to deal with the prob-lems in Indian Territory. The Cherokees established light-horse companies, "very summary dealers in justice," to patrol each district in response to continuing factional violence in the mid-1840s. The Creek light-horse police in the 1850s acted with good effect upon a tribal mandate to destroy the liquor traffic. The Choctaws, their crops withered from drought, altered their farming methods and managed to produce respectable corn yields under dry conditions. Tribal govern-ments sought—and sometimes gained—peace within the tribe, with other immigrant tribes, and with western Indians and independent remnants of eastern tribes who raided within Indian Territory bound-aries.

In fact, the tribal governments of the Cherokees and Choctaws, the Creeks and Chickasaws showed real strength and staying power. Their white agents had "nominal" duties, while the intertribal councils "made compacts regulating such matters as the requisition of criminals and intertribal naturalization." They also continued to fight for lands lost, the Cherokees in the mid-1850s sending a representative to Washington "to petition Congress for permission to sue the state of Texas for the return of 1.5 million acres in east Texas."

Such unity was born of both departure from tradition and adherence to it. The Cherokees continued to develop a model democratic system fashioned after that of the United States government, while the Creeks, "adher[ing] to their old system of government, by national and town chiefs" throughout the period, could show that "their laws are respected and obeyed by the people."

Again white encroachment threatened to undermine everything. Anglos "wandered" across the Indian boundaries, contributing to or creating disorder and often bringing charges against the Indians of the territory in Anglo courts in Arkansas. These incidents were part of a larger pattern, which was apparent to the *Cherokee Advocate* in 1845: "Our comfortable cabins, productive farms, valuable mineral resources, clear streams and beautiful prairies excite the cupidity and moisten the lips of those who have not failed to filch by fraud, or rob by superior power of their native inheritance, every Indian community with whom they have come in contact."

Twelve years later, John Ross, still principal chief of the Cherokees, made the same point, warning that the long, hard years of rebuilding would be for naught if views such as those of Kansas Governor Robert J. Walker prevailed. Walker wanted the United States to appropriate the Oklahoma lands as it had those in Kansas. He spun out a fantasy in which the Oklahoma Indians would "most cheerfully" agree to relinquish the lands on which they were living—"valueless to them"—in exchange for money and smaller, less fertile tracts to the west.

Even had the Indians consented to such a plan—and they were prepared to fight it in the courts—the United States could no longer ignore the fact that the American West beyond Indian Territory boundaries was already populated by native peoples. They, like the Cherokees in their homelands some thirty years earlier, had no intention of moving aside or away.

* * *

In the nineteenth century the native West was an incredibly diverse place, both geographically and culturally. Most of the Pueblo peoples, peaceful southwestern farmers, lived along the Rio Grande and the New Mexico streams feeding into it—this was a country of stark mountain ranges and desert expanses, but with enough summer rainfall to sustain careful agriculture. The westernmost group, the Hopi, inhabited the high mesas of the Colorado Plateau.

Around these natives many centuries before had settled the nomadic, warlike Apaches and their Athapascan relatives, the Navajos, the latter having adapted well to agrarian practices. Farther toward the setting sun, in what is now western Arizona, resided such desert farmers as the Pimas, Papagos, Mojaves, Havasupais, and Yavapias, who irrigated their crops with water from the Gila and Colorado rivers and their tributaries.

Crossing the Colorado into southern California and working northward on the west side of the Sierra Nevadas, a traveler in the first half of the nineteenth century would have encountered among the coastal ranges and in the central valley a variety of hunting-and-gathering tribes, often called "tribelets" because of their small size—Serrano and Yokut, Miwok and Pomo. Beyond the northern California groups—the Pomos and Wiyoks and Yuroks and Karoks, among others—lay the rugged yet lush northwest coastal country of such tribes as the Siletz, the Clapsop, the Chinook and Puyallup, who lived on a bounty of salmon and wild foods.

Moving inland along the salmon-choked Columbia River, the traveler would enter the Columbia Plateau, "Inland Empire of the Northwest," fifteen hundred square miles encompassing northeastern Oregon, eastern Washington, northern Idaho, and western Montana. Here lived the hunting-and-gathering Yakimas and Palouses, the Walla Wallas and Cayuses, the Nez Perces and Flatheads. To the south, between these groups and the southwestern tribes, stretched the Great Basin, a 200,000-square-mile area, dominated by deserts and mountains and ringed by uplands—southeastern Oregon, southern Idaho, western Wyoming, all of Nevada and Utah, western Colorado. Here dwelt the desert foragers: the Paiutes, the Utes, the Shoshones.

To the east, in a region stretching from present-day Canada to Texas—between the tribes of the Columbia Plateau, the Great Basin, and the Southwest on one side and the advancing white and immigrant Indian frontier on the other—lived the Great Plains Indians, sedentary tribes, such as the Arikara, Mandan, and Omaha, and nomadic hunters and gatherers, such as the western Sioux, the Pawnees, and the Kiowas.

All of these groups had had some contact with European and American adventurers, their animals, and their technologies long before the advent of the wagon trains. Many had already undergone major transformations as a result of that contact.

For example, the Spanish introduction of the horse into North America had long since given rise to distinctive Plains cultures in which the horse figured prominently, enhancing and significantly altering Plains Indian mobility, prosperity, political leadership, and warfare. This European-introduced horse culture also had drawn neighboring tribes such as the Cheyenne and the Comanche into the region.

In California coastal tribelets had adapted to a determined eighteenth-century Spanish colonizing thrust by becoming "Mission Indians," and they continued to assimilate into the Spanish frontier culture after the missions were secularized.

In the Southwest, Santa Fe, founded a mere three years after Jamestown, had stabilized as a trading center for the Spanish, Mexicans, Indians, and European Americans, the Santa Fe Trail linking the town with the Missouri settlements in the 1820s. In the early nineteenth century, the British had established a fur-trading foothold in the Northwest, while American "mountain men" out of St. Louis had traversed (and roughly mapped) the western interior, living with, trading with, and fighting with the natives.

Inevitably, European diseases had also preceded the wagons west. "I cannot see the enemy who is killing us," declared a Cheyenne warrior, afflicted with what was probably cholera, early in the century. "When I see an enemy I never stay back, but I cannot protect the people from this thing; they just fall and die." In 1833, Hudson's Bay Company trappers carried malaria into California's valleys, the disease quickly wiping out "an estimated twenty thousand Indians" and continuing to scourge the remaining population for years as the homes of the dead, "filled with skulls and bones," collapsed around them.

The most massive epidemic—or perhaps, as demographer Russell

Thornton says, only the best recorded—occurred in the late 1830s. Smallpox swept across the Plains from the Missouri River frontier, extending to the Pacific Northwest and all the way into Canada and Alaska. As in New England two centuries before, the epidemic devastated and weakened whole native populations shortly before the advent of any significant number of Anglo immigrants.

An American Fur Company steamboat navigating the Missouri River in 1837 with smallpox-carrying passengers left an appalling wake, as many as ten thousand Plains Indians dying of smallpox within a few weeks. The Blackfeet, who ranged the northern Plains from present-day Montana into Canada, lost two thirds of their population, or some six thousand people. The Mandans, who had long farmed along the river in present-day North Dakota, dropped from an estimated total of as many as 2,000 to 138 within four months. The painter George Catlin had found the Mandans a handsome, healthy people only a short time before; in the wake of the epidemic, he learned, the living had fallen into "too appalling despair," while the dead lay "in horrid and loathsome piles in their own wigwams, with a few buffalo robes, etc. thrown over them, there to decay and be devoured by their own dogs."

Despite such cataclysmic misfortunes, up until about midcentury, western Indians in general managed to keep changes that resulted from contact with Europeans and European Americans "evolutionary" and largely "within the bounds of traditional culture." However, to the ravages of disease were added further dependence on trade and troubling changes in the natural world. By 1845, buffalo were already growing scarce on the eastern Plains, forcing the Lakota Sioux to extend their hunting area "west of the Laramie mountains of Wyoming, far beyond their normal range." Historian Elliott West has traced this early decline to the increase in Indian numbers and to increased Indian hunting for market on the Plains. The Cheyennes, for example, having migrated onto the Plains in response to what appeared to be abundant hunting opportunities, "watched the steady disappearance of what had brought them into this new country in the first place."

Indian overhunting was not the only cause of the decline in the buffalo herds, of course. Non-Indian hunters and repeated withering droughts on the Central Plains (1848–1862)—even diseases carried by westering immigrants' livestock—contributed to a significant drop in bison numbers even before the notorious Anglo overhunting of the post–Civil War period. Further, both Indians and whites were already using up the land's resources at an accelerating rate.

The times called for new strategies for survival, but unlike the whites, the Indians had "no alternative source of support" when land resources failed them.

Perhaps the least vulnerable of western Indian cultures to the coming of white treaty makers and immigrants were the Pueblos of the Southwest—the Hopis, Zunis, and a handful of other indigenous groups. Peaceful irrigation farmers with well-defined villages and ancient claims to them, they aligned first with the Hispanic occupiers of the land, then with the Anglo-Americans, against their more warlike native neighbors.

When the United States claimed the Southwest from Mexico in the 1848 Treaty of Guadalupe Hidalgo, it actually upheld the Pueblos' land claims—under Spanish title—but, like the Hispanic government before it, "could not protect them from Apache, Navajo, and Ute raiders and would not protect them from Hispanic and Anglo squatters." The Pueblos watched with some resentment as the United States negotiated with and offered concessions to the more aggressive southwestern tribes.

These tribes would have happily done without such government attention. But the United States was intent on gaining military control over their regions, winning treaty concessions to establish forts in 1849 and creating New Mexico Territory (present-day New Mexico and Arizona) the next year. Even though few whites—primarily gold prospectors—had a desire to tackle the corrugated desert country where Apaches and Navajos thrived, the government wanted to push the natives as far into that country as possible to eliminate the raiding eastward and to ensure safe travel routes.

Both the Apaches and the Navajos at first proved approachable. Veterans of a combative but often cooperative world of ethnic diversity, they were willing to work with the trickle of newcomers to their mutual advantage. The renowned Chiricahua Apache leader Cochise "even contract[ed] to supply firewood for the Butterfield stage line."

The whites, however, kept bombarding the natives with treaties that were puzzling in their attempted restrictions on Indian land and freedoms. The New Mexico territorial governor, David Meriwether, acting in line with the new federal emphasis on clearly bounded reservation lands for western Indians, negotiated a series of such treaties with Apaches, Navajos, and Utes.

The southwestern tribes were no strangers to the concept of a reservation, for the Spanish had in the late 1700s established a string of eight *establecimientos de paz,* or peace establishments. Here Indians could settle under Spanish military protection against the various warring interests in the Southwest; here they would receive weekly rations and training in farming, the Spanish still hoping to assimilate them as colonists.

But the peace establishments had been a voluntary—and often temporary—choice for only a portion of the natives. Meriwether was talking about confining all onto a reduced land base, and he dangled before them the promise of annuities. At an 1855 conference with the Navajos, the white man's strange map unfurled before him, Navajo leader Manuelito "made enough objections to the [proposed] boundaries to show that he grasped at least some of the implications," but probably not the fact that "about two-thirds of [the Navajos'] traditional homeland, almost fifteen thousand square miles, was to be yielded and that they were all now to live within an area about half that size," where the whites could install "such wagon roads, railways, and military posts as might be needed at any time."

Nor could they be expected to grasp all the implications of the government's annuity promises, for the $96,000 to be paid to them over the next twenty years would remain under control of the president of the United States, who could use the funds "for such beneficial objects as in his judgment will be calculated to advance them in civilization."

The persuasive Meriwether did obtain the Navajo leaders' signatures, but the United States Senate refused to ratify this and the governor's other treaties, complaining that the monetary cost would be too high. So the Indians were not bound by the Meriwether treaties. New Mexico officials nonetheless would use their continued presence on the land identified for cession as a "pretext for subsequent aggressive measures." The Southwest had not yet reached the point of open warfare between Indians and whites insisting on their retreat or removal—but it was imminent.

In California the situation was different—even unique—for four reasons. First, the massive 1849 American gold rush precipitated California into statehood in 1850, and set thousands of adventurers and immigrants thronging into the valleys west of the Sierras and the mountains themselves all through the 1850s. Second, the tribelets of California "unlike Indians in other parts of the Far West . . . did not form large and powerful nations with warrior societies that fought the U.S. Army," subsisting instead "in smaller groups and often quickly accommodat[ing] to white incursions." Third, the Anglos initially saw the benefits in following the Spanish and Mexican practice of incorporating the Indians into the labor force. And fourth, California became a "testing ground" for midcentury American reservation policy as conceptualized by Commissioner of Indian Affairs William Medill.

The Indians whom gold seekers encountered inland and in the northwestern portion of the state had remained relatively isolated and independent, and would prove most hostile. Those in southern California and along most of the coastline had already adapted to the exploitative but relatively limited Spanish and Mexican incursions. The Spanish, recognizing the distinction between usufruct rights and ownership, had instructed their missionary priests "to administer lands for the benefit of the Indians" until the latter could manage European-style land management on their own. With Mexican independence, the Mexican government had granted the Indians citizenship and started a process whereby the missions would be secularized and land be granted outright to native inhabitants.

In actual practice, with the secularization of the missions, Indians moved into the lower strata of Mexican society in California as servants and "rancho" workers. The earliest European and Anglo-American immigrants used them in this way as well, chief among them being the Swiss John Sutter, who was building his agriculture-and-trade empire of New Helvetia on Indian labor until the frenzied disorder of the gold rush spoiled his plans.

Indian labor continued to be valued in early Anglo California, as the natives showed "a remarkable independence" by rejecting low wages and confidently asking for cash for work. But here, as elsewhere, "permanent white settlement irrevocably changed the conditions of native survival," eventually forcing Indians to the periphery of the labor force. Also as elsewhere, Indians became superfluous and

bothersome to Anglos—especially when technological innovations—
"steam-powered threshers, horse-driven headers"—lessened the need
for laborers.

At the same time, in a familiar development, the presence of growing numbers of Anglos, as well as gold-struck adventurers from all
over the globe, wrecked Indian subsistence patterns. The salmon were
disappearing from streams silted, dammed, and diverted by mining
activity. Game became hard to find, and Anglos were pushing natives
off productive foraging lands, not even allowing them to harvest
acorns or grass seed, elements of a traditional diet. As they had done
on previous frontiers, the whites outlawed native burning of the prairies, forcing them "to forgo a resource management strategy that enhanced the productivity of the environment" and effectively barring
them from "us[ing] their meagre resources in the most productive
ways they knew."

Anglo officials dealt inconsistently with California Indian land
claims. At first, there was some sentiment for recognizing Indian
rights. In 1850, Senator John Frémont introduced a bill calling for
three commissioners to make treaties with California Indians, arguing,
"Spanish law clearly and absolutely secured to Indians fixed rights of
property in the lands they occupy. . . . Some particular provision will
be necessary in order to divest them of these rights," which were
being breached "by the strong hand alone."

Thus, the first three Indian agents sent to California—a doctor, a
lawyer, and a businessman—came as treaty commissioners and succeeded in confining a number of Indian bands on loosely defined reservation tracts. However, the U.S. Senate would not confirm the
treaties the agents obtained, members of a special committee arguing
that the United States had already acquired California from Mexico.

The climate in newly established Anglo California was extremely
hostile for natives off and on reservations. In 1851, after a group of
white men killed nine Indians and fatally wounded two on the fledgling Kings River reservation, the leader of the Kings River residents,
Pasqual, asked, "What shall we do? We try to live on the lands the
commissioners gave us, in friendly relations with the white man, but
they kill our women and our children, and, if we flee to the mountains,
then they hunt and kill us, and we have no peace."

In California—as in Oregon Territory to the north—natives were both hunted for sport and killed with impunity. One of the more chilling incidents occurred off the coast of northern California in 1860. When a band of Wiyots returned to Indian Island, "the center of their universe from time immemorial," for their annual ceremonies, they were attacked and massacred by white settlers from nearby Eureka. Historian Jack Norton has provided a compelling rationale for the Indians' return, despite their knowledge of the danger involved:

> The ceremony they had come to perform was comparable to the high mass. If you believe that you are responsible for keeping the world in balance, you have a duty to do it no matter what. They must have looked around themselves and seen the collapse of everything they knew. The most natural thing for them was to go to the center, to go to God.

The state and federal governments did not sanction wanton killing and did periodically make some attempts to safeguard Indian lives. But Albert Hurtado's remark on the 1850 California Act for the Government and Protection of the Indians is apt: it "protected them very little and governed them quite a lot."

The state hemmed the natives about with restrictions that went beyond even Georgia's excesses, "legaliz[ing] the indenture of children and adults, authorizing any justice of the peace to sell their services to the highest bidder, and depriv[ing] them of all recourse by making their testimony inadmissible in court." This indenture system affected "as many as ten thousand Indians" before it was altered in 1863, "as a result of the Emancipation Proclamation."

An extensive California reservation plan created in 1851 seemed to offer an alternative to such exploitation. Although it located some of the proposed reservations near massive ranches so as to provide as a ready labor force, it did so as a means of ensuring a market for Indian labor rather than as a means of indenturing natives. It also offered a measure of Indian freedom from state control and economic deprivation by creating reservations that promised to be "federally subsidized livestock ranches with Indian proprietors."

White Californians, loath to allow the natives the twelve thousand square miles of potentially valuable land included in the plan, scuttled the whole proposition in the United States Senate in 1852. The next year, the newly appointed California Indian Affairs superintendent, Lieutenant Edward F. Beale, won congressional approval of an alternate plan: to establish five military reservations on land not occupied by whites and shifting, if necessary, to meet white demands, the tracts "not to exceed twenty-five thousand acres each." On these, he would put the Indians to work according to Anglo ideas of efficient production, their surplus crops to be sold to recoup the military expense.

This scheme, so accommodating to white interests—and the failure and disorder that followed—would characterize much of the western reservation experience as it developed in the next few decades. J. P. Dunn's wry description of some of the early California reservations is instructive: Nome Lackee reservation "had no game, no acorns, no fishery, and no rain, and hence, being useful for nothing else, was eminently fitted for a reservation." At Mendocino, the fish and mussels that could provide subsistence disappeared with the construction of a sawmill by "white friends of the agency," for the river became jammed with logs. The Tejon reservation of southern California "was a nice, dry place where the Indians were never bothered by rain or crops." And over all of these locations presided "one of the ablest Indian rings ever known in America."

In the 1850s, some of the Indians on the eight California reservations that were established on a mere two or three thousand acres as a result of Beale's plan managed to produce good crops. But "no reservation provided enough work to absorb the total Indian labor pool," making "unemployment and underemployment . . . the lots of most reservation Indians," especially since employment opportunities for laborers were disappearing outside the reservation boundaries as well. In 1858, a special Indian agent found only about forty men on the Nome Lackee reservation engaged in farming; most of the 2,500 residents were out foraging for traditional foods. He reported that some Nisenan girls were employed weaving straw hats, but, blind to any value in the traditional subsistence activities, judged that "the real mass of the Indians appeared to have no occupation whatever."

The special agent found the reservations "simply Government Almshouses where an inconsiderable number of Indians are insufficiently fed and scantily clothed, at an expense wholly disproportionate to the benefits conferred." Farming could not feed the entire Indian population, most of which still preferred and practiced traditional methods of gathering food. Their continued foraging had validity, too, in the face of such setbacks as the drought of 1858 at the Fresno farm reservation. The drought reduced foraging opportunities, of course, but it obliterated food crops and severely damaged hay crops.

Often, the natives knew better what the land would support. The Yuroks on the Klamath reservation continued to hunt and gather rather than to heed their agent's urgings to plant crops within the canyons of the Klamath River, where "a single flood could wipe out a year's work."

Subsistence was not the only precarious aspect of life on the reservations. With lack of sufficient protection, reservation boundaries did not stop whites who "continued to attack tribal members even after they had come under [an] agency's protection." Often, the very people charged with taking care of the natives exploited them unmercifully. On one reservation, agents and other white employees "daily and nightly engaged in kidnapping the younger portion of the females for the vilest of purposes . . . the wives and daughters of the defenseless [men] . . . prostituted before the very eyes of their husbands and fathers." Agents also misappropriated funds, used Indian labor for their own advancement, and engaged in corrupt contracting practices, foisting poor supplies on their charges or providing no supplies at all.

All in all, as one exasperated army officer put it, the California reservation system was "turned into a speculation for the benefit of the Agents." By any standard, the whole idea failed dismally for a variety of reasons, yet—significantly for future efforts—"failures were almost always portrayed as the result of corruption rather than any fundamental unsoundness of design."

The Indians themselves managed to hang on through these years by *not* staying on the reservations. Unlike many of their fellows some years later, they had freedom of movement for two reasons: first, because Beale's plan was based on their voluntary participation, and second, because even when they were occasionally forced onto reservations, the borders proved as porous for them as they did for white marauders.

Many learned to use the reservations to their advantage without locating permanently on them. The Mono Indians, for example, in the 1850s combined seasonal work for white farmers with their own gold mining and wild food gathering in the mountains, on occasion coming into the Fresno River Farm subagency for food and clothing to supplement their efforts. When the reservations did offer work, some, like the natives from Tuolumne and Mariposa counties, came just for this opportunity. In order to retain some freedom within their homelands, Indians were willing to stay for part of the year on reservations or on white farms and ranches as laborers and servants.

Still, the changes in native life and fortunes had been devastating. In eighty years with the Spanish among them, the California Indian population had dropped from 300,000 to 150,000. Now in a mere fifteen years, from 1845 to 1860, the population collapsed from 150,000 to 35,000. "Where can we go now that the Americans will not follow us?" asked one Miwok. "Where can we make our homes, that you will not find us?"

California Indians did mount armed resistance. The Miwoks and Yokuts of the central interior had fought the gold-seeker influx in the Mariposa War of 1850 and 1851. Many in the north had retreated into the mountains with the coming of the whites, and by 1860 they were engaged in a series of small battles with a United States military determined to subdue them. In this struggle, they had been preceded by the natives of Oregon Territory.

As early as 1844, white immigration into the Willamette Valley had rendered natives unable to feed their families. Cultivated fields and livestock pastures replaced the abundant stands of wild plants; immigrants fished the streams and hunted deer and elk. The white invasion quickly grew, affecting most of the Indians of the coastal Pacific Northwest and the Columbia River Plateau. In 1847, the Cayuse War exploded in the latter region when Cayuse Indians attacked a Presbyterian mission station overseen by missionaries Marcus and Narcissa Whitman. This site had become a way station for swelling numbers of westering immigrants. The measles virus the immigrants carried, barely affecting them, had wiped out many of the Cayuses.

Both of these developments created deep suspicions among the Cayuses, who killed the Whitmans and eleven other people at the mission and took almost fifty hostages. Volunteer troops sent to deal with the situation exacerbated it by slaughtering a band of Cayuses not involved in the raid. The war ended with the execution in 1850 of six Cayuse leaders who reportedly hoped by their sacrifice to salvage Indian lands and lives. One, Tilokaikt, was said to have reasoned, "Did not your missionaries teach us that Christ died to save his people? Thus die we, if we must, to save our people."

The Cayuses were driven from their Walla Walla Valley homelands, removing to the Umatilla Valley or joining other Plateau tribes. Meanwhile, officials of the new Oregon Territory began pushing for Indian land-cession treaties, their goal at first being to free up for settlement the alluring and fertile coastal valleys by removing natives raised amid forests and streams to the "hot, dry country"—plateau, plain, and basin—east of the Cascade Mountains.

The officials scrambling to effect these treaties could not say exactly where they should go, for the land was already occupied by the Yakimas, the Cayuses, and other tribes, many of whom saw the coastal groups as disease carriers and "did not want the strangers in their midst." Further, settlers were out locating lands both west and east of the evergreen-clad Cascades under the Oregon Donation Land Law of 1850, which allowed each adult male citizen 320 acres of the "public domain." While Indians were not considered citizens, neither was their territory regarded as "public domain"—a fact the government recognized when it passed an Indian treaty act to begin divesting the Northwest natives of their land. This distinction between Indian land and "public domain" did not stop the white settlers.

In Oregon tensions led to the Rogue River War, which erupted in 1853 and again in 1855, as village bands, collectively known as the Rogue River Indians, rose up against gold hunters and settlers in the mountainous coastal regions between the Willamette Valley and the California border. These natives had been harassed unmercifully by "vigilantes" eager to attribute to them any and every bloodthirsty action or plot.

As a result of the 1853 troubles, the Indians relinquished "roughly two thousand square miles," retaining a temporary reservation of "about one hundred square miles" until the government decided where else it might choose to locate them. Whites continued to charge the most peaceable Indians with the crimes of both white marauders and "the more reckless of the Indians." There were open calls for extermination of the natives. The reservation proved no refuge against violent vigilantes—nor did it afford its unfortunate residents enough to eat, especially since they were not allowed to buy firearms and ammunition to hunt, and "white farmers and cattlemen had 'greatly diminished the substance derived from native roots and seeds.' " In 1855, the diminishing Rogue River bands fled to the mountains and mounted defensive warfare through midsummer 1856.

Meanwhile, a large portion of the Northwest became Washington Territory, its first governor—and by extension its first superintendent of Indian Affairs—the energetic, confident, and callous Isaac Stevens. He set about to extinguish the land titles of the northern coastal Indians, his methods revealing much about the ways in which natives were compelled to sign treaties. Stevens hurried them through the complexities, offered extravagant promises to overcome objections, hinted at dire consequences for not signing, browbeat and divided Indian leaders, and "in at least one instance" reportedly "forged the 'X' mark of a chief who had refused to sign."

By these means, he obtained their grudging consent to inhabit reservations within their home regions. Seattle, leader of the Suquamish and Duwamish, noted that "should we accept [the reduced land base,] I here and now make this condition that we will not be denied the privilege without molestation of visiting at any time the tombs of our ancestors, friends, and children." He and most others were surely unaware of the clause allowing the government "the right to move the Indians to other reservations at any time 'when the interests of the Territory require it.' "

Stevens then turned his attention to the Indians east of the Cascades, on the Columbia Plateau. These tribes knew of both distant events, such as the forced marches of southern Indians to Indian Territory, and the ones nearer to home—what was happening to the coastal Indians and what had already happened in their own region with the Cayuses. In 1854 or 1855, the leaders of various Plateau tribes agreed to hold firm in defining the boundaries of their lands when the officials appeared.

Stevens came bearing his treaties in 1855. Peopeomoxmox of the Walla Wallas rejected his offer of trade items for land, arguing, "Goods and the Earth are not equal; goods are for using on the Earth. I do not know where they have given land for goods." A Yakima named Owhi summed up the delegates' dilemma: "What shall I do? Shall I give the lands that are a part of my body and leave myself poor and destitute? Shall I say I will give you my lands? I cannot say.''

Chief Joseph of the Nez Perces was more assertive: "I will not sign your paper. You go where you please, so do I; you are not a child. I am no child; I can think for myself. No man can think for me. I have no other home than this. I will not give it up to any man. My people would have no home. Take away your paper. I will not touch it with my hand.''

Isaac Stevens—plugging for a northern railroad route and for extended Anglo settlement—nonetheless quickly prevailed upon Joseph and other Nez Perce leaders to sign, along with influential Yakima leaders, by drawing out for these tribes "sizeable reservations encompassing much of their traditional hunting and gathering ground.'' Smaller tribes had to take what they could get; the Cayuses, Walla Wallas, and Umatillas would share a reservation.

The hasty treaties only deepened Indian divisions and resistance. "My people, what have you done?'' demanded Looking Glass, a Nez Perce war chief who had been hunting on the Plains at the time of Stevens's treaty sweep. "While I was gone, you have sold my country. I have come home, and there is not left me a place on which to pitch my lodge.''

Problems stemmed from the fact that Stevens, and invading settlers, considered the treaties a *fait accompli,* but the U.S. Senate had not yet ratified them. The natives, who had been promised a gradual transition, found instead that whites were pouring into the area, ignoring Indian land claims while reservations went unsurveyed and other promises went unfulfilled. Nonetheless, Stevens hurtled onward, coercing the long-friendly Flatheads, Pend d'Oreilles, and Kutenais into reservation treaties as well.

The Yakimis tried to lead a pan-Indian resistance in the Yakima War of 1855 and 1856. Pressed by Stevens to declare their allegiances, even those Indians who had long pledged peace to the white man showed understandable resentments. "When I speak you do not understand me,'' declared a Spokane native, known as the friendly "Spokan Garry,'' to Stevens. "It is as if we have been talking for nothing.'' He urged Stevens to treat Indian leaders as proud people deserving of the truth and explained, ''The Indians are not satisfied with the land you gave them. . . . If all those Indians had marked out their own Reservation, this trouble would not have happened. . . . If I had the business to do I could fix it by giving them a little more land.''

The Yakima War "petered out inconclusively" in early fall 1856, but the Yakimas soon threw themselves into a second significant resistance effort that drew wider native support, especially from the Spokanes, the Palouses, the Coeur d'Alenes, and the northern Paiutes. The series of confrontations that resulted in 1858, called both the Coeur d'Alene War and the Spokane War, ended with the execution of Indian leaders and the further reduction of tribal movement and freedoms.

By 1860, "all the Oregon and Washington treaties had been ratified, eight reservations established, and the noble experiment of converting Indians into Christian farmers begun." As on previous frontiers, Indians had the choice of trying to eke out a living on the periphery of white culture or going onto the fledgling reservations. Sometimes they had no choice at all, for the military periodically responded to white pressure by forcing natives within reservation boundaries, where they were to intermingle with members of other unfortunate indigenous groups.

Here they could enjoy no sense of safety. Napoleon, a Tulalip of Puget Sound, would recall with bitterness, "We never saw any agent on the reservation who had pity on the Indians, they all frighten them." With whites telling reservation Indians, "You will all be killed soon," he reported, their hearers did not "care to work the land."

In the Great Basin, too, the overwhelmingly peaceful foraging natives were subjected to rapidly growing Anglo control. In 1850, the United States government created what it called "Utah Territory"— present-day Nevada, Utah, and western Colorado. The Mormons had already established themselves at Salt Lake; soon other settlers began to appear, taking up the best locations in the midst of native hunting grounds.

With the growing influx of settlers, Chief Winnemucca of the northern Paiutes was disturbed by dreams of massive white migration and warfare: "I saw the blood streaming from the mouths of my men that lay all around me"—and tried to retreat to the mountains during the peak immigrant travel months in the summer. But such moves disrupted the Indians' ability to collect essential wild plant foods as they ripened.

Further, the discovery of "Comstock lode" silver in Nevada in 1859 brought adventurers scurrying all over the Paiute lands, cutting down for their wood the piñon trees on which the Paiutes depended for fall pine-nut harvests. The immigrants brought in livestock to graze the grasslands and appropriated precious water from the region's meager streams, altering their flow for mining purposes. Many of the Paiutes were reduced to near-starvation and treated as nonentities to be ignored, laborers to be exploited (Anglos found them hardworking and adaptable), or hostiles to be eliminated.

A series of tensions culminated with the Paiute War, or Pyramid Lake War, of 1860. Accounts of its origins vary. Paiute Sarah Winnemucca, who became a spokesperson for her people, traced the conflict to the Paiutes' discovery of two missing Paiute girls held and abused by traders in the cellar of a Carson River trading post. A white resident of the region at the same time noted that hostilities began when whites started grazing their cattle on the reservation. Indians butchered and ate some of the beeves, claiming they were "get[ting] their pay for the use of their lands because the whites have driven their game away and were eating up their fish." In this version of the war's origins, ranchers shot the "rustlers" and Indians retaliated.

After two battles, the second ending in Indian defeat, the Paiutes' fate—and that of other Great Basin tribes—remained uncertain. Tensions ran so deep that many settlers did not even want to allow the natives to inhabit a reservation. The Indians, for their part, found it difficult to trust even the most sympathetic of whites, and they had no illusions concerning treaties; as Ouray, a Ute, put it, "Agreements the Indian makes with the government are like the agreement a buffalo makes with the hunter after it has been pierced by many arrows. All it can do is lie down and give in."

East of the Paiutes, most of the Indians of the prairies and Plains—still "unorganized" territory—continued to claim and occupy large western expanses. They looked with dismay on the burgeoning number of westering adventurers scrambling across these expanses, contributing in the process to the erosion of the land base. "We have to live on these streams and in the hills," the Arapaho Cut Nose announced at a Plains treaty negotiation in 1851, "and I would be glad if the whites would pick out a place for themselves and not come into our grounds."

The land could only sustain so much activity, even among Indian populations. Yet by the mid-nineteenth century, Indians "were keeping as many as 100,000 to 150,000 horses year-round on the west central plains." The Plains Indian movements were dictated not only by pursuit of the bison, but by pursuit of forage for their animals: "They spent the year chasing grass, basically."

Now non-Indian immigrants harvested precious prairie timber for campfires. Their livestock "stripped bare the valley grasses and ate their way up the benches," destroying animal habitat and the wild plants upon which the Indians still depended, forcing some into "planting and harvesting the species needed for medicinal and religious use."

The wild game, hunted by both Indians and whites, could not be replenished in this way, and Plains residents began to struggle at certain points in the year against the specter of starvation. One facet of the problem was that the non-Indian immigrants descended on the most fertile portions of the Plains—the river lowlands—in the summer, while the Indians depended on these locations for winter camps.

Increasingly, Indians found the grasses trampled and eaten by livestock and the trees cut, "leaving little fuel or cottonwood sprigs to help feed their horses." Yet what could they do but use up what remained?

The land never had a chance to recover: "Indians, white travelers, and their horses and oxen and mules were gobbling and burning the very bejabbers out of one of the most vital, vulnerable, and limited habitats of the Great Plains."

Such debilitating changes were accompanied by the inevitable white pressure upon the Indians to give way. In the early 1850s, the United States government with great ceremony and "mountain[s] of presents" made treaties with both northern and southern Plains tribes in which the natives pledged perpetual peace with the whites and assented to a *fait accompli*—the presence of government forts and immigrant roads in their lands. The tribes were confirmed in their territorial rights, their lands "not called reservations and . . . not, as elsewhere, intended as instruments for the control and civilization of the Indians.''

Yet the treaties—all too ominously, in light of the direction that federal Indian policy was taking—''laid the foundations for future reservations.'' And the invaders were no longer simply travelers. By 1858, trader William Bent was reporting the Arapahos and Cheyennes ''very uneasy and restless about their country, the whites coming into it, making large and extensive settlements and laying off and building Towns all over the best part.''

On the Plains, as elsewhere in the West, the mid- to late 1850s were marked by flaring Indian-white violence. In 1854, a young and soon-to-be-notorious West Point lieutenant named John L. Grattan escalated a simple dispute over a butchered cow into a series of violent clashes between Sioux and army troops; in 1857, the Cheyennes battled army troops sent to halt Indian raids on travelers.

These incidents were mere preludes to more bitter conflicts. Even as the American nation plunged into a long and brutal civil war, across the West such diverse groups of Indians as the farm-dwelling Cherokees and the buffalo-hunting northern Cheyennes would plunge into their most desperate bid yet for autonomous survival as they ''entered a new and more traumatic phase of their relations with white people.''

Chapter Six

→←

"Run Them About"
(1861–1886)

I think you had better put the Indians on wheels. Then you can run them about whenever you wish.
   —Sioux leader Red Dog to treaty commissioners, 1876

The Poncas of the eastern Plains had fared better than many tribes in their dealings with white officials, a treaty of 1865 having retained for them 96,000 acres of their homeland in what was about to become the state of Nebraska. Here the Poncas were periodically set upon by their old enemies and neighbors the Brule and Oglala Sioux, but they lived as peacefully as possible, accepting a mission and schools for their children.

Scant years after the treaty agreement, however, the United States government inadvertently included Ponca land within the reservation promised to the Brule Sioux, and both the government and the Sioux meant to have it sooner or later. In 1877, Indian inspector Edward C. Kemble appeared and announced that the Poncas must sell out and move to Indian Territory.

The natives protested, then reluctantly agreed to send ten leaders with Kemble to examine three Indian Territory sites. Their journey led to a land they found deficient in good water sources and subsistence opportunities. When they refused to accept it, Kemble unsuccessfully pressured the group, then abandoned them to a rough return trek across a harsh winter landscape.

Kemble himself hurried back to the Ponca reservation and convinced ten of the Nebraska families to submit to a small soldier force and board wagons for the journey southward. Even when threatened with guns and bayonets, most of the Poncas refused to move without seeing and hearing from their absent leaders. These leaders, who had nearly frozen to death before receiving aid and horses from the Oto Indians and their agent, finally reached home.

Then more soldiers arrived. "We locked our doors, and the women and children hid in the woods," remembered Standing Bear, one of the returnees. But the soldiers forced them out and took Standing Bear and his brother Big Snake to a jail in their fort. Here the two talked with the officers and found the commander sympathetic and willing to query the president of the United States regarding the Poncas' fate.

Standing Bear was told that the president claimed ignorance of the matter. In a scene reminiscent of the removal of the southern tribes some forty years earlier, soldiers gathered all the people, "broke open the houses," and assembled the Poncas' possessions—"reapers, mowers, hay rakes, spades, ploughs, bedsteads, stoves, cupboards, everything we had on our farms"—loading into wagons whatever would fit.

"We told them that we would rather die than leave our lands," said Standing Bear, "but we could not help ourselves." Almost seven hundred Poncas began the five-hundred-mile march to Indian Territory. More than two hundred died along the way. Others would quickly succumb on the inhospitable land their leaders had tried to reject, but still others—chief among them Standing Bear—would live to gain a victory.

The years 1861–1886, beginning with the disruptions of the Civil War that affected Indians as well as whites and ending with "the collapse of the last armed resistance to the reservation system," encompass a dizzying range of struggles among tribes facing dispossession—or further dispossession—in the West. Western Indians could now be divided into three broad groups. First, there were the already "subjugated" immigrant and native Indians of Kansas, Indian Territory, and Nebraska, most of whom were simply trying to hold on to well-established reservations that now represented "the base of their economy, their self-government, and their cultural institutions." Whatever these reservations' limitations and problems, their residents inhabited sustainable land bases, enjoyed some freedom to live independently and govern themselves, and had gradually adapted to aspects of Anglo culture while retaining much of their traditional cultures.

The second group consisted of those western Indians still new to the reservation system but at least nominally accepting it. This acceptance stemmed from the generally peaceful and militarily weak nature of these native societies, the fact that the government allowed them to remain in their home regions, and their recognition of the reservations' potential advantages: limited security from white and Indian aggressors and the possibility of using the reservation as a base for cultural and economic survival as the more acculturated tribes were doing. Representative of this group were the California natives and the sporadically resistant but generally peaceful Great Basin Indians.

The third group was made up of highly resistant Indians who were trying to stay outside the bounds of reservations or to escape them. In general, these natives, primarily of the warrior societies of the Great Plains and Southwest, had been or were being forced into especially unpalatable situations. Some were being removed from home regions; most were being pressed onto only the poorest land—or a small fragment of a fair land—and then subjected to newly intensified coercive and authoritarian measures to remake them in an Anglo-American mold.

In fact, whatever their previous freedoms, western Indians in general were coming under heightened Anglo control in this era. Distant federal officials worked more assiduously than ever before to shape the fate of the Indians, with soldiers, agents, and the superintendents who oversaw clusters of agencies carrying out their designs, along with missionaries and teachers. The experiences of the first two Indian groups in maintaining their reservations—outlined in this chapter— and of the warring natives in resisting and surviving theirs—examined in the next two chapters—were inextricably tied to United States events and policies.

The Civil War detonated among the nearly 100,000 Native Americans in Indian Territory with such force that "the casualties and destruction . . . were probably proportionately greater than anywhere else in the United States." As the hostilities commenced, most tribal leaders attempted to avoid taking sides. "We have done nothing to bring about the conflict in which you are engaged with your own people," Cherokee John Ross explained, "and I am unwilling that my people shall become its victims." He vowed "to do no act that shall furnish any pretext to either of the contending parties to overrun our country and destroy our rights.''

Yet, as one Shawnee in Indian Territory would recall, ''It was almost impossible to remain neutral.'' A Cherokee would remember his father attempting to stay out of the conflict, as ''he did not believe in fighting . . . [or] in slavery.'' But a company of Confederate soldiers rode up to their cabin, the captain announcing, ''Get ready, Watt, and let's go. You will have to fight.''

The federal government, which had already been serving the territory's tribes poorly, had immediately shifted its attention and resources elsewhere, leaving tribes with little opportunity to communicate with federal Indian Bureau personnel.

At the same time, the Confederacy made a concerted effort to bring the Indian Territory tribes under its authority. Southern Representative Albert Pike negotiated treaties with the Choctaws and Chickasaws, the Seminoles and Creeks. The first two groups were overwhelmingly pro-southern, the latter two less so, with Creek leader Opothleyaholo leading a substantial Union faction. However, the South had an advantage not only in its active wooing of the Indians but in the southern ties these Indians possessed. Despite a bitter history of relations with white southerners, they had roots in the region, had intermarried with southern whites, and, until the war, had had mainly southern men serving as federal agents and exerting influence among them. Thus, many Indians welcomed the South's annexation of Indian Territory in May 1861. Others departed for Union Kansas.

The Cherokees continued to split along the old acrimonious lines: Stand Watie immediately led a Cherokee regiment into the southern ranks as John Ross struggled to keep the Cherokees out of the fray. After a decisive Confederate victory in Missouri in August 1861, however, Ross had to yield to the strong southern sympathies in the Cherokee Nation or face an internal war.

The Confederacy was offering recognition of Cherokee land title and self-government, agreeing to restrictions on the Cherokee agent and trader, and accepting greater Cherokee self-rule. Citing these welcome developments, as well as his people's longstanding southern ties and the present state of war, Ross capitulated, and his government raised a Cherokee regiment as well.

Yet Ross was unable to head off a civil war within Indian Territory.

In November and December 1861, Confederate Indian troops repeat-edly attacked their neutral or pro-Union neighbors even as the latter—Cherokees, Choctaws, Shawnees, Kickapoos, Seminoles, Delawares, and Comanches—attempted to flee to Kansas in a caravan of "car-riages, ox teams, covered wagons, [and] buggies." Injured and debil-itated, the exiles, their tools, blankets, and extra clothing abandoned, left a trail of blood across the frozen prairies and attempted to create a refuge from blizzards with "aprons, handkerchiefs, and scraps of cloth . . . stretched over saplings for makeshift tents."

In Kansas a military commander fed the refugees as best he could from his limited stores, but could provide little relief. Some were fortunate in reuniting with their established tribespeople: the "Absen-tee Shawnees" who had been living among the Creeks now were welcomed by the Kansas Shawnees. Most lived in refugee camps, without the most basic cooking and camping tools, subsisting on raw beef and uncooked meal, and suffering from "inflammatory diseases of the chest, throat, and eyes," as well as "mumps, diphtheria, mea-sles, smallpox, frostbite, consumption, and pneumonia."

Meanwhile, non-Indian guerrilla bands and other marauders from Kansas and Texas laid waste to homesteads in Indian Territory and openly stole livestock. At the same time, Indian troops under Stand Watie continued to harry those loyalists and neutralists remaining, also razing houses and obliterating crops. A secret society—the Ketowahs, or Nighthawks, arose to protect families against depredations from both sides, but Watie's troops forced some six thousand refugees to cluster around Fort Gibson for protection. Here they, like their com-patriots in Kansas, suffered horribly from disease and deprivation as the Union military officials at Fort Gibson struggled to deal with the influx.

As Union forces began to gain ground in the broader conflict, with federal troops reclaiming Indian Territory, pro-southern Indians be-came the refugees. The Confederacy had laid better plans than had the United States government by providing for refugee camp inspec-tors, for supply and distribution agents, even for physicians and schoolteachers. But the plans quickly foundered in the realities of losing a war. More and more refugees gathered in pro-southern Choctaw-Chickasaw country and spilled into northern Texas. Their presence and needs placed tremendous strains on the Choctaws, Chickasaws, and local military officials, and the refugees suffered many of the same deprivations as their former neighbors in Kansas.

Indian groups remained deeply split politically as well as geographically. The Creeks, Seminoles, and Cherokees all had both Union and Confederate governments, with the ubiquitous Stand Watie, the only Indian to achieve the rank of brigadier general in the Civil War military, serving as chief of the Confederate Cherokees.

Before war's end, the U.S. Congress appropriated money to aid the refugees in Kansas to return to Indian Territory, and they began the homeward exodus. They—and the others who followed, from south and north—found most of their decades-long efforts to establish comfortable homes and fields had been erased. "When we returned to our old home, we found one chair ... in the potato cellar under the house," recalled a Cherokee returnee. "We also found our old black mottled-faced cow who had escaped being eaten by the soldiers. . . . That is all we had to start our home again."

The Cherokee, Creek, and Seminole nations had been so badly split that there was serious talk of dividing each permanently in what would have been an ironic outcome to a war to preserve federal union. But only the Seminoles remained divided into northern and southern governments, and only for a dozen years. Other tribes rediscovered their commonality in the face of the punitive treaties pressed by the Reconstruction government of the United States. Just as John Ross had feared, the United States used the Confederate allegiance of some of the territory's Indians—including Ross himself, who, honor-bound, stayed with the Confederacy to the end—to wrest land concessions and cessions from all.

The former southern tribes were compelled to allow railroad rights-of-way and to relinquish control of their western regions so that the government might relocate immigrant tribes—those living in Kansas and certain Plains tribes. The cessions represented a big chunk of Choctaw, Chickasaw, Creek, and Cherokee holdings. The Cherokees made two cessions—the north central and northwestern portion of the territory, known variously as the "Cherokee Outlet" and the "Cherokee Strip," and a rectangle known as the "Neutral Lands," lying across the border in Kansas. The Seminoles, who had only obtained a separate land base in 1856, "relinquished all their land for fifteen cents an acre," and under federal direction bought a corner of the reduced Creek territory at $1.25 an acre.

With the exception of Seminole country, the ceded lands had not been settled or had been only sparsely settled by their tribal owners before the war—the acreages were too remote from markets, too difficult to farm, and too exposed to hostile western Indians. So, despite the trauma of the losses at the "bargaining" table, the Five Tribes had retained their heartlands.

Now they showed the same resiliency they had demonstrated in previous upheavals. They rebuilt their mud-chinked log cabins, barns, and fences, often working communally to clear timber or enclose a garden. They found that the fish were still thick and lively in the streams, the game—"wild pigeons, turkeys, quail, prairie chickens, deer, opossum, raccoon, fox coyotes, mink, muskrat, squirrel, rabbits, etc."—still plentiful. Livestock could forage in the wild, and the corn and wheat grew tall in the fields.

The tribes continued to rely on old herbal remedies and native "conjurers" for healing. They maintained their clan distinctions—including the prohibition against couples from the same clan marrying—and cultivated some of their ancient traditions, chief among them the Green Corn Ceremony tied to the late-summer harvest. During this celebration, the former southeastern tribes "extinguished and re-kindled their ceremonial fires to symbolize the end of the old year and the beginning of the new."

Throughout the year, the people of Indian Territory moved about freely upon their lands. "Visiting was much enjoyed," recalled one Shawnee youth returned from Kansas, who happily remembered men forming hunting parties, then gathering around campfires in the evenings and elaborating on traditional stories. The inhabitants of the territory also played ball games, patronized horse races, and danced. A Creek would recall the popular stomp dance as "an Indian's heaven," explaining, "The Bible says there are just two places for a person to go after death. There would have to be a stomp ground for me to be happy." Some of the more Christianized Indians avoided the traditional dances, but others incorporated native and Christian beliefs and practices, and religious camp meetings were as popular among the territory's Indians as they were among their rural white southern counterparts.

For their livelihood, most Indians continued subsistence farming and hunting. A Cherokee summed up prevailing attitudes well: "The Indians probably originated the theory, let every day provide for itself, as each morning the man would get out early in the morning and bring in enough game for that day only." Yet the acquisitiveness and entrepreneurship of Anglo culture were making themselves felt. "Our people no longer were satisfied with the meager necessities of existence, that formerly had seemed sufficient," Shawnee Thomas Wildcat Alford explained, noting that the traders' stores offered "so many things" and that "civilization" seemed "nothing more or less than a multiplication of man's needs and wants."

Some entrepreneurial Indians adapted so well to the Anglo market system that they were able to take advantage of their special status as holders in common of inalienable lands. Without having to put money into land ownership, they gained "a share of the profits from outside corporate investments," primarily through land leasing to ranchers, loggers, and miners. But these were the exception rather than the rule. Other ambitious natives—particularly those who had received an Anglo education—found themselves stymied.

Thomas Wildcat Alford is representative of this latter group. As one of two young men selected by Indian Territory Shawnee leaders to attend Hampton Institute in Virginia in 1879, he seemed well on his way to his goal of a chieftainship. His elders had encouraged him to learn everything he could about the white man's ways and culture and to come back and use this knowledge as a leader for the tribe's benefit. This he was eager to do, but he violated the old chiefs' one stipulation: not to embrace the white man's religion.

Both because he did choose Christianity and because his education in general set him off from his community, Alford found his return "a bitter disappointment," with "no happy gathering of family and friends, as I had so fondly dreamed there might be." Instead, his family and friends "gave me to understand very plainly that they did not approve of me."

A logical move for Alford was to seek local employment with the Indian Bureau, and he did sporadically obtain teaching, clerical, and administrative jobs. But educated Indians watched in frustration as appointments were doled out to whites through a political spoils system. "Capability, efficiency, or fitness had little to do with securing an appointment," Alford testified; a dedicated worker developing a coherent plan would suddenly be replaced with a political hack "who had no training or special interest in Indian work." Alford and his wife, in their time with the Bureau, "never knew when we would be discharged, or for what reason."

While Alford did gradually regain the trust of many of his people, internal divisions continued to develop in each tribe, pitting traditionalist against progressive. Yet never had it been more imperative for the tribes to show unity in order to preserve their self-government and their land.

With the end of the Civil War, the major Indian Territory tribes had reestablished their republican governments, "rely[ing] heavily on these national political institutions to meet the challenge of maintaining order" in a region plagued with the war's aftershocks in the form of "rampant crime and violence." Overall, the tribes policed their own members well, sometimes relying on community censure, sometimes on mild restraining actions—such as tying up drunken men— and sometimes on harsh physical punishments—such as whippings and hangings.

However, the tribes found they had little power to meet the formidable external challenges to their own systems of law and order. When Comanches, Kiowas, and Apaches stole Chickasaw livestock, Chickasaw volunteer militias searched the Plains Indians' territory for their stolen animals. But in general, the Indian residents of the territory had to depend upon the United States government to control outside aggressors, both Indian and white.

How complicated and fruitless this was is evidenced by the procedure necessary to remove intruders from a reservation: "The local tribal officials reported [the intruders] to the federal agent; the agent reported them to the Indian Office; the Indian Office reported them to the secretary of the interior; the secretary requested the War Department to act; and the secretary of war relayed an order through army channels down to the commander at Fort Gibson." Troops were then dispatched to convey the intruder to the Kansas or Texas boundary:

"Then he turned around and came back, and the whole process had to be repeated."

The number of non-Indians living in the territory soared in the decades following the Civil War; it would reach 70 percent of the entire territorial population by 1890. Among this group were many men living with or married to Indian women, and these derisively termed "squawmen" often added immeasurably to troubles on the reservation as "disturbers of the peace, who profited shamelessly from their special situation and made life miserable for anyone who opposed their schemes." Governance headaches abounded, for the non-Indians "were not subject to tribal law," either its protection or its punitive power. Yet after 1880 the United States government appeared to give up any attempt to keep them out, and settlers continued to appropriate land, while outlaws operated with impunity, stealing livestock, dealing in whiskey, robbing and murdering.

As individual actions undermined tribal authority, so, too, did the policies of the United States government. When Congress sought to impose law and order on the reservations in the late 1870s and the 1880s, such action was badly needed, and it led to the appointment of Indian police forces and Indian judges. But ultimately the law-and-order measures buttressed white control. The Indian agent, growing in power, chose the police force, while Indian judges were charged with "enforc[ing] a list of 'Indian offenses' compiled by the Indian Bureau and aimed . . . at feasts and dances, the practices of medicine men, and a large body of customs judged 'demoralizing and barbarous.' "

Furthermore, under the auspices of law and order, Indians found their movements restricted. An 1873 order by the secretary of the interior forbade tribal members nationwide to depart their reservations "without a special permit in writing from the Agent" when it appeared to the agent "that the issuance of same will inure to the benefit of the applicant." An 1885 act extending federal jurisdiction to "major" crimes on the reservations promised greater order and security, but further eroded Indian self-governance.

These developments reflected a general legislative movement away from recognition of Indian political sovereignty in the 1870s and 1880s. A congressional directive of 1871 flatly stipulated that the government would make no more treaties with tribes. This meant that the tribes had lost even their "domestic dependent nation" status as articulated by Chief Justice John Marshall four decades earlier.

The government pledged to abide by previous treaties and did continue to enter into "agreements" with Indian leaders, but any pretense of a politically equal relationship on the part of the United States— and any but the slightest Indian bargaining power—had disappeared. Congress or the president unilaterally established reservations or changed their boundaries. Further, an 1874 Supreme Court ruling gave the government possession of reservation timber resources, the Indians "only a right of occupancy."

Another disturbing development was the presence of railroad construction in Indian country; not only did the disorderly construction camps add an element of instability and violence, but railroad speculators bombarded Congress with legislation that would allow them to appropriate more reservation land. Tribes had to fight constantly against further encroachment by these and other speculators, the major Indian Territory tribes "[keeping] delegations in Washington" for this purpose.

Of even greater immediate concern, the federal government was pressing for the one thing most inimical to a continued tribal identity and land base: the breaking up of the reservation. On certain reservations, Indian lands were to be "allotted," divided into individually owned plots, the "surplus" to be bought at a pittance by the government and sold. With the division would come the elimination of tribal governments and the unraveling of tribal culture. The Indians whose land had been promised to them forever were to be subsumed—sink or swim—into the population of a federally sanctioned territory. They had only to look to their Kansas neighbors to see the dimensions of this threat.

While the Indian Territory tribes faced increasing encroachments from non-Indians in the post–Civil War years, the tribes of eastern Kansas and Nebraska—immigrant and native—were simply overrun. Most clung tenaciously to their reservations, but white settlers, speculators, and reformers all pushed them to accept removal, allotment, or some combination thereof.

Reservation residents were worn down in a variety of ways. On the

Pawnees' remaining land in Nebraska—a thirty-mile-long strip along the Loup River—whites openly and repeatedly stole the timber the Indians needed "for cooking, heating, and building." At one point, a number of Pawnee men gave up their winter hunt in order to guard the timber, but still the brazen theft continued. The Pawnee agent managed to collect some fines from the timber takers, but tribal members did not see the money. Despite their request that the funds be used to buy needed staples such as flour and beef, especially for the poorest among them, "the money went its bureaucratic way into the treasury."

The situation became particularly maddening when the Indians were blamed for any theft or destruction suffered by their white neighbors and forced to pay damages from annuity funds. By the time two men demanded payment for hay lost in a prairie fire they said was set by a Pawnee, chiefs "said that the Pawnee must be identified or they would not pay."

A further complication occurred as the Pawnees, despite a record of peaceful relations with whites, became increasingly restricted to the reservation in response to white fears regarding their movements. Not only were they unable to search out timber sources to replace the lost ones, but they were prevented from "journeying at will over their ancient lands to hunt; to visit ancestral graves near abandoned villages; to seek visions on high, grassy hills; and to take the Sacred Pipe to visit and adopt members of other tribes and thus establish and maintain bonds between the tribes."

Nor could they respond to repeated raids by the Sioux and by whites, or simply enjoy an excursion. The mayor of Omaha complained about Indians on the street, and Pawnee army scouts lost their much-prized free passes to ride the tops of the railroad cars to various towns to shop and visit. Whites tried to rescind the tribe's treaty rights to hunt off the reservation, even with an official escort, but the Pawnee agent successfully backed his charges in the matter.

The Osages of Kansas, who in 1865 had agreed to sell most of their lands, were experiencing a range of similar pressures. In 1869, they were still awaiting the annuity promised them as interest on the sale; the Indian Bureau "had failed to open an account to disburse the funds." When the Osages tried to hunt to the west, Kiowas, Comanches, Arapahos, and Cheyennes pushed them back.

At home on their reduced lands, settlers were pouring in unimpeded and taking up the best locations for farming. The attitude still prevailed among most westering European Americans that the land was theirs to take by right of their superior culture and plans for land use. One invader petitioned his congressman: "Hurry up the removal of these lazy, dirty vagabonds. . . . It is folly to talk longer of a handful of wandering savages holding possession of land so fair and rich as this. We want this land to make homes. Let us have it."

Nebraska immigrants engaged in similar rhetoric. "We deny the so-called original rights of the aborigine to the soil," the state legislature declared in March 1870, advocating Indian removal to "more congenial and advantageous localities where their presence will not retard settlement by the whites." To make the Indians' current locality even less "congenial and advantageous," in 1874, a bill was introduced into Congress "allow[ing] white citizens to carry guns for protection against the [remaining] Nebraska Indians."

Such talk and actions seemed out of line with the "Peace Policy" then being promoted by the Grant administration. Many white Americans had come to agree with William Tecumseh Sherman's definition of "reservation" as "a parcel of land, set aside for Indians, surrounded by thieves." Taking office in 1869, Ulysses S. Grant had replaced the political-patronage agents who had prevailed for so long with men recommended through church mission organizations. He had created a Board of Indian Commissioners, made up of reforming philanthropists and charged with overseeing part of the ration and annuity process. He had even appointed an Indian, the highly acculturated Seneca chief Ely Parker, as commissioner of Indian Affairs.

Not only would the Peace Policy flounder as the Grant administration sagged under its own corruption and ineptitude, but the policy was still based upon white understanding of the Indian "problem," upon continued removal of the Indians to lands not desired by the whites, there to be "civilized" under white control.

So the Nebraskans' attitudes boded ill for those Indians who chose to take allotted land rather than succumb to removal pressures. When most of the Osages left for Indian Territory in 1871, "about thirty mixed-bloods and a few full-bloods decided to stay on their allotments in Kansas and become citizens of the state." But half of them had fled to Indian Territory within three months, driven out by their white neighbors' threats, the firing of their homes and barns, and the killing or theft of their livestock. When a Quaker agent appealed to settlers who had pledged to help the remaining Indians, he received a damning response: "the Osages have signed the Bill [of removal] and we have got the land, let the half breeds go to hell."

One way or another, allotted land simply slipped through Indian hands. The Citizen Potawatomis, Delawares, and Ottawas of Kansas quickly plunged into debt and had to sell their farms, then depart for Indian Territory. As early as 1871, Commissioner of Indian Affairs Enoch Hoag was seeking to halt the "ruinous" practice of allotment, noting that the Indians couldn't "withstand the corrupting influences which are thrown around them by designing and dishonest men, who cling to them like leeches, until they have possessed themselves of all their property."

In particular, those Indians who had been persuaded off a still-viable land base looked on their choice with deep regret. The Kickapoos who held their land in common were doing well farming and stock raising in the mid-1870s, when "the allotted Kickapoos announced that they no longer wanted American citizenship and petitioned to rejoin their tribe on the common reserve."

Allotment also created mammoth legal tangles. When some Potawatomis fled Kansas in hopes of participating in a Kickapoo attempt to settle in Mexico, self-interested tribesmen declared them dead and got themselves appointed executors of their estates. Meanwhile, white traders claimed that the Potawatomis in Mexico had sold their land rights to them. Then the exiles returned, further complicating the picture.

In the East, similar complications over land management and division led to allotment as well. The Massachusetts Mashpees, a group "believed to have been part of the Wampanoag tribe," struggled with complex land issues, but most did not agree with the state legislature's 1870 directive to divide their common lands. They watched "many valuable cranberry bogs and shorefront properties" quickly pass into white hands. By 1880, the Narragansetts of Rhode Island were ready to give up the attempt to maintain tribal lands, wearily relinquishing them for $5,000 or $15.41 per tribal member.

In the West, removal remained a cleaner solution to the "Indian problem" as far as most white immigrants were concerned. The

Osages were removed to Indian Territory in 1871, the Pawnees in 1872. While the move was traumatic for both tribes—the Osage departure being marked by "the cries of the old people, especially the women, who lamented over the graves of their children, which they were about to leave forever"—they at least relocated on familiar hunting lands.

In fact, the Osages adapted well, carefully devising a republican form of self-government resembling that of the Cherokees and of the United States. Many of these "wandering savages" also proved industrious and astute enough farmers and ranchers that by 1878 a new agent found them employing a fair-sized white labor force.

However, Indian self-determination was cut off at every turn. Although their Quaker agent testified that the Osage government worked well in its first year, "the Bureau of Indian Affairs and the Department of the Interior refused to recognize the tribal government officially, and for years remained ambivalent about its worth," only grudgingly releasing funds for its operation "from the tribe's own account in the United States Treasury."

Money—the earning of it, the disbursement of it, the spending of it—remained a bitter point of contention. On the Pawnee reservation in Indian Territory, after a "devastating grasshopper invasion and failure of the hunt" in 1875, tribal members were denied permission to sell their downed timber in order to buy food. On the Osage reservation, the men complained of being "fed like dogs" on "a weekly dole from an agency warehouse." They won the right to receive cash rather than rations, but unscrupulous neighbors then charged them inflated prices for goods—or simply robbed them.

As the Pawnees, Osages, and other former Kansas and Nebraska tribes struggled to survive the latest uprooting, some leaders mounted a strong resistance to removal. Among them were Standing Bear and many of the Poncas who had reluctantly trudged from Nebraska to Indian Territory under soldier guard.

Poncas were seeking to return to their former reservation both because it was home and because they, like many western Indians, were being forced into the bleakest of living conditions. "After we reached the new land, all my horses died," recalled Standing Bear. "The water was very bad [a fact the leaders had noted in earlier rejecting the location]. All our cattle died; not one was left." Standing Bear and other Ponca leaders met with President Rutherford B. Hayes and Secretary of the Interior Carl Schurz and requested that they be allowed to return to their Nebraska reservation, or to join Omaha kinspeople in Nebraska. The officials refused, as they were pursuing a policy of "concentrating tribes on larger reservations."

Then, Standing Bear recalled, malaria struck the tribe: "I stayed till one hundred and fifty-eight of my people had died. Then I ran away with thirty of my people, men and women and children." Standing Bear's own son was among the dead, his last wish to be buried back in the land in which he was born.

The Ponca band fled to the Omaha reservation, where the inhabitants gave them a piece of land to farm. General George Crook was dispatched to take them back to their barren reserve. The Poncas were putting in a crop of wheat when the reluctant Crook and his soldiers arrived. "Half of us were sick," Standing Bear explained. "We would rather have died than have been carried back; but we could not help ourselves." They were taken to nearby Fort Omaha.

The Poncas' treatment—to make room for the Brule Sioux, whom the government did not succeed in settling in Ponca country—attracted both regional and national attention and sympathy. Crook himself wrote of the irony inherent in "an Irishman, German, Chinaman, Turk, or Tartar [being] protected in life and property," when a native of America could "command respect for his rights only so long as he inspires terror for his rifle." Whites had helped the Poncas in their flight and aided them in the filing of a landmark lawsuit. "They are right & we are wrong," New Englander Helen Hunt Jackson announced firmly in 1879. A prominent advocate of Indian rights, Jackson welcomed "our one chance for decency as a nation in our treatment of them . . . in this movement toward the courts."

Standing Bear and his band had offered to give up their official tribal identity in order to remain, but they also asked for this right of choice in United States district court. Judge Elmer Dundy in 1881 ruled in their favor: the Poncas, as individuals, possessed the same right to "life, liberty, and the pursuit of happiness" as did other Americans, and "federal officials could not force them to return to the reservation."

The Poncas had scored a decisive victory, even winning a congressional appropriation "as an indemnity for losses sustained" in their relocation. But such justice was not extended to other tribes, as illustrated by the experience of the Sacs. A leader named Mokohoko had already proven resistant to white acculturation efforts, rejecting the stone-and-frame houses built by federal employees on the Kansas Sac reservation by pitching his bark wickiup "right under [their] very eaves."

In 1869, when most of the Mississippi River Sacs departed for Indian Territory, sold out by former chief Keokuk's son Moses, Mokohoko and about a hundred tribespeople remained, insisting that to depart "would be like putting our heads in the mouth[s] of great Bears to be eaten off."

Instead, the remaining Sacs adopted a survival strategy by living on a part of their previous lands not coveted by whites, by being as pacific and unobtrusive as possible, by hunting and raising crops, by foraging for nuts and berries, and by hiring themselves out to whites, the men as seasonal farm workers, the women as household help. They simply resisted any attempts by officials to break their resolve, and the officials—influenced by Grant's Peace Policy—hesitated to force them. Soon, many of the Sacs who had been removed began returning, giving up their government annuity payments in order to do so.

For six years, Mokohoko's community held out, adapting as necessary. With the buffalo disappearing as a major form of subsistence, they learned to look to "smaller game such as deer, rabbits, raccoons, and prairie chickens." They maintained a rich ceremonial life, but like the Poncas were willing to relinquish official tribal status rather than leave their homes along the banks of the Marias des Cygnes River.

The government refused them even this. In late 1875, United States infantrymen arrived to take them to Indian Territory. Most of the Sac men were away on their winter hunt, and the remaining men, women, and children offered no resistance, the leaders among them simply asking that "they be allowed to remain behind briefly in order to conduct religious rites," as "their houses rested on sacred ground and could not be abandoned without the proper rituals."

So the Sacs went—and immediately filtered back, picking up their old living patterns and endearing themselves to the whites and the Chippewa Indians for whom they periodically worked. Their quiet form of passive resistance would buy them another decade on the Marias des Cygnes. Yet they still fell under a government removal edict as "a roving band of ignorant vagabond trespassers . . . without any means of support whatever."

A lieutenant sent in the 1886 removal force found the reality far from the rhetoric. The Sacs were "hardly the 'Ignoran[t] vagabond trespassers, naked and starving without any means of support' " which he had been led to expect, but quiet, peaceful inhabitants of a small strip of riverbank, people whose departure would be mourned "with few exceptions" by their white neighbors. They accompanied the soldiers without resistance, if reluctantly and morosely, and insisted on paying for their own goods on the journey southward. They would not come back again.

Even the Poncas' victory came late. Despite the poor conditions, most were adjusting to their new land in Indian Territory and chose to stay there. In Kansas the biggest victory had been won by a band of Kickapoos under a strong religious and political leader named Kenekuk. They had used the same strategies as had Mokohono and the Sacs, but with greater success. Peaceful resistance, adaptability to white culture, and luck led them to be "among the few Indians left in Kansas."

As most of the Kansas and Nebraska tribes made the transition to new reservations, some western tribes and bands were moving with little or no resistance onto the lands designated for them by government officials. The government won a certain acquiescence by locating these reservations within the tribes' homelands. The new reservation Indians also had hopes that the bounded land would prove a haven from the land hunger and general aggression of whites and enemy tribes, from the disorder and deprivation they were experiencing off the reservation, and—ironically—from Anglo attempts to control and "civilize" them.

Like previous tribes, western Indians were willing to go to great lengths of accommodation to remain in their homelands. A resident of the Paiutes' Pyramid Lake reservation in 1875 announced, "Anything the Government says, we will do—if we can keep our homes." But even as Anglo officials attempted to create places where Indians "would become *like* whites," many Indians, eager to retain their cultures and shape their own destinies, no doubt "envisioned the reservation as the place where they could become independent *from* whites," or at least "survive . . . with as little interference in their daily lives as possible."

Few of their hopes would be realized, but this does not mean that they became passive victims once they were on the reservation. Even among the most peaceable tribes, "the circumstances of the struggle may have changed, but the struggle itself did not."

Land remained the biggest point of contention. For one thing, the U.S. government left the reservation boundaries ambiguous or failed to take into account varying claims. When the Wind River reservation of the Shoshones was created, officials inadvertently included a gold-mining town and white homesteads, leading to endless wrangling. Further, the Shoshones and Plains tribes continued to fight over the territory, so that the reservation "resembled a battleground rather than a homeland."

In another case, the government lured many California Indians onto the Round Valley reservation in the early 1870s with promises of enlargement of the reservation, and a congressional edict to back those promises up. Yet white settlers blocked the plan. "The Indians are getting tired of waiting . . . ," wrote their agent in 1878. "They see the horses, cattle, and sheep of the settlers occupying the very lands long ago promised to them." One native group used money earned picking hops to buy a piece of this Anglo-held acreage and—with the help of a lawyer—successfully resisted the agent's attempts to induce them to move back.

The Paiutes, who had given up any concerted violent resistance after their war of 1860, had reason to be happy with their two reservations surrounding Pyramid and Walker lakes, as these were some of their best and most familiar subsistence lands. They knew how to catch the fish and migratory birds that came to the lakeshores, how to collect the berries and rice grass and other wild foods that the lake regions produced. Yet the federal government had no sooner unofficially established the reservations (after claiming the Great Basin without any mention of compensation for the natives) than whites were trying to strip the Paiutes of them.

To many whites, natives were simply "given" a reservation on sufferance. This viewpoint was fed by the existence after 1871 of the

This portrait of Pacific Northwest natives netting whitefish in the Columbia River rapids appeared in *Frank Leslie's Illustrated Newspaper* in 1871. Although it reflects romanticized Anglo perceptions of natives, it also reflects the fact that Indians used natural resources to live self-sufficiently, an ability that dispossession dramatically reduced or destroyed. *Courtesy Denver Public Library, Western History Department*

The white settler takes center stage in this Thomas Davenport drawing "Indian Neighbors," produced as a National Life of Vermont ad in the early twentieth century. The Indians recede, in line with a common late-nineteenth-century American perception that Indians were vanishing from the American scene. *Courtesy National Life of Vermont, Montpelier, Vermont*

The trauma of relocation and survival shows in the appearance of this young Navajo woman at Fort Sumner, New Mexico Territory, in 1866. Like thousands of others, she had been forced out of Navajo country to the inhospitable confines of Bosque Redondo. *Courtesy Museum of New Mexico*

By 1890, the western Indians who had fought the longest to maintain their lands and way of life found themselves reduced to bleak dependency. Here, "Ration Day" on South Dakota's Pine Ridge reservation in 1891 reinforces that grim reality. *Courtesy Denver Public Library, Western History Department*

On the reservations, Indians found ways to maintain tradition while acceding to pressure by officials to conform to Anglo lifeways, as evidenced by the living quarters shown in this late-nineteenth-century photograph on the Rosebud reservation in South Dakota. *Courtesy John Anderson Collection, Nebraska State Historical Society*

The boundaries of Indian Territory kept crumbling. With the extinguishing of Cherokee claims to the "Cherokee Outlet," or "Cherokee Strip," the "boomers" rushed in, September 16, 1893. *Courtesy Western Historical Collections, University of Oklahoma Libraries*

Removals continued. In this 1903 exodus the Cupeno Indians of California, having lost a legal fight to retain their traditional homes on the Warner Ranch, depart for a reservation. *Courtesy Southwest Museum, Los Angeles*

The allotment that began in the 1890s posed a new threat to the Indian land base. Here, an allotment crew posed along with the family of half-Indian, half-white interpreter William Garrett before the dividing of the Pine Ridge reservation in South Dakota. *Courtesy Denver Public Library, Western History Department*

Indians continued to observe and creatively adapt their own traditions. Here, Ute Indians at the Garden of the Gods in Colorado in 1911 wear finery for a traditional dance. *Courtesy Denver Public Library, Western History Department*

This tranquil photograph appears to depict an earlier era, but it was taken in 1912 at a Ute camp in Colorado. *Courtesy Denver Public Library, Western History Department*

Indians welcomed the mobility of the automobile, but continued to juxtapose the old ways with the new, as in this photograph of a woman shelling green corn on the Standing Rock reservation in North Dakota. *Courtesy Denver Public Library, Western History Department*

Over and over, Indian representatives made their way to Washington to press their tribal claims and concerns. They often found it advantageous to appear both in the storied Plains dress familiar to non-Indians and in business suits. In this 1926 council with U.S. senators, Chief Eugene Little (*seated left*) and Chief William Spotted Tail (*seated right*) are dressed in full regalia, in contrast to other delegation members. *Courtesy Denver Public Library, Western History Department*

Ironically, one of the most poignant and powerful images of Indian land loss is captured in this standard bureaucratic portrait. George Gillette, chairman of the Fort Berthold tribal council, weeps as Secretary of the Interior J. A. Krug signs a 1948 contract relinquishing 155,000 acres of Fort Berthold reservation land for the Garrison Dam. *Courtesy AP/Wide World Photos*

Indians protested against the water projects. Here, William Rickard (*left*) and Wallace "Mad Bear" Anderson (*bottom right*) attempt to keep the New York State Power Authority from flooding the Tuscarora reservation. *Courtesy Buffalo and Erie County Historical Society*

In the 1960s, life on a reservation for most Indians still involved an overwhelming, inescapable dependence on the Bureau of Indian Affairs. Here, a Sioux couple waits outside a BIA office in 1968. *Courtesy Denver Public Library, Western History Department*

The War on Poverty had little or no impact on the lives of many reservation residents, including this Pine Ridge woman, photographed in 1970. *Courtesy Denver Public Library, Western History Department*

Indians continued to challenge their dispossession. In November 1982, Dennis Banks leads an "unthanksgiving ceremony" at Alcatraz Island, highlighting Indian efforts to regain lost lands. *Courtesy AP/Wide World Photos*

"executive order" reservations created by presidential mandate, for Indian title to the land was not as clear as on reservations established by treaty.

What this added up to for the northern Paiutes, whose Pyramid Lake reservation had been established in 1859 but only made official under executive order in 1874, was a world of trouble. Many agents and superintendents as well as settlers openly advocated—or conceded the inevitability of—white use of Paiute resources and further taking of Paiute lands.

The Paiutes protested repeatedly, but were virtually ignored. They did have champions. Major Henry Douglas in 1869 replaced an agent who wanted to appropriate a Paiute location called Goat Island for an Anglo cashmere goat–raising operation. In rejecting the idea, Douglas pointed out that the island was located "in the *heart* of the Reservation," where a white enterprise "could not but be detrimental to the interests of the Indians," that it was "just as available for the raising of goats (cashmere or otherwise) for the benefit of *Indians,* as it is for the aggrandisement of any one white man," and that "the withdrawal of the Island from the Reservation" would set a precedent encouraging other interlopers. Douglas further noted that the previous agent's attempt to portray the Paiutes as "good hands for white men" glossed over the fact that they would, "with proper assistance and good management, *be good hands for themselves.*"

Government approval of railroad rights-of-way across the reservation in 1864 and again in 1873 created havoc. Whites assumed that the common practice of allotting alternate sections of land along the route to railroad companies would be followed, thus opening these tracts for speculation. "Is Pyramid Lake reservation abandoned or to be?" a desperate agent telegraphed Washington in the second excitement. "White men are rushing upon it and I am powerless through ignorance of facts to prevent them. Indians are full of anxiety which I can't allay. I beg for instructions. Answer."

The secretary of the interior finally ruled that the railroad would be limited to the right-of-way, the reservation preserved. But such governmental victories for the Indians only stimulated greater machinations by those whites covetous of their land. Interlopers challenged the boundaries of the reservation, but even many years after it was surveyed in 1865, beleaguered agents had no maps or official land markings to show them. Some whites argued that the survey itself was invalid. The upshot, as an 1884 inspector explained, was that "unless a person is found trespassing upon the waters of [Pyramid] Lake in a boat, it appears impossible to convict any one before a Court of Justice, of trespassing, on the Reserve."

This meant, of course, that even when the government sought to aid them in keeping intruders out, natives could not feel safe and protected within the reservation boundaries. Whites still drove their livestock into Indian fields and gardens, and threatened and assaulted the natives and even their agents.

The intruders reacted violently to any real or imagined sign of Indian hostility. As had their westering predecessors, they used the transgressions or supposed transgressions of individual tribespeople as justification for attacking others and divesting a whole tribe of land, even though in the Great Basin "practically all native resistance had ended" by 1865.

Paiute numbers shrank by as much as two thirds in the decade of the 1860s, in large part due to white aggression "in isolated attacks on Indian camps or individuals [on and off the reservations] by organized paramilitary forces and by unauthorized white citizens." The Indians' very adaptability to white culture made them targets. A Paiute named Truckee John had established a good farming and ranching operation on the lower Truckee River, earning the approbation of agents, but he was murdered by white men in July 1867 in a plot to take his spread.

Intruders simply moved brazenly onto reservation lands. In 1862, Nevada Governor James Nye reported that "a series of trespasses makes [the Paiutes] testy and uneasy." By 1865, white squatters had streamed onto the Pyramid Lake reservation in such numbers that "whites controlled over half of the agricultural lands"; by 1869, the figure would be 80 percent for the relatively fertile river bottoms on the southern portion of the reservation. When a new agent in 1873 tried to oust a man holding two hundred acres, the man told him that every agent had ordered him off in the nine years he had been there, but that "he had convinced them that he was not on the reserve at all."

The Paiutes and their agents were bedeviled by other invasive tactics. Unencumbered by fences, cattlemen grazed their herds on reservation grass, which the Indians recognized as an important resource. They were already complaining vociferously of this practice in the early 1860s; a quarter-century later, nothing had changed, an inspector in 1886 noting, "The Stockmen allow their Stock to come here and break into [the Paiutes'] fields. When Indians complain the cattlemen tell them to show the lines, which they cannot do."

More than grazing, however, the presence of white fishermen at Pyramid Lake and along the Truckee River threatened Indian subsistence. Governor Nye won undying gratitude from Paiute activist Sarah Winnemucca in 1865 when he responded to Paiute complaints by sending soldiers to chase the fishermen off. But they came back again and again, wearing down both the Paiutes and the government with their intransigence. In 1869, a federal inspector reported, "The Indians very justly complain of interference with their fisheries by parties of white men who have been located on the reservation for some time— from one to two years—near the mouth of the river." These intruders not only took fish belonging to the Paiutes by treaty, but employed commercial fishing methods that left the Indians, who were unfamiliar with a market economy and unable to pay for better boats and equipment, at a competitive disadvantage in making something of their resources.

The situation only grew worse. In 1877, Paiute agent A. J. Barnes called the white fishermen an aggravation "almost beyond endurance." He reported: "The Indians *are very much excited* concerning this matter and are making complaints to me daily that these white men will supply the market with fish from the lake and thus deprive them of their *only means of making a livelihood*" during half the year, October to April.

Barnes, like many another agent, found that he had no control over the intruders and that local and state courts tended to be sympathetic to the invading whites. He finally sent for a federal marshal, then notified the commissioner of Indian Affairs: "The marshal has been fired on and declares his inability to clear the Reservation without military assistance. The Indians are enraged." Just as troops were being sent from San Francisco, the fishermen agreed to leave. But they quickly returned and began claiming that the reservation itself was illegal. A federal court ruled this argument invalid, which angered most of the white citizenry, and the wholesale invasion continued, even while troops periodically tried to rid Pyramid Lake of unauthorized fishermen.

Meanwhile, the appropriation of Indian land by squatters was allowed to continue, the whites on the reservation buying and selling land and paying taxes on it. "I want this reservation to stay," a Paiute named Captain Jim had announced in 1870 when asked his opinion on squatters. "I want to live here and do what the Government tells me. Don't want any white men on the reserve." But the Paiutes' refuge had turned out to be no refuge at all.

Even had the whites not trespassed and appropriated land and resources, Indians could not have realized their hopes of freedom from deprivation. For one thing, they were dependent to a large extent on government annuities and goods. Winnemucca would remember one meager "issuing day": "It was enough to make a doll laugh. A family numbering eight persons got two blankets, three shirts, no dress-goods. Some got a fishhook and line; some got one and a half yards of flannel, blue and red. . . . It was the saddest affair I ever saw." Further, the agent distributed the limited and sporadic goods as he saw fit, often shortchanging those who resisted his authority or dared to disagree publicly with his management.

Many Indians on the relatively new reservations teetered close to starvation, and those who attempted to move outside the boundaries in traditional hunting-and-gathering forays faced white hostility and changes in the land and its resources. This situation allowed the more resistant to gain sway within the tribes and turned initially acquiescent Indians hostile, as exemplified by the Santee Sioux of Minnesota and the Bannocks of Idaho.

The Santee, or eastern, Sioux, unlike their western cousins had been pressed with limited resistance onto a ten-mile-wide strip along the Minnesota River, where they waited in vain in 1862 for promised government goods and annuities. Supplies they desperately needed were sitting in the agency warehouse, but the agent would not distribute them until the cash portion of the annuity arrived as well—cash that traders were ready to seize "to satisfy credit they said, and nobody could disprove, had already been extended."

When the Santee Sioux ventured out to hunt, they found that the game had been severely depleted by the settlers crowding them along the banks of the river. Trader Andrew Myrick's callous remark regarding their condition—"If they are hungry let them eat grass or their own dung"—fanned the flames of the young men's resentment, and their desperate condition drew even those who had begun adopting an Anglo lifestyle to rebel.

The result was "the most disastrous Indian uprising white Americans had experienced since the attacks of Opechancanough and Philip on the Virginia and Massachusetts frontiers two centuries before." The Santee Sioux killed some four hundred immigrants, including Myrick, who was found with his mouth stuffed with grass.

In a similar situation sixteen years later, the peaceful Bannocks of Idaho and Wyoming were nearing starvation on their western reservation. They still had one important food resource: the camas roots that they were allowed by treaty to dig on the Idaho prairies. When they went out to do so, they found that the settlers' hogs had uprooted the valuable plants and cattle had trampled and denuded the soil in which they grew.

The Bannocks, too, began killing settlers, leading Indian fighter General George Crook to muse, "I do not wonder . . . that when these Indians see their wives and children starving, and their last source of supplies cut off, they go to war. And then we are sent out to kill them."

Both revolts were summarily crushed. The Santee Sioux—like the Pequots of an earlier era—were scattered and reduced, some continuing a bare survival on a Nebraska reservation. The United States government, responding to expanding Minnesota settlement, seized the opportunity to remove the still-peaceful and oft-pressed Winnebagos as well, to an "all dust" South Dakota tract.

What the government wanted on the reservations was Indians supporting themselves through farming. In fact, the government did not recognize any activity but Anglo-style farming as honest subsistence work. Yet it failed repeatedly to provide Indians with the promised tools and expertise, it failed to recognize that western reservation Indians could not put enough acres into cultivation quickly enough to feed even a portion of their population, and it failed to recognize that other subsistence efforts better suited both the land and the natives. Field agents reported that much of the country was suited for stock raising, an occupation that most western Indian men took to more readily than farming. Nevada's Governor Nye pointed out that the natives "were familiar with the characteristics and curing of wild grasses after hundreds of years of their own food-gathering, and that they would work well with hay and pasturage."

Instead, officials in Washington persisted in issuing directives to turn the western Indians into Anglo-style farmers, and some agents followed through ruthlessly, again turning initially peaceful natives to hostiles. On the Ute reservation in Colorado in 1879, agent Nathan Meeker ignored his charges' cattle-raising skills, "plowed up their winter pasture," told them "the government would take away their reservation if they would not cultivate it," and called in troops to back him up. The Utes killed him.

For even these overwhelmingly "peaceable" Indians remained remarkably resistant to all attempts to make them exchange their native identity for an Anglo-approved one. An historian studying the Indians of Round Valley reservation in California looked for evidence of "cultural disintegration" under overwhelming pressures and instead found the natives "not only stoutly resist[ing] white domination, but also pursu[ing] their own goal of self-sufficiency." Another historian in examining the Shoshones of the Wind River reservation in the 1870s found "even [this] nominally receptive tribe" doggedly resisting "acculturation to white ways."

It should be noted that white officials did occasionally mandate more humane treatment of tribespeople by their own. For example, they forbade the Apache practice of cutting off the nose of an adulterous woman, and they outlawed some tribes' custom of helping themselves to the possessions of a recently deceased person, a practice that by their own testimony left family survivors—especially children—traumatized and in need.

But Anglos also continued to impose cultural standards that were unjustifiable by any but the most ethnocentric reckoning. Tensions grew from the fact that, as in the praying towns of the eastern frontier two centuries earlier, agents and missionaries tried to hold Indians to a standard not shared by the white population in general. For example, the Paiutes' agent tried to outlaw the games of chance that "had a central place in Paiutes' culture throughout historic and apparently prehistoric times" even as the Anglo mining frontier expanded nearby in a dizzying orgy of betting and speculation.

In addition, there was the maddening paternalism of the whole reservation system. Carl Schurz, appointed secretary of the interior in 1877, blandly assured one Indian group questioning a local agency action, "The Great Father is a very wise man. He knows everything. If there is anything wrong with your agent, he will know it before either you or I know it."

The western Indians who assented to reservations continued to assert their independence in a number of ways. Some, such as the large traditional faction of Kickapoos, waged a "cold war" against the officials placed over them, one characterized by "constant criticism, fault-finding, and open defiance of agency rules."

Like African Americans on southern plantations, reservation Indians moved slowly through work imposed by autocratic or patriarchal agents and caused further delays by breaking tools. Despite off-reservation discrimination, many Indians shifted between reservations and western towns, making use of whatever resources and limited economic opportunities existed for them in both environments. They quietly resisted proselytizing attempts—two years of missionary work among the Shoshones at Wind River yielded only fourteen converts, all children. They continued to hold traditional rites, such as feasts and sweathouse ceremonies. They refused to send their children to white day schools, and particularly to white boarding schools.

This does not mean that these Indians were resistant to all change. Most simply wanted to adapt in ways that seemed comfortable and appropriate for them. Many of the Paiutes, for example, proved competent farmers, but they preferred to do the work communally, cultivating each plot in turn.

The United States government had an opportunity to meet these western natives halfway. It did not, becoming instead more coercive in its resolve to remake generally peaceful natives in a model Anglo mold. Meanwhile, it faced far more sustained and serious challenges to its plans by militaristic Indians of the Southwest and the Plains, and even by less war-oriented northwestern Indians unhappy with government dictates as to where and how they should live.

←——————→

Chapter Seven

"I Hope to God You Will Not Ask Me to Go to Any Other Country"
(1861–1875)

I hope to God you will not ask me to go to any other country
except my own. It might turn out another Bosque Redondo.
—*Navajo chief Barboncito to peace commissioners, 1867*

Of the Ponca removal to Indian Territory, Standing Bear had mourned that his people lacked power to mount an effective resistance—"We could not help ourselves." Indeed, the Poncas and many others were simply overwhelmed, the advance of Anglo-dominated settlement barely slowing with the coming of the Civil War. Five new territories—Colorado, Dakota, Idaho, Arizona, and Montana—emerged during the war years, while Nevada with its silver mines gained statehood. Yet various tribes and bands of the Southwest and Plains used the American government's distraction with the struggle for union to mount bold, bloody frontier resistance.

After the war, Anglo settlement and enterprise spread with explosive force across the western landscape, along the way creating the states of Nebraska and Colorado and the territory of Wyoming. Tribes responded with their own explosive attempts to repel the advance and thwart the boundaries set for them by a government intent on corraling Indians in out-of-the-way locations. Clash after clash, including "virtually every major war of the two decades after Appomattox" centered on government attempts "to force Indians on to newly created reservations or to make them go back to reservations from which they had fled.''

The chronicle of direct resistance during this quarter-century is studded with names that have become familiar in American mythology: Cochise, Red Cloud, Crazy Horse, Chief Joseph, Sitting Bull, Geronimo. From the mountains of the Mexican border to the northern Plains, western Indians rallied around such leaders, engaging with whites and sometimes with members of other tribes in the most sweeping struggles yet for native land rights and freedoms.

The Apaches and Navajos of the arroyos and mesas of the Southwest had fought readily with each other, with other tribes, and with Mexican troops and Mexican settlers through the early decades of the nineteenth century. As the Civil War began, the initial peaceful relations with immigrants to New Mexico Territory from the United States had broken down in the press of settlement and in such bloody strong-arm incidents as the "Bascom affair."

A young lieutenant named George Bascom accused Chiricahua Apache chief Cochise of raiding a ranch. When Cochise protested that this was the work of other Apaches (there were at least a dozen distinct bands), Bascom attempted unsuccessfully to take him prisoner, then held five of Cochise's relatives. Cochise seized captives as well— a Butterfield stage agent and two travelers—and tried to exchange them for his family members. When he was rebuffed, Cochise killed his captives, and Bascom hanged his. Cochise then led a series of murderous raids against troops, settlers, and miners.

Both the Apaches and the Navajos became hopeful when troops began pulling back to meet war needs in the East. Perhaps they were succeeding in driving out the land-hungry and combative newcomers.

Instead, United States Army troops from the West rebuffed a Confederate bid for the territory and joined New Mexico volunteers in wartime operations to "pacify" the Indians and get them out of the whites' way. General James Carleton, commander of the military department of New Mexico, enlisted famed frontier scout Kit Carson in an offensive to force first the Mescalero Apaches of southern New Mexico—some five hundred to a thousand people—then the far more populous Navajos, onto a "forty-mile-square tract of semi-arid land" on the Pecos River in New Mexico Territory.

Carson and the troops harried the Mescalero Apaches so fiercely that they could not visit a water hole without encountering soldiers, and the Indians' ammunition supplies quickly dwindled. By spring 1863, most had surrendered and had begun moving northward under army guard to Carleton's reservation, called Bosque Redondo, or "round grove of trees," for its distinguishing feature—a ring of large cottonwoods.

Here Carleton, operating out of the adjacent Fort Sumner, hoped to establish a model reservation and show the Bureau of Indian Affairs, normally in charge of such efforts, what proper military control could do. He would "civilize" the Indians in a no-nonsense authoritarian program that would turn them into white-educated Christian farmers. For the virtually captive Apaches, Bosque Redondo offered some faint hope of being a place of refuge from war and want. But both Carleton and his charges were to be disappointed.

Upon arrival, the Mescaleros found only a few rough adobe shelters housing the troops for the fledging fort. Under the direction of military overseers and of their Bureau of Indian Affairs agent, Lorenzo Labadie, with whom Carleton often quarreled, the natives began the laborious task of clearing the mesquite-studded land to construct their own shelters and to plant seeds. Scarcely had they started than the food ran out. Accompanied by an army officer, the men were allowed to go antelope hunting with bow and arrow, but tribal members were not allowed to range in search of mescal, the bulb of the century plant, which they had cooked as a food staple for generations.

Carleton did work hard to keep his charges fed, at one point lessening the rations of his troops rather than cut the Indians' portion. But constant supply problems would plague the reservation. Soon after goods started arriving, the Mescaleros insisted that someone was attempting to poison them with the government-issue flour. Checking it, Labadie found "bits of slate, broken bread, and something that resembled plaster of paris." This cheating tactic used by contractors to line their pockets naturally fostered deep suspicions among the Indians, who had no say regarding who was to be their contractor or even what would be provided.

Carleton's long-term plan was the standard bureaucratic fantasy: to get the natives to feed themselves through Anglo-style farming. The Mescaleros planted corn, beans, and melons and dug irrigation ditches, but only under constant supervision. For one thing, they had such limited tools that many were "work[ing] the soil with . . . bare hands." For another, they were disheartened with and unenthusiastic about farming, being accustomed to a highly mobile life hunting game—primarily deer and rabbit—and gathering wild foods—primarily mesquite seeds and the mescal cactus.

An official who visited the Mescaleros in their early days on the reservation sensed among them "a deep sadness" and an urge "to flee the reservation at the first opportunity." However, they produced respectable crops in that summer of 1863. They also brewed their native liquor, *tiswin,* from the ripening corn, and drunkenness became a problem.

Meanwhile, Carleton and Carson were pursuing the Navajos with the same determination that had subjugated the Mescaleros. Arizona Territory was split off from New Mexico Territory in 1863. The Navajos had been hitting hard against settlements within or bordering their northeastern Arizona Territory and northwestern New Mexico Territory homelands—particularly against Fort Defiance, planted deep in their country of piñon-juniper woodlands and sagebrush plains. A major at the fort had recommended that the Navajos "be removed to several, small, isolated reserves, where they could be instructed in agricultural pursuits and learn to become self-sufficient." While the major was thinking of the Navajos' welfare as well as the settlers', he exhibited blindness to an Indian self-sufficiency that had not yet been compromised by the white invasion: the Navajos, unlike the more nomadic Mescaleros, had a long record of productive farming and livestock raising, and many still boasted rich fields and vast herds.

In April 1863, as the Mescaleros began their life at Bosque Redondo, Carleton informed two Navajo chiefs, Barboncito and Delgadito, that peace could only come when the Navajos agreed to removal to the same site, well east of Navajo territory.

Both chiefs were seeking a peace, but not on these terms. "When the Navajos were first created four mountains and four rivers were pointed out to us, inside of which we should live," Barboncito would later explain. "That was to be our country and was given to us by the first woman of the Navajo tribe. It was told to us by our forefathers, that we were never to move east of the Rio Grande or west of the San Juan Rivers."

So the chiefs refused. Then in June, Carleton issued a chilling order: "Tell them they can have until the twentieth day of July of this year to come in—they and all those who belong to what they call the peace party; *that after that day every Navajo that is seen will be considered as hostile and treated accordingly*." An army captain relayed the message to one Navajo band: "My Government has given orders to kill you all unless you come in and surrender. So come in to the fort today or else take your families and flee to the wildest mountains."

Suddenly the troops were striking all the way to the western border of Navajo land. The soldiers carried out their orders to kill the Indians they discovered but concentrated primarily on wiping out their crops and stealing or slaughtering their sheep, goats, cows, and horses. Adding to the Navajos' predicament were raids by other groups who "scented plunder": New Mexico citizen militias, Utes and Paiutes from the north, Pueblo Indians from the east, "even the normally mild Hopis" from the west. "Now from every side other Indians came in to fight them," one Navajo would sadly relate.

Then the troops under Carson penetrated the deep oasis of Canyon de Chelly, where once the Anasazi culture had flourished and where the "ancient ones" had left their traces in structures, burial sites, and petroglyphs. For generations the canyon had been Navajo stronghold, sanctuary, and home. On the sandy floor, they had grown their corn and wheat, tended their fruit orchards, watched their sheep herds flourish. In January 1864, the soldiers cut the corn and the peach trees, and rounded up the sheep "as shouting, cursing Indians rained arrows from the rims of the sheer red sandstone walls."

Some twelve thousand Navajos lived on the land, from Canyon de Chelly in the north to the Little Colorado River to the south. By mid-March, half of that number had come in to the army forts in the eastern portion of their territory. Most were near destitution, but a fair number who still possessed respectable herds had been drawn in by Delgadito, who had seen the reservation and thought they could subsist there. He also felt they had no other choice.

Bosque Redondo still lay 250 to 300 miles to the east, and so was born the Navajo equivalent of the Trail of Tears—the Long Walk. Soldiers organized and oversaw the migration. There was much suffering along the route, and many deaths from exposure and dysentery. But another two thousand Navajos followed this trail by year's end.

The Cebolletan Navajo band entered the reservation first. They had proven particularly friendly to whites, the men serving as army scouts, but were now "technically prisoners of war." Almost immediately, hostile Navajos began raiding their sheep, as well as the Mescalero livestock and provisions.

With the influx of other Navajos onto the reservation, the situation—already precarious—deteriorated. The internees enjoyed no freedom from either deprivation or hostilities, and the forced work and white cultural standards fed their confusion and resentment.

The Bureau of Indian Affairs superintendent for the region argued that the forty acres would sustain at most three major Apache bands—the Mescalero, Mimbres, and Chiricahua, totaling some 2,500 people. Instead, Carleton had as many as 8,577 Navajos and hundreds of Mescaleros trying to subsist on this tract. After the first Mescalero harvest, problems plagued the farming efforts. The Navajos were good workers when adequately fed, but they seldom if ever received enough food to live on. The crops repeatedly failed—"insects, hail, floods, drought—something every year." At one point, as yet another corn crop fell victim to the ravaging "army" worm, Carleton conceived the idea of having both soldiers and Indians go through the fields opening each husk, removing the bugs, and then closing the husk.

Nothing stemmed the destructive forces—which extended to intertribal warfare. Navajos raided Apache corn fields, destroying their crops. Apaches responded in kind, members of both tribes battling "with hoes and shovels among the tall green stalks," even ignoring soldiers' warning gunshots in their enmity and frustration. Nor did they trust the government; in 1865, the rumor spread that the soldiers were trying to kill their charges with a poison coating on the beef rations, and later that same year Indians avoided a harvest feast because of similar fears of poisoning.

Meanwhile, government rations continued to be poor and inadequate, forcing Carleton to cut individual portions repeatedly. In fall 1864, as the reservation faced massive crop failure, both military overseers and residents learned that "swindlers had made off with one-half of the Congressional appropriation for the Navajos." Although expenses for Carleton's experiment repeatedly topped a million dollars a year, the Indians never received enough to remotely meet their basic needs.

The effects of the swindle were apparent at a supply distribution on Christmas Eve 1864, one much anticipated by the Indians, who lacked provisions for winter: as "nearly 7,800 Navajos . . . sat quietly on the cold ground," the Indian Bureau superintendent and his assistants tried to ascertain that everyone got something, but "badly needed blankets and cloth rapidly ran out, and many . . . ended up with awls, buttons, or beads."

The military did try carefully to determine what provisions to obtain and when to obtain them, but bureaucrats and contractors continued to appropriate money without providing adequate amounts or quality of provisions. Healthy livestock herds would have helped allay some of their needs. "We try and keep our sheep for their milk," explained a Navajo named Herrero to members of an 1865 congressional investigation team, "and [we] only kill them when necessary, when the rations are short or smell bad." But the animals brought by Navajos to the reservation were dying off for lack of adequate forage, and the animals promised by the government never arrived. By the winter of 1865–1866, guards had to be placed around the herds that were being held by the military for meat distribution, as the reservation Indians were resorting to secret cattle raiding.

Supply and livestock problems intensified as Kiowas and Comanches to the east raided supply trains bound for Bosque Redondo and even swept onto the reservation, raiding the government herds and Navajo horses.

Navajos on the reservation were also killed by the raiders, or warned that they were on Comanche and Kiowa land. This is perhaps the most overlooked and most psychologically frustrating aspect of the Bosque Redondo experience for the Navajos: having been forced from their own territory onto the reservation, they soon found that their presence drew resentment from all directions. The Mescaleros hated them. Agent Labadie even told them that they were "trespassing on an Apache reservation and that soon they would be forced to move elsewhere." Some of the soldiers mistreated them. The citizens of New Mexico hated them and blamed them—perhaps with increasing accuracy—for incursions off the reservation. New Mexicans tried to argue both that the reservation was on private land and that the Navajos belonged in Arizona Territory, where the bulk of their homelands were located.

Both Mescaleros and Navajos were also suffering from lack of fuel for cooking and warmth. The cottonwood grove quickly fell under the ax, and natives were sent out in replanting work details. But the trees they planted would take decades to develop; the natives had to travel in widening circles to collect mesquite wood, devoting whole days to finding it and hauling it home on their backs.

Illnesses—malaria, exposure, measles, venereal disease—plagued reservation residents. Carleton established a Navajo hospital, but one surgeon described it as "only fit to keep pigs in." Besides, the Navajos were suspicious of any place in which a death occurred, and were particularly so of the hospital, site of numerous deaths; it was "permeated with the spirits of death and therefore taboo." But the Navajos' own healing traditions depended on herbs and roots not found at Bosque Redondo.

Added to all of these problems was the struggle between Carleton, with his plans to turn the Indians into pseudowhite farmers, and the Indians, who searched for autonomous ways to survive. Like many of the civilian agents, Carleton thought he knew best. He wanted the Navajos to inhabit Pueblo-style adobes. This plan the natives ignored, building traditional hogan-style huts from which they could move easily if a death within the structure made it taboo. Thwarted, Carleton then instructed a subordinate to show the Navajos how to construct a "model" hut for warmth. The subordinate reported that the Navajo huts "were too warm already."

Seldom did government officials, military or civil, show sensitivity to Indian self-determination. In the midst of the reservation's myriad problems, the military officials at Bosque Redondo in 1865 developed a plan for reorganizing the Navajos that simply reinforced Anglo control; chiefs, who were to keep "a record of absent Indians," were to be appointed by the post commander and subject to dismissal by him at any time.

The reservation routine became increasingly regimented, the workers summoned by the peal of a giant bell—purchased with money in an account supposedly the Indians' own—"to commence work in the fields, to eat, and to cease laboring in the evenings."

Naturally, many Indians saw getting off the reservation as the only way to gain any freedom. "Cage the Badger and he will try to break from his prison and regain his native hole," explained one Navajo leader. "Chain the Eagle to the ground, and he will strive to gain his freedom and though he fails, will lift his head and look up to the sky which is his home."

This escape impulse was heightened by the privations on the reservation. "We have lost a good many of my people, and many are now sick," the Mescalero chief Cadette noted in 1865 to congressional investigators. "All but one of my horses have died from starvation. We could live better in our old country than in this. The water and grass are better there. Tell the Great White Father that we would like to go back to our old country."

Many just slipped away—including, in 1866, the whole Mescalero tribe, splitting into small groups and fleeing under cover of darkness. As many as five hundred Navajo escaped in one night, despite escalating military attempts to cut off movement. Indians had to have passes to depart the reservation; eventually, the order was handed down that "every reservation Indian found off the Bosque without a pass be killed."

Ironically, as Indians slipped away, others arrived upon the reservation for the first time, worn down by the constant enmity they faced outside. Manuelito, who had objected to territorial Governor Meriwether's boundary maps eleven years earlier, finally surrendered and arrived at Bosque Redondo in late 1866, just as the crops failed yet again.

By 1867, reservation buildings were crumbling, livestock continued to dwindle, farming operations were declining—and hail destroyed the fall crops. Furthermore, the reservation had become a bottomless hole for government expenditures. In spring 1868, General William Tecumseh Sherman and Samuel Tappan arrived from Washington as peace commissioners and, anxious for an alternative solution, actually listened to what the remaining Indians had to say about their situation.

Barboncito was one of those who spoke. "Our Grand-fathers had no idea of living in any other country except our own and I do not think it right for us to do so . . . ," he announced. "I think that our coming here has been the cause of so much death among us and our animals." He reported that the crops did not grow at Bosque Redondo as they did in the Navajo homeland to the west, and that people were now having to travel twenty-five miles for firewood, in the winter succumbing to exhaustion and cold on the journey. This world the

Navajos had entered was inhospitable and alien, rattlesnake bites proving fatal, while "in our own country a Rattlesnake before he bites
gives warning which enables us to keep out of its way and if bitten
we readily find a cure—but here we can find no cure."

The peace commissioners came with a hope that the Navajos would
accept the idea of going to Indian Territory. Sherman broached the
subject: "We have heard you were not satisfied with this reservation
and we have come here to invite some of your leading men to go and
see the Cherokee country and if they liked it we would give you a
reservation there."

Barboncito's response was to the point: "I hope to God you will
not ask me to go to any other country except my own. It might turn
out another Bosque Redondo." Repeatedly, he responded directly and
unequivocally: "We do not want to go to the right or left, but straight
back to our own country." If only they could return to their own land,
the Navajos expressed a willingness, even an eagerness to obtain
schools—which had been a failure at Bosque Redondo—and to have
blacksmith and carpentry shops. They also agreed to allow a railroad
to run through their home territory.

The commissioners' acquiescence reflected a new emphasis on
peaceful terms, exasperation with Carleton's experiment, fear that the
Navajos would violently resist other plans, and the fact that the Navajo
homelands were not attractive to settlers. Congress appropriated
$150,000 for the exiles' return. "After we get back to our country it
will brighten up again and the Navajos will be as happy as the land,"
Barboncito enthused. "Black clouds will rise and there will be plenty
of rain. Corn will grow in abundance and everything look happy."

So they turned westward, journeying back to the region within their
beloved four mountains in the summer of 1868. "When we saw the
top of the [first peak] . . . we wondered if it was our mountain, and
we felt like talking to the ground, we loved it so," reported the former
resistance chief Manuelito, "and some of the old men and women
cried with joy when they reached their homes."

The Navajos mounted no further warfare. Struggling on government
rations their first year back in their homelands, they soon received
sheep and goats from the United States government and resumed their
herding traditions. They would never throw off the demands of Anglo
government and culture, but they did have enough space—a large

reservation, although only a fraction of their former country—and breathing room to work out lives that combined tradition and adaptation.

Meanwhile, the Apaches had grown tired of the guerrilla warfare that characterized their relations with whites in the 1860s. Objects of white hostility, they had grown more hostile themselves, especially after the Chiricahua leader Mangas Coloradas was tortured and murdered by soldiers, his head cut off and "boiled . . . in a cauldron to prepare the skull for 'scientific study.' " Under the leadership of Mangas Coloradas's son-in-law Cochise and others, the Apaches had forced the government to expend millions of dollars in trying to chase and subdue them, with paltry results.

But Apache resources were diminishing as Anglo resources in the region expanded. As one Chiricahua noted, the invaders "seemed to have unlimited supplies of necessities furnished them, while the Indians were compelled to rustle everything they obtained."

Yet the alternative to warfare was life on a reservation. Such a choice drew Cochise to despair: "When I was young I walked all over this country, east and west, and saw no other people than the Apaches. After many summers I walked again and found another race of people had come to take it." Now, he reported, "the Apaches wait to die," their desolation so great that "they roam over the hills and plains and want the heavens to fall on them."

Cochise was being pressed in 1866 to leave the southern Arizona mountain ranges for a reservation at Tularosa in New Mexico. "I want to live in these mountains; I do not want to go to Tularosa," he insisted. "That is a long ways off. . . . I have drunk of these waters and they have cooled me; I do not want to leave here."

After a few more years of wearing resistance, Cochise, and his counterpart among the Mimbres Apaches, Loco, tried to negotiate with the United States government to let them establish reservations within their best subsistence lands, but the government kept them hanging, then again offered only Tularosa. As the Navajos settled onto their home reservation, the Apaches' situation remained confused and inflammatory. Some reluctantly moved onto poor, peripheral tracts sectioned off for them by the government. They would not stay; they would wage further extended resistance. During the 1870s, United

States officials would be more preoccupied with the fiery and often concerted resistance mounted by the Indians of the Plains.

The natives of the Great Plains had grown increasingly uneasy—and angry—with white incursions. A group of Yankton Sioux in 1858 had relinquished fifteen million acres of what would soon become Dakota Territory, over the objections of their own band members and of other Indians who protested that the Yanktons had only been inhabiting this region on the sufferance of other Sioux. In the same year, the discovery of gold in the Rockies had given birth to Denver and had caused immigrants and adventurers to spread along the Rocky Mountain chain immediately to the west of the Plains. Then, with Colorado becoming a territory in 1861, white officials began pushing to get the natives there to stay north of the Platte River and south of the Arkansas.

Some Cheyenne and Arapaho leaders agreed to remove across the southern river boundary. Many others refused. South of the Arkansas was Comanche and Kiowa country, where the antelope and buffalo essential to Plains cultures would not be as plentiful, especially with a growing concentration of native groups. Seeing their kin continue in old patterns of movement within their heartlands, even those natives who had agreed to move south of the Arkansas continued to cross freely. Various Plains bands clashed with settlers and the military, which led the commissioner of Indian affairs in 1863 to conclude that the Union under Lincoln "had upon [its] hands, in addition to the great rebellion, an Indian War of no mean proportion."

To white officials, the only "good" Indian was one who would remain contained within whatever boundaries the government had prescribed. However, matters were never that simple. In 1864, a band of Cheyennes—five hundred men, women, and children under peace chief Black Kettle—camped on Sand Creek in Colorado, just north of the Arkansas, under instructions from the military at nearby Fort Lyon to remain there and continue their late-fall hunt until the troops received orders from Washington regarding them.

On November 29, Colorado volunteers under Colonel John M. Chivington rode up to the camp. Black Kettle emerged from his tipi. "I looked toward the chief's lodge and saw Black Kettle had a large American flag tied to the end of a long lodgepole and was standing in front of his lodge holding the pole . . . ," southern Cheyenne

George Bent would recall. "I heard him call to the people not to be afraid, that the soldiers would not hurt them; then the troops opened fire."

Forced to retreat under the barrage, Black Kettle managed to return for his fallen wife, shot repeatedly but still alive. He lifted her onto his back and joined the other survivors in a straggling escape as some two hundred of the band lay dead and dying—most of them women and children.

The Chivington massacre exemplified the "only-good-Indian-is-a-dead-Indian" frontier philosophy that often brazenly superseded government policy. White Colorado immigrants had been unnerved by the Santee Sioux uprising in Minnesota and by Indian depredations, real and fantasized, in the territory. They had a common frontier tendency to assume that all Indian bands were hostile and therefore somehow deserving of the most extreme penalty: extermination.

"After the massacre, other Cheyennes who had been on the Arkansas River came over to Sand Creek. My grandmother was with that party," Cheyenne John Stands-in-Timber would relate. "None of them ever forgot what they saw there. The Cheyennes were almost all in raids after that. When the chiefs tried to prevent it they would ask, 'Do you want the white men to kill our people like that?' They wanted to get even."

In early 1865, Cheyennes, Arapahos, and Sioux scourged the territory, "burning virtually every ranch and stage station on the South Platte, twice sacking the town of Julesburg, ripping up miles of telegraph wire, plundering wagon trains, running off cattle herds, and completely cutting off Denver from the East." On the southern Plains, Comanche and Kiowa warriors continued their raids against any and all invaders. On the northern Plains, armed Indian resistance was crystallizing around a particular trail—the Bozeman route to the Montana goldfields—and around a particular leader, the Oglala Sioux Red Cloud.

The Bozeman Trail cut deep into the territory claimed by the western Sioux and their allies, the northern Cheyennes and Arapahos. This was territory formerly claimed by the Crows and other tribes, and a Crow chief's words provide a counterpoint to the general story of Indian dispossession by Anglos:

These are our lands by inheritance. The Great Spirit gave them to our fathers, but the Sioux stole them from us. They hunt upon our mountains. They fish in our streams. They have stolen our horses. They have murdered our squaws, our children. What white man has done these things to us?

The Crow-Anglo alliance would hold, and the Crows would eventually obtain one of the broader and more appealing reservation tracts in their home country. But in 1866, despite a worsening shortage of food and provisions and a treaty capitulation by some of their fellows, most of the Sioux were ready to defy Crows, Anglos, and anybody else to hold on to what they had won.

The government was making a show of consulting them regarding the road and the forts along it, but the Sioux knew this for a sham. Red Cloud, who had stripped a government surveying party and sent them ''naked in[to] the wilderness,'' reminded the Sioux and their allies of the government's early promises—''We were told that they wished merely to pass through our country, not to tarry among us.'' But now the soldiers' axes were ringing ''upon the Little Piney,'' their presence ''an insult and a threat.'' Red Cloud asked, ''Are we then to give up [our ancestors'] sacred graves to be plowed for corn?'' By September 1866, he had amassed an army that proceeded virtually to shut down the Bozeman Trail.

The United States government repeatedly sent troops into the field against the Sioux-Cheyenne-Arapaho alliance, the resulting battles ''not simply the helpless armed resistance of the Sioux to white intrusion'' but '' 'the clash of two expanding powers.' ''

These clashes pointed up the differences in warfare tactics between the U.S. military and western natives. European-American officers and troops saw battle in terms of extended large-scale clashes, while Indians relied primarily on sudden raids, ''sparring with enemies rather than engaging in toe-to-toe combat.''

Indians had good reason to favor guerrilla-warfare tactics. They needed to keep their own casualties at a minimum—''A dozen men lost from a company of soldiers could easily be replaced with recruits, but a generation was required to replace Indian warriors killed in battle.'' Indians seldom had the firepower of the frontier regulars, and with the element of surprise they could rout large numbers while keeping their own casualties low.

Soldiers learned to travel in the open as much as possible, to draw Indians to open ground for battle. Many learned this lesson in the wake of the Fetterman Massacre. Captain William J. Fetterman, an aggressive Civil War veteran, was said to boast that "with only eighty men, he could ride through the entire Sioux nation." He had been stationed at Fort Phil Kearny, one of the three Bozeman Trail forts, less than two months before Crazy Horse and other Sioux decoys lured him and exactly the number of men he had confidently projected— eighty—into an ambush. The warriors killed all but two officers, who in a common frontier pact shot each other rather than be taken prisoner. The encounter became known as the "Battle of the Hundred Slain" to the Sioux.

Both the Indians and the whites had their war and peace factions. On the central Plains, Black Kettle was again signing away land, although he emphasized that his signature was only one of many that treaty commissioners would have to collect. Other Cheyennes continued to hold out against restriction to the southern Plains, but periodically the peace party held sway, and a respected agent, Edward Wynkoop, convinced some important leaders of the wisdom of making concessions.

The natives recognized that changes beyond their control were shifting the world under their feet, but in the 1860s they clung to the traditional resources that remained. As Little Raven of the Arapaho explained of his desire to stay in his homeland, "Where the antelope and buffalo live is country where I want to live; that is what I raise my children on, and the way I get my support: hunting." Further, he was understandably uneasy about being pushed onto lands occupied by other tribes, diplomatically announcing that "we . . . accept [the government-specified lands], but we prefer to leave them there for the present . . . until you have acquired such a title to them from other Indians as will enable us to live on them in peace."

In Washington, D.C., a peace faction of humanitarian reformers was clamoring to decrease or abandon the aggressive military operations against the Indians. They were just as eager as the most pugnacious soldier or land-hungry settler to get the Indians out of the way of Anglo settlement and development—and more eager to control them using Anglo reform standards—but they at least favored negotiation over warfare. It was partly their influence, and partly the effective continuing resistance of the Plains tribes, that brought about the Medicine Lodge Council of 1867 and the Fort Laramie Council of 1868.

The United States government invited tribes from across the southern and central Plains to the October 1867 meeting, and they came—some five thousand strong, Comanches and Cheyennes, Kiowas and Arapahos, erecting their tipis and grazing their pony herds in a valley beside Medicine Lodge Creek in Kansas. Their leaders listened impatiently to the government officials' plans to restrict their movements and to provide them with Anglo-style housing and provisions for agriculture.

"This building of homes for us is all nonsense," announced the formidable Kiowa leader Satanta. "We don't want you to build any for us. . . . I want all my land, even from the Arkansas south to Red River. My country is small enough already. If you build us houses the land will be smaller." As for farming, he asserted, "land doesn't want to be worked. Land gives you what you need if you are smart enough to take it. This is good land but it is our land. We know how to take what it gives us."

Ten Bears of the Comanches also rejected the officials' blandishments: "I was born upon the prairie, where the wind blew free, and there was nothing to break the light of the sun. I was born where there were no enclosures, and where everything drew a free breath. I want to die there, and not within walls. . . . Why do you ask us to leave the rivers, and the sun, and the wind, and live in houses?"

Yet even as they resisted, the leaders recognized that their earlier lives were being irretrievably lost. "I know every stream and every wood between the Rio Grande and the Arkansas," Ten Bears explained. "I have hunted and lived over that country. I lived like my fathers before me, and like them, I lived happily." Now whites had appropriated "the places where the grass grew the thickest and the timber was the best," leading Ten Bears to conclude, "The white man has the country which we loved and we only wish to wander on the prairie until we die."

The Indians could not be impervious to the mass of enticing trade goods government representatives had brought with them, nor to the promise of annuities, nor to the assurances that they "could continue to hunt anywhere south of the Arkansas River.'' Most leaders signed the Medicine Lodge Treaty, which ''established three large reservations in western Oklahoma for the Cheyennes, Arapahos, Kiowas, Comanches, Caddos, and Wichitas.''

Still, the troubles continued. In July 1868, the Cheyennes began raiding and killing after being denied arms as part of their annuities. Black Kettle tried again in vain to bring peace, but could not control the young men. A soldier killed him with a shot to the back as he tried to flee an army raid on his village in November 1868.

To the north, the Sioux and their allies continued their warfare against the Bozeman Trail and white incursions in general. Red Cloud had refused to meet with the peace commissioners in the spring, instead sending a message: ''We are on the mountains looking down on the soldiers and the forts. When we see the soldiers moving away and the forts abandoned, then I will come down and talk.''

The Hunkpapa Sioux leader Gall came into Fort Rice on the upper Missouri River, in present-day North Dakota. There he met with the peace commission made up of army generals, and spoke plainly and forcefully: ''You fought me and I had to fight back: I am a soldier. The annuities you speak of we don't want. Our intention is to take no present.'' Gall did not believe the commission's offers of peace: ''If you want to make peace with me, you must remove this Fort Rice, and stop the steamboats.''

If the native leaders seemed to be expressing impossible hopes, the northern Indian alliance nonetheless seemed on its way to victory with the Bozeman Trail. The United States government pronounced itself willing to give up the road and its forts—in part because the route had lost its prime importance for immigration and in part because the Indian resistance had been so strong. Furthermore, peace commissioners were willing to confirm the Sioux in possession of their heartlands, ''the western half of South Dakota'' and a small section of North Dakota, as their reservation. The Powder River country, the massive region ''between the north Platte and the Yellowstone'' and reaching westward through southern Montana and northern Wyoming, would remain unceded as well.

In November 1868, after the Bozeman Trail forts had been abandoned per Red Cloud's wishes, peace commissioners and Indian resistance leaders met at Fort Laramie on the Oregon-California Trail.

The Sioux were promised "absolute and undisturbed use of the Great Sioux Reservation" and a key safeguard: lands within the reservation could only be ceded under treaties "executed and signed by at least three-fourths of all the adult male Indians, occupying or interested in the same."

Further, the Indians were to control the unceded lands of the Powder River country: "No white person or persons shall be permitted to settle upon or occupy any portion [of these lands] . . . or without the consent of the Indians . . . to pass through the same."

It was the best deal any tribe had won in a long, long time, and Red Cloud signed the treaty. Yet almost immediately, the army began trying to force the Sioux to stay within the boundaries of the reservation land. General Phil Sheridan made it a matter of policy that Indians on the unceded lands would be considered hostile. Thus, "barely a year after it was signed, the Fort Laramie Treaty became worthless."

The tumultuous 1860s had brought no real relief against white land pressures. In 1870, pursuing a new survival strategy, Red Cloud traveled to the East, met President Grant in Washington, D.C., and made an appeal for assistance in the continuing struggle with the government to an audience at New York's Cooper Institute. "You hear of us only as murderers and thieves," he noted. "We are not so. If we had more lands to give you, we would give them, but we have no more. We are driven into a very little island."

In 1867, the Kiowa leader Satanta had brushed aside government offers to provide for the Kiowas: "Time enough to build us houses when the buffalo are all gone. . . . This trusting to agents for food I don't believe in." The words both acknowledged an inevitable loss and projected it into the distant future. But no one, Indian or white, could have projected how rapidly the loss would take place.

In 1871, tanners in the East discovered that buffalo hide could be transformed into commercial leather. It was another of those seemingly innocuous industrial developments, like Eli Whitney's cotton gin, that helped enslave a people, for the wholesale slaughter of the buffalo in the 1870s, aided by the availability of high-powered telescopic rifles, would leave "no alternative to the reservation" for those who had depended upon the buffalo for their sustenance. By 1878, the southern herd would disappear, and a few years later "a scientific expedition could find only two hundred buffalo in all of the West." Crow chief Plenty-Coups would lament, "When the buffalo went away, the hearts of my people fell to the ground, and they could not lift them up again."

Satanta's "time enough," then, was little more than a decade—less for the southern tribes—but in that fleeting period the Plains tribes continued their fierce resistance both to the government's reservation plans for them and to the continued taking of their lands.

By 1870, military troops had pushed most members of the recently resistant southern tribes onto the western Indian Territory tracts designated for them by the Medicine Lodge Treaty: Comanches and Kiowas together in the southwest, with the southern Cheyennes and Arapahos sharing a reservation just to the north of them. Despite the Grant administration's policy of sending church-appointed agents to reduce the corruption in the Indian service, these reservations continued to be places where the Indians felt deprived, coerced, and invaded at every juncture, and where all concerned felt tremendous frustration. The Comanches and Kiowas ignored their earnest Quaker agent's "fine plans for their salvation," by locating "distant from the agency," only "riding in . . . to draw the rations due them under the Medicine Lodge Treaty," and refusing to farm or to send their children to the agency school.

Even worse from the Anglo standpoint, these two groups used the reservation as a base for bloody forays into Texas, where they took out their wrath against the Texans who had settled much of their former territory. Charged with a particularly grisly murder—the Salt Creek Massacre of 1871, in which a small group of teamsters hauling freight had been tortured and killed in North Texas—the Kiowan Satanta openly and defiantly stated that he had led the raid. He was convicted, then pardoned through the efforts of peace policy advocates, and returned to raiding. Among the Comanches, Quanah Parker, the son of a chief and a white woman taken captive as a girl, led in resisting confinement to the reservation and harrying whites in his Texas homelands, particularly the buffalo hunters, who were depleting the herds.

In the Red River War of 1874–1875, the military convinced peace advocates to allow the army to pursue the warring natives aggressively. In a scene reminiscent of Kit Carson's destructive ride through the Navajos' Canyon de Chelly thirty years before, Colonel Ranald Mackenzie penetrated the Comanches' natural fortress in the Texas Panhandle, Palo Duro Canyon, his troops tearing down tipis and shooting most of the Indian horse herd. The military also confronted hostile factions on the reservations, and shipped the leaders off to the grim confines of Fort Marion, Florida.

In this way, they broke the resistance. After 1875, the southern Plains tribes could mount no further direct armed challenge. Satanta had been returned to Texas for breaking parole. Incarcerated in a state prison in the alien, enclosing East Texas woodlands, he would dive from a second-story hospital balcony to end his life in 1878.

There had been plenty of bloodshed inflicted by and upon both Indians and non-Indians in the southern Plains conflict. Perhaps the most poignant comment—and the most revealing of the roots of the tumult—had come from Buffalo Good, a Wichita, in 1871: "I want you to stop the white men from killing the Indians after this," he said. "The Indian loves to live as well as the white men. [Indians] are there, and they can't help being there."

Chapter Eight

"Cornered in Little Spots of the Earth"
(1875–1886)

We . . . are cornered in little spots of the earth, all ours by right—cornered like guilty prisoners, and watched by men with guns who are more than anxious to kill us off.

—*Washakie, Shoshone*

On the northern Plains, as on the southern, the early 1870s had been marked by active Indian resistance to the government's attempts to move them permanently onto reservation land. Even when Red Cloud had capitulated, many Sioux, northern Cheyennes, and northern Arapahos had refused to have any part of the treaty process.

These "nontreaty" Indians moved on and off the reservation at will, flouting all the agent's rules and periodically drawing to them their reservation kin. They occasionally raided "along the Platte and among the Montana settlements," but not with the intensity of their southern counterparts. Their attitude was summed up by one of their number, destined for the most fame and notoriety, a veteran of various skirmishes with soldiers. Sitting Bull told his reservation kin, "You are fools to make yourselves slaves to a piece of fat bacon, some hardtack, and a little sugar and coffee."

Such statements carried a sting when viable choices existed, yet increasingly the northern Plains Indians were compelled to put their energies into survival at any cost, especially after a military expedition headed by George Armstrong Custer discovered gold within the boundaries of the Sioux reservation itself, in the sacred Black Hills.

"Of all our domain we loved, perhaps, the Black Hills the most," Luther Standing Bear would explain. The dense Ponderosa pines on the lower elevations from a distance gave the appearance of blackness, while on the upper elevations, white spruce and birch spiked the sky. Within the hills—mountains, really—deer, elk, and antelope roamed, myriad springs gushed forth, and broad meadows offered campsites ''shelter[ed] from the storms of the plains.''

The Fort Laramie Treaty of 1868 had allowed the United States government a wedge into Sioux territory by ''permitting the construction of rail and wagon roads and 'other works of utility and necessity,' '' an open-ended insertion that the natives had probably overlooked in their jubilation at getting the hated forts removed from Montana. Now Custer and his small force were roaming the Black Hills in search of a site for yet another fort—at least, that was their official purpose. Their golden find, although recorded almost nonchalantly, sparked a struggle over Sioux land that continues to reverberate into the modern era.

The gold seekers began pouring onto the Sioux reservation in 1875. In a by now predictable pattern, the United States government at first tried to stop, then to accommodate them—''it seemed easier to displace [the Indians] than the intruders.'' Thus, the Indians had to try to defend not only their unceded land to the west but the reservation itself.

Since the 1871 congressional ruling had unilaterally demoted tribes from ''nation'' status, the Indians had very little political power. The United States government was to look out for their interests and its own, an obvious conflict of interest in this and other cases. Nonetheless, Sioux delegates went to Washington in summer 1875 and met with President Grant, who equivocated in true Jacksonian style. If the Sioux didn't sell their land, the government might not be able to keep the invaders out—or might not even be inclined to. The secretary of the interior warned that rations might be cut at the agencies, and ''hinted that the Indians might want to give up their land altogether'' and go to Indian Territory, where they could share land with the Creeks.

As was often the case, it was a military man in the field who had the most telling comments. General George Crook's aide-de-camp, John Gregory Bourke, noted the difficulty in explaining to an Indian ''why it is that as soon as his reservation is found to amount to anything he must leave and give up to the white man.'' He judged that the "whole policy of the American people has been to vagabondize the Indian, and throttle every ambition he may have for his own elevation." Why, he asked, "should not Indians be permitted to hold mining or any other kind of land?"

It wasn't a question many whites wanted to ask or answer. Commissioners were sent to Sioux country in fall 1875 to get the natives to sell or lease the land. They were met with outright defiance from the nontreaty Indians—"I will kill the first chief who speaks for selling the Black Hills!" declared Little Big Man. Others knew they had to try to negotiate. Some were willing to think the unthinkable, outright sale, if they could actually obtain enough money to purchase a fair degree of security. But the government offered $6 million in fifteen separate payments, and installment payments that were promised to Indians had a way of shrinking or failing to materialize. The Indians refused the offer.

Then the secretary of the interior issued an order: all Sioux were to come in to the six reservation agencies by January 31, 1876. This move has been interpreted, with justification, as a patent attempt to gain an excuse to treat the Sioux and their allies as hostile. It included the nontreaty Indians who had never agreed to live on a reservation, as well as those who had departed the reservation—often with their agents' blessings—on winter hunts, food being extremely scarce at the agencies. This edict ignored the fact that the Indians were moving about on lands still accessible to them by treaty—the unceded region to the west and hunting lands to the south. Officials also ignored the fact that the winter weather precluded travel—either to distant camps to give them the word or from distant camps. "It was very cold," one young Oglala Sioux would remember, "and many of our people and ponies would have died in the snow. We were in our own country and doing no harm."

In the spring, reservation Indians joined their free-roaming kin, escaping "worsening conditions at the agencies" and attempts to restrict and intimidate them regarding the Black Hills sale. The Sioux and their Cheyenne allies found the buffalo still plentiful enough for their needs. Meanwhile, army troops moved into the field to "subdue" them.

The result was the Great Sioux War. Crazy Horse's men effectively repelled a cavalry attack on the Powder River in an initial engagement in March. This was followed by another Indian victory over General George Crook's forces in June along Rosebud Creek.

Custer's storied June 25 attack at the Little Bighorn "did not surprise the Indians as much as many people think," John Stands-in-Timber would relate. "They knew the soldiers were in the country looking for them, and they expected trouble, though they did not know just when it would come." Sitting Bull, who with Crazy Horse had assumed a position of leadership in the swelling Indian encampment along the river, had received a vision of soldiers on horses riding upside down through the sky toward an Indian village. As he explained to the gathered people, the vision had told him, "These soldiers do not possess ears. They are to die, but you are not supposed to take their spoils."

When the soldiers arrived, Sioux and Cheyenne warriors poured from their family camps on the Little Bighorn River and obliterated Custer's five companies of the Seventh Cavalry, some 265 men, also engaging and punishing detachments that Custer had dispatched under Captain William Benteen and Major Marcus Reno.

In the wake of the Indian victory among the rolling hills of Montana Territory—a stunning national defeat from the Anglo perspective—the United States government would quickly justify ruthless retaliation. The frontier army was given the resources to turn the tide, and it went after the warriors—"damn soldiers everywhere," recalled one native. With the help of Indian scouts, the army collected a string of victories, including Ranald Mackenzie's November attack on a camp in the Bighorn Mountains, where Cheyenne resistance leaders Dull Knife, Little Wolf, and Wild Hog had brought their people. Troops killed forty and left the surviving occupants without food, shelter, or clothing as the temperature dropped to thirty below zero, babies "[freezing] to death at their mothers' breasts."

Meanwhile, a commission headed by George Manypenny, a peace policy advocate, had arrived on the Great Sioux Reservation bearing the government's new and disheartening terms. Manypenny and his associates knew that the terms were unjust, but they saw no other way to salvage the Indians' future, and they wanted their own opportunity to "civilize" the Indians. The Sioux were to relinquish the Black Hills, some 7.3 million acres, plus their rights to "22.8 million acres of surrounding territory." They were to allow three more roads across the reduced reservation and—chillingly for most—to consider removal to Indian Territory. They were also to move to the eastern border of the reservation for their annuities, along the Missouri River, where it was easier for the government to deliver supplies. (The Sioux had earlier convinced officials to move this agency into the interior, as they found the river location unhealthy and too close to white settlements.)

In exchange, the natives would receive 900,000 acres of grazing land on the reservation's northern boundary, all the accoutrements of civilization that had already been promised to them in the 1868 treaty—the blacksmiths and schoolhouses and farming implements so beloved of the white humanitarians and so unappealing to the majority of Indians—and "life-sustaining rations until they became self-supporting," although "even this . . . had qualifications attached to its distribution."

The Sioux correctly saw this choice as "sign, or die" through starvation. "Whatever we do, wherever we go, we are expected to say yes! yes! yes! yes!" exclaimed Standing Elk, "and when we don't agree at once to what you ask of us in council you always say, You won't get anything to eat! You won't get anything to eat!"

They signed. "At the door was a company of soldiers with guns with bayonets," recalled Joseph Black Spotted Horse. "Further back towards the fort, all the cannon were turned toward us." There was no attempt to get the approval of three fourths of the adult males, as specified in the Fort Laramie Treaty.

On February 28, 1877, Congress ratified the document. Just over two months later, both Dull Knife and Crazy Horse surrendered with almost nine hundred people, bringing the Great Sioux War to an end. In the same week, Sitting Bull began his escape to Canada with about one thousand exiles. He had told General Nelson Miles, one of the leaders of the military offensive, "that God Almighty made him an Indian and did not make him an agency Indian either, and he did not intend to be one." The Plains wars had ended, but the Sioux never forgot the wrong done them in the treaty of 1877.

Even as the Sioux, Cheyennes, and Arapahos were finally forced within reservation boundaries, one of the most peaceful Indian tribes in the Northwest rose up to fight the same fate. Chief Joseph and the

Nez Perces captured both the attention and sympathy of the nation in 1877, on the heels of the Great Sioux War. Joseph was the son of the elder chief of the same name, who after his 1855 experience with Washington Governor Isaac Stevens had resisted all further treaties, including one in 1863 in which the Nez Perce leader Lawyer signed away the family's beloved Wallowa Valley, a stretch of rich grazing land bordered by mountains thick with pine, spruce, and fir.

Father and son continued to live there with their people, the elder Joseph from his deathbed in 1871 instructing the younger, "Always remember that your father never sold his country. You must stop your ears whenever you are asked to sign a treaty selling your home. . . . This country holds your father's body. Never sell the bones of your father and your mother."

His son Joseph learned well, repeatedly telling white officials that the Nez Perces who lived in the Wallowa Valley had never assented to be moved and would never do so. Neither did they accept gifts or annuities. When settlers began encroaching on the valley land, he succeeded in convincing an investigating committee that the Wallowa should be made a formal reservation. But this "protected" status lasted only from 1873 to 1875, when the government yet again gave in to the demands of settlers, who continued to appropriate the valley land and threaten the Indians.

For the next two years, settlers were free to enter the valley, and the Nez Perces were free to remain there. Tensions developed, especially after settlers shot and killed a peaceable young Indian named Wilhautyah. The whites feared violent retaliation from the Nez Perces, but Joseph used the death as a means of reasserting ownership: Wilhautyah's body was buried in the valley, which was consequently "more sacred to [Joseph] than ever before, and he would and did claim it now as recompense for the life taken," planning to "hold it for himself and his people from this time forward forever."

The government in Washington vacillated, but General Oliver Howard formed a commission to nudge or shove the Indians onto the Lapwai reservation, north of the valley. The nontreaty Nez Perces—Joseph's band and other bands with Toohoolhoolzote as their spokesman—met with Howard and his commission in November 1876.

The meeting did not go well. Howard was autocratic and impatient, Toohoolhoolzote defiant: "The Great Spirit Chief made the world as it is, and as he wanted it, and he made a part of it for us to live upon. I do not see where you get authority to say that we shall not live where he placed us.''

Howard told him to shut up and threatened him with punishment. ''Who are you, that you ask us to talk, and then tell me I sha'n't talk?'' asked Toohoolhoolzote. ''Are you the Great Spirit? Did you make the world? Did you make the sun? Did you make the rivers to run for us to drink? Did you make the grass to grow? Did you make all these things, that you talk to us as though we were boys? If you did, then you have the right to talk as you do.''

An irate Howard threw Toohoolhoolzote in jail for five days, and continued to press Joseph and other Nez Perce leaders, taking them to Lapwai to look at the land the government wished them to inhabit. Joseph found it ''good land'' but ''already occupied by Indians and white people.'' When officials made noises about moving some of these residents, he responded, ''No. It would be wrong to disturb these people. I have no right to take their homes. I have never taken what did not belong to me. I will not now.''

Officials read Joseph's peaceful and persistent refusal to leave his home as obtuseness and hostility, charging him—inaccurately—with being a member of the Pacific Northwest ''Dreamer'' religious movement, which whites considered dangerous. Like previous Indian religious revitalization movements, this one—led by the Wanapum medicine man Smohalla—was indeed based in part on a belief that the Great Spirit meant the natives to hold on to or reclaim their ancestral lands.

Sometimes an agent would provide some much-needed perspective and champion his ''charges,'' but when the commission recommended that Joseph and the others be forced to go to Lapwai, Nez Perce agent John Monteith simply requested aid ''in the removal of Joseph's and other roving bands of Nez Perce Indians to and locate them upon proper lands . . . by the use of such troops as you may deem necessary.''

Overwhelmed, Joseph and the other nontreaty Nez Perces began to make their way independently to the reservation in May 1877, compelled by the threat of military force and a mid-June deadline to gather their stock and possessions and ford the seasonally swollen streams.

On the way, however, a few of the young men, riddled with anger and humiliation, rode from their camp and killed four white men known for their hostile actions against Indians. This led other young men of the tribe to ride out in vengeance, too, and Joseph realized that any prospect of peace had vanished.

There followed a series of skirmishes and battles between the non-treaty bands fleeing eastward and the volunteer militia and troopers pursuing from both west and east. Despite the Anglo perception that Joseph was masterminding the Nez Perces' repeated successful escapes, a number of warriors led the effort, among them Joseph's brother Ollikut, Toohoolhoolzote, and Looking Glass, the latter having tried to stay neutral until cavalry troops assaulted his village.

Joseph wanted to return to the Wallowa to fight—"I love that land more than all the rest of the world," he would declare. But he acceded to the majority's wish to try to reach Crow country in hopes of allying with them. They crossed into Montana, traversed the Bitterroot River Valley, and passed through the Bitterroot Mountains into Yellowstone National Park, which had been established five years earlier. Here they scooped up a few befuddled tourists and an old prospector who said he knew how to get to Crow country.

Now the Nez Perces turned northward, into the Crow heartlands, but when Crow army scouts tried to sabotage their desperate flight, the Nez Perces concluded they could not look for sanctuary in this quarter. General Howard was following with all the ire of a man badly thwarted, and telegraphing ahead to rush other troops into the field. The Indians were forced to fight again and again, and they did so gamely, the men moving the women and children and horses ahead and holding off the pursuers. Now they hoped to get to Canada, to the camp of the self-exiled Sitting Bull.

They almost made it. Less than forty miles from the Canadian border, they camped on chill and barren flats in the ravines of the northern Bear Paw Mountains. General Nelson Miles, dispatched from a Tongue River camp, found them here, and in the ensuing battle Ollikut, Toohoolhoolzote, and Looking Glass were all killed.

Joseph's surrender speech is justly famous, encapsulating the agony and despair of many a doomed resistance: "I am tired of fighting. Our chiefs are killed. . . . It is cold and we have no blankets. The little children are freezing to death. . . . Hear me, my chiefs! I am tired. My heart is sick and sad. From where the sun now stands, I will fight no more forever.''

Yet both Joseph and Yellow Wolf, a tribesman with him at the end, testified that they would never have surrendered had not Miles promised they could return to their own region, at least to the Lapwai reservation. ''That was how he got our rifles from us,'' reported Yellow Wolf. ''It was the only way he could get them.'' Joseph would note, ''I have heard that [Miles] has been censured for making the promise to return us to Lapwai. He could not have made any other terms with me at the time.''

Miles, a humane and sympathetic officer, no doubt wanted to return the Nez Perces to their own country, but officials had other plans. They moved the surviving Indians—some 350 women and children and 80 men—to Fort Leavenworth, where, Joseph reported, ''we were placed on a low river bottom, with no water except river water to drink and cook with.'' Longing for their cool mountain water, ''many sickened and died, and we buried them in this strange land.''

The government then moved the Nez Perces to Indian Territory, which they called Eeikish Pah, or Hot Place. Here they had some success in cattle raising, ''but they continued to pine for their mountains—and to die.'' Joseph captured the conscience of many Americans with his continued eloquent protests. In 1879, he said, ''I can not understand why so many [Anglo] chiefs are allowed to talk so many different ways, and promise so many different things. . . . I am tired of talk that comes to nothing. It makes my heart sick when I remember all the good words and all the broken promises.''

Joseph's stance did not change. Neither he nor his father had ever sold their land in the Wallowa Valley. No one had explained satisfactorily to him ''where [white chiefs] get their authority to say to the Indian that he shall stay in one place, while he sees white men going where they please.'' He asked simply for freedom to make his own choices, and ''if I can not go to my own home,'' then to be allowed to go to ''a home in some country where my people will not die so fast.''

Public sympathy for Joseph and his people continued to grow. If such sympathies sparked only faint and belated attempts at justice, as members of the dominant culture clung to a romantic and convenient image of the doomed "red man" fading away, at least they called attention to terrible dislocations and living conditions. In 1885, by a special act of Congress, half the Nez Perces who wanted to return home were allowed to go back to the Lapwai reservation for which they had reluctantly been heading eight years earlier. The others, Joseph among them, "were dumped with some unrelated Columbia River tribes on the Colville Reservation in Washington."

As more and more western natives were pushed within reservation boundaries during the 1870s, the very reasons that they had resisted—the loss of the most basic freedoms and the precarious nature of reservation life—pressed in with dull reality upon them. Not that all western reservations shared the grimness of a Bosque Redondo. Some natives benefited from a large and familiar reservation base that supplied at least part of their needs and an agent who listened to them and tried to assist rather than coerce them. Such factors enabled them to move about freely within the borders, to locate with kin or friends, and to continue or adapt many of their traditional ceremonies and lifeways as they saw fit. A visitor to the Crow reservation in 1877 found the natives living well in their old ways, going on weekly buffalo hunts, practicing their own ceremonies, managing their large horse herds, and visiting back and forth with each other and nearby tribes.

In addition, natives began making the reservations bearable and workable through resilience and adaptability. For example, Cheyenne members of military societies, veterans of the northern Plains wars, shifted their communal identity to that of farmers, "all gather[ing] at the farthest place up the river and work[ing] together until that was done, and then mov[ing] to the next," because this was both quicker and "more fun."

But the whole thrust of government policy during the 1870s and early 1880s was to force the Indians—especially the tribes who had given the most resistance—into a subordinated and Anglicized cultural mold, with an emphasis on individual striving. Officials did not want creative adaptation, but conformity to their directives. These were quite clear, Bureau of Indian Affairs regulations in 1884 specifying, "The chief duty of an agent is to induce his Indians to labor in civilized pursuits." Since an agent was to be judged on how well he did this, sensitivity to the natives' real wants and needs continued to be something of a drawback.

Thus, agents banned such "heathen" rituals as the Sun Dance, "once the centerpiece of the social and religious fabric of the Sioux." They withheld rations from those Indians "who did not 'labor' by white definition of the word, or whose children were not in school." They prohibited as "savage and filthy" Indian consumption of the intestines and blood of annuity cattle. They used Indian police forces and Indian courts, established in the late 1870s and early 1880s, to enforce "civilizing" rules, "all the decrees of the court . . . subject to the approval or disapproval of the agent."

On the horribly underfunded reservation schools, "head shaving and even shackling with a ball and chain were common punishments for Indian pupils who ran away or spoke in their native tongue." Teachers, though often well-meaning, condemned, punished, and ridiculed Indian ways in encounters that deeply confused and humiliated many of their charges.

As the tensions between this forced Anglicization and the students' home life became apparent, Anglo authorities established off-reservation boarding schools to remove the children from Indian influences. Young charges were forcibly separated from their parents and sent to such faraway institutions as Carlisle Indian School in Pennsylvania, where director Richard Pratt believed in "killing the Indian to save the man." Their Indian dress was taken away, their hair cut. "Among our people short hair was worn by mourners, and shingled hair by cowards!" Sioux Gertrude Bonnin would recall bitterly of her own boarding-school initiation. Anglo educators imposed a highly regimented routine, including plenty of manual labor. Eager to keep the students separated from their families and tribes, Pratt and other boarding-school directors even sent the children to work for white families over school holidays, ostensibly to learn these families' "civilized" ways.

On the reservation, agents and missionaries bypassed traditional leaders in favor of natives more responsive to their "civilizing" agenda. It should be noted that traditional structures often reasserted themselves, and often unbeknownst to the agent. For example, many reservation policemen were members of the old native soldier societies. But under the reservation regimes of the late nineteenth century, they were enforcing white regulations, and they and the judges walked a fine and bitter line between competing Indian and Anglo interests and traditions. They also had to navigate the inevitable intertribal rivalries—or rivalries among tribes crammed together on the same land base. The split between traditional and progressive factions widened, helped along by the actions of government officials, continuing pressure from interlopers, and the confused state of jurisdictional issues in general.

Some of these problems were brought to light as a result of an incident on the Great Sioux Reservation in 1883. Crow Dog shot longtime chief Spotted Tail in cold blood. Under tribal law, relatives of the dead man accepted cash and goods in settlement. Nonetheless, Crow Dog was convicted and sentenced to die by the Dakota territorial court.

The Supreme Court overturned the sentence, freeing Crow Dog and ruling that the United States "had no jurisdiction over crimes committed by one Indian against another." Congress responded in legislation enacted in 1885 "extending jurisdiction over Indians for seven major crimes," but this, of course, both further closed off possible native self-regulation and "still left great legal needs uncovered."

Another problem grew out of the infighting between the War and Interior departments, which had varying ideas for controlling and civilizing the Indian. This wrangling "resulted in bungled plans and jurisdictional squabbles" that both undercut help getting to the Indians and Indians helping themselves.

Nor had President Grant's "peace initiative" worked. Corruption in the Indian service remained, and agents tended to be either tyrannical or ineffectual—through ignorance and ineptitude or through circumstances that pitted them against white interests. "No Agent who discharged his whole duty . . . could possibly avoid trouble, vexations, and opposition when brought in conflict with the white element," one army officer observed. Further, "whether or not an agent was a crook, a benevolent tyrant, or a fatherly administrator," he almost inevitably appropriated the power that had rested in the chiefs.

Governance issues palled, however, beside the challenges of physical survival on many of the reservations. For one thing, the government continued to control the money that was due the natives, highhanded and paternalistic officials spending it as they saw fit for their "children."

Indians were compelled to adjust to life on the reservation in myriad ways. Luther Standing Bear's recollection of the first delivery of cattle to his reservation indicates the degree of change necessary. Since buffalo were growing harder to find, he and his friends welcomed a trip to the agency for distribution of the "spotted buffalo," but on arrival the youths were quickly enveloped in a foul smell.

"I asked my father what was the matter around there, as the stench was more than I could stand," he would recall. "He told me it was the odor of the spotted buffalo. Then I asked him if we were going to be obliged to eat those terrible animals. 'The white people eat them,' was his reply." Standing Bear could not yet bring himself to do so. For one thing, he discerned too much difference between "meat that is killed while in a contented state" and "meat that is carried in trains day after day on the hoof."

To add to the wrenching challenges of reservation adjustment, the government's "communication and procurement system" continued to work poorly at best, most of the money going to corrupt, negligent, or inefficient contractors. The result for the Indians was more skimpy and unpalatable rations, cheap blankets, clothing "devoid of appearance, warmth, or durability," and tools that hindered rather than helped, such as tin shovels that simply bent under pressure.

"The agency issued rations, but not nearly enough to keep a person alive," a Blackfoot named White Calf would recall. Thursday was "Nothing Happens Day because by then all the people would be starving and just sitting around waiting for the next rations." Moreover, Fridays brought only "a little flour and sugar and sometimes a small piece of meat," the butchering of a few cows being considered adequate for a population of three thousand.

Always, too, there was the possibility that even sorry provisions might fail to appear. Blackfoot, a Crow leader, observed in 1873, "The commissioners told us at Laramie if we remained good friends of the whites we would be taken care of for forty years. You are in a hurry to quit giving us food." Ten years later, Sitting Bull, who had tired of the fugitive life in Canada and returned unhappily in 1881 to become an "agency Indian," expressed a willingness to follow the white man's way if he could get tools and provisions to do so, for "I want to tell you that our rations have been reduced to almost nothing, and many of the people have starved to death."

Brigadier General John Pope, too, chafed at the Plains tribes' situation, concluding, "It is an injustice to the character of the government and a wrong to the Indians that they should be compelled to remain on their reservations and there slowly starve"—and that troops should be stationed among them "with no power or authority except to force them to starve tranquilly."

Many natives regarded tools and provisions as a continuing entitlement, "not as a bridge to self-reliance but as a well-merited substitute for it" in light of their overwhelming concessions. In particular, the Sioux resented the forced exchange of the Black Hills for nothing more than rations, some grazing land, and the standard and often unwanted promises of "civilizing" support personnel such as carpenters, teachers, and farm "bosses." Dakota natives were not blind to the mineral riches pouring out of the Black Hills, with George Hearst's Homestake Mining Company on its way to becoming the richest mining operation in the Western Hemisphere.

Further, Indian farming efforts continued to come to naught, sometimes through lack of interest, more often through a dearth of proper tools, equipment, and know-how, and even more often through the unsuitability of the reservation land for the traditional Anglo farming being promoted. "The drawbacks to successful agriculture are so great as not to be overcome with any reasonable amount of labor," one Plains agent would conclude in 1887.

Plains stock raising did not prove viable in this period, either— small efforts did not flourish due to disease, drought, and theft. And as on the reservations in Indian Territory, any government jobs almost inevitably went to whites.

All of this meant that many western Indians found their reservations "mammoth poorhouses," their environment progressively deteriorating. "We preferred hunting to a life of idleness on the reservations, where we were driven against our wills," Crazy Horse reportedly told an agent as he lay dying of a bayonet wound inflicted by a Sioux guard at Fort Robinson, Nebraska, a few months after his surrender. He noted the lack of food on the reservation, and the fact that hunters were not allowed to go beyond the borders to obtain meat, concluding,

"We preferred our own way of living. We were no expense to the government then. All we wanted was peace and to be left alone."

These sentiments, hunger, and the lure of homelands led some to bolt. The Modoc War of 1872–1874 erupted when troops tried to dislodge some sixty or seventy Modoc families from their remote homeland on Lost River in northern California after they escaped the southern Oregon reservation they shared with the Klamaths. "The Indians say there was but one of two deaths left to them, by starvation on the reservation, or a speedier death by the bullet in the lava-beds," reported an official. "They chose the latter."

The Modocs' determined and extended resistance among the lava beds bordering Tule Lake ended with the hanging of Kintpuash, or Captain Jack, and three other Modoc leaders and the banishing of the rest to Indian Territory.

The resistant Modocs—arguing among themselves as to how to continue the fight—had urged Kintpuash to kill Brigadier General Vincent Canby in a peace conference. He did so, and a fellow Modoc killed a second commissioner. Kintpuash later offered in his own defense that he felt trapped, both by the demands of his own people and by the demands of Anglo officials. After capture, he insisted that Canby had repeatedly "fooled" him, and he noted pointedly that his own father and a number of other Modocs had been slaughtered at an earlier peace conference, their Anglo attackers going unpunished. Underlying all of this was the desperation of trying to find a place the Anglos would not invade: "You white people have driven me from mountain to mountain, from valley to valley, like we do the wounded deer."

With the killing of Canby, Kintpuash could expect little sympathy from the American citizenry, whatever the circumstances. By contrast, a similar case of exiles attempting to return both captured and held public support in 1878.

The northern Cheyennes had thought they would be allowed to remain in their home region on the short-grass Plains around the Northern Platte River after the Great Sioux War. Instead, they were moved in with their southern kin and suffered terribly from what was to them a hot and unhealthy climate in Indian Territory. In 1878, they implored their Quaker agent, John D. Miles, to let them move back north.

Miles held out some hope of a return the following year, but, with malaria raging and rations short, as one Cheyenne would note, "The Indians thought in another year they would all be dead." Cheyenne leader Wild Hog would recall, "We were *always* hungry; we *never* had enough. When they that were sick once in a while felt as though they could eat something, we had nothing to give them."

Finally, some of the chiefs simply told Miles they were planning to leave. Miles himself had written forcefully of the folly of trying to transplant northern Indians to the Indian Territory climate, but he followed policy and attempted to dissuade the Cheyennes.

Military leader Little Wolf, a veteran of the Great Sioux War who no doubt knew the possible consequences of leaving, responded, "I am moving everyone back home. I will not do any harm. If you want to fight, wait until we get away from the reservation. Let's not talk about it any more. We are going to carry out our plan." As John Stands-in-Timber relates, Little Wolf then shook Miles's hand and called him a "good man."

On September 9, they left, Little Wolf and Dull Knife leading some three hundred Cheyennes, about a third of the reservation population. They journeyed hundreds of miles "through an open country, with soldiers attacking them from all sides," called into battle from the various frontier forts. The group then split, Little Wolf's hardier band heading for the distant Tongue River area of Montana Territory, Dull Knife's for the Red Cloud agency in northern Nebraska, which he did not know had been relocated to South Dakota.

Dull Knife's band reached Fort Robinson, former site of the Red Cloud agency, where he vowed "we will no more fight or harm white people." Content to be in their familiar region, they did not resist the military control at Fort Robinson. Then an officer read them a presidential letter saying that they would have to go back to Indian Territory. "Great Grandfather sends death in that letter," announced Dull Knife. "You will have to kill us and take our bodies back down that trail. We will not go."

Dull Knife's band—149 men, women, and children—was kept in army barracks, without rations or fuel, and even without water, all in hopes of breaking their resistance. None would give in. Dull Knife told the fort commander, "The only way to get us [to Indian Territory] is to come in here with clubs and knock us on the head and drag us out and take us down there dead.''

At last, they burst forth, but only because they determined to die on the open prairie rather than in the fort. Soldiers pursued them over the snowladen winter landscape, killing almost half of them and capturing most of the others. A few, Dull Knife among them, escaped, plunging northward, eating roots to stay alive, and finally reaching the Great Sioux Reservation, where they found refuge.

Meanwhile, Little Wolf's escape proved much the better one, as his group enjoyed the freedom of a winter hunting in the sand hills of western Nebraska. Then—on their way to Powder River country in March—they encountered an army officer with whom they were friendly. With him, they traveled to Montana's Fort Keogh, where General Miles enlisted some of the men as scouts and allowed the other returnees to go up the Tongue River. "It was a good place for the Cheyennes to go," one would remember. Whites had not yet moved into the area, which still abounded in grass and water and even harbored some of the remaining buffalo. Further, the American public had been roused to acknowledge the desperation and courage that had propelled the Cheyennes northward. Miles was able to follow through on a promise to secure for them some of this good land as a reservation.

By 1881, with Sitting Bull's return to the Great Sioux Reservation, armed Plains Indian resistance to reservations had crumpled under the weight of the forces brought to bear against them. Sitting Bull remained defiant, his relationship with the autocratic Sioux agent James McLaughlin a constant struggle of wills. "I consider that my country takes in the Black Hills, and runs from the Powder River to the Missouri," Sitting Bull was still insisting forcefully in 1883. However, he now lacked the power to force even a token consideration of such views by those in control.

This left one last group offering concerted, persistent armed resistance to the reservation: the Apaches of the Southwest.

Three years after the final failure of Bosque Redondo, a prominent reformer named Vincent Colyer, member of the Board of Indian Commissioners, had arrived in Arizona Territory with a self-generated mandate to lay out reservations for the Indians. Something certainly needed to be done; only a few months before Colyer's arrival, a Tucson "Committee of Public Safety," accompanied by Papago Indians, sworn enemies of the Apaches, had attacked a large camp of Pinal and Araviapa Apaches living near Camp Grant. The vigilantes, citing isolated raids attributed to Apaches, made a mockery of the asylum granted the overwhelmingly peaceful group by the Camp Grant commander and "slaughtered, raped, and mutilated scores of victims," as well as seizing twenty-nine children to become slaves.

Colyer had wanted to secure protected spaces for the natives—and, like other reformers of his day, he was there to ensure that they learned the nobler of the white man's ways. Following on his heels had been General Oliver Howard, not yet assigned to the Northwest and his fateful negotiations with Chief Joseph. Both men rather haphazardly and autocratically had outlined reservation lands, but at least they had consulted with the natives and confirmed many in preferred portions of their homelands, among them the Chiricahuas under Cochise in the southern Arizona mountains and the Coyoteros in the White Mountains of the Fort Apache reservation.

General George Crook had been dispatched in 1872–1873 to harass the Apaches into confining their movements to the reservation lands. His punishing campaign had ensured that most of them would cluster within reservation borders—but not that they would stay. At the Fort Apache reservation, some had tried to exercise initiative and autonomy by saving their ration tickets to buy cattle; the beef contractor, wanting to keep his business, "offered only steers." When the Apaches protested, government officials did bring in some cattle for them, but they were of such poor quality that one recipient termed them "older than this world."

With Crook's departure to fight in the Sioux campaigns to the north—and with the government's decision to consolidate most of the Apaches onto one reservation—the stage was set for further conflict.

Pressure for white settlement and for the economic development of Arizona's copper resources led the United States government in early 1875 to begin consolidating the Apaches at the San Carlos reservation bordering the Gila River. Officials uprooted the Tonto Apaches and other southwestern bands from the Verde reservation near Prescott, where they had worked with the aid of army troops to cultivate and irrigate fields, the year before "produc[ing] forty acres of vegetables."

The farms were abandoned, the Indians herded over the mountains to the southeast. Many simply slipped away; others completed the 180-mile trek to San Carlos. Soon the Fort Apache Indians were compelled to turn toward the Gila as well, relinquishing the clear, cool air and water of the White Mountains. Cochise having died of natural causes, most of the Chiricahuas too were coaxed and intimidated out of their mountains to go to San Carlos.

San Carlos was Apache country, but, in the words of one Chiricahua, "the worst place in all the great territory stolen from the Apaches." The bands had never tried to live for any length of time in this bleak desert land with its bedraggled cottonwoods and "dry, hot, dust-and gravel-laden winds," its brackish water and searing heat, its monotonous stands of cacti and multitude of "insects and rattlesnakes . . . tarantulas, Gila monsters, and centipedes."

In the mid-1870s, a young Apache agent from New England named John Clum succeeded in concentrating at this site five thousand Indians—those formerly served by five agencies and those who, like the Chiricahua leaders Victorio and Geronimo, remained resistant to the reservation system. Clum effectively pioneered an Indian police force on the reservation, in part by having different bands select the policemen from their ranks. He also gave the Indians freedom "to check out guns and travel to other parts of the reservation to hunt."

Like Lorenzo Labadie at Bosque Redondo, Clum often clashed with military officials; at one point, he and the local military commander directed the Indians to line up for separate but simultaneous roll calls, the commander "threaten[ing] to attack any Apache who failed to appear."

The Indians found other relationships confusing and dangerous as well. Neighboring whites often simply wanted natives eliminated from the area; one Arizona newspaper proclaimed that Apaches ought to be either "out of Arizona or under it." For many citizens, the only reason to tolerate an Indian presence was as an opportunity for lucrative government contracting work, and they were therefore hostile to any plans to make the Indians self-sufficient or—worse yet—economically competitive, as when an officer bought crops for the garrison from the natives.

On the reservation itself, different bands had to sort out their own relationships, some of them continuing old hostilities against each other as they jockeyed for whatever political and economic advantage they could grasp under Anglo control. But the main aim remained basic physical survival. The war leader Victorio was drawn onto San Carlos in the late 1870s, and one of his band would recall the experience as "that horrible summer" of "nothing but cactus, rattle-snakes, heat, rocks, and insects," with people starving to death all around him.

Victorio's band bolted, wandered about looking for refuge, and in September 1879 began the Victorio War with an attack on cavalry. Troops responded by pushing the group into Mexico, where Victorio was killed in a battle with Mexican soldiers in 1880.

Meanwhile, conditions at San Carlos worsened. Some of the agents who followed Clum proved notoriously corrupt. The Apache medicine man Noche-do-klinne, who seemed to threaten Anglo power with a new spiritual movement, was shot and killed in a botched military attempt to arrest him in 1881. Arizona citizens continued to charge Apaches with any random violence in the territory: "much that was done by mean white men was reported at Washington as the deeds of my people," Geronimo would complain.

The military tried to intensify its control. By the early 1880s, San Carlos males over fourteen were required always to wear or carry brass identification showing the number assigned them within their band. The Apaches were not allowed to brew their native beer, *tiswin,* and one young man who defied the edict was sent to Alcatraz.

All of these factors and more combined with General Crook's re-newed pursuit of nonreservation Indians to keep many natives bounc-ing between desolate San Carlos and the perilous world outside its boundaries. Chief among these—in the public imagination and in re-ality—was Geronimo, leader of the southernmost band of Chiricahuas, who ranged through northern Mexico and southeastern Arizona. Clum had arrested him and brought him to San Carlos in 1877. Long a skilled warrior, primarily against Mexicans after a Mexican massacre of his family in 1858, Geronimo escaped the reservation and began raiding in 1881. The next year he returned and at gunpoint compelled others of his divided band to join the resistance.

Crook eventually talked Geronimo into returning to the reservation for a period during 1884 and 1885, but Geronimo escaped again to lead the last significant armed resistance to Anglo domination. The extent of this accomplishment is captured in the words of a young lieutenant who participated in the final campaign against Geronimo's band: "thirty-five men and eight half-grown or older boys, encumbered with the care and sustenance of 101 women and children, with no base of supplies and no means of waging war or of obtaining food or transportation other than what they could take from their enemies, maintained themselves for eighteen months, in a country two hundred by four hundred miles in extent, against five thousand troops, regulars and irregulars, five hundred Indian auxiliaries of these troops, and an unknown number of civilians.''

In March 1886, Crook met with Geronimo in a northern Mexican canyon and again won a verbal surrender. The fighting men of the band were now facing prison time, but they capitulated "on the condition that, after no more than two years imprisonment, they would be allowed to join their families at Turkey Creek north of San Carlos.''

Crook left in advance of the Apaches, who were to enter Fort Bowie in southern Arizona the next day, accompanied by the Indian scouts. Then a whiskey trader named Bob Tribolett showed up. Tribolett, suspected of "acting on behalf of the infamous Tucson Ring of contractors who profited from the Apache conflict,'' plied both warriors and scouts with mescal liquor and convinced them they would be murdered if they entered the fort. Again, they fled. "We were reckless of our lives, because we felt that every man's hand was against us,'' Geronimo would recall. "If we returned to the reservation we would be put in prison and killed; if we stayed in Mexico they would continue to send soldiers to fight us; so we gave no quarter to anyone and asked no favors.''

General Miles took over from Crook, and dispatched Lieutenant Charles B. Gatewood with a new set of terms: "the Apaches must go to Florida and wait for the President to decide their ultimate fate.'' Geronimo insisted he would only return to the Chiricahuas at San Carlos. Then came the stunning news that broke the band's resolve: the government had taken their people at San Carlos—even Crook's Chiricahua scouts—and loaded them on railway cars for Florida.

So they all went, more than five hundred total, to the humid lowlands of Florida, the fighting men to prison at Pensacola, the others to Fort Marion. There they dreamed of snow in the high desert mountain ranges, of game hunting and root gathering and the coyote's wail. In 1888, they were reunited on another alien site, in huts at Mount Vernon Barracks in Alabama, where they died off in distressing numbers. The children, taken from their parents and sent to Carlisle, Pennsylvania, declined as well, almost a third dying within the first three years there.

After eight years of far exile, the Chiricahuas would be moved to Fort Sill in Indian Territory. The people would gain permission to travel forty-five miles to the nearest mesquite grove, there to collect the mesquite beans that had been a staple of their old lives, and the women would cry to hear the coyote's wail once more. None would live to see their homeland again, although this would be Geronimo's persistent wish until his death in 1909. Instead, in 1913, the government would allow those who wished to do so—more than one hundred people—to join the Mescalero Apaches in New Mexico.

By the time the remnant Chiricahuas made their way to New Mexico, government allotment policy—"a mighty pulverizing engine for breaking up the tribal mass"—had accomplished far more damage to Indian country than even hard-charging military forces had inflicted. For with the subjugation of Geronimo's band, the U.S. government had established its hegemony over Indians in general: "Congress could, according to the courts, dictate the fates of hundreds of thousands of people in the American West and control tens of millions of acres of Indian land."

Western Indian reservations, 1900

Chapter Nine

← →

"Gumbo with Greasewood on It" (1887–1910)

Gumbo with greasewood on it. There were cracks in it so big you could almost see China.
—*Assiniboine from Montana, on his allotment under the 1887 Dawes Act*

They made us many promises, more than I can remember, but they never kept but one; they promised to take our land and they took it.
—*Sioux elder, 1891*

Day after day the people danced, wearing circles on the earth. They had plaited eagle feathers in their hair, painted their faces, and donned sacred garments, white muslin with painted symbols of the natural world—"a crow, a fish, stars." As the pace quickened from a slow, steady shuffle to a free-form frenzy, many fell to the ground and had visions of a world restored—dead loved ones revived, the wild game replenished, the Plains and prairies reclaimed as free domain of the Indian. In these visions, whites had simply vanished or had sunk under the revitalized soil, while new invaders had found the seas blocked when they set out in their ships.

"There was no hope on earth and God seemed to have forgotten us," the old Sioux leader Red Cloud would recall. Thus, on reservation after reservation the natives of the prairies and Plains grasped at the teachings of the Paiute prophet Wovoka. Like Tenskawatawa and other Indian prophets before him, Wovoka had combined elements of native spirituality and Christian teachings to nurture hope and strength among those feeling hopeless and helpless. As transmitted across the

West, Wovoka's Ghost Dance religion resonated with peaceful mysticism and with simple and fantastic visions of escape, some believers encouraged to prepare for a group ascension to a glorious "country of the Dead."

Inevitably this religion also carried the seeds of direct rebellion. Casting off the dictates of the United States government, Indians abandoned their reservation cabins or camps near the agencies to gather in tipis and sweat lodges beside streams and in groves of trees. Emerging to dance the Ghost Dance, they dared hope for an alternative to the future laid out for them by their subjugators.

"The craze is spreading like a prairie fire, and the chiefs who are encouraging it do not even come to the agency," the new Pine Ridge agency doctor, Charles Eastman, himself half Sioux, was told soon after his arrival in 1890. "They send after their rations and remain at home. It looks bad."

And it would end badly for the people who danced and sought a miraculous reversal of three centuries of United States expansion. For one thing, effective armed group resistance had ended with Geronimo's surrender in the mountains far to the south. For another, a new era would require not a retreat to the past in hopes of creating a more desirable future, but an ability to challenge the white man's world from within.

Between 1887 and 1900, intruders continued to stream onto the western reservations. The Bureau of Indian Affairs (BIA), still often referred to as the Indian Bureau or Indian Office, had given up trying to control the influx in Indian Territory, while efforts were spotty and ineffective elsewhere. At the Paiutes' Pyramid Lake reservation, cattlemen by 1890 were not only illegally grazing their herds but building corrals and sheds, while whites extended their occupation of the reservation's cultivatable land until "only the delta and river mouth, directly under the windows of the agency house, [remained] in Indian hands." In 1895, even a determined agent backed by fifty added policemen could not remove white intruders on the Omaha and Winnebago reservations.

The greatest challenge to the remaining native land base—and therefore to cultural survival—began in 1887 with the passage of the Dawes Allotment Act. Reformers such as the act's sponsor, Senator

Henry Dawes, felt that Indians had to be assimilated into American citizenship and culture. To do this—and to alleviate the bleak dependency into which most western Indians had recently been forced—the reformers advocated dividing the reservation lands into family and individual holdings—160 acres allotted to heads of family, 80 acres to single natives over eighteen, 40 acres to minors. They hoped thereby to reduce the natives' reliance upon the government for subsistence, then to sever that reliance altogether. To this end, the government would renew its efforts to educate Indian children and to provide farming supplies and experts for the Indians.

Across the span of more than a century, one can see why this plan would have appeared progressive. It acknowledged that the oft-reviled Indians were potential American citizens who should not be bound in oppressive and often degrading relations with the federal government as its wards. In reality, however, the act—which authorized both the president and the U.S. Congress to allot most Indian lands—was based on four troubling assumptions.

First, the reformers were judging tribal culture and custom of no value and Anglo cultural values as supreme. Many tribes had been adapting to their circumstances in ways that were familiar and workable to them, on the reservation "successfully using the family and tribal structure to organize land use distinctions." But government officials recognized only formal plats based on individual ownership. Thus, although the Cherokees were generally thriving, avoiding the poverty of many other reservations, a visiting Senator Dawes found as a roadblock to "civilization" their holding of common lands, even when farmed Anglo-style. "The common field is the seat of barbarism," explained one like-minded agent, while "the separate farm [is] the door to civilization." Dawes chafed at the Cherokees' lack of desire to possess and achieve more than their fellows, for he shared with many prominent Americans of the era a conviction that selfishness "lay at the root of advanced civilization."

Second, the reformers assumed that the Indians would abandon their own values for those of "advanced civilization." In this, they ignored or failed to discern a constant expressed by an old Sioux on the Cheyenne River reservation many years after the Dawes Act had failed: "We Indians will be Indians all our lives, we never will be white men. We can talk and work and go to school like the white people but we're still Indians.'' With any say in the matter—and even without—western Indians continued to group in old kinship and community networks, to forsake the cabins that many found unhealthy in favor of native structures, to move about as much as possible following seasonal routines, to use traditional medicinal remedies, to share property, to reject Anglo schools, and to worship and celebrate in their own ways, adapting freely from some norms of white culture and from those of other Indian cultures.

Third, the act's framers assumed—very conveniently for white expansion purposes—that any acreage left over after allotment to eligible tribal members could be deemed ''surplus'' land for the federal government to appropriate or buy cheaply, ostensibly with tribal agreement. In this way, the government could accommodate a rapidly swelling citizenry—as Indian numbers declined, the American population would show almost a 70 percent increase between 1890 and 1910. In wanting to free up more land for white settlers and entrepreneurs, the reformers inadvertently but firmly fell in with the basest of land speculators to reduce Indian country further, for as much as nine tenths of the acreage on some Indian lands could be taken in this way.

Fourth, the reformers assumed that allotment would lead to Indian self-sufficiency on the allotted tracts. In this, not only were they very wrong, but they ignored or downplayed the testimony of those who had seen the negative results of some eleven thousand earlier piecemeal allotments. These observers anticipated even more negative results from the new directive, given its ''compulsory'' nature, its conveyance of tremendous discretionary powers to the president, and its usefulness as ''a process of reduction of Indian lands'' through ''surplus'' land sales.

Enoch Hoag, who had reported in 1871 how ''designing and dishonest men'' would ''cling . . . like leeches'' until they gained Indian allotments, was only one voice in a disturbing chorus. In 1880, a minority report from the House Indian Affairs Committee had baldly noted of an allotment proposal: ''The real aim . . . is to get at the Indian lands and open them up to settlement. . . . If this were done in the name of greed it would be bad enough; but to do it in the name of humanity, and under the cloak of an ardent desire to promote the Indian's welfare by making him like ourselves, whether he will or not, is infinitely worse." Seven years later, Senator Henry Teller, a former secretary of the interior, opposed the Dawes Act, arguing that the legislation might as well be titled "A bill to despoil the Indians of their lands and to make them vagabonds on the face of the earth."

Other opponents were former Indian Commissioners Manypenny and Parker, the latter speaking from experience in both white and Indian worlds. "Our wise legislators at Washington, the Indian Aid and Indian Rights Associations are all advocating with a red hot zeal the allotment and citizenship schemes," Parker noted, ". . . [but] the Indians as a body are deadly opposed to the scheme for they see too plainly the certain and speedy dissolution of their tribal and national organizations."

Some Indians did favor allotment. These tended to be mixed-bloods, more acculturated to Anglo ways and hopeful that gaining title to land and becoming citizens would alleviate the feeling of being, in the words of one, "strangers in the land where we were born." Some had even taken advantage of an earlier, related initiative, the Indian Homestead Act of 1876, which allowed Indians, like white homesteaders, the opportunity to "prove up" a piece of the western tracts the government now claimed and controlled as "public domain" and win title to it.

Most Indians, however, distrusted this newest white plan, worried about the loss of identity and livelihood without the bond of community holdings, and were particularly concerned about what would happen to the more "improvident or thriftless" among them with the loss of traditional community care. They also found alien and disturbing the idea of dividing into separate tracts the surface of the earth, particularly in regions already familiar to them through long residence. Indian delegations arrived in Washington to try to head off passage of the act—at least one group was there in defiance of an agent's threat to arrest them for leaving the reservation.

In fairness to Dawes and other reform advocates of allotment, they envisioned the government helping tribal members develop farming and stock-raising operations as part of the divisions. The reformers also tried to build in a necessary, albeit paternalistic, safeguard against Indian land loss by stipulating that the government would hold all allotments in trust for twenty-five years, the divided plots not to be sold, leased, or taxed during this time. In other words, Indians would not hold "fee patents," which would allow them to manage and dispose of the land as they saw fit and require them to pay property taxes, until they had accumulated experience as citizens and individual landholders.

In reality, however, the Indian Bureau would "[fail] to provide enough training, equipment, and capital to prevent thousands of Indian farmers and stockraisers from sinking into poverty," and land-trust relationships would quickly be breached.

Even had these failures not occurred, the Dawes Act was a full-frontal attack on tribal identity, an attempt at cultural genocide, however well-intentioned from an Anglo perspective. It is in this context—as well as in the broader context of the government and white settlers hacking and whittling away at Indian country through various means—that the Ghost Dance religion took hold, especially among the corraled, humiliated, hungry, and smoldering western Sioux occupying the Great Sioux Reservation.

The siege to break up this reservation had begun in 1882, when Dakota Congressman Richard F. Pettigrew inserted a rider to a successful congressional appropriations bill. The rider authorized a commission to visit the Sioux and determine whether they would cede almost half the region in return for "clear title" to six smaller reservations carved from it.

The commission head, former Dakota Territory Governor Newton Edmunds, had traveled from agency to agency, pressing and confusing the Indians, intimidating them with talk of possible ration cuts and removal to Indian Territory, repeatedly glossing over the massive land loss that the agreement would entail, and thereby obtaining 384 signatures of acceptance. One reluctant signer, Yellow Hair, offered the commissioners a clod of dirt, announcing, "We have given up nearly all our land, and you had better take the balance now, and here I hand it to you."

With the document going to Washington for congressional confirmation, the Sioux had protested so vociferously that the government sent a fact-finding mission to investigate why. They found the Sioux Nation "practically unanimous in its opposition to this proposed agreement," insisting that the signers had been coerced and misdirected. Some of the Sioux had understood that they were simply carving the reservation into segments, not losing half of it. Aided by reformer friends in the East, Indian protesters also pointed out that Edmunds had not obtained the requisite approval of a three-fourths majority of adult males.

The reservation had remained intact. But now, in the wake of the Dawes Act, another commission appeared, led by rigid Carlisle Indian School educator Richard Pratt. The government wanted to buy nine million acres from the Sioux for white settlement. It offered fifty cents an acre, promise of a cattle herd, and a few of the standard farm-and-school benefits. The rest of the reservation—six different tracts surrounding the existing agencies—would later be broken into allotments.

The promise of a cattle herd carried some weight, for the Sioux, like other Plains residents and like the Indians of Oklahoma and the Southwest, had some affinity for ranching. Yet they would not trade their land for this or any other promise, nor would they give in to intimidation and deteriorating conditions on the reservation. Pratt found that ''only a few could be induced to give their approval; many refused even to accept copies of the act and the map, and large numbers would sign no document, not even the one indicating rejection of the proposal.''

So, in 1889, the government sent the Sioux's former military foe, George Crook, to treat with them, trusting to his reputation among the Indians as a respected fighter and man of his word.

Crook carried a modified proposal for breaking up the remaining land base, including provisions that ''a majority of the adult males at each of the separate reservations would have to approve allotment before the Dawes Act could be applied, and ... family heads would receive 320 acres—twice the established quota.'' He acted forcefully and shrewdly, prevailing on key leaders one by one and telling them all the raw and frightening truth: ''Last year when you refused to accept the bill Congress came very near opening this reservation anyhow. It is certain that you will never get any better terms than are offered in this bill, and the chances are that you will not get so good.''

The Sioux tried to master the agreement wording, ''twelve pages of ... fine print,'' with convoluted talk of ''acreage, graduated prices, trust funds, and property rights,'' daunting even to the white-educated younger progressives. Finally, they capitulated, more than three fourths of the 5,678 eligible men putting their marks to the paper.

Despite this apparent consensus, Crook "left behind a badly divided and thoroughly demoralized people," all too aware that they had not acted as they wanted and that their future had become further jeopardized.

Indeed, despite repeated promises that the agreement would not affect the flow of desperately needed treaty rations, the government immediately made deep cuts in beef provisions. Through the winter of 1889–1890, many western Sioux lived close to starvation, and fell ill with whooping cough, measles, and influenza. They regarded with suspicion the government's newest initiatives to establish stronger agency control, build schools, and make farmers of them. The next summer, those who had planted crops saw them wither in a bitter drought. And as the crops withered, the Ghost Dance religion flourished on the now fragmented Sioux reservations, where the Ghost Shirts took on a special power: they were, the believers claimed, impervious to bullets.

By late fall, the Ghost Dance fervor and devotion of Sioux bands at the Pine Ridge agency, at Rosebud, at Cheyenne River, and at Standing Rock were worrying agents, other civil officials, military commanders, and nearby whites. Agents tried to ban the dances, but still they continued as Indians increasingly chose to camp away from the agencies and to ignore or reject official demands. The situation was particularly tense on the Pine Ridge reservation, where a recent political appointee, Daniel F. Royer, exerted little control as agent, the natives calling him Young-Man-Afraid-of-Indians.

There is no question that the Sioux bands were growing increasingly independent—and therefore defiant—under the leadership of such men as Kicking Bear, Short Bull, Hump, Big Foot, and Two Strike, but the whites' response, in the form of a show of force from government troops, only served to exacerbate matters, with the "hostiles" deserting the agencies and dividing over whether to hold out—at least defensively—or try to bargain with the military officers.

Sitting Bull remained at Standing Rock reservation, still fiercely resistant to Agent McLaughlin's authority and increasingly a supporter of the Ghost Dance movement. Both McLaughlin and the military authorities regarded Sitting Bull with deep distrust, and in December Indian police were sent to arrest the venerable old warrior. "We all felt sad," one of the contingent, John Lone Man, would recall.

At first, Sitting Bull agreed to come peacefully with them; then, as his supporters gathered around, he refused. A melee broke out, Sioux fighting Sioux. As policeman Bull Head went down with a fatal bullet in his right side, both he and fellow policeman Red Tomahawk fired on Sitting Bull. The chief—long the primary symbol of Indian resistance to the American nation—died there, in front of his reservation cabin, and was buried in the graveyard of Standing Rock's Catholic mission church.

Meanwhile, General Nelson Miles had been dispatched to Dakota. Miles saw all too well the source of the troubles: "We have taken away their land and the white people now have it. The Indians have been half fed or half starved. Neither I nor any other official can assure the Indians that they will receive anything different in the future. They say, and very justly, that they are tired of broken promises."

But Miles knew his job; he sought to bring into the agencies all of the "hostiles," and to this end he deployed both troops and Sioux willing to convince their tribespeople to return to reservation control. Many of the Ghost Dancers were doing so, or starting to, within two weeks of Sitting Bull's death. The army was particularly anxious to snare a band living on the Cheyenne River under the leadership of another venerable old chief, Big Foot, whom they saw as a major troublemaker. Ironically, Big Foot himself had already abandoned the Ghost Dance religion and was eager to maintain peace, although some of his young men were not.

An officer elicited Big Foot's promise to come into Camp Cheyenne for a council. But then, on the advice of his counselors, the ailing chief instead led some 350 men, women, and children toward the Pine Ridge agency. Cavalry troops caught up with them on December 28, and the pneumonia-racked Big Foot followed orders to camp on Wounded Knee Creek and prepare to go with the soldiers the next morning.

When morning came, however, the Seventh Cavalry's attempts to disarm the Indians before traveling ended in bloodshed. One Sioux, Black Coyote, testily refused to relinquish the rifle for which he insisted he had paid dearly, and as he struggled with two soldiers, the rifle fired.

Immediately, a few of the other young Indian men drew Winchesters, and for a long and desperate moment Indian and cavalryman stared at each other. Robert Utley has argued cogently that neither side was seeking a violent confrontation, but the firing quickly poured from both. For the Indians—most of whom had clearly been surrendering peacefully—the altercation could only prove deadly, as 470 soldiers ringed them and 4 Hotchkiss guns were trained upon them. The cavalrymen killed almost 150 of the Sioux, about a third of them women and children. The Sioux managed to kill 25 soldiers, some of them in hand-to-hand combat.

Wounded Knee was simply a coda to the violent Indian resistance of the nineteenth century, for with it "the reality of [the Indians'] political subordination could no longer be denied or ignored." The Ghost Dance had hinged not on "armed challenge to the reservation," but on a fierce and forlorn longing for a lost world divinely renewed. Now Native Americans faced more fully and frighteningly than ever a world of someone else's making.

For most tribes in the West, that world consisted of continually shrinking boundaries. As in the case of the Sioux, the government was eager to divest the Indians of large amounts of "surplus" land even before any allotment began. Congress appropriated half of Washington State's Colville reservation for white settlement in 1891 by insisting that its status as an "executive order" reservation meant that natives could live there only at the government's will. (A few years later, officials would open up the rest for mineral exploration, unleashing a swarm of prospectors on the residents.) The Paiutes of Walker River and Pyramid Lake were repeatedly threatened with loss of large portions of these reservations, especially where whites had already intruded. At one point, a presidential commission offered the Pyramid Lake Paiutes $20,000 worth of cattle for an estimated 18,700 acres of land, "the total value of the proposed cattle herd" being "significantly less than the value of the crops removed illegally from the reservation by . . . squatters in any two-year period." In addition, those Paiutes who lived in a primarily white town in the southern portion of the reservation were to remove to a mini-reserve surrounding the town's Indian school, with no compensation for their abandoned homes, gardens, and other improvements.

Meanwhile, the government coerced residents of Indian Territory into giving up all rights to the "unassigned" western lands, which the tribes had earlier agreed the government could use for other Indian bands undergoing relocation. A federal district court in 1880 had ruled that the lands remained Indian country whether or not Indians lived upon them, but cattlemen had kept moving in and legislators had introduced bill after bill to open the lands.

Finally, with a commission headed by David Jerome pressuring them as a prelude to allotment, the tribes involved "saw that they must choose between a forced sale and seizure." The Creek and Seminole sale in early 1889 sparked a frenzied land rush among whites, but the Cherokees clung to rights to the much coveted six-million-acre Cherokee Strip, the long, rectangular region bordering the upper western portion of their reservation. They collected grazing lease money from the white cattlemen there.

In response, President Benjamin Harrison in 1890 "declared the grazing leases illegal and ordered the area vacated of all cattle." Oklahoma Territory was born of the western Indian Territory lands the same year; in late 1891, the Cherokees reluctantly sold the strip and another land rush ensued in 1893.

The Jerome Commission continued its work, providing a hearing for, but ultimately overriding, Indian objections because both groups knew that the commissioners had "the authority to put the policy into effect without [the Indians'] consent." An Osage leader named Strike Axe reminded the commission in 1893 that the government had promised "when we came here that we would be the fartherest [sic] west and . . . at the fartherest edge of Indian country and it was impossible to be bothered." Now, "as you say, we have more whites than Indians, but where shall we go?" The quick, dismissive answer—"On your farm"—demonstrated the hopelessness for the Indians of such negotiations.

By 1894, the Jerome Commission had secured "the cession of more than fifteen million acres of 'surplus' Indian lands," and Oklahoma, the "permanent" refuge of some sixty tribes and tribal remnants, was well on its way to statehood, no matter what the Indians might say or do. In addition, allotment was proceeding slowly but surely.

It began on the reservation of the Sisseton and Wahpeton Sioux in present-day northeastern South Dakota, the pattern quickly becoming established. Surveying crews from the General Land Office appeared on the reservations, their detailed mapping paid for with Indian Bureau funds, "which the Indians were theoretically to repay." The government drew up rolls of the various tribes, and special allotment agents were dispatched to oversee the apportioning of the tracts among the members.

The agents were encouraged to allow natives to select the better lands—with heads of family identifying parcels for minor children—and to confirm in possession those who already occupied or had made improvements on a particular homestead. In the early years of allotment, many agents did work to carve out good lands for allottees and to aid them in the transition. Shawnee Thomas Alford remembered the allotment agent with whom he worked, N. S. Porter, as a "patient and sympathetic man" advising the confused allottees judiciously on the most promising farming tracts.

But for those Indians who did not want any part of this new scheme, there was no escaping the fact that the agent was present to see that they took part. "The Indian people don't want their allotments," one Cherokee noted, "but at the same time some of them take them, for [government agents] scared them into it."

Some of the political appointees in charge of allotment showed favoritism to the mixed-blood progressives or ignored established claims. Tracts were assigned with no attention either to the Indians' wishes or to the acreage's agricultural potential. Some allotments were located in riverbeds, others in high, dry country that could never be irrigated. As a matter of policy, agents also avoided allotting to Indians any potentially valuable mineral lands, which were to be reserved for white development and exploitation, and wrangled with natives over allowing them valuable timber stands.

Further, the size of the parcels presented a problem. A generation of immigrant homesteaders had already discovered how difficult and often impossible it was to make a living on 160 or 320 acres in the West; while the Blackfeet received 320-acre plots, it is instructive to note that "today [1995], in this region, the size of the average farm is greater than 1500 acres." And despite the "surplus" lands on large reservations, the holdings of some tribes had already shrunk to the point that there was not enough land to be allotted—or whites coveted so much of the reservation that they got the allotment amounts reduced. Shoshone families in Wyoming were being assigned eighty "often arid and worthless" acres, Papagos in the Southwest a scant ten "irrigable" acres.

The Paiutes, whose better lands were desired by whites, were allotted a mere five acres each in a 1905 bill. Their agent responded with the obvious—"Neither Indian nor white man can make a living upon 5 acres of land in Nevada"—and the allotment was not carried out, but it hung like a Damoclean sword over the tribe for decades. The Turtle Mountain Chippewas in North Dakota, who had ceded millions of acres of "good wheat land" for "two six-mile-square townships of untillable brush-covered hills," had to venture onto the public domain to obtain allotments. They then gravitated back to live with kin, the far-flung "farms" falling into white hands.

When Indians had a choice, they tended to select parcels close to kin and previous neighbors, thereby creating a sense of continuity in the midst of change. They sought to maintain some kind of communal land base beyond the cemetery and agency tracts usually set aside by the government. For example, the Nez Perces tried unsuccessfully to hold on to "surplus" land for a communal grazing area. The Chippewas and Munsees of Kansas did succeed in buying their "surplus" lands back, but at a high cost. These natives, unusual in their high degree of assimilation, had agreed to terminate their relationship with the federal government as tribes—"they had retained their lands, but they were no longer Indians."

Perhaps the most maddening aspect of allotment for western Indians was the government's blithe assumption that they could and would support themselves as families by farming. "God damn a potato," declared one Shoshone chief being regaled with the virtues of the family vegetable garden.

The Mescalero Apache agent argued successfully that allotment wouldn't work on the Mescalero reservation because the land would better support communal grazing and timber operations. An official at Pine Ridge made a similar argument—the Sioux and the land itself favored stock raising, while to carve the land into farms would mean "the degradation of this people and their speedy extinction." He did not stop allotment, but with a supportive superintendent, the Sioux at Pine Ridge developed a healthy cattle industry in the first decade of the twentieth century.

Still, tribal members would recall preallotment stock raising as the best, with family needs adequately met and a pleasant round of communal chores. Besides, it was hard to make even stock raising viable if the land was being partitioned off: as Cheyenne John Wooden Legs argued, "Sensible people knew it would be wrong to take cattle land like ours and divide it up into little pieces—big enough for grazing rabbits, but not cattle."

Indian resistance to allotment took a variety of forms. The strong traditionalists in particular exuded hostility to allotment officials. Thomas Alford, who had obtained a job surveying the land of his uncle Big Jim's Shawnee band, reported that even his own generally good relationship with his kinsman failed to stop Jim and the others from "pull[ing] up my corner stakes as fast as I could establish them."

Defiant natives warned other tribespeople against cooperating with the allotment officials. They refused to meet with those sent to enroll them or to accept their allotments, and in communities as diverse as those of the Yuma and Cherokee, people went to jail rather than do so.

Even most of the progressives were strongly antiallotment, and leaders of various political persuasions tried different delaying tactics, including ordering allotment agents off the land. In Kansas, where allotment was mandated in 1890, the remaining tribes rallied around the Potawatomi activist Wahquahboshkuk. He argued against taking annuities, lest they be tied to allotment. The Kansas tribes, after all, had already seen and felt the devastation of an earlier allotment. Trying to work within the system that controlled their destinies, they sent leaders and legal advisers to Washington in an attempt to stave off this newest threat, but without success.

The allotment threat had mobilized the Hopis, whose villages had always operated as independent political units. When allotment officials began dividing up the tribe's mesa domain without any understanding of clan claims to parts of it, leaders in 1894 managed to unite and petition the "Washington Chiefs" with their arguments, including a reminder of the tribe's considerable corn-cultivation skills based on a true knowledge of the southwestern soil and climate.

Indians tried to impress upon white officials that they had their own land laws. For example, among the Choctaws, one pointed out, "an Indian could settle on a piece of land . . . and improve it, and if he did not get within a quarter of a mile of someone else's improvements, the land was his to use as long as he wished," although still a part of the common holdings. The Hopis explained that changes in agricultural landholdings had traditionally been "effected by mutual discussion and concession among the elders, and among all thinking men and women of the family groups interested."

The Hopis' insistence on being heard and the fact that they lived in a region still remote and forbidding to whites staved off allotment, but anywhere settlers clamored for land, the reservation's outlines were destined to crumble despite the fiercest resistance. For one thing, whether or not it was pushing allotment policies, the United States government consistently used its power during this period to undermine tribal attempts at self-determination. Reservation residents were encouraged to look to the agent, the federal government, and state and local courts for decision making, rather than to traditional tribal governments.

As forced allotments became the rule in the mid-1890s, these tribal governments kept trying to assert some authority or at least to be included in the process. When the Choctaws' council tried to become involved in the allotment process, offering to send a commission "to visit every settlement with maps, plats, and field notes to assist in the selections," President Teddy Roosevelt rejected the plan.

Nowhere was the impact of allotment more keenly felt than among the Choctaws and the other groups in Indian Territory. At first, the government exempted the Five Civilized Tribes—Choctaw, Cherokee, Chickasaw, Creek, Seminole—along with the Osages, Miamis and Peorias, and Sacs and Foxes, and concentrated on groups like the Kickapoos who had been pressed into Oklahoma. The Kickapoos occupied the small but fertile Deep Fork reservation coveted by whites— so much so that the Jerome Commission, three times rebuffed by the Kickapoos, resorted to trickery. John T. Hill, a white rancher whom the Kickapoos knew, told them he might be able to protect their common lands and obtain funds supposedly held for them in Washington. With the aid of a mixed-blood Cherokee interpreter, he cajoled and coerced some of the Kickapoos into signing what turned out to be a power of attorney, with which he and the interpreter accomplished an allotment agreement, complete with forged signatures of tribal members.

The Kickapoo Allotment Act stripped the Indians of 188,000 acres of "surplus" land, awarding them a paltry thirty cents an acre—at a time when nearby tribes were receiving $1.50 an acre—and leaving enrollees allotments of only eighty acres each.

The Kickapoos refused to move from the "surplus" land or to accept the government payment for it. For a couple of years, they held off the deluge, but finally officials simply opened up the land to homesteaders, the high-noon stampede on May 18, 1895 "surpass[ing] anything previously seen in Oklahoma land rushes." Those Kickapoos who had not accepted allotments—and some fifty who had been away hunting when the allotment rolls were prepared—scattered, many following earlier Kickapoo migrations to Mexico.

Meanwhile, Senator Henry Dawes led a concerted attempt to convince the Five Tribes to allot their land. When they refused, Congress in 1895 gave the Dawes Commission the authority to survey and allot land without any pretense of obtaining tribal consent. Nearly twenty million acres were at stake—almost half of Oklahoma, "an area enormously rich in agricultural land, timber, coal, asphalt, oil, and natural gas." Extralegal resistance movements began to build—the revival of the Keowah, or Nighthawk, secret society among the Cherokees, the "Snake Indian" resistance among the Creeks—but the tribes' best hope lay in their councils. Yet when the tribal councils tried to fight the allotment edict, Congress first extended federal controls over the reservations and the councils, then—in the 1898 Curtis Act—simply overrode any authority of the long-term tribal governments and began phasing them out.

Stripped of any remnants of sovereignty and of most means of legal recourse, many tribal members simply withdrew as much as possible from any interaction with the United States government and its representatives. Some, "forced to accept allotments," responded by continuing in their old patterns; the Sacs of Oklahoma "still lived in a village and farmed their contiguous lands 'without regard to individual ownership.' "

But wherever the government had decided to allot the land, Indians could not escape some consequences. "We have never wanted allotments," a delegation of Yumas would announce, "and all our troubles have come since we had it." "Grafters," men eager to obtain tracts through whatever trickery proved necessary, swarmed over the allotted or soon-to-be-allotted reservations, their capacity to create havoc and hardship unlimited. Even the most careful and frugal progressive Indian found himself unprepared for the onslaught, and for the tangled web of deeds and mortgages that represented the dominant culture's way of doing things. The government added a further troubling complication in 1891 when it acknowledged that some Indians, at least, would be unable to make the land economically viable on their own, and it began to allow limited leasing of the allotted land by whites.

That same year, President Harrison announced sanguinely that "it is . . . gratifying to be able to feel . . . that this work has proceeded upon lines of justice toward the Indian, and that he may now, if he will, secure to himself the good influences of a settled habitation, the fruits of industry, and the security of citizenship."

Yet the decade brought further dwindling of tribal power and the loss of half the reservation land base—some 28,500,000 acres—as "surplus." Some tribal members received small per-capita payments, but many realized nothing for the loss of these lands, which tended to be the well-watered and richly timbered tracts desired by whites.

By 1900, Indian numbers were at an all-time low—237,000—and most of these individuals lived on "171 steadily shrinking land areas scattered throughout twenty-one different states and territories." Their conditions varied, as did their legal status, for they were subject to a confusing array of treaty terms, legislative acts, and state jurisdictional mandates. Thirteen percent of the already allotted land was leased out to white farmers and stockmen, giving the Indian families involved a small, precarious income, but effectively cutting them off from their one clearly identifiable asset as they moved in with relatives or resumed camp life.

If the intact reservation had had the characteristics of a "poorhouse" and "prison" for many, it had also carried at least the hope of remaining or becoming a communal base for survival. The Dawes Act and subsequent legislation undermined even this possibility, and with the new century would come the most intense assault on Indian country yet. If the Indians were going to accommodate the whites by disappearing—as many whites supposed they would—the early years of the twentieth century would have been the logical time to do so.

Instead, Indian America held on, took its grievances to Washington and to the courts, adapted in major ways, and refused to adapt in others. Indians would "remain a tribal people" and they would continue to seek a renewed land base even as most of their reservation land passed into other hands.

Between 1900 and 1910, not only did allotment reach its peak, but a "policy of . . . exploitation" overrode plans to assimilate Indians into white society. "The Indian Bureau administers as if the Indian was selected for their benefit, to exploit them, and not that they were created for the benefit of the Indian," Omaha Thomas Sloan would protest at the first national conference of the Society of American Indians in 1911.

Federal emphasis had been shifting from a simple policy of removing and restricting Indians so that whites could settle on the land. Now the emphasis was on "managing" western resources, and Commissioner of Indian Affairs Francis Leupp in 1905 judged Indians as "primitive peoples" to be "wasteful of their natural resources." Such wastefulness, of course, should not be allowed to continue. Americans were waking up to the mineral and industrial potential of the West, and Indians were to be pushed onto the sidelines to fulfill an old Anglo yeoman ideal as farmers. Whether or not they could survive in this way, Leupp reasoned, "it is our duty to set [the Indian] upon his feet or sever forever" his economic ties to tribe and government.

"Humanitarian" reformers chimed in with perhaps the most brutally uncomprehending pronouncements of the era, when Board of Indian Commissioners member Albert K. Smiley intoned, "Work is the saving thing for the Indians. We have coddled them too much. . . . Put them on their mettle; make them struggle, then we will have some good Indians."

To accommodate such sentiments, the government continued to change the rules of the game of Indian survival. The Burke Act of 1906 made provisions for "competent" Indians to receive fee patents to their allotments, thereby removing safeguards against loss and freeing the government from any further trust responsibility toward the recipients. "Competent" Indians were also allowed to lease their lands, with few restrictions. In response, grafters only redoubled their efforts to control the Indian land base.

A grafter would lease an allotment for a pittance, then rent it at a higher rate to a tenant farmer; on the Winnebago reservation in Nebraska, one grafter outfit "paid the Indians from 10 cents to 25 cents per acre and ... sublet to white farmers for one to two dollars per acre." Or, knowing that many Indians would be allowed to sell parts of their individual allotments as "surplus," the grafter would offer to help in the selection of an allotment tract, in the process obtaining the uncomprehending allottee's signature on a lease for the "surplus" with "an illegal contract to sell it as soon as it should become alienable."

Grafters quickly learned how to gain legal control of allotments that Indians had refused to accept, and they would check other allotments to see if the owners were physically present, filing homestead claims if they were away. "Much land was illegally secured in this way by unscrupulous persons," Thomas Alford would recall from his days working in various facets of the allotment process.

The guardianship racket became the "most profitable" type of grafting. In 1903, county probate courts began assigning white guardians for Indian minors, ostensibly to protect the minors' interests, as Indian parents were known to have "sold or leased their children's allotments for a pittance." Now grafter guardians ravaged the Indian estate.

As the government began to loosen some of its trust policies, the grafters became further emboldened. They would "secure special legislation removing the trust status from a full-blood's allotment without the owner's knowledge, and then purchase the land." They had adult Indians declared incompetent so that they could take over their assets and affairs.

Whole "rings" of opportunists developed to capitalize on the natives' ignorance of the European-American legal system. In Oklahoma a lawyer and judge named Ed Baker led a duplicitous group of "livestock dealers, merchants, bankers, county officials, four or five Cheyennes and Arapahos, and at least one agency superintendent" in defrauding Cheyennes and Arapahos. Anticipating the natives' fee-patent ownership of land—with the accompanying freedom to sell it or lose it to debt—Baker would win their confidence by representing them in local courts and loaning them money. For the loans he required that they sign undated mortgages. The loan recipients would use the money to buy goods from other members of the ring, who inflated the prices so that the loan money wasn't enough—Indians had to sign promissory notes for the difference. When the notes came due, the Indians could not pay and the sellers could reclaim their merchandise. Meanwhile, Baker harassed the Indians for repayment of the mortgages, eventually obtaining their deeds to patented land.

The most notorious attempts to part Indians from their land at the turn of the century centered on the Oklahoma Kickapoos. This group had had an agent, an opportunistic lawyer named Martin Bentley, who had endeared himself to most of them by protecting many of their rights and allowing them a great deal of cultural and religious freedom. At the same time, he was extending his control over his charges' land.

Bentley promised the discontented tribespeople a refuge in Mexico. Collaborating with local speculators, he could then realize handsome profits from the sale of their lands. A suspicious commissioner of Indian Affairs replaced Bentley in 1901, but the former agent had friends in high places, including Senator Henry Teller. Bentley continued to represent himself as the Kickapoos' champion, both to them and to Congress, much to the consternation of the hardworking new agent, Frank Thackery.

Playing on the Kickapoo fears of the U.S. government and their hopes to escape its control, Bentley continued with his plans to move them to Mexico, escorting a number of them south of the border to temporary sites. Many of these immigrants drank heavily; all lived in impoverished conditions, unwelcomed by Mexican authorities who were on good terms with previous Kickapoo immigrants.

Bentley was investigated in 1905 after a Kickapoo woman returned from Mexico to find him selling to a townsite company the land she had leased to him. The former agent nonetheless proceeded with his plan to get the Kickapoos out of the way in Mexico, while pushing through Congress in 1905 and 1906 acts that would remove the restrictions on their lands.

Bentley and his confederates were not the only speculators interested in Kickapoo acreage. As restrictions were lifted, some Oklahomans who saw their chance began harassing the Kickapoos in both Mexico and Oklahoma. At first, these speculators competed with each other, but a group of "about fifteen" came together and became known as the "Shawnee Wolves," so named because they also harassed Shawnees sharing the Kickapoos' dreams of removal and independence.

The Wolves would stop at nothing to get the remaining Deep Fork properties. They got Bentley jailed in Mexico, rounded up the Oklahoma Kickapoos there, and had them "herded to Eagle Pass under close guard, held incommunicado in a wagon yard, and taken out a few at a time to sign deeds before Texas notaries and courts of record." Indians who did not cooperate were "arrested, placed in chains, and put to work on the streets," some beaten in front of their families. When even these methods did not work, the Wolves simply forged signatures. They also kidnapped Kickapoos who were still residing in Oklahoma and took them to Mexico to sign deeds.

The abuses became too flagrant to be ignored, and when Bentley got out of the Mexican jail, he positioned himself as tribal attorney to lead the fight against the Wolves. A congressional subcommittee in December 1907 concluded that the Wolves' conduct "has never been equalled in the history of any dealings to secure lands from American Indians." The United States sued to recover the lands the Wolves had taken, but allowed Bentley to continue holding acreage and funds in trust for many of the Kickapoos.

The government also awarded the Kickapoos a settlement for the fraudulent 1893 treaty that had been obtained by rancher Hill. Frank Thackery continued to try to break Bentley's hold on the tribe, convinced it was as destructive to them as the machinations of the Wolves. Indeed, a Bentley confederate, testifying in a 1909 investigation, would reveal the goal underlying their actions: "to get hold of as much of the land as we could and make a profit out of it along with other people who might be in the same business."

Yet in 1907 more than half the remaining allottees chose to turn over to Bentley their portions of the settlement money, almost $90,000 to go to the shaky Mexican Kickapoo colony in Sonora. Meanwhile, Thackery and attorney John Embry worked to restore and secure the Kickapoos' Oklahoma allotments and to ensure that those who stayed had an adequate living, bolstered by their share of the settlement.

The Kickapoos who removed to Mexico under Bentley experienced extreme poverty and a dissolution of the very traditional values they had attempted to preserve. Their dreams of full and independent living on a new land base had been rudely dashed, and although they eventually sued in court, they did not recover the $90,000.

Fortunately for these exiles, the governmental investigations and Thackery's and Embry's tenacity had restored many of their allotments. But government policy in general repeatedly made it easier for speculators to snap up pieces of Indian country. A 1902 congressional act allowed both heirs of a deceased allottee and minors to sell allotments, the latter through court-appointed guardians. This was a compelling proposition for the heirs, who often "lacked the capital to develop" the land or found it impossible to create viable holdings from their fractions. The proposition was also a bonanza for speculators, who could get hold of the heirship shares and—as guardians or buyers—of the minors' property. These operators obtained most of the 775,000 acres that passed out of Indian hands as a result of these legislative changes from 1902 to 1910.

The Burke Act and subsequent legislation—such as the 1907 Indian Appropriation Act—also made it far easier for speculators to obtain land. More and more Indians were deemed "competent" and given fee patents. They had little or no concept of the land's true value— or the ability to demand to know what it was. Officials cheated them with low appraisals—or gave fair ones that were undermined by grafters who could bring the amount down by "conspir[ing] to lessen competition in bidding." In this way, the grafters bought tracts for a song, or they dangled "worthless securities and credit in return for land," in the latter case, like Ed Baker, luring the owners into debt in order to confiscate the acreage. All around Indian country, bankers and merchants "extended credit in the hope of getting land at bargain rates."

At about the same time that the government allowed competent Indians to sell their allotments, it also liberalized leasing laws. A "progressive" Indian could lease his or her own land. Nonetheless, leasing abuses continued and multiplied. Indians rented land to obtain ready money, often to pay debts or get loans or credit. Just after the turn of the century, Indian Commissioner William Jones had reduced rations sent to reservations as part of the prevailing work-like-a-white-man-or-suffer-the-consequences philosophy.

Indians' lease money soon disappeared—in loan interest payments totaling as much as 3,000 percent, in purchase of essential supplies, in purchase of enticing items and liquor—and owners often had trouble collecting further rent payments. Meanwhile, lessees who had promised to improve the tracts as part of the bargain instead often reduced their value—for example, by planting only one crop, thereby robbing the soil of its vitality.

It seemed that everything the government did to "set [the Indian] upon his feet" had the opposite effect. For example, after 1900, BIA officials became committed to seeing that western natives had enough water to make irrigation farming viable. But the cumbersome irrigation projects, financed by appropriated tribal funds from "surplus" land sales, were poorly planned.

Further, non-Indians often refused to recognize Indian water needs and rights. One congressman sought to divert Truckee River water, thereby drastically reducing the flow to the Paiutes' much-valued Pyramid Lake, with the argument that it and Winnemucca Lake "existed 'only to satisfy the thirsty sun.' " Through such specious reasoning—or simply through physical appropriation—vital water supplies were diverted, leaving high and dry the people of the reservations, who recognized all too well that "water is to the land what blood is to the body."

Conflicts led to a landmark Supreme Court case regarding water rights. In 1905, the superintendent at the Fort Belknap reservation in Montana, home to some thirteen hundred Gros Ventre and Assiniboine Indians, complained to the commissioner of Indian Affairs, "So far this Spring we have no water in our ditch whatever. Our meadows are now rapidly parching up. The Indians have planted large crops and a great deal of grain." He predicted crop failure and a winter of starvation for the Indians "unless some radical action is taken at once to make the settlers above the Reservation respect our rights" regarding water from the Milk River.

The superintendent argued on the basis of "prior appropriation"— the fact that an earlier superintendent had in 1898 laid claim for the natives to a specified amount of the river's flow. Another oft-used argument in the West was that of riparian rights, whereby those owning land beside a stream could divert the water. But when the Fort Belknap case made it to the Supreme Court as *Winters* v. *United States,* the Court used neither standard. Instead, in January 1908, it upheld Indians' rights in what would become known as the Winters

Doctrine on the basis that "the creation of an Indian reservation carried with it the setting aside of water as well as land."

This victory was significant, as over half the reservations—and most of the tribal population—were and are located in the driest areas of the West. But the government did not clarify the ruling or put muscle into it. How much Indians should receive and how water use should be administered remained open to debate, and the Bureau of Indian Affairs often fell back on state prior-appropriation laws.

Paternalism lay at the core of many of the government's failures. The Indians themselves were seldom consulted about plans that involved their livelihood, except in the most perfunctory way.

Of course, the tribes lacked complete unanimity; in fact, the gap between members who resisted aspects of Anglo control and those who acquiesced to them continued to widen. By 1906, one Hopi village, Oraibi, was literally torn apart after decades of growing tension between the progressives and the traditionalists, who resisted sending their children to Anglo schools. The progressives, or "Friendlies," goaded traditionalist leader Yokeoma into a "pushing match" as a means of deciding "who should go and who should stay." When a rival leader forced Yokeoma across a line in the sandrock, four hundred members of the traditional faction had to flee immediately. After a week's journey, they stopped and established another village, Hotevilla.

In a milder but no less irrevocable instance, one Cherokee would remember that after his great-aunt traveled among the relatives to urge them not to allot, his grandfather cut off communication with all those who did.

Among the Creeks, who by a majority had reluctantly agreed to allotment in 1899, the antiallotment faction in 1901 established its own government and police force at Hickory Grove, a small community near Checotah, Oklahoma. Led by an accomplished orator, Chitto Crazy Snake Harjo, these "Snake" Indians drew in dissidents from other tribes, carried out their own sometimes harsh law around Hickory Grove, and sought to replace the Creek government at Okmulgee with their own. Arrested for threats against Creek principal chief Pleasant Porter, Harjo and almost one hundred followers were given two-year suspended sentences, but the orator and nine companions who continued to agitate went to jail to serve their sentences in 1902.

This cooled the movement somewhat, but did not end it. Harjo continued to fight against allotment, appearing before a Senate committee in 1906 and seeing his resistance grow in 1908 into the activist Four Mothers Nation, an Oklahoma pan-Indian group. The next year, Harjo was wounded in an altercation with some sheriff's deputies. He eluded capture, but the injury proved fatal.

Many Indians found fault only with some of Harjo's more radical methods. A Choctaw named Crawford Anderson harked back to predictions in Mississippi seventy years earlier that if the Creeks "moved to the new Indian Territory they would again . . . be asked to give it over to the white man," and cited the frustration the Creeks felt "when they realized that the warnings given to their fathers in Mississippi . . . were well founded."

Others simply refused to accept their allotments, removing to remote locations where they could live independently. Despite poverty, they returned the per-capita payments authorized them, almost two thousand Cherokees still standing firm in this way in 1912.

Others tried to maintain their Indian identity through a unified peaceful separation of their own. A faction among the Choctaws in 1906 requested unsuccessfully that Congress allow them to sell their allotments so they could buy land in South America or Mexico and start over, just as the whites who had emigrated to America had done. Another group of Indian Territory residents sought to create an Indian state of Sequoyah, but Congress "tabled the measure."

Still others simply made their voices heard within the system so as to expose allotment's effects. Dewitt Clinton Duncan, a Dartmouth-educated Cherokee from Oklahoma, told a Senate committee in 1906 that he had previously had a promising three-hundred-acre farm, but then received a sixty-acre allotment. "Let me tell you, Senators," he announced, "I have exerted all my ability, all industry, all my intelligence, if I have any, my will, my ambition, the love of my wife— all these agencies I have employed to make my living out of that 60 acres, and, God be my judge, I have not been able to do it. I am not able to do it. I can't do it. I have not been able to clear expenses." He reported that it would take the proceeds from his whole "pretty good crop'' just to cover ''the debts that I have incurred to eke out a living during the meager years just passed.''

Indians especially protested the turning loose of those allottees whom white officials deemed ''competent'' by giving them fee patents to tracts. ''It isn't right for old Indians and young ones to draw patents in fee,'' Cheyenne chiefs told officials in 1908. ''It makes [them] worse and poor.'' Mower, a member of a Cheyenne-Arapaho delegation to Washington in 1909, told the acting commissioner of Indian Affairs that restrictions should be strengthened, not weakened: ''Speculators take money from us. . . . They are standing ready to grab our land and money the moment it is in our possession.''

Indeed, allotted acreage passed through Indian hands with the swiftness of a spring freshet. Surveys in 1908 showed that ''over 60 percent of the Indians who received fee patents quickly lost their land'' through sale or mortgage, and within a few years of allotment on many reservations percentages would range between 75 and 95.

Meanwhile, Indians also had to continue to fight the removal of more and more of their reservation lands as ''surplus,'' whether allotment was tied to the reduction or not. In this struggle, they were severely hampered by the outcome of the 1903 Supreme Court case *Lone Wolf* v. *Hitchcock*. The Kiowas, Comanches, and Kiowa Apaches had gone to court to protest both an 1892 agreement procured from some tribal members to relinquish a massive tract and its modification by Congress without any attempt at Indian approval, despite the terms of an earlier 1868 treaty. The Supreme Court ruled in *Lone Wolf* v. *Hitchcock* that Congress ''had [full] authority over tribes and could alter treaty provisions without Indian consent.''

In other words, the United States could now appropriate Indian land without any pretense of an agreement—and without any attempt at payment. This hit particularly hard on reservations such as the Rosebud in Sioux country, where a 1901 agreement to sell ''surplus'' land in 1903 turned into a giveaway. Within the boundaries of the already reduced and fragmented Great Sioux Reservation, between 1904 and 1912 the Sioux had taken from them, by congressional land statute, five million acres, leaving the total acreage for the western Sioux reservations at eight million.

The Sioux protested the whole way. Ironically, the United States government itself had given them one means to do so: through their business council.

The business councils were instituted by the government in 1898 to replace the old tribal leadership with progressive white-educated cadres. Thomas Alford, who never realized his dreams to be Shawnee chief but did become head of that tribe's business council, remembered his major duties as representing the tribe "in all dealings with the United States," advising tribal members, certifying "the identity of grantors of sales of land," and "act[ing] for the tribe in other matters." Council members served without pay, although they occasionally were allowed to keep small fees for specific services.

The business council progressives were more readily accepting than many of their tribespeople of the government's assistance in—and pressure regarding—educational, religious, and agricultural "advancement." But the council members balked at land cessions, and at the prospect of complete loss of communal identity. Although Alford and others of the new "progressive" generation had returned from white schools too acculturated for their traditional neighbors' tastes, most had the interests of their people at heart. They developed and continued to develop exactly what the Shawnee elders had hoped for when they sent Alford away: the ability to operate within the white man's world—and to challenge it not with guns but with words and papers.

The business council on the Cheyenne River reservation in Sioux country responded to congressional bills to reduce their reservation by calling upon the Indian Rights Association for aid and by speaking out forcefully to officials. Chair James Crow Feather fought against one of two 1907 bills to open parts of the reservation to homesteaders using the following arguments:

1. Our consent was never asked.
2. In our reservation we think the lands are rich in mineral deposits. We want these lands to be examined before opening for settlement.
3. The bill is not satisfactory to us.
4. What former treaties promise is not fully carried into effect yet.

The Cheyenne River Sioux sent a delegation to Washington to advance these arguments and to offer instead a smaller tract, reserving mineral rights. While the delegates were unsuccessful—President Roosevelt signed a bill authorizing the opening of half the reservation to white settlement in May 1908—they nonetheless were "gaining valuable experience in dealing with assaults on [their] territory."

Indians in general were becoming too vocal to be ignored regarding lands lost. In 1904, the Turtle Mountain Chippewa of North Dakota won a payment from the government for ten million acres that had been seized from them in the 1880s. The payment amounted to a paltry ten cents per acre, but any recognition of land rights was welcome, and it also fed hopes in some quarters of the possible return of homelands.

In this regard, the western Sioux were particularly active. As early as 1891, an Oglala Sioux council had formed to keep alive a protest over the government's taking of the Black Hills. The Sioux were hamstrung by the fact that Congress had dictated that Indian tribes could not sue the government and by the BIA's reserving for itself the right to hire and direct lawyers for tribes. But they were getting louder and smarter regarding "the processes that controlled their collective fate."

So, even as allotment and fee patenting played havoc with the Indian land base, even as trespassers continued to plague reservation residents, even as economic opportunities failed to develop, Indians began actively redefining themselves from the periphery of the white world. And there were a few substantial victories, chief among them that of the Osages, who managed to hold on to oil rights when the black gold was discovered on their land in 1895. They enjoyed a relatively secure economic position, thanks to the oil and gas income, farming and grazing leases, and "interest payments from the sale of [their] Kansas reservation." They kept under allotment all of their reservation lands, and tribal mineral rights as well, maintaining "a semblance of the continuation of traditional group living" by designating three tracts of land "where any Osage could stay without cost as long as he desired."

But the Osages' stronger economic position also brought a greater influx into their territory of non-Indians, especially liquor sellers and rustlers, and their oil-lease income stagnated far below what whites would expect or demand. Indians throughout the United States in 1910 lived overwhelmingly on checkerboarded and permanently breached reservations, 60 to 75 percent of the fee-patented land in white hands, along with ''surplus'' acreage. What control Indians had over the circumstances of their lives—economic, political, social—had been further reduced, as had federal protection. Even the Five Tribes of Oklahoma had been brought under county jurisdiction in 1908. It would be another quarter-century before the United States government officially acknowledged that Indians had a right to be Indian or to plan a tribal future.

Chapter Ten

"Where Are We Now?"
(1911–1930)

> I live upon a reservation now. . . . My people do not know when
> they are citizens or when they are not. They send word to the
> Department, "We wish this and so." The Department sends word
> back, "You are citizens of the United States. We can't do that for
> you." They send in for something else. The word comes back,
> "Why you are wards of the government. We cannot grant you
> that." Where are we now?
> —*"Miss Johnson," at the first convention of the Society of*
> *American Indians, 1911*

Every summer, the elderly man called Puts-on-His-Shoes erected the
tipi of his dead brother beside the frame government home in which
he lived with his extended family on the Cheyenne River reservation
in South Dakota. Every summer, he furnished the interior in the old
way—with buffalo robes and willow back rests—and there he slept
and entertained friends who came to sit and smoke and talk of days
gone by.

Through the early twentieth century, most Indians—like Puts-on-
His-Shoes—alternated and navigated between two worlds in their
daily lives. Even the Osages who built comfortable Anglo-style houses
from their oil royalties left them standing empty for months at a time
as they traveled about the reservation and camped with kin and friend.
Tribes sent their young men off to fight in World War I, but welcomed
them back with purification rites and celebration feasts, as they had
their warriors in increasingly distant days.

Tribal members consulted both medicine men and doctors. Despite
the assaults on tribal governance structures, they balanced these old,
fluid forms of decision making, in which numerous delegates came
together and worked through issues at length, with the necessity to

acknowledge and adopt Anglo-style authority structures. They tried to balance old ways of hunting, gathering, producing, and preserving with wage employment and trips to the store or trading post. They shifted as necessary between their native tongues and the English words laboriously learned in Anglo schools.

Throughout most of this era, officials continued trying to force Indians to be like whites, frequently resorting to intimidation and coercion to wipe out "heathen" ways. "I have almost completely broken up the practice of the Indian 'Doctors' on this Reservation," a Paiute agent wrote with satisfaction in 1914, noting his hope that one or two could be banished to the penitentiary as an example to all.

Indians maintained a spirit of resistance. The Sioux conducted their outlawed Sun Dance ceremony "in remote parts of their reservations," choosing "open places where winds would disperse the sounds of singing and drums" and posting mounted guards. Children who were beaten with "big long rubber hoses" for "talking Indian" at the government schools still clung to their language identities; Neola Walker, a Winnebago student, would conclude, "[I]t wasn't wrong to talk Indian. That's the only way I could talk to my grandma and them. So I just made up my mind I was going to talk Indian."

Some Indians continued to resist altogether the move to Anglo-style houses. In 1912, a government official reported that more than half the tribal population at the Cantonment agency on the Cheyenne-Arapaho reservation remained, apparently by choice, "in tipis and in camps consisting of from two to fifteen families." Not only was this way of life familiar, but it provided a measure of freedom and reflected deeply held beliefs; some tribes placed great emphasis on the power of circles, including circular dwellings. A Lakota Sioux mourned that the "little gray houses of logs" provided by the government offered "a bad way to live, for there can be no power in a square." An Oglala Sioux compelled to exchange his circular tent for a house in the 1920s raged, "I don't want no son-of-a-bitch house. I don't want to live in a box. . . . There's no tomorrow in this goddam box!"

The fact that white officials had the power to dictate such changes naturally galled many tribal members. The "Beautiful Mountain Uprising" of 1913 in Navajo country demonstrated continuing resistance to Anglo culture and to official control. The Bureau of Indian Affairs superintendent at Shiprock Agency, a man named Shelton, had called for a young Navajo named Hatot'cli-yazzie, or Little Singer, to be brought to the agency, along with his three wives, to answer the charge of engaging in plural marriage. The three women were found and brought to Shiprock, but Hatot'cli-yazzie and his father, the medicine man Bi-joshii (or Bizoche) rode into the compound with a few companions and "freed the three women by armed force." The band then retreated to the Beautiful Mountains to the southwest.

Other Navajos and a missionary respected by the natives tried to arrange a peace, but Shelton obtained arrest warrants, stirred up the white population, and vowed to "make an example" of Bi-joshii's group.

Under these circumstances, the Navajos were not inclined to surrender. Nor would the local federal marshal accommodate Shelton by forming a posse. Secretary of the Interior Franklin K. Lane sent negotiator James McLaughlin, who also worked as a competency commissioner, judging allottees' competency to receive the fee patents that allowed them to dispose of their property. Like Shelton, McLaughlin recommended using force to capture the band—its adult males numbering twelve to fifteen—and bring them in to face charges.

Lane dispatched General Hugh Scott with a 261-man contingent. Scott was a good choice, for he arranged a meeting with Bi-joshii and dealt as fairly as he could with him, outlining the consequences of holding out and pledging to help keep the band safe. Indeed, when Bi-joshii and the others appeared in court, they were sentenced to only ten to thirty days in jail, to Shelton's disgust.

Yet there were more Sheltons than Scotts, and even the Scotts told independent tribespeople to submit, and to submit again. This fact of life for Indians in general—being constantly under the control of representatives of another culture—had perhaps been captured most painfully and poignantly in an exchange between Oto chiefs from Nebraska and Commissioner of Indian Affairs Edward P. Smith some forty years before the Beautiful Mountain Uprising. The Indians had learned with dismay that Smith could control the monies due them for sale of lands. "How would . . . white men feel to have their property used in this way?" an Oto named Stand By had asked.

Smith had responded, "If the white men [were] children and you [were] their guardians, you [could] do what you please with their money—provided you do what is good for them." To this, another Oto, Medicine Horse, had retorted, "We are not children. We are men. I never thought I would be treated so when I made the Treaty." Smith had not budged: "It takes you a long time to find out that I am going to do what I think best for you."

Nothing had changed since this bitter confrontation. When the Paiutes on the Pyramid Lake reservation formed their own council and asked for information of vital importance to reservation residents, including "the Indian position relative to state game laws" and "the extent of their legal rights in the reservation lands," their agent and the BIA simply refused to acknowledge them as having any authority even to inquire.

In particular, Anglo government and religious officials of the 1910s and 1920s sought to wipe out a variety of "heathen" religious practices. John Lame Deer, a Sioux, complained after struggling to give his mother an Indian burial in 1920, "they wouldn't even allow us to be dead in our own way."

Especially the officials targeted "peyotism," which centered on the eating of the peyote cactus to induce healing and visions. This practice, which had ancient indigenous roots, had been developed by the Comanches, the Mescalero Apaches, and the Kiowas in the late nineteenth century. Despite officials' efforts, in 1918, devotees of peyotism incorporated as the Native American Church and continued to draw believers. "It's the last thing of the Indian that is Indians'," Winnebago Sterling Snake would explain some fifty years later. "And it's something they want to hang on to."

The Native American Church combined Christian and native teachings in the rich synthesis that Indians often drew from their changing and changed situations. In large part, Indians survived culturally by combining old and new. For example, the Osages now buried their dead with a peyote ceremony, with the traditional rite of painting the corpse's face and leaving food at the grave, and with "Latin prayers recited by a Catholic priest." Officials either failed to recognize the ways in which Indians *had* adapted, or reacted with horror to their combining of Anglo beliefs and symbols with "primitive" ones. A few sympathetic agents, however, supported the natives in their religious practices.

By the second decade of the twentieth century some Indians coming out of Anglo boarding schools did clearly evidence more affinity for Anglo beliefs and lifeways than for native ones. Modern historians find in these tribal members' lives and words evidence of a continuing or revived pride in at least some traditional Indian values, but the Indians who represented the success of Carlisle and other off-reservation schools often decisively and permanently became part of the dominant culture—what Indians of a later generation would derisively call ''Uncle Tomahawks'' or ''apples,'' red on the outside and white on the inside. For example, Geronimo's cousin Jason Betzinez, a graduate of Carlisle, rejected his past as an Apache guerrilla fighter and, as a farmer married to a white woman, resisted what Geronimo had dreamed of but had not lived to see: the opportunity to return to the Southwest in 1913.

Of course, such acculturation—or even the simple willingness to acculturate—fit well with United States government plans for the Indian. Thus it was that on a spring morning in 1916, a crowd of two thousand, a few reporters, and a movie company gathered for a ''citizenship ceremony'' at the Yankton Sioux agency on the north bank of the Missouri River in South Dakota.

Officials in Woodrow Wilson's administration—most notably, Secretary Lane and Indian competency Commissioner McLaughlin—were pursuing Dawes's policies with fresh vigor. Every Indian landholder was to receive an unrestricted fee patent to his acreage, thereby gaining American citizenship and leaving his Indian identity behind. On the Yankton reservation, Lane and McLaughlin had two hundred Sioux who had professed a willingness to do so.

Lane and McLaughlin designed the ceremony so that the Sioux would step one by one from a tipi set up on the agency grounds and shoot an arrow into the South Dakota skies as a farewell to the old life. One by one, they placed their hands upon a plow and received from the officials a purse in which to save their earnings. And, holding the American flag, each vowed to ''give my hands, my head, and my heart to the doing of all that will make me a true American citizen.''

Many of the participants were soon to be landless American citizens, for they had already succumbed to the blandishments of speculators, committing themselves to selling the tracts as soon as they had fee patents in hand. Nothing was as simple and secure as the symbolism of the ceremony suggested. Indian rights and status—particularly land rights and status—remained riddled with confusion and inequities, even after all Indians, not just those with fee patents to land, were finally granted citizenship in 1924. Through the 1910s and 1920s, almost every Indian in America had ample reason to ask, "Where are we now?"

A quarter-century after the Dawes Act, most of the desirable farming and grazing lands on reservations had already passed into white hands. When the Woodrow Wilson administration began to set policy in 1913, Indians faced three heightened and interrelated challenges to their remaining land rights and livelihoods.

First, western congressmen were gaining power in national politics; Lane, for example, was a Californian, BIA Commissioner Cato Sells, a Texan. Such westerners eagerly sought to develop their regions by downplaying or disregarding Indian claims and rights; Sells "perhaps more than any other commissioner . . . [would expedite] the separation of Indians from their land base." Second, the legislation spawned by the Dawes Act over the previous two decades had "provided all administrative statutory authority" for them to do so. Third, the assault on Indian lands continued by other means as well. While the practice of dividing the land into allotted tracts slowed, the pattern of dispossession continued and even accelerated.

Competency commissions continued to grant fee patents to allottees without interviewing them or without taking into account such obvious disadvantages as a holder's inability to speak English. Further, officials revived the forced fee patent, thereby cutting loose those Indians who realized that it was wiser to continue to claim government protection for their holdings. "I didn't want any deed to my land, but they gave me my deed to the land anyway," Sam Robertson, a Sisseton Sioux of South Dakota, would recall. Hoxie Simmons, a Siletz Indian who had voluntarily taken a fee patent for his own 80 acres, asked a competency commission that he not be forced to take fee patent on 160 additional acres he had inherited, "hilly land, no cultivated land at all." The competency commission nonetheless awarded the patent, and Simmons mortgaged the inheritance land, using the $500 mortgage loan in an attempt to improve his original allotment, which was "only slightly more promising" in agricultural potential. He soon lost the 160 acres to foreclosure.

Over and over, Indians testified to the detrimental effects of losing federal trust status, even voluntarily. "Some of our school boys thought they were educated enough to manage their own affairs," noted Carlisle graduate Alfrich Heap, but as soon as they received their fee patents, "the white man . . . jumped on them and took all their land and money," leaving them with nothing.

Grafters continued their old tricks, luring Indians into sales and mortgage agreements before their allotted tracts were even out of trust status, offering meager amounts of money and worthless securities, and often lubricating the deals with liquor. The government had wisely decreed that Indian lands could not be taken for debts incurred before the issuing of fee patents, but in actual practice, many whites acquired Indian acreage by extending credit until they could step in and seize the land in payment.

Once Indians had fee patents in hand, the speculators heightened their efforts. For a few weeks after the ceremony on the Yankton Sioux reservation, the superintendent found it overrun with "land buyers, automobile agents and fakers of all kinds . . . busy day and night," targeting the "most susceptible" with the help of "smooth tongue[d] mixed bloods" who received a cut on each deal.

The bright and shiny automobiles, symbols of status and mobility, lured those who could ill afford to give up their one clear asset. A superintendent notified Commissioner Sells that a number of younger Indian men with families mortgaged their lands before receiving fee patents in order to obtain cars, often over the protests of their worried wives. The practice of trading land rights for cars became so pervasive that one Cheyenne River Sioux deemed highly "competent" considered an offer of citizenship, then responded "that he did not know how to drive a car."

Indians protesting the dangers of fee patenting made the journey to Washington to plead for continued trust status—"I don't know how to write, I don't know how to manage my affairs the white man's way," explained the Cheyenne leader Wolf Chief on one such journey.

Sells and Secretary Lane overrode all arguments. They also ignored such evidence as that contained in a 1914 study of liberal fee patenting on the Omaha reservation in Nebraska: 80 percent of the patentees "had little or nothing to show for their land," grafters having wormed the patents from them with liquor and "false promises."

In 1916, Sells did extend the trust restrictions for many of the early allottees who were approaching their twenty-five-year cutoff, but in 1917 he announced a "Declaration of Policy" in which all individual tribal members who possessed one half or more European-American blood would automatically be deemed "competent." This racist rule-of-thumb was supported by reformers as well as speculators, and the next three years saw 17,716 fee patents issued, "twice the number [the government] had issued from 1906 to 1916." Whole groups refused to accept them, including both full-bloods and mixed-bloods on the Umatilla, Flathead, and Yakima reservations, but those who resisted received the documents by registered mail.

As Alfrich Heap noted of his educated fellows, even the most competent not only had trouble making the land pay enough to cover taxes, but they lost in any financial dealings with whites. Sam Robertson would recall how his uncle tried to hold a local banker to a careful contract for the uncle's eighty acres—$2,000 down and another $4,400 in payments. But when the payments were not forthcoming and the uncle threatened foreclosure, the banker mortgaged the land with a Sisseton bank, and the uncle held only a second mortgage. He never saw anything beyond the down payment.

With the advent of World War I, the government, concerned with land productivity for the war effort, encouraged Indians to sell at least part of their allotments and use the proceeds to improve what was left. While some managed to do this, others quickly foundered amid the strange and complex realities of surviving on one's own as a small farmer in an age of growing agribusiness. Many sold allotments or remaining allotments because they simply "could not make enough money off [these tracts] to meet their taxes."

Meanwhile, struggles over the "surplus" reservation lands continued. Having already lost half their reservation as "surplus," the Sioux of Cheyenne River repeatedly fought efforts by South Dakota Senator Robert Gamble and others to take away the remaining unallotted acreage. Gamble's periodic introduction of congressional bills to do so brought fierce opposition. If a "Gamble bill" passed, Sioux John Last Man argued, "this reservation is opened up and gone and used to the benefit of the white men and for them until the Indians die of starvation.''

The Cheyenne River Sioux were supported by their BIA superintendent and their boarding-school administrator, the latter writing that the loss of the remaining land would ''be disastrous to these Indians.'' But it was the Sioux themselves who took the fight to Washington in April 1911 with a set of counterproposals.

Frederick Hoxie has argued persuasively that the Gamble bills stimulated unity and the development of more effective strategies for resistance and survival among the residents of the Cheyenne River reservation. First, the threat ''heightened their commitment to the reservation.'' It also stimulated the development and acceptance of leaders well versed in both white and Indian ways, among them the business council originally mandated by whites, but which was now operating according to native goals and concerns.

The Sioux delegation to Washington succeeded in staving off Gamble's bid to ''authorize the sale of all unallotted land'' on the Cheyenne River reservation, but the Indian land base in general was hemorrhaging. By 1920, nine out of every ten Turtle Mountain Chippewas who had received fee patents had lost their tracts. By 1921, ''more than one-half of the individuals within tribes affected by the Dawes Act were landless . . . and economically devastated people.'' These increasingly included those born after the allotment rolls had closed, although the government belatedly attempted to provide some of them with ''surplus'' land. Many heirship allotments had become virtually worthless, the pennies the heirs earned yearly from their fractions only a shadow of the administrative costs involved.

Where did the people without land go? They retreated deeper into the reservation's most undesirable regions, subsisting as best they could. Or they moved in with relatives and friends, taxing their meager resources as well. Some ventured outside the reservations, fighting racism and poor-to-nonexistent employment opportunities. Many came to depend upon state and county provisions for the needy.

By the 1920s, the situation had become so acute that only the most obtuse official could fail to see the devastation Dawes Act policies had wrought. Indians still had little or no voice in policies affecting their own fate, but they fought back as best they could, two Coeur d'Alene Indians taking their refusal to accept fee patents to a United

States circuit court of appeals, which ruled that they could not be taxed on the land for which the fee patents were issued. The Board of Indian Commissioners in 1921 weighed in with the judgment that competency boards' actions appeared "a shortcut to the separation of freed Indians from their land and cash."

Reformers became vocal, among them a Georgia-born social worker named John Collier who was spearheading a separate legal fight for Pueblo Indian land and water rights. Collier argued that fee-patent recipients "had not received individual or group training in modern business life or citizenship, did not have enough land to live on, had no experience in getting or using credit, and were heavily indebted to the government for reimbursable funds."

As such criticisms gained prominence, BIA Commissioner Sells's successor, Charles Henry Burke, sought to correct some of the worst excesses of allotment and fee patenting and tried to bring some of the fee-patented land back into trust. He also continued the damaging policies, including the discredited allotment. Burke targeted some of the small "Mission reservations" of California. Their residents resisted fiercely, driving off surveyors and arguing that communal identity and communal enterprise were essential to their successful farming communities. Burke not only disagreed, but contended that the Indians really had no say in the matter, and marshaled Indian police to see that the work proceeded.

Elsewhere, agricultural land had fallen in value, but Indian sellers had trouble collecting even the small amounts due them. BIA representatives often refused to help, allowing the buyers to default. Or officials behaved highhandedly; in 1927, an elderly Fort Peck reservation Indian named Circling Eagle charged the BIA agent with selling his 320-acre allotment "without his consent and against his wishes." The agent presented Circling Eagle with a two-room house, but the Indian, who did not receive a penny in payment, "could not discover what his land had sold for, what the house cost, or if there was any balance due him."

Further problems stemmed from the fact that the original allottees were dying off, either leaving more fractionated shares for multiple heirs who had no hope of making the land productive, or opening up the opportunity for superintendents to dispose of the land through sales. Between 1911 and 1926 alone, two million acres of heirship land passed into non-Indian hands, along with three million acres of fee-patented land. "Just leave the restrictions on and not let anybody, the State or anyone else, take the restrictions off the land," one Cherokee would implore a Senate committee in 1930. "We have not very much land left now. If we keep on selling it piece by piece, after a while the Indians will not have any land in this country, not one piece left. Now what are we going to do? Are we going to be turned out like hogs or something like that?"

By 1928, Commissioner Burke was admitting to the House Indian Affairs Committee, "Those who were responsible for the allotment act were not farseeing. They did not realize that it was, in the last analysis, going to work out by leaving the Indian landless."

In the same year, the Meriam Report, the results of a massive Rockefeller family–funded investigation led by Lewis Meriam of the Institute for Government Research, also deemed allotment an abysmal failure, having caused Indians "to lose much of their land without improving their economic ability" and the BIA to "neglect ... field work and vocational guidance" in favor of the red tape involved in increasingly complex property issues.

The government was taking some measures to remedy the situation. In 1927, the BIA had "adopted a policy of allotting land only to those Indians who applied in writing," and Congress had approved an act allowing the cancellation of forced fee patents, some ten thousand of which had been issued. The act did little good, however, for it exempted those who had subsequently sold or mortgaged any portion of the allotment, and many of the Indians who had received the forced patents could not even be located.

The cataclysmic effects of the Dawes Act partially obscured the fact that non-Indians continued to challenge Indian land ownership in other ways as well. For example, the "Ute uprising" of 1915 had nothing to do with legislation and everything to do with the old ploy of non-Indians using a "crisis" to run Indians out—and off desirable lands.

White residents of southwestern Colorado and southeastern Utah regarded natives of the area with suspicion, attributing to them not only the modest amount of rustling some actually committed, but numerous acts of theft and violence. A Ute named Tse-ne-gat, who lived with his band outside the Ute reservation, stood accused of killing a

Mexican sheepherder, and the local marshal sent a posse after him with a murder warrant. This posse, a white area resident informed Interior Secretary Lane, consisted in large part of "boozefighters, gamblers and bootleggers" who "talked as though they were going rabbit hunting." Indeed, when they arrived at the Ute camp, they opened fire without even identifying themselves, killing and injuring women and children. The Utes fought back, with the help of a nearby band who rode to their aid.

With possemen killed as well, it was easy enough for those who wanted the Utes gone to justify wartime measures; "the people of this section will feel easier when the Indians have been driven out of the country," the *Rocky Mountain News* flatly announced.

Utes who had nothing to do with the altercation were rounded up and disarmed, even manacled and jailed. A reconstituted posse began driving both Utes and Navajos from homes in the "Four Corners" area—the intersection of Colorado, Utah, New Mexico, and Arizona— homes which were legally theirs under the Indian Homestead Act, homes in well-watered canyons, where the Indians had labored like whites to make numerous improvements.

With the Navajos understandably becoming perturbed as well, Lane again sent General Hugh Scott to ease the situation. And he did, arranging for Tse-ne-gat's peaceful surrender along with three other Ute leaders. "My problem was to prevent them from being legally murdered," Scott would explain. "White men had been killed and the trial would be in the hands of white men, possibly prejudiced against the Indian, whose land incidentally was wanted."

Scott obtained the freedom of all but Tse-ne-gat, who was eventually acquitted by a white jury. However, some 160 Indians were permanently driven off their legal property, which dealt a tremendous blow to the goal of Indian adaptation the government professed to want. As a chronicler of the "uprising" asked, "For what Indian, on the Ute or any other reservation, would risk filing on a nonreservation homestead on the public domain, would invest his time and labor building a home, fences and irrigation ditches, when he faced the possibility of being run off his land by whites whose only authority was a Winchester?"

Unfortunately, reservation Indians often faced the same dilemma. The central economic question for them—how to make a living upon the land remaining—was often accompanied by an equally pressing one—how to keep whites from appropriating whatever resources were left.

Predictably, the United States government continued to push farming as the chief economic activity of the reservation. In conjunction with allotment, it had deployed a cadre of "government farmers," men designated to work with and train reservation Indians in Anglo farming practices. There were some 249 of these federal employees in 1913, and the government was trying to upgrade their quality and their role. Agents and superintendents frequently diverted the farmers' services, making each a "man of all work." The farmers received scant pay and often proved to be poorly prepared to advise natives on agricultural practices, even when given the opportunity to do their designated job. Some depended on payoffs from traders in exchange for orders of seed and equipment. The government tried to eliminate these problems, but with little success.

Government officials also instituted agricultural fairs on the reservations, and during the good harvest years, these were fine, satisfying events for many hardworking Indian farm families. Paul Robertson, a Santee Sioux born in 1904, would recall his childhood and youth on the Santee Sioux reservation in Nebraska as a time when "those early Indian farmers really did well," despite lack of education and ignorance of the English language. Like their white neighbors, they staged elaborate fairs, displaying "potatoes, corn, beans, squash, and watermelon," examples of the women's sewing and quilting, and a variety of prize farm animals—"poultry, swine, cattle, turkeys, ducks."

Such abundance could seldom be sustained. The government's own reclamation work with white farmers in the West had shown that "they needed a minimum capital of $2,000 and two years of farming experience" to have much chance of success. The Indians were almost invariably operating without enough cultivated land or capital to gain a firm base of self-sufficiency. They had been pushed off the better farming lands, even on the reservation, as the government continued to be ineffective in removing squatters. Indians didn't have the funds or the technological or financial know-how to create the working capital that would lead to self-sufficiency through "financing additional purchases of land, equipment, seed, and livestock." They lacked tools and machines, the northern Cheyennes losing much of their 1912 grain crop when threshing machines did not arrive as promised.

Further, the environment "often posed an insurmountable obstacle for Indian and white farmers alike as crops perished under the blazing sun." Plains Indians who harvested respectable crops during World War I found themselves floundering in postwar drought, exacerbated by an accompanying postwar depression that drove farm prices down.

Such conditions would be daunting to the most motivated and determined farmer, but many Indians were neither. Members of tribes that had not depended on agriculture, or had depended upon it only minimally, continued to show a marked lack of interest in it, while others continued to believe—with reason—that it was foolish to make farming one's sole, or even primary, livelihood.

Yet the government in 1923 responded to increased farming woes by initiating "Five Year Programs" of agricultural development on fifty-five of the reservations, and Indians set to work planting according to government guidelines. On one Sioux reservation, farmers dutifully sowed "one acre of potatoes, one acre of garden, and ten acres of corn." Some Indian farmers produced good crops under the Five Year Programs, and many kept trying. However, agricultural conditions, never consistently good since the era of dispossession, became "worse . . . than ever before by the mid 1920s," and there were soon reports of Indians on western reservations subsisting primarily on horsemeat and prairie gophers.

Not surprisingly, part of the problem in the arid West remained the demand for water. Here, too, the government had proceeded with its own plans to develop and aid Indian farmers, continuing to mount ambitious irrigation projects without consulting the Indians who would be affected.

By the midteens, irrigation ditches extended through about 600,000 acres of Indian country, primarily the reservations of the Southwest, the Rocky Mountains, and the Pacific Northwest. These ditches were extremely costly to the Indians, since their tribal funds were appropriated by the U.S. government to create them. By 1914, $7 million of the $9 million that had been expended on irrigation in Indian country had come from tribal accounts. Furthermore, despite the Winters Doctrine, the conduits remained more likely to provide a boost to white farmers than Indian ones; non-Indians living on or around the reservations were irrigating five acres for every acre irrigated by an Indian from these ditches.

In light of these facts, the secretary of the Board of Indian Commissioners, Frederick Abbott, recommended that the government "give the Indians a voice in the matter" of irrigation. This was too radical an idea for officials, who instead sought to create greater parity by charging Indian tribes for both completed and pending projects based on ability to pay—again, despite the fact that Indians had not asked for these projects.

This step was followed in 1920 by an act stipulating that "all owners of irrigable land, Indian or white" would be responsible for partially reimbursing the government from "personal funds." By this point, whites were cultivating nine out of every ten acres ostensibly made irrigable for the Indians. The natives cultivating the other 10 percent were highly resistant to any charges, the Walker River reservation agent estimating that three fourths or more of the Indians affected there would "stop making improvements . . . and abandon their homes" rather than attempt to pay charges on land they had only recently laboriously cleared in hopes of obtaining a subsistence.

Indians came to look upon the irrigation projects as yet another means of taking the land from them, for the government would charge for irrigation "until [the charges] exceeded the value of the land" and would place a lien on the acreage, "requir[ing] that payment be satisfied when the land was sold." The projects remained ill-suited for Indian users accustomed to dry farming, anyway. As a "high-technology, resource-intensive form of agriculture," the projects better suited the whites, who wound up using them the most.

Whites did this in two ways—first, by taking occupation (either through purchase of fee-patent and "surplus" land or through squatting) and second, by leasing. Leasing—both of individual allotments and of reservation lands still held in common—swelled into the biggest obstacle yet to a viable economic land base for the Native American population.

Why, in light of the various leasing abuses—low rents, unpaid rents, leasing without the owner's approval, terms unmet—did the practice continue and even grow? Resistance flared among both Indians and government officials, but for many of the former, it still seemed the only way to realize anything from their land, and for many officials—particularly those in the Wilson administration—it seemed the best way to make the land productive and to hasten Indian acculturation. Officials justified the connection of leasing and acculturation with arguments that Indians would benefit from the income, especially if they held other property and could use the funds to develop it. At the least, they would learn from the lessees how to run a successful operation, and would benefit from the improvements left when the lease expired.

Of course, this was a very flawed fantasy. In actuality, leasing simply gave whites—increasingly, speculators and corporations—access to Indian land. As early as 1912, eight out of every nine acres of trust lands on the Cheyenne-Arapaho reservation were leased to non-Indians, and abuses only intensified in the second decade of the century.

First, Indians often had trouble even getting their hands on any of the rental money. Leasing became a fact of life on the Pyramid Lake reservation in 1911, and the grazing lease fees were set very low. Still, white cattlemen simply turned their herds loose on the Paiute range without paying, even after repeated warnings. On the Osage reservation, lessees grazed their cattle free of charge for months; taken to court, they delayed, then simply conceded that "the grazing contracts had been forfeited owing to nonpayment" and "drove their well-nourished herds off the Osage pasturage." To add insult to injury, the departing cattlemen often added Indian stock to their own.

Even when the lessees paid, the Indians did not necessarily receive the money. The Paiutes had been given vague assurances that leasing payments from their communal lands would come directly to those who needed it most, but instead, the Bureau cited a regulation directing that "any profit from reservation enterprises had to be used first to meet the administrative costs of operating the reserve," and they used the precious funds "to pay white agency employees."

Property improvements also failed to materialize. Of course, Indian landowners may or may not have been interested in the improvements that the Bureau was trying to encourage the lessees to provide, but the latter ignored their contractual obligations anyway, even removing buildings when the leases expired.

The Interior Department did try again to build in some safeguards—such as a 1916 stipulation that farming and grazing leases be limited to three years. But the U.S. entry into World War I made the government eager to use Indian lands in ways that would support the war effort. For one thing, it simply appropriated parts of reservations. On the Nisqually reservation in Washington State, 3,300 acres—"more than 70 percent" of the Nisquallies' land base—were seized "for use by the Army's Fort Lewis." (The Indians later received compensation of almost $170,000, and at least received trust status for some of the nearby land they managed to buy.)

The government also put pressure on the Indians either to use the land effectively by white standards—for farmers, this meant producing large harvests—or to allow non-Indians to take over. At the same time, the limited support personnel the government had provided— irrigation workers, government farmers, home extension agents—were being pulled away in a wartime reallocation of resources. The "Great Plow-up" of reservation lands as part of the war effort was accomplished largely by lessees who had gained "greater access to reservation lands" because of wartime needs or projected needs.

This left the Indians out of the picture, often not even able to collect on the leases. At Pine Ridge, payments were held up for one or two years, residents charging that some of their number died of starvation before the funds arrived.

Wartime grazing leases also wreaked havoc in Indian country. For one thing, the lessees' cattle wandered at will, damaging the crops of those Indians who were still trying to farm their own lands, or at least to grow food for their families. "It is pretty hard for us on the reservation," reported Pine Ridge resident James Red Cloud. "The reservation is covered with cattle like a whole lot of worms on it. I cannot raise a garden and cannot do anything." Yet when Indians attempted to drive the cattle off, local officials arrested them.

An even bigger problem was caused by the way in which cattle prices and leasing affected Indian ranching during the years of the First World War. Ranching had been the most natural economic enterprise for many western tribes, a promising "strategy to confront changing times" that still allowed them some self-definition, and there had been some ranching successes, such as that of the Pine Ridge Sioux. Further, the government had encouraged some of these efforts by providing tribal herds, the idea being that the money would be recouped and the communal herd broken up, after individual stock raisers had built their own herds from the breeding stock made available.

The government put a lot of money into these efforts even as it undercut any advances by actively encouraging Indians—especially the northern Plains ranchers—to sell their cattle when prices were high and to lease their lands to the non-Indian cattlemen. This process started before the United States' entry into the war, as white cattlemen began moving onto the Sioux range with leasing agreements, but it accelerated with the government's move to wartime footing. Again, white officials were primarily concerned with how much the land could produce, and Indians could not be expected to engage successfully in the kind of extensive commercial ranching favored by whites.

Indians who had been developing herds sold their cattle, even the breeding stock, and they turned the land over to the cattlemen for leasing money. One historian has called this "the greatest disaster that had befallen the Pine Ridge Indians since the vanishing of the buffalo," for the Indian ranching economy was decimated. The short-sightedness of the trade became all too apparent after the war when general economic conditions deteriorated. White cattlemen begged for relief from lease payments, and the Bureau of Indian Affairs acquiesced. Many Indians were now left without use of their land and without income from it.

To make matters worse, the BIA was administering the lands with less and less pretense of consulting the Indians themselves. Sometimes Indians forced the issue. In 1918, Crow leaders bowed to the inevitability of leasing, but successfully set terms on the length of leases and the method of payment. In 1919, the Pimas, with the help of the Indian Rights Association, fought a "done deal" by Commissioner Sells: the leasing of five thousand acres of their Gila River reservation to Phoenix businessman W. R. Elliot for a ten-year period in exchange for various improvements, including installation of wells and electricity. The Pimas successfully argued that Elliot would be getting use of the land at a fraction of its value, and that "if the government gave the Indians the water it had promised . . . they could farm the land themselves."

The Pimas had a clear view of the nature of leasing, judging that it destroyed an Indian's sense of ownership, "his sense of appreciation of land value," and "his responsibility as a homemaker and producer." However, the liberal World War I leasing practices bred major troubles. The Crows, who earlier had agreed to leasing only with the greatest reluctance, in 1918 found that a corporation was simply taking over whole sections of the reservation, ripping down fences and plowing up unleased lands as well. When the Crows complained to their superintendent, he responded, "As long as it has been plowed, you better sign a lease."

The abuses on the Crow reservation resulted in a congressional investigation in 1919. It was found that the superintendent had leased land without the Indian owners' consent, and had also appropriated for leasing the lands of allottees when they died. Further, the corporation was subletting some of the Crow land—for, of course, a handsome profit.

Despite the investigation, abuses continued to spiral, superintendents intimidating Indians into leasing land the Indians wanted to work themselves, or renewing leases without the owners' consent and keeping them in the dark as to terms and payments. Such practices were helped along by a 1923 government directive that superintendents could "sign leases for allottees who were 'clearly incapable of acting for their best interests by refusing to lease their lands.' "

Whether an Indian owner had a say in the leasing of his or her lands or not, rentals remained hard to collect. In 1921, more than seven of every ten acres on the Yuma reservation were leased, but payments arrived erratically or not at all, and "Indians who complained to the superintendent rarely received their money." Tribes tried to cancel leases for which they were receiving no money, but the BIA overrode their attempts. An Oklahoma Indian woman who traced a lessee owing her back rent in the late 1920s was laughed at by agency personnel to whom she appealed for aid in collecting. More conscientious local BIA employees felt powerless to press prominent whites for payment.

The failures of leasing to protect Indian land were only part of a larger disregard for native land rights. For example, "prospectors" were allowed to enter reservations to stake mining claims, and covetous whites used this invitation to snatch up some of the more desirable locations for other uses. In 1919, Congress further legitimized this practice in a bill authorizing the interior secretary "to grant mineral entry on reservations on the same terms as on the public domain" and to lease Indian mineral lands. In the debates that preceded the bill's passage, "not once . . . had the opponents of the bill questioned the basic assumption that the federal government had complete authority over Indian land."

On the Crow reservation, this meant that Superintendent Calvin Asbury handled oil leases, and the tribe knew he was not handling them to their advantage. They "had been offered more favorable leases than those arranged by Asbury," who appeared to depend upon graft and intimidation of any Indian questioners or critics. The tribal council "unanimously passed a resolution requesting [his] removal . . . and the cancellation of all oil leases made without the owner's consent," judging that "if Asbury was not a crook, 'then he is so incompetent as to appear one.' "

The climate continued hostile for Indian mineral rights with the appointment of Franklin Lane's replacement as interior secretary, Albert Fall. When oil was found on Navajo reservation land in 1922, Fall "ruled that it belonged to the government"—indeed, he maintained that all "executive order" reservations were government land, their resources to be administered by a division of the Department of the Interior, with the Indians to be allowed only a share (in the case of the Navajos, a third) of any royalties. The Navajos protested, and were upheld by a 1924 attorney general's decision and by Congress, in the form of the 1927 Indian Oil Leasing Bill. This legislation affirmed Indian title to executive order lands "and their rights to the proceeds of mineral leases."

The Osages could have testified, however, that such assurances did not remove all problems from oil and gas leasing. This tribe on its oil-rich Oklahoma land had been receiving lease money for many years and were the envy of Indian and non-Indian alike, as all families "shared equally rather than a lucky few whose allotments happened to coincide with the locations where producing wells were drilled, as was the case elsewhere in Oklahoma." Further, the Osage fields just kept producing after others had declined.

But the oil income—a total of about $20 million a year in the early 1920s—had further marked the Osages as targets of aggression and fraud. Osage women were married for their mineral rights, then killed by their erstwhile husbands or their accomplices. Liquor traders flooded the reservation during Prohibition, no matter what Indian leaders and BIA officials did to stop them, and alcoholism "became the biggest health problem among the Osages," who "all too often turned to alcohol for short-range and long-range surcease from the puzzlements and confusions of life intensified by the oil boom." The towns surrounding the reservation fed off it, storekeepers marking up their goods, lawyers grabbing Osage legal business even when this business could and should have been conducted by the local BIA agency, bankers eagerly lending money in order to charge astronomical interest.

Guardianship rackets multiplied as well until Congress in 1925 "gave the Osage Agency joint supervision with the county court in the appointment and the expenditures of guardians." This step went a long way toward countering graft, but the Osages themselves still had little control over their lives. Because they were able to pay most of their agency expenses, they "had always felt the government was being paid to watch over them," but this arrangement nonetheless fostered dependency. For its part, the government gradually improved in its trust responsibility toward the Osages and their holdings, but its performance in their behalf was uneven at best.

Most tribes could only wish for the economic base that provided the Osages a regular cash income, whatever the vicissitudes that came with it. BIA positions on the reservation continued to be filled by whites, as did jobs in nearby towns. The best most Indians could hope for was a low-level job at the trader's store, or perhaps a stint with the agency. Fools Crow, a Sioux, would recall, "In the winter of 1916 the agency people offered me a job as a lineman. I was to service the line . . . from the main agency office to the farm agent's branch offices. . . . I received no money for the job, just rations, and worked at it for about eighteen months."

Some tribes that had always depended heavily on fishing for subsistence had continued to do so, but this livelihood was seriously challenged by the 1920s, for white officials "continued to ignore the value" of Indian fishery operations.

In 1913, the Paiutes of Pyramid Lake had petitioned the BIA to stop "the white people com[ing] down from City of Wadsworth and Fallon, Nev. + some other place[s] and haunt [sic] and fishing on the reservation," but still they came. In 1915, young Paiute men had removed white-owned boats from the lake, shoving them into the sagebrush. The agent had sent the protesters home; the sheriff then came out and fished with one of the boat owners.

Six years later, the Paiutes again tried to save their fishing industry by mounting a delegation to visit lawmakers. But their superintendent ordered them home and instructed his agent, "You must discourage 'meetings' of Indians that take them away from their work and do nothing but excite them. . . . The 'talk habit' must be stopped wherever possible."

The BIA soon instituted a Pyramid Lake day-use fee that non-Indian fishermen were supposed to pay. Not only did this give legitimacy to "the omnipresent trespass," but it also "was continuously avoided by whites who believed that they had a just right to fish anywhere they pleased." Even had the lone tribal policeman been able to patrol the various roads leading to the lake and its circumference, he had no power over non-Indians to make them comply.

By the late 1920s, state laws and the continuing encroachments of white fishermen had "gutted their fishing enterprise," and Paiutes reluctantly left the reservation for uncertain lives outside or transferred their efforts to farming on the marginal reservation land not appropriated by whites. At about the same time, the Quinault tribe of the Pacific Northwest lost their traditional fishing site, Peacock Split on the Columbia River, when Washington State leased the fishing rights to a fishing company for a $36,000 yearly fee.

Timber, too, provided a potential source of income, although great swaths of old-growth forest had already been destroyed by interlopers. By the 1920s, the home region of the Sinkyone Indians of coastal northern California was "all but denuded of living adult tan oaks." The Sinkyones had for generations carefully harvested the tan oaks, burning under them to promote their health, but non-Indians had removed the trees' bark to use in tanning leather and "left the husked trees to rot." In Sinkyone legend, the creator Nagaicho mourned, "It looks just like my people lying around, lying around with all their skin cut off."

A conservation ethic was at work in the U.S. government under Teddy Roosevelt's administration, but it clashed with the principle of Indian rights when Roosevelt attempted unilaterally to appropriate fifteen million acres of trees on executive order reservations in order to add them to the national forests.

Roosevelt's sweeping mandate was overturned in the courts. Meanwhile, the Bureau of Indian Affairs began trying to build in some safeguards and incentives for Indians who had had to watch helplessly as interlopers ravaged their trees. The Omnibus Act of 1910 provided some much-needed guidelines, "for the first time [giving] Indians title to live timber" and also "permit[ting] the sale of timber on trust allotments with the receipts credited to the allottees."

Despite such small strides, Indians, unable to depend either on traditional forms of subsistence or wages from reservation work, remained increasingly compelled to leave the reservations in search of employment. This phenomenon was already becoming apparent during and after World War I as some of the BIA services that had been started for Indians were scaled back or abandoned.

One long-term economic success story in Indian country was that of native ranchers of the Southwest. With strong stock-raising abilities and agents who did not push leasing upon them, the San Carlos Apaches, the Papagos, and the Navajos all gradually developed their herds, bearing out historian Peter Iverson's judgment that ranching offered "the best chance" for many native communities to develop their own economic base. When whites pressing on the reservation boundaries tried to undermine these efforts, such men as Superintendent James Kitch, at San Carlos in the 1920s, fought to preserve and extend the native ranching base. BIA employee H. W. Shipe told a congressional committee, "[I]t is [the Indians'] property and we want them to develop their property to their own best advantage." If some did not manage their property as well as others, well, that was "just as is the case with the white men."

The Navajos in particular continued to be both excellent farmers and stock raisers. They endured years of drought and harsh winter, but they usually managed to rebound, and even to prosper by Indian standards, abundantly meeting their own needs for such staples as wool, mutton, corn, and squash, and engaging in limited trading.

Meanwhile, Anglo and Mexican stockmen moved closer and closer to the perimeters of the reservation, taking up lands on which Navajo cattle grazed and challenging the public-domain allotments some Navajos had taken. The Navajo superintendent in 1922 complained regarding these off-reservation allotments under siege: "Is it right to let the white men have this country just because they are asking for it and trying in every way to get it, regardless of what the Indians might say?"

At the same time, the long-term southwestern erosion problem was becoming more apparent—"gullies carried away prime farmland and lowered the water table so that farming the remaining land was impossible." By the 1920s, the Navajos clearly needed to depend more heavily on their livestock, but other cattlemen were "successfully restricting Navajo access to traditional off-reservation ranges," cutting off "the older Navajo response to rising population—dispersion into new areas."

The Navajos adapted as best they could. Horses required more forage than sheep, so they reduced the number of horses they owned. They also "improved their shearing methods," thereby "increas[ing] the wool yield of their flocks." The government tried to help with stock improvement and water projects, but it increasingly pointed a finger at the Navajos themselves, citing overgrazing alone as the source of their problems, and thereby downplaying white incursions and the effects of drought. In 1928, the BIA introduced a plan for a grazing tax to be paid by the Navajos and to be used for "stockwater development." This would be the beginning of the end of Navajo economic autonomy.

Meanwhile, the Papagos had won a significant victory. Like their neighbors the Navajos, by 1915 the Papagos were being squeezed by non-Indian cattlemen. Unlike the Navajos, they lived overwhelmingly on lands that the federal government had designated as public domain, with no reservation line to stop encroachers—or, at least, to give them pause. The Papago Indian League successfully lobbied President Wilson for new executive order tracts, which were then created in both 1916 and 1917 on the land they already occupied.

White westerners reacted so severely, however, that Congress "blocked the creation of any more executive order reservations." The trend was away from allowing Indians to own any part of public-domain lands. At the same time, too many whites regarded reservations as essentially the same as public-domain lands: the government's to do with as it saw fit, and white Americans' to possibly claim for their own.

In the face of such challenges, Indians continued to seek compensation for lands lost, the return of these lands, or validation and security for the lands on which they now resided. The 1910s and 1920s were marked by a number of other land-rights struggles in addition to the Papagos'. The Sioux continued to argue their claim to the Black Hills. Nine hundred heirs of Texas Cherokees tried to bring a $100-million lawsuit against the state of Texas for lands lost in the nineteenth century, but the U.S. Supreme Court would not allow them to sue. By contrast, the Arapahos were allowed in 1927 to petition the Court of Claims for their lost territory and won a judgment of more than $6 million, "the appraised value of half of their land."

While the Arapahos could celebrate at least a monetary victory, Indians—and their defenders in and out of government service—repeatedly found themselves undercut, yanked this way and that, by the very government agencies that were supposed to provide aid, protection, and counsel.

In New Mexico, the Taos Pueblos' land battle is a case in point. The Pueblo Indians of the Southwest had survived for decades without even the modest protection and aid of the federal government, thanks to an 1876 Supreme Court ruling that identified them as independent landholders neither bound nor protected by the federal restrictions relating to tribal lands. Trespassers had flooded Pueblo holdings, almost precipitating an uprising in 1910. Taos Pueblo leaders had seen the government seize much of their land, including their sacred site of Blue Lake, to create a national forest, and some twelve thousand non-Indians claim pieces of the rest. Again and again the Pueblos asked for an executive order reservation with Blue Lake as its heart.

The Supreme Court in 1913 reversed the 1876 ruling that had denied the Pueblos a tribal basis for hanging on to their territory. The court now concluded that "the Pueblos had the same legal status as other Indians, that they could not alienate their lands without the approval of the federal government, and that they were entitled to reclaim lands that had passed out of their hands, legally or illegally."

The Interior Department itself tried to circumvent the ruling with the "Bursum Bill," a Senate proposal validating non-Indian claims to at least sixty thousand acres of Pueblo land. But the Indians mobilized. Aided by a host of reformers—chief among them John Collier—they lobbied in Washington and won an alternate measure, the Pueblo Lands Act, which created a Pueblo Lands Board "to review the value of each claim and compensate either the Indians or the non-Indians for the lands they gave up.''

The board did its job in settling up claims and restoring sections of Pueblo land, but it served the Taos Pueblo poorly in regard to Blue Lake. Tribal members proposed to waive a land-settlement payment of almost $300,000 from the town of Taos if they could regain the Blue Lake region. The board acquiesced without any authority to return Blue Lake, and "the Indians were out both their money and the lake."

The Taos Pueblo continued to fight for the sacred area's return, but in the late 1920s long-term dispossession had left its mark on every remaining corner of Indian country. The Indian land base had become so reduced, fractionated, and "checkerboarded"—and in various cases so eroded, overgrazed, and devoid of water and resources—that even a subsistence living on it seemed a distant dream.

The situation was compounded, of course, by economic depression, its effects being felt on reservations and in other segments of American society well before the stock market crash of 1929. In the 1920s, Indians could simply not expect to gain much from sales of remaining lands or from leasing of farm and cattle lands. Nor could they command the resources to make a living off the land or improve their situation through steady outside employment.

In 1928, "over half the nation's Indian population had per capita incomes of less than $200 annually"—about 30 percent of the average American's per-capita income at the time—"and only 2 percent made more than $500 a year." With the Great Depression soon to make itself felt throughout America, those numbers were unlikely to rise. But major changes lay ahead for the residents of Indian country.

Chapter Eleven

←——————→

"Who's Got the Button?"
(1930–1950s)

It has been a matter of something like the game of "Button,
button, who's got the button?" They give us an opportunity and
we begin to advance; then they take it away and give us something
else, depending on who happens to be in Washington. . . .
                                              —*Johnson Holy Rock, Sioux*

With the advent of the Great Depression, Indian communities—like
other depressed rural communities—did not have as far to fall as did
other segments of society. As one reservation resident told his BIA
superintendent, "We're all on the same level now. The white man is
in the same shape we are."

The early Depression years nonetheless further eroded Indian livelihoods as already limited resources, jobs, and leasing opportunities
dried up. The "dust bowl" in Oklahoma affected Indian farmers as
well as white; the blizzards and bone-cold of 1931–1932 in the Southwest wiped out Navajo livestock, the people collecting wool from the
corpses of their sheep in an attempt to have something to trade.

Congress did appropriate money for Indian relief and increased the
BIA's funding, although most of the latter went into the salaries of
BIA workers. Early Depression relief efforts were simply not far-
sighted enough, or were not directed where the need was greatest.
Indians had naturally come to depend upon "Uncle Sam" in many
ways, and now asked if "Uncle Sam had gone broke."

The degree of need felt by Indian Americans and the frustration in
meeting it is demonstrated by the experience of the Paiutes at Pyramid
Lake early in the Depression. With even their low ration payments in
danger of being cut off, they enlisted the aid of the local press and of
concerned whites, but with achingly meager results.

One neighbor of the Paiutes in particular, a mining engineer named John Reid, undertook to aid them by writing to government officials. The senior Nevada senator, Tasker Oddie, responded by taking up the case of an elderly Paiute, Gilbert Natches, who supported a blind mother and disabled nephew. Under pressure, the BIA allowed Natches $10 a month in supplies. When Reid forcefully argued how inadequate this was, the Bureau increased the amount to $20 worth of "government subsidized farm produce" per month. But the government did nothing for other Paiutes in the same situation. It had taken "the mobilization of senatorial influence" and Reid's continuing efforts to secure severely limited assistance for only one family.

As the struggle for survival intensified in Indian country, allotment continued to splinter the land base. A 1931 congressional act tried to build upon the 1927 act allowing cancellation of the fee patents issued to Indians without their acquiescence. Both measures led, however, to the rescinding of only about one in twenty of the forced patents that had brought taxation woes and intensified pressures to relinquish allotment tracts.

At least patenting had slowed down. Yet by 1934, the United States government "had allotted 118 out of 213 reservations and brought over three-fourths of the Indians under the provisions of the [act]." Between sales of surplus lands and of allotments, Indian country had diminished considerably—from 138 million acres in 1887 to an estimated 52 million in 1934. In the Five Tribes area of Oklahoma alone, holdings had shrunk from nearly twenty million acres to one and a half million. As historian Janet McDonnell reports, "two-thirds of [America's] Indians were either completely landless or did not own enough land to make a subsistence living."

Many of the old ways had disappeared along with the land, and many Indians had given in to despair. Some tribes saw a significant rise in alcoholism—and a corresponding unraveling of tribal social organization—as the rural depression of the 1920s mushroomed into the pervasive national depression of the 1930s.

Indians nonetheless maintained connections with territory lost and held, and with their own essential tribal identities, still growing and evolving in relation to their circumstances. Assimilation had failed. It had failed so consistently and spectacularly that the United States government finally began to reverse its policies regarding Native Americans. The reversal would offer hope of cultural survival on a renewed land base—but only on the government's terms, and for a brief time.

Sentiment for drastic changes in Indian policy had burgeoned among Anglo reformers through the 1920s and early 1930s, fed by a new acknowledgment of and appreciation for cultural pluralism. Increasingly, the reformers "demanded a more enlightened policy under which the Indian Service would keep the reservations intact, preserve Indian culture, and give Indians the same rights as other citizens." Before Franklin Delano Roosevelt took office in 1933, hundreds of civic leaders petitioned him to implement such changes.

Roosevelt acted by appointing Pueblo land-fight veteran John Collier as commissioner of Indian Affairs. With his background in anthropological training and fieldwork among the Pueblos, Collier had remained a particularly outspoken and effective critic of allotment, enough of a visionary to conceive of radical reform before many of his fellows did. He wanted the BIA truly to protect Indian interests. Further, he found great value in Indian cultures, seeing in them a community health and land-based vitality that offered a necessary counterpoint and example to modern western industrial society.

Collier succinctly summarized his main objectives as commissioner: "Economic rehabilitation of the Indians, principally on the land. Organization of the Indian tribes for managing their own affairs. Civil and cultural freedom and opportunity for the Indians."

Collier's "Indian New Deal" became embodied in the Wheeler-Howard Act of 1934, also known as the Indian Reorganization Act. The IRA completely rejected previous policies in favor of three basic initiatives, each intimately tied to the other. First, it provided for the Indians' holding on to and regaining their land base by banning further allotment, extending the trust period for restricted allotments, allowing for the return of "surplus" lands, authorizing $2 million in funding for land acquisition, and beginning consolidation programs to regain a communal land base.

Second, the act set up a blueprint for new Indian tribal governments with constitutions and extended powers, among them a limited power to hire their own legal counsel, authority "to negotiate with federal, state, and local governments," and ability to halt "the sale, lease, or encumbrance of tribal lands and other assets without tribal consent."

The tribal governments would include "special Indian courts, using traditional law, to exercise original jurisdiction on reservations."

Third, the IRA sought to support the creation of a healthy Indian economy by establishing a means by which Indian business corporations could form and by providing a revolving loan fund of $10 million for their use.

Implicit in all of these measures was the idea that Indian cultures would again be able to flourish in ways that combined traditional and progressive worldviews and lifeways.

The bill did not pass without a storm of opposition and various amendments. The consolidation program would allow the secretary of the interior to require Indians to sell or swap individual landholdings in order to re-create Indian land bases. Congressional members saw this as "a violation of personal property rights."

Indians, too, were uneasy about this aspect of the proposed bill. Those who had retained individual holdings and made improvements upon them resented the idea that "the lands were going to be taken away from them and put into common ownership." Despite the communal nature of much Indian life, many of the tribes had roots in smaller units—independent or semi-independent villages—and communal identity as a tribe had brought them little or no power on the reservations, where the government and its agents reigned. In resisting government-directed communal ownership, most Indians were trying to adhere to their survival traditions rather than "reacting selfishly."

In the final bill, the controversial land-consolidation program had become an option, and the Indian court system had been scrapped, with the administration of justice to be addressed in tribal constitutions. The bill still offered an acknowledgment of tribalism and a degree of self-government that would have been unthinkable only a decade before. For the first time since their subordination, Indians were being encouraged to enter *"as groups"* into the political life of the nation, to become genuine participants "in the decision-making process."

Now it was up to the residents of the reservations—still the bulk of the Indian population—to decide in special elections within a year whether to come under the IRA provisions or not. Considering the history of Indian-white relations in the United States, it is understandable that a deep suspicion pervaded Indian country in regard to the bill, despite the good intentions of Collier and his supporters. Resistant Indians told their friends, "This is the action of the white man, that he's going to close on you. This is a law, a legal way to bleed you to death and bring you to an end."

Even if an Indian could get past such generalized fears, at bottom there was no denying that the secretary of the interior retained the ultimate power over Indian affairs in the final version of the bill as well as in the original, whatever the new Indian governments and corporations might decide. "I think many of them looked at this as another way for government to take over more control," Brule Sioux Alfred DuBray would muse. Or, as another Brule, Ramon Roubideaux, would cogently put it, "It's not self-government, because self-government by permission is no self-government at all."

Anglo religious leaders resisted the bill as well, but for a different reason: they opposed Commissioner Collier's acknowledgment of the value of traditional cultures. "The Bureau in conjunction with these various denominations [had] set up regulations," Brule Sioux Antoine Roubideaux would recall. "Like stopping Indians from growing long hair, stopping the Sun Dance or other ceremonial dances, and . . . making sweat baths their own way." Superintendents strictly controlled where and when Indians could hold dances. Then "Mr. Collier came along and said, 'No, you're denying the freedom of worship. Let the Indians exercise these traditions, cultural, any ceremony he wants like he used to. Leave him go.' "

While these were welcome, even undreamed-of words for many Indians, among the tribes there were people who felt that Collier was trying to wipe out acculturation gains—to send them "back to the blanket." Clarence Foreman of the Yankton Sioux would later insist that the IRA wasn't needed, that his tribe was making good progress as farmers and citizens of an already established tribal government.

The whole governance issue was a sore one for many Indians. Not only did federal control continue, but also the governments the Indians were being asked to set up differed so completely in most cases from those to which they gravitated. Most Indians had continued to value the slow, deliberative, inclusive, and flexible nature of their old governance structures, in which individuals were chosen for specific leadership roles on the basis of generosity, courage, appropriate skills, ceremonial knowledge, and other traditional values. Even though traditional Indian leadership had long been effectively undermined by white dominance, Indians still valued the old forms; as Sioux Ben Reifel, an IRA promoter, would note, "They didn't have much, if any, power at all, but they did have an opportunity to express their views and to give vent to some of their feelings. I think they saw themselves losing this, what little influence it had—at least their participation in the Indian system."

Collier worked hard to overcome such objections, targeting some of the major tribes in hopes of winning approval from others as well. He and his representatives—including acculturated Indian leaders such as Reifel—traveled around the reservations explaining and arguing and cajoling. "Nobody really understood it too well," Sioux Alfred DuBray would recall, and people interpreted what was said to them in different ways, often not really grasping the extent of Collier's program "for probably several years ... until they got into the change."

Ultimately, 181 tribes—with a total membership of almost 130,000—voted to accept the legislation, including many in the Great Lakes and northern Plains regions. Seventy-seven tribes—with a total membership of more than 86,000—voted to reject the plan, prominent among them the residents of the Klamath, Crow, Sisseton, Turtle Mountain, and Fort Peck reservations.*

Collier could count the influential Sioux among the affirmatives, but in the most bitter blow for him, the largest tribe—the Navajos—voted against the plan. This defeat was tied to other events in Navajo country—most directly, to the fate of Navajo goats.

When John Collier took office in 1933, the government had become determined to force the Navajos to reduce their livestock. Erosion now threatened not only southwestern farming and ranching, but also the Boulder Dam project then being mounted, for engineers anticipated problems with silt from the rivers that ran through the Navajo reservation. From the beginning of his term, Collier found himself doing

---

*Figures vary somewhat. These are from Terry L. Anderson, *Sovereign Nations or Reservations? An Economic History of American Indians,* pp. 143–144.

the very thing he had deplored: trying to coerce Indians into accepting a foreordained government decision, in this case by giving up the stock which represented much of their livelihood.

He met fierce resistance. "This is the second day at the meeting which is supposed to be our meeting," Navajo Jim Shirley announced at an extended 1933 conference. "It seems that the officials are talking most of the time in discussing the way this work should be done. We know something about that by nature because we were born here and raised here and we knew about the processes of nature on our range."

Gradually, however, the tribal council was pressed into approving a sheep reduction program in which government officials would pay the Indians for their "surplus," then remove or kill the animals. The program was poorly executed, exacerbating ill feeling, but what followed was even worse. In late 1934, government officials came for the Navajos' goats.

To the Navajos, the targeting of goats showed an abysmal lack of understanding—these animals "were hardier than sheep," more likely to survive a harsh winter, and "critical especially for owners of small herds since they could eat their goats and save their sheep." Yet people were systematically intimidated into selling, and most of the goats were slaughtered, some 3,500 carcasses piled in one canyon. This government action "deeply shocked the Navajos," with "only the Long Walk equal[ing] its emotional impact." Immediately, the poor got poorer, having to rely on sheep for food instead of wool.

The goat slaughter occurred in late 1934; the Navajos voted against the IRA in June 1935. Other factors were reflected in the negative vote—for example, the opposition of relatively well-off, acculturated Navajos—but livestock reduction would remain the bitterest point of contention in Navajo relations with the government.

Meanwhile, Collier's reforms drew an uneven response from other tribes as they debated each stage of the reforms. "The law was accepted at Pine Ridge, but they didn't take the corporate charter," Reifel would remember in reviewing the Sioux reservations. "I guess at Rosebud they took all three.... Lower Brule accepted all three. Crow Creek didn't accept anything.... Cheyenne River accepted all three, as I recall." In all, ninety-five reservations adopted constitutions, most of these also taking the third step: corporate charters.

The IRA and its options had a number of effects—good and bad, short-term and long-term—on the tribes that accepted it, and even on those that did not, for Collier tried to extend some of the reforms to them anyway. The legislation did validate and support Indian identity, community, and cultural values. The western Sioux, for example, had never really lost their strong tribalism, but through the IRA "it began to take on new institutional expression" through "the establishing of the tribal councils, the restoration of rituals such as the Sun Dance, and in general, a much more favorable attitude toward Indian nativism."

The IRA also gave tribes some legal voice in protecting their lands. The Paiutes of Pyramid Lake, for example, used their right to hire lawyers, the federal government's new commitment to the self-governance of the tribal council, and the aid of Indian rights groups to stave off Senator Pat McCarran's "numerous attempts to give their lands to white squatters."

Further, the IRA enabled both the government and Indians themselves to extend their land base—not as fully as either the Indians or Collier might wish, but significantly nonetheless. Congress appropriated funds that added 400,000 acres to Indian country, while more than twice that was added by special legislation. The government turned over to Indian populations public-domain grazing lands and some of the "surplus" lands it had earlier taken. Tribes "using their own funds" bought about 390,000 acres. The Sioux at the Rosebud reservation set up a Tribal Land Enterprise, and heirs could sell their interests to the tribe. The program continued, leading one Sioux later to note proudly, "Of course, every time we buy land, it becomes tribal land. So we're building up again what we lost."

Benefiting from a new BIA adherence to "bring[ing] the entire reservation into use by Indians," tribes also used the IRA to mount initiatives that would increase their abilities to subsist and thrive on their land bases. With help from the government's revolving credit fund, they finally could obtain enough capital to get started in an enterprise without enduring ruinous interest rates, and they developed individual and communal farming and ranching projects, taking back thousands of acres of formerly leased lands.

In particular, the Apaches at the San Carlos and White Mountain reservations further developed vital stock-raising operations, while

Sioux ranching, decimated during World War I, revived. At Pine Ridge, cattle ownership would jump "by more than seven times" between 1935 and 1945. The northern Cheyennes developed a successful steer enterprise, run largely by a tribal board of directors. In each case, the cattle industry increased opportunities and living standards for tribal members in general.

To aid in these transformations, the government provided a limited number of technical advisers, or extension agents. It also, in the Johnson-O'Malley Act of 1934, "permitted state agencies to extend social services to reservations for the first time," leading to some improvements in health care and other services.

Collier also saw that federal New Deal policies were brought to the reservations in the form of the Indian arm of the Civilian Conservation Corps, the Indian Emergency Conservation Work Program. In this program, Indians worked to improve their own lands. For example, Navajos worked on reservation irrigation projects. Although again they experienced the frustration of not being listened to—workers warned correctly that the dams they were constructing across arroyos would wash away in the next flood—the infusion of wage labor, the "most significant" to date on the reservation, was most welcome.

Overall, however, Collier's well-meant and enlightened policies had their limitations. They ignored water and fishing rights, failed to "extend the civil liberties of Indians or to remove oppressive and obsolete legislation," did not attempt to meet treaty obligations, and allowed exploitative leases on oil, gas, and mining to continue.

The IRA itself failed to take into account the very cultural differences it was designed to encourage and preserve. For example, on the Mescalero reservation, Apaches were assigned farms and BIA-built houses that separated them into a grid, "distances between houses and land assignments [breaking] the tradition of shared work and thus reduc[ing] household efficiency."

The IRA also failed to halt the pattern of dispossession. For example, despite their legal gains and hard work in taking advantage of them, the Pyramid Lake Paiutes continued to importune the government unsuccessfully to remove long-term reservation squatters.

With few exceptions, the IRA also failed to improve the Indian economy to the extent Indians had been led to believe would occur. "There were farming loans; we had farming loans," a Mdewakanton

Sioux named Amos Owen would recall. "That was the only benefit we got out of the Wheeler-Howard Act."

The long-term effects of economic depression—and of the Great Depression itself—could not be easily overcome, nor could a debilitating pattern of economic and political dependence born of previous government policies. It is clear from Indian accounts of the 1930s that many families survived through cutting timber, cutting posts, and doing as much traditional work—trapping, hunting, fishing, gathering— as their current environment would support. If the IRA made any difference at all, it was, as Sioux activist and author Vine Deloria, Jr., recalls, simply as a means of moving "from absolute deprivation to mere poverty."

Even then, many Indians felt forced to leave the reservation in search of work, "almost half" of the Kansas reservation Indians journeying to state urban areas and beyond during the Depression in hopes of getting a job. One Winnebago, Noah White, reflected this trend; after completing a yearlong commercial course in Pierre, South Dakota, he reported, "I went back to the reservation for a couple of years. From there on, I just went out to seek jobs wherever I could find employment, and returned to the reservation when I was unemployed."

Despite John Collier's zealous efforts, by the late 1930s, government funding and commitment to Indian programs was waning. Between 1931 and 1941, the average income on the Pine Ridge Sioux reservation actually declined—for a family of five from $152.80 to $120, "one-sixth the figure for the rest of South Dakota and one-third that of Mississippi, the poorest state in the nation."

Although Collier remained in office until 1945, most of the IRA programs were swept away with the advent of World War II. Antoine Roubideaux, recalling a Sioux wheat-growing cooperative, would note, "That was a good program. It was operating smoothly until the war . . . broke out. Then they just jerked the program out."

The war drew even more Indians off the reservation into the military or into support industries. "The war dispersed the reservation people as nothing ever had," Vine Deloria, Jr., would note. "Every day, it seemed, we would be bidding farewell to families as they headed west to work in the defense plants on the Coast." This exodus, and new government appropriation of land for military activities, along with the wartime cutback in overall government services for the reservation, undercut Collier's and the Indian leaders' vision of a viable reservation economic base.

Reservations did survive and even improve economically during the war as wage earners returned or sent money home, and as Indian farmers and ranchers redoubled their efforts, this time protected by stronger policies regarding leasing. Yet the BIA reported in 1945 that "one-third of reservation families had annual incomes of under $500, and nearly all of the remainder earned under $1,000."

Returning military veterans and other wage earners could not find reservation work and left again, moving with increasing adaptability in the Anglo-dominated world and becoming both more acculturated to it and more aware of the distinctiveness of their tribal identities. For many, the reservation was no longer their day-to-day home, but a home base.

Anglo leaders began capitalizing on this shift with calls to end federal trust relations with the tribes—in the popular phrase of the day, to "get the government out of the Indian business." As early as 1943, a Senate committee recommended abandoning IRA policies and dismantling the Bureau of Indian Affairs. Individual and tribal funds were to be divided and paid out; services were to be reduced and transferred to states or to other federal agencies.

Again, Indians would be confronted with a major change not of their making. This time, however, they were becoming more savvy and outspoken in relation to the dominant culture. In 1944, tribal leaders gathered in Denver and created the National Congress of American Indians as a means of safeguarding Indian lands and Indian cultures.

If the IRA had encouraged such a strong and unified voice, it had also—sadly and inadvertently but undeniably—undercut it. Ramon Roubideaux, reflecting in 1968, judged it "possibly one of the best intentioned but unfortunate happenings that could have possibly taken place as far as the Indian people are concerned," for, as Indians had perceived from the beginning, it was "a white man's idea of how they should live—rather a paternalistic type of government."

While some superintendents had tried to maintain an advisory role, others had "used job patronage, credit and budget decisions, and a host of informal pressures to dominate the tribal councils," and even the most sympathetic often yanked the reins of authority on matters they considered of crucial interest. As the distinguished Indian-rights lawyer Felix Cohen would recall, "While every official was in favor of self-government generally, by the same token he was opposed to self-government in the particular field over which he had any jurisdiction."

All of this had contributed to deepening divisions within the reservation populations themselves. Collier, as a product of the anthropological training of his day and as an observer of one of the more cohesive native cultures, had assumed "greater cultural cohesion and more group orientation than often existed" among the Indian population in general. The people had fought over whether to accept the legislation, how to go about setting up constitutional governments and corporate charters, and who would claim the powers the BIA was willing to delegate. Indians with mixed blood had quickly "gained an unfair advantage over full bloods in the new governments because of superior linguistic skills and political manipulations." Those who would most easily accept and adopt Collier's plans were rewarded; they were "the favorite sons of the Bureau of Indian Affairs," Cecil Provost would remember. "It was just a handful. They got everything. They got all the benefits and everything."

What the IRA had done, then, was to affix "unrepresentative minority governments on many reservations." Even though the Collier-inspired Indian governments were nominally democratic, they were by no means representative of the people they ostensibly led and served. This fact would have bitter long-lasting consequences on reservations.

In 1945, however, the biggest threat to Indian country was still external. Growing from the Senate recommendations of 1943, what came to be known as the "federal policy of termination" would lend force to D'Arcy McNickle's observation that "to appreciate Collier" one needed to look at not only "what had happened before him"— allotment—but "what happened after he left."

The possibility of terminating the federal trust relationship with tribes came to dominate Indian-government relations by 1950. Collier's successor as commissioner, William A. Brophy, labored to protect Indian rights, but members of Congress were becoming increasingly eager to "get out of the Indian business."

As one way of doing this, they cited the Indian Claims Commission formed in 1946. Hadn't it been established to settle once and for all the Indians' proliferating complaints over land loss? True, there had been opposition, one Republican congressman declaring, "Why must we buy America from the Indians all over again?" But the measure had passed, and tribes could now abandon the old, difficult process of trying to get bills before Congress; instead they could now file claims and bring suits in the special court.

Further, congressmen reasoned, hadn't Indian military and defense workers shown during the war that they could work and live within the larger culture? Didn't at least some of the tribes have a large number of educated, acculturated, business-minded members who should be able to support themselves individually or tribally? (The Menominees, owners of a successful timbering operation, were often cited as an example.) Didn't everyone agree that something needed to be done about the growth and expense of the BIA, a bureaucratic monster from anybody's perspective?

When ill health forced Brophy to relinquish control of the agency, his assistant commissioner, William Zimmerman, cooperated with the congressmen who were pressing him on these questions by preparing the 1947 "Zimmerman Plan," a tentative attempt to identify which tribes were acculturated enough to be cut loose from federal trust status. The idea was to "terminate" selected tribes, one by one; "the federal government would end its administrative responsibilities as soon as each tribe's circumstances permitted, transfer these to state and local governments, and distribute tribal assets either to tribes or individual members." In this way, the Bureau could be streamlined and perhaps eventually abolished—the government could indeed divest itself of the Indian business.

The idea of termination appealed to some Indians who had adapted strongly to Anglo culture. Reservation-born Sioux and BIA official Ben Reifel, for example, maintained, "The United States is the Indian citizen's 'Reservation' today," with the old reservation "fast becoming just a place where some Indians were born."

Even if other Indians did not subscribe to this view, the idea of getting a lump-sum settlement from tribal assets and of getting rid of the BIA—informally known to the recipients of its ministrations as "Bosses Indians Around"—had definite appeal.

Yet most could not help but be troubled by the implications of a policy that sought to deny their native identity and their special relationship with the federal government, making them subject to state and local governance. The BIA had at least served as a buffer, however imperfect, against grasping reservation outsiders. While its officials had often tried to remake Indians according to Anglo rules and norms, its existence had acknowledged the distinctiveness of Indian culture in general, and the need to maintain a separate land base.

Termination would, they feared, destroy tribal groups. It would open the remaining Indian land base to taxation and, with the tracts now unrestricted, to the machinations of non-Indians who wanted to claim Indian country and/or its resources. Indians also wondered whether those "terminated" could count for assistance upon state and local governments. Iroquois leader Clinton Rickard argued, "Those white people who live closest to Indians are always the most prejudiced against them and the most desirous of obtaining their lands." Would state and local governments be willing to serve the needs of Indian citizens? Did they have the resources to do so?

Dillon Myer cared nothing for such considerations. The former director of the War Relocation Authority, which oversaw the Japanese internment camps in the West, Myer received appointment as commissioner of Indian Affairs in 1950. The terminationists had their dream official, and American Indians had a nightmare.

Myer halted the money for economic development that was still trickling into the reservations. He replaced holdovers from the Collier BIA era with his own bureaucrats, unversed in Indian affairs. He "ordered BIA personnel to devise withdrawal plans for all groups and institutions" without requiring them to consult those affected.

Myer did occasionally show some sensitivity—for example, in stipulating that Indians fifty years old or older receive lifetime tax exemptions when released from trust status. But overall, he lived up to former Secretary of the Interior Harold Ickes's assessment of him: "a Hitler and Mussolini rolled into one." When Superintendent E. R. Fryer at Pyramid Lake backed the Paiutes in their legal victory over whites using their grazing land, Myer—spurred by the Paiutes' archenemy McCarran—simply had the superintendent transferred. This caused such an outcry from the Paiutes and their supporters that President Truman reinstated Fryer. But Myer himself stayed into the next administration—in fact, he was given even greater latitude under Dwight Eisenhower.

Most significant to the history of Indian dispossession, Myer "did not believe that a better Indian future was in the land." Indians had not "[met] the standards of the dominant society" on their remaining and often submarginal tracts; thus, "the Indian-land relationship . . . had to be dissolved," along with tribal governments and separate Indian services such as hospitals and schools.

With the aid of conservative Utah Senator Arthur Watkins, these ideas came to fruition in the infamous House Concurrent Resolution 108 in August 1953. Setting in motion the termination process, the resolution talked glowingly of bestowing upon Indians the "rights" and "privileges," as well as the responsibilities, of other American citizens.

George Pierre, a chief of the Colville Confederated Tribes of Washington State, would remember varying reactions among his friends and kin. "The great majority . . . feared the consequences," he related, for "the action of Congress, accompanied by the phrase 'as rapidly as possible,' sounded to them like the stroke of doom."

In truth, termination would take a number of years and would descend upon a limited number of tribes. Nonetheless, like allotment, it was a "pulverizing engine" that threatened all of Indian country and left its mark even on still-viable reservations. Angie Debo has characterized the 1950s as "mark[ing] the most concerted drive against Indian property and Indian survival since the removals following the act of 1830 and the liquidation of tribes and reservations following 1887."

Under Myer, the Bureau of Indian Affairs proceeded with the idea of "first ending federal services and then making the tribes self-sufficient." Others saw the shortsightedness of such a policy, Acting Secretary of the Interior Oscar Chapman arguing that Indian groups could only be hurt economically by "withdrawal of guarantees protecting Indian property rights or the termination of federal services before state services were made available." Myer, however, found plenty of allies in the Eighty-third Congress. Pointing to the more visible acculturated Indians and anxious to shed the government's obligations to Indians in general, they worked to begin "liberating" Indians from federal control.

As termination bills began to mount in this Congress—in January 1954 they reached their zenith—it was hard to discern the principles of selection at work. Certainly, the choices did not reflect a careful assessment of a tribe's or band's readiness to be removed from federal trust. Neither did they necessarily reflect a "land grab" mentality. Although there might be truth to such a charge in the targeting of Menominees, Klamaths, and Flatheads, "other groups had little worth grabbing," as evidenced by tribal-asset payments totaling only $37 per person on the small Turtle Mountain reservation when termination was enacted there.

In general, legislators targeted two kinds of Indian communities: very small tribal groups such as the Oklahoma Wyandots and Quapaws, usually among the more acculturated and possessing only meager land and few other resources to apportion, and certain larger tribal groups—notably the Menominees and Klamaths—who had attained a degree of economic success as tribes on the reservations.

As Congress held hearings on the various termination bills, Indians came to Washington and protested, even though their delegations had to fight restrictions imposed by Myer in order to do so. They made clear that while they "did not want to be wards of the government . . . neither did they want to be flung suddenly into the sea of the larger American society." The government had insisted decade after decade on making their decisions for them; now it wanted to drop them like unwanted stepchildren. "Everything we wanted to do, we had to go to the Bureau and ask them. Can we do this? Can we do that?" a Menominee named Gordon Keshena pointed out. "You cannot ask the people to go on their own and govern themselves now when for all those years they have not been permitted to do anything for themselves."

Senator Watkins responded, "All you have to do is to agree now to grow up—that you are no longer children; and that you are able to look the world in the face as free Americans, and ask to be regarded as first class citizens."

Watkins conveniently ignored the fact that the government had forced dependency upon Indians and had reinforced that dependency at every turn, even as it periodically attempted to reinvent them as assimilating Americans. "We are not children. We are men," the Oto Medicine Horse had protested eighty years before these hearings were held, and his agent had told him, "It takes you a long time to find out that I am going to do what I think best for you." Now the government was renouncing the responsibility it had demanded—and at the same time, continuing to do "what I think best for you" with little regard for Indian views and perspectives.

Indians nonetheless continued fighting to be heard. To Senator Watkins's remark that "the federal government was getting tired of acting as guardian to the Indian peoples," Mohawk journalist Ernest Benedict responded that Indians were tired, too—"tired of poverty and ignorance and disease," of "neglect and broken promises and fruitless hoping." He asked, "Can an honorable Nation, just because it is tired, shrug off its responsibilities regardless of the wishes and condition of the ward?"

Indians again argued how crucial a tribal land base was to them. "I want the committee to know that this land is the most important part of my life and the Indian people that live on it for existence and happiness," wrote a resident of the Colville reservation in Washington to members of a Senate hearing. At least the reservation, whatever its problems, was something Indians could call their own—"Owning this reservation gives me pride and the feeling of importance and respect." Potawatomi John Wahwassuck similarly said, "The only thing that I am proud of is that we have got a home, whether the land is worth anything or not, we have got a place to go."

The land base still provided some sustenance. "I can go fishing and hunting when I get hungry," explained a Colville resident. "I can cut my own wood whenever I run out of wood; sell some. My folks go out and dig roots, for my medicine and berries to eat."

Traditionalists in particular saw the reservation as a place where, despite government dictums, they could still be Indian, and where they could remain at least partially insulated from the confusion and discrimination they encountered in the non-Indian world. It would be catastrophic to them to lose this haven, however imperfect: "when this bill ever goes through," a Colville resident mourned, "I will have no place to go. The only place I have now is the reservation."

When the 1954 hearings concluded, Congress approved six termination bills: those of the Menominees, the Klamaths, the Alabama Coushattas who had migrated to Texas, the "Mixed-Blood Utes" (those with one half or less Ute blood) on the Uintah-Ouray reservation, the southern Paiutes in Utah, and a constellation of small western Oregon tribes and groups.

As with allotment, the government sought official acceptance of termination from the people affected, but didn't let dissent stand in its way. In some tribes a majority of those voting on the issue favored termination. However, in a pattern that was deeply ingrained in many Indian groups, and one that obscured the realities for non-Indians, significant numbers of reservation residents showed their dissent by "avoiding the politics of the termination debate and refusing to participate in surveys, polls, public meetings, and so forth."

Among those who did vote for termination were individuals who felt that the rewards—getting the government out of their lives and receiving financial benefits—were worth the loss of trust status. Others voted for it because once again it seemed as if the government were offering them no other choice. For example, when the Menominees won an $8.5 million judgment from the Indian Claims Commission, Senator Watkins flatly told them that they would not receive their per-capita payments unless they agreed to termination.

The government, then, wielded its power to withhold funds and to withdraw other supports in the early 1950s. Most significantly, a companion bill to House Concurrent Resolution 108, Public Law 280, authorized California and Nebraska "to exercise civil and criminal jurisdiction over all Indian lands within their boundaries," and granted Minnesota, Oregon, and Wisconsin the same controls over most reservations within these states.

States were neither prepared to take over these responsibilities nor particularly inclined to do so, yet the law was extended to include other states and tribes. The result was further deprivation and confusion on Indian reservations. For example, the Omahas, who had policed themselves in cooperation with the Bureau of Indian Affairs on their Nebraska reservation, were thrown into a legal limbo. The state was now supposed to provide police services, but did not do so for eight long years in which crime increasingly gripped the reservation.

Meanwhile, the Department of the Interior was removing trust restrictions on 12 percent of the lands still held in allotment by Indians, and the Bureau of Indian Affairs was handling the sales that inevitably followed. Bit by bit, the reservations continued to shrink.

As tribes dealt with such unsettling changes, the government's push for termination continued. Many tribes unilaterally resisted termination, citing bitter experience with previous absence of trust protection. Certain Kansas groups—Potawatomis, Kickapoos, Sacs, and Iowas—all had seen tribal allotments disappear to tax debts and "each passed resolutions opposing the plan." When the Osages discovered that they were on the government's termination list, they pointed to their "continual harassment and exploitation from grafters since the 1920s" as reason to be removed from the list; with the help of other Oklahomans who also anticipated the worst, they were.

Other termination bills, however, continued to advance through Congress. In the late 1950s, various Oklahoma tribes—including the Peoria, Ottawa, and Wyandot—would receive the government edict, as would a number of California *rancherías*. The Catawbas of South Carolina would follow—most of them willingly, it should be noted, as they had assimilated to a high degree and felt hamstrung whenever they tried to make financial deals and obtain home loans.

Through these years, tribes grappled with the possibility of termination without getting a clear idea of its dimensions, for government policy was inconsistent and inadequate "for successfully assisting Indian people through the troublesome process." On the Colville reservation, the Indians were compelled to draw up a termination plan; they responded with a proposal "directed toward keeping the reservation intact, to be operated by themselves as communally owned property." In 1958, they would vocally oppose termination, arguing that "the American Indians must have an adequate land base if they are to continue to exist." A few years later, one tribally elected council—disgusted with both the BIA and the previous tribal government—would vote for termination, but antiterminationists soon regained control.

As this brief example illustrates, termination—or even the threat of it—inevitably bred further factionalism among reservation residents as they struggled to determine what courses to take and how to meet the needs of both the termination-ready and the termination-resistant.

In all, 109 tribes or groups, many of them weakened by factionalism, lost their trust status in the termination era. However, the figure is misleading, as many of these groups were quite small, the combined population involved being estimated at just over thirteen thousand. Strong Indian opposition to termination stymied further inroads. But the threat to all had been significant, and the effects on those who were terminated cannot be ignored. For one thing, almost 1,366,000 acres of trust land would be lost.

Those tribes receiving termination mandates from Congress were granted two to five years to make the transition. Early in the process, tribal rolls had to be updated and the Indians had to decide to do one of two things: "to organize into a corporation for continued management under a trustee of their choice" or "to sell all properties and assets with the proceeds to be distributed among tribal members." The Menominees took the first option, most of the Klamaths the second. Both choices would have overwhelmingly negative consequences.

The Menominees had avoided allotment at the turn of the century. Their 234,000-acre reservation was rich in timber, and they had capitalized on this by operating a successful sawmill enterprise, overseen by the Bureau of Indian Affairs and employing many tribal members. In addition, one third of the Menominee work force had found employment off the reservation. For these reasons, the Menominees looked to terminationists like an ideal group to be removed from wardship status. Strong-armed by Senator Arthur Watkins, and no doubt hoping to attain self-sufficiency, the Menominees themselves had even voted for termination.

They quickly and decisively changed their minds, but once a move had even a whisper of Indian assent, the government had seldom been loath to bulldoze onward. President Eisenhower signed the Menominee termination bill in June 1954, to become effective December 1958. In those three and a half years, the Menominees had to work out a host of complex matters. Should they merge into one of two already established Wisconsin counties or form their own? To what extent should they retain the communal timbering operation, especially in light of the fact that state taxes would now take almost half the profits? If they established their own county, what about a tax system for it? What about the need to establish municipalities, to provide social services, police, and courts? How and where did they need to align with Wisconsin state law?

In keeping with their distinctive identity, the Menominees did decide to create their own county, and further, to create a private corporation that "would invest in various business enterprises without any assistance or control from the government." These were bold and promising moves, but the Bureau of Indian Affairs failed miserably in providing the kind of transitional advice and support the Menominees needed. Bureau representatives worked well and closely with some of the smaller terminated groups, but even Wisconsin non-Indians noted the BIA's lack of response to repeated Menominee requests for consultation. The state "could be of only limited assistance since the tribe was still controlled by federal red tape until December 1958."

With some help from the state legislature, the Menominees proceeded with the planning of their new county and corporation, Menominee Enterprises, Inc., its board of directors tribally elected. As the tribe worked through the organizational complexities, the government extended their termination deadline to 1960. But the long transition period, however necessary, became a liability: "social services were disrupted; their logging and lumbering industry was at a standstill, with resulting unemployment, and bitter factionalism grew out of their natural dissatisfaction" with the whole weighty and troubling process.

The Klamaths had even greater timber resources than the Menominees—"some 590,000 acres capable of producing 3.8 billion board feet of commercial lumber" out of total holdings of almost a million acres. The Bureau of Indian Affairs had been managing this resource through sustained-yield cuttings.

Unlike the Menominees, many Klamaths—especially the 10 percent who lived off the reservation—wanted to sell the bulk of the forested area and split the proceeds, which everyone recognized would be considerable. There was wrangling over the official tribal roll, with names stricken and names added. There was also concern on the part of both Klamath and non-Indian Oregon residents that the forests would not be managed properly when sold and that the whole regional economy would suffer.

The government tried to establish safeguards regarding the timber-lands offered for sale: if the tracts did not draw buyers willing to pay fair-market value and to use sustained-yield harvesting techniques, the secretary of agriculture "would make the land part of the National Forest program and the Klamaths would be paid the government-appraised value of the property."

Of the 2,133 Klamath tribal members (which included some Mo-docs and another northwestern band), 23 percent chose to retain their tribal affiliation, and along with it about 145,000 acres, an average of more than 250 acres per person. Once the rest of the land was opened up, the terminating Klamaths—each of whom would receive a liqui-dation payment of $43,700—would obtain only about 80,000 acres, an average of approximately 50 acres each. If the cash payments ap-peared to offset the significantly smaller land base and loss of trust status, they also would prove fleeting, given the Klamaths' financial inexperience and the intensified pressures they would face.

As the Menominees and Klamaths struggled to meet termination demands, Glen Emmons, who had replaced Myer as Bureau commis-sioner in 1953, oversaw most of the termination activity. Fortunately, he differed from Myer in seeking gradual, carefully planned dissolu-tion of the federal-Indian bond, bolstered by economic assistance for Indians *before* they were released from government trust. Unfortu-nately, he was unable to improve relations with Indians who had been alienated by Myer, to create a consistently well-funded and well-run program, or to ensure that state and local governments could meet the new demands put upon them by the termination of federal services on the selected reservations.

Also unfortunately for the future of an Indian America, Emmons believed in the termination policy, despite his problems in imple-menting it. Like Myer, he saw relocation—the movement of Indians from the reservations to urban areas—as an important component. Like Myer, he vigorously sought to remove Indians from their land bases.

◄───────►

Chapter Twelve

"Our Land Is Everything to Us"
(1950s–1964)

Our land is everything to us.... It is the only place where
Cheyennes remember the same things together.
                                        —*John Wooden Legs*

The BIA brochures and posters glittered with pictures of the 1950s
American dream. "Come to Denver," urged one poster, citing "Good
Jobs," "Happy Homes," "Training," and a beautiful location. Photos showed Indian men doing office work, operating machinery, and
receiving vocational training; they pictured Indian families embarking
on a middle-class life in neat white frame homes.

Young Indians on the reservations of the early 1950s looked around
them and saw uninterrupted or renewed poverty and insecurity. They
saw ramshackle housing, tainted water supplies, inadequate sewage.
They saw pervasive illness, with hepatitis, tuberculosis, pneumonia,
influenza, alcoholism, and other diseases keeping Indian life expectancy to about forty-four years at a time when white Americans on
the average could expect to live to about seventy. Many saw family
disintegration and violence born in part of the coercion and physical
punishment that parents of the fifties had been subjected to as children
in government boarding schools.

They saw the land base continuing to erode as the government
withdrew more trust restrictions from Indian allotments and as officials allowed one or more heirship holders to sell the whole tract,
even if it meant the removal of another heirship holder.

Of such actions one Blackfoot woman explained, "We had to sell our land to live." Employment and entrepreneurial prospects were growing bleaker as the administration in Washington withdrew economic development money from the reservations and hired outside contractors, with their own labor forces, to do reservation work. Even seasonal farm laborer jobs were evaporating as agribusiness depended more and more upon farm machinery rather than human labor. Meanwhile, inflated prices at the monopolistic reservation trading posts gobbled up meager and erratic incomes and encouraged a life of debt.

Federal social services had never been adequate on the reservation, but reservation residents saw these, too, diminishing as the Eisenhower administration sought to turn welfare matters over to the states. And even though the government agency that had controlled many aspects of their lives, the Bureau of Indian Affairs, was supposedly being scaled back, they observed that it still maintained legalistic control over a host of Indian matters. Further, the young Indians witnessed continuing debilitating factionalism among reservation residents.

So—curious, hopeful, sometimes spurred by stories of those who had already departed the "rez"—reservation residents went to their local BIA agency or area office and volunteered to "relocate." Most preferred to go to the cities closest to their reservations, even if some distance away, but the BIA wanted them to sever ties with the reservation as completely as possible. Further, the Bureau had quotas for each urban area, so "most people were lucky if they ended up with their third choice, unless they were willing to wait—sometimes years."

With bus and train tickets provided by officials, the relocatees journeyed to distant cities. Chicago and Los Angeles absorbed the largest numbers, but the urban destinations dotted twenty states. In each, relocation agents met the newcomers and helped them get set up, seeing that the first month's expenses were covered.

Like most rural dwellers, the relocatees found city life foreign and often jarring. Unlike other rural dwellers, they often lacked even the most basic urban survival skills. Many learned to tell time by a clock only after their arrival. "They don't even understand where you board a bus, how to pay, and how to open and close the doors," one acculturated Indian, a young Sioux named Richard McKenzie, would comment of the relocatees in San Francisco. Another young Sioux who relocated and began attending college recalled, "I nearly went crazy during the first two weeks. . . . No matter where I was, I always had to be somewhere else at a certain time. There was no rest.''

There was, however, hope of a better future—an item in short supply back on the reservation. To Anglo authorities, of course, realization of the hope would mean total assimilation of relocatees into the dominant culture, including total separation from their land base. To the relocatees themselves, matters were not that black-and-white. Nor did the better future seem to be assured.

Relocation had actually started in 1948, after a particularly brutal winter had further impoverished Navajo and Hopi reservation residents. Men from these tribes had been dispatched by the BIA to do railroad and agricultural work in other western locations. To Commissioner Dillon Myer and other government officials, relocating Indian workers, usually to urban areas, seemed both a promising solution to the reservations' persistent economic woes and a powerful means of assimilation—''once the new urban migrants had adjusted to living in the cities there would be no need for reservations.''

In the early 1950s, then, Indians began relocating in significant numbers—some of them were BIA-sponsored, some departed the reservation for urban work centers on their own. Congress appropriated increased funds for urban relocation offices in 1952, and when Glen Emmons became commissioner in 1953, he gave the program priority. By the middle of 1956, more than 12,600 Indians had relocated through the BIA.

With lengthy waiting lists for government-sponsored relocation on some reservations, tribal councils entered into the process as well, seeking ''ways to improve relocation services among their people.'' Both they and the federal government recognized the need to make the relocatees more employable. To this end, the government in 1956 started vocational training programs, using financial incentives to lure companies to set up factories near reservations—not as a means of strengthening the reservation economy, but to provide low-level training for the jobs that the relocatees would fill in the cities. These programs lurched along shakily, employing fewer Indians than officials had hoped and offering only limited and negligible skills training.

Meanwhile, in 1957, the government-sponsored migration hit its zenith, with almost seven thousand reservation residents officially leaving for the cities. By 1960, "a total of 33,466 had been relocated," spread across twenty states. The number of those who went on their own far exceeded this figure, although it is hard to determine by how much. There are estimates that as many as 100,000 Indians relocated or were relocated between 1945 and 1957.

Not surprisingly, the most successful of these migrants shared a combination of characteristics: youth, greater educational level, experience with the wartime military or support industry, and a high motivation to assimilate. Even among this group, however, the realities could be daunting. Most jobs—even the BIA-secured ones—were intermittent and low-paying. Not only did the migrating Indians have to adjust to the different pace of the urban environment, but—accustomed to low-cost living on the reservation—they were swamped by unanticipated expenses. Facing discrimination, exploited by employers or out of work for long periods, many could not extricate themselves from urban ghettos without the aid of other Indians who had created community Indian centers.

Some had intended to return to the reservation anyway, seeing the sojourn in the city simply as an opportunity to boost their incomes. Despite its problems, the reservation exerted a strong pull on both those who planned to return and those who did not. It was home, and individual and tribal roots ran deep.

"I have noticed that very few that went on relocation stayed and made good," a South Dakota Sisseton Sioux named Jonas Keeble would recall in 1969. "Most of them always come back—I don't know why—come back to the reservation. It's just a habit I guess or something; they come back and are unemployed." Brule Sioux Alfred DuBray felt that people had been pushed into the program. "This is the reason the returnee rate was so high to begin with, probably 50 percent or more. . . ."

Many Indians saw or came to see relocation as an "extermination program" in which "the Indians would be integrated by taking all the youngsters off the reservation, the old would die off, the young would be integrated, and the land would become free for public domain, and all the [other] people could grab it." A California Indian named George Woodward mused, "At the very outset, we thought it would be a good thing. It would give Indians an opportunity to spread their wings and gain education and employment and generally become equal." But, he noted, "after about a year or two years, at the outside, we discovered . . . it was designed . . . to get all Indians off all reservations within X number of years." So, he concluded, "we started digging in our heels to prevent total assimilation, assimilation to the degree that we would lose our identity as Indian people."

By the late 1950s, non-Indians, too, were vociferously questioning the wisdom of the termination and relocation policies that had reflected national postwar pressures toward conformity, homogeneity, and acceptance of prescriptive authority. The Democrats in Congress in particular now argued against involuntary termination. In 1957, Senator James Murray and Congressman Lee Metcalf, both of Montana, introduced Senate and House resolutions that required Indian consent for termination policies and for other policies involving their lives and livelihoods: "Indian participation had now become a factor in the policy activities of the government."

Such initiatives were increasingly joined by westerners, "a sizeable portion of western leaders" now "assum[ing] a more tolerant and sympathetic attitude toward Indians." This shift reflected a new generation and new economic realities as westerners in general faced attempts by national and international corporations to control western resources.

Washington's attitudes toward Indians continued to change for the better as well. Philleo Nash, an anthropologist and experienced government administrator, became commissioner of Indian Affairs in 1961, early in the Kennedy administration. Nash proved sensitive and effective in the role, reversing some of the termination policies in favor of stressing Indian economic development and cultural survival. Relocation he saw as too often "merely a program to transport people from one pocket of poverty to another," concluding, "Not everyone likes city living—not everyone is suited to it. To combat poverty successfully will require programs that relate people to jobs wherever they choose to live."

Like allotment before them, however, termination and relocation took far too long to grind to a halt. The termination of the Menominees and Klamaths in particular continued to expose the serious problems inherent in prior government policies.

Menominee County started its existence at the bottom of the state's seventy-two counties "in total population, family income, employment, adequate housing, high school graduates, and farmland.'' Although the Menominees' corporation would manage to climb out of debt by 1965, lack of guaranteed federal lumber contracts and the cost of maintaining a county infrastructure would prove too debilitating. The county had to tax the Menominee corporation in order to provide services, and the corporation in turn placed economic burdens on its shareholders, the Menominee people. Many sank into debt, failed to pay property taxes, lost homes and farms, and went on welfare. With inadequate funds to meet state licensing requirements, the only county hospital closed even as serious tuberculosis outbreaks developed. As a result of termination, ''a relatively prosperous Indian community [had] collapsed into poverty and ill-health.''

The Klamath termination became an extremely expensive enterprise for the government, which eventually wound up buying over half the released land. And it was a frustrating experience for the Klamaths, despite the lucrative final payoffs awarded to more than three fourths of the tribe. The payoffs flowed right through their hands, even as their trust relationship with the government was severed.

Thus, for most of the Klamaths, including those who had refused to participate in the breakup of tribal assets, ''termination meant a shift in trust from the BIA to a Portland bank,'' a situation that satisfied no one with the possible exception of the bank's executives. Meanwhile, lumber companies gradually moved onto the former Klamath timberlands.

The early sixties saw final termination proceed against other tribes as well, including the Uintah-Ouray mixed-blood Utes and the Oklahoma Choctaws. Congress passed an act in 1964 targeting the Poncas of Nebraska for termination, and over the next few years they, too, lost their reservation and their trust status with the government.

Further, reservations continued to offer so little hope that residents kept leaving for opportunities elsewhere. Among this number were people whom other community members considered important or potentially important to the reservation's future. As Cato Vanandra, a Brule Sioux on the Rosebud reservation, would note in 1967: ''The drain-off of potential leadership from reservations is terrific. Because what happens when a guy goes out and gets a degree in business administration? There's nothing here for him. There are elective offices; but you've got to go out and continually campaign.''

Yet the exodus, far from leading to complete assimilation, led to the formation of new pan-Indian identities as Native Americans grouped together in cities, learned to navigate in the dominant culture, started Indian centers to meet their needs, launched their own newsletters and newspapers, and traveled freely about the country—including back to the reservation, thereby lessening its isolation. Some developed or participated in conferences on Indian issues; many joined "the growing powwow circuit," in which Indians came together in ritualized singing, dancing, and drumming events. The sixties would see the development of a dynamic Indian activism.

Even among urban Indians, however, this activism was grounded in the recognition that Indian identity was tied to Indian land. And termination had not been the only threat to this land in the 1950s and early 1960s. The new Indian militancy was growing in part as a result of the other ways in which Indian country was being reduced and reshaped in mid-twentieth-century America.

"We were contented to let things remain as the Great Spirit Chief made them," Chief Joseph had mused in 1879. But the people who came and took the land were not; they "would change the rivers and mountains if they did not suit them." In the mid-twentieth century, Anglos did just that with a series of major dam projects designed to reduce flooding, to enhance navigation, to provide water for irrigation, and/or to produce hydroelectric power.

These projects would rob some tribes of their best remaining lands. Many had clung to the areas most desired by the engineers—the river-valley portions of their homelands—because these tracts still abounded in familiar natural resources.

The onslaught occurred among some of the nearly forgotten tribes of the East as well as those in the West. In New York State in the late 1950s, both the Tuscaroras and the Senecas still inhabiting reservations fought tenaciously against dam projects that would further reduce those reservations. Both tribes cited a 1794 treaty that guaranteed the lands for their use. The Tuscaroras were battling the New York State Power Authority, and did so all the way to the U.S. Supreme Court, which in 1960 rejected their claims. Three justices—Earl Warren, William O. Douglas, and Hugo Black—dissented, the latter protesting in writing that the Court had failed to keep the American nation's covenant with the tribe.

Even as the Tuscarora case wended its way through the judicial system, the U.S. Army Corps of Engineers was moving ahead with plans for the Kinzua Dam in Pennsylvania. This dam would cause the Allegheny River to flood some ten thousand acres of Seneca land—most of Pennsylvania's Cornplanter reservation and one third of the Allegany reservation near Salamanca, New York. The deluge would cover "ancestral homes, farms, hunting grounds, fishing sites, community buildings, and burial plots." Yet the Senecas were not included in any of the preliminary planning or in the congressional hearings that resulted in appropriations for the dam.

When they belatedly learned of the project, the Senecas asked for an injunction to stop the army engineers, and they suggested another dam site that would be less destructive. As planned, on the Allegany reservation the dam would require not only digging up and reburying about three thousand Seneca dead, but also relocating more than one third of the population, or some seven hundred individuals.

"On paper, this does not seem like very many people," Seneca Nation President George D. Heron testified before the House Subcommittee on Indian Affairs. "Other lands, substitute houses can be found, say the supporters of the project." However, he argued, "if you knew these Senecas the way I do ... if you knew how much they love that land—the last remnant of the original Seneca country—you would learn a different story. To lose their homes on the reservation is really to lose a part of their life."

With the Corps emphasizing that only one third of this reservation would be inundated, Heron responded, "What the Corps does not say is that this ... includes almost all of the flat lowlands and fertile riverbanks, while the remainder of the reservation is inaccessible and thus virtually uninhabitable mountainside." Further, he noted all too accurately that the flooded land "during the dry season ... will not be a lake but rather muck and mud flats."

The Corps of Engineers did not give an inch; they possessed authorization from Congress and the right of condemnation. Further, the United States Court of Appeals in Washington ruled in their favor when the Senecas brought suit; yes, the taking of land broke the 1794 treaty, the court conceded, but Congress had the power to do so.

Not all members of Congress were comfortable with this situation, or with the Corps' ruthless approach, which included refusing to allow the Senecas a part in choosing grave-relocation sites. The Corps even appropriated a small private gift of land intended as a community base for the dispossessed Cornplanter residents, reserving it instead as a public recreation site. Such tactics led Congressman John P. Saylor of Pennsylvania to respond to a Corps representative testifying before him in 1964, "Apparently you have become so calloused and so crass that the breaking of the oldest treaty that the United States has is a matter of little concern to you." He saw no indication the Corps had ever "intended to do anything whatsoever to the Seneca Indians" except leave them "only their recourse in the courts."

The situation had proven much the same in the West, although Indians along the Columbia River in the Pacific Northwest did win a large settlement for the loss of their one remaining abundant fishing site, Celilo Falls. On the northern Plains, along the upper Missouri River, dam projects had the greatest impact. Here in the 1950s and early 1960s a series of projects made up the Missouri River Basin Development Program. This program was the result of the Pick-Sloan Plan of 1944, which gave the Corps and the United States Bureau of Reclamation the green light to construct an elaborate series of levees and dams along the Missouri and its tributaries. The Corps had the primary role, constructing massive dams on the main river course in order to prevent flooding and improve navigation, while the Reclamation Bureau busied itself with smaller tributary dams to help irrigate and generate power.

Indians and non-Indians alike often acknowledged a need or desire for such improvements, and a few of the dams had already been authorized before Pick-Sloan. But the whole attempt to harness the Missouri would prove to be of less value than anticipated—historian Michael Lawson points out that the projects flooded "the most potentially irrigable lands" and established an enormously expensive navigation route that would be of limited usefulness. Further, Indians would receive few of the irrigation or hydroelectric benefits, and the efforts of the two agencies would play varying degrees of havoc with the residents of twenty-three reservations, primarily in the Dakotas, Wyoming, and Montana.

Most affected would be the residents of the Fort Berthold reservation in North Dakota, and five Sioux reservations, part of whose acreage would be flooded by the major Corps dams of the upper Missouri. Garrison Dam would impact the Fort Berthold reservation's Three Affiliated Tribes—the Mandan, Arikara, and Hidatsa peoples. These reservation residents would be railroaded into meager per-capita payments, and they would watch 94 percent of their farming land slip under the waters, with 80 percent of the population forced to move.

In Sioux territory, Pine Ridge and Rosebud reservations were not affected, but the Oahe Dam threatened both Standing Rock and Cheyenne River reservations. Fort Randall Dam would impact the Yankton reservation, and both the Fort Randall and Big Bend dams promised to flood parts of the Crow Creek and Lower Brule reservations.

None of these Sioux reservations would lose as large a percentage of its farming land as would Fort Berthold, but sliding under the waters would be some of the best riverside acreage, home to as many as nine hundred families, many of whom would be asked to move to "places so barren that even 'the jackrabbit carries a box lunch.' " By 1962, the Sioux would lose almost 205,000 acres, "more Indian land than was taken for any other public works project in the United States."

Of course, the Sioux—also involved in pressing their Black Hills claims before the Indian Claims Commission—did not sit idly while even more land slipped from their grasp. They did, however, face a number of momentous obstacles.

First, like the Senecas, the Sioux on the targeted reservations had remained too long unaware of the plans so vitally affecting them, even though "existing treaty rights provided that land could not be taken without their consent." The Bureau of Indian Affairs as well as the Corps of Engineers failed to include them in the planning process, the BIA finally giving them an inkling in the late 1940s of the changes to come. The Corps brought earth-moving equipment onto the reservations and commenced construction before even meeting with tribal leaders to discuss settlement terms. No wonder tribal leader Frank Ducheneaux greeted the start of negotiations on the Cheyenne River reservation in 1953 with despair: "We are here to participate in the gutting of our reservation."

Second, the Corps ignored or inadequately addressed the "checkerboarded" nature of the reservation. How could they condemn or buy heirship allotments? The situation had gotten so complex that, as one allottee would tell the House Committee on Interior and Insular Affairs in 1960, he and his three surviving siblings had each received a 960/20160 share of his sister's allotment, with cousins receiving shares as small as 35/20160.

Further, what about all those people—Indian and non-Indian—who lived on the reservation, and even owned property there, but did not fall under trust status and therefore were excluded from the negotiations going on between tribal leaders and Corps officials? In the case of the Crow Creek and Lower Brule Sioux, Congress would allow payments for nontrust owners, but they came out of the trust owners' settlement.

The Corps was no more willing truly to negotiate along the Missouri than they had been in New York, "consistently refus[ing]" to compromise. They offered financial settlements without attempting to justify the amount, and if owners said no, the Corps simply started condemnation proceedings. Once the property was condemned in federal court, owners not ready to leave had to rent the land from the Corps "at variable rates" and to pay salvage fees on any "houses, improvements, or other resources" that they removed. In addition, any personal items not removed by Corps deadlines became Corps property.

It should be pointed out that people who lived on reservations were not the only ones facing dispossession; the Corps operated just as cavalierly with other landowners whose property stood in the path of dam projects and it drew vehement protest from them as well. In a sense, the Indians had an advantage, for the fact that they were still a distinct population in a unique relationship with the federal government made them more united in their opposition and possessing some government safeguards. A 1950 law required the BIA, as well as the Corps, to prepare appraisals on Indian property, and it allowed tribal members to appeal these appraisals "in federal district court at army expense." However, such safeguards were inadequately and unevenly applied, Indians were disproportionately affected by the construction and flooding, and they did not have "the same opportunity [as non-Indian property owners] to move to land of comparable value."

They also remained at a disadvantage in dealing with the Anglo power structure. Many were unaware or unsure of their legal rights and how to pursue them. Bureaucrats and politicians tended to ignore their concerns and complaints or to demonstrate "split allegiances and shifting loyalties." The BIA controlled any hiring and payment of lawyers to represent Indians in the courts, and even if a sympathetic lawyer was appointed, he faced a formidable array of government attorneys representing the Corps.

Increasingly, Indians insisted that they needed both to be allowed to fight their own battles and to hire their own independent counsel. Frank Ducheneaux and the Cheyenne River Sioux took their protests to Washington, paying their own expenses because the BIA would only pay for "official visits up to five days"—inadequate time to "cut through the white tape." The Standing Rock Sioux sent a delegation to Washington to lobby for the right to hire their own lawyer with their own funds, a move Commissioner Myer had blocked. The delegates camped in Interior Secretary Oscar Chapman's office for almost a month in 1951, garnering support from influential officials, civic and professional groups, and journalists. In May Chapman capitulated, overruling Myer and ensuring that "for the first time tribes could select their own attorneys and could make contracts with them on their own terms."

Yet the whole episode demonstrated the truth of the axiom "The price of freedom is eternal vigilance," for Myer continued to try to undercut the victory, and the Standing Rock Sioux had to fight again in Washington to keep him from rendering it virtually meaningless.

They and the other reservation residents affected also had to fight for the value not only of the land but of its resources. The Lower Brule Sioux, in calculating a settlement, included a six-dollar-per-bushel estimate for the value of their "mouse beans," wild peas from which they made a much-favored soup. But Lower Brule Chairman Richard LaRoche, Jr., would remember congressmen "laughed like hell and said we had never heard of such a damn thing." The Sioux had to get confirmation of the food value of the beans from a University of Maryland botany professor.

As negotiations continued, problems arose in regard to the communal nature of Indian claims as reservation residents argued for both tribal and individual settlements. Despite nominal tribal unity, people on the Sioux reservations were often strongly divided in outlook and affiliation. There were various dimensions to this factionalization.

Blackfeet, classified as Teton Sioux, resided on both the Standing Rock and Cheyenne River reservations—in the first instance with Hunkpapa (Teton) and Yanktonai (Middle) Sioux, in the second with Miniconjous, Two Kettles, and Sans Arcs. Yanktonais resided not only at Standing Rock but also at Crow Creek. Even though most Indians had come to identify with other residents of their own reservations, some of these old divisions remained, along with the debilitating splits between the traditionalists and the progressives.

These splits were aggravated by resentments growing out of the Collier years against progressive governments that acceded to Anglo interests more than they represented the people. And wherever individual Sioux fell along the traditional-progressive spectrum, many distrusted the BIA-sanctioned leadership as federal officials began to talk of relocation and "rehabilitation" funds in payment for the land, the idea being that the relocatees would receive communal money to reestablish themselves. Who would control this money? One group of Lower Brule residents, anticipating tribal payment for flooded lands, gave notice that "under no circumstances will we consent to the use of these funds for experimental reservation programs or projects instituted by either the Tribe or the Bureau of Indian Affairs."

Some on each reservation simply wanted "river money" payments to be divided equally among reservation residents. "Give me the money," a Standing Rock Sioux named John Gates announced, "and I will rehabilitate myself."

Others still felt it important to try to gain advantages as a group. This meant winning communal payments that reflected both the present and future value of the land, as well as relocation, reconstruction, and "rehabilitation" costs for all. It also meant pressing for such benefits as trust status for the land to which they moved, reduced rates on the hydroelectric power produced by the dams, and "shoreline rights" allowing the relinquishers to hunt, fish, and graze cattle along the new waterline.

As all of these things were debated both on the reservations and in meetings with government officials, the Corps proceeded with condemnation notices and dam construction. In 1958, the Standing Rock Sioux tried in U.S. District Court to stop construction on the Oahe Dam until an "adequate settlement" had been reached. Even the Sioux's own counsel initially thought the move futile and advised against it, but this reservation group won a second significant ruling: that only Congress had the power of eminent domain over Indian land, and the Corps had to get authorization from Congress to do what it was doing.

Unfortunately, this ruling didn't help much. Congress had only added to the Sioux's problems by dragging its heels even in confirming those settlements that had been reached. Ultimately, all of the reservation populations affected received inadequate settlements, although each successive one was a little better. The Standing Rock Sioux received the best, but it took eight years of hard fighting and still did not approach what the land was worth to them or what they needed to start over again.

The actual removals echoed those of the Five Tribes more than a century before, the Standing Rock people in the Oahe flood basin having to vacate the land "in the midst of a fierce Dakota winter, with temperatures falling as low as thirty degrees below zero." By the terms of their settlement, the government was either to build new homes or to relocate the old ones, but as nothing had been done, the dislocated were shuttled into temporary trailers.

The evicted Sioux faced a number of new and continuing problems. Both tribal and individual redevelopment monies that were agreed upon in the settlements were meager, reflecting the government's early-fifties terminationist stance. They were also slow in coming and were tangled in "white tape." Although both the Standing Rock and Cheyenne Sioux won some control over their tribal funds, the BIA continued to clutch the purse strings, its precautions appearing "designed not so much to protect the Indians from monetary problems as to protect the settlement funds from Indians."

Many relocatees lived for months in the temporary trailers. They often had to pay their own relocation costs; the displaced Crow Creek and Lower Brule Sioux waited two years after the move before even receiving their settlement. (By this time, some of them had had to move again, Fort Randall Dam relocatees having become victims of government bumbling that placed them on lands that were scheduled to be flooded by the Big Bend Dam.)

Any who received settlement money on a per-capita basis quickly spent it trying to get reestablished in an inflated market. Non-Indian merchants and ranchers, as well as other Indians, tried to separate them from their payments with the least return possible. Whether or not sellers were taking advantage, it was hard to buy comparable land. Chairman Ducheneaux at Cheyenne River had owned a productive, well-established 1,400-acre ranch; his Oahe Dam settlement enabled him to buy 200 acres on which to start over.

The new ranches on the upland prairies, unlike those on the river border, offered little in the way of shelter, water, and grass for the herds. Indian livestock owners had to build artificial shelters, to dig "artesian wells, cisterns, and stock water ponds," and to buy feed supplements in order "to replace the natural water and food sources of the old habitat." Farmers had to work with poorer soil and to figure out how to water the crops.

The well-being and self-sufficiency of everyone who moved was affected in subtle but significant ways. People no longer had easy access to wood, a source of heat, lumber, and a modest sale income. They had fewer hunting-and-gathering opportunities away from the watercourses. Their homes were more exposed to the elements, more expensive to heat and cool, and "new sources of fuel, lumber, food, and water had to be developed or purchased."

At the same time, the land loss and relocations disrupted the reservation as a whole. The natural resource base had been reduced; both the Cheyenne River and Standing Rock Sioux lost 90 percent of their forested land to the Oahe Dam. Government services for all were thrown into a state of flux, particularly when BIA agencies had to be moved out of the water's path. Other vital structures, such as churches, hospitals, and community centers, had to be moved as well.

The people on the reservations had little say in where all of these buildings would go, or even if they would be grouped together. On the Crow Creek reservation, where the most substantial community was flooded, the BIA agency moved to South Dakota's capital, Pierre, and the Indian Health Service hospital moved to another location, while tribal offices were located at a third. Both the Crow Creek and Lower Brule Sioux lacked fast, dependable means of travel yet faced journeys of as much as ninety miles to reach one of these facilities. Once there, they could "no longer . . . take care of their BIA, public-health, and tribal business needs on the same day at the same location."

The promise of paved roads, streetlights, and gutters had disappeared in the negotiation process, although the Corps remained responsible for relocating the buildings and for seeing that there were appropriate roads, adequate water, and other community necessities. At best, the Corps provided these minimally, employing non-Indian labor. Both the Standing Rock and Cheyenne River Sioux protested, but Congress typically delayed action until the point was moot. It did the same with Standing Rock appeals to uphold lumber salvage rights on their lost land, confirming them in these rights only when no time was left to harvest the trees.

Meanwhile, the tribes tried with limited settlement money and limited control of it to address their remaining needs. These were so many and so pressing that in general they, too, "failed to provide for such crucial items as development of satisfactory water supplies, construction of sufficient housing, or reestablishment of lost sources of income."

All in all, the relocations proved confused, traumatic, even devastating. "I'd been hard up and I was waiting for my money, never realizing what we were losing," Gib LeBeau, a Cheyenne River leader, would recall. "We look back now to see that we lost everything . . . we had the best part of our life in that area." The government did not even honor its promises to return to tribal ownership any condemned land that had not been inundated.

There were, however, some successes, in that stronger, more assertive tribal leaderships were coalescing. Cheyenne River leaders had fought the BIA over where to relocate their agency and had won. At both Cheyenne River and Standing Rock, residents had gained control over "rehabilitation" money and had started farm and ranching programs, business and industrial development, and various forms of assistance for families. The farm and ranch initiatives would prove uneven, and business and industrial development initiatives would create little long-term tribal enterprise or employment opportunities. But tribal administration of funds did improve many families' quality of life on the remaining reservation lands—and it fed a growing sense of Indian pride and possibility. Indians were not simply being done *to;* they were doing.

One avenue for Indian activity was the Indian Claims Commission, which handled so many requests for compensation that its life had to be extended repeatedly; between its creation in 1946 and its end in 1978, it would merge 852 suits "into 370 dockets," completing most of these and awarding millions of dollars to tribes.

Those tribes that brought suits first had to, with the help of an attorney or attorneys, demonstrate their claims to the lands specified. If they could do so to the commission's satisfaction, it would estimate "the value of the land at the time of cession" and determine the difference between this and the amount actually paid. This difference was what the government owed—minus whatever officials could show that the government had spent "for the benefit of the claimants." Congress then appropriated a net payment to the tribe, but held the money in the U.S. Treasury while determining "how it should be distributed among various tribal members."

The commission rejected a number of petitions, among them that of the Texas Cherokees who, undaunted, "petitioned the state of Texas for redress of grievances nearly 125 years old." Here, too, the validity of their claims was rejected. The Sioux lost their bid for the Black Hills claims before the Indian Claims Commission (ICC) in 1956, obtained new lawyers and won a reinstatement of their claim before the commission, only to have the case drag on for another twenty years.

Some tribes won substantial settlements. Three thousand Utes obtained a $31.7 million settlement for six million acres of western Colorado land that had been seized in 1868. But settlement figures are misleading, for the Indians had to shoulder the cost of their litigation, and the government used its power to hack away at the awards by claiming large expenditures on the tribes. Thus, "a tribe might receive only 8 to 10 percent of its original claim."

Besides, some tribes did not want even to consider monetary compensation; they wanted the land. The ICC, in hearing the claims of the Taos Pueblo, acknowledged "that the tribe still held legal title to the 130,000 acres that the government had taken from it in 1906," but could and would only offer them money in compensation. As the Sioux would later do with their Black Hills claim, the Taos Pueblo kept fighting for the land itself, or at least for the fifty thousand acres that included Blue Lake.

In the fifties and early sixties, then, the biggest challenge for Indians as Indians remained how to retain or regain land and how to be self-sufficient upon it. Even when not threatened with termination or with a dam project, tribes in the 1950s could never feel that their lands were free from attack. Senator Pat McCarran repeatedly tried to turn Paiute territory over to squatters' legal ownership, and the tribal council had to work constantly against this. Commissioner Emmons's land policies "went beyond even Dillon Myer's" in releasing Indian lands from trust. In response, the tribal councils became more vocal regarding "the right to buy land offered for sale, especially 'key tracts' vital to land management."

As in the case of termination, they were helped by Washington's improving attitudes toward Indian rights as the decade neared an end. In 1959, Congress actually donated to western reservations "346,370 acres of federally owned submarginal lands, located next to tribal lands," thereby enhancing "both the size of the reservations and the amount of natural resources available for tribal advancement." And in 1961, Secretary of the Interior Stewart Udall declared, "I firmly believe that the Indians' land base is essential to a sound economic future. I intend to support Indian effort to acquire more land where they need it and use it productively." If "use it productively" smacked of the old paternalism, Udall's statement nonetheless signaled a major shift in government policy.

At the same time, it was primarily the Indian tribes themselves who worked to bring about a renewed and enlarged land base. Beginning in the mid-fifties, as trust allotments expired, the northern Cheyenne worked to buy up the pieces of their reservation "that foolish or desperate members put up for sale." Council President John Wooden Legs explained why: "Our land is everything to us. . . . It is the only place where Cheyennes remember the same things together." One of the things they remembered there, he explained, was "that our grandfathers paid for it—with their lives."

The tribe was particularly interested in sixty reservation tracts the BIA planned to sell; the "Bixby Tracts" offered some of the best water resources on the reservation. Tribal members sold part of their cattle to raise $40,000 for this purpose, only to have the BIA hold the money up in an audit as the tracts went on the auction block in 1957. A white bidder snapped them up for $22,485, then—a year later—

tried to sell them to the Cheyennes for about $48,000. By then, however, "they had to use their money to bid on other allotments as they were offered."

In 1959, the tribe prepared an "unallotment" plan and gave it to the interior secretary, declaring their determination to buy back every piece of reservation land they could and asking for first rights to any reservation tracts and a $500,000 loan "to be repaid over a long-term period by the income from their tribal holdings." In particular, they were eager to get thirteen tracts close to the Bixby Tracts, and they received some encouragement from Washington.

Then came the news that the government was putting the tracts on the open market. "The Cheyennes could not talk—they were so angry and sad," Wooden Legs would recall. However, some officials in Washington stopped the sale—Wooden Legs "never saw the Cheyennes as happy as that"—and finally, in 1962, the government approved a Cheyenne consolidation plan, providing loans for cattle production and craft and tourism enterprises.

Another land-consolidation success story was that of the Cheyenne River Sioux, who parlayed their "rehabilitation" funds from the Oahe Dam project into a tribally controlled exchange system "whereby allotted interests were traded for individually held tribal lands." By 1970, they would "increase the amount of tribally owned land by 117,000 acres and their individual holdings by 107,000 acres," also canceling leases and significantly limiting non-Indian land ownership and use.

The Cheyenne River Sioux demonstrated what a tribe could do with money and motivation in order to stay and survive on their land. They made some mistakes along the way, such as putting funds into small family ranches when a single tribally owned cattle program would have been more effective. But then, as a Lower Brule tribal councilman put it, "The government has been making programs for us for years, and all of them have failed. I think it's time they gave us the right to fail."

The degree of tribal autonomy remained unclear during this period, although Indians made a number of gains. In 1956, white ranchers took the Oglalas at Pine Ridge to court over a new three-cents-an-acre leasing tax the tribal council had imposed. United States District Court Judge George Mickelson ruled that "permittees had a choice.

They could pay the tax or not use Native land." In 1959, the Supreme Court told a plaintiff that he must sue in a tribal court to get money he claimed was owed him by Navajos with whom he had contracted on the reservation. The idea behind the judgment was "that tribes were largely autonomous bodies subject to federal but not state control," and that these tribes "held power that existed independent of Congress."

But the courts had also judged at various times that "tribes possessed only delegated authority," and any legal gains always threatened to evaporate. Tribes also felt pressure to create governance structures in line with Bureau expectations. For example, the Navajos devised their own Court of Indian Offenses, but the court and its codes have been judged to reflect Anglo expectations rather than "an internal Navajo demand."

Struggles over power and privilege among reservation residents continued to sour and further complicate life. Even at Cheyenne River, the Sioux expressed great dissatisfaction with their own government, one woman insisting that the tribal council was "corrupt" in its handling of the livestock program, with its cash, cattle, and supply disbursements: "the full bloods who were on the program didn't have a chance. [The council] just went in and took them over and took over the leases on their lands." On the Osage reservation in 1964, disaffected tribal members started an alternative to the tribal government. The Osage Nation Organization existed, they vowed, "to promote Osage unity, Osage economic development, to better transact our nonmineral business affairs, to protect our religious rights, to protect and maintain our lands, and to further the general welfare of the Osage tribe."

Such actions were a response to a generalized feeling of oppression, whether by BIA officials or one's own tribespeople. "Everything is pretty well controlled by local authorities so that individuals can't do as they would like to do," a Sisseton Sioux named Titus Goodbird would explain. "They have to get consent from the superiors for everything they want to do. They have to ask, and they say 'No.' Well, that's it. Most of the time, whatever we ask, it's 'No.' "

Yet at least the reservation remained a place where an Indian could practice Indian ways, such as traditional food gathering. Reuben Snake would remember his Winnebago grandmother in Wisconsin picking cranberries and blueberries and wading into ponds, feeling with her toes for the water-lily roots, which she would dry and then fry.

Indians also continued to be adept at fashioning and refashioning their own rituals and ceremonies. The Native American Church kept growing. Plains Indians secretly practiced the Sun Dance, which again drew official censure, and despite the government's disapproval, members of many tribes engaged in elaborate giveaways of their limited goods to celebrate a holiday or other special event, such as a homecoming. Tribes with ranching enterprises developed rodeos, and pow-wows continued to draw Indians together in celebration of their heritage.

Occasionally, tribal governments had enough power delegated by the BIA and support from the reservation population to alter white policy so as to reflect Indian values. On the Mescalero Apache reservation in the 1950s and 1960s, the leadership worked with the BIA and other federal agencies to help residents relocate their homes and build new ones according to the old matrilineal groupings. To facilitate this change, the leaders worked to emphasize the types of jobs "that would reduce the need for dispersed land assignments and residences."

Jobs of any kind remained in short supply on reservations. At Standing Rock in 1955, "74 percent of the heads of families were unemployed," and those who had jobs worked primarily as "cowboys, farmers, or construction workers or in nonsupervisory positions with the BIA." Almost half the reservation population received some kind of welfare. In the early sixties, reservation unemployment rates in general were reported at 40 to 90 percent—some rising to 95 percent during the winter months. Family income naturally reflected these dismal statistics. In 1960, monthly income for families on Pine Ridge reservation "averaged . . . less than 100 dollars per family, and most of that amount came from public assistance."

Some of the tribes that won ICC judgments were able to brighten this picture and provide jobs and enhanced services. The Utes chose to spend their settlement money "through the BIA on schools, livestock, and hospitals," rather than take per-capita payments. And tribal ranching enterprises continued to prove strong and promising. In particular, Peter Iverson has argued that the San Carlos Apaches "through the 1960s, at least . . . used the business of cattle ranching to remain San Carlos Apaches," investing the activity with their own meanings and using it "to remain on the land" and "to promote family and extended family ties."

However, as Standing Rock's unemployment figures show, most tribes that had promising cattle enterprises still could not parlay them into self-sufficiency. Given the land and money constraints, tribal ranching for them could involve only "a small proportion of the reservation population," who could not be expected "to compete with neighboring white ranchers who used feedlot methods and more modern equipment."

It isn't hard to see, then, why relocation—either government-sponsored or individual—held appeal. Military veterans in particular felt the lack of opportunities—and the sting of discrimination. A Mdewakanton Sioux of Minnesota would recall "some of our Indian boys," high school graduates and veterans of the "air police" in the 1950s, coming back to the reservation and trying to obtain jobs as policemen in a nearby town, only to see the employment go to "somebody that didn't even finish high school." So, he concluded, "they had to go someplace else." When Reuben Snake returned to the Winnebago reservation in 1958 from service as a Green Beret, he learned that "the only way . . . to get work" was to go sit on the "employment log" early in the morning and wait for local farmers to come by and hire day laborers. Mary Crow Dog characterized the settlements on the Rosebud reservation, where she grew up in the fifties and sixties, as "places without hope," where "there was nothing for the men to do . . . but hit the bottle."

How much good was the land going to be to Indians as long as the economic picture remained blighted and encouraged social deterioration as well? BIA Commissioner Dillon Myer had "consistently opposed tribal control of their own resources" even as he pushed termination; Commissioner Glen Emmons had "concentrated on attracting private manufacturers to reservations" rather than supporting tribal enterprise. Under his programs, Indians were offered only the opportunity "to join the lowest segments of the industrial order by becoming wage earners in factories owned and managed by non-Indians."

These industrial enterprises were tenuous, made more so by the poor match between the industrial jobs and the Indian work force, whose noncompetitive tribal and kinship relationships and "concepts of time and patterns of land use" were at odds with industrial organization and goals. By 1961, of the ten firms Emmons had managed to draw to reservations, four were still in business; "none had flourished, and they employed relatively few Indians."

A similar attempt to attract manufacturers by the Kennedy administration, 1961–1963, brought equally disappointing results. This administration developed a commitment to minorities and the poor—the 1961 Area Redevelopment Act recognized tribes as potential economic players by identifying them as "recipients of aid on the same basis as other units of government." But officials took a "one size fits all" approach to aid programs, the emphasis continued on "exten[ding] the industrial network on reservations," and the BIA still administered economic programs, since few Indians possessed the business and economic background necessary for these endeavors. Further, a study at Pine Ridge showed that in most cases, even Sioux families with members employed by a plant there remained below the poverty line.

Oil and coal companies promised a greater economic boost. While the Osages' rich oil fields remained exceptional, many other western reservations included within their boundaries significant natural resources. Indians were in no position to develop these resources themselves, nor did they receive the least encouragement from the government to work toward doing so. Instead, they had to be content with the lease monies offered by the extractors and trust to the BIA to protect their interests.

The BIA, however, failed to monitor the companies, either at all or in any effective, consistent way. The Shoshones and Arapahos of the Wind River reservation in Wyoming would lose substantial income on their oil for four decades as "some thirty different oil companies" employed "a variety of shabby methods" to cheat them. The enterprises did bring jobs to the reservation, but at a cost to the land and its occupants, who did not share in the advantages produced—"virtually all the power generated on or near reservations was for the use of cities far away from the reservations." Nor were reservation residents told of the environmental consequences of some of this industrial activity. They were, however, figuring some things out for themselves—or beginning to demand responses to long-held concerns. Most of the new awareness and new militancy was fomenting among the urban Indians, but ''red power'' was coming to the reservation as well.

Chapter Thirteen

"Until We Have Regained Our Rightful Place"
(1964–1979)

Now, we shall not rest until we have regained our rightful place.
—*Declaration of the Five County Cherokees of Oklahoma*

Nothing . . . keeps Native Americans more wary of the rest of American society than their realization that they must continue to struggle defensively for the little land that is left to them.
—*Alvin Josephy,* Now That the Buffalo's Gone

In 1970, the Winnebago navy ceremoniously launched its vessels from the backwaters along the west bank of the Missouri River. A borrowed fourteen-foot runabout led the procession into the main channel, a war-bonneted Winnebago named Louie LaRose occupying the prow. Tied to the runabout was a twelve-foot aluminum rowboat. "This was the magnificent fleet of the Winnebago Navy," participant Reuben Snake would recall with humorous relish, for he thought that the wind whipping LaRose's eagle-feathered headdress forward made him look "like a Mormon pioneer woman in a sun bonnet," and the corpulent Snake himself sank in the back of the rowboat with each acceleration of the runabout.

The mission, however, was a serious one. The Army Corps of Engineers again was trying to condemn Indian land, this time the Winnebagos'. Most of the tribe's reservation lay on the west bank of the Missouri, in northeastern Nebraska, but they owned more than six hundred acres across the river, an Iowa tract coveted by the Corps for a water recreation complex. The "navy" was transporting signs declaring THIS IS WINNEBAGO INDIAN LAND BY TREATY OF MARCH 8, 1865. NO TRESPASSING.

The Winnebago action pales beside some of the more spectacular Indian activism of the 1960s and 1970s—the Pacific Northwest "fish-ins," the militant walks, the occupations of Alcatraz Island, Mount Rushmore, and Wounded Knee. But it also symbolizes the pervasive spirit of a new Indian assertiveness. Indians had never stopped seeking to be heard, but had been ignored or patronized for generations—ever since they lost the power of armed warfare. Now they were demanding attention to their land claims and their rights to live upon the land in ways that did not reflect the goals and values of the dominant culture.

This activism had its roots in a number of developments. The existence of the Indian Claims Commission had made tribes more aware of the provisions of the old treaties, some 370 "between 1789 and 1868." Ironically, these documents, which were crafted to part Indians from most of their lands, could now be used as a "basis for claiming land and just compensation, and for tribes' distinct relationship with the federal government." Even if a tribe failed to win its suit, members had gained valuable knowledge of their historical rights and of the workings of the judicial system.

This knowledge complemented the continually growing exposure of Indians to a wider world. More moved into urban areas, where, being "neither protected nor restricted by the Bureau of Indian Affairs," they became "more independent and more outspoken." Many moved back and forth between reservation and city. They began to advance in school in greater numbers; between 1960 and 1970, the number of Indian high school and college students more than doubled. They became more confident in questioning and in moving between Indian and white worlds.

They found social ferment enveloping the United States itself as other ethnic groups—chiefly African Americans—asserted their own rights and ethnic pride, and as "mainstream" youth questioned the values of the dominant culture. These developments fed a tenuous but growing general interest in Indian perspectives regarding land use and American history. As a nationwide environmental movement burgeoned, Americans romanticized, but at least began recognizing, the value of traditional Indian land stewardship. The public was reading Alvin Josephy's popular historical accounts of Indian resistance and making a best-seller of Dee Brown's 1971 *Bury My Heart at Wounded Knee,* a narrative of the 1890 South Dakota massacre that is sympathetic to the Sioux.* Hollywood was producing movies that challenged old frontier myths of whites as civilization bearers and Indians as barbarians.

Of special significance, Indian voices were emerging in mainstream publishing. In 1969, Yankton Sioux Vine Deloria, Jr., offered a blistering, widely read challenge to non-Indian America with *Custer Died for Your Sins.* That same year, the awarding of the Pulitzer Prize to Kiowa N. Scott Momaday for his lyrical novel *House Made of Dawn,* dealing with Indian identity in mid-twentieth-century America, showed that not only could an Indian voice break into the literary marketplace, but Indian experience could be recognized as rich, complex, and meaningful.

Through such developments, a stronger sense of unity, purpose, and hope emerged among Indians in regard to their essential identity as indigenous peoples. Of course, many of them had never lost this sense: Seminole leaders had told President Eisenhower quite plainly in 1954 that they were "not White Men but Indians," and did not wish "to become White Men" but wished to share the "land of all of our Tribe" in time-honored fashion. Such assertions were now also fed by a growing Indian awareness of their right to a distinctive identity— and of a global and national context for their struggles.

In the sixties, Indian Americans were making connections between their experiences and those of other "indigenous, traditional, ethnic, and colonized peoples throughout the world." Within the political sphere of the United States, they were becoming more aware of each other's struggles, including those of their fellow colonized Americans, the natives of Alaska and Hawaii. Within the conterminous United States, they were becoming more likely to form alliances across geographical boundaries, as did the Iroquois from reservations in New

---

*Brown followed in a tradition of such non-Indian champions as Helen Hunt Jackson, whose 1884 *Ramona* generated popular interest with its romantic depiction of California Indians; Oliver LaFarge, whose *Laughing Boy,* a novel on Navajo life, won the Pulitzer Prize in 1930; and Mari Sandoz, whose 1953 *Cheyenne Autumn* chronicled the desperate flight of the northern Cheyennes in 1878.

York State who joined and led western "red power" activities. They also drew strength from the discovery of various "disappeared" Indian groups, pockets of nearly forgotten tribes or remnants of relocated tribes, people who had clung quietly and persistently to their indigenous identity.

Indians, then, brought their own hopes and values to a new national dialogue on American identity, and these hopes and values centered on land and tradition. The groundbreaking American Indian Chicago Conference in June 1961 had drawn "at least 420 Indians from sixty-seven tribes." Their "Declaration of Indian Purpose" reminded the nation of how they felt about the land: "When Indians speak of the continent they yielded, they are not referring only to the loss of some millions of acres in real estate. They have in mind that the land supported a universe of things they knew, valued, and loved." Now, delegates vowed, they meant "to hold the [remaining] scraps and parcels as earnestly as any small nation or ethnic group was ever determined to hold to identity and survival."

Tied into this determination was an affirmation of the "old ways," the often nearly lost rituals and languages and laws and celebrations. Young educated Indians were increasingly drawn to what the traditional elders of the tribe had to say. Although the dynamic varied from reservation to reservation, young people who would previously have been alienated or caught up in the progressive factions now energized Indian country with a revitalized and hopeful traditionalist perspective. "I suggest that tribes are not vestiges of the past, but laboratories of the future," Vine Deloria, Jr., declared.

The United States government in many ways encouraged such thinking. The Economic Opportunity Act that inaugurated Lyndon Johnson's "War on Poverty" in 1964 provided for tribal governments "the beginning of a meaningful voice in the decision-making process" and for reservations "a flow of funds exceeding even the New Deal." The primary vehicle for change, the Community Action Program (CAP), included a range of self-help programs, from Head Start for children to legal aid. Funded by grants from the Office of Economic Opportunity, it was originally to be administered by the BIA. However, Indians won an important victory when seventeen tribes successfully "protested that this would violate the legislative intent of maximizing local participation" and won the right to identify themselves as Community Action Agencies and to form these agencies with other tribes.

As the War on Poverty progressed, this action made Indians eligible for "a variety of public works grants and loans, business development loans, technical assistance grants, and planning grants." A number of government agencies, including the Small Business Administration and the newly created Economic Development Administration, offered planning assistance and funds.

In 1966, Johnson appointed the first Indian BIA commissioner since Ely Parker, Wisconsin Oneida Robert Bennett. The administration's National Council on Indian Opportunity, created in 1968, consisted of the vice president, six Indian members appointed by the president, and seven Cabinet members, all of whom were to help facilitate Indian-related federal programs and to ensure that Indians had a say "in the highest levels of the federal policy and program formulative process."

Further, under President Johnson the government began moving more decisively away from termination policies, the president's 1968 special message on Indian affairs affirming that Indians should be able "to remain in their homelands, if they choose, without surrendering their dignity." To this end, the government began expressing a commitment to aid residents in developing "human and natural resources on reservations."

Johnson's successor, Richard Nixon, also encouraged greater Indian involvement in policies affecting them and in the preservation of their land base. His administration instituted a National Tribal Chairmen's Association, made the National Council on Indian Opportunity more useful "as a coordinating center for the improved delivery of federal programs to the reservation," and provided tribal leaders with a direct line to the White House by appointing a domestic affairs aide, Bradley Patterson, to act "as a sort of overall trouble-shooter for the Indians' complaints."

Nixon appointed another Indian, Sioux-Mohawk Louis Bruce, as BIA commissioner, and Bruce amassed a "New Team" of "well-educated, young Native American leaders who shared many of the goals of the new Indian movement and, in many cases, had experience in Great Society agencies." They worked to change the BIA "from a management to a service organization," with stronger input from the Indian population. In addition, Nixon urged Congress to create a trust council Indians could turn to for legal representation regarding their land and resources, and he backed the Taos Pueblo in its continuing battle to regain Blue Lake.

The Supreme Court heard a number of cases involving Indian rights, with more court victories for tribal authority than defeats. For its part, Congress provided increased funding for reservation health care, education, and economic development. It passed the Indian Civil Rights Act of 1968 affirming tribal authority in tribal matters, thereby staving off the threat of states' control of Indian country. In 1973, Congress authorized an American Indian Policy Review Commission, its members overwhelmingly Indian. A year later, Congress also passed the Indian Self-Determination and Education Assistance Act, designed to provide more needed funds and local authority for Indian communities; this "initiated a continuing shift of practical authority to tribal governments." The act was followed in 1978 by a joint resolution affirming American Indian religious freedoms.

All of this governmental activity to address Indian problems and concerns actually fed activism rather than defused it in the sixties and early seventies. The basic, long-term injustices remained and festered. "Where did you get the money for your government programs? And your riches? From us!" declared tribal Chairman Roger Jourdain of the Red Lake Chippewas. "You acquired the richest resource we had. It was our land that made you rich."

Further, Indians saw many of their problems and concerns as the direct outcome of even the most well-intentioned federal government efforts—"God help us from those who want to help us!" as Vine Deloria, Jr., expressed it. They distrusted the government's attempts to include Indians in policy discussions. For too many years, the situation had been what Cherokee activist Finis Smith described as Indians being "called to assemblies to be berated for not cooperating in our own destruction."

Indian activists looked on the Nixon administration's National Tribal Chairmen's Association as yet another attempt to co-opt and control Indian leadership. Most also saw little movement in Bruce's "New Team" commitment to changing BIA-Indian relations and allowing for greater self-determination.

Tribal councils chafed against top-down government economic plans for Indian welfare, especially since these plans often did not take into account tribal differences. "We do not want development to be something which is done *to* us, but something done *by* us," the United Southeastern Tribes explained in 1969. "We want our own goals, attitudes, and cherished beliefs to be expressed in the way in which we develop. Indeed, all Indian tribes are not alike, and some of our tribes may seek one form of development, while others seek another."

It did not help that Indians still had to worry about a variety of old problems. One was retaining their land base. Prior to President Johnson's message supporting the continuation of a distinctive Indian country, legislation in Congress had again threatened to erode Indian lands by further removing trust status, and the mechanisms for tribal termination were still in place. Indian delegates who were called to Washington for talks refused to "cooperate in their own destruction" by rubber-stamping such policies.

Instead, they boldly proposed that Indian tribes receive from the United States "foreign aid" in the manner of colonial nations elsewhere, and they asked the president to reconfirm "our rights to continue to occupy the lands remaining to us" without threat of termination and under continued tax-exempt status—"founded on agreement by the Indians and the United States . . . [in] recognition that the Indian people paid more than adequate consideration when they gave up valuable land in exchange for smaller, less valuable parcels." While all their proposals were not met, their demands contributed heavily to the demise of trust-removal legislation.

As the Winnebago example demonstrates, however, Indians still had to fight against government appropriation of reservation tracts. In 1969, the Interior Department tried to push legislation that would eliminate even the pretense of tribal approval for the construction of highways, dams, and power lines in Indian country.

With increasing legal savvy and sympathetic court hearings, Indians effectively fought such moves. After their foray across the Missouri River, the Winnebagos won their case against the U.S. Army Corps of Engineers in both district and circuit courts, retaining and eventually building a bingo hall on their Iowa land. The Taos Pueblo, so firm in its resolve that it had rejected a related 1965 cash settlement so as not to jeopardize its Blue Lake claims, celebrated a stunning victory in late 1970 when the Senate overwhelmingly voted to restore to them the lake and 48,000 acres. The Senecas of the Allegany reservation in New York, still reeling from the flooding of much of their territory by the Kinzua Dam, in the 1970s resisted New York State plans to extend a four-lane superhighway through the remaining land. Their effort did not keep the highway off their land, but they won the right to bargain with the state as one sovereign to another, eventually garnering "795 acres of state land and $2 million in cash in exchange for a permanent easement to 795 acres in the reservation."

But Native Americans could never rest easy. The eastern Cherokees found themselves fighting to keep their Little Tennessee Valley homeland from being flooded by the Tennessee Valley Authority's Tellico Dam project. These Indians lived on a nearby North Carolina reservation, often visiting the valley, which contained their ancient town sites—those "old Beloved Towns" cited by the Cherokee visionaries in 1811—as well as their "medicine gathering places, shrines, and cemeteries." In 1979, the Cherokees would attempt to stop the dam under the terms of the 1978 American Indian Religious Freedom Act, arguing for the valley's continuing centrality to their being. "If the homeland of our fathers is covered with this water," explained Cherokee Lloyd Sequoyah, "it will cover the medicine and spiritual strength of our people because this is the place from which the Cherokee people came." In 1980, the place from which the Cherokee people came would be inundated, since the Cherokees lost the fight.

Even when Indians retained land, they still found they had little power or say regarding the use of its natural resources. Cherokee anthropologist Robert Thomas in the 1960s described the "hidden colonialism" at work in this regard. "Let's say the U.S. government is in charge of the resources on an Indian reservation and cuts the timber," he postulated. "You have a 'tribal sawmill,' which is tribal only in the sense that it is located on the reservation, but the people in the government bureaucracy actually run it." They did so, he explained, because that was simply their job, and they were naturally going to hire "responsible" Indians, those "who [were] most like whites in many ways."

These, then, were the Indians who gained control—"insofar as anybody on the Indian reservation has control of anything"—over whatever money from the sawmill entered the tribal treasury, after the government "deduct[ed] from the sale of these resources the costs of providing social services to the reservations."

If the picture on surface resources was this bleak, that on mineral resources was worse. Indian country contained "about 3 percent of the nation's total reserves of oil and natural gas," as well as "7 to 13 percent of American coal reserves and a large proportion of uranium reserves." Energy companies struck secret deals to mine these resources. In 1970, the Hopis discovered that the head of their tribal council had signed a strip-mining agreement, "under pressure from the Interior Department and the tribe's non-Indian lawyer." Even the members of the council "did not know the terms of the leases or to whom the coal company was making its payments."

If the Indians did know, they seldom knew enough. As energy prices escalated in the early seventies, tribes learned that the flat rates they had accepted as compensation for resource extraction allowed the energy companies to pocket all the soaring profits. The Navajos in the 1950s had locked into a contract with Utah International, Inc., in which they would receive royalties of 15 to 37½ cents a ton for strip-mined coal. Twenty years later, with coal selling at retail for $15 to $20 per ton, the Navajos would still be "receiving the same royalties."

Companies were laying waste to Indian land, establishing "highly pollutant power and coal gasification plants," gouging out highway and railroad rights-of-way, laying "transmission, pipe, and slurry lines," and using up valuable water supplies.

The coal strip-mining activities on and around the Hopis' sacred mesas bore graphic witness to the despoliation of the land. The landscape became bound about with mining roads and railroad tracks, dotted with power stations and drilling rigs. Excavating equipment tore into the earth, exposing great raw expanses. Power plants belched toxins into the desert air. Deep wells were drilled, "sucking up the pure, precious water of the desert aquifers in order to wash the 'slurry' of particulate coal to the Mojave power plant in Nevada."

As painful as it was to see the land denuded in so many different ways, Indians realized that the wells—and other appropriations of water—represented the most harrowing environmental challenge. In the West, survival could not be separated from water rights. Yet in 1967, the BIA, "without regard to the prior and paramount rights of the Wind River Indians in Wyoming and the Crow and Northern Cheyenne tribes in Montana," sold the "surplus" water of their reservations to a dozen energy corporations, leaving the tribes "with virtually no water for their own future development."

Tribes were also living with the legacy of the dam projects. Irrigation promised from the Pick-Sloan projects that were so disruptive to upper Missouri reservations was now deemed too costly. Further, in the wake of these projects, Indians found that their new shorelines were eroding so severely as the water fluctuated that they could not "develop fully their shoreline land and resources." Plant and animal habitats had been altered or ruined, so Indians were again left to deal with grim long-term ecological consequences.

There also remained the problem of how to meet the needs of both reservation Indians and urban Indians. Forty-five percent of Indians were living in urban areas by 1970. The migrants continued to experience substandard urban living conditions and uncertain employment with exploitative companies in the cities. The exodus did slow in the seventies, with only another 4 percent residing in cities by the end of the decade, but the Indian population had increased "116 percent in urban centers," as compared with only 62 percent on the reservations. Many of these new urbanites moved back and forth between the two worlds. All these factors led Indian leaders to identify a need to consider "migration to and from urban areas when planning reservation programs."

Tied to the shifts in Indian numbers was the problem posed by the rediscovered and federally "nonrecognized" tribes. Federal protection had at least ensured that other Indian groups would retain some land, but a 1976 task force found that the land base for most of the Indians who lacked government recognition had eroded completely or almost completely.

Now who was to evaluate these peoples' identity and claims, and how? These questions led to a host of complexities. The Lumbees of Robeson County, North Carolina, who had previously been classed as "free Negroes" and had tried to be classed as Cherokees—to the Cherokees' displeasure—"lacked a clear Indian history," as well as "formal organization, explicit membership criteria, [and] distinctive cultural paraphernalia." Even federally recognized tribal groups opposed the Lumbees' being admitted to federal recognition along with reservation-based Indians. Yet the Lumbees insisted on their Indian identity, took part in the Indian activism of the sixties, and maintained their own schools and community base in the Carolina swamplands, living on tracts that had proven undesirable to whites.

In 1978, a Federal Acknowledgment Project, "mandated to determine an Indian group's eligibility for recognition," would begin sorting the Lumbees' and other claims. But the project would stimulate its own share of controversy and bitterness among Indians who were resistant to the idea that one's native identity hinged on quantum blood standards for a particular tribe and federal government approval of one's "Indianness."

Yet another continuing problem was the specter of state control over aspects of Indian welfare. Although the 1968 Indian Civil Rights Act blocked states from extending jurisdiction, the federal government soon renewed its efforts to shift some reservation-welfare responsibilities to the states. "Almost without exception, state and local governments [have] failed to provide adequate education, health services, or even protection under the law," the United Southeastern Tribes protested in 1969. Just as the federal government was becoming "increasingly responsive to Indian participation in decision making," Indians faced a shift to state and local control, "which could end Indian participation and return our people to the domination of non-Indian local governments with which we are all too familiar."

All in all, Indians continued to feel a host of constraints. "We don't control any facet of our lives," Oglala activist Lehman Brightman told an audience at the University of South Dakota in 1970. "The Bureau of Indian Affairs, HEW, the Federal Government, they even tell how many cattle you can raise on your land, how much timber you can cut, how much hay you can cut, who you can lease your land to, how much you can lease it for. Well, hell, this is our land, we should be able to do with it as we please."

Brightman's words touched on a contradiction at the heart of much Indian activism, for few were willing to relinquish the federal protection of their land base that conflicted with Indian control over individual landholdings. Still, grass-roots organizations were formed that sought ways to increase Indian self-determination while holding the government to previous promises of support and safeguarding of Indian land.

A number of national Indian activist organizations flourished, chief among them the National Indian Youth Council, which had emerged from the 1961 University of Chicago Conference; the American Indian Movement (AIM), founded in 1968 in Minneapolis by urban Indians George Mitchell and Dennis Banks; and Americans for Indian Opportunity, created by Comanche tribal member and congressional spouse LaDonna Harris after the 1968 and 1969 public hearings on urban Indian problems.

In 1974, Indians convened a massive meeting of representatives from ninety-seven tribes at the Standing Rock Sioux reservation and formed the International Indian Treaty Council. The group established a New York office, and began producing a newsletter and "sending delegations of traditionalist spokesmen and medicine men to international meetings concerned with the rights of indigenous peoples." They drew international support, particularly from Europe.

Whether part of an activist organization or not, Indians in the 1960s and 1970s overcame some of the traditional aversion to Anglo political structures and began to develop political clout. Indian voters helped elect two of their own to the New Mexico state legislature in 1964, thus challenging a pattern of white political dominance that stretched back to the Spanish conquistadors. Tribes became more resistant to BIA involvement in tribal political issues, causing local BIA officials to move warily in such cases. And by the early 1970s tribal leaders had developed "increasingly more sophisticated and precise definitions of tribal autonomy," as well as the ability to lobby effectively on their behalf.

The basic goal of Indian activists remained simple—"red power" as defined by Vine Deloria, Jr.: "We want power over our own lives. . . . We simply want the power, the political and economic power, to run our own lives in our own way." The land base was so central to this goal that, as the Taos Pueblo had done, Indians repeatedly rejected cash settlements in order to fight for lands lost. In California in 1969, the impoverished Pit River Indians turned down an ICC settlement of $29 million; "all checks were returned."

To develop and demonstrate "red power," activists staged a variety of protests and demonstrations. They boycotted stores where Indians were cheated and treated badly. "Maybe we didn't change their attitudes," Reuben Snake would recall of one such effort, the Winnebago boycott of stores in Walthill, Nebraska. "But at least they became more respectful of us."

Native Americans demonstrated against substandard reservation housing and against firms that hired non-Indians to do reservation work at a higher rate of pay than Indian workers. They pulled their children out of schools to protest educational inequities. They tracked and protested instances of police harassment and brutality against Indians. They disrupted pageants and parades celebrating Anglo accounts of America's beginnings, in 1970 smearing red paint on Plymouth Rock.

Some of the most dramatic demonstrations centered around the Indians' right to hunt, harvest, and fish on and off the reservation "in usual and accustomed places," in the standard phrase of the old treaties. This form of activism was a natural outgrowth of the renewed emphasis on and celebration of traditional lifeways, as well as of simple dietary and economic need. In Oklahoma, where state Department of Wildlife officials in 1966 arrested ex-marine John Chewie, a member of the Five County Cherokee Movement, for hunting without a license, he argued both that he had the right as a full-blood Cherokee to hunt on Cherokee trust land and that his family was hungry.

In the sixties, Indian hunters defiantly penetrated New England forests and Florida swamps, western prairie habitats and mountain fastnesses in search of game. State wardens and Department of Wildlife officials tried to make them adhere to Anglo regulations, but usually without success. Court rulings, while often ambiguous, proved encouraging to the Indians as when the Red Lake Band of Chippewas in Minnesota "fought for and won their 'ancestral right' to hunt wild ducks without licenses from the state or the United States."

Even more portentous, the terminated Menominees of Wisconsin won a 1968 Supreme Court ruling that they did not have to abide by state hunting and fishing laws because this would violate a treaty and require that the Menominees be paid for the loss of these resources. The ruling was "an extraordinary defense of tribal authority," in that the Menominees had officially been brought under state law with their termination as a tribe.

Fishing rights generated the most controversy and drama, particularly in the Pacific Northwest. It is hard to overemphasize the importance of fish and fishing to many of the Pacific Northwest indigenous groups. "My strength is from the fish," a Yakima named Meninick had proclaimed. "My blood is from the fish, from the roots and berries. The fish and game are the essence of my life."

Northwest Indians no longer depended as heavily as they once had upon the resources of the streams and lakes, but fish still had both an economic and a symbolic value to the tribespeople. In the mid-sixties, it was estimated that one fourth of "the income of the Yakimas and the Columbia River tribes" came from their fishing activities. Fish continued also to play a central role in the culture of northwest Indians, whose ancestors had greeted the annual return of the salmon "with ceremonies of thanksgiving."

The most explosive battles over this resource had started with the January 1961 arrest of two Muckleshoot Indians, James and Louis Starr, Jr., along with a Puyallup named Leonard Wayne, as they checked their gill nets on the Green River in western Washington State. The charges: fishing out of season and using nets.

The three had appealed their conviction, and in November 1962 a superior court judge had determined that "they had been fishing legally in accordance with rights contained in a treaty which their ancestors had made with the federal government." This legal victory had been quickly followed by another: a San Francisco appeals court ruled in a case involving the Umatilla reservation in Oregon that the state could only restrict Indian fishing by citing the need for conservation methods. Further, the state needed to show that other methods—such as restricting non-Indian fishermen—had been tried.

These early victories for the Indians had brought a storm of protest from commercial and sport fishermen, and the next court ruling set the stage for a long and sometimes violent struggle over fishing rights. The Washington State Supreme Court ruled that the state could restrict Indian fishing for conservation reasons, by implication without having to use other conservation methods first. The justices argued that the original treaty makers had not been able to consider the effect of gill netting, which Indians and non-Indians now used and which could entrap fish that would otherwise be left free to spawn.

The Indians countered that their careful use of gill nets did not signal wastefulness, and certainly not on the scale of non-Indian fishermen. Their tribally owned lands were tiny—the Puyallups' were only thirty-three acres, the Nisquallies' a mere two acres—and they depended upon the "usual and accustomed grounds" treaty provisions simply to survive.

These meager tribes on their meager lands had trouble being heard, but they were determined, and they found a champion in the National Indian Youth Council, which with the tribal elders in 1964 organized a series of "fish-ins." These were media events in which Indians exercised their treaty rights in defiance of state law. In both orchestrated and spontaneous actions, men, women, and children gathered along the Puyallup and Yakima rivers—the Nisqually, the Quillayute, the Columbia, and the Green rivers. They fought the game wardens who came to arrest the fishermen, and dozens—eventually hundreds— of Indians went to jail.

The protests exposed the fracture lines between the activists and some of the tribal governments, intent on maintaining good relations with the white power structure. Even when tribes were unified on the issue, the challenges were formidable. State agencies refused even to talk with Indian leaders about possible conservation plans that would be equitable to all. Oregon and particularly Washington game and fish authorities cracked down on Indian fishermen, and the courts continued to hand down rulings that could easily be interpreted in ways that undermined Indian fishing rights.

Undaunted, Indian activists threw themselves into the fight. The Nisquallies, who fished and lived along the river of the same name south of Puget Sound, "formed an organization, issued a newsletter, sought legal aid from the National Association for the Advancement of Colored People, and called in the media to cover arrests" at Frank's Landing and other fishing spots on the Nisqually River. From their reservation base on the east side of the Cascade Mountains, the Yakimas, citing the treaties made with Isaac Stevens in 1855, repeatedly defied the game wardens by fishing for chinook salmon with set-nets at Cooks Landing above Bonneville Dam. At one point a Yakima named Clarence Tahkeal even turned the tables by making a citizens' arrest of wardens for trespassing.

In 1968, Sidney Mills, a Yakima and Cherokee serving in the U.S. military, summed up his frustrations and those of his friends: "Why can't an Al Bridges or Lewis Squally fish on the Nisqually without placing their lives and property in jeopardy, when 45,000 non-Indian citizens of this State draw their income from the commercial salmon industry. . . . Why must the life patterns of a Richard Sohappy be altered and the subsistence of a family be denied, when two to three times the total annual salmon catch by Indians of this State are alone escaping past Bonneville Dam and as many being caught by non-Indians below it?''

The BIA, in its usual bureaucratic torpor, had been slow to involve itself in the controversy, but by 1968 it was taking some responsibility for the Indians' welfare in this matter. Court decisions continued to be contradictory and confusing. The Supreme Court left Washington State quite a bit of leeway when it ruled in 1968 in *Department of Game* v. *Puyallup Tribe* that the tribe did have treaty rights for ''usual and accustomed places off the reservation,'' but that ''the state had the power to regulate the fishing, providing the regulation was reasonable and necessary and did not discriminate against the Indians.''

A more promising decision for the Indians came the next year, when the U.S. district court in Oregon echoed and enhanced the 1963 Umatilla decision: the state had to use other conservation measures before restricting Indian fishermen, and it had to include Indians in the regulation-setting process.

Although direct protest would give way to further courtroom battles in the 1970s, the issue remained one of the most bitterly contested in Indian country and in Indian-white relations. The government stepped up to represent the Puyallups in a key Washington State case in 1974, one in which U.S. District Court Judge George H. Boldt ruled strongly for the Indians' rights.

By this point, the non-Indian backlash had become formidable, with opposition coming not only from fishermen but from conservationists, from any who depended in some way on the tourist industry, and from other residents of fishing areas. Washington State officials refused to enforce Boldt's ruling, and non-Indian fishermen and other state residents mounted a concerted campaign to resist and overturn it. When the U.S. Supreme Court heard the case in 1979, it would make only minor modifications to Boldt's decision. Other tribes won similar decisions, and a Washington district court judge would soon take the victories one step further by ruling that the state also was responsible for seeing that Indian fishing spots were protected against "environmental degradation." Still, the battles for enforcement continued.

Just as the confrontations on western waterways called attention to and dramatized Indian claims and complaints, so did the tactic of occupying unused land and buildings, the occupiers citing obscure federal regulations allowing certain tribes to reclaim unused land or to claim "excess" land. An early occupation that most dramatized the Indian struggle for Americans in general occurred in 1969 on a grim, rocky island jutting out of San Francisco Bay. On November 20, seventy-eight Indians, mostly college students and residents of the bay area, captured the attention of all America by taking over the empty, forbidding prison site of Alcatraz. Calling themselves the "Indians of All Tribes," they sent out a proclamation reclaiming the island and offering in payment $24 in glass beads and red cloth, consciously echoing the white man's payment for "a similar island"—Manhattan—almost three centuries earlier. "We must start somewhere," they declared after about a month on the island. "We feel that if we are going to succeed, we must hold on to the old ways. *This is the first and most important reason we went to Alcatraz Island.*"

News of the occupation stimulated other Indians to travel to Alcatraz or to engage in other forms of activism. Many non-Indians, too, responded with sympathy and encouragement. The Nixon administration attempted to negotiate with the Alcatraz occupants, in the process exposing the gulf between Anglo economic-oriented solutions and Indian goals. The government considered leasing the island to the protesters for "an Indian trading post or Indian-oriented amusement park, or for some other income-producing scheme." The occupiers flatly rejected this as making them "tourist attractions or public curiosities" rather than moving them toward "self-determination, the chance to do for ourselves what the government of these United States . . . neglected to do since its inception."

The occupation of Alcatraz would drag on for a year and a half, Indians ferrying back and forth to school and jobs. Federal marshals finally performed a daytime sweep and removed the handful of people occupying the island during the day.

National interest had turned elsewhere, but the Indians of All Tribes had made a point about who could lay claim to the land, and especially about the difficulties Indians faced on the land base left them. From the beginning, plagued by inhospitable living conditions, they had compared Alcatraz to "most Indian reservations" in its isolation "from modern facilities" and transportation, in its lack of palatable water and adequate sanitation, in the dearth of employment opportunities, of health care and educational services. They had also noted tellingly that on Alcatraz, as on Indian reservations, "the population has always exceeded the land base" and "has always been held as prisoners and kept dependent upon others."

The Alcatraz occupation stimulated similar takeovers well into the 1970s. Some were largely symbolic, such as the two occupations at Mount Rushmore in the early seventies. The Oglala Sioux and AIM highlighted the continuing Sioux claims to the Black Hills by camping upon the mountain above the great stone expanse carved into a glorification of American political leaders.

Others combined the symbolic and the practical, as did the AIM takeover of the abandoned Minneapolis Naval Air Station. The station had been declared "excess property," and AIM members had petitioned the Department of Defense for permission to occupy it as a national headquarters. When the government said no, AIM members determined, "If they don't want to turn it over to us, let's just go and occupy the damn place and take it over ourselves." They climbed the fences and declared the station AIM headquarters. Although the occupation lasted only a few days and ended peacefully, it, too, called national attention to Indian demands and concerns.

Still other site occupations simply reflected a real Indian frustration at seeing land and structures sit unused when tribal needs were so pressing, their claims so ancient and still ignored. In 1970, irate Indians in the Seattle area tried to take over federal acreage that was being declared "surplus." In early 1975, a group of Menominees spent thirty-five days in a reservation church building, demanding that they be allowed to appropriate it and convert it into a much-needed hospital. The Seattle protesters were arrested, their attempt defeated, but the Menominees got their building.

Some occupations centered on BIA offices, which had come to stand for all that was most paternalistic and controlling in the dominant culture. Ironically, these takeovers—in cities as far-flung as Cleveland and Albuquerque, Philadelphia and Alameda, California— came during a time when the BIA, headed by Indian commissioners, was finally introducing Indians into its employment ranks at varying levels and in increasing numbers. The targeting of the BIA also came during a time when the agency had lost its almost exclusive control over Indian life. In the War on Poverty and thereafter, the BIA shared administrative duties with other federal agencies. By 1984, it would be responsible for "only 33 percent of total Federal expenditures on Indians."

Nonetheless, the Bureau had so long trapped Indians in a "cumbersome bureaucracy" that "inhibited, socially crippled, and demoralized the tribes" that it stood as the chief target of Indian ire in the late sixties. "The only thing to do with the B.I.A. is to abolish it," an Indian announced on a televised 1970 discussion. "I want to make something right now certain, that I am not for termination, I am for the abolishment of the Bureau of Indian Affairs."

Such frustrations partially explain what happened at the end of the "Trail of Broken Treaties," a protest march via caravan from Minneapolis-St. Paul to Washington, D.C., in 1972. A Rosebud reservation leader named Robert Burnette had proposed the march as a peaceful demonstration that would garner the support of American citizens and officials. But the march took a more militant turn with the involvement of AIM leaders, who saw that the petition carried to Washington included such demands as "full recognition of tribal sovereignty," as well as "an increase in the Indian land base to 110 million acres and the cancellation of most existing leases held by non-Indians." When the marchers reached BIA headquarters, they occupied the building and created havoc and destruction, despite Commissioner Louis Bruce's attempts to defuse the situation.

The Trail of Broken Treaties and the occupation of the BIA headquarters helped bring about the creation of the American Indian Policy Review Commission, but the trashing of the BIA building revealed a schism between more moderate Indians and the militants and tempered non-Indian sympathy for Native American demands. Although the AIM tactics reflected those of Vietnam war protesters and other militant groups of the era, the image of AIM as a group of out-of-control radicals would unfortunately obscure the facts of the next occupation; the most explosive one yet—even though it would occur on land indisputably Indian.

To understand what happened on the Pine Ridge Sioux reservation in February 1973—the second "Battle of Wounded Knee"—it is necessary to look again at tribal governance issues. Despite the emerging alliance between traditional elders and educated youth, the old, ugly split between traditionalists and progressives had continued to widen on many reservations. This split, of course, could be traced all the way back to the early reservation days, to those who continued to resist white domination and often paid for it by being excluded from the few benefits available, and those who accommodated to it—out of desperation, out of an affinity for white ways, out of hope of personal gain, or out of some combination of these. The Indian Reorganization Act of 1934 had further split the two groups, as the "progressives" adapted most readily to an Anglo-style form of government, enhanced their own political power, and left the traditionalists—and even those progressives outside the power structure—feeling more isolated and oppressed than ever.

Then the money from President Johnson's War on Poverty and the Nixon administration programs began pumping into the reservations, and for the first time tribal governments had some real autonomy in dispensing the funds. Suddenly the stakes in tribal power struggles had been raised.

There were many ethical tribal political leaders who walked a fine line, weighing the diverse wants and needs of their people against government expectations and their own desire for personal advancement. However, to some of their constituents, at least, no matter what they did, they were "Indian puppets of the government" or selfish opportunists.

Some filled the bill all too well, among them Pine Ridge tribal Chairman Richard Wilson, who took office in 1972. Wilson quickly alienated a large number of his constituents by establishing his own rigid political fiefdom, complete with what his opponents called a "goon squad"—an auxiliary police force paid from federal funds. Through intimidation and violence—the very antithesis of traditional Sioux governance—the goon squad effectively suppressed any complaints about Wilson's administration and calls for his impeachment, despite "more signatures on one petition to impeach Wilson than people who had voted for him in the first place."

The people of Pine Ridge were in a quandary. "Nothing like this has ever happened before, where we have guns all over the reservation," Sioux Ellen Moves Camp noted in early 1973. "Threatening people, hitting people, putting them in the hospital—you don't have no protection at all."

Yet the U.S. government continued to recognize Wilson as legitimate leader; despite the advances it had made in its relations with Indians, the Nixon administration clung to a comfortable—for the government—sense that it need only work with established tribal authorities. A group calling itself the Oglala Sioux Civil Rights Organization (OSCRO) formed upon the Pine Ridge reservation under the leadership of a slight, energetic man named Pedro Bissonnette. OSCRO enlisted the aid of the leaders of AIM, fresh from the controversial BIA occupation in Washington and a courthouse melee over the murder of an Indian man named Wesley Bad Heart Bull in nearby Custer, South Dakota.

The volatile situation led government officials to station U.S. marshals on the reservation. Since they were there to reinforce Wilson's regime—and arguably in violation of true tribal jurisdiction—their presence angered the beleaguered Wilson challengers. On February 28, protesters, led by AIM activists Russell Means and Dennis Banks and OSCRO's Bissonnette, took over the reservation town of Wounded Knee, near the site of the 1890 massacre. They rejected the blatant extension of federal control and called for the right to oust Wilson and establish a more traditional tribal government that better reflected the needs and goals of the majority of the Oglala Sioux.

Almost immediately, the FBI, U.S. marshals, and BIA police surrounded the community, and there followed weeks of erratic negotiations, cease-fires, and firefights. As the government stepped up pressure on the activists, Russell Means insisted, "We haven't demanded any radical changes here, only that the United States Government live up to its own laws" by respecting the terms of the 1868 Sioux treaty acknowledging the tribe's right to govern itself. "You're going to have to kill us," Means announced, insisting that he would not die as yet another Indian drunk in a car crash or another senseless victim of Wilson's goon squad. ''I'm going to die fighting for my treaty rights. Period.''

The occupation of Wounded Knee again drew national attention to Indian country. Like the occupation of Alcatraz, it immediately stimulated many Indians to assume a more active political identity, and it garnered strong support from among the non-Indian activists also challenging American values and policies.

Meanwhile, however, the government brought such an array of firepower against the occupiers that, Indian commentators have since noted, the overuse of federal force at Waco and Ruby Ridge in the 1990s pales by comparison. The entrenched protesters grew weary and discouraged, especially after the sniper death of one of their own, Buddy Lamont. The siege ended peacefully on May 9, 1973, when FBI agents and federal marshals arrested those who remained.

The aftermath of the confrontation proved even more disheartening as the activists faced prosecution, and Wilson only heightened his campaign of control and bloody retaliation. He won reelection in 1974, with his opponents charging vote fraud. The situation at Pine Ridge continued to deteriorate, leading to the murder of two FBI agents in June 1975, a case that would make Indian activist Leonard Peltier, convicted of the crime on flimsy evidence, an enduring cause célèbre in Indian country.

Wounded Knee had some positive outcomes. It called attention to the unsettled and oppressive state of reservation affairs, although Wilson's excesses were obscured in the government and media by the perceived threat of the AIM militants. It made more responsible tribal governments pay greater attention to their constituents, and it united the urban and reservation Indians who participated.

AIM leaders had already determined that Indian strength would grow best with a general return to the reservations, and the Wounded Knee experience had heightened the lure of homelands, however troubled they might prove. Dennis Banks predicted what would happen to urban Wounded Knee participants: ''They'll go back to their cities. . . . They'll look at the city streets and buildings and cars and they're going to hate it. They're really going to hate it. So they're going to go back home to their people more and more.''

Indians would continue to use various forms of organized protest throughout the 1970s, the most notable being the ''Longest Walk'' in

July 1978, in which some fifteen hundred Indians, accompanied by a large number of sympathizers, flooded onto the grounds surrounding the Washington Monument "to protest against pending anti-Indian bills and corporate interests that wanted access to Indian water and mineral resources." But as the reasons for the march suggest, protests were only one reflection of the central story of Indian survival: how people were surviving upon the land base left to them.

By the 1960s, reservations had developed long and complex histories. For the Anglo-Americans in power, they remained primarily places to get Indians out of the way of expansion and development, and to keep them out of the way until they died off or were transformed into "civilized" Americans. Genuinely concerned Anglos had also seen reservations as places of relative safety for beleaguered Indians, and the most enlightened—far too few—had seen them as places where Indians could survive and thrive as Indians.

To Native Americans themselves, the reservation had remained both prison and refuge, the proof of their degraded status as marginalized people and a place of hope and renewal. This paradox is reflected in their attitudes toward the reservation in the sixties. Lehman Brightman's conclusion that "we don't control any aspect of our lives," which appeared in Stan Steiner's 1968 *The New Indians,* was echoed by Steiner himself, who concluded that the individual Indian's only freedom lay in leaving the reservation: "If he wishes to be a tribal Indian, he has to have permission. Paternalism governs only those things the Indian does as an Indian. On his reservation. In the tribal way."

Yet just by their existence, reservations fed Indian pride and independence, especially if the land had been retained or regained. "Our reservation is more than a reservation to us . . . ," the tribal council of the northern Cheyennes declared. "Our land is the home of our people, and that is why our grandfathers broke out of prison in Oklahoma and died and starved and froze and fought all the way back to this good place." A young Red Lake Chippewa declared: "I feel freer on the reservation. Ever since I came home I feel no one is telling me what to do, how to act, where to go. Tribal life is freer."

The young man's words carried as much truth as Brightman's and Steiner's. For those who had lived in the larger culture—where they often had to fight racial prejudice, almost inevitably experiencing confusion and stress in maintaining a dual identity—being on a reservation meant that they could simply be at home in their "Indianness." Further, despite tangled and often overwhelming problems, reservations continued to offer opportunities to live in the old ways and in creative blendings of the old and new, reflecting Indian principles of sufficiency, harmony, and order.

Tradition still infused many Indian lives. Hosts of Navajos carried their babies on cradleboards, lived in hogans, visited their shaman when sick, watched over their sheep herds, ate traditional foods such as mutton and corn dishes, participated in a variety of cherished dances, and continued to speak in their native language. In Florida, where the Seminoles, their cousins the Miccosukees, and a variety of "independent traditionalists" still held doggedly to land tracts, many continued to observe their Green Corn ceremony, spoke "little or no English," and resided in "chickees," their traditional "raised-platform buildings without walls and with poles supporting thatched roofs."

This does not mean that traditional Indian groups were frozen in time. Rather, they consciously worked to retain and refashion as much of the old as possible. They were not always successful in stopping cultural loss; by the 1970s, the Hopis were having trouble mounting their elaborate and ancient four-step initiation into Hopi adulthood. But traditionalists continued to think and act in contrast to acquisitive, future-oriented Anglo culture. "The majority of the Indian people are content to remain 'status quo' on a reservation," announced Oglala Sioux Matthew High Pine. He rejected the idea that traditionalists were isolationists or socialists; they were simply "content now to live on the reservation, the wide-open spaces, where hospitality still reigns and the atmosphere is friendly."

"Friendly" did not, of course, describe the bitter factionalism that sparked the second Wounded Knee conflict. But traditional value systems did include an emphasis on interrelationships and sharing. The interrelationships had always been traced through the clans or through kinship systems. By the sixties, clan lines were blurring and crossing as more Indians intermarried with those from other tribes or with non-Indians. However, kinship relationships still played a vital role in most tribes, and many who moved outside the kinship networks did so with a stronger sense of their identity as tribal members or simply as Indians.

This pan-Indian consciousness helped shape a pan-Indian revitalization of some of the old ceremonies. The Plains Indians' Sun Dance had never really been abandoned, even under the most autocratic Anglo attempts to stifle it. In the sixties, it reemerged as an event of significance on various reservations.

The realities of reservation life, however, undercut the ability of many to perceive the value of or to follow traditional lifeways. It took a strong sense of one's own identity, determination, and a fair degree of luck in one's location to live traditionally in a rapidly modernizing world. There were many who did so—to the point of resisting such dependency-producing innovations as electricity and telephones, one "very old [Hopi] woman [following] the telephone crew around, filling in the holes as fast as they were dug."

But there were many Indians who saw this behavior as did the dominant culture: a strange contrariness—quaint at best, stupid at worst. Besides, too many Indians lived not simple but impoverished lives. They did not live on sustainable land in hogans or chickees or tipis, or even in minimally decent Anglo-style housing. They lived instead on badly eroded tracts in tar shacks and dirt hovels—some with dirt walls—or shoddily constructed government dwellings that reflected someone's vision of urban rather than rural renewal. The rain and snow came right into the often crowded living quarters.

In 1969, although government housing projects had been greatly expanded, "only 3 percent of the houses on Cheyenne River [Sioux reservation] could be classified as suitable for human occupancy." Their residents faced unending sewage and garbage problems. Fewer than one in four households had good working toilets. Just over one in three had electricity—and no doubt most of the others would have embraced its advantages. Fewer than one in five had running water, but on some reservations no one had it, and the water sources used by the residents, such as irrigation ditches and ponds, were full of contaminants.

Not surprisingly, health statistics were grim. In 1966, it was estimated that approximately three out of every ten babies born to reservation families died before reaching their first birthdays. Those who survived could expect to live on average about forty-three years. A host of diseases winnowed the Indian population at a far higher rate than that of non-Indians: tuberculosis, hepatitis, alcoholism, influenza, meningitis, gonorrhea, pneumonia, dysentery.

The 1960s War on Poverty and subsequent Nixon administration programs helped alleviate these conditions somewhat, but they were insufficient and not meaningful and satisfactory to many of the recipients. First, despite the welcome federal dollars, there was never enough money to go around, as it had to be divided among the various tribes and CAP programs. Second, Indians repeatedly pointed out that top-down programs and initiatives did not reflect Indian realities or aspirations. "Community development must be just what the word implies, Community Development," Mel Thom protested in 1967. "It cannot be packaged programs wheeled into Indian communities by outsiders which Indians can 'buy' or once again brand themselves as unprogressive if they do not 'cooperate.' " Programs, he concluded, "must be Indian creations, Indian choices, Indian experiences"—and, if necessary, Indian failures, through which they could learn and grow.

Indians did gain at least some control, tribal community assistance programs extending the range of aid to include ranch management programs and classes in tribal politics. In particular, the sixties saw promising strides in Indian education. The Rough Rock Demonstration School, established in 1966 on the Navajo reservation, "featured community control and teaching English as a second language." Indians who had been ridiculed and beaten for speaking their own language, for behaving in Indian ways, now planned curriculum around those once outlawed activities. "We started introducing [small children] to their native language . . . ," Reuben Snake, who participated in a Winnebago Head Start program, would recall. "We started teaching them how to speak their language, and started teaching them about Native American music and dance."

Indians also won concessions regarding housing. As the government persisted in building urban apartments on reservations, Indian people, however impoverished, often remained reluctant to move in. "Why is it that practically every housing program the Indians have with government funding is an adaptation of urban programs?" asked Vine Deloria, Jr. "Why don't they ask us what we want?" Indian groups hammered at government officials until some tribes, such as the Chippewas and the San Carlos Apaches, gained control over housing projects and began shaping them according to Indian priorities.

Two tribes—the Miccosukees of Florida and the Zunis of New Mexico—won unprecedented control over a range of tribal affairs, but the BIA retained the power to "reassert its authority" and control quickly eroded back to the agency. Most tribes won power only over Office of Economic Opportunity (OEO) programs. This was no small advance—tribes strengthened reservation health and legal services and learned how bureaucracies worked, especially in the administering of funds.

Unfortunately, however, some of the most selfish and acquisitive tribal members found ways to extend their own power, heightening problems rather than relieving them. Leadership troubles on the Sioux reservations predated the rise of Richard Wilson. Tribal housing authorities, other Sioux charged, "enriched themselves in corrupt deals with white contractors who threw together substandard housing units." Some observed that the OEO programs seemed to spark a "tidal wave of theft, embezzlement, graft, and corruption."

Despite such misappropriations, the government was pouring enough money into the reservations—more than $70 million from the Economic Development Administration (EDA) alone by 1970—that living standards were rising. Much of the money, however, was going into economic development plans that had yet to prove workable.

Everyone recognized that reservation residents had to have a means of making a living; without this, none of the debilitating conditions would change. "It doesn't take all kinds of experts, social scientists, or government bureaucrats to figure out what Indian communities need," announced Mel Thom. "Any Indian will tell you he needs a steady income; he needs a job."

But what kind of a job? The Johnson administration, like the Eisenhower and Kennedy administrations, thought it knew the answer: factory work, with perhaps some tourism and crafts thrown in. Unlike previous administrations, to this end it was willing to commit substantial funds to improve the reservation "infrastructure." This meant that a lot of money went into public works projects such as road improvement and water and sewer lines for industrial parks.

These projects at least had the potential to benefit residents as well, but they did not reflect Indian perspectives on land and resource use. "Instead of starting where the tribal people are, from how they think, and trying to develop industries they understand, the government brings in these multimillion-dollar projects," Vine Deloria, Jr., argued. "The government takes an urban ideology and they try to put it into a rural, tribal setting."

Then again, the programs did bring employment to reservations still routinely suffering a lack of paid work opportunities. "Here we have ninety percent of the men without jobs," a tribal OEO director noted. "So even a no-good job, doing a no-good job on a no-good project is better than nothing. It feeds someone's kids."

The BIA and other federal agencies worked with tribal governments, training Indian leaders to "sell" reservation sites to labor-intensive manufacturers. Results were evident by 1970, when almost 3,500 Indians were employed in manufacturing on "the twenty-four most heavily populated reservations," the factories thereby giving employment to almost one fourth of the reservation wage earners. Many of the operations produced "low weight items like electronic components" under contract to the Department of Defense.

At best, the factories reduced unemployment rates to one in three workers—no small feat when some reservations had had close to nine out of ten unemployed. And the government showed itself willing to work with Indians to make the industries more their own; the Small Business Administration coordinated with tribes on a plan to attract corporations with low-interest loans, training and moving Indians into managerial roles and allowing tribes gradually to buy the enterprises.

However, most of the industrial initiatives faltered and failed, for a variety of good reasons. Again, the geographical remoteness of many reservations proved a disadvantage. Planning had been "shallow," technical assistance limited, consultants lacking "knowledge of Indian culture." Those companies that could be lured tended to be shaky themselves, especially since Congress specified that incentives to locate on or near the reservation should be offered only to new companies. The national economy as a whole suffered in the early seventies, and defense spending fell.

Indians chafed at the jobs offered. Not only did they pay low wages, but, as David Vinje explains, they often proved temporary, required a strict Anglo-oriented work routine, and promised little in the way of advancement. Non-Indian managers failed to take into account cultural differences, for example "encouraging competition among workers" when Indian cultures "dictated against intragroup rivalry."

Even when the match of Anglo industry and Indian workers seemed successful, Indian activism exposed fault lines; in 1975, a semiconductor plant on the Navajo reservation closed down after twenty armed AIM activists occupied it, charging exploitation and protesting layoffs. In addition, the factories often had a negligible impact on reservation incomes overall, especially since the reservation labor force was growing faster than the number of jobs.

In the late 1960s, tribal councils began taking more control of their funds by moving money out of the U.S. Treasury into mutual funds and stocks and bonds. However, funds for tribal enterprise remained tight. In fiscal year 1970, tribes requested from the BIA's revolving loan fund almost eight times what the fund contained. Yet they could not go elsewhere for loans, for their trust lands—usually the one clear asset—"could not be used as collateral," nor did most want them to be so used, for then they could be seized.

The Comprehensive Employment and Training Act (CETA) of 1973 gave tribes a boost by allowing them administrative control over manpower training. But Indians still found themselves limited to "small-scale, under-financed, labor-intensive operations that [could] easily be jeopardized by a small change in technology or a small change in . . . import laws." And they sometimes added to their own problems—for example, by putting as many people as possible on the payroll when jobs were few.

In addition to industrial development, the government pushed tourism as an income-producing strategy. This emphasis brought in funds for reservation improvement. The Blackfeet received "$576,000 in grants and $144,000 in loans for street improvements in the reservation town of Browning" in an attempt to lure vacationers from Glacier National Park, just to the west. The results were disappointing. Both the Standing Rock Sioux and the Crows built elaborate tourist complexes with EDA funds, but both languished, not only because business was slow, but because the Indians themselves were not comfortable with the enterprise or actively resented it. Like the occupiers of Alcatraz, they "had no wish to become tourist attractions or public curiosities''—or to have a steady stream of non-Indians moving through a homeland over which they still lacked much control.

Although the government kept pushing one economic activity or another, the best strategy seemed to be an update on the Indians' ability to mix different subsistence strategies. The White Mountain Apaches in the 1960s developed a tourism industry, but combined it successfully with tribal ranching and farming cooperatives.

Another bright spot in the economic picture was that of the Indian Action Teams (IATs) in the early to mid-1970s. Commissioner Bruce worked to get money circulating on the reservations, not escaping from them. To this end, the BIA trained the IAT construction teams who built everything from tribal administrative offices to roads linking the more remote areas of the reservation. They installed guard rails, buried septic tanks, and performed other necessary services. The program "started with three teams and an annual budget of $800,000 in 1972, and grew to eighty-six IATs and $23,500,000" in 1976.

Then funding began to dry up. Reservation employment had already peaked in 1973. As the reservations started to feel the impact of a faltering national economy in the late seventies, as industries withdrew and tribal businesses failed, Indians still had reason to ask in frustration, "Where are we now?" However, the strong Indian activism of the sixties and early seventies—and the government programs of the Johnson, Nixon, and Ford administrations—had transformed Indian country. Residents had experience in shaping their environments in significant ways and in making themselves heard in the world beyond.

With growing expertise and confidence, Indians of the seventies asserted their rights to lost tribal status, to lost lands and appropriated resources. Terminated tribes, such as the Menominees and the Siletz of western Oregon, won congressional restoration acts. Being recognized by the federal government had distinct advantages; for one thing, tribes could use federal loans to buy back acreage. In this way, the Kickapoos "managed to reacquire more than twenty-four hundred reservation acres that had previously fallen into white hands," and by the early 1980s they could claim "about thirty-five hundred acres in common."

Other tribes continued to bring suit before the Indian Claims Commission (ICC). Although the commission was only empowered to pay money for lands taken—and then only "based on land values at the time of cessions"—some tribal groups continued in the hope of parlaying the admission of wrongdoing into land restoration as well. When the ICC disbanded in 1978, after thirty-two years and 342 cases decided, it "transferred over sixty unresolved cases to the Court of Claims."

Indians not only brought suit in federal courts, but petitioned the courts to represent them in other land suits. Among the more sensational—and successful—of these cases was that of the Passamaquoddies and the Penobscots, nonrecognized tribes who fought to require the United States to file suit against the state of Maine "for the loss of approximately twelve million acres of tribal land under a 1794 treaty." Their case—well publicized in the mid-seventies because of their demand for more than half of Maine's area and $25 billion in damages and recompense—led to a 1980 settlement in which "each tribe dropped its claims in exchange for $13.5 million in funds and $26.5 million to purchase 150,000 acres as trust land."

Just as the Indians reclaimed land, they also reclaimed resources. Some, such as the northern Cheyennes, imposed "a moratorium on all energy development until they could control energy contracts," thereby negotiating better terms and payments based on their own valuation of the resources. Comanche LaDonna Harris and Osage Charles Lohah, whose tribal income had again soared as a result of the Arab oil embargo of 1973, created the Council of Energy Resources Tribes to provide Indians with information and to help with negotiations.

Such actions were buttressed in part by the previously mentioned Indian Self-Determination and Education Assistance Act, implemented in 1975, which empowered tribes to continue to assume management of their own affairs and to receive federal funds for improving reservation life and programs. A spirit of hopefulness pervaded many of the reservations. The Kickapoos not only bought back land, but greatly strengthened their community services, adding everything from a water-treatment plant to a day-care center. As they instituted a tribal farm and other enterprises, "the rapid development . . . led to expanded economic opportunity" and drew urban Kickapoos back to the "rez."

Tribes recognized the importance of creating economic opportunities not based on federal grants and contracts. Too many of the reservation-based industries produced items exclusively for government agencies, especially the military. This left reservation enterprise caught in a ''self-contained system with little connection to private markets,'' a system that ''stood like a house of cards with a foundation dependent upon government spending.''

Under the self-determination act, tribes sought, in the words of Winnebago Reuben Snake, to ''develop our economic base so that we were generating our own income and creating our own jobs.'' This was a tall enough order, but the tribal activities under Snake, who became chairman in 1977, show the scope of Indian self-determination in this time period. The Winnebagos made economic development part of a four-point self-sufficiency plan, also concentrating on ''cultural enhancement and cultural revitalization,'' sovereignty issues, and ''problems of alcoholism and health.'' They centralized the tribal program management, taking over the administration from federal agencies. They contracted with the Indian Health Service to create ''a tribal health department with programs for home health care, community health representatives, emergency medical service, and alcohol and drug abuse treatment.''

For the first time, tribal governments had freedom to develop programs according to the wishes of the Indian community. ''They wanted a wake and a burial program,'' Snake recalled, ''so we created [one].'' Like the Kickapoos, the Winnebagos also began buying back land—using Farmers Home Administration loan funds—and they both witnessed and actively cultivated the return of younger, educated urban members to the reservation.

Perhaps the best thing to come out of the Indian self-determination act was that tribal leaders continued to accelerate their education in how to get things done within the dominant culture, learning how to ''operate in a much broader political and economic environment than the traditional relationship with the BIA.'' In centralizing the Winnebago programs and building an organizational structure for them, Reuben Snake would remember, ''We began to understand where the money came from and who was responsible to whom for the administration of each program, the dispensation of the funding, and the accountability of the funding.'' Such knowledge—and the skills developed with it—contributed to a sense of power and control.

However, old problems festered. No amount of local control could disguise the fact that Indians continued under ''the bonds of wardship'' to the government. Further, the act, like the antipoverty programs of the sixties, stimulated self-interested Indians to seize positions of power; ''charges of graft, corruption, and mismanagement, this time on a larger scale, were again rampant.''

The 1970s had exposed three troublesome and interrelated dilemmas. First, how could Indian cultural values be reconciled with economic development? The government had pressured the Indians to build industrial parks and tourist facilities because to whites these seemed the most feasible economic routes to Indians retaining and building upon a land base. Not only had these ventures failed to draw outsiders, but they had failed to engage Native Americans in a sense of meaningful enterprise.

This failure led to the second dilemma: what role the federal government should play in Indian affairs. The trend had clearly been toward greater self-determination, Richard Nixon announcing in 1970, ''The time has come to . . . create the conditions for a new era in which the Indian future is determined by Indian acts and Indian decisions . . . we must make it clear that Indians can become independent of Federal control without being cut off from Federal concern and Federal support.''

Was it realistic to think Indians could be independent of federal control when receiving federal money? Could they have self-determination without self-sufficiency? A 1970 Smithsonian Institution study had argued that tribal governments should receive federal funds with no strings attached in recognition of their loss of most of their land base. But even if the government did manage to divorce itself from the control and administration of funds, should it fork money over even when tribal leaders in authority were clearly misusing it?

One could argue, of course, that the government routinely handed over federal funds to corrupt white politicians, but it also had ways to hold those politicians accountable. Its ability to do so was not so clear-cut in relations with tribal leaders, yet Indians under oppressive regimes looked to the federal government to restore balance.

Such situations led to the third dilemma: defining Indian sovereignty in general. If tribes retained discrete powers outside the purview of federal, state, and county governments, what were those powers? How extensive were they? And what were the implications for Indians and for other Americans? The 1980s and early 1990s would bring some answers, but answers that inevitably led to more questions.

← →

Chapter Fourteen

"There Is No Place but Here"
(1980–1996)

> I am well known among the hills, among the ditches, rivers, streams, plants. I have touched them in various ways and they have touched me the same. There is no place but here.
> —*Asdzaa Yazhi Bedoni, Navajo, about 1985*

> Had our forefathers spurned you from [the region] when the French were thundering at the opposite end to get a passage through and drive you into the sea . . . the Iroquois might still have been a nation; and I, instead of pleading for the privilege of living within your borders—I . . . might have had a country!
> —*Waowowanoonk, or Peter Wilson, Cayuga, to the New-York Historical Society, May 1847*

Seventy miles south of Buffalo, New York, the town of Salamanca sits beside the Allegheny River on the Allegany reservation of the Seneca, just northeast of the lands flooded by the Kinzua Dam. Despite Salamanca's location on the reservation, its citizens have always been overwhelmingly non-Indian. The town developed in the late nineteenth century as a center for white farmers leasing Seneca lands, for railroad people working on leased rights-of-way through the thirty-thousand-acre reservation, and for employees of the non-Indian "Seneca Oil Company" that leased acreage in the 1890s and proceeded to extract for the company a handsome profit in oil and natural gas. By the turn of the century, "Salamanca's white residents outnumbered the Indian population on Allegany by five to one."

Town residents enjoyed the most nominal of leases from the tribal council—as little as a dollar a year for up to ninety-nine years. But many of Salamanca's citizens, counting on the lands being broken up for allotment or otherwise opened up to white claims, delayed in paying the meager rentals—or simply refused to do so.

In 1942, with more than eight hundred Salamanca leaseholders delinquent on their rent, the tribal council went to court and won the right to renegotiate unpaid leases. This sparked grudging payments from lessees, and the situation rocked uneasily along for almost another half-century. Then, in 1991, most of the leases expired.

The tribal council offered new forty-year leases at a higher but not exorbitant rate—up to $300 a year—and all but sixteen of the 2,500 non-Indian Salamanca homeowners signed. However, in overseeing the new lease terms, Congress also granted the Senecas rights to "improvements" on the rented land. Many non-Indian residents in late 1996 joined a suit against the federal government, charging that it "negotiated on our behalf without our approval" in the new lease arrangement, which, residents asserted, enabled the Senecas to "claim possession of homes and buildings on the land," leaving homeowners "little recourse."

The evolving story of Salamanca—including possible evictions of recalcitrant homeowners by the federal government—illustrates the significance of Indian landholdings near the century's end. The bits and pieces of land that Indians retained—and the tracts they were winning or buying back—now more than ever represented the promise of achieving political, cultural, and economic clout in a non-Indian society.

Even a mere ten years earlier, this trend might have been hard to spot. In the mid-1980s, residents of Indian country were reeling under the Reagan administration's federal budget cuts, reductions that were "ten times greater than those affecting their non-Indian fellow Americans." Unemployment rates on reservations soared, community services for both urban and reservation Indians were scaled back or closed down, roads and buildings on the reservations deteriorated. As federal funds disappeared, it became all too clear that the self-determination efforts of the 1970s had not led to self-sufficiency. A 1986 Department of the Interior report concluded that Indians were "perhaps even more dependent than before on the Federal government for income, employment and general provision for their economic welfare."

As even the report pointed out, however, this was in large part due to the dizzying swings in federal policy to which reservation Indians had always been subject. In the wake of the early Reagan administration budget cuts, William Morgan, a Navajo official, complained, "Just when we were starting to get our hands on the ledge, to pull ourselves up—whack! We're dropped right back where we were before."

In its attempt to shift responsibility for tribal welfare to state and local authorities, as well as in its draconian budget cuts—from $3.5 billion to $2.5 billion in the first two years—the Reagan administration echoed the termination policies of thirty years before. And with Secretary of the Interior James Watt overseeing the Bureau of Indian Affairs, western Indians found themselves and their reservations regarded as "stumbling blocks in the development of the West."

At the same time, the self-help philosophy espoused by Reagan and his officials translated into a movement toward greater tribal self-determination, somewhat paralleling the greater powers granted to state and local governments. The Reagan administration instituted a Presidential Commission on Indian Reservation Economies whose goal was to "identify obstacles to economic development." Reservation Indians were consulted on federal programs, and were even "encouraged to modify national programs to fit their particular needs."

Yet Indians found themselves in an increasingly complex bureaucratic maze, which drained their interest in "assuming responsibility for activities on the reservations." And scandals plagued federal reservation programs in the late Reagan and early Bush years, the most prominent being the case of the Native American Construction Company on the Navajo reservation. With federal contracts in hand, "a non-Indian construction company actually performed the work and siphoned off profits."

With the change from a Republican to a Democratic administration in the early nineties, funding for federal reservation programs continued to be shaky and problematic, but the emphasis on Indian empowerment increased.

In the first term of the Clinton administration, the government took numerous initiatives to protect Indian interests and encourage self-determination. Drastic federal budget cuts promoted by Republican leaders in the mid-1990s could have left reservations devastated, but the Senate Committee on Indian Affairs worked to ensure continuing funds for social services and economic development. Clinton issued a series of executive orders affirming Indian rights. The Department of Justice committed to "strengthening tribal justice systems" as "the most appropriate institutions for maintaining order in tribal communities," and began providing money and technical aid to that end. The Environmental Protection Agency turned over some of its controls to the tribes. At the Bureau of Indian Affairs, Assistant Secretary of the Interior and Menominee tribal member Ada Deer actively provided tribes with the opportunity to administer their own programs with federal grants.*

Any history of late-twentieth-century Indian-white relations, however, is less and less an account of government doing to and for tribal people, and more and more one of what tribes themselves were doing. In the Reagan years, Indians showed they had grown "more politically astute," better versed at generating funds, at lobbying Washington officials, at focusing attention on issues critical to them. During the Bush years, and in Clinton's first term, tribal governments became more forceful, more assured, "determined to remake the entire relationship between Indians and the United States."

This determination took various forms. Indians campaigned against the use of negative or trivializing Indian stereotypes, rejected non-Indian gurus who presented themselves as authorities on Indian spirituality, and demanded the return of Indian skeletons and artifacts from museums and dealers—an action given legal muscle in 1990 by the Native American Graves Protection and Repatriation Act. In 1984, the Papagos reverted to their traditional name of Tohono O'odham, or Desert People, while other tribes reasserted their own rights to use traditional names for themselves and for the places cherished in their histories. Their reaffirmation of the old place names reflected the fact that as groups, they remained most concerned with the land itself.

Some tribes were fighting to gain or extend a land base. Some were asserting rights to special and even exclusive uses of off-reservation lands. Many were fighting to make the base they had—the reserva-

*In 1977, the head BIA position became that of assistant interior secretary rather than commissioner.

tion—economically, politically, and socially viable, and to do so on their own terms. In all of these endeavors, they were redefining and reclaiming Indian country in ways that challenged all Americans to consider anew the relationship between Indian tribes and the rest of society.

To the old warrior Sitting Bull, the Standing Rock reservation on which he lived from 1883 to his violent death in 1890 had become the most barren of lands, his impoverished and dependent people clustered under the iron control of an agent, James McLaughlin, and a government that seemed both indifferent to their welfare and determined to strip them of their identity. "When I was a boy the Sioux owned the world," he mourned. "The sun rose and set in their lands. They sent 10,000 men to battle. Where are the warriors to-day? . . . Where are our lands?"

With what wonder, then, would this despairing nineteenth-century leader greet the words of South Dakota Governor Bill Janklow in summer 1995? Speaking to a county Republican organization, Janklow warned that the Standing Rock Sioux had "a master plan . . . to acquire all of western South Dakota," primarily through profits from casino operations.

Tribal leaders themselves marveled—no doubt with both satisfaction and some trepidation—that they were being perceived as such a potent threat to white interests in the state. Standing Rock and the other South Dakota reservations were still struggling to extricate themselves from a legacy of poverty and powerlessness. Reservation lands were still passing out of protected trust status—more than 42,000 acres in South Dakota in the preceding decade.

In the same period, however, Indians had indeed managed to restore almost fifteen thousand acres to South Dakota reservations. They were gaining in economic and political power. If Janklow's assertion was hyperbolic, it nonetheless carried a germ of truth. Against all odds, Indian country was once again growing, both in physical size and in Indian jurisdictional control over the "checkerboarded" reservations.

Some of this growth resulted from the Indians' pressing of old claims. Terminated tribes continued to win restoration of federal recognition and renewed rights at least to a part of their pretermination land bases. Allotted tribes also won significant victories, the northern

Utes in the 1980s regaining "legal jurisdiction to four million acres that had comprised their preallotment reservations in Utah." This meant that despite the convoluted trust/nontrust ownership situation on reservations—despite the fact that almost 50 percent of the land on the thirty-nine largest reservations was held independently by Indians and non-Indians—tribes were winning important powers over reservations as a whole.

Some victories were more modest and outside the United States court system. The Episcopal Church in 1995 acceded to the request of Virginia's Monacan Indians, a group numbering about 700, for the return of seven wooded acres containing a tribal meeting center, a former mission school, and a log cabin. The Hia-Ced O'odham, or Sand Papagos, a group the government had ignored because of their apparent near-extinction, in late 1996 convinced the Bureau of Land Management to transfer to them twenty acres, including an old Papago cemetery. Although the 1,400 tribal members had asked for almost 104,000 acres of traditional lands, the victory was significant, for the Sand Papagos obtained the tract despite the fact that they lacked "formal tribal recognition" and a reservation.

In court, Indian groups traditionally needed federal recognition to present their land claims—and to obtain federal aid funds. The whole issue of recognition remained confused, so confused that the unfortunate Samish tribe of Washington State existed from 1969 to 1996 "in legal limbo" after a BIA clerk mistakenly omitted them from the state's roster of federally recognized tribes.

Some groups had long been recognized as distinct tribes by the states in which they resided, but not by the federal government. Some recognized tribes actively fought against state and federal recognition for other Indian groups who might challenge and confuse their own land and other claims. The Cherokee Nation in the mid-nineties contested federal recognition of the Delawares, who were folded into the nation in 1979 but now wanted separate status; the Cherokee Nation, along with the Eastern Band of Cherokees, also contested Georgia's recognition of one Creek and two Cherokee groups.

Land claims continued to pit Indian against Indian. Two of the most tangled struggles were those of the Navajos and Hopis in Arizona and the Oneidas in Wisconsin and New York.

The Navajo-Hopi dispute had deep roots. In 1882, President Chester

Arthur established an executive order area for the Hopis within their mesa homelands—and within the vast Navajo reservation area. But the boundaries were never clearly marked nor explained, and both Hopis and Navajos continued their traditional lifeways without reference to lines on a map. The Hopis tended to stay in their mesa villages, but used the rugged grasslands surrounding them for traditional subsistence activities such as wood gathering. They looked with growing concern on Navajo homes and sheep herds in these areas, which the Hopis understood to be their own by both tradition and government fiat.

With the Navajos also having strong claims based on long-term use, the U.S. government tried to establish a "joint use" policy for the two tribes in the disputed lands. When this attempt failed, the 1974 Navajo-Hopi Indian Land Settlement Act split the disputed areas surrounding the Hopis' mesas into Hopi Partition Lands and Navajo Partition Lands. All Hopis who lived on the Navajo side—some one hundred of them—were to move back across the line. The same would apply to the Navajos, who by contrast numbered about ten thousand.

This "solution" led to more than twenty years of acrimony, legal maneuvering, and suffering, as Navajos refused to move or exchanged their traditional hogans on land they had inhabited for generations for substandard government housing and dismal dependence across the border line. The controversy split loyalties within the two tribes. It also fed bitterness and suspicion against the United States government and against the coal companies who wield power on the Navajo reservation. Many Indians, in fact, saw the whole controversy fueled more by the energy-leasing plans of these companies than by a genuine Navajo-Hopi enmity.

In a 1996 "accommodation agreement," the Hopis accepted a federal payment to be used to extend their reservation, and they agreed to extend seventy-five-year leases to Navajos remaining on the Hopi Partition Land. But the situation remained volatile as some Navajos refused to sign the leases, provoking another wave of negotiations with the federal government and the Hopis.

The Oneida case represents a different aspect of the land-claim wars. Before their dispossession by whites, the Oneidas occupied what would become New York State. Under removal pressure, some went to Canada, some relocated in the 1830s in Wisconsin, and others stayed on a reservation in their homeland. In the mid-1980s, a century and half after their removal, the Wisconsin Oneidas sued for ''about 250,000 acres of land in central New York,'' which they claimed had been promised the Oneidas by George Washington in return for Oneida assistance in the Revolutionary War. The United States Supreme Court in 1985 recognized the Oneida groups in all three locations—Wisconsin, New York, and Canada—and upheld their right to negotiate a settlement for the New York land.

The New York Oneidas joined in the negotiations, but in 1993 they split from the Wisconsin group and began trying to negotiate a settlement on their own. In late 1996, the New York and Wisconsin Oneidas were mired in accusations and counteraccusations, the latter insisting that they had always planned to return home and would do so even if ''forced . . . to reestablish ourselves in the homeland separate and apart'' from New York kin.

The Wisconsin Oneidas had considered simply buying land in New York, and as Indian tribes gained in economic power, this strategy promised to become more popular, although tribes had to work with and win the approval of the Interior Department to ensure that purchases could be added to federal trust lands.

Some were able to buy land out of settlement money won from the U.S. Court of Claims. Others used money generated through private enterprise, chiefly gambling. In this respect, the Mashantucket Pequots of Connecticut blazed the way spectacularly, using funds from their lucrative Foxwoods Resort Casino, opened in early 1992, to extend their reservation base. By mid-1995, this small group had accumulated about fifteen hundred acres and planned to more than quadruple that amount.

Other Indian groups without the Mashantucket Pequots' financial resources were acting innovatively to reclaim Indian country. Along California's rugged northern coastal mountain range, a nonprofit consortium of ten small, federally recognized tribes, including the Pomos and the Yukis, in late 1996 had pooled their funds to create the Intertribal Sinkyone Wilderness Project, purchasing a 3,800-acre upland tract for an intertribal park. On this landscape covered by ''rolling second-growth Douglas fir, scrubby ceanothus, and resurgent tan oak,'' they were working to reestablish some traditional lifeways, such as fishing and wild-food gathering, and to develop earth-friendly enterprises, such as a native-plants nursery and limited logging designed to maintain "a sustainable, mature forest."

Even as Indians worked to reclaim and restore lands previously lost, they found themselves for the first time also having some environmental control over lands not likely to revert to their legal ownership. Members of the Intertribal Sinkyone Wilderness project were also at work in adjoining Sinkyone Wilderness State Park, where they had contracted to help renew an old logging road. They not only planted native trees and grasses, but had authority to stop earth-moving equipment if it appeared to threaten an Indian burial ground or other historic site. "Ten years ago Indians were totally excluded from projects like this," said one. "The attitude was: What? Indians? What do they have to do with this? Well, we're defining how this thing needs to go forward because this is really Indian land, and state parks are starting to acknowledge that."

Federal officials were arriving at this acknowledgment, too, in the wake of an executive order "directing federal land managers to protect American Indian sacred sites." In Wyoming the U.S. Park Service worked with the Lakota Sioux to reserve Devil's Tower, a volcanic-rock landmark in the state's northeast corner, for exclusive Indian use for ceremonial observance in June each year.

To the west, in Wyoming's Bighorn National Forest, two predominantly Indian-led alliances joined with historical preservation organizations, the U.S. forestry service, and county officials to devise a preservation plan that not only protected the ancient native Medicine Wheel, a massive stone circle in the forest, but also restricted "timber harvesting, mining, and tourism development" on the mountain on which it sits. The plan also specified "24 days of exclusive use for enrolled Native Americans," as well as the opportunity to close the Wheel area to the general public at other times "for short ceremonials."

These gains by Native Americans brought them into direct conflict with non-Indians, who saw the issue as unfair preferential treatment. Commercial guides refused to abide by a voluntary ban on climbing Devil's Tower in the month of June, a busy period for their enterprises. Other non-Indians not only resented being excluded on the basis of ethnicity, but questioned where such policies would lead, arguing that under such precedents, any group may choose to "discover transformational spiritual power in land over which they would like to exert control.''

A wrinkle was added to the land-control debate by the Mount Graham telescope controversy, where Native American perspectives and scientific inquiry collided head-on. A consortium that was planning to place giant telescopes atop the peak, in the Pinaleno Mountains of Arizona, in order to extend astronomical knowledge ran into concerted resistance from San Carlos Apaches, who argued that the telescope construction would destroy the sacred nature of the mountain and would endanger its old-growth forest. The project lurched forward, but Apache activists repeatedly forced halts and delays that left the outcome in question.

If the Indians' renewed influence over off-reservation sacred sites stimulated conflict, their extended hunting and fishing rights stimulated even more. The conflicts and court decisions of the 1970s in the Pacific Northwest—especially the Boldt decision of 1974—had ignited a white backlash that continued through most of the 1980s. Sport and commercial fishermen agitated against enforcement of court rulings favorable to Indians, and law officers refused to protect Indians exercising those rights. The situation grew so severe that comparisons were made between Washington State in the late 1970s and early 1980s and ''the resistance of southern states to civil rights during the 1960s.'' Finally, in the late 1980s, Washington State officials acknowledged and pledged to uphold the tribes' hard-won court rights.

Indians continued to go to court to argue for the right to hunt and fish under their own rules both off the reservation and on it. In the courtroom, much depended on the agreements that had been made when reservations were established. The Menominees, for example, lost a battle over the right to fish and hunt across their former territory—''10 million acres of public land in eastern and central Wisconsin''—and to fish off-shore in Lake Michigan, the Wisconsin River, Green Bay, and Lake Winnebago. District Court Judge Barbara Crabb ruled that an 1831 treaty ''allowed hunting and fishing until the lands were 'surveyed or sold by the president,' '' and this had been accomplished in 1834.

By contrast, the Abenakis of Vermont won an acknowledgment of their independent fishing rights from a Vermont district court judge in 1989. The decision was based on the state's lack of proof that the

Abenakis had ever "abandoned or ceded" their homeland or lost these rights through any clear act of extinguishment. But in 1992, the Vermont Supreme Court reversed the decision, concluding that the Abenakis' claims "had been extinguished by 'the increasing weight of history.'"

Conclusions like these could negate many gains or potential gains in Indian country, but other judgments have run counter to this one. In early 1996, federal Judge Richard Kyle decreed "that the Fond du Lac Band of Chippewa have permanent rights to hunt, fish and gather over a large area of eastern Minnesota . . . under rules set by their own people and not the state's." With this ruling, the state was limited to "regulat[ing] the band's harvest when it is necessary for public safety, public health and conservation."

Difficulties in enforcing uneven judgments abounded both for tribes and state and local officials whether the hunting and fishing was occurring off or on the reservations. In fall 1996, the Sisseton-Wahpeton Sioux of South Dakota opened their deer-hunting season a week before the state did, amid warnings from South Dakota officials that nontribal members hunting with Sioux licenses during this week would be arrested.

The central issue is not whether a tribe can issue its own licenses to nonmembers, but to what extent the tribe can and will be regarded as a separate, sovereign political entity. It is this question that bedevils the residents of Indian country—both Indian and non-Indian—as well as the officials who deal with Indian policy matters and—to an extent—the urban Indians who look to their homelands for renewal. It is a question that has implications even for those Americans who live far from any reservation.

In February 1995, the Western Shoshone National Council sent a notice to city, county, and state officials—and to the president of the United States: "Your office lacks jurisdiction within the Territory of the Western Shoshone Nation. . . . Your office is hereby put on notice by the Western Shoshone National Government."

Tribes were asserting their sovereignty to an extent undreamed of through most of the history of Indian-white relations. They did so with a clear understanding of the importance of their land, estimated at 54 million acres in the late 1980s. Even though this land often remained splintered through sales and allotment, even though the number of Indians actually living on reservations dropped to 35 percent by 1990, the presence of a separate land base and the heritage and hopes that it represented continued to draw others back for short or long periods.

In sum, reservations were being transformed politically from the barren lands of the late nineteenth century and most of the twentieth century to the locus of power for tribes, "defin[ing] the unique status of Indians in modern America." As Suquamish tribal leader Georgia C. George put it when she addressed a tribal leaders' conference in 1991: "Without a land base, how can we keep from eventually being swallowed up? Without land 'sovereignty' becomes just an old word that our grandfathers told us about."

Tribal independence was buoyed by a series of court decisions acknowledging tribes' jurisdictional powers, their "residual sovereignty," which was first affirmed in the 1832 Supreme Court ruling *Worcester* v. *Georgia*. A pivotal ruling had occurred in the 1959 *Williams* v. *Lee* case, when the Supreme Court had decided that a non-Indian storekeeper on the Navajo reservation must go through the Navajo court, and not the state courts, in order to seek collection of a debt from a Navajo couple. In subsequent rulings, the U.S. courts upheld tribes' rights to set their own membership standards, to extend their jurisdiction over both Indian and non-Indian reservation residents, and to tax corporations—including energy companies—wishing to do business on the reservation.

Those tribes with a better economic base, strong leadership and unity, and most of their reservation still in trust were best able to build upon this opportunity for political self-determination. But the lines between tribal sovereignty and federal and state authority were not clearly and consistently drawn.

Many complications stemmed from the question "Who comes under tribal jurisdiction and when?" Non-Indians living on reservations were now supposed to abide by tribal ordinances, but many resisted, citing their long fee-simple ownership of the tracts within the reservation boundaries and resenting tribally imposed taxes and restrictions that seemed arbitrary and exploitative, a form of "racial separatism" to people who did not share in tribal membership or benefits.

Even routine police matters on reservations unleashed a host of jurisdictional questions. A case making its way through the U.S. courts in late 1996 centered on whether the tribal government at the Fort Berthold reservation in North Dakota had jurisdiction over a traffic accident that occurred on the reservation between two non-Indians, one living there and one visiting on business.

When tribes did have clear and extended powers, there was always the danger that leaders would mishandle the power, violating members' own civil rights. As John Stricker, a Yankton Sioux, had observed in the 1960s, "We say the white man is violating our rights, but we as Indians, ourselves, we have ambitious Indians that would become dictators on the reservation and deny us our own rights."

Indians advocating greater sovereignty were quick to point out that these same dangers existed in the American political system in general, and even critics of Indian sovereignty agreed that "tribal governments as a whole are probably no more mismanaged or corrupt than many municipal administrations elsewhere in the United States." However, many tribes were still struggling toward creating an effective system of checks and balances, toward true accountability on the part of their leaders.

Marina Ortega, an environmental activist from the Santa Ysabel reservation northeast of San Diego, California, noted that tribal governments were "capable of making your life very difficult if you live on the reservation." She explained, "If you don't support the current political party, you can be denied housing, you can be denied electricity, you can be denied sanitary facilities, water."

Opposition to the tribal government in power sometimes sparked violence. Political factionalism on the Senecas' Cattaraugus reservation in early 1995 led to a shootout in which three people died. The elected president of the Seneca Nation, Dennis Bowen, Sr., had been impeached and reinstated, but a faction refused to recognize his reinstatement and elected another president, Karen Bucktooth. The three who were slain were Bucktooth supporters, shot "after storming [an] administrative building occupied by Bowen supporters."

More often, reservations were simply thrown into political turmoil for long periods. Various factions mounted recall drives, and council seats repeatedly changed hands. Tribal leaders were charged with corruption, many convicted and sent to jail. Among those sentenced in 1996 were former Three Affiliated Tribes Chairman Wilbur Wilkinson of Fort Berthold on embezzlement and other charges, and former White Earth tribal Chairman Darrell "Chip" Wadena on a host of charges, including conspiracy, theft, misapplication of funds, and embezzlement. Former Navajo Chairman Peter MacDonald was serving a fourteen-year sentence on bribery and conspiracy convictions growing in part out of his participation in the Native American Construction Company fraud. The Navajos—whose own district court had found MacDonald guilty—and the National Congress of American Indians were nonetheless seeking a pardon for him. Meanwhile, his successor, Albert Hale, was facing a recall attempt on charges that he had misused funds.

Indian governance problems became more critical with the rise of Indian gaming. Proponents of tribal casinos called gaming the new buffalo. Just as the animal provided for a range of Plains needs—food, clothing, tools, shelter—so the money from tribal gaming, coupled with sales of cigarettes at tax-free Indian shops, promised to provide a steady and even abundant flow of cash to reservation governments and to individual Indians. The Seminoles of Florida started the gaming trend in 1979 with a high-stakes bingo operation, but it was not until the 1988 passage of the Indian Gaming Regulation Act that the enterprise began to seem possible and profitable to many tribes.

The act outlined three classes of gaming: the first was "traditional Indian low-stakes gambling done as part of ceremonies"; the second encompassed "bingo and several similar forms of gaming"; and the third included "slot machines, baccarat, blackjack, and other casino games." The second and third classes were subject to regulation by a commission, and to enter into them, tribes had to work out agreements with state governments based on the types of gambling already state approved.

Many states were reluctant to "allow" Indian gaming, both because of the legal and moral issues involved and because tribes could not be taxed on the proceeds. In New Mexico, Governor Gary Johnson signed gambling compacts with fourteen tribes in 1995, but the state supreme court ruled casino gambling illegal. By the end of the year, the tribes were ordered to shut down their casinos. Some won exemptions until an appeal could be heard; others did not. At the Mescaleros' Casino Apache in Lincoln County, layoffs from the forced closure in 1996 "nearly doubled the unemployment rate" in the county. Meanwhile, fourteen states "ask[ed] an appeals court to support New Mexico's contention that its tribally operated casinos are illegal."

Many Indians argued that the states should have no part in approving or regulating Indian gaming, that these matters fell under Indian-federal relations. Even with the wrangling between state and tribal governments, however, Indian gaming grew phenomenally. By 1991, tribes were operating "more than 130 legal operations," which garnered "more than 500 million tax-free dollars." By the mid-nineties, tribal gaming was grossing $5 to $6 billion annually, in large part through "forty full-fledged casinos, in twenty states." While this still represented only a small fraction of the $330 billion a year spent on gambling in America, the net income produced nonetheless represented a significant windfall.

How significant can be demonstrated by the rapid rise of the Mashantucket Pequot fortune, their gross gaming revenues estimated at $1 billion in 1995. They had borrowed money from investors for a series of rapid expansions, but were already retiring their debts and were reported as candidates for the Fortune 500. With fewer than 350 tribal members, the Pequot wealth might be "considered more from the perspective of a family fortune," in which case the tribe seemed destined to be "on a par with some of the most famous wealthy Americans," such as the Kennedy family.

The Pequot group overcame state officials' resistance by agreeing to put "25 to 30 percent of its gross gambling revenues into a special state fund to aid local governments." Still, non-Indian state residents resented the group's growing power based in large part on its unique relationship with the federal government. When land is added to the reservation, it continues to be exempted from property taxes and from local and state zoning and environmental regulations. Thus, a planned Pequot reservation extension in 1995 led the mayor of nearby Ledyard, Connecticut, to fume, "Here's the world's richest Indian tribe . . . and [Interior Secretary] Bruce Babbitt feels they need to have another 247 acres to avoid zoning and environmental regulations."

As the Pequots and their neighbors attempted to deal with the tribe's phenomenal success, gaming initiatives across Indian country yielded mixed results. The enterprise was simply not feasible for many tribes because of isolated locations and/or existing competition for gambling dollars. Some tribes were deeply split whether to mount a gaming enterprise; the Seneca troubles that led to the deaths of the three Bucktooth supporters resulted in part from hostilities between progaming and antigaming factions. And compacts with states were only as valid as the latest court ruling allowed them to be.

However, the advantages for tribes with a viable location were clear. Gambling greatly eased reservation unemployment and "reverse[d] or at least slow[ed] the normal flow of dollars from reservations to border towns," its revenues in the early 1990s filling the void caused by budget cuts and faltering energy royalties.

In short, the revenues were a godsend to many tribes. While some simply divided the proceeds among individual members, many used the money to improve the reservation base, building "the kind of infrastructure that most American towns take for granted, but that many Indian communities conspicuously lack: fire and police departments, clinics, child care centers, roads, sewage systems and power plants, and new housing." Near El Paso, Texas, the Tigua Indians used the proceeds from their gaming hall and tax-free cigarette shop to erect a center where Tigua youth learned about their traditional culture. The Winnebagos of Nebraska earmarked gaming money for a variety of initiatives, including a reservation nursing home and a dialysis clinic, youth programs, and wildlife restoration.

Yet troubles were escalating on some reservations with gambling operations. On the Oneida Nation Territory in Madison County, New York, tribespeople in 1995 protested that their government had shut them out of both the decision making and the benefits in setting up the Turning Stone Casino, the Oneida Nation Smokeshop, and the Oneida Nation Bingo Hall. They charged that the tribe as a whole had not been involved in the gambling agreement with the state, "nor were they informed as to massive capital expenditures, such as the new bingo hall, hotel or the slotless slots." Further, they were not receiving any public accounting of the gambling income, they saw many of the jobs generated filled by non-Indians, and they continued to live in substandard housing, with limited access to health care.

The presence of gaming, then, could increase frictions and inequities on the reservation—so much so that in fall 1995 about half the residents of the Lake County Pomo reservation in California fled their homes as gun battles flared among tribal members "over control of the tribe's land and its casino," the Pomo Palace, north of San Francisco.

In November 1996, Colorado Senator Ben Nighthorse Campbell was the keynote speaker at the Western Indian Gaming Conference in Reno, Nevada. He warned that the lucrative nature of Indian gambling was creating conflict over who benefited and how much, as well as provoking white resentment and luring young Indians into thinking they didn't need to continue their educations because they could live off gaming proceeds.

Other Indian leaders voiced similar concerns, and many saw gaming as only a temporary and fragile vehicle for economic independence. But as Gaiashkibos, the Ojibway president of the National Congress of American Indians, explained to a congressional subcommittee, "Gaming is all that many tribes have today that can work. . . . We had no competitive edge to attract non-Indian business nor the financial resources to create our own businesses and employ our people."

Reservation statistics remained grim, with an unemployment rate far above that of the national population. In the decade of the 1980s, the overall reservation unemployment rate climbed from 27 percent to 40 percent, "while the unemployment rate for the nation as a whole hovered between 5 and 7 percent."

These numbers, of course, translate to low incomes, something that urban Indians shared with their reservation kin. In 1990, almost a third of Indian households received public assistance money, and almost a fourth fell "below the poverty line." In the mid-1990s, Indian family income in general averaged less than $22,000, short of two thirds of the $35,000 national average.

On some reservations, the average income lingered much lower. "I've seen these people cry," said tribal administrator Robert De La Garza of the Kickapoos of Eagle Pass, Texas, in September 1996. Having won federal recognition, most of the tribe had moved from shanties under the Eagle Pass bridge between Texas and Mexico to substandard housing on a stark 125-acre reservation near the town. Few could afford the government's new brick houses or obtain low-cost loans. "The only money we have comes from there," De La

Garza told a reporter, indicating a soft-drink machine in the tribal government building. "In peak season, we've been getting $60 a month."

Government support was more extensive on many reservations, but federal funding efforts continued to meet with mixed and generally disheartening results. Since the days of John Collier's programs in the 1930s, the federal government, through its agencies, had repeatedly attempted to "provide capital to reservation economies under the assumption that economic growth would follow." In far too many cases, it had not or had provided only a temporary economic boost.

Further, the federal government in the form of the Bureau of Indian Affairs had been as remiss in its handling of funds as the most careless and corrupt tribal leader—and on a far larger scale. In 1993, auditors were attempting to make sense of a financial system "in such disarray that they could not audit $3.2 billion of $4.4 billion in BIA assets." Moreover, the $2.1 billion Indian trust fund containing individual and tribal incomes from mineral royalties, claims settlements, and other sources had been woefully administered, with no systematic filing or auditing for decades.

Even though the BIA had become far more sensitive to Indian issues—and was now largely Indian-staffed—it remained something of a bureaucratic black hole, with both the traditional Washington-centered administration of Indian programs and the more recent regionally centered approach having their problems. The end result was that "remarkably little of the agency's money," including funds held in trust, reached those for whom it was crucial. BIA officials in 1994 admitted that perhaps "less than 20 cents of each dollar" from the 1994 $1.8 billion BIA budget would make it to the reservations.

Economic woes were fed and compounded by the fact that school dropout rates for Indians both on and off the reservation remain higher than for other segments of the population, despite some remarkable initiatives in Indian-administered education.

Indians also continued to have more health problems than other American groups. High rates of alcoholism led to a disproportionate number of children born with fetal alcohol syndrome. Almost four in ten Indian men were still dying "before reaching age 45, many from diabetes complications" common to Indian populations. In South Dakota the counties with the highest cancer rates were those containing reservations. In Arizona, Navajo youth were reported having "a cancer rate 17 times the national average."

Indian activists pointed to the intense environmental pollution present on many reservations, created or exacerbated by "oil wells, strip mines, timber clear-cuts, power plants, and industrial wastes." In Navajo country, the massive strip-mining of coal, with all of its attendant health hazards, continued, while more than a thousand abandoned uranium mines sat "leaking radioactive contaminants into the air"—and into the earth and water supplies. Toxic waste dumps abound in or near Indian country, "an estimated 1,200 hazardous waste sites . . . located on or adjacent to reservations."

These toxic-waste sites stimulated an economic controversy in Indian country as well as an environmental one. Like other low-income minority groups, Indians had had little or no say over the locating of waste sites and received little or no compensation for their presence. Then in the late eighties, waste company officials began soliciting tribal approval to locate "national landfills, toxic waste incinerators, or nuclear waste repositories on their lands."

Since tribal members held land in common, any leasing deals that were struck would mean money for the whole tribe, "to be distributed per capita or invested in tribal projects such as subsidized housing or other economic development ventures." In addition, tribes could create or expand reservation employment by specifying that their members have preference for the jobs which resulted.

These advantages rapidly diminished if the tribe was large. The Rosebud Sioux, with eighteen thousand members, rejected a landfill project on their reservation, one commenting, "How dumb do they think we are? They say we have 85 percent unemployment. So we get a megadump and what do we have? 84.5 percent."

For some, however, such as the three-hundred-member Campo tribe, the proposals were more than tempting, even though they put the tribal government at odds with Indian and non-Indian neighbors, who sounded the familiar refrain "not in my backyard."

In 1987, the Campo tribe, with an unemployment rate of 79 percent and an annual tribal budget of $15,000, began entertaining landfill proposals for their reservation in southeastern San Diego County, California. In 1989, the tribe announced plans to develop a six-hundred-acre commercial landfill that would hold solid waste from the cities in San Diego County. The Campos immediately ran afoul of their non-Indian and Indian neighbors, who feared water contamination, and of Indian and non-Indian environmental activists from across the West.

Still, the tribe moved forward with its plans, requiring the developer to cover all the costs of starting the program and establishing and meeting stringent regulatory standards. By 1992, thanks to waste company funding as the project developed, "tribal unemployment had been reduced to thirty percent, and annual tribal government revenues had skyrocketed to $700,000." The next year, Interior Secretary Bruce Babbitt approved the Campos' lease with the waste company, at the same time setting forth guidelines to guard against exploitation and environmental damage.

As the project moved forward, the Campos stood to gain as much as $3 million a year in income and 100 percent employment. To them, the landfill provided "real hope, the first hope [they'd] had since the coming of the whites, that their children's lives [could] be better than their own." Again, however, this economic solution would work only for certain tribes. Besides, troubling environmental implications remained.

Indians, then, thought and worked creatively to build reservation economies that did not depend on gambling income or waste dumps, toxic or otherwise. Despite its myriad problems, the Indian country of the mid-1990s was more than ever since the days of dispossession a place of creative economic possibility.

There were some acknowledged advantages in pursuing new economic programs. Since the tribes did not have to pay local, state, or federal taxes—and since they had access to "millions of dollars in government grants"—they could offer cost-effective packages to business partners. Oregon's Colquille tribe, which gained federal recognition in 1989, by the mid-1990s was pursuing a variety of business options, knowing that they could offer a manufacturer such incentives as "12 million in cut-rate government financing" if the manufacturer hired "30 tribal members at $20,000 apiece."

However, tribes also continued to operate at a disadvantage, in part as a result of their trust status. They still could not use their most valuable asset, the federal trust land that comprises more than half the reservation land base, as collateral for loans, for this land was protected by the federal government against seizure by creditors. "No one wants to do business with you unless you can be sued," explained one tribal attorney. Trust lands remained underutilized, often as grazing tracts.

Sovereignty also complicated economic development initiatives. In the 1980s, U.S. courts upheld tribes' rights "to tax and regulate as sovereigns," but this made companies wary of doing business with them, for it added an element of uncertainty to partnerships of any duration.

In addition, federal funds and tax breaks often did not offset the lack of other advantages sought by companies. To lure them, tribes sometimes created "enterprise zones" with the "less restrictive regulations" that opponents of toxic waste dumps feared.

There was also the problem of combining the traditional values tribes were trying to retain or regain with the realities of the marketplace, with what constitutes entrepreneurship in a capitalistic, commodity-based economy. Louie Pitt of Oregon's Warm Springs tribe argued, "Being Indian means that you stay home and take care of your people, and that you're not out to max profits." By contrast, a consultant to the Mississippi Choctaws in their successful climb from privation to diversified industry, noted, "Our philosophy is, if it's good business, if it's legitimate, if it makes a profit, there ain't nothing wrong with it."

In a study of development plans of three different tribes in the early 1980s, David Vinje found that they resembled those of other rural or nonurban economic planning groups; in other words, they did not reflect a distinctive Indian identity. However, the diversity and potential of the plans led him to conclude that Indian cultural values and economic development might coexist, particularly if tribes adopted "small-scale tribally operated economic activity of a labor-intensive nature."

Some tribes have proven successful at mounting such manageable, productive enterprises. The Choctaws used a grant and a BIA loan to establish a factory assembling wired parts for General Motors cars and trucks. Although the enterprise faltered shortly after opening, it soon grew stronger and allowed the tribe to gain financing for other assembly plants, as well as for an elaborate resort complex.

The best-known example of Indian enterprise remains that of the Cherokee Nation, which, despite its lack of a reservation base, boasts various manufacturing plants and other businesses—"a motel, gift shops, a ranch, a lumber company, [and] a greenhouse business with satellite stores in dozens of regional shopping malls." Such initiatives do present dangers in the changing American economy; in fiscal year 1995–1996, Cherokee Nation Industries, "one of the oldest subsidiaries the tribe possesses," ran into financial troubles and had to lay off employees. It revived, thanks to a loan from the Cherokee Nation Tribal Council and new contracts "to manufacture cables, fiber optics accessories and other products."

Light manufacturing—from the eastern Cherokees' mirror industry to the Sioux Manufacturing Corporation's production of "radar-absorbing tank camouflage"—remains the most obvious route into the economic mainstream. Tribes are also developing and extending tourism operations, which have gained in appeal as Indians assert control over their land bases and the terms of the tourism. Reservation hotels, conference centers, recreation areas, and gift and specialty craft shops are becoming popular.

A new emphasis on "culturally appropriate" economic programs is also having an effect. The Nez Perces of Idaho have launched a horse-breeding operation with funds from the tribal coffers, from the U.S. Department of Health and Human Services, and from the First Nations Development Institute. They are cross-breeding Appaloosas with rare central Asian horses. "We were once horsemen, we once raised cattle and worked our own land," says Rudy Shebala, a Navajo who married into the Nez Perces and runs the breeding program. "These horses will help us get the old way back."

One of the most promising economic avenues for tribes is management of their own natural resources. In 1993, Indians were reported controlling "approximately 30 percent of the coal west of the Mississippi River, over 40 percent of uranium sources, 4 percent of known oil and gas reserves, and other mineral resources of indeterminate value," as well as "millions of acres of forest land and the rights to an unquantified amount of water."

Since the passage of the Indian self-determination act of 1975, tribes have been assuming the management of these resources. The Navajos and the Jicarillas of Arizona have "their own tribal oil and gas commissions to regulate production on their lands," and the Jicarillas have also entered into "risk-sharing joint ventures with petroleum companies." Representatives of various tribes continue to work together for control and management of energy resources in the Council of Energy Resources Tribes; by 1993, fifty-three tribes belonged to this organization.

Energy-related reservation jobs for Indians and tribal income from direct revenues, royalties, and severance taxes have grown handsomely, and the potential for further economic gain is enormous—the Crow reservation alone "sits on $2.5 billion in mineral resources." Of course, that potential exists only for those tribes whose lands contain exploitable resources. And these natural riches bring their own problems. For one thing, tribal governments have had trouble "managing and reinvesting windfall resource royalties" because they feel obliged to meet the pressing needs of reservation residents, either through per-capita payments or through direct funding of reservation improvements.

For another, there is also the question of how to honor and maintain traditional values regarding the land. In the 1980s, the Navajo tribal government reluctantly concluded that members must live with the effects of "coal gasification plants, electrical generating plants, etc." in order to generate "jobs and income." At the Warm Springs reservation in the Oregon Cascades, tribal officials overrode residents' protests against extensive tribal logging by arguing that the jobs gained are worth the loss of natural habitat for wildlife.

There is also the temptation to sell hard-won water rights. The history of water rights in the West—and Indian water rights in particular—has only become more convoluted with the growth of competing interests. One recent water project "pit[ted] southern and Ute Mountain Utes against Navajos, and non-Indian environmentalists against both groups."

Indians have won some recent victories—most notably the affirmation of the Pyramid Lake Paiutes' control of water in a chunk of northern Nevada—and with dwindling western water supplies and thirsty, mushrooming western cities, "converting Indian water into money could become a major source of new revenue."

The treatment of natural resources as commodities—and the effect of this on the reservations—strikes at the core of many Indians' understanding of trust land as preserved "homeland" and "sanctuary." Vine Deloria, Jr., has noted that tribes need to determine "whether the reservation is to be considered a homeland or a resource," but Indian country before dispossession was both. Many tribes are now committed to seeking out "culturally appropriate" economic activities and experimenting with less invasive resource extraction (such as sustained yield logging) in hopes of making the "rez" both.

Many are also speaking out forcefully against the environmental degradation accompanying the activities of some non-Indians and of their own tribespeople. "The Yakima Indian Nation is not interested in discussing with you or anyone how [many] toxic chemicals can be dumped into the Columbia River by the pulp-and-paper industry," Yakima Councilman Harry Smisken told the Oregon Environmental Quality Commission regarding a 1990 Yakima resolution against chlorine bleaching by the industry.

"The Yakima Indian nation does not want to debate mixing zones for toxic pollution, nor do we want to debate whether a mile, two miles, or the entire Columbia River is water-quality-limited. . . . Those topics wrongly assume that it is okay to dump pollution into the river that can impact the health of our fish and the health of our people."

Hundreds of Indian environmental groups exist and operate on local and international levels. One of the most prominent of these groups is Citizens Against Ruining Our Environment (CARE), formed by Navajos in 1989. In 1990, CARE offered a conference on toxic threats to Indian country and drew "over two hundred Indian delegates from thirty tribes." CARE has not only participated in the fight against waste dumps on Indian land, but has also stopped clearcutting in the Chuska Mountains by the Navajo Nation's own logging operation.

Other native groups have halted mining at sacred sites, have challenged the presence and efficacy of dams, and have "reassert[ed] treaty rights to dictate stream flows." Sometimes their environmentalism has led to previously unheard-of alliances, as in the Black Hills

Alliance, when "the cowboys and Indians got together" to fight for pure groundwater.

Like the members of the Intertribal Sinkyone Wilderness project, others also are tackling formidable land-restoration projects. The Pomos are at the forefront of an effort to clean up northern California's Clear Lake, where herbicide poisoning has ravaged the purple tule plants that have served as a Pomo food source for centuries. With grants from the EPA, they are "leading a multi-agency local, state and federal effort." The Puyallup tribe in Washington has received a grant to restore and develop a polluted area bordering the Port of Tacoma. The White Earth Chippewas of Minnesota inhabit a reservation that was virtually stripped of its forests by non-Indian lumber companies during the allotment era, a reservation where most of the land has passed out of Chippewa hands. Yet their White Earth Land Recovery Project by late 1996 had "restored over 1,000 acres of land within the reservation, defeated several ecologically and culturally destructive development proposals, and begun to restore the traditional land-based economy that depended on local products like maple syrup and wild rice." In 1996, an estimated 200,000 pounds of wild rice was being processed through the project's mill.

Indian activism does not change the fact that Indians are still vastly outnumbered—in the 1990 census they made up less than 1 percent of the American population—and that much of Indian tradition has been or is being lost. "It's probably 99 and 44/100ths gone," says one Tonkawa of her tribal tradition, which a Tonkawa historian is trying to re-create with travels to archives to study early historical accounts on Tonkawa ways.

Native American languages are fading as well; while more than two thirds of North America's three-hundred-odd native languages are still spoken, fewer and fewer children speak them. Even the Navajos— who still have Navajo-language radio stations—have undergone a sea change, with "90 percent of Navajo children entering school speak[ing] English, but not Navajo," as opposed to a generation ago, when "the reverse [was] true."

Indians have attempted to stem such cultural loss in part by borrowing traditions from other tribes with stronger continuing identities and by creating pan-Indian ones. They do not agree on the rightness or efficacy of such attempts at creative survival. Longtime Lakota Sioux activist Russell Means decries the appropriation by other tribes of Plains Indian songs, the vehicles for knowledge of "where we came from and why, where we're going and why," arguing that with the "mixing" the songs "have been corrupted." He also thinks that the burgeoning powwows offer a weak, easy, and garbled imitation of tribal traditions.

Means has a point. Yet powwows have emerged as the most common and accessible vehicle for pan-Indian identity. Indian publications devote page after page to listings of these events nationwide. Clearly, many Native Americans find the powwows a meaningful and affirming form of self-expression, whatever has been diluted or borrowed.

Indian identity continues to assert itself in a variety of ways. The Native American Church and other Indian religious groups remain vital, despite some freedom-of-religion setbacks in the courts. Native American literature has flourished in the late twentieth century, writers such as James Welch, Leslie Marmon Silko, Louise Erdrich, Michael Dorris, and Sherman Alexie articulating both the commonalities and distinctly native dimensions of twentieth-century life.

Evidence of Indian cultural persistence and determination filters into the mainstream news of the day, from a report that a Seminole family convinced Florida officials to bypass building codes and allow them to remain in their traditional chickee to a note that the U.S. Department of Veterans Affairs has begun reimbursing the Navajo Nation's Department of Veterans Affairs for veterans' use of medicine men and traditional healing ceremonies.

Whatever growth and changes do occur, it is primarily the land itself—the fragile, divided land—that supports and sustains Indian identity and culture. "Who we are is our land, our trees, and our lakes," says Winona LaDuke. Such pronouncements may occasionally sound like self-serving romanticism, but they are an expression of centuries of Indian reality. And they reflect an environmental consciousness that cannot be ignored in an era of rapidly vanishing species, of troubling climatic shifts and widespread pollution. As Asdzaa Yazhi Bedoni said, there is no place but here. And Indians occupy this "here" in increasingly vital and visible ways.

*   *   *

The Indian experience of dispossession is rife with heartache and horrors. At the same time, as apologists point out, the federal government
has striven over the decades to make good on some of its promises.
As early as 1947, it had paid an estimated $800 million for Indian
lands. Since 1936, it has appropriated billions more for Indian economic development. It has attempted, however imperfectly, to meet
Indian social-service needs. But throughout most of the history of
Indian-white relations, the government did not listen to the Indians
themselves.

Few officials—and other cultural representatives, such as missionaries—ever took into account the differences among Indian groups,
the fact that "no single policy can be devised that will successfully
serve all Indians."

Fewer still were able to look or function outside a system that
attempted to coerce the Indian into an Anglo mold. One can argue
that the representatives of Anglo culture were simply people of their
era, their actions and attitudes consistent with the understandings and
standards of the day, but that does not alter the fact of their debilitating
effect on Indian lives. "If you have come to help me, you are wasting
your time," an aboriginal Australian woman once told a visitor. "But
if you have come because your liberation is bound up with mine, then
let us work together." Representatives of Anglo culture repeatedly
came to "help" Indians, to do to and for them, and therein lies a
painful record of missed opportunities.

For Indians were adapting all along, adapting so well that many of
the problems in Indian-white relations today might not exist if the
Indians had been allowed to continue to "evolve at their own pace
according to their own standards." For example, the Five Tribes of
the Southeast had made major adjustments in their lifeways before
being uprooted and forced into Indian Territory. Here they again made
major adaptations, only to be fragmented by allotment. Tribes in various locales developed ways of living on the reservation that worked
for them, amalgamations of old and new, only to lose much of this
independence as more dictatorial Anglo control became the norm. Indian agriculturists had some success in combining their own methods
and those of Anglo farmers, only to have the good agricultural lands
taken away from them and to be subjected to a confused variety of

government initiatives. Indians began integrating their own beliefs with those of Christianity, only to be told that anything outside the Anglo canon was heathen. Without this rejection, "the history of Christianity among the Indians might have been quite different."

In short, representatives of United States policy have, throughout most of the history of Indian-white relations, consistently sabotaged Indian adaptation. This includes those who acted in the utmost good faith, such as the 1930s liberal John Collier with his Anglo-style tribal governments and the Kennedy and Johnson administrations, which sought to impose generic minority assistance programs and Anglo economic-development models on the reservations.

Now, as the twenty-first century nears, Indians face renewed opportunities to work out their own liberation. With these opportunities, however, come a number of formidable challenges, chief among them the still-thorny issue of governance.

Indian governments have been crippled for too long by scarcity, factionalism, and white control. These patterns allow the ascendance of native leaders who "manipulate tribal resources for their and their supporters' benefit," or who are suspected of doing so. When this occurs, Indians have been compelled to look to federal, state, or local governments for assistance in assessing and righting the situation, thereby further undercutting any genuine political self-determination.

This is not to imply that Indian country seethes with dissension and corruption. Many tribal governments act as wisely and fairly as they can for the good of all who are affected by their policies. Some have shown tremendous initiative in remaking their political structures along lines appropriate to them. The Flathead tribal council in the 1970s began creating a government that was both independent of the BIA and clearly accountable to the Flathead people. It adapted freely between traditional ways and newer ones, simplifying tribal committee organization and devising a chain of command that reinforced responsible performance of duties. The Flatheads continue to succeed governmentally with "a blend of traditional and borrowed rules that encourage productivity."

Still, tribal sovereignty in general remains "ill-defined and ill-regulated." It is problematic for the Indians themselves, in part because it involves extended, draining legal battles over "land and resources, services and taxation, jurisdiction and politics," in part because any legal gains may evaporate if federal courts choose to cite judicial precedents that favor greater federal or state control. And tribal sovereignty is problematic for the American population as a whole because this affirmation of separateness invests groups with indeterminate independent powers in the national political and legal systems.

The problems of sovereignty focus attention on the very concept of Indianness. Who is an Indian and who is not? On a continental scale, the definition is expanding, especially as people classified as "Hispanic" and "Latino" question the significance of a Spanish heritage and look to their indigenous origins.

After centuries of interaction and intermarriage with other ethnic groups, some federally recognized tribes in the United States have no "full-bloods." Survival of Indian groups as tribes involves two opposing strategies: keeping the blood-quantum requirement fairly high "in order to protect the [tribe] as an entity" or widening the tribal base by taking in people with minimal blood connections. Those at the more exclusive end may require proof of a one-fourth bloodline to confirm an individual's tribal membership; those at the other extreme are represented by the Cherokee Nation of Oklahoma, which requires only "descent along Cherokee lines."

Then there are related and often shifting judgments: whether stepchildren can be entered on the tribal rolls, whether bloodlines can be traced through both the father and the mother. Tribes hold full power in these matters, as a U.S. Supreme Court decision made clear in 1978. Julia Martinez, a native of the Santa Clara Pueblo of New Mexico who married outside the tribe, sued for her daughter's right to become an enrolled member, but the court upheld the pueblo's right to enforce a 1939 ordinance that allowed the enrollment of children of men who married outside the pueblo while excluding the offspring of women in the same circumstances.

If such determinations—and blood-quantum levels in general— seem "based on obsolete ideas of race and ethnicity," the situation promises to grow only more complex. As historian David Rich Lewis notes, "Intermarriage and the emergence of mixed-blood groups . . . will continue to generate social and political factionalism within tribes," requiring "the periodic and painful redefinition of tribal identity and Indianness."

These redefinitions will be increasingly necessary as Indians who are trying to build upon their political and economic gains confront anew the old vexing question of who can speak for a tribe, or for Indians in general.

The questions, then, gain in urgency. What kinds of tribal membership standards are feasible and fair as Indians continue to intermarry with people from other tribes and with non-Indians? How does one test for "Indianness," especially when the economic and cultural stakes may be high? How do tests for Indianness fit into an American society that is attempting to move away from discrimination based on race and ethnicity?

Further, how can Indian sovereignty best be realized? How can tribal governments avoid or minimize a non-Indian backlash as they exert powers on the reservation and off? How far should they try to extend these powers? How can they govern reservations splintered both by non-Indian landholders and by deep-seated differences among Indian residents? How can they overcome "persistent social disorganization," building mature, accountable governments that draw upon the support of those governed and offer effective resolution of disputes?

In particular, how can they extricate themselves from the contradiction of depending upon, even seeking, a unique federal trust relationship while seeking or demanding self-determination? Decades of bureaucratic paternalism have brought them to this impasse—wanting freedom, and wanting and needing the federal aid many feel is still their due. Yet, as historian Francis Paul Prucha noted in 1984, "It is impossible to expand trust responsibility without also expanding paternalism, however devoutly the Indians and their spokesmen in government wish it were not so."

Indians recognize this reality, of course, and see many of their new economic initiatives as a means to true self-determination. Meanwhile, groups fight to get on the roll of federally recognized tribes in order to gain political and economic benefits, and the struggle for a balance "between federal trust and true tribal authority" will continue.

This struggle is not exclusive to the United States. For example, the indigenous people of Canada and the national and provincial officials there face many of the same dilemmas. But wherever the struggle is played out, it strikes at the roots of national identity.

In this sense, Indians as a minority group pose a major challenge to America's concept of itself, both in the old sense of a "melting pot" and in the new sense of a multicultural society. Historically, most Indians resisted full assimilation into the dominant culture. They retained both a distinctive cultural identity and a distinctive political one. They retained and regained portions of their former country.

Now, with these land bases—representing 3 to 4 percent of the nation's acreage—and with increased control over them, Indians can claim "an economic and political significance beyond that of other ethnic groups in shaping the present and future history of the American West," while once forgotten tribal groups gain prominence in the East as well. Indians' presence and growing power both reinforce the multicultural nature of American society and put it to the test. How can diversity be balanced with a commitment to legal and social equality? How can it be reconciled with the idea of American identity and community?

Scorned and driven to "the edge of the earth," hunted and coerced, Indians have survived to contribute significantly to the working out of such questions. They have survived to write a new chapter in the history of this ancient land, this United States, in myriad places and myriad ways Indian country still.

Notes

PREFACE

vii "It is, of course . . .": Angie Debo, *A History of the Indians of the United States* (Norman: University of Oklahoma Press, 1970), p. v.

viii "myriad mutations": Nancy Turner McCoy, "Perry or Seattle? What Difference Does It Make?" May 1, 1997, paper for Theories of Rhetoric course, New College, St. Edward's University, Austin, Texas. McCoy traces the fabrications, especially those made to reflect a 1960s ecological consciousness, and the public's acceptance of them.

viii "The critical edge . . .": Daniel K. Richter, *The Ordeal of the Longhouse: The Peoples of the Iroquois League in the Era of European Colonization* (Chapel Hill: University of North Carolina Press, 1992), p. 6.

viii "American Indian": See Deborah Locke, "American Indian or Native American?" *News from Indian Country* X, 24 (late December 1996): 16A.

ix "Even as late as . . .": Robert M. Utley, *The Indian Frontier of the American West 1846–1890* (Albuquerque: University of New Mexico Press, 1984), p. 12.

INTRODUCTION

xix "The *Natives* are very . . .": Qtd. in William Cronon, *Changes in the Land: Indians, Colonists, and the Ecology of New England* (New York: Hill and Wang, 1983), p. 60.

xix "experienced in the . . .": William Wood, qtd. in Neal Salisbury, *Manitou and Providence: Indians, Europeans, and the Making of New England, 1500–1643* (New York: Oxford University Press, 1994 ed.), p. 32.

xix "My people do not want . . .": Qtd. in Lee Miller, ed., *From the Heart: Voices of the American Indian* (New York: Vintage Books, 1995), p. 300.

xix "The Crow country . . .": Miller, p. 231.

xxi "If we are wounded . . .": Miller, p. 41.

xx "humans and animals . . .": Peter Nabokov, ed., *Native American Testimony: A Chronicle of Indian-White Relations from Prophecy to the Present, 1492–1992* (New York: Penguin Books, 1992), p. 50.

xx "Everything on this . . .": Mark St. Pierre, *Madonna Swan: A Lakota Woman's Story* (Norman: University of Oklahoma Press, 1991), p. 29.

xx "the number of workers . . .": Terry L. Anderson, *Sovereign Nations or Reservations? An Economic History of American Indians* (San Francisco: Pacific Research Institute for Public Policy, 1995), p. 58.

xx "carefully husband[ing] . . .": Richard White, *The Roots of Dependency: Subsistence, Environment, and Social Change Among the Choctaws, Pawnees, and Navajos* (Lincoln: University of Nebraska Press, 1988 ed.), p. 159.

xx "not to overcollect": David J. Wishart, *An Unspeakable Sadness: The Dispossession of the Nebraska Indians* (Lincoln: University of Nebraska Press, 1994), p. 25.

xx "could go . . .": Qtd. in Terry Anderson, p. 39.

xxi "an all-inclusive . . .": White, *Roots of Dependency,* p. 236.

xxi "I think of it . . .": Qtd. in Nabokov, p. 50.

xxi "the people of . . .": David Rich Lewis, "Still Native: The Significance of Native Americans in the History of the Twentieth-Century American West," *Western Historical Quarterly* XXIV, 2 (May 1993), p. 209.

xxi "stand for a . . .": In Arnold Krupat, ed., *Native American Autobiography: An Anthology* (Madison: University of Wisconsin Press, 1994), p. 311.

xxi "This country holds . . .": Nabokov, p. 132.

xxii "Our lands are . . .": Debo, p. 89.

xxii "The earth is . . .": Debo, p. 4.

xxii "no people owns . . .": Arlene Hirschfelder and Martha Kreipe de Montano, *The Native American Almanac: A Portrait of Native America Today* (New York: Prentice Hall, 1993), p. 273.

xxii "too sacred to . . .": Utley, *Indian Frontier,* p. 341.

xxii "I claim a right . . .": Miller, p. 341.

xxii "gave the white . . .": Qtd. in Nabokov, p. 97.

xxii "We fought and bled . . .": Miller, p. 233.

xxiii "should not be disturbed . . .": Qtd. in Alvin M. Josephy, Jr., *The Nez Perce Indians and the Opening of the Northwest* (New Haven: Yale University Press, 1971), p. xvi.

xxiii "seemed large . . .": Debo, p. 221.

xxiii "When they are taken . . .": Debo, p. 8.

xxiii "I don't want . . .": Debo, pp. 219–220.

xxiv "turn to water . . .": Debo, p. 229.

xxiv "Everything is X'ed . . .": Qtd. in Alvin M. Josephy, Jr., *Now That the Buffalo's Gone: A Study of Today's American Indians* (New York: Alfred A. Knopf, 1982), p. 132.

xxiv "also means history...": Qtd. in Peter Matthiessen, *Indian Country* (New York: Penguin Books, 1992 ed.), p. 119.

xxiv "Wherever we went...": John G. Neihardt, *Black Elk Speaks: Being the Life Story of a Holy Man of the Oglala Sioux* (New York: Pocket Books, 1972), p. 112.

Chapter One

2 "a people come...": Jamestown leader John Smith reported a Mannahoac Indian's words. See James H. Merrell, *The Indians' New World: Catawbas and Their Neighbors from European Contact through the Era of Removal* (Chapel Hill: University of North Carolina Press, 1989), p. 8.

3 "almost one people": General Thomas Gage, qtd. in Richard White, *The Middle Ground: Indians, Empires, and Republics in the Great Lakes Region, 1650–1815* (Cambridge, England: Cambridge University Press, 1991), p. 316.

3 "more zealous...": David J. Weber, *The Spanish Frontier in North America* (New Haven: Yale University Press, 1992), p. 22.

3 "had a place...": Wilbur R. Jacobs, *Dispossessing the American Indian: Indians & Whites on the Colonial Frontier* (New York: Charles Scribner's Sons, 1972), p. 153.

4 "cumberers of the ground": Debo, p. 257.

4 "integrate," "sought to...": Albert L. Hurtado, *Indian Survival on the California Frontier* (New Haven: Yale University Press, 1988), p. 213.

4 "elimination of...": Hurtado, p. 28.

5 "have the worst...": See Francis Jennings, *The Invasion of America: Indians, Colonialism, and the Cant of Conquest* (Chapel Hill: University of North Carolina Press, 1975), p. 66.

5 "a fowle trouble...": Qtd. in Jennings, p. 116.

6 "I know not...": Qtd. in Miller, p. 52.

6 "rather than submit...": Qtd. in Miller, pp. 105–106.

6 "abandoning whatever...": J. Leitch Wright, Jr., *The Only Land They Knew: The Tragic Story of American Indians in the Old South* (New York: The Free Press, 1981), p. 78.

7 "by right...": Jennings, p. 80.

7 "contagious 'crowd'...": Weber, p. 28.

7 "prone to carry": Richter, p. 58.

7 "dry and well-nourished": Richter on the Iroquois, p. 59.

8 "What could they...": Charles M. Segal and David C. Stineback, *Puritans, Indians & Manifest Destiny* (New York: G. P. Putnam's Sons, 1977), p. 33.

8 "vast disaster zone": Salisbury, *Manitou*, p. 103.

8 "for a distance...": Jennings, pp. 28–29.

9 "without acknowledging . . .": Salisbury, *Manitou,* p. 200.

9 "any of the . . .": Salisbury, *Manitou,* p. 200.

9 "deed[s] of . . .": Jennings on the Wampanoag agreement, p. 131.

9 "use an area . . .": Cronon, p. 62.

9 "began to be . . .": Russell J. Thornton, *American Indian Holocaust and Survival: A Population History Since 1492* (Norman: University of Oklahoma Press, 1990 ed.), p. 75.

9 "When the Christians . . .": Weber, p. 28.

10 "All those . . .": Qtd. in Richter, p. 169.

10 "since that you . . .": Virgil J. Vogel, *This Country Was Ours: A Documentary History of the American Indian* (New York: Harper & Row, 1972), p. 43.

10 "enforce their [own] . . .": Sidney L. Harring, *Crow Dog's Case: American Indian Sovereignty, Tribal Law, and United States Law in the Nineteenth Century* (Cambridge, England: Cambridge University Press, 1994), p. 5.

10 "justified reprisals": Jennings, p. 158.

10 "the total war . . .": Jennings, p. 153.

11 "very bowstrings," "entertained with . . .": Captain Underhill, qtd. in Laurence M. Hauptman, "The Pequot War and Its Legacies," in Laurence M. Hauptman and James D. Wherry, eds., *The Pequots in Southern New England: The Fall and Rise of an American Indian Nation* (Norman: University of Oklahoma Press, 1990), p. 73.

11 "the English were . . .": Qtd. in Salisbury, *Manitou,* p. 202.

11 "relied upon . . .": Salisbury, *Manitou,* p. 225.

11 "interdependent," "dependent": See Neal Salisbury, "Indians and Colonists in Southern New England after the Pequot War: An Uneasy Balance," in Hauptman and Wherry, p. 82.

12 "became an . . .": Salisbury, *Manitou,* p. 151.

13 "I am going . . .": Richter, p. 86.

13 "suppl[ied] them . . . ," "be well able . . .": James Adair, qtd. in Michael Green, *The Politics of Indian Removal: Creek Government and Society in Crisis* (Lincoln: University of Nebraska Press, 1982), p. 19.

13 "to maintain . . .": Sacvan Berkovitch, foreword in Segal and Stineback, pp. 27–28.

14 "clam banks . . .": Cronon, p. 63.

14 "to take and . . .": Qtd. in D'Arcy McNickle, *Native American Tribalism: Indian Survivals and Renewals* (London: Oxford University Press, 1973), p. 32.

14 "by craft . . .": Qtd. in McNickle, p. 33.

14 "for the comforts . . .": Salisbury, *Manitou,* pp. 226–227.

15 "exclusive and . . .": Salisbury, *Manitou,* p. 227.

15 "just lawes . . .": Qtd. in Jennings, p. 241.

15 "comely, as . . .": Jennings, pp. 243–244.

16 "transitional . . .": White on the Choctaws in *Roots of Dependency*, pp. 18–19—an observation applicable to Anglo perceptions of other "mixed hunting-horticultural groups."

16 "living apart . . .": Qtd. in James Axtell, *The Invasion Within: The Contest of Cultures in Colonial North America* (New York: Oxford University Press, 1985), p. 170.

16 "They can live . . .": Qtd. in Axtell, p. 161.

16 "Which of these . . .": Miller, p. 44.

16 "cooperated only . . .": Weber, p. 115.

17 "rescued": Jennings, pp. 144–145.

17 "threat of violence": Ibid.

17 "[We] have let . . .": Miller, p. 69.

18 "flit[ted] about . . .": Merrell, p. 107.

18 "should be used . . .": Cronon, p. 163.

19 "Since these Englishmen . . .": Thornton, p. 60.

19 "exploiting resources . . .": Salisbury, *Manitou,* p. 85.

19 "probably consumed . . .": Cronon, p. 120. Cronon's insights regarding ecological change inform much of my discussion in this section.

19 "stream levels . . .": Cronon, p. 126.

19 "competed with . . .": Colin G. Calloway, *The Western Abenakis of Vermont, 1600–1800: War, Migration, and the Survival of an Indian People* (Norman: University of Oklahoma Press, 1990), p. 53.

19 "Your hogs . . .": Qtd. in Frank W. Porter III, ed., *Strategies for Survival: American Indians in the Eastern United States* (Westport, CT: Greenwood Press, 1986), p. 142.

20 "letting their . . .": Cronon, p. 150.

20 "new seasonal routines": Merrell, p. 179.

20 "English fixity," "Indian mobility": Cronon, p. 53.

20 "took to . . .": Cronon, p. 101.

20 "permanently fortified sites": Ibid.

20 "all lands in . . .": Qtd. in Cronon, p. 70.

20 "border guards": Merrell, p. 58.

20 "to strengthen . . .": Calloway, p. 96.

21 "hint[ing] at . . .": Merrell, p. 27.

21 "great uneasiness . . .": Qtd. in Marshall Becker, "The Okehocking Band of

Lenape: Cultural Continuities and Accommodations in Southeastern Pennsylvania,'' in Porter, p. 52.

21 "Removed a . . .'': Qtd. in Axtell, p. 165.

21 "there Chiefest . . .'': Axtell, p. 165.

21 "appeared . . . deserted . . .'': Porter, p. 145.

21 "Pitiful Situation . . .'': Qtd. in Porter, p. 144.

22 "Discreet persons," "to have . . .'': Laurie Weinstein, " 'We're Still Living on Our Traditional Homeland': The Wampanoag Legacy in New England,'' in Porter, pp. 87–88.

22 "not cede . . .'': Atiwaneto in Miller, p. 51.

23 "adopted whole . . .'': Jennings, p. 152.

24 "staved and spilled . . .'': Colonial records, qtd. in Thomas Wildcat Alford, *Civilization and the Story of the Absentee Shawnees* (Norman: University of Oklahoma Press, 1979 ed.), pp. 48–49.

24 "it would be . . .'': Qtd. in Utley, *Indian Frontier,* p. 51.

25 "some ingrained . . .'': Willard Rollings, *The Osage: An Ethnohistorical Study of Hegemony on the Prairie-Plains* (Columbia: University of Missouri Press, 1992), on the Osages, p. 3.

25 "practically all . . .'': Carl Waldman, *Atlas of the North American Indian* (New York: Facts on File, 1985), p. 105.

26 "There is not . . .'' Calloway, pp. 91–92.

26 "not for him . . .'': Calloway, p. 172.

26 "by 1700 . . .'': Green, p. 18.

26 "[kept] their . . .'': Green, p. 23.

26 "the strength . . .'': Qtd. in White, *Middle Ground,* p. 224.

26 "the Virginians . . .'': White, *Middle Ground,* p. 235.

26 "demanded that . . .'': Jacobs, p. 81.

27 "had as good . . .'': Qtd. in Miller, pp. 107–108.

27 "Brethren, you . . .'': Richter, p. 44.

27 "Now, Brother . . .'': Qtd. in White *Middle Ground,* p. 239

28 "We are ashamed . . .'': Jacobs, p. 76.

28 "Almost surrounded'': Merrell, p. 171.

28 "landlords upon . . .'': Merrell, p. 210.

28 "tuck [a sample] . . .'': Qtd. in Merrell, p. 164.

29 "without the . . .'': Ethel Boissevain, *The Narragansett People* (Phoenix, AZ: Indian Tribal Series, 1975), p. 41.

29 "even with . . .'': Qtd. in Merrell, p. 223.

30 "drive[n] away . . .'': Qtd. in White, *Middle Ground,* p. 245.

30 "draw back . . .": Qtd. in White, *Middle Ground,* p. 254.

30 "Why don't you . . .": Qtd. in White, *Middle Ground,* p. 252.

31 "he did not . . .": Jacobs, p. 79.

31 "rather than . . .": Weber, p. 139.

32 "eroding economic status . . .": Weber, p. 175.

CHAPTER TWO

33 "or they would . . .": Qtd. in Jacobs, p. 76.

33 "If you add . . .": Ibid.

35 "double the . . .": George Croghan, qtd. in White, *Middle Ground,* pp. 319–320.

35 "When a fort . . .": Miller, p. 133.

35 "a lawless . . .": Qtd. in White, *Middle Ground,* pp. 315, 322.

36 "distressed . . .": Qtd. in White, *Middle Ground,* p. 396.

36 "The Elks . . .": Qtd. in White, *Middle Ground,* p. 341. White provides insights into the parallels between the two "village worlds" of native and immigrant.

36 "The English come . . .": Qtd. in White, *Middle Ground,* p. 307

36 "We only . . .": Rollings, pp. 129–130.

36 "Rum will . . .": Qtd. in White, *Middle Ground,* p. 281.

37 "carr[ying] it to . . .": White, p. 334.

37 "When our chiefs . . .": Qtd. in Miller, pp. 105–106.

38 "hemmed in . . .": Qtd. in White, *Middle Ground,* p. 356.

38 "almost constant . . .": Thornton, p. 14.

38 "We have no . . .": Debo, pp. 85–86.

39 "take[n] full . . .": Waldman, p. 109.

39 "with more . . .": White, *Middle Ground,* p. 407.

39 "In endeavoring . . .": Qtd. in White, *Middle Ground,* p. 408. White notes that the Iroquois in complaining of British treachery in handing over Indian lands were "forgetting . . . their own actions at Fort Stanwix."

40 "an opportunity . . .": White, *Middle Ground,* p. 369.

40 "noting that . . .": Merrell, p. 217.

41 "controlled backcountry . . .": White, *Middle Ground,* p. 395.

41 "there was no . . .": Merrell, p. 223.

41 "often had . . .": Calloway, p. 235.

41 "found themselves . . .": Calloway, p. 224.

41 "a swamp . . .": Porter, p. 17.

41 "We have scarcely . . .": W. C. Vanderwerth, *Indian Oratory: Famous Speeches by Noted Indian Chiefs* (Norman: University of Oklahoma, 1971), p. 47.

42 "to take care . . .": Vanderwerth, pp. 38–39.

42 "be[coming] an . . .": Green, p. 50.

42 "one Dish . . .": Axtell, p. 167.

43 "new stance . . .": White, *Middle Ground,* p. 457.

43 "their lands . . .": Qtd. in Hirschfelder and de Montano, p. 10.

44 "could restore . . .": White, *Middle Ground,* p. 435.

44 "stuffed the . . .": White, *Middle Ground,* p. 454.

45 "cuts off . . .": Qtd. in Miller, pp. 184–185.

45 "even asked . . .": White, *Middle Ground,* p. 472.

46 "less than . . .": Gregory E. Dowd, "Thinking and Believing: Nativism and Unity in the Ages of Pontiac and Tecumseh," *American Indian Quarterly* XVI, 3 (Summer 1992), p. 321.

46 "If we do . . .": Qtd. in Josephy, *Now That,* p. 135.

46 "We can retreat . . .": Lenape delegation, qtd. in Miller, p. 180.

47 "Now if a . . .": White, *Middle Ground,* p. 502.

47 "If we are not . . .": Qtd. in White, *Middle Ground,* pp. 489–490.

47 "at almost every . . .": Dowd, pp. 315–316.

47 "poison'd the land": Dowd, p. 313.

47 "half a tree's . . .": Dowd, p. 314.

48 "Where today . . .": Vanderwerth, p. 63.

48 "no tribe . . .": Qtd. in Miller, p. 189.

48 "neither buy . . .": Dowd, p. 327.

49 "We are determined . . .": Vanderwerth, p. 68.

49 "too incompetent . . .": William G. McLoughlin, *Cherokees and Missionaries, 1789–1839* (Norman: University of Oklahoma Press, 1994), p. 25.

50 "We had hoped . . .": Qtd. in Miller, p. 135.

50 "after receiving . . .": Ibid.

50 "We are neither . . .": Ibid.

50 "Under what kind . . .": Nabokov, pp. 122–123.

50 "the law of . . .": Ibid.

51 "the older brother . . .": Arcowee, Qtd. in McLoughlin, p. 38.

51 "ploughs, horses . . .": Qtd. in McLoughlin, p. 16.

51 "as [nothing] . . .": Peter Iverson, *When Indians Became Cowboys: Native*

Peoples and Cattle Ranching in the American West (Norman: University of Oklahoma Press, 1994), p. 16.

51 "government-built . . .": McLoughlin, p. 42.

51 "the tribe's . . .": Ibid.

51 "implements of . . .": Dianna Everett, *The Texas Cherokees: A People Between Two Fires, 1819–1840* (Norman: University of Oklahoma Press, 1990), p. 6; "declare war . . .": McLoughlin, p. 15.

52 "virtually subjugated": Everett, p. 6.

52 "the tribe's demographic . . .": McLoughlin, p. 14.

53 "condemned [the] . . .": Everett, p. 11.

53 "19,500 cattle . . .": As reported by Elias Boudinot in Theda Perdue, ed., *Cherokee Editor: The Writings of Elias Boudinot* (Athens: University of Georgia Press, 1996 ed.), p. 72.

53 "if you put . . .": Qtd. in McLoughlin, p. 82.

54 "unauthorized and . . .": Green, p. 34.

54 "The land belongs . . .": Qtd. in Debo, p. 97.

54 "hoes, axes . . .": Green, p. 38.

55 "to remove the . . .": Green, p. 74.

55 "for every . . .": Green, pp. 51–52.

55 "over-zealousness . . .": Qtd. in Green, pp. 51–52.

56 "edge habitat": Rollings, p. 68.

56 "to control . . .": Rollings, p. 7.

56 "seminomadic plains hunting": Rollings, p. 64.

57 "consolidate": Rollings, p. 216.

57 "50,000 Squar[e] . . .": Negotiator William Clark, qtd. in Rollings, p. 224.

57 "a blacksmith . . .": Rollings, p. 225.

58 "right to remain . . .": Green, p. 50.

58 "no tribe or . . .": Qtd. in Warren A. Beck and Ynez D. Haase, *Historical Atlas of the American West* (Norman: University of Oklahoma Press, 1989), p. 51.

58 "Our views . . .": Qtd. in Green, p. 46.

Chapter Three

60 "I was of . . .": Krupat, p. 159.

60 "Not to settle . . .": Krupat, p. 159.

60 "expected . . . they . . . ," "agreed that . . .": Krupat, p. 160.

61 "cheat[ing] them . . .": Krupat, p. 161.

61 "took his team . . .": Krupat, p. 160.

61 *denied,* positively . . .": Krupat, p. 162.

62 "ancient village . . .": Black Hawk in Vanderwerth, pp. 86–87.

62 "that land . . .": Krupat, p. 160.

63 "We never . . .": Miller, p. 203.

63 "transfer any . . .": Porter, p. 15.

63 "The evil . . .": Qtd. in Vogel, p. 111.

65 "surveyed the . . .": Krupat, p. 149.

65 "not to neglect . . .' ": Joseph B. Herring, *The Enduring Indians of Kansas: A Century and a Half of Acculturation* (Lawrence: University of Kansas Press, 1990), p. 23.

65 "an immense . . .": Herring, pp. 24–25.

65 "The President . . .": Qtd. in Herring, pp. 24–25.

66 "nearly 100,000,000 . . .": Terry P. Wilson, *The Underground Reservation: Osage Oil* (Lincoln: University of Nebraska Press, 1985), pp. 8–9.

67 "was never . . .": Qtd. in Grant Foreman, *The Five Civilized Tribes* (Norman: University of Oklahoma Press, 1934), pp. 164–165.

67 "good treaty," "that something . . .": Foreman, *Five Tribes,* pp. 164–165.

67 "Our last two . . .": Qtd. in Cecile Elkins Carter, *Caddo Indians: Where We Come From* (Norman: University of Oklahoma Press, 1995), p. 268.

67 "sorrowful solution," "offering all . . .": Qtd. in Carter, p. 268.

67 "Are you not . . .": Carter, p. 280.

68 "if they did not . . .": Carter, pp. 279–280.

69 "we beg leave . . .": Vogel, pp. 106–107.

69 "Where have we . . .": Perdue, *Cherokee Editor,* pp. 95–96.

70 "for the purpose . . .": Fergus M. Bordewich, *Killing the White Man's Indian: Reinventing Native Americans at the End of the Twentieth Century* (New York: Doubleday, 1996), p. 44.

70 "who sought . . .": Grant Foreman, *Indian Removal: The Emigration of the Five Civilized Tribes of Indians* (Norman: University of Oklahoma Press, 1972 ed.), p. 229.

70 "a political . . .": Debo, p. 121.

70 "not known . . .": Fred L. Ragsdale, Jr., "The Deception of Geography," in Vine Deloria, Jr., ed., *American Indian Policy in the Twentieth Century* (Norman: University of Oklahoma Press, 1985), p. 67.

70 "Whoever really . . .": Perdue, *Cherokee Editor,* p. 114.

71 "The Cherokee Nation . . .": Qtd. in Debo, pp. 121–122.

71 "Since the decision . . .": Edward Everett Dale and Gaston Litton, *Cherokee*

Cavaliers: Forty Years of Cherokee History as Told in the Correspondence of the Ridge-Watie-Boudinot Family (Norman: University of Oklahoma Press, 1995 ed.), p. 10.

72 "John Marshall . . .": Qtd. in Foreman, *Indian Removal,* p. 235.

72 "how, if he . . .": Foreman, *Indian Removal,* p. 247.

72 "well-dressed . . .": Herman J. Viola, *Diplomats in Buckskins: A History of Indian Delegations in Washington City* (Bluffton, SC: Rivilo Books, 1995), p. 79.

72 "the institutions . . .": Viola, p. 79.

72 "wholly undeserving . . .": Qtd. in Foreman, *Indian Removal,* p. 249.

73 "average Cherokee . . .": Douglas C. Wilms, "Cherokee Land Use in Georgia Before Removal," in William L. Anderson, ed., *Cherokee Removal: Before and After* (Athens: University of Georgia Press, 1991), p. 23.

73 "turning . . . with . . .": Qtd. in Foreman, *Indian Removal,* p. 254.

74 "Sir, that paper . . .": Qtd. in Foreman, *Indian Removal,* p. 270.

74 "It is . . . vain . . .": Qtd. in Foreman, *Indian Removal,* p. 271.

74 "entitled to . . .": Qtd. in Foreman, *Indian Removal,* p. 270.

74 "I know that . . .": Dale and Litton, p. 7.

74 "for back rents . . .": Qtd. in Foreman, *Indian Removal,* p. 272.

74 "living upon . . . ," "Many have . . .": Qtd. in Foreman, *Indian Removal,* p. 271.

75 "brought hard-core . . .": Green, p. 54.

75 "to dispose . . .": Green, p. 74.

76 "to promote . . .": Qtd. in Miller, p. 139.

76 "the irreducible . . .": Green, p. 74.

76 "On no . . .": Green, pp. 76, 80.

76 "the northern . . .": Green, p. 88.

77 "if property . . .": Qtd. in Green, p. 117.

77 "that this was . . .": Debo, p. 116.

77 "readily lay . . . ," "I trust . . .": Qtd. in Green, p. 111.

77 "appearance . . . remarkable . . .": Viola, p. 162.

78 "You know that . . .": Qtd. in Green, p. 135.

78 "$27,491 plus . . .": Green, p. 138.

78 "many of them . . .": Qtd. in Green, pp. 142–143.

79 "set a dangerous . . .": Green, p. 155.

79 "It is idle . . .": Qtd. in Green, p. 163.

79 "spoil": Qtd. in Green, p. 168. This was a pattern recognized by restless

frontiersmen as well as by Indians, one Georgian, Gideon Lincecum, commenting on his own decision to remove westward that "the immigrants were pouring in with their shot-guns and hounds and it was very plain to be seen that the game would soon be gone."

79 "they had been . . .": Qtd. in Green, p. 168.

80 "grantees could not . . .": Green, p. 171.

80 "any State . . .": Ibid.

80 "Instead of . . .": Qtd. in Foreman, *Indian Removal,* p. 113.

81 "I have never . . .": Qtd. in Foreman, *Indian Removal,* p. 130.

81 "You cannot have . . .": Qtd. in Foreman, *Indian Removal,* pp. 119–120.

81 "They linger . . .": Qtd. in Foreman, *Indian Removal,* p. 126.

81 "borne with . . .": Qtd. in Foreman, *Indian Removal,* p. 132.

81 "You place . . .": Ibid.

82 "the white man . . .": Qtd. in Green, p. 184.

82 "it was with . . .": Alexander Cornell, Creek, in Miller, p. 112.

82 "The war with . . .": Qtd. in Foreman, *Indian Removal,* p. 151.

83 "We rely . . .": Qtd. in Foreman, *Indian Removal,* pp. 318–319.

85 "My Brothers . . . ," "When the agent . . .": Qtd. in Nabokov, p. 125.

85 "a fine and . . .": Qtd. in Foreman, *Indian Removal,* p. 357.

85 "till the last . . .": Qtd. in Foreman, *Indian Removal,* p. 327.

85 "I shall never . . .": Qtd. in Miller, p. 186.

86 "would thankfully . . .": Qtd. in Foreman, *Indian Removal,* pp. 359–360.

86 "we have committed . . .": Qtd. in Foreman, *Indian Removal,* p. 360.

86 "retire to . . .": Foreman, *Indian Removal,* p. 372.

86 "if the Indians . . . ," "I now come . . .": Qtd. in Foreman, *Indian Removal,* pp. 377–378.

87 "to tell her . . .": Qtd. in Foreman, *Indian Removal,* p. 383.

87 "in nearby . . .": John R. Finger, "The Impact of Removal on North Carolina Cherokees," in William Anderson, p. 106.

87 "If we should . . .": Nabokov, pp. 151–152.

CHAPTER FOUR

88 "sadness of the heart": William Shorey Coodey, qtd. in Foreman, *Indian Removal,* p. 290. Coodey relates the scene described here.

90 "Long time we . . .": Miller, p. 153.

90 "32 million . . .": Utley, *Indian Frontier,* p. 37.

91 "men shot . . .": Qtd. in Thornton, pp. 116–117.

92 "the loss of . . .": Qtd. in Foreman, *Indian Removal,* p. 288.

92 "preyed upon . . .": Qtd. in Foreman, *Indian Removal,* p. 167.

92 "The property of . . .": Qtd. in Foreman, *Indian Removal,* p. 288.

93 "They are generally . . .": Qtd. in Foreman, *Indian Removal,* p. 60.

93 "6 or 7 . . . ," "I used . . .": Qtd. in Foreman, *Indian Removal,* p. 127.

94 "the earth . . .": Qtd. in Foreman, *Indian Removal,* p. 335.

94 "stroking the . . .": Nabokov, p. 151.

94 "The feeling . . .": Qtd. in Foreman, *Indian Removal,* p. 56.

94 "the people are . . .": Qtd. in Foreman, *Indian Removal,* p. 303.

94 "have refused . . .": Qtd. in Foreman, *Indian Removal,* pp. 210–211.

94 "They have not . . .": Qtd. in Foreman, *Indian Removal,* pp. 210–211.

95 "refused to . . .": Qtd. in Foreman, *Indian Removal,* p. 216.

95 "Nocowee has . . .": Qtd. in Foreman, *Indian Removal,* p. 303.

95 "the most brutal . . .": Qtd. in Foreman, *Indian Removal,* p. 170.

95 "Death was . . .": Qtd. in Foreman, *Indian Removal,* p. 93.

96 "A crude . . .": Qtd. in Debo, p. 120.

96 "There is a dignity . . .": Qtd. in Foreman, *Indian Removal,* p. 258.

96 "carrying reeds . . .": Qtd. in Debo, p. 120.

96 "Tell our people . . .": Qtd. in Foreman, *Indian Removal,* p. 176.

97 "When I read . . .": Qtd. in Foreman, *Indian Removal,* pp. 306–307.

97 "the remnant . . .": Qtd. in Foreman, *Indian Removal,* p. 154.

97 "the most dirty . . .": Qtd. in Foreman, *Indian Removal,* p. 365.

97 "the degree . . .": Qtd. in Foreman, *Indian Removal,* p. 333.

99 "a pacifying . . .": Everett, p. 31.

100 "it will be . . .": Qtd. in Everett, p. 41.

100 "because [it] . . .": Everett, pp. 71–72.

101 "The Indian lands . . .": Qtd. in Everett, p. 88.

101 "The white man . . . ," "push[ing] a . . .": Qtd. in Steve Russell,
"The Legacy of Ethnic Cleansing: Implementation of NAGPRA in Texas," *American Indian Culture and Research Journal* 19, 4 (1995), p. 199.

101 "improvements, crops . . .": Everett, pp. 108–109.

102 "People sometimes . . .": Miller p. 153.

103 "usually represented . . .": Brad Agnew, *Fort Gibson: Terminal on the Trail of Tears* (Norman: University of Oklahoma Press, 1980), p. 4, in comments that are applicable to other frontier forts.

103 "How are we . . .": Herring, p. 26.

105 "I am here starving . . .": Qtd. in Foreman, *Indian Removal,* pp. 222–223.

105 "spoiled and . . . ," "scraped and . . .": Foreman, p. 70.

107 "near civil . . .": Dale and Litton, p. xviii.

107 "quarrelled constantly . . .": Herring, p. 36.

108 "more political . . .": Foreman, *Five Civilized Tribes,* p. 153.

108 "for several . . .": Foreman, *Five Civilized Tribes,* p. 256.

108 "caus[ed] irreparable . . .": Foreman, *Five Civilized Tribes,* p. 51.

109 "in a deplorable . . .": Qtd. in Foreman, *Five Civilized Tribes,* p. 176.

109 "We have employed . . .": Foreman, *Indian Removal,* p. 50.

110 "not secured . . . ," "*this labor* . . .": Foreman, *Five Civilized Tribes,* p. 19.

110 "We don't want . . .": Foreman, *Five Civilized Tribes,* p. 179.

110 "Both the Creeks . . .": Foreman, *Five Civilized Tribes,* p. 164.

111 "enjoyed a . . .": Renard Strickland and William M. Strickland, "Beyond the Trail of Tears: One Hundred Fifty Years of Cherokee Survival," in William Anderson, p. 112.

111 "sell, cede . . .": Qtd. in Jane Lancaster, *Removal Aftershock: The Seminoles' Struggles to Survive in the West, 1836–1866* (Knoxville: University of Tennessee Press, 1994), p. 47.

CHAPTER FIVE

112 "wild animals . . .": Nabokov, p. 83.

112 "Why do you . . .": Nabokov, pp. 83–84.

114 "I will go . . .": Nabokov, p. 84.

114 "the United States . . .": Utley, *Indian Frontier,* p. 4.

115 "more Indian acreage . . .": Hirschfelder and de Montano, p. 53.

115 "the whites . . .": Utley, *Indian Frontier,* p. 46.

115 "taught to . . .": Utley, *Indian Frontier,* p. 63.

115 "as long as . . .": Hurtado, p. 126.

116 "several English . . .": Boissevain, p. 57.

116 "All Lands . . .": Qtd. in Boissevain, p. 50.

116 "alarming rates . . .": Qtd. in Weinstein, in Porter, p. 99.

117 "living everywhere . . .": Merrell, p. 253.

117 "the acts of . . . ," "We have had . . .": Foreman, *Five Civilized Tribes,* p. 75.

118 "all cattle . . .": Foreman, *Indian Removal,* p. 384.

118 "We did not . . .": Foreman, *Five Civilized Tribes,* p. 249.

118 "saw how . . .": Foreman, *Five Civilized Tribes,* p. 254.

118 "rather be killed . . .": Miller, p. 169. Wild Cat was a member of a "branch" Seminole group, the Miccosukees.

118 "I asked for . . .": Qtd. in Nabokov, p. 176.

119 "transported to . . .": Qtd. in Debo, pp. 125–126.

119 "We used to . . .": Qtd. in Nabokov, pp. 163–164.

119 "in exchange . . .": Utley, *Indian Frontier,* p. 76.

119 "thousands of . . .": Herring, p. 27.

120 "The poor Indians . . .": Qtd. in Herring, p. 87.

120 "the Iowas consented . . .": Herring, pp. 76–77.

120 "that their own . . .": Herring, p. 50.

120 "Protestant-like work ethic": Herring, p. 44.

121 "obtained land . . .": Debo, p. 147.

121 "signed away . . .": Herring, p. 48.

122 "there is not . . .": Qtd. in Herring, p. 47.

122 "sadly mistaken": Herring, p. 8.

122 "Washington bureaucrats . . .": Herring, p. 33.

122 "arranged a deal . . .": Herring, p. 9.

123 "far surpassed . . .": Bordewich, p. 55.

123 "improvement societies," "[becoming] the . . .": Ibid.

123 "good cabins . . .": Foreman, *Five Civilized Tribes,* p. 84.

123 "horse mills . . .": Ibid.

123 "mak[ing] more corn . . .": An 1847 agent's report in Foreman, *Five Civilized Tribes,* p. 113.

123 "enumerated by . . .": Debo, p. 8.

123 "All that can . . ." Qtd. in Foreman, *Five Civilized Tribes,* p. 217.

124 "summer, game . . .": Lancaster, p. xiii.

124 "active guardians . . .": George Klos, " 'Our People Could Not Distinguish One Tribe from Another': The 1859 Expulsion of the Reserve Indians from Texas," *Southwestern Historical Quarterly* (April 1994), p. 607.

125 "there is to be . . .": Qtd. in Klos, p. 611.

125 "I have this day . . .": Qtd. in Walter Prescott Webb, *The Texas Rangers: A Century of Frontier Defense* (Austin: University of Texas Press, 1985 ed.), p. 171.

125 "and this has . . .": Qtd. in Foreman, *Five Civilized Tribes,* p. 211.

126 "For some days . . .": Qtd. in Foreman, *Five Civilized Tribes,* pp. 192–193.

126 "politically well-connected . . .": Utley, *Indian Frontier,* pp. 45–46.

126 "very summary...": An 1846 observer in Foreman, *Five Civilized Tribes,* p. 344.

127 "made compacts...": Debo, p. 148.

127 "to petition...": Everett, p. 120.

127 "adher[ing] to...": An official in 1860, qtd. in Foreman, *Five Civilized Tribes,* p. 219.

127 "Our comfortable cabins...": Foreman, *Five Civilized Tribes,* p. 340.

127 "most cheerfully...": Qtd. in Foreman, *Five Civilized Tribes,* p. 417.

129 "I cannot see...": Qtd. in John Stands in Timber and Margot Liberty, *Cheyenne Memories* (New Haven: Yale University Press, 1967), p. 121.

129 "an estimated...": Hurtado, p. 46.

130 "too appalling...": Qtd. in Thornton, p. 98.

130 "evolutionary...": Utley, *Indian Frontier,* p. 30.

130 "west of the...": Charles M. Robinson, III, *A Good Year to Die: The Story of the Great Sioux War* (New York: Random House, 1995), p. 10.

130 "watched the...": Elliott West, *The Way to the West: Essays on the Central Plains* (Albuquerque: University of New Mexico Press, 1995), p. 41.

131 "no alternative...": West, p. 33.

131 "could not...": Utley, *Indian Frontier,* p. 58.

131 "even contract[ed]...": Richard J. Perry, *Apache Reservation: Indigenous Peoples & the American State* (Austin: University of Texas Press, 1993), p. 97.

132 "made enough...": Utley, *Indian Frontier,* p. 51.

132 "for such beneficial...": Qtd. in Utley, *Indian Frontier,* p. 50.

132 "pretext for...": Utley, *Indian Frontier,* p. 51.

133 "unlike Indians...": Hurtado, p. 7.

133 "testing ground": Hurtado, p. 5. Hurtado rejects the view that the California reservation system "was significant because it foreshadowed the creation of reservations elsewhere in the American West," instead calling it "exceptional" but noting that it did prove "a difficult testing ground for Indian policy." While I find Hurtado's analysis insightful, I do think the California system "foreshadowed" other western reservations.

133 "to administer...": Hurtado, p. 36.

133 "a remarkable independence": Hurtado, p. 162.

133 "permanent white...": Hurtado, p. 54.

134 "steam-powered threshers...": Hurtado, p. 30.

134 "to forgo...": Hurtado, p. 131.

134 "Spanish law...": Qtd. in George Harwood Phillips, *Indians and Indian*

Agents: The Origins of the Reservation System in California, 1849–1852 (Norman: University of Oklahoma Press, 1997), p. 11.

134 "What shall we . . .": Qtd. in Phillips, p. 147.

135 "the center of . . .": Jack Norton in Bordewich, pp. 51–52.

135 "The ceremony . . .": Qtd. in Bordewich, pp. 51–52.

135 "protected them . . .": Hurtado, p. 131.

135 "legaliz[ing] the . . .": Debo, p. 164.

135 "as many as . . .": Bordewich, p. 51.

135 "federally subsidized . . .": Hurtado, p. 138.

136 "not to exceed . . .": Hurtado, p. 142.

136 "had no game . . . ," "white friends . . . ," "was a nice . . . ," "one of the . . .": Dunn, qtd. in Miller, p. 301.

136 "no reservation . . .": Hurtado, p. 165.

136 "the real mass . . .": G. Bailey, qtd. in Hurtado, pp. 150–151.

136 "simply Government . . .": G. Bailey, qtd. in Hurtado, pp. 150–151.

137 "a single flood . . .": Hurtado, p. 152.

137 "continued to attack . . .": Todd Benson, "The Consequences of Reservation Life: Native Californians on the Round Valley Reservation, 1871–1884," *Pacific Historical Review* 60 (May 1991), p. 225.

137 "daily and nightly . . .": San Francisco newspaper, qtd. in Bordewich, p. 50.

137 "turned into . . .": Qtd. in Utley, *Indian Frontier,* p. 53.

137 "failures were . . .": Hurtado, p. 150.

138 "Where can we go . . .": Miller, p. 300.

139 "Did not your . . .": Qtd. in Josephy, *Nez Perce Indians,* p. 276.

139 "hot, dry country": Josephy, *Nez Perce Indians,* p. 279.

139 "did not want . . .": Ibid.

139 "roughly two thousand . . .": E. A. Schwartz, *The Rogue River Indian War and Its Aftermath, 1850–1980* (Norman: University of Oklahoma Press, 1997), p. 59.

139 "the more reckless . . .": Qtd. in Schwartz, p. 85.

140 "white farmers . . .": Schwartz, p. 65.

140 "in at least . . .": Josephy, *Nez Perce Indians,* p. 303.

140 "should we accept . . .": Vanderwerth, p. 121.

140 "the right to . . .": Josephy, *Nez Perce Indians,* p. 304.

140 "Goods and the Earth . . .": Miller, p. 332.

140 "What shall I . . .": Miller, p. 333.

141 "I will not sign . . .": The younger Chief Joseph remembering his father's words, qtd. in Nabokov, p. 131.

141 "sizeable reservations . . .": Carlos A. Schwantes, *The Pacific Northwest: An Interpretive History* (Lincoln: University of Nebraska Press, 1989), p. 118.

141 "My people, what . . .": Qtd. in Josephy, *Nez Perce Indians,* p. 319.

141 "When I speak . . .": Josephy, *Nez Perce Indians,* p. 343.

141 "The Indians are not . . .": Ibid.

142 "petered out . . .": Utley, *Indian Frontier,* p. 54.

142 "all the Oregon . . .": Utley, *Indian Frontier,* p. 55.

142 "We never saw . . . ," "You will all . . .": Miller, p. 329.

142 "I saw the blood . . .": Qtd. in Martha C. Knack and Omer C. Stewart, *As Long As the River Shall Run: An Ethnohistory of Pyramid Lake Indian Reservation* (Berkeley: University of California Press, 1984), p. 37.

143 "get[ting] their . . .": Qtd. in Knack and Stewart, p. 150.

143 "Agreements the Indian . . .": Miller, p. 287.

143 "We have to . . .": Debo, p. 166.

144 "were keeping . . .": West, p. 32.

144 "They spent . . .": West, pp. 32, 22.

144 "stripped bare . . .": Utley, *Indian Frontier,* p. 47.

144 "planting and . . .": White on the Pawnees, in *Roots of Dependency,* p. 193.

144 "leaving little . . .": West, p. 37.

144 "Indians, white . . .": West, p. 27.

144 "mountain[s] of presents," "not called . . .": Utley, *Indian Frontier,* p. 61.

145 "laid the . . .": Ibid.

145 "very uneasy . . .": Qtd. in West, p. 46.

145 "entered a new . . .": Utley, *Indian Frontier,* p. 72.

CHAPTER SIX

147 "We locked . . .": Qtd. in Nabokov, p. 168.

147 "broke open . . .": Nabokov, p. 169.

147 "We told them . . .": Ibid.

147 "the collapse . . .": Utley, *Indian Frontier,* p. 257.

147 "the base of . . .": Utley, *Indian Frontier,* p. 236.

148 "the casualties . . .": Lancaster, p. 155.

148 "We have done . . .": Qtd. in Debo. p. 171.

149 "It was almost . . .": Alford, p. 7.

149 "he did not . . . ," "Get ready . . .": Qtd. in Theda Perdue, *Nations Remem-*

bered: An Oral History of the Cherokees, Chickasaws, and Seminoles in Oklahoma, 1856–1907 (Norman: University of Oklahoma Press, 1993), p. 7.

150 "carriages, ox . . .": Lancaster, p. 138.

150 "aprons, handkerchiefs . . .": Lancaster, p. 40.

150 "inflammatory diseases . . .": Lancaster, p. 140.

151 "When we returned . . .": Qtd. in Perdue, *Nations Remembered,* p. 8.

151 "relinquished all . . .": Perdue, *Nations Remembered,* p. 17.

152 "wild pigeons . . .": Cherokee remembrance in Perdue, *Nations Remembered,* p. 48.

152 "extinguished and . . .": Perdue, *Nations Remembered,* p. 85.

152 "Visiting was . . .": Alford, p. 66.

152 "an Indian's . . .": Qtd. in Perdue, *Nations Remembered,* p. 90.

153 "The Indians probably . . .": Qtd. in Perdue, *Nations Remembered,* p. 61.

153 "Our people no . . .": Alford, p. 84.

153 "a share . . .": Perdue, *Nations Remembered,* p. 143.

153 "a bitter . . . ," "gave me . . .": Alford, p. 111.

154 "Capability, efficiency . . . ," "never knew . . .": Alford, p. 129.

154 "rely[ing] heavily . . .": Perdue, *Nations Remembered,* p. 19.

154 "The local tribal . . .": Debo, p. 306.

155 "Then he turned . . .": Ibid.

155 "disturbers of . . .": Francis Paul Prucha, *American Indian Policy in Crisis: Christian Reformers and the Indian, 1865–1900* (Norman: University of Oklahoma Press, 1976), p. 214.

155 "were not subject . . .": Utley, *Indian Frontier,* p. 263.

155 "enforc[ing] a list . . .": Utley, *Indian Frontier,* p. 220.

155 "without a . . .": Benson, pp. 233–234.

156 "only a right . . .": Donald L. Parman, *Indians and the American West in the Twentieth Century* (Bloomington: Indiana University Press, 1994), p. 26.

156 "[keeping] delegations . . .": Debo, p. 203.

157 "for cooking . . .": Martha Royce Blaine, *Pawnee Passage: 1870–1875* (Norman: University of Oklahoma Press, 1990), p. 12.

157 "the money went . . .": Blaine, p. 14.

157 "said that the . . .": Blaine, p. 16.

157 "journeying at will . . .": Blaine, p. 25.

157 "had failed . . .": Wilson, p. 14.

158 "Hurry up . . .": Qtd. in Wilson, p. 11.

158 "We deny . . .": Qtd. in Blaine, p. 5.

158 "more congenial and ...": Blaine, p. 7.

158 "a parcel of ...": Qtd. in Nabokov, p. 189.

158 "about thirty ...": Wilson, p. 17.

159 "the Osages have ...": Ibid.

159 "ruinous ...": Herring, p. 131.

159 "the allotted ...": Herring, p. 135.

159 "believed to have ...": George Cantor, *North American Indian Landmarks: A Traveler's Guide* (Detroit: Visible Ink Press, 1993), p. 17.

159 "many valuable ...": Weinstein in Porter, p. 97.

160 "the cries of ...": Newspaper account, qtd. in Wilson, p. 1.

160 "the Bureau ...": Wilson, p. 34.

160 "devastating grasshopper ...": Blaine, p. 14.

160 "fed like ...": Wilson, p. 29.

160 "After we reached ...": Qtd. in Nabokov, pp. 168–169.

161 "concentrating tribes ...": Valerie Sherer Mathes, "Helen Hunt Jackson and the Ponca Controversy," *Montana the Magazine of Western History* 39, 1 (Winter 1989), p. 45.

161 "I stayed ...": Qtd. in Nabokov, pp. 168–169.

161 "Half of us ...": Ibid.

161 "an Irishman ...": Qtd. in Mathes, p. 46.

161 "They are right ...": Qtd. in Mathes, p. 42.

161 "life, liberty ...": Herring, p. 114.

162 "as an indemnity ...": Mathes, p. 52.

162 "right under ...": Qtd. in Herring, p. 100.

162 "would be like ...": Qtd. in Herring, p. 99.

162 "smaller game ...": Herring, p. 109.

162 "they be allowed ...": Herring, p. 112.

163 "a roving band ...": Qtd. in Herring, p. 115.

163 "hardly the ...": Qtd. in Herring, p. 116.

163 "among the few ...": Herring, p. 54.

163 "Anything the ...": Knack and Stewart, p. 116.

163 "would become ...": Benson, p. 244, in reference to the Indians of California's Round Valley reservation.

164 "survive with ...": Knack and Stewart, p. 116, in reference to the Paiutes of the Pyramid Lake reservation.

164 "the circumstances ...": Benson, p. 244.

164 "resembled a ...": Henry E. Stamm, "The Peace Policy at Wind River: The

James Irwin Years, 1871–1877," *Montana the Magazine of Western History* 41, 3 (Summer 1991), p. 61.

164 "The Indians are . . .": Qtd. in Benson, p. 230.

165 "in the *heart* . . .": Qtd. in Knack and Stewart, pp. 128–129.

165 "good hands . . .": Qtd. in Knack and Stewart, p. 130.

165 "Is Pyramid Lake . . .": Qtd. in Knack and Stewart, p. 137.

166 "unless a person . . .": Qtd. in Knack and Stewart, p. 147.

166 "practically all . . .": Waldman, p. 221.

166 "in isolated . . .": Knack and Stewart, p. 84.

166 "a series . . .": Qtd. in Knack and Stewart, p. 151.

166 "whites controlled . . .": Knack and Stewart, pp. 181, 183.

166 "he had convinced . . .": Qtd. in Knack and Stewart, p. 186.

167 "The Stockmen . . .": Qtd. in Knack and Stewart, p. 153.

167 "The Indians very . . .": Qtd. in Knack and Stewart, p. 160.

167 "almost beyond endurance," "The Indians . . .": Qtd. in Knack and Stewart, pp. 164, 165.

167 "The marshal . . .": Qtd. in Knack and Stewart, p. 165.

168 "I want this . . .": Qtd. in Knack and Stewart, p. 187.

168 "It was enough . . .": Qtd. in Nabokov, p. 200.

168 "to satisfy . . .": Utley, *Indian Frontier,* p. 76.

169 "If they are hungry . . .": Utley, *Indian Frontier,* p. 76.

169 "the most disastrous . . .": Debo, p. 189.

169 "I do not wonder . . .": Debo, p. 265.

169 "all dust . . .": Winnebago Little Hill in Nabokov, pp. 163–164.

170 "were familiar . . .": Knack and Stewart, p. 104.

170 "plowed up . . .": Debo, p. 265.

170 "cultural disintegration . . .": Benson, p. 224.

170 "even [this] . . .": Stamm, p. 69.

170 "had a central . . .": Knack and Stewart, p. 109.

171 "The Great Father . . .": Qtd. by Felix Cohen in Alvin M. Josephy, Jr., *Red Power: The American Indians' Fight for Freedom* (Lincoln: University of Nebraska Press, 1985 ed.), p. 27.

171 "cold war . . .": A. M. Gibson, *The Kickapoos: Lords of the Middle Border* (Norman: University of Oklahoma Press, 1963), p. 277.

CHAPTER SEVEN

172 "virtually every...": Utley, *Indian Frontier,* p. 166.

173 "forty-mile...": Debo, p. 199.

174 "bits of slate...": Gerald Thompson, *The Army and the Navajo* (Tucson: University of Arizona Press, 1976), p. 18.

175 "work[ing] the soil...": Ibid.

175 "a deep...": Thompson, p. 17.

175 "be removed...": Qtd. in Thompson, p. 9.

175 "When the Navajos...": Qtd. in "The Navajo Treaty-1868" (Las Vegas, NV: K. C. Publications in cooperation with the Navajo Tribe, 1968), p. 2.

176 "Tell them they...": Carlton to the commander of Fort Wingate, qtd. in Utley, *Indian Frontier,* p. 83.

176 "My Government has...": Qtd. in Nabokov, p. 160.

176 "scented...": Utley, *Indian Frontier,* p. 84.

176 "Now from every...": Qtd. in Nabokov, p. 161.

176 "as shouting...": Utley, *Indian Frontier*, p. 84.

177 "technically prisoners...": Thompson, p. 21.

177 "insects, hail...": Debo, p. 199.

177 "with hoes...": Thompson, p. 43.

177 "swindlers had...": Thompson, p. 46.

178 "nearly 7,800...": Thompson, p. 66.

178 "We try and...": Qtd. in Nabokov, p. 197.

178 "trespassing on...": Thompson, p. 35. Instead, the military forced Labadie off the reservation; when he relocated about twenty miles north, they would not allow the Mescaleros to visit him, even though he was still the Apache agent.

179 "only fit...": Qtd. in Thompson, p. 80.

179 "permeated with...": Thompson, p. 81.

179 "were too warm already": Thompson, p. 71.

179 "a record of...": Thompson, p. 82.

179 "to commence...": Thompson, p. 94.

179 "Cage the Badger...": Qtd. in Thompson, p. 100.

180 "We have lost...": Qtd. in Thompson, p. 84.

180 "every reservation...": Thompson, p. 93.

180 "Our Grand-fathers...": "The Navajo Treaty–1868," p. 2.

181 "in our own country...": "The Navajo Treaty–1868," p. 3.

181 "We have heard...": "The Navajo Treaty–1868," p. 5.

181 "I hope to God . . .": "The Navajo Treaty," pp. 5–6.

181 "We do not want . . .": Barboncito, qtd. in Thompson, p. 155.

181 "After we get back . . .": "The Navajo Treaty–1868," p. 9.

181 "When we saw . . .": Qtd. in Thompson, p. 140.

182 "boiled . . . in . . .": Perry, p. 104.

182 "seemed to have . . .": Qtd. in Perry, p. 99.

182 "When I was young . . .": Qtd. in Vanderwerth, p. 153.

182 "I want to . . .": Ibid.

183 "had upon . . .": Qtd. in Edward Lazarus, *Black Hills White Justice: The Sioux Nation Versus the United States 1775 to the Present* (New York: HarperCollins, 1991), p. 28.

183 "I looked toward . . .": Qtd. in Miller, pp. 218–219.

184 "After the massacre . . .": Stands-in-Timber and Liberty, p. 170.

184 "burning virtually . . .": Utley, *Indian Frontier,* pp. 93–94.

185 "These are our lands . . .": Qtd. in Robinson, p. 130.

185 "naked in [to] . . .": Lazarus, p. 33.

185 "upon the . . . ," "Are we then . . .": Peter Matthiessen, *In the Spirit of Crazy Horse* (New York: Penguin Books, 1992 ed.), p. 3.

185 "not simply the . . .": Susan Badger Doyle, "Indian Perspectives of the Bozeman Trail, 1864–1868," *Montana the Magazine of Western History* 40 (Winter 1990), p. 67; Richard White is quoted.

185 "sparring with . . .": Don Rickey, Jr., *Forty Miles a Day on Beans and Hay: The Enlisted Soldier Fighting the Indian Wars* (Norman: University of Oklahoma Press, 1963), p. 282.

185 "A dozen men . . .": Rickey, p. 282.

186 "with only eighty . . .": Robinson, p. 19.

186 "Where the antelope . . .": Qtd. in Vanderwerth, pp. 141–142.

186 "we . . . accept . . .": Ibid.

187 "This building of homes . . .": Qtd. in Debo, pp. 219–220.

187 "land doesn't want . . .": Qtd. in Miller, p. 230.

187 "I was born upon . . .": Qtd. in Vanderwerth, p. 161.

187 "I know every . . .": Ibid.

187 "the places where . . .": Ibid.

187 "could continue . . .": Utley, *Indian Frontier,* p. 116.

188 "established three . . .": Parman, p. 7.

188 "We are on . . .": Utley, *Indian Frontier,* p. 119.

188 "You fought me . . .": Qtd. in Vanderwerth, p. 184.

188 "If you want...": Qtd. in Vanderwerth, pp. 184–185.

188 "the western half...," "between the...": Debo, pp. 234–235.

189 "absolute and...": Qtd. in Matthiessen, *In the Spirit,* p. 7.

189 "No white person...": Qtd. in Robinson, p. 22.

189 "barely a year...": Robinson, p. 23.

189 "You hear of us...": Qtd. in Vanderwerth, p. 188.

189 "Time enough...": Qtd. in Debo, pp. 219–220.

189 "no alternative...": Utley, *Indian Frontier,* p. 229.

190 "a scientific...": Ibid.

190 "When the buffalo...": Qtd. in Krupat, pp. 241–242.

190 "fine plans...": Utley, *Indian Frontier,* p. 143.

191 "I want you to...": Qtd. in Miller, p. 219.

CHAPTER EIGHT

192 "along the Platte...": Utley, *Indian Frontier,* p. 180.

192 "You are fools...": Qtd. in Robinson, p. 36.

192 "Of all our...," "shelter[ed] from...": Qtd. in Matthiessen, p. 4.

193 "permitting the...": Debo, pp. 234–235.

193 "it seemed easier...": Debo, p. 236.

193 "hinted that...": Lazarus, p. 78.

193 "why it is that...": Matthiessen, *In the Spirit,* p. 10.

194 "I will kill...": Qtd. in Lazarus, p. 81.

194 "It was very cold...": Qtd. in Lazarus, p. 85.

194 "worsening conditions...": Utley, *Indian Frontier,* p. 180.

195 "did not surprise...": Stands-in-Timber and Liberty, p. 191.

195 "These soldiers...": Qtd. in Robert Utley, *The Lance and the Shield: The Life and Times of Sitting Bull* (New York: Henry Holt, 1993), p. 138.

195 "damn soldiers everywhere": Qtd. in Utley, *The Lance and the Shield,* p. 180.

195 "[freezing] to death...": Utley, *Indian Frontier,* p. 184.

195 "22.8 million...": Matthiessen, *In the Spirit,* p. 13.

196 "life-sustaining rations...": Lazarus, p. 91.

196 "Whatever we do...": Qtd. in Lazarus, p. 91.

196 "At the door...": Qtd. in Lazarus, p. 92.

196 "that God Almighty...": Miles's account, qtd. in Robinson, p. 267.

197 "Always remember...": Qtd. in Vanderwerth, pp. 269–270.

197 "more sacred...": Qtd. in Josephy, *Nez Perce Indians,* p. 467.

197 "The Great Spirit . . . ," "Who are you . . .": Qtd. in Vanderwerth, pp. 268–269.

198 "good land . . . ," "No. It would . . .": Qtd. in Vanderwerth, pp. 269–270.

198 "in the removal . . .": Qtd. in Josephy, *Nez Perce Indians,* pp. 484–485.

199 "I love that . . .": Qtd. in Nabokov, p. 132.

199 "I am tired . . .": Qtd. in Utley, *Indian Frontier,* p. 193.

200 "That was how . . .": Qtd. in Krupat, p. 202.

200 "I have heard . . .": Qtd. in Vanderwerth, p. 279.

200 "we were placed . . . ," "many sickened . . .": Qtd. in Vanderwerth, p. 280.

200 "but they continued . . ." Debo, p. 264.

200 "I can not understand . . .": Qtd. in Vanderwerth, pp. 282–283.

200 "where [white . . . ," "if I can not . . .": Ibid.

201 "were dumped . . .": Debo, p. 264.

201 "all gather[ing] . . ." Stands-in-Timber and Liberty, p. 278.

201 "The chief duty . . .": Qtd. in Prucha, *American Indian Policy,* p. 195.

202 "once the centerpiece . . .": Utley, *Indian Frontier,* p. 243.

202 "who did not . . .": Robinson, p. 253, referring to the Sioux reservation, but true of other reservations as well.

202 "savage and filthy": Prucha, *American Indian Policy,* p. 212.

202 "all the decrees . . .": Prucha, *American Indian Policy,* p. 209. Decisions could be appealed to the BIA commissioner, but Indians doing so would have to continue to live with the agent whose authority they had challenged—and with delays and uncertainty.

202 "head shaving . . .": Lazarus, p. 103.

202 "Among our people . . .": Qtd. in Krupat, pp. 290–291.

203 "had no jurisdiction . . . ," "extending jurisdiction . . .": Utley, *Indian Frontier,* p. 220.

203 "resulted in . . ." Stamm, pp. 68–69.

203 "No Agent who . . .": Qtd. in Stamm, p. 66.

203 "whether or not . . .": Nabokov, p. 191.

204 "I asked my father . . .": Qtd. in Krupat, pp. 300–301.

204 "meat that is . . .": Krupat, pp. 300–301.

204 "communication and procurement system": Stamm, p. 68.

204 "devoid of . . .": Government official, qtd. in Bordewich, p. 116.

204 "The agency issued . . .": Qtd. in Miller, p. 234.

204 "The commissioners told . . .": Vanderwerth, p. 196.

205 "I want to tell . . .": Qtd. in Vanderwerth, p. 231.

205 "It is an injustice . . .": Qtd. in Miller, p. 349.

205 "not as a bridge ...": Lazarus, p. 103.

205 "The drawbacks ...": Lazarus, p. 104.

205 "mammoth poorhouses": Francis Paul Prucha, qtd. in Stamm, p. 63.

205 "We preferred hunting ...," "We preferred our own ...": Qtd. in Nabokov, p. 179.

206 "The Indians say ...": Qtd. in Miller, p. 311.

206 "You white people ...": Qtd. in Miller, pp. 314–315.

207 "The Indians thought ...": Stands-in-Timber and Liberty, pp. 232–233.

207 "We were *always* ...": Qtd. in Miller, p. 248.

207 "I am moving ...": Stands-in-Timber and Liberty, pp. 232–233.

207 "through an open ...": Debo, p. 241.

207 "we will no more ...": Qtd. in Debo, pp. 241–242.

207 "Great Grandfather sends ...": Qtd. in Stands-in-Timber and Liberty, p. 235.

207 "The only way ...": Qtd. in Debo, p. 242.

208 "It was a good ...": Stands-in-Timber and Liberty, p. 238.

208 "I consider that ...": Qtd. in Vanderwerth, p. 231.

209 "slaughtered, raped ...": Utley, *Indian Frontier*, p. 139.

209 "offered only ...," "older than ...": Qtd. in Iverson, *When Indians*, p. 96.

209 "produc[ing] forty ...": Perry, p. 132.

210 "the worst place ...": Qtd. in Perry, p. 120.

210 "dry, hot ...," "insects and ...": Army officer and Chiricahua, qtd. in Perry, p. 20.

210 "to check ...": Perry, p. 130.

210 "threaten[ing] to ...": Perry, p. 132.

210 "out of Arizona ...": Qtd. in Perry, p. 121.

211 "that horrible ...": Qtd. in Utley, *Indian Frontier*, p. 196.

211 "much that was done ...": S. M. Barrett, ed., *Geronimo: His Own Story* (New York: Ballantine Books, 1971), p. 131.

212 "thirty-five men ...": Lt. Britton Davis, quoted in Perry, p. 125.

212 "on the condition ...": Perry, p. 126.

212 "acting on behalf ...": Ibid.

212 "We were reckless ...": Barrett, pp. 150–151.

212 "the Apaches must ...": Utley, *Indian Frontier*, p. 201.

213 "a mighty ...": The phrase is often attributed to Teddy Roosevelt, but Janet McDonnell, *The Dispossession of the American Indian, 1887–1934* (Bloomington: Indiana University Press, 1991), p. 6, cites Indian Commissioner William Jones as the originator.

213 "Congress could...": Richard White, *It's Your Misfortune and None of My Own: A New History of the American West* (Norman: University of Oklahoma Press, 1991), p. 117.

CHAPTER NINE

214 "a crow, a fish, stars": Anonymous Pine Ridge Sioux account in Nabokov, p. 254.

214 "There was no hope...": Qtd. in Lazarus, pp. 113–114.

216 "The craze is...": Qtd. in Krupat, p. 278.

216 "only the delta...": Knack and Stewart, p. 192.

217 "successfully using...": Terry L. Anderson, p. 9.

217 "The common field...": Qtd. in Nabokov, p. 233.

217 "lay at the root...": Bordewich, p. 118.

217 "We Indians...": Qtd. in Frederick E. Hoxie, "From Prison to Homeland: The Cheyenne River Indian Reservation Before World War I" in Peter Iverson, ed., *The Plains Indians of the Twentieth Century* (Norman: University of Oklahoma Press, 1985), p. 72.

218 "compulsory...": Schwartz, p. 215.

218 "The real aim...": Qtd. in Debo, p. 300.

219 "A bill to...": Qtd. in Herring, p. 136.

219 "Our wise legislators...": Qtd. in Nabokov, p. 234.

219 "strangers in...": Omaha Joseph La Flesche et al., in requesting Omaha allotment in 1881, qtd. in Nabokov, p. 240.

219 "improvident or thriftless": The New York Senecas, resisting allotment in 1881, qtd. in Nabokov, p. 237.

220 "[fail] to...": McDonnell, p. 26.

220 "We have given...": Qtd. in Lazarus, p. 107.

220 "practically unanimous...": Qtd. in Prucha, *American Indian Policy,* p. 176.

221 "only a few...": Prucha, *American Indian Policy,* p. 182.

221 "a majority of...": Lazarus, p. 110.

221 "Last year when...": Qtd. in Lazarus, p. 110.

221 "twelve pages...": Lazarus, p. 111.

222 "left behind...": Utley, *Indian Frontier,* p. 251.

222 "We all felt...": Qtd. in Robert M. Utley, *The Last Days of the Sioux Nation* (New Haven: Yale University Press, 1963), p. 157.

223 "We have taken...": Qtd. in Robinson, p. 333.

224 "the reality...": Utley, *Indian Frontier,* p. 261.

224 "armed challenge...": Utley, *Indian Frontier,* p. 257.

224 "the total value . . .": Knack and Stewart, pp. 196–197.

225 "saw that they . . .": Debo, p. 297.

225 "declared the grazing . . .": Utley, *Indian Frontier,* pp. 265–266.

225 "the authority . . .": Debo, p. 305.

225 "when we came here . . .": Wilson, p. 40.

225 "the cession . . .": Utley, *Indian Frontier,* pp. 265–266.

226 "which the Indians . . .": McDonnell, p. 7.

226 "patient and . . .": Alford, p. 137.

226 "The Indian people don't . . .": Qtd. in Nabokov, p. 257.

226 "today [1995] in . . .": Terry L. Anderson, p. 122.

227 "often arid . . .": McDonnell, p. 19.

227 "Neither Indian nor . . .": Qtd. in Knack and Stewart, p. 201.

227 "two six-mile-square . . .": Debo, p. 354.

227 "they had retained . . .": Herring, p. 150.

227 "God damn . . .": Qtd. in Nabokov, p. 237.

227 "the degradation . . .": Debo, p. 313.

228 "Sensible people . . .": Debo, p. 314.

228 "pull[ing] up my . . .": Alford, p. 138.

228 "an Indian could . . .": Qtd. in Perdue, p. 184.

229 "effected by . . .": Qtd. in Nabokov, p. 250.

229 "to visit every . . .": Debo, p. 325.

230 "surpass[ing] anything . . .": Debo, p. 321.

230 "an area enormously . . .": Parman, p. 52.

230 "forced to . . .": Herring, p. 152.

230 "We have never . . .": McDonnell, p. 22.

231 "It is . . . gratifying . . .": Vogel, p. 188.

231 "171 steadily . . .": Nabokov, p. 261.

232 "remain a . . .": Hoxie in Iverson, *Plains Indians,* p. 62. Hoxie is speaking of the Cheyennes and Arapahos, but his remarks relate as well to Indians in general.

232 "policy of . . . exploitation": McDonnell, pp. 3–4.

232 "The Indian Bureau . . .": Josephy, *Red Power,* p. 11.

232 "primitive peoples . . . ," "it is our duty . . .": Qtd. in McDonnell, p. 7.

232 "Work is the . . .": Qtd. in Donald J. Berthrong, "Legacies of the Dawes Act: Bureaucrats and Land Thieves at the Cheyenne-Arapaho Agencies of Oklahoma," in Iverson, *Plains Indians,* p. 37.

233 "paid the Indians . . .": Parman, p. 5.

233 "an illegal . . .": Debo, p. 325.

233 "Much land was . . .": Alford, p. 180.

233 "most profitable": Bordewich, p. 122.

233 "sold or leased . . .": Parman, p. 54.

233 "secure special . . .": Ibid.

233 "livestock dealers . . .": Berthrong in Iverson, *Plains Indians,* p. 46.

234 "about fifteen": Debo, p. 320.

235 "herded to . . .": Gibson, p. 340.

235 "has never been . . .": Qtd. in Gibson, p. 344.

235 "to get hold . . .": Qtd. in Gibson, p. 354.

236 "lacked the capital . . .": McDonnell, p. 55.

236 "conspir[ing] to . . .": McDonnell on allotment on the Uintah and Ouray reservation, p. 57.

236 "worthless securities . . .": Bordewich, p. 122.

236 "extended credit . . .": Parman, p. 17.

237 "existed 'only . . . ' ": Knack and Stewart, p. 272.

237 "water is to . . .": Qtd. in Josephy, *Red Power,* p. 177.

237 "So far this . . . ," "unless some . . .": William R. Logan, qtd. in Norris Hundley, Jr., "The Winters Decision and Indian Water Rights: A Mystery Reexamined," in Iverson, *Plains Indians,* p. 80.

238 "the creation of . . .": Hundley in Iverson, *Plains Indians,* p. 78.

238 "who should go . . .": Qtd. in Nabokov, p. 271.

239 "moved to the . . .": Qtd. in Perdue, pp. 189–190.

239 "tabled the measure": Perdue, p. 177.

239 "Let me tell you . . . ," "pretty good . . .": Nabokov, p. 267.

240 "It isn't right . . .": Qtd. in Berthrong in Iverson, *Plains Indians,* p. 38.

240 "Speculators take . . .": Qtd. in Berthrong in Iverson, *Plains Indians,* p. 39.

240 "over 60 percent . . .": McDonnell, p. 89.

240 "had [full] . . .": Parman, p. 14.

241 "in all dealings . . .": Alford, p. 160.

241 "Our consent was . . .": Qtd. in Hoxie in Iverson, *Plains Indians,* p. 63.

242 "gaining valuable . . .": Hoxie in Iverson, *Plains Indians,* p. 65.

242 "the processes that . . .": Lazarus, referring to further attempts to reduce the Cheyenne River reservation, p. 127.

242 "interest payments . . .": Wilson, p. 99.

242 "a semblance of . . .": Wilson, p. 94.

Chapter Ten

245 "I have almost . . .": Knack and Stewart, p. 101.

245 "in remote parts . . .": Russell Means with Marvin J. Wolf, *Where White Men Fear to Tread: The Autobiography of Russell Means* (New York: St. Martin's Press, 1995), p. 186.

245 "big long . . .": Qtd. in Joseph H. Cash and Herbert T. Hoover, *To Be an Indian: An Oral History* (St. Paul: Minnesota Historical Society Press, 1995 ed.), p. 79.

245 "in tipis . . .": Berthrong in Iverson, *Plains Indians,* p. 42.

245 "little gray . . .": Neihardt, p. 164, quoting Black Elk. Again, although there is now controversy regarding the veracity of *Black Elk Speaks,* the line conveys a valid Indian perspective.

245 "I don't want no . . .": Qtd. in Nabokov, p. 313.

246 "freed the three . . .": Frank McNitt, *The Indian Traders* (Norman: University of Oklahoma Press, 1962), p. 349.

246 "How would . . . ," "If the white . . . ," "We are not . . . ," "It takes you . . .": Nabokov, p. 139.

247 "the Indian position . . .": 1920 effort, reported in Knack and Stewart, p. 232.

247 "they wouldn't even . . .": Nabokov, p. 312.

247 "It's the last . . .": Qtd. in Cash and Hoover, p. 37.

247 "Latin prayers . . .": Wilson, p. 200.

248 "give my hands . . .": Qtd. in McDonnell, p. 95. McDonnell describes the ceremony, pp. 95–96.

249 "perhaps more than . . .": Iverson, *When Indians,* p. 68.

249 "provided all . . .": Berthrong in Iverson, *Plains Indians,* p. 42.

249 "I didn't want . . .": Cash and Hoover, p. 92.

249 "hilly land . . . ," "only slightly . . .": Schwartz, p. 233.

250 "Some of our school . . .": Qtd. in Berthrong in Iverson, *Plains Indians,* pp. 42–43.

250 "land buyers . . .": Qtd. in McDonnell, p. 101.

250 "that he did not know . . .": McDonnell, p. 113.

250 "I don't know how . . .": Qtd. in Berthrong in Iverson, *Plains Indians,* 42–43.

251 "had little or . . .": McDonnell, pp. 92–93.

251 "twice the number . . .": McDonnell, p. 110.

251 "could not make . . .": McDonnell, p. 113.

251 "this reservation is . . .": Qtd. in Hoxie in Iverson, *Plains Indians,* p. 66.

252 "be disastrous . . .": Qtd. in Hoxie in Iverson, *Plains Indians,* p. 66.

252 "heightened their . . .": Hoxie in Iverson, *Plains Indians,* p. 68.

252 "authorize the . . .": Hoxie in Iverson, *Plains Indians,* p. 65.

252 "more than one-half . . .": Berthrong in Iverson, *Plains Indians,* p. 42.

253 "a shortcut to . . .": Qtd. in Berthrong in Iverson, *Plains Indians,* p. 48.

253 "had not received . . .": McDonnell, p. 119.

253 "without his consent . . .": McDonnell, p. 58.

253 "could not discover . . .": Ibid.

254 "Just leave the restrictions . . .": Qtd. in Debo, p. 330.

254 "Those who were . . .": Qtd. in McDonnell, p. 25.

254 "to lose much . . .": McDonnell, p. 25; Debo, p. 336.

254 "adopted a policy . . .": McDonnell, p. 24.

255 "boozefighters, gamblers . . .": Qtd. in Forbes Parkhill, *The Last of the Indian Wars* (New York: The Crowell-Collier Press, 1962), p. 67.

255 "the people of this . . .": Parkhill, p. 73.

255 "White men had . . .": Parkhill, p. 89.

255 "For what Indian . . .": Parkhill, p. 113.

256 "man of all work": R. Douglas Hurt, *Indian Agriculture in America: Prehistory to the Present* (Lawrence: University Press of Kansas, 1987), p. 157. On pp. 155–157 Hurt provides the information on government farmers summarized here.

256 "those early Indian . . .": Qtd. in Cash and Hoover, p. 76.

256 "potatoes, corn . . .": Ibid.

256 "they needed . . .": McDonnell, p. 41.

256 "financing additional . . .": Hurt, p. 165.

257 "often posed . . .": Hurt, p. 157.

257 "one acre of . . .": McDonnell on the Standing Rock reservation, p. 140.

257 "worse . . . than . . .": Hurt, p. 167.

258 "give the Indians . . .": McDonnell, p. 77.

258 "all owners . . .": McDonnell, p. 79.

258 "stop making . . .": Ibid.

258 "until [the charges] . . .": McDonnell, p. 84.

258 "requir[ing] that . . .": Hurt, p. 170.

258 "high-technology . . .": McDonnell, p. 81.

259 "the grazing contracts . . .": Wilson, p. 137.

259 "any profit . . .": Knack and Stewart, p. 155.

260 "more than . . .": Josephy, *Now That,* p. 185.

260 "greater access . . .": Parman, p. 68.

260 "It is pretty hard . . .": Qtd. in McDonnell, pp. 65–66.

260 "strategy to . . .": Iverson, *When Indians,* p. 14.

261 "the greatest disaster . . .": Gordon Macgregor, qtd. in Parman, p. 70.

261 "if the government . . .": McDonnell, p. 64.

261 "his sense of . . .": Qtd. in McDonnell, p. 60.

262 "As long as . . .": McDonnell, p. 65.

262 "sign leases . . .": McDonnell, p. 49.

262 "Indians who complained . . .": McDonnell, p. 69.

262 "to grant mineral . . .": McDonnell, p. 50.

263 "not once . . . had . . .": McDonnell, p. 51.

263 "had been offered . . . ," "unanimously passed . . .": McDonnell, pp. 68–69.

263 "ruled that . . .": Debo, p. 295.

263 "and their rights . . .": McDonnell, p. 54.

263 "shared equally . . .": Wilson, p. 127.

264 "became the biggest . . .": Wilson, p. 133.

264 "gave the Osage . . .": Debo, p. 333.

264 "had always felt . . .": Wilson, p. 184.

264 "In the winter . . .": Krupat, p. 460.

264 "continued to ignore . . .": Knack and Stewart, p. 108.

264 "the white people . . .": Knack and Stewart, p. 176.

265 "You must discourage . . .": Bordewich, pp. 133–134.

265 "the omnipresent . . .": Knack and Stewart, p. 177.

265 "gutted their . . .": Knack and Stewart, p. 110.

265 "all but denuded . . .": William Poole, "Return of the Sinkyone," *Sierra* 81:6 (Nov./Dec. 1996), pp. 54–55.

265 "left the husked . . . ," "It looks just like . . .": Ibid.

266 "for the first . . .": Parman, p. 27.

266 "the best chance": Iverson, *When Indians,* p. 84.

266 "[It] is [the Indians'] . . . ," "just as . . .": Qtd. in Iverson, *When Indians,* p. 114.

266 "Is it right . . .": McDonnell, p. 17.

267 "gullies carried . . .": White, *Roots of Dependency,* p. 227.

267 "successfully restricting . . .": White, *Roots of Dependency,* pp. 230–231.

267 "improved their . . .": White, *Roots of Dependency,* pp. 232, 248–249.

267 "blocked the creation . . .": McDonnell, p. 17.

268 "the appraised value . . .": Debo, p. 241.

268 "the Pueblos had . . .": Josephy, *Now That,* p. 117.

268 "to review . . .": Ibid.

269 "the Indians were . . .": Josephy, *Now That,* p. 120.

269 "over half . . .": Wilson, p. 130.

CHAPTER ELEVEN

270 "We're all . . .": Qtd. in Cash and Hoover, p. 152.

270 "Uncle Sam had . . .": Qtd. in Parman, p. 91.

271 "government subsidized . . .": Knack and Stewart, p. 116.

271 "the mobilization . . .": Ibid.

271 "had allotted 118 . . .": McDonnell, p. 10.

271 "two-thirds of . . .": McDonnell, p. 121.

272 "demanded a more . . .": McDonnell, p. 119.

272 "Economic rehabilitation . . .": Qtd. in White, *Roots of Dependency,* p. 255.

272 "to negotiate . . .": Stephen Cornell, *The Return of the Native: American Indian Political Resurgence* (New York: Oxford University Press, 1988), p. 92.

273 "special Indian . . .": Parman, p. 94.

273 "a violation . . .": Ben Reifel, qtd. in Berthrong in Iverson, *Plains Indians,* pp. 109–110.

273 "the lands were . . .": Reifel in Cash and Hoover, p. 122.

273 "reacting selfishly": Schwartz, p. 239. Schwartz provides these insights into Indian reaction.

273 "*as groups* . . .": Cornell, pp. 93, 92.

274 "This is the action . . .": Naysayers' view, qtd. in Cash and Hoover, p. 146.

274 "I think many . . .": Berthrong in Iverson, *Plains Indians,* pp. 126–127.

274 "It's not self-government . . .": Cash and Hoover, p. 132.

274 "The Bureau in . . . ," "Mr. Collier came . . .": Qtd. in Berthrong in Iverson, *Plains Indians,* p. 124.

275 "They didn't have . . .": Berthrong in Iverson, *Plains Indians,* p. 112.

275 "Nobody really . . .": Qtd. in Berthrong in Iverson, *Plains Indians,* pp. 126–127.

276 "This is the second . . .": Qtd. in White, *Roots of Dependency,* p. 260.

276 "were hardier . . .": White, *Roots of Dependency,* p. 263.

276 "deeply shocked . . .": White, *Roots of Dependency,* pp. 263–264.

276 "The law was accepted . . .": Berthrong in Iverson, *Plains Indians,* p. 113.

277 "it began to take . . .": Robert White, qtd. in Cornell, p. 97.

277 "numerous attempts . . .": Knack and Stewart, p. 324.

277 "using their own funds": Debo, p. 341.

277 "Of course, every . . .": Qtd. in Berthrong in Iverson, *Plains Indians,* p. 123.

277 "bring[ing] the . . .": Iverson, *When Indians,* p. 146.

278 "by more than . . .": Iverson, *When Indians,* p. 140.

278 "permitted state . . .": Michael L. Lawson, *Dammed Indians: The Pick-Sloan Plan and the Missouri River Sioux, 1944–1980* (Norman: University of Oklahoma Press, 1994 ed.), p. 36.

278 "most significant": White, *Roots of Dependency,* p. 256.

278 "extend the civil . . .": Lawson, pp. 36–37.

278 "distances between . . .": Martha L. Henderson, "Settlement Patterns on the Mescalero Apache Reservation Since 1883," *Geographical Review* 80 (July 1990), p. 232.

278 "There were farming . . .": Cash and Hoover, pp. 140–141.

279 "from absolute . . .": Qtd. in Lawson, pp. 36–37.

279 "almost half": Herring, p. 158.

279 "I went back . . .": Cash and Hoover, p. 104.

279 "one-sixth the figure . . .": Bordewich, p. 123.

279 "That was a good . . .": Qtd. in Berthrong in Iverson, *Plains Indians,* p. 122.

279 "The war dispersed . . .": Qtd. in Josephy, *Red Power,* p. 210.

280 "one-third of . . .": Parman, p. 117.

280 "possibly one of . . .": Cash and Hoover, p. 132.

280 "used job patronage . . .": Parman, p. 100.

281 "While every official . . .": Qtd. in Josephy, *Red Power,* p. 23.

281 "greater cultural . . .": Iverson, *When Indians,* p. 122.

281 "gained an unfair . . .": Parman, p. 100.

281 "the favorite sons . . .": Cash and Hoover, p. 132.

281 "unrepresentative minority . . .": Josephy, *Now That,* p. 219.

281 "to appreciate . . .": Qtd. in Iverson, *When Indians,* p. 150.

282 "Why must we . . .": Qtd. in Donald L. Fixico, *Termination and Relocation: Federal Indian Policy, 1945–1960* (Albuquerque: University of New Mexico Press, 1986), p. 30.

282 "the federal government . . .": Parman, p. 135.

282 "The United States is . . .": Qtd. in Iverson, *When Indians,* p. 161.

283 "Those white people . . .": Laurence M. Hauptman, *The Iroquois Struggle for Survival: World War II to Red Power* (Syracuse: Syracuse University Press, 1986), p. 22.

283 "ordered BIA personnel . . .": Parman, p. 133.

283 "a Hitler . . .": Robert M. Kvasnicka and Herman J. Viola, eds., *The Commissioners of Indian Affairs, 1824–1977* (Lincoln: University of Nebraska Press, 1979), p. 293.

284 "did not believe . . .": Fixico, p. 67.

284 "The great majority . . .": Qtd. in Fixico, p. 184.

284 "mark[ing] the most . . .": Debo, p. 349.

284 "first ending . . .": Lawson, p. 127.

284 "withdrawal of . . .": Fixico, p. 56.

285 "other groups . . .": Parman, p. 138.

285 "did not want to . . .": Kathleen A. Dahl, "The Battle Over Termination on the Colville Indian Reservation," *American Indian Culture and Research Journal* 18, 1 (1994), p. 42.

285 "Everything we wanted . . .": Qtd. in Fixico, pp. 95–96.

285 "All you have . . .": Qtd. in Fixico, p. 96.

286 "We are not children . . .": Nabokov, p. 139.

286 "the federal government . . . ," "Can an honorable . . .": Qtd. in Hauptman, *Iroquois Struggle,* pp. 49–50.

286 "I want the committee . . .": Qtd. in Dahl, p. 43.

286 "Owning this . . .": Ibid.

286 "The only thing . . .": Qtd. in Herring, p. 162.

286 "I can go . . .": Qtd. in Dahl, p. 43.

286 "when this bill . . .": Ibid.

287 "avoiding the politics . . .": Dahl on Colville reservation residents, p. 46.

287 "to exercise civil . . .": Fixico, p. 119.

288 "each passed . . .": Herring, p. 160.

288 "continual harassment . . .": Fixico, p. 39.

288 "for successfully . . .": Fixico, p. 132.

288 "directed toward . . .": Dahl, p. 33.

288 "the American Indians . . .": Qtd. in Dahl, p. 34.

289 "to organize . . .": Fixico, pp. 103–104.

290 "would invest in . . .": Fixico, p. 132.

290 "could be of . . .": Fixico, p. 115.

290 "social services were . . .": Debo, p. 374.

290 "some 590,000 . . .": Fixico, p. 102.

291 "would make the land . . .": Fixico, p. 127.

CHAPTER TWELVE

292 "We had to sell . . .": Debo, p. 376.

293 "most people were . . .": Means, p. 77.

293 "They don't even . . .": Lazarus, p. 221.

293 "I nearly went . . .": Qtd. in Fixico, p. 136.

294 "once the new . . .": Fixico, p. 134.

294 "ways to improve . . .": Fixico, p. 142.

295 "a total of . . .": Parman, p. 143.

295 "I have noticed . . .": Qtd. in Cash and Hoover, p. 62.

295 "This is the reason . . .": Cash and Hoover, p. 139.

295 "extermination . . .": California Indian Joseph Vasquez in Fixico, p. 149.

295 "At the very . . .": Qtd. in Fixico, p. 157.

296 "Indian participation . . .": Fixico, p. 161.

296 "a sizeable . . .": Parman, p. 147.

296 "merely a program . . .": Qtd. in Stan Steiner, *The New Indians* (New York: Dell, 1968), p. 180.

296 "in total population . . .": Lazarus, p. 223.

297 "a relatively . . .": Ibid.

297 "termination meant . . .": Parman, p. 140.

297 "The drain-off of . . .": Cash and Hoover, p. 170.

298 "We were contented . . .": Vanderwerth, p. 267.

299 "ancestral homes . . .": Josephy, *Now That,* p. 128.

299 "On paper . . .": Qtd. in Vogel, pp. 218–219.

299 "What the Corps . . .": Ibid.

300 "Apparently you have . . .": Qtd. in Josephy, *Now That,* p. 143.

300 "the most potentially . . .": Lawson, pp. 57, 187.

301 "places so barren . . .": W. L. Gipp in Lawson, p. 75.

301 "more Indian land . . .": Lawson, p. 134.

301 "existing treaty . . .": Lawson, p. 45.

301 "We are here . . .": Qtd. in Lawson, p. 80.

302 "consistently refus[ing]": Lawson, p. 68.

302 "at variable . . .": Lawson, p. 77.

302 "in federal district . . .": Lawson, p. 65.

302 "the same opportunity . . .": Lawson, p. 79.

303 "split allegiances . . .": Lawson, p. 69.

303 "official visits . . .": Lawson, p. 94.

303 "for the first . . .": Lawson, p. 71.

303 "laughed like hell . . .": Qtd. in Lawson, p. 125.

304 "under no circumstances . . .": Lawson, pp. 124–125.

304 "Give me the money . . .": Ibid.

304 "adequate settlement": Lawson, p. 116.

305 "in the midst . . .": Lawson, p. 145.

305 "designed not so . . .": Lawson, p. 136.

306 "artesian wells . . .": Lawson, p. 57.

306 "new sources . . .": Lawson, p. 57. Lawson's description of the change in conditions underpins my own.

306 "no longer . . .": Lawson, pp. 48–49.

307 "failed to provide . . .": Lawson, p. 146.

307 "I'd been hard up . . .": Qtd. in Lawson, p. 159.

308 "into 370 dockets": Parman, p. 127. Figures vary on number of dockets and total amount awarded; Parman says $800,000,000.

308 "the value of . . . ," "for the benefit . . .": Parman, p. 127.

308 "how it should . . .": Hirschfelder and de Montano, p. 25.

308 "petitioned the state . . .": Everett, pp. 120–121.

308 "a tribe might . . .": Hirschfelder and de Montano, p. 25.

308 "that the tribe . . .": Josephy, *Now That,* p. 120.

309 "went beyond . . .": Parman, p. 146.

309 "the right to . . .": Ibid.

309 "346,370 acres . . .": Fixico, p. 172.

309 "I firmly believe . . .": Debo, p. 407.

309 "that foolish . . .": John Wooden Legs in Debo, p. 378.

309 "Our land is . . .": Qtd. in Lazarus, p. 223.

310 "they had to use . . .": Debo, p. 378.

310 "to be repaid . . .": Debo, pp. 379–380.

310 "The Cheyennes . . .": Qtd. in Debo, pp. 379–380.

310 "never saw . . .": Debo, pp. 379–380.

310 "whereby allotted . . .": Lawson, p. 142.

310 "increase the amount . . .": Ibid.

310 "The government has . . .": Qtd. in Lawson, p. 172.

310 "permittees had . . .": Iverson, *When Indians,* p. 163.

311 "that tribes were . . .": Parman, p. 163.

311 "tribes possessed . . .": Ibid.

311 "an internal . . .": Ragsdale in Deloria, p. 71.

311 "the full bloods . . .": St. Pierre, p. 155.

311 "to promote . . .": Wilson, p. 190.

311 "Everything is pretty . . .": Cash and Hoover, p. 85.

312 "that would reduce . . .": Henderson, p. 234.

312 "74 percent . . .": Lawson, p. 41.

312 "averaged . . . less . . .": Fixico, p. 174.

312 "through the BIA . . .": Fixico, p. 43.

312 "through the 1960s . . .": Iverson, *When Indians,* p. 187.

313 "a small proportion . . .": Lawson, p. 43.

313 "some of our Indian . . .": Anonymous, in Cash and Hoover, p. 193.

313 "the only way . . .": Reuben Snake, as told to Jay C. Fikes, *Reuben Snake, Your Humble Serpent: Indian Visionary and Activist* (Santa Fe: Clear Light Publishers, 1996), p. 82.

313 "places without . . .": Qtd. in Lazarus, p. 258.

313 "consistently opposed . . .": Lazarus, p. 224.

313 "concentrated on . . .": Parman, p. 144.

313 "to join . . .": Larry Burt, "Western Tribes and Balance Sheets: Business Development Programs in the 1960s and 1970s," *Western Historical Quarterly* XXIII, 4 (Nov. 1992), p. 478.

314 "concepts of time . . .": Burt, p. 478.

314 "none had flourished . . .": Parman, p. 145.

314 "recipients of aid . . .": Burt, p. 480.

314 "exten[ding] the . . .": Ibid.

314 "some thirty . . .": Josephy, *Now That,* p. 223.

314 "virtually all the . . .": Joseph O'Neal, December 1996 notes to author.

CHAPTER THIRTEEN

316 "This was the magnificent . . .": Snake, pp. 150–151.

317 "THIS IS WINNEBAGO . . .": Ibid.

317 "between 1789 . . . ," "basis for . . .": Lewis, p. 217.

317 "neither protected . . .": Steiner, pp. 188–189.

318 "not White Men . . .": Josephy, *Now That,* p. 28.

318 "indigenous, traditional . . .": Burt, p. 479.

319 "at least 420 . . .": Hauptman, *Iroquois Struggle,* p. 208.

319 "When Indians speak . . . ," "to hold the . . .": Qtd. in Vogel, p. 212.

319 "I suggest that . . .": Qtd. in Steiner, p. 155.

319 "the beginning . . .": Josephy, *Now That,* p. 225.

319 "a flow of funds . . .": Parman, p. 151.

319 "protested that . . .": Burt, p. 482.

320 "a variety of . . .": Burt, p. 483.

320 "in the highest . . .": Josephy, *Red Power,* p. 143.

320 "to remain in . . .": Qtd. in Debo, p. 411.

320 "human and . . .": Fixico, p. 195.

320 "as a coordinating . . .": Josephy, *Now That,* p. 231.

320 "well-educated, young . . .": Burt, p. 490.

320 "from a management . . .": Josephy, *Red Power,* p. 144.

321 "initiated a . . .": Bordewich, p. 84.

321 "Where did you get . . .": Qtd. in Steiner, p. 196.

321 "God help us . . .": Steiner, p. 256.

321 "called to assemblies . . .": Steiner, p. 12.

322 "We do not want development . . .": Qtd. in Josephy, *Red Power,* p. 149.

322 "our rights to . . .": Qtd. in Josephy, *Red Power,* pp. 68–69.

323 "795 acres . . .": Josephy, *Now That,* p. 150.

323 "medicine gathering . . .": Josephy, *Now That,* p. 122.

323 "If the homeland . . .": Matthiessen, *Indian Country,* p. 116.

323 "hidden colonialism," "Let's say . . . ," "insofar as . . .": Qtd. in Steiner, p. 255.

324 "about 3 percent . . .": Parman, p. 169.

324 "under pressure . . . ," "did not know . . .": Josephy, *Now That,* p. 234.

324 "receiving the same . . .": See Josephy, *Now That,* p. 222.

324 "highly pollutant . . .": Lawson on the Navajo reservation, p. 43.

324 "sucking up . . .": Matthiessen, *Indian Country,* p. 97.

325 "without regard . . .": Lawson, p. 192.

325 "develop fully . . .": Lawson, pp. 182–183.

325 "116 percent . . .": See Parman, p. 149.

325 "migration to . . .": Vine Deloria, Jr., *Custer Died for Your Sins* (New York: Macmillan, 1969), p. 257.

325 "lacked a clear . . .": Karen I. Blu, *The Lumbee Problem: The Making of an American Indian People* (Cambridge, England: Cambridge University Press, 1980), p. 2.

326 "mandated to determine . . .": Porter, p. 3.

326 "Almost without . . . ," "increasingly responsive . . .": Qtd. in Josephy, *Red Power,* pp. 147–148.

326 "We don't control . . .": Cash and Hoover, p. 199.

327 "sending delegations . . .": Josephy, *Now That,* pp. 254–255.

327 "increasingly more . . .": Parman, p. 168.

327 "We want power . . .": Qtd. in Steiner, p. 269.

327 "all checks . . .": Matthiessen, *Indian Country,* p. 251.

328 "Maybe we didn't . . .": Snake, p. 112.

328 "fought for . . .": Steiner, p. 8.

328 "an extraordinary . . .": Parman, p. 164.

329 "My strength is . . .": Qtd. in Miller, p. 338.

329 "the income of . . .": Steiner, p. 51.

329 "with ceremonies . . .": Josephy, *Now That,* p. 180.

329 "they had been fishing . . .": Josephy, *Now That,* p. 177.

330 "formed an organization . . .": Parman, pp. 153–154.

330 "Why can't an . . .": Qtd. in Josephy, *Now That,* pp. 83–84.

331 "usual and accustomed . . .": Josephy, *Now That,* p. 200.

332 "environmental degradation": Josephy, *Now That,* p. 208.

332 "a similar island": Vogel, p. 228.

332 "We must start . . .": Josephy, *Red Power,* p. 188.

332 "an Indian trading . . . ," "tourist attractions . . .": Josephy, *Now That,* p. 229.

333 "most Indian . . . ," "the population has . . .": Vogel, pp. 228–229.

333 "If they don't want . . .": Snake, p. 121.

334 "only 33 percent . . .": U.S. Department of Interior 1986 report, qtd. in Terry L. Anderson, p. 147.

334 "inhibited, socially . . .": Steiner, pp. 262–263.

334 "The only thing to . . .": Qtd. in Fixico, p. 196.

334 "full recognition . . .": Parman, p. 156.

335 "Indian puppets . . .": Robert Burnette, head of American Indian Civil Rights Council, qtd. in Steiner, p. 257.

336 "more signatures . . .": Matthiessen, *In the Spirit,* p. 61.

336 "Nothing like this . . .": Matthiessen, *In the Spirit,* p. 62.

336 "We haven't demanded . . .": Qtd. in Matthiessen, *In the Spirit,* p. 76.

373 "They'll go back . . .": Qtd. in Matthiessen, *In the Spirit,* p. 81.

338 "to protest . . .": Parman, p. 162.

338 "If he wishes . . .": Qtd. in Steiner, p. 265.

338 "Our reservation is . . .": Steiner, p. 169.

338 "I feel freer . . .": Steiner, p. 142.

339 "independent . . .": Josephy, *Now That,* p. 28.

339 "the majority of . . .": Qtd. in Steiner, p. 168.

340 "very old [Hopi] . . .": Matthiessen, *Indian Country,* p. 94.

340 "only 3 percent . . .": Lawson, p. 176.

341 "Community development must be . . .": Qtd. in Josephy, *Red Power,* p. 76.

341 "featured community . . .": Parman, p. 166.

341 "We started introducing . . .": Snake, p. 108.

341 "Why is it that . . .": Steiner, p. 137.

342 "reassert its authority": Josephy, *Now That,* p. 227.

342 "enriched themselves . . .": Parman, p. 151.

342 "a tidal wave . . .": Anonymous Sioux leader, qtd. in Parman, p. 151.

342 "It doesn't take . . .": Qtd. in Steiner, p. 133.

343 "Instead of starting . . .": Qtd. in Steiner, p. 134.

343 "Here we have . . .": Qtd. in Steiner, p. 206.

343 "the twenty-four . . .": David L. Vinje, "Cultural Values and Economic Development on Reservations," in Deloria, *American Indian Policy,* p. 155.

343 "low weight . . .": Burt, p. 484.

343 "shallow . . .": Burt, p. 485.

344 "encouraging competition . . .": Burt on the Zunis and the AIRCO Corporation, p. 487.

344 "could not be . . .": Burt, p. 488.

344 "small-scale, under-financed . . .": Vinje in Deloria, *American Indian Policy,* p. 157.

344 "$576,000 in grants . . .": Burt, p. 483.

344 "had no wish . . .": Alcatraz activist in Josephy, *Now That,* p. 229.

345 "started with three . . .": Burt, p. 491.

345 "managed to reacquire . . .": Herring, p. 164.

346 "based on land . . .": Parman, p. 128.

346 "transferred over . . .": Hirschfelder and de Montano, p. 25.

346 "for the loss . . .": Porter, p. 32.

346 "each tribe dropped . . .": Harold Prins in Mary B. Davis, ed., *Native America in the Twentieth Century: An Encyclopedia* (New York: Garland Publishing, 1994), p. 436.

346 "a moratorium . . .": Parman, p. 171.

346 "the rapid development . . .": Herring, p. 164.

347 "self-contained system . . .": Burt, p. 495.

347 "develop our . . .": Snake, p. 144.

347 "cultural enhancement . . .": Ibid.

347 "a tribal health . . .": Snake, pp. 148–149.

347 "They wanted a . . .": Snake, p. 144.

347 "operate in a . . .": Terry L. Anderson, p. 149.

347 "We began to understand . . .": Snake, p. 143.

348 "the bonds of wardship": Terry L. Anderson, pp. 148–149.

348 "charges of graft . . .": Josephy, *Now That,* pp. 256–257.

348 "The time has come . . .": Qtd. in Bordewich, p. 83. Bordewich also questions the implications of this stance.

CHAPTER FOURTEEN

350 "Salamanca's white . . .": Hauptman, *Iroquois Struggle,* p. 17.

351 "negotiated on our behalf . . .": "Seneca lease holdouts want $115M," *News from Indian Country* X, 23 (mid-December 1996): 6A.

351 "ten times greater . . .": Josephy, *Now That,* p. 258.

351 "perhaps even more . . .": Qtd. in Terry L. Anderson, p. 18.

352 "Just when we . . .": Qtd. in Josephy, *Now That,* p. 258.

352 "stumbling blocks . . .": Lewis, p. 205.

352 "identify obstacles . . .": Burt, pp. 475–476.

352 "encouraged to modify . . .": Deloria, *American Indian Policy,* pp. 3–4.

352 "assuming responsibility . . .": Deloria, *American Indian Policy,* p. 12.

352 "a non-Indian . . .": Burt, pp. 475–476.

353 "strengthening tribal . . .": "Lack of effective dispute resolution causes turmoil on most reservations," *News from Indian Country* X, 18 (late September 1996): 18A.

353 "more politically astute": David Wilkins, "Four More Years," *News from Indian Country* X, 23 (mid-December 1996): 18A.

353 "determined to . . .": Bordewich, pp. 10–11.

354 "When I was a boy . . .": Qtd. in Miller, p. 254.

354 "a master plan . . .": Qtd. in "Governor claims tribes have 'master plan' to buy western South Dakota," *News from Indian Country* IX, 17 (mid-September 1995): 1.

355 "legal jurisdiction . . .": Lewis, p. 210.

355 "formal tribal recognition": "Extinct Indian group given land," *News from Indian Country* X, 22 (late November 1996): 6A.

355 "in legal limbo": "Samish restored," *News from Indian Country* X, 22 (late November 1996): 7A.

357 "about 250,000 . . .": Joel Stashenko, "Federal official says Oneida claim resolution 'vanishing,' " *News from Indian Country* X, 24 (late December 1996): 7A.

357 "forced . . . to reestablish . . .": Deborah Doxtator, Wisconsin Oneida chairwoman, in "Oneida Nation of Wisconsin Chairwoman's reply to ad run by Oneida Nation of New York," *News from Indian Country* X, 24 (late December 1996): 14A.

357 "rolling second-growth . . .": Poole, pp. 54, 72.

358 "Ten years ago . . .": Poole, p. 72.

358 "directing federal . . .": Karen Coates, "Stairway to Heaven," *Sierra* 81, 6 (November/December 1996): 27–28.

358 "timber harvesting . . .": "Medicine Wheel agreement reached," *News from Indian Country* X, 21 (mid-November 1996): 1A+.

358 "24 days of . . .": Ibid.

358 "discover transformational . . .": Bordewich, p. 234.

359 "the resistance of . . .": Parman, p. 176.

359 "10 million acres . . . ," "allowed hunting . . .": Michael C. Buelow, "Court: No to reconsideration," *News from Indian Country* X, 23 (mid-December 1996): 1A+.

360 "abandoned or ceded": Calloway, p. 250.

360 "had been extinguished . . .": Ibid.

360 "that the Fond du Lac . . .": "Judge upholds off-rez rights," *News from Indian Country* X, 7 (mid-April 1996): 1A.

360 "Your office lacks . . .": "Shoshones serve notice on feds," *News from Indian Country* IX, 7 (mid-April 1995): 12.

361 "defin[ing] the unique . . .": Bordewich, p. 19.

361 "Without a land . . .": Bordewich, p. 111.

361 "residual sovereignty": Ragsdale in Deloria, *American Indian Policy,* p. 69.

361 "racial separatism": Bordewich, p. 313.

362 "We say the white . . .": Cash and Hoover, p. 148.

362 "tribal governments as a whole . . .": Bordewich, p. 88.

362 "capable of making . . .": Qtd. in Dan McGovern, *The Campo Indian Landfill Wars: The Fight for Gold in California's Garbage* (Norman: University of Oklahoma Press, 1995), p. 245.

362 "after storming . . .": "Seneca Nation Chronology: Power Struggle," *News from Indian Country* IX, 7 (mid-April 1995): 2.

363 "traditional Indian . . .": Parman, p. 177.

364 "nearly doubled . . .": "Cino backs down: casino will be closed," *News from Indian Country* X, 20 (late October 1996): 1A.

364 "ask[ed] an appeals . . .": Deborah Baker, "States want casino compacts illegal," *News from Indian Country* X, 21 (mid-November 1996): 1A.

364 "more than 130 . . .": Lewis, p. 215.

364 "forty full-fledged . . .": Bordewich, pp. 107–108.

364 "considered more from . . .": "Pequots ready to burn casino mortgage," *News from Indian Country* IX, 6 (late March 1995): 6.

364 "25 to 30 percent . . .": Bordewich, pp. 107–108; a $130 million figure for 1995 was projected in "Interior gives go-ahead for Mashantucket land buy," *News from Indian Country* IX, 11 (mid-June 1995): 4.

364 "Here's the world's richest . . .": Qtd. in "Interior gives go-ahead for Mashantucket land buy," *News from Indian Country* IX, 11 (mid-June 1995): 4.

365 "reverse[d] or at least . . .": Parman, pp. 176–177.

365 "the kind of infrastructure . . .": Bordewich, p. 108.

365 "nor were they informed . . .": Doug George Kanentiio, "Oneidas raise serious leadership questions," *News from Indian Country* IX, 11 (mid-June 1995) : 34.

366 "over control . . .": "Gunfire erupts on California reservation," *News from Indian Country* IX, 20 (late October 1995): 1.

366 "Gaming is all . . .": Qtd. in Bordewich, pp. 107–108.

366 "while the unemployment . . .": Terry L. Anderson, p. 1.

366 "below the poverty . . .": Ibid.

366 "I've seen these . . .": Qtd. in David Pego, "We Are Moving Forward," *Austin American-Statesman* (September 2, 1996): E1.

366 "The only money . . .": Ibid.

367 "provide capital . . .": Terry L. Anderson, pp. 15–16.

367 "in such disarray . . .": Michael Satchell, "The worst federal agency: critics call the Bureau of Indian Affairs a national disgrace," *U.S. News & World Report* 28 (November 1994): 61+.

367 "remarkably little . . .": See Satchell.

367 "before reaching . . .": David Pego, "It's O.K. to Be Indian Now," *Austin American-Statesman* (August 31, 1996): E1.

368 "a cancer rate . . .": Winona LaDuke, "Like Tributaries to a River: The Growing Strength of Native Environmentalism," *Sierra* 81, 6, (November/December 1996): 41.

368 "oil wells . . .": Lewis, p. 216.

368 "leaking radioactive . . .": LaDuke, p. 41.

368 "an estimated 1,200 . . .": Parman, p. 173.

368 "national landfills . . .": McGovern, p. xix.

368 "to be distributed . . .": Ibid.

368 "How dumb . . .": Qtd. in McGovern, p. xix.

369 "tribal unemployment . . .": McGovern, p. 24.

369 "real hope . . .": Ibid.

369 "millions of dollars . . .": Jeff Barnard, "Coquille look at diversity to drive tribal economy," *News from Indian Country* IX, 8 (late April 1995): 8.

369 "12 million in . . .": Barnard, p. 8.

370 "No one wants . . .": Richard Wilks, Pima-Maricopa tribal attorney, in Bordewich, p. 126.

370 "to tax and regulate . . .": Terry L. Anderson, p. 174.

370 "enterprise . . .": Lewis, p. 213.

370 "Being Indian means . . .": Qtd. in Bordewich, p. 135.

370 "Our philosophy is . . .": Qtd. in Bordewich, p. 309.

370 "small-scale tribally . . .": Vinje in Deloria, *American Indian Policy,* p. 172.

371 "a motel . . .": Bordewich, p. 56.

371 "one of the oldest . . .": "CNI nets profit, rehires laid-off employees," *News from Indian Country* X, 23 (mid-December 1996): 11A.

371 "to manufacture . . .": Ibid.

371 "radar-absorbing tank camouflage": Lewis, p. 213.

371 "We were once horsemen . . .": Jim Robbins, "Nez Perce see the future in their past," *News from Indian Country* X, 24 (late December 1996): 13A.

371 "approximately 30 percent . . .": Lewis, pp. 212–213.

372 "their own tribal . . .": Bordewich, p. 134.

372 "sits on $2.5 billion . . .": Richard Oppel, editorial, *Austin American-Statesman* (August 25, 1996): D3.

372 "managing and reinvesting . . .": Lewis, p. 216.

372 "coal gasification . . .": Vinje in Deloria, *American Indian Policy,* p. 169.

372 "pit[ted] southern . . .": Lewis, p. 219.

373 "converting Indian water . . .": Parman, p. 173.

373 "whether the reservation . . .": Deloria, *American Indian Policy,* p. 11.

373 "The Yakima Indian Nation . . .": Qtd. in LaDuke, "Like Tributaries," p. 42.

373 "over two hundred . . .": McGovern, p. 18.

373 "reassert[ed] treaty rights . . .": Lewis, p. 219.

374 "the cowboys and . . .": Cheyenne River Sioux Madonna Thunderhawk, in McGovern, p. 19.

374 "leading a multi-agency . . .": George Snyder, "Fighting for another 10,000 years of living in balance," *News from Indian Country* X, 23 (mid-December 1996): 23.

374 "restored over . . .": LaDuke, p. 40.

374 "It's probably 99 . . .": Qtd. in Pego, "We Are Moving."

374 "90 percent of . . .": Nancy Lord, "Native Tongues," *Sierra* 81, 6 (November/ December 1996): 68.

375 "where we came from . . .": Means, p. 69.

375 "Who we are is . . .": LaDuke, p. 43.

376 "no single policy . . .": Fixico, p. 197.

376 "If you have come to . . .": I recorded this quote years ago, source unknown.

376 "evolve at their . . .": Bordewich, p. 123.

377 "the history of Christianity . . .": Steiner, p. 109.

377 "manipulate tribal . . .": Terry L. Anderson on situation in mid-nineties, p. 151.

377 "a blend of traditional . . .": Terry L. Anderson, p. 152.

377 "ill-defined and ill-regulated": Bordewich, p. 88.

377 "land and resources . . .": Lewis, p. 220.

378 "in order to protect . . .": Thornton, p. 198.

378 "descent along . . .": Thornton, p. 199.

378 "based on obsolete . . .": Bordewich, p. 13.

378 "Intermarriage and . . .": Lewis, p. 207.

379 "persistent social disorganization": "Lack of effective dispute resolution causes turmoil on most reservations," *News from Indian Country* X, 18 (late September 1996): 18A.

379 "It is impossible . . .": Prucha, "American Indian Policy in the Twentieth Century," *Western Historical Quarterly* XV, 1 (January 1984): 17–18.

379 "between federal . . .": Lewis, p. 218.

380 "an economic and . . .": Lewis, p. 211. Lewis (1993) says 3 percent, LaDuke (1996) 4 percent. These percentages include Alaska lands, which are outside the scope of this narrative.

Selected Bibliography

Not only is the literature on Indian history large and varied, but new perspectives and new insights—as well as previously obscured ones—are constantly emerging. The following list does not do justice to the wealth of information and interpretation available, but includes materials I found most useful on my journey of discovery, among them classic texts, helpful reference works, and some of the most intriguing and provocative studies by current examiners of American Indian experience.

For further visual aids that show the process of Indian dispossession, I recommend that the reader consult maps in Carl Waldman's *Atlas of the North American Indian* (New York: Facts on File, 1985), and *Historical Atlas of the American West* (Norman: University of Oklahoma Press, 1989).

To cultivate an awareness of the issues emanating from and affecting Indian country today, I recommend *News from Indian Country,* a newspaper published twice a month by Indian Country Communications, Inc., Rt. 2, Box 2900-A, Hayward, WI 54843.

Agnew, Brad. *Fort Gibson: Terminal on the Trail of Tears*. Norman: University of Oklahoma Press, 1980.

Alford, Thomas Wildcat. *Civilization and the Story of the Absentee Shawnees*. Norman: University of Oklahoma Press, 1979 ed.

Anderson, Terry L. *Sovereign Nations or Reservations? An Economic History of American Indians*. San Francisco: Pacific Research Institute for Public Policy, 1995.

Anderson, William L., ed. *Cherokee Removal: Before and After*. Athens: University of Georgia Press, 1991.

Axtell, James. *The Invasion Within: The Contest of Cultures in Colonial North America*. New York: Oxford University Press, 1985.

Barrett, S. M., ed. *Geronimo: His Own Story*. New York: Ballantine Books, 1971.

Beck, Warren A., and Ynez D. Haase. *Historical Atlas of the American West*. Norman: University of Oklahoma Press, 1989.

Benedek, Emily. *The Wind Won't Know Me: A History of the Navajo-Hopi Land Dispute*. New York: Vintage Books, 1993 ed.

Benson, Todd. ''The Consequences of Reservation Life: Native Californians on the

Round Valley Reservation, 1871–1884.'' *Pacific Historical Review* 60 (May 1991): 221–244.

Blaine, Martha Royce. *Pawnee Passage: 1870–1875*. Norman: University of Oklahoma Press, 1990.

Blu, Karen I. *The Lumbee Problem: The Making of an American Indian People*. Cambridge, England: Cambridge University Press, 1980.

Boissevain, Ethel. *The Narragansett People*. Phoenix, AZ: Indian Tribal Series, 1975.

Bordewich, Fergus M. *Killing the White Man's Indian: Reinventing Native Americans at the End of the Twentieth Century*. New York: Doubleday, 1996.

Burt, Larry. ''Western Tribes and Balance Sheets: Business Development Programs in the 1960s and 1970s.'' *Western Historical Quarterly* XXIII, 4 (November 1992): 475–495.

Calloway, Colin G. *The Western Abenakis of Vermont, 1600–1800: War, Migration, and the Survival of an Indian People*. Norman: University of Oklahoma Press, 1990.

————, ed. *The World Turned Upside Down: Indian Voices from Early America*. Boston: St. Martin's Press, 1994.

Camp, Gregory S. ''Working Out Their Own Salvation: The Allotment of Land in Severalty and the Turtle Mountain Chippewa Band, 1870–1920.'' *American Indian Culture and Research Journal* 14, 2 (1990): 19–38.

Canfield, Gae Whitney. *Sarah Winnemucca of the Northern Paiutes*. Norman: University of Oklahoma Press, 1988 ed.

Cantor, George. *North American Indian Landmarks: A Traveler's Guide*. Detroit: Visible Ink Press, 1993.

Carter, Cecile Elkins. *Caddo Indians: Where We Come From*. Norman: University of Oklahoma Press, 1995.

Cash, Joseph H., and Herbert T. Hoover. *To Be an Indian: An Oral History*. St. Paul: Minnesota Historical Society Press, 1995 ed.

Churchill, Ward. *Indians Are Us? Culture and Genocide in Native North America*. Monroe, ME: Common Courage Press, 1994.

Cornell, Stephen. *The Return of the Native: American Indian Political Resurgence*. New York: Oxford University Press, 1988.

Cronon, William. *Changes in the Land: Indians, Colonists, and the Ecology of New England*. New York: Hill and Wang, 1983.

Crow Dog, Mary, with Richard Erdoes. *Lakota Woman*. New York: HarperPerennial, 1991 ed.

Dahl, Kathleen A. ''The Battle Over Termination on the Colville Indian Reservation.'' *American Indian Culture and Research Journal* 18, 1 (1994): 29–53.

Dale, Edward Everett, and Gaston Litton. *Cherokee Cavaliers: Forty Years of Cherokee History as Told in the Correspondence of the Ridge-Watie-Boudinot Family*. Norman: University of Oklahoma Press, 1995 ed.

Davis, Mary B., ed. *Native America in the Twentieth Century: An Encyclopedia*. New York: Garland Publishing, 1994.

Debo, Angie. *A History of the Indians of the United States*. Norman: University of Oklahoma Press, 1970.

Deloria, Vine, Jr., ed. *American Indian Policy in the Twentieth Century*. Norman: University of Oklahoma Press, 1985.

———. *Custer Died for Your Sins: An Indian Manifesto*. New York: Macmillan, 1969.

Dowd, Gregory E. "Thinking and Believing: Nativism and Unity in the Ages of Pontiac and Tecumseh." *American Indian Quarterly* XVI, 3 (Summer 1992): 309–330.

Doyle, Susan Badger. "Indian Perspectives of the Bozeman Trail, 1864–1868." *Montana the Magazine of Western History* 40 (Winter 1990): 56–67.

Everett, Dianna. *The Texas Cherokees: A People Between Two Fires, 1819–1840*. Norman: University of Oklahoma Press, 1990.

Fikes, Jay C. (as told to). *Reuben Snake, Your Humble Serpent: Indian Visionary and Activist*. Santa Fe: Clear Light Publishers, 1996.

Fixico, Donald L. *Termination and Relocation: Federal Indian Policy, 1945–1960*. Albuquerque: University of New Mexico Press, 1986.

Foreman, Grant. *The Five Civilized Tribes*. Norman: University of Oklahoma Press, 1934.

———. *Indian Removal: The Emigration of the Five Civilized Tribes of Indians*. Norman: University of Oklahoma Press, 1972 ed.

Gibson, A. M. *The Kickapoos: Lords of the Middle Border*. Norman: University of Oklahoma Press, 1963.

Green, Michael. *The Politics of Indian Removal: Creek Government and Society in Crisis*. Lincoln: University of Nebraska Press, 1982.

Hauptman, Laurence M. *The Iroquois Struggle for Survival: World War II to Red Power*. Syracuse: Syracuse University Press, 1986.

Hauptman, Laurence M., and James D. Wherry, eds. *The Pequots in Southern New England: The Fall and Rise of an American Indian Nation*. Norman: University of Oklahoma Press, 1990.

Harring, Sidney L. *Crow Dog's Case: American Indian Sovereignty, Tribal Law, and United States Law in the Nineteenth Century*. Cambridge, England: Cambridge University Press, 1994.

Henderson, Martha L. "Settlement Patterns on the Mescalero Apache Reservation Since 1883." *Geographical Review* 80 (July 1990): 226–238.

Herring, Joseph B. *The Enduring Indians of Kansas: A Century and a Half of Acculturation*. Lawrence: University Press of Kansas, 1990.

Hirschfelder, Arlene, and Martha Kreipe de Montana. *The Native American Almanac: A Portrait of Native America Today*. New York: Prentice Hall, 1993.

Hurt, R. Douglas. *Indian Agriculture in America: Prehistory to the Present*. Lawrence: University Press of Kansas, 1987.

Hurtado, Albert L. *Indian Survival on the California Frontier*. New Haven: Yale University Press, 1988.

Iverson, Peter, ed. *The Plains Indians of the Twentieth Century*. Norman: University of Oklahoma Press, 1985.

———. *When Indians Became Cowboys: Native Peoples and Cattle Ranching in the American West*. Norman: University of Oklahoma Press, 1994.

Jacobs, Wilbur R. *Dispossessing the American Indian: Indians & Whites on the Colonial Frontier*. New York: Charles Scribner's Sons, 1972.

Jaimes, M. Annette, ed. *The State of Native America: Genocide, Colonization, and Resistance*. Boston: South End Press, 1992.

Jennings, Francis. *The Invasion of America: Indians, Colonialism, and the Cant of Conquest*. Chapel Hill: University of North Carolina Press, 1975.

Josephy, Alvin M., Jr. *The Nez Perce Indians and the Opening of the Northwest*. New Haven: Yale University Press, 1971.

———. *Now That the Buffalo's Gone: A Study of Today's American Indians*. New York: Alfred A. Knopf, 1982.

———. *The Patriot Chiefs: A Chronicle of American Indian Resistance*. New York: The Viking Press, 1969.

———. *Red Power: The American Indians' Fight for Freedom*. Lincoln: University of Nebraska Press, 1985 ed.

Klos, George. " 'Our People Could Not Distinguish One Tribe from Another': The 1859 Expulsion of the Reserve Indians from Texas." *Southwestern Historical Quarterly* XCVII, 4 (April 1994): 599–619.

Knack, Martha C., and Omer C. Stewart. *As Long As the River Shall Run: An Ethnohistory of Pyramid Lake Indian Reservation*. Berkeley: University of California Press, 1984.

Krupat, Arnold, ed. *Native American Autobiography: An Anthology*. Madison: University of Wisconsin Press, 1994.

Kvasnicka, Robert M., and Herman J. Viola, eds. *The Commissioners of Indian Affairs, 1824–1977*. Lincoln: University of Nebraska Press, 1979.

LaDuke, Winona. "Like Tributaries to a River: The Growing Strength of Native Environmentalism." *Sierra* 81, 6 (November/December 1996): 38–45.

Lancaster, Jane. *Removal Aftershock: The Seminoles' Struggles to Survive in the West, 1836–1866*. Knoxville: University of Tennessee Press, 1994.

Lawson, Michael L. *Dammed Indians: The Pick-Sloan Plan and the Missouri River Sioux, 1944–1980*. Norman: University of Oklahoma Press, 1994 ed.

Lazarus, Edward. *Black Hills White Justice: The Sioux Nation Versus the United States 1775 to the Present*. New York: HarperCollins, 1991.

Lewis, David Rich. "Still Native: The Significance of Native Americans in the History of the Twentieth-Century American West." *Western Historical Quarterly* XXIV, 2 (May 1993): 203–227.

Lindquist, Mark, and Martin Zanger, eds. *"Buried Roots and Indestructible Seeds": The Survival of American Indian Life in Story, History, and Spirit*. Madison: Wisconsin Humanities Council, 1993.

McDonnell, Janet A. *The Dispossession of the American Indian, 1887–1934*. Bloomington: Indiana University Press, 1991.

McGovern, Dan. *The Campo Indian Landfill War: The Fight for Gold in California's Garbage*. Norman: University of Oklahoma Press, 1995.

McLoughlin, William G. *Cherokees and Missionaries, 1789–1839*. Norman: University of Oklahoma Press, 1994.

McNickle, D'Arcy. *Native American Tribalism: Indian Survivals and Renewals*. London: Oxford University Press, 1973.

McNitt, Frank. *The Indian Traders*. Norman: University of Oklahoma Press, 1962.

Malinowski, Sharon, ed. *Notable Native Americans*. New York: Gale Research, Inc., 1995.

Mankiller, Wilma, and Michael Wallis. *Mankiller: A Chief and Her People*. New York: St. Martin's Press, 1993.

Mathes, Valerie Sherer. "Helen Hunt Jackson and the Ponca Controversy." *Montana the Magazine of Western History* 39, 1 (Winter 1989): 42–53.

Matthiessen, Peter. *Indian Country*. New York: Penguin Books, 1992 ed.

———. *In the Spirit of Crazy Horse*. New York: Penguin Books, 1992 ed.

Means, Russell, with Marvin J. Wolf. *Where White Men Fear to Tread: The Autobiography of Russell Means*. New York: St. Martin's Press, 1995.

Merrell, James H. *The Indians' New World: Catawbas and Their Neighbors from European Contact Through the Era of Removal*. Chapel Hill: University of North Carolina Press, 1989.

Miller, Lee, ed. *From the Heart: Voices of the American Indian*. New York: Vintage Books, 1995.

Nabokov, Peter, ed. *Native American Testimony: A Chronicle of Indian-White Relations from Prophecy to the Present, 1492–1992*. New York: Penguin Books, 1992.

"The Navajo Treaty–1868." Las Vegas, NV: K.C. Publications, in cooperation with the Navajo Tribe, 1968.

Neihardt, John G. *Black Elk Speaks: Being the Life Story of a Holy Man of the Oglala Sioux*. New York: Pocket Books, 1972.

Parkhill, Forbes. *The Last of the Indian Wars*. New York: The Crowell-Collier Press, 1962.

Parman, Donald L. *Indians and the American West in the Twentieth Century*. Bloomington: Indiana University Press, 1994.

Perdue, Theda, ed. *Cherokee Editor: The Writings of Elias Boudinot.* Athens: University of Georgia Press, 1996 ed.

———. *Nations Remembered: An Oral History of the Cherokees, Chickasaws, and Seminoles in Oklahoma, 1856–1907.* Norman: University of Oklahoma Press, 1993.

Perry, Richard J. *Apache Reservation: Indigenous Peoples & the American State.* Austin: University of Texas Press, 1993.

Phillips, George Harwood. *Indians and Indian Agents: The Origins of the Reservation System in California, 1849–1852.* Norman: University of Oklahoma Press, 1997.

Poole, William. "Return of the Sinkyone." *Sierra* 81, 6 (November/December 1996): 52–55ff.

Porter, Frank W., III., ed. *Strategies for Survival: American Indians in the Eastern United States.* Westport, CT: Greenwood Press, 1986.

Prucha, Francis Paul. *American Indian Policy in Crisis: Christian Reformers and the Indian, 1865–1900.* Norman: University of Oklahoma Press, 1976.

———. "American Indian Policy in the Twentieth Century." *Western Historical Quarterly* XV, 1 (January 1984): 5–18.

———. *Atlas of American Indian Affairs.* Lincoln: University of Nebraska Press, 1990.

Richter, Daniel K. *The Ordeal of the Longhouse: The Peoples of the Iroquois League in the Era of European Colonization.* Chapel Hill: University of North Carolina Press, 1992.

Rickey, Don, Jr. *Forty Miles a Day on Beans and Hay: The Enlisted Soldier Fighting the Indian Wars.* Norman: University of Oklahoma Press, 1963.

Riley, Patricia, ed. *Growing Up Native American: An Anthology.* New York: William Morrow, 1993.

Roberts, David. *Once They Moved Like the Wind: Cochise, Geronimo, and the Apache Wars.* New York: Simon & Schuster, 1993.

Robinson, Charles M., III. *A Good Year to Die: The Story of the Great Sioux War.* New York: Random House, 1995.

Rollings, Willard. *The Osage: An Ethnohistorical Study of Hegemony on the Prairie-Plains.* Columbia: University of Missouri Press, 1992.

Russell, Steve. "The Legacy of Ethnic Cleansing: Implementation of NAGPRA in Texas." *American Indian Culture and Research Journal* 19, 4 (1995): 193–211.

St. Pierre, Mark. *Madonna Swan: A Lakota Woman's Story.* Norman: University of Oklahoma Press, 1991.

Salisbury, Neal. *Manitou and Providence: Indians, Europeans, and the Making of New England, 1500–1643.* New York: Oxford University Press, 1994 ed.

Schwartz, E. A. *The Rogue River Indian War and Its Aftermath, 1850–1980.* Norman: University of Oklahoma Press, 1997.

Segal, Charles M., and David C. Stineback. *Puritans, Indians & Manifest Destiny.* New York: G. P. Putnam's Sons, 1977.

Snipp, C. Matthew. *American Indians: The First of This Land.* New York: Russell Sage Foundation, 1989.

Stamm, Henry E. "The Peace Policy at Wind River: The James Irwin Years, 1871–1877." *Montana the Magazine of Western History* 41, 3 (Summer 1991): 56–69.

Stands-in-Timber, John, and Margot Liberty. *Cheyenne Memories.* New Haven: Yale University Press, 1967.

Steele, Ian. *Warpaths: Invasions of North America.* New York: Oxford University Press, 1994.

Steiner, Stan. *The New Indians.* New York: Dell, 1968.

Thompson, Gerald. *The Army and the Navajo.* Tucson: University of Arizona Press, 1976.

Thornton, Russell J. *American Indian Holocaust and Survival: A Population History Since 1492.* Norman: University of Oklahoma Press, 1990 ed.

Utley, Robert M. *The Indian Frontier of the American West 1846–1890.* Albuquerque: University of New Mexico Press, 1984.

———. *The Lance and the Shield: The Life and Times of Sitting Bull.* New York: Henry Holt, 1993.

———. *The Last Days of the Sioux Nation.* New Haven: Yale University Press, 1963.

Vanderwerth, W. C. *Indian Oratory: Famous Speeches by Noted Indian Chiefs.* Norman: University of Oklahoma, 1971.

Viola, Herman J. *Diplomats in Buckskins: A History of Indian Delegations in Washington City.* Bluffton, SC: Rivolo Books, 1995.

Vogel, Virgil J. *This Country Was Ours: A Documentary History of the American Indian.* New York: Harper & Row, 1972.

Waldman, Carl. *Atlas of the North American Indian.* New York: Facts on File, 1985.

Washburn, Wilcomb. *Red Man's Land/White Man's Law: The Past and Present Status of the American Indian.* Norman: University of Oklahoma Press, 1994 ed.

Weber, David J. *The Spanish Frontier in North America.* New Haven: Yale University Press, 1992.

West, Elliott. *The Way to the West: Essays on the Central Plains.* Albuquerque: University of New Mexico Press, 1995.

White, Richard. *It's Your Misfortune and None of My Own: A New History of the American West.* Norman: University of Oklahoma Press, 1985.

———. *The Middle Ground: Indians, Empires, and Republics in the Great Lakes Region, 1650–1815.* Cambridge, England: Cambridge University Press, 1991.

———. *The Roots of Dependency: Subsistence, Environment, and Social Change Among the Choctaws, Pawnees, and Navajos.* Lincoln: University of Nebraska Press, 1988 ed.

Wilson, Terry P. *The Underground Reservation: Osage Oil.* Lincoln: University of Nebraska Press, 1985.

Wishart, David. *An Unspeakable Sadness: The Dispossession of the Nebraska Indians.* Lincoln: University of Nebraska Press, 1994.

Wood, Peter H., Gregory A. Waselkov, and M. Thomas Hatley. *"Powhatan's Mantle" Indians in the Colonial Southeast.* Lincoln: University of Nebraska Press, 1989.

Wright, J. Leitch. *The Only Land They Knew: The Tragic Story of American Indians in the Old South.* New York: The Free Press, 1981.

Wright, Ronald. *Stolen Continents: The Americans Through Indian Eyes Since 1492.* Boston: Houghton Mifflin, 1992.

Index

Page numbers in *italics* refer to maps.

Abbott, Frederick, 258
Abenaki, xxi, *xxviii,* 22, 23, 26–28, 41, 359–
    360
acculturation (Anglicization), 174–175, 201–
    203, 217, 244–248, 280–284, 376–
    377
Ackowanothic, 30
Acoma Pueblo, xvi
Adams, John, 46, 52
Adams, John Quincy, 77–78, 83
Adams-Onis Treaty (1819), 98
African Americans, 7, 83, 84, 171, 317
agriculture, 36, 51, 56, 66, 68, 73, 115, 128,
    163, 222, 270, 293, 376–377
  of Apache, 174–175, 177, 209–210
  in California, 136, 137
  in colonial period, xix, 2, 6, 8, 9, 13, 14,
    16, 19–20, 21, 25
  government emphasis on, 169–170, 174–
    175, 205, 227, 256–258, 260
  in Indian Territory, 103, 104, 106, 110,
    120, 123, 124, 126, 152, 153
  of Navajo, 175, 176, 180
  on Rock Island, 59, 61, 62
  of Seminole, 83, 85
Alabama, xxiii, 49, 55, 87, 117, 213
  Creek in, 53, 54, 75–78, 80, 81, 82, 92,
    97
Alaska, xvii, xviii, 130
Albany, N.Y., 20–21
Alcatraz Island, occupation of, 317, 332–
    333, 344
alcohol, 13, 17, 29, 30, 61, 95, 250, 251
  in Indian Territory, 107, 111, 116, 126
  trade in, 24, 36–37, 46, 126, 212, 263–
    264
  treaties and, 46, 59
alcoholism, 264, 271, 292, 341, 367
Alford, Big Jim, 228
Alford, Thomas Wildcat, 153–154, 226, 228,
    233, 241

Algonquian, 13, 23, 26, 30, 56
  Iroquois and, 27, 37, 44
  land use alternative of, 33, 35
Allegany reservation, 299, 323, 350–351
Allegheny River, 31, 299, 350
allotment, 225–240, 242, 256, 271, 272, 284,
    287–288, 292, 302, 309, 354–355,
    376
  Dawes Act and, 215, 216–221, 231, 249,
    252, 254
  exploitation and, 232–236, 249–254
  grafters and, 230–232, 250, 251, 288
  resistance to, 228–229, 230, 238–239
allotment agents, 226, 228
Amathla, Eneah, 83
American Fur Company, 130
American Indian Chicago Conference (1961),
    319
American Indian Movement (AIM), 327, 333–
    337, 344
American Indian Policy Review
    Commission, 321, 334
American Indian Religious Freedom Act
    (1978), 323
American Indians, use of term, viii
American Revolution (1775–1783), 37–41,
    43, 45, 49, 57, 357
Americans, use of term, ix
Americans for Indian Opportunity, 327
Amherst, Jeffrey, 24
Anadarko, *88*
Anderson, Crawford, 239
Anderson, Terry L., 275*n*
Anglo-Americans (Anglos), use of term, ix
animals:
  diseases of, 130–131
  hunting of, *see* hunting
  Indian removal and, 92, 93–94
  livestock, *see* livestock
  population of, xx, 18–19
annuities, 46, 47, 48, 84, 90, 115, 117, 121,
    132, 187, 228
  of Creek, 54, 84, 109

annuities (*continued*)
  of Osage, 66–67, 157
  problems with, 66–68, 109, 124, 125–126, 168
  of Sioux, 168, 188, 196
annuity chiefs, 47
Apache, ix, xviii, xxiii, 128, 131–132, 154, 170, 248, 359
  Araviapa, 209
  Chiricahua, 131, 173, 177, 182, 209–213
  Coyoteros, 209
  Indian Reorganization Act and, 277, 278
  Jicarilla, *113*, 372
  Kiowa, *113*, 240
  Lipan, *88, 112*
  Mescalero, xvi, 173–175, 177–180, 213, 227, 247, 278, 312, 363–364
  Mimbres, 177, 182
  Pinal, 209
  reservations of, 174–175, 177–180, 182, 209–211, 227, 266, 277, 312–313, 342, 345
  resistance of, 173, 182, 208–213, 248
  Tonto, 209–210
  western, *88, 112*
Apalachee, *xxviii*, 25
Appalachians, 6, 25, 30, 31, 49, 52
  Proclamation of 1763 and, 32, 35
Arapaho, *88, 112*, 144, 145, 157, 183–188, 190, 192, 196, 240, 245, 259, 268, 314
  Baker ring and, 233–234
Area Redevelopment Act (1961), 314
Arikara, 129, 301
Arizona, xvi–xvii, 98, 114, 131, 255, 359, 368, 372
  Navajo-Hopi dispute in, 355–356
Arizona Territory, 172, 175
  reservations in, 178, 208–212, *214*
Arkansas (Arkansas Territory), xv–xvi, 52, 55, 56, 99, 106, 110, *214*
  Cherokee removal to, 50, 53, 68, 69
  Indian removal in, 90–91, 97, 105–106
Arkansas *Gazette,* 97
Arkansas River, 56, 102, 104, 109, 183, 187, 188
Army, U.S., xvi, 64, 65, 77, 103, 121, 133, 154, 173–176, 178, 183–186, 189, 190–191, 207–208
  Chivington massacre and, 183–184
  Creek and, 78–79
  in Great Sioux War, 194–195
  Seminoles and, 83, 85–87
  at Wounded Knee, 223–224
Army Corps of Engineers, U.S., 299–305, 316–317, 322
Army Department, U.S., 91
Arthur, Chester, 355–356
Asbury, Calvin, 263
assimilation, 217, 227, 232, 271–272, 288
  relocation and, 293–298
Assiniboine, *112*, 215, 237
Assunwha, 118

Atakapa, *112*
Austin, Stephen F., 99–100
automobiles, land traded for, 250

Babbitt, Bruce, 364, 369
Bad Heart Bull, Wesley, 336
Baker, Ed, 233–234
Ballew, Bennett, 50
Banks, Dennis, 327, 336, 337
Bannock, *112*, 168, 169
Baptists, 122
Barboncito, 172, 175–176, 180–181
Barnes, A. J., 167
Bascom, George, 173
Bascom affair, 173
"Battle of the Hundred Slain," 186
Beale, Edward F., 136, 137
Beautiful Mountain Uprising (1913), 245–246
Bedagi (Big Thunder), xx
Bedoni, Asdzaa Yazhi, 350, 375
Benedict, Ernest, 286
Bennett, Robert, 320
Bent, George, 184
Bent, William, 145
Benteen, William, 195
Bentley, Martin, 234–235
Betzinez, Jason, 248
Big Bend Dam, 301, 305
Big Foot, 222, 223
Bighorn National Forest, 358
Big Snake, 147
Bi-joshii (Bizoche), 246
Biloxi, *xxviii*
Bissonnette, Pedro, 336
Bixby Tracts, 309–310
Black, Hugo, 298–299
Black Coyote, 223
Black Elk, xxiv
Black Elk Speaks (Neihardt), viii, xxiv
Blackfoot (Crow leader), 204
Blackfoot Indians, *112*, 130, 226, 292–293, 304, 344
Black Hawk (Ma-ka-tai-me-she-kia-kiak), 60–66
Black Hawk War, 64–65, 68
Black Hills, 192–195, 205, 208, 242, 268, 301, 308, 333
Black Hills Alliance, 373–374
Black Kettle, 183–184, 186, 188
Black Spotted Horse, Joseph, 196
Bloody Fellow, 51
Blue Lake, 268, 269, 308, 321, 322–323
boarding schools, 202, 213, 248, 292
Board of Indian Commissioners, U.S., 158, 159, 208–209, 232, 253, 258
Boldt, George H., 331, 359
Bonnin, Gertrude, 202
Boquet, Henry, 31
Bosque Redondo, 174–181, 201, 208
Boudinot, Elias, 69–72, 106–107
Boulder Dam, 275

Bourke, John Gregory, 193–194
Bowen, Dennis, Sr., 362
Bozeman Trail, 184–186, 188
Bradford, William, 8, 11
Brazos Reservation, 124
Brightman, Lehman, 326, 338
Brophy, William A., 281–282
Brown, Dee, 318
Bruce, Louis, 320, 321, 334, 345
Bucktooth, Karen, 362
buffalo, 36, 130–131, 183, 208
    hunting of, xx, 56, 130, 131, 162, 189–
        190, 194
Buffalo Good, 191
Bull Head, 223
Bureau of Indian Affairs, U.S. (BIA; Office
        of Indian Affairs; Indian Office;
        Indian Bureau), 62, 155, 157, 160,
        220, 225–226, 232, 242, 245–246,
        249–254, 264–267, 272–283, 287–
        295, 309, 311, 312, 314, 317, 343,
        344, 345, 353, 355, 367
    activism and, 319, 320, 321, 327, 333–
        334, 336, 342, 347
    Bosque Redondo and, 174, 177, 178
    Collier and, 272–281, 283
    dam projects and, 301–307
    Depression and, 270, 271
    1884 regulations of, 201–202
    Indian Territory and, 103, 149, 153–154,
        216
    leasing and, 259, 261, 262
    Myer and, 283–285, 291, 294, 303, 313
    Sells and, 249–251
    water rights and, 237, 238
Bureau of Land Management, U.S., 355
Bureau of Reclamation, U.S., 300
burial sites, burials, xxi–xxii, 66, 96, 176,
        197, 223, 247, 353, 355
    dam projects and, 299, 300
Burke, Charles Henry, 253, 254
Burke Act (1906), 232, 236
Burnette, Robert, 334
burning, 6
    in resource management, xix, 8, 19, 47,
        134
Bursum Bill, 268
Bury My Heart at Wounded Knee (Brown),
        318
Bush, George, 352, 353
business councils, 241–242, 252

Caddo Nation, 56, 57, 67–68, *88, 112,* 124,
        125, 188
Cadette, 180
Calhoun, John C., 58
California, xxi, 25, 52, 98, 114, 133–138,
        206, 318*n,* 357–358, 374
    gold in, 114, 133, 134, 137–138
    Indian activism in, 327, 332–333
    reservations in, 133–138, 164, 170, *214,*
        253, 265, 366, 368–369

    termination policy in, 287, 288
    tribelets in, 128, 129, 133
California Act for the Government and
        Protection of the Indians (1850), 135
Calusa, *xxviii,* 25
Campbell, Ben Nighthorse, 366
Camp Grant, Ariz., 209
Camp Moultrie, Treaty of (1823), 83, 84
Campo, 368–369
Canada, xviii, xxi, 130, 357, 379
    colonial period in, 2, 18, 21, 26, 32, 40,
        49
    Indian migration to, 21, 41, 196, 199, 356
Canadian River, 101–102
Canby, Vincent, 206
Cannesatego, 28
Cantonment agency, 245
Canyon de Chelly, 176, 191
Captain Jack (Kintpuash), 206
Captain Jim, 168
Carleton, James, 173–177, 179, 181
Carlisle Indian School, 202, 213, 248
Carolina colony, 12, 13, 23, 24, 25, 26, 31,
        38
Carson, Kit, 173–176, 191
casinos, 357, 363–366
Catawba, xv, *xxviii,* 21–24, 28, 29, 40, 42,
        105, 116–117, 288
Catlin, George, 85, 130
Cattaraugus reservation, 362
cattle:
    of Indians, 51, 53, 66, 73, 94, 151, 169–
        170, 202, 204, 209, 221, 224, 227–
        228, 266–267, 278, 311, 312–313
    leasing and, 259–261
    of non-indians, 7, 18, 19, 28, 166–167,
        216, 225, 242, 259–260
Cayuga, 12–13, 39–40, *88,* 350
Cayuse, *112,* 128, 138–141
Chapman, Oscar, 284, 303
Cheraw, 21
Cherokee, xv, xvi, xxiv, *xxviii,* 49–54, 59,
        66, *88,* 94–103, 117, 325, 355, 378
    activism of, 316, 321, 323, 328
    adaptations of, 50, 53, 68–69, 106, 123,
        126–127, 217
    allotment and, 226, 228, 229, 230, 238,
        239–240, 254
    American Revolution and, 38, 39, 40
    Civil War and, 148–151
    in colonial period, 22, 37, 38
    Creek compared with, 77, 78, 79
    in final struggle to stay in East, 68–75, 87
    in Indian Territory, 53, 71, 73, 102–103,
        105–107, 110, 111, 123, 126–127,
        148–151, 217, 225, 229, 230
    Iroquois ceding of land of, 37
    mixed-blood, 50, 69–70, 107
    raids of, 56–57
    removal of, 75, *88,* 90, 91, 92, 94–98, 100–
        101, 105–106
    in Texas, 99–101, 106, 268, 308

Cherokee (*continued*)
  western, 53, 71, 73, 105–107
  written language of, vii, 68
Cherokee Advocate, 127
Cherokee Nation Industries, 371
Cherokee Nation Tribal Council, 371
Cherokee Nation v. *Georgia,* 70
Cherokee Phoenix, 70–71
Cherokee Strip, 151, 225
Chewie, John, 328
Cheyenne, *88,* 129, 130, 145, 157, 201, 245, 250, 259
  Baker ring and, 233–234
  northern, *112,* 145, 192, 194–196, 206–208, 278, 309–310, 318*n,* 325, 338, 346
  southern, *112,* 190, 183–188, 190
Cheyenne Autumn (Sandoz), 318*n*
Cheyenne River reservation, 217–218, 222, 223, 241–242, 244, 250, 251–252, 276, 310, 311, 340
  dam project and, 301, 303–307, 310
Chickasaw, xv, *xxviii,* 22, 39, 41, 48, 54, 68, 87, *88*
  allotment and, 229, 230
  in Indian Territory, 101, 102, 105, 108, 110, 123, 124, 126–127, 149–151, 154, 229, 230
  removal of, 90, 91, 92, 94, 95
Chinook, *112,* 128
Chippewa (Ojibway), *xxviii,* 45–46, 48, 64, 162, 321, 328, 338, 360, 374
  allotment and, 227
  in Indian Territory, 103–104, 119, 122
  Turtle Mountain, 227, 242, 275, 285
Chivington, John M. 183–184
Chivington massacre, 183–184
Choctaw, *xxviii,* 37, 48, 54, 68, 87, *88,* 117, 370–371
  allotment and, 228–229, 230
  in Indian Territory, 101, 104, 105, 108–110, 117, 123, 124, 126–127, 149–151, 229, 230
  raids of, 56–57
  removal of, 87, 90, 91, 93–94, 97, 98
cholera, 7, 66, 95, 129
Christianity, 3, 15–17, 26, 41–42, 47, 116, 152–153, 214, 247, 377
  see also missionaries
Chumash, *112*
Circling Eagle, 253
Citizens Against Ruining Our Environment (CARE), 373
citizenship, 248–249, 250, 253
Civilian Conservation Corps, 278
Civil War, U.S., 40, 91, 145, 147–151, 172, 173–174
Clapsop, 128
Clark, George Rogers, 39, 40
Clark, William, 65
Clear Fork Reservation, 124
Clinton, Bill, 352–353

Clum, John, 210, 211
Coacoochee (Wild Cat), 118–119, 124
coal, 324, 368, 371
Coast Salish, *112*
Cochise, 131, 173, 182, 209, 210
Coeur d'Alene, *112,* 142, 252–253
Coeur d'Alene War (Spokane War) (1858), 142
Cohen, Felix, 281
Collier, John, 253, 268, 272–281, 283, 367, 377
colonial period, 1–32
  accommodation in, 5, 15–16
  adoption of captives and refugees in, 22–23
  disease and epidemics in, 2, 4, 7–10, 13, 22–25
  map of tribes in, *xxviii*
  reservations in, 14–15, 17, 20, 21, 28, 29, 132
  trade in, 2–6, 9, 12–13, 18–19, 22, 23, 24, 27, 30, 31–32
  war in, 6–7, 10–11, 17, 20, 21, 23, 25, 26, 29–30, 38
colonists, use of term, ix
Colorado, 52, 98, 128, 142–143, 254–255
  reservations in, 170, *214,* 308
Colorado Territory, 172, 183–184
Colquille tribe, 369
Columbia Plateau, 128, 138, 140
Columbia River, xx, 128, 265, 300, 329, 330, 373
Colville Confederated Tribes, 284
Colville reservation, 201, 224, 286, 288
Colyer, Vincent, 208–209
Comanche, xvi, 66, *88,* 99–100, *112,* 129, 157, 183, 184, 187, 188, 190–191, 240, 247, 327
  Bosque Redondo attacked by, 178
  in Indian Territory, 124, 125, 150, 154
Community Action Agencies, 320
Community Action Program (CAP), 319–320, 341
competency, competency commissions, 232, 240, 249, 250, 251, 253
Comprehensive Employment and Training Act (CETA), 344
Confederacy, Confederates, 149–151, 173
Congress, U.S., xxiv, 46, 121, 127, 158, 181, 203, 224, 234, 236, 242, 264, 267, 271, 308, 309, 320–321, 322, 343, 351
  allotment and, 220–221, 230, 239, 254
  Creek and, 77, 79, 109
  dam projects and, 299–300, 302, 305, 307
  1871 directive of, 155–156, 164–165, 193
  Indian removal and, 63–64
  Indian Reorganization Act and, 273, 280
  leasing and, 262–263
  Lone Wolf v. *Hitchcock* and, 240
  Ponca victory and, 161–162
  relocation and, 294

termination policy and, 280, 281, 284–289, 297
see also House of Representatives, U.S.; Senate, U.S.
Connecticut, 42, 357
  colonial period in, 14, 15, 20, 34
conservation, xx–xxi, 116, 265–266, 329
Coos, 112
Cornplanter, 6, 37, 42, 46
Cornplanter reservation, 299, 300
Cornstalk, 35
Corn Tassel, 50–51
Coronado, Francisco Vasquez, 3
Council of Energy Resources Tribes, 346, 372
Court of Appeals, U.S., 299
Court of Claims, U.S., 268, 346, 357
Court of Indian Offenses, Navajo, 311
cows, see cattle
Crabb, Barbara, 359
Crawford, Thomas Hartley, 103
Crazy Horse, 173, 186, 194–196, 205–206
Cree, 13
Creek, xv, xxviii, 39, 48, 49, 59, 66, 75–84, 88, 355
  allotment and, 229, 230, 238–239
  in colonial period, 13, 22, 24, 26, 29, 31
  Coushatta, 54, 287
  in Georgia, 29, 31, 53–55, 75–80, 82, 355
  in Indian Territory, 101–105, 107–111, 123–127, 149–152, 193, 225, 229, 230
  removal of, 82, 90–93, 95–98
  Seminoles and, 82–84
  Shawnee merger with, 109
Creek War (1813–1814), 54, 75
Creek War (1836), 82, 91
Crook, George, 161, 169, 193, 195, 209, 211–212, 221–222
Crow, xix, xxii–xxiii, 112, 184–185, 199, 325, 344, 372
  leasing and, 261, 262, 263
  reservation of, 185, 201, 261, 262, 263, 275
Crow Creek reservation, 301, 302, 304–306
Crow Dog, 203
Crow Dog, Mary, 313
Crowell, John, 77
Crow Feather, James, 241
Cupeno, 112
"Curly" (Absaroka Crow), xxii–xxiii
Curtis Act (1898), 230
Cusabo, xxviii
Custer, George Armstrong, 192, 193, 195
Custer Died for Your Sins (Deloria), 318
Cut Nose, 144

Dakota Territory, 172, 183, 223
dams, 275, 298–307, 310, 323, 325
Davis, W. M., 74
Dawes, Henry, 217, 219, 230, 248

Dawes Allotment Act (1887), 215, 216–221, 231, 249, 252, 254
Dawes Commission, 230
Debo, Angie, vii, 284
"Declaration of Indian Purpose," 319
"Declaration of Policy" (Sells), 251
Deep Fork reservation, 229
Deer, Ada, 353
deer, xix, 2, 18, 28, 36, 193
Defense Department, U.S., 333, 343
De La Garza, Robert, 366–367
Delaware Indians, xx, xxviii, 30, 34, 36, 40, 44–47, 63, 88, 159, 355
  in Indian Territory, 111, 119, 122, 150
  raids of, 56–57
  in Texas, 99, 101
Delgadito, 175–176
Deloria, Vine, Jr., 279, 318, 319, 321, 327, 341, 343, 373
Denver, Colo., 183, 280, 292
Department of Game v. Puyallup Tribe, 331
Detroit, Mich., 39, 40
Devil's Tower, 358
discrimination, 110, 154, 171, 205, 264, 295, 313, 328, 379
District Court, U.S., 304, 310–311
Douglas, Henry, 165
Douglas, William O., 298
Dragging Canoe, 50
"Dreamer" religious movement, 198
Drinks Water, xxv
drought, xviii, 84, 87, 96, 130, 137, 177, 257, 266, 267
DuBray, Alfred, 274, 275, 295
Ducheneaux, Frank, 301, 303, 306
Dull Knife, 195, 196, 207–208
Duncan, DeWitt Clinton, 239–240
Dundy, Elmer, 161
Dunmore, Lord, 38
Dunn, J. P., 136
Durham, Jimmie, xxiv
Dutch, 12, 14
Duwamish, 140

earth, as mother, xix–xx, xxiii, xxiv
Eastman, Charles, 216
Eaton, John, 79, 80
Economic Development Administration (EDA), 320, 342, 344
Economic Opportunity Act (1964), 319
Edmunds, Newton, 220–221
education and training, 28, 54, 110, 116, 120, 123, 153, 217, 238, 245, 293–294, 328, 341
  boarding schools and, 202, 213, 248, 292
Eisenhower, Dwight D., 284, 289, 293, 318
Eliot, John, 15
Elliot, W. R., 261
"Eloheh," xxiv
Emancipation Proclamation (1863), 135
Embry, John, 235, 236
Emmons, Glen, 291, 294, 309, 313–314

employment, 264, 265, 279, 280, 293, 312–
        314, 342–347, 366, 368–372
    relocation and, 294, 295
    see also agriculture; livestock;
        unemployment
encomienda system, 31
England, see Great Britain
environmental change, environment, 267,
        275, 314, 317–318, 324–325, 368–
        369, 370, 372–374
    in colonial period, 18–20
Environmental Protection Agency (EPA),
        353, 374
epidemics and disease, 7–10, 24–25, 66, 116,
        150, 161, 176, 222, 292, 341, 367–
        368
    of animals, 130–131
    Indian removal and, 95–96, 98
    in West, 129–131, 138
Episcopal Church, 355
Eshtonoquot, Chief, 103–104
establecimientos de paz (peace
        establishments), 132
Everett, Edward, 63–64

Fall, Albert, 263
Fallen Timbers, Battle of (1794), 45, 46, 49,
        52
FBI (Federal Bureau of Investigation), 336,
        337
Federal Acknowledgement Project, 326
fee-patent ownership, 232–236, 240, 242,
        248–254, 258, 271
Fetterman, William J., 186
Fetterman Massacre, 186
"First Nation," use of term, ix
First Seminole War (1817–1818), 83
fishing, xix, xx, 42, 164, 167–168, 264–265,
        279, 286, 300, 360
    activism and, 328–332, 359
    in colonial period, 2, 8, 14, 20
Five County Cherokee Movement, 316, 328
Five Year Programs, 257
Flathead, 112, 113, 128, 141, 251, 285, 377
Florida, xxiii, 39, 53, 54–55
    Apache in, 212–213
    in colonial period, 3, 13, 15, 25, 26, 32,
        34
    Seminole in, 55, 82–87, 118, 339, 363,
        375
Fools Crow, 264
Foreman, Clarence, 274
Fort Apache reservation, xvi, 209, 210
Fort Belknap reservation, 237–238
Fort Berthold reservation, 300–301, 362
Fort Bowie, Ariz., 212
Fort Defiance, 175, 176
Fort Gibson, 105, 108, 110, 150, 154
Fort Harmar, 44
Fort Keogh, Mont., 208
Fort Laramie Council (1868), 187, 188–189
Fort Laramie Treaty (1868), 189, 193, 196

Fort Leavenworth, 200
Fort Lewis, Wash., 260
Fort Lyon, 183
Fort Marion, Fla., 212–213
Fort Miami, 45, 49
Fort Omaha, 161
Fort Osage, 57, 66
Fort Peck reservation, 253, 275
Fort Phil Kearny, 186
Fort Pitt, 31
Fort Randall Dam, 301, 305
Fort Rice, 188
Fort Robinson, Neb., 205–206, 207–208
forts:
    Bozeman Trail, 186, 188
    English, 26–27, 30, 32, 35, 45, 49
    French, 24
    in Indian Territory, 103, 105, 108, 110
Fort Sill, 213
Fort Stanwix, Treaty of (1768), 37, 45
Fort Sumner, xvi, xvii, 174
Fort Wayne, Treaty of (1809), 46
"Four Corners" area, 255
Fox, xxviii, 23, 46, 48, 59, 63, 88, 229
Fredonian Rebellion (1826), 100
Frémont, John, 134
French, France:
    colonialism of, 2–3, 5, 8, 12, 18, 21, 22,
        24, 26–32, 36, 98
    trade of, 2–3, 12, 24, 27, 30, 31, 55, 56,
        98
French and Indian wars, 29–30, 32, 38
Fresno farm reservation, 137
fryer, E. R., 283
fur trade, 2, 3, 12, 13, 19, 56, 129

Gaiashkibos, 366
Gall, 188
Gamble, Robert, 251, 252
Gamble bill, 251–252
gambling, 170, 357, 363–366
Garrison Dam, 301
gas, natural, 324, 350, 371, 372
Gates, John, 304
Gatewood, Charles B., 212
gathering, xix, xxii, 9, 14, 83, 115, 136, 137,
        162, 164, 168, 174, 175, 245, 279,
        286, 311–312
General Land Office, 225–226
George, Georgia C., 361
Georgia, 39, 49, 52–55, 83
    Cherokee in, 49, 68–75, 87, 355
    colonial period in, 3, 29, 31, 34, 38
    Creek in, 29, 31, 53–55, 75–80, 82, 355
    militia of, 77, 82, 83
Geronimo, xxiii, 173, 210–213, 216, 248
Ghost Dance religion, 214, 216, 220, 222–
        224
Gila River, 128, 209
Gila River reservation, 261
Goat Island, 165
goats, 51, 181, 275, 276

gold, 70, 72, 114, 131, 133, 134, 183, 184, 192, 193
Goodbird, Titus, 311
grafters, 230–232, 250, 251, 288
Grant, Ulysses S., 158, 162, 189, 190, 193, 203
Grattan, John L., 145
grazing, 36, 216, 225, 227–228, 242, 259–260, 283
Great Basin, 128, 142, 143, 148, 164, 166
Great Britain, 8, 55, 56
  American Revolution and, 3–41, 43, 45, 49, 57
  colonialism of, 1–22, 24, 26–32, 111
  Fort Stanwix Treaty and, 37, 45
  Proclamation of 1763 and, 32, 34, 35
  in War of 1812, 49, 57–58
Great Depression, 269, 270–271, 279
Great Lakes, 2, 5, 31, 37, 43, 45, 48, 63, 275
  Algonquians of, 26, 30, 37
Great Plains, xviii, xx, xxi, 31, 143–145 *see also* Plains Indians
Great Plow-up, 260
Great Sioux Reservation, 188, 189, 192–196, 203, 208, 220, 240
Great Sioux War, 194–196, 206, 207
Great Spirit, xix, xxii, 47, 62, 85, 197–198, 298
Green Corn Ceremony, 152, 339
Green River, 329, 330
Greenville, Ohio, 45, 48
Greenville, Treaty of (1794), 45–46, 48
Gros Ventre, *112*, 237
Guadalupe Hidalgo, Treaty of (1848), 114, 131
guardians, for Indian minors, 233, 236, 264

Hadjo, Hallec, 86
Hainal, *88*
Hale, Albert, 363
Harjo, Chitto Crazy Snake, 238–239
Harmer, Josiah, 44
Harris, LaDonna, 327, 346
Harrison, Benjamin, 225, 231
Harrison, William Henry, 46, 47, 48
Harrod, James, 35–36
Hatot'cli-yazzie (Little Singer), 246
Havasupai, 128
Hayes, Rutherford B., 161
healing, xix–xx, xxii, 152, 244, 245, 247, 375
Heap, Alfrich, 250, 251
Hearst, George, 205
Heron, George D., 299
Herrero, 178
Hickory Grove, Okla., 238
Hidatsa, *112*, 301
High Pine, Matthew, 339
Hill, John T., 229, 235
History of Indians of the United States, A (Debo), vii

Hitchcock, Ethan Allen, 86–87
Hoag, Enoch, 159, 218
hogs, 19, 21, 25, 53, 66, 73, 169
Holy Rock, Johnson, 270
Homestake Mining Company, 205
Hopi, xviii, *112*, 128, 176, 238, 294, 324, 339, 340
  allotment and, 228, 229
  Navajo dispute with, 355–356
  reservation of, xvii, 356
horses, 7, 19, 28, 36, 51, 53, 67, 191, 267, 371
  Indian removal and, 92, 93–94
  Plains Indians and, 55, 129, 144
Hotevilla, 238
House Made of Dawn (Momaday), 318
House of Representatives, U.S., 72, 296
  Committee on Indian Affairs of, 70, 218–219, 254, 299
  Committee on Interior and Insular Affairs of, 302
  Concurrent Resolution 108 of, 284, 287
housing, 16, 244, 245, 253, 255, 278, 312, 340, 342, 366
Houston, Sam, 100–101
Howard, Oliver, 197–198, 199, 209
Howard, O. O., xxiii
Hoxie, Frederick, 252
Hudson's Bay Company, 129
hunting, xviii, 2, 8, 9, 14, 28, 30, 36, 50, 66, 67, 115, 152, 162, 168, 245, 279, 286, 328, 359, 360
  of Apache, 174, 175
  buffalo, xx, 56, 130, 131, 162, 189–190, 194
  of Omaha, 113, 114
  trade and, 12, 13, 18–19, 24, 44
Hupa (Natinook-wa), xxi, *112*
Huron, 23, 44, 45–46
Hurtado, Albert, 135
hydroelectric power, 298, 300, 304

Ickes, Harold, 283
Idaho, 114, 128, 172, *214*, 371
  Bannocks of, 168, 169
identity, Indian, xvi, 4, 15, 42, 116, 244–249, 271–278, 374–375
  activism and, 318–319, 325–326, 327, 337–340
  occupation and, 169–170
  place-based, xxii, xxiv, 162–163, 271, 283, 284, 286, 298, 353
  political, 11, 14, 16, 23, 26, 27, 37, 53, 68–75, 106, 272–275, 327, 337, 377
Illinois, 37, 40, 123
Illinois Indians, *xxviii*, 30
Illinois Territory, 48, 59–62, 64, 65
immigrant, use of term, x
income, 279, 280, 312, 366, 372
Indiana, 37, 40, 123
Indian Action Teams (IATs), 345

Indian agents, 22, 42, 61, 62, 68, 155, 160, 166–171, 203, 206–208, 222
of Apache, 174, 178, 210, 211
in California, 134, 136, 137
of Catawba, 28, 42, 117
civilizing function of, 201–202, 245
Creek and, 55, 75, 77
in Grant administration, 158, 159, 190
Paiute and, 166, 167, 168, 245
sympathetic, 42, 66–67, 103, 117
Indian Appropriation Act (1907), 236
Indiana Territory, 46, 48, 64, 65
Indian Civil Rights Act (1968), 321, 326
Indian Claims Commission (ICC), 282, 287, 301, 307–308, 312, 317, 327, 345–346
Indian country, mid-nineteenth century, four types of, 115
Indian Department, U.S., 40
Indian Emergency Conservation Work Program, 278
Indian Gaming Regulation Act (1988), 363
Indian Health Service, 306, 347
Indian Homestead Act (1876), 219, 255
Indian Island, 135
Indian Oil Leasing Bill (1927), 263
Indian removal, 63–65, 88–98, 115–122, 146–147, 156–163, 220
disease and epidemics during, 95–96, 98
in Nebraska, 120–122, 146–147, 156–158
in Texas, 100–101, 125, 127
in West, 115, 172–182
Indian Removal Bill (1830), 63–64, 68, 70, 84, 90
Indian Reorganization Act (IRA; Wheeler-Howard Act) (1934), 272–281, 335
Indian Rights Association, 241, 261
Indian rings, 122, 136
Indian Self-Determination and Education Assistance Act (1974), 321, 346, 347
Indians of All Tribes, 332–333
Indian Springs, Treaty of (1825), 77, 78
Indian Territory, xvi, 90, 101–111, 119–127, 146–156, 181, 193, 220
allotment and, 229–230
Cherokee in, 53, 71, 73, 102–103, 105–107, 110, 111, 123, 126–127, 148–151, 217, 225, 229, 230
Cheyenne in, 206–207
Civil War in, 148–151
Creek in, 101–105, 107–111, 123–127, 149–152, 193, 225, 229, 230
discrimination in, 110, 154, 205
location and size of, 88, 98, 214, 224–225
Modoc banished to, 206
Nez Perce in, 200
Osage in, 160
Pawnee in, 160
Ponca in, 160–161, 163
Proclamation of 1763 and, 32, 34, 35, 37
Sac in, 119, 120, 121, 162, 229

Seminoles in, 102, 103, 104, 108, 111, 118–119, 124, 149–152, 225, 229, 230
supply problems in, 103–105
"unassigned" lands in, 224–225
influenza, 7, 66, 222, 292, 341
Institute for Government Research, 254
Interior Department, U.S., 160, 161, 171, 203, 268, 303, 322, 324, 351–352, 357
leasing and, 259–260, 262–263
termination policy and, 284, 287
International Indian Treaty Council, 327
Interstate 40 (I-40), xv–xvii
Intertribal Sinkyone Wilderness Project, 357–358, 374
invaders, use of term, ix, xviii
Iowa (Iowa Territory), 52, 60, 65, 101, 119, 214
hunting grounds in, 113, 114
reservations in, 214, 317, 322
Iowa Indians, 88, 112, 119, 120, 288
Iroquois Confederacy, viii, xxviii, 22, 28, 41, 88, 115
activism of, 318–319
in American Revolution, 39, 40
group displaced by, 12–13, 23
Kahawake, 10
lands ceded by, 27, 29, 37, 38, 44
refugees and captives adopted by, 23
warfare of, 17, 21, 23, 25
see also Cayuga; Mohawk; Oneida; Onondaga; Seneca; Tuscarora
irrigation, 257–258, 278, 298, 300
Iverson, Peter, 33, 266, 312

Jackson, Andrew, 54, 58, 67, 79, 83, 84
Cherokee and, 70, 72, 74
Indian removal and, 63, 84, 90–91, 97
Jackson, Helen Hunt, 161, 318n
James I, king of England, 5
James River, 2, 6
Jamestown, Va., 2, 4–7, 11, 18
Janklow, Bill, 354
Jefferson, Thomas, 52–53, 57
Jerome, David, 225
Jerome Commission, 225, 229
Jesuits, 6, 26
Jesup, Thomas, 86
Johnson, Gary, 363
Johnson, Lyndon B., 319–320, 322, 335, 342–343, 345, 377
Johnson-O'Malley Act (1934), 278
Jones, William, 236
Joseph, Chief (father), xxi–xxii, 113, 141, 197, 200, 298
Joseph, Chief (son), xxi–xxii, 173, 196–201, 209
Josephy, Alvin, 316, 318
Jourdain, Roger, 321
Justice Department, U.S., 353

Kansa, 55, 56, *88, 112*
Kansas, 52, 55, 63, 67, 147, 156–160, 163
  allotment in, 227, 228
  Civil War and, 149, 150, 151
  as Indian Territory, 65, 101, 103–104,
    107, 119–122
  reservations in, *214,* 242, 279
  termination policy in, 288
Kansas-Nebraska Act (1854), 122
Karankawa, *112*
Karok, 128
Kaskaskia, 119
Kaske, Charlot, 36
Keeble, Jonas, 295
Kemble, Edward C., 146
Kenekuk, xxii, 120, 163
Kennedy administration, 296, 314, 377
Kentucky, 35–36, 38, 40, 42–43
  Indian removal in, 90, 96–97
Keokuk, 60, 61, 64, 66, 162
Keshena, Gordon, 285
Ketowahs (Nighthawks), 150, 230
Kichai, *88*
Kickapoo, xxii, *xxviii, 64, 88,* 150, 159, 288,
  347
  allotment and, 229–230, 234–236
  Bentley's exploitation of, 234–236
  Prairie, 107
  removal of, 65, 120
  reservation of, 119–122, 163, 171, 345,
    346, 366–367
  in texas, 101, 107
  treaties and, 45–46, 48, 63
  Vermillion, 107, 120–121, 122
Kickapoo Allotment Act, 230
Kicking Bear, 222
Kicking Bird, xxiv
kidnappings, 1, 6, 8, 137, 143
King Philip's War, 17, 20
Kings River reservation, 134
Kintpuash (Captain Jack), 206
Kinzua Dam, 299, 323, 350
Kiowa, xxiii, xxiv, 66, *88, 112,* 129, 154,
  183, 184, 187–190, 240, 247
  Bosque Redondo attacked by, 178
Kitch, James, 266
Klamaths:
  reservation of, 137, 206, 275, 290–291
  termination policy and, 285, 287, 289, 290–
    291, 296, 297
Kutenai, 141
Kyle, Richard, 360

Labadie, Lorenzo, 174, 178, 210
LaDuke, Winona, 375
LaFarge, Oliver, 318*n*
Lamar, Mirabeau, 101
Lame Deer, John, 247
Lamont, Buddy, 337
land, Indian vs. European view of, xxii–xxiii,
  9, 13–15, 17

Lane, Franklin K., 246, 248, 249–250, 255,
  263
language, xx, 4, 5–6, 245, 249, 341, 374,
  Cherokee, vii, xxiv, 68, 117
Lapwai reservation, 197, 198, 200, 201
LaRoche, Richard, Jr., 303
LaRose, Louie, 316
Last Man, John, 251–252
Laughing Boy (LaFarge), 318*n*
law, legal system:
  English, 10, 12, 17, 20, 35
  Indian, 10, 16, 154, 155, 203, 228–229
  Indian rights and, xxiii, 3, 4, 9, 12, 14, 15–
    16, 20, 28–29, 35, 70–72, 134, 135,
    155, 161, 247, 302–303
Lawson, Michael, 300
leasing, 236–237, 258–265, 269, 324, 350–
  351, 356, 368
LeBeau, Gib, 307
Leupp, Francis, 232
Lewis, David Rich, 378
Lewis, Meriwether, 57
life expectancy, 292, 341, 367
Lincoln, Abraham, 183
Little Bighorn, attack at (1876), 195
Little Big Man, 194
Little Hill, 119
Little Prince, 78
Little Raven, 186
Little Singer (Hatot'cli-yazzie), 246
Little Turtle, 44, 45, 47
Little Wolf, 195, 207–208
livestock, 44, 51, 117, 143, 144, 169–170,
  205, 275–278, 311
  in colonial period, 2, 7, 14, 17, 18, 19, 20
  in Indian Territory, 104, 105, 110, 123
  of Navajo, 175, 176, 178, 181, 266–267,
    270, 275–276
  theft of, 124, 154, 155, 159
  see also cattle; hogs; horses; sheep
Loco, 182
Lohah, Charles, 346
Lone Man, John, 222
Lone Wolf v. *Hitchcock,* 240
Longest Walk, 337–338
Long Walk, 176, 276
Looking Glass, 141, 199
Louisiana, 52, 56, 67, 96, 98, 214
  colonial period in, 2, 26, 31, 32, *34*
Louisiana Purchase, 52, 98–99
Lower Brule reservation, 301–306, 310
Lower Towns:
  Cherokee, 52
  Creek, 54, 75, 76, 107–108
Lumbees, 325–326

McCarran, Pat, 277, 283, 309
MacDonald, Peter, 363
McDonnell, Janet, 271
McIntosh, Roley, 108
McIntosh, William (White Warrior), 76–77,
  108

MacKenzie, Ranald, 191, 195
McKenzie, Richard, 293
McLaughlin, James, 208, 222, 246, 248, 354
McNickle, D'Arcy, xxiv, 281
Mahican, *xxviii*
Maine, *34,* 346
Ma-ka-tai-me-she-kia-kiak (Black Hawk), 60–66
malaria, 7, 129, 161, 179
Manahoac, *xxviii*
Mandan, *112,* 129, 130, 301
Mangas Coloradas, 182
Manhattan Indians, 12
Manhattan Island, 12, 332
Manifest Destiny, xxiii, 58, 114
Manuelito, 132, 180, 181
Manypenny, George, 195, 219
maps, *xxviii, 34, 88, 112, 214*
Marias des Cygnes River, 162–163
Mariposa War (1850–1851), 138
Marshall, John, 70, 71–72, 156
Martinez, Julia, 378
Maryland, colonial period in, 10, 19, 21, 23, *34*
Mashpee, 159
Massachuset, *xxviii*
Massachusetts, 40, 116, 159
   colonial period in, 8, 15–16, 18, *34*
Massachusetts Bay Company, 9
Masters, John, 85
Mather, Increase, 9
Mattagund, 19
Mattaponi, 115–116
Means, Russell, 336–337, 375
measles, 7, 138, 150, 179, 222
Medicine Horse, 247, 286
Medicine Lodge Council (1867), 187–188
Medicine Lodge Treaty (1867), 188, 190
Medill, William, 115, 133
Meeker, Nathan, 170
Meninick, 329
Menominee, *xxviii,* 23, 48, 65–66, 282, 328, 333, 353, 359
   termination policy and, 285, 287, 289–290, 291, 296–297, 328, 345
Menominee Enterprises, Inc., 290, 297
Meriam, Lewis, 254
Meriam Report, 254
Meriwether, David, 132, 180
mescal, 174, 175, 212
Metacom (King Philip), 17
Metcalf, Lee, 296
Mexican War, 114
Mexico, Gulf of, 31, *34,* 37, 48
Mexico, Mexicans, 4, 9, 133, 173, 211–212, 266
   independence of, 99, 133
   Indian migration to, 68, 107, 124, 126, 159, 211, 230, 234–236, 239
   Kickapoo in, 234–236
   Texas claimed by, 99, 100
   U.S. relations with, 99, 114

Miami, *xxviii,* 30, 44–47, 63, *88,* 229
Miantonomo, 18, 19
Miccosukee, 339, 342
Michigan, 37, 45, 48
Michigan Territory, 64, 65
Mickelson, George, 310–311
Micmac, *xxviii,* 16
Miles, John D., 206–208
Miles, Nelson, 196, 199–200, 212, 223
militancy (activism), Indian, 298, 315–342, 344–347, 353–363
Mills, Sidney, 330–331
mineral lands, 224, 226, 232, 241, 242, 324
   leasing of, 262–264
mining, 70, 72, 143, 170, 172, 205, 358
Minneapolis Naval Air Station, 333
Minnesota, 13, 37, 52, 287, 328, 360
   reservations in, *214,* 374
Minnesota Indian Affairs Council, viii
Minnesota Territory, xviii, 119, 168–169, 184
missionaries, 1, 6, 15–16, 26, 30, 41, 120, 122, 246, 376
   Cherokee and, 52, 71
   in Indian territory, 102, 109–110
   in West, 133, 138, 139, 170, 171, 223
Mississippi, 87, 117, 279
Mississippi River, xv, 2–3, 31, 32, 42, 48, 49, 50, 52, 55, 56–57, 59, 60, 63, 64, 90, 98, 99, 119, *214,* 371
Mississippi Territory, 54
Missouri, 52, 63, 65, 90, 99, 114, 123, *214*
Missouri Indians, *112*
Missouri River, 56, 63, 90, 98, 99, 113, 119, 130, 188, 196, 208, *214,* 248, 316–317, 322
   dam projects on, 300–302, 325
Missouri River Basin Development Program, 300
Mitchell, David, 55, 75, 76, 77
Mitchell, George, 327
Miwok, xix, *112,* 128, 138
Modoc, *88, 112,* 206
Modoc War (1872–1874), 206
Mohawk, 1, 10, 12–13, 27, 39–40, 48, 286
Mohegan, *xxviii,* 11, 42
Mojave, *112,* 128, 324
Mokohoko, 162, 163
Momaday, N. Scott, 318
Monacan Indians, 355
Monmouth, sinking of, 98
Mono, 137–138
Monroe, James, 58, 63, 69, 77
Montana, 52, 128
   reservations in, *214,* 237–238, 300, 325
Montana territory, 172, 184, 188, 192–196, 199
   Cheyenne in, 207, 208
Monteith, John, 198
Montgomery *Advertiser,* 82, 97
Moravians, 30, 52
Morgan, William, 352
Mormons, 142

Moses, 112, 162
Mount Graham telescope controversy, 359
Mount Vernon Barracks, 213
Moves Camp, Ellen, 336
Mower, 240
Muckleshoot, 329
Munsee, 119, 122, 227
Murray, James, 296
Mushulatubbe, 109
Myer, Dillon, 283–285, 291, 294, 303, 309, 313
Myrick, Andrew, 168–169
"Mystic Fort," 10–11

Nacogdoches, 100
Nagaicho, 265
Nanticoke, 21
Napoleon, 142
Narragansett, *xxviii*, 8, 10, 11, 17, 29, 48, 116, 159
Nash, Philleo, 296
Natches, Gilbert, 271
Natchez, *xxviii*
Natinook-wa (Hupa), xxi, *112*
National Association for the Advancement of Colored People, 330
National Congress of American Indians, 280, 363, 366
National Council on Indian Opportunity, 320
National Creek Council, 75–82
National Indian Youth Council, 327, 330
National Tribal Chairmen's Association, 320, 321
nations, use of term, ix
Native American Church, 247, 312, 375
Native American Construction Company, 352, 363
Native American Grave Protection and Repatriation Act (1990), xxi, 353
Native Americans, use of term, viii
Navajo, xvi, xviii, xxi, *112*, 128, 131–132, 173, 175–182, 255, 294, 311, 318*n*, 324, 339, 341, 350, 363, 374
    appropriations swindle and, 177–178
    Beautiful Mountain Uprising of, 245–246
    Bosque Redondo and, 172, 175–181
    Cebolletan, 177
    Hopi dispute with, 355–356
    Indian Reorganization Act and, 275–276
    livestock of, 175, 176, 178, 181, 266–267, 270, 275–276
    oil rights of, 263
    reservation of, xvi–xvii, 263, 266–267, 344, 352, 356, 361, 372, 373
Navajo-Hopi Indian Land Settlement Act (1974), 356
Nebraska, xx, 52, 55, 101, 112, 172, 207–208, 328
    reservations in, 120–122, 146–147, 156–158, 160–161, 169, *214*, 232–233, 250–251, 316
    termination policy in, 287, 297

Neighbors, Robert Simpson, 125
Neihardt, John, viii, xxiv
Neolin, 30, 47
Nevada, 128, 142–143, 172, 324
    reservations in, 163, 165–168, *214*, 216
New Echota, Ga., 68–69, 123
New Echota, Treaty of (1835), 74–75, 100, 107
New England, colonial period in, xix, 8–11, 13–20, 22, 23
New Hampshire, *34*
New Indians, The (Steiner), 338
New Jersey, *34*
New Mexico, xvi–xvii, xxi, 15, 98, 114, 128, 131, 255, 327, 378
    casinos in, 363–364
    Taos Pueblo in, 268–269, 308, 321, 322–323, 327
New Mexico Territory, 131–132, 173–181, 213
    reservations in, 174–181, *214*
New Orleans, La., 2, 31, 32
New York City, 189
New York *Observer*, 72
New York State, 20–21, 39, 115, 350–351, 355, 356–357, 365
    colonial period in, 12, 20–21, 22, 23, 29, *34*
    dam projects in, 298–299, 302, 323, 350
New York State Power Authority, 298–299
Nez Perce, ix, xxi–xxii, *112*, 113, 128, 141, 227, 371
    uprising of, 196–201
Nicholson, Joseph, 42
Nipmuc, 17
Nisqually Indians, *112*, 260, 330
Nisqually River, 330, 331
Nixon, Richard, 320–321, 332, 335, 336, 341, 345, 348
Noche-do-klinne, 211
Nocowee, 95
Nome Lackee reservations, 136
non-Indians, use of term, ix
"nonrecognized" tribes, 325–326, 355
Nopkehe, Chief, 28, 105
North Carolina, xv, 25, *34*, 39, 40, 325–326
    Cherokee in, 49, 72, 87, 117, 323
    see also Carolina colony
North Dakota, 52, 130, 188, 227
    reservations in, *214*, 227, 242, 300–301
Northwest Ordinance (1787), 43
Norton, Jack, 135
Nottoway, 21
Now That the Buffalo's Gone (Josephy), 316
Nye, James, 166, 167, 169–170

Oahe Dam, 301, 304–305, 306, 310
Occaneechee, 20
Ockehocking Lenape, 21
Oddie, Tasker, 271
Office of Economic Opportunity (OEO), 319, 342

Ogden Land Company, 115
Oglala Sioux Civil Rights Organization
    (OSCRO), 336
Oglethorpe, James, 29, 31
Ohio, 37, 45, 48, 55
Ohio River, 31, 45, 48
Ohio River Valley, 2, 5, 28, 36, 40, 43, 63
    Algonquian in, 26, 27, 30, 33, 37, 44, 56
oil rights, 242, 244, 263–264, 314, 324, 346,
    350, 371, 372
Ojibway, see Chippewa
Oklahoma, xv–xvi, 52, 55, 56, 63, 101, 122–
    124, 127, 188, 234–235, 238–239,
    243, 270, 271, 328
    Baker ring in, 233–234
    Creek in, 238–239
    leasing in, 262, 263–264
    termination policy in, 288, 297
Oklahoma Territory, 214, 225, 229–230
Old Northwest, 37, 39, 42–46, 52, 56, 59–66
Old Tassel, 38
Ollikut, 199
Omaha Indians, 55, 112, 114, 129, 161, 216,
    250–251, 287
Omnibus Act (1910), 216
Oneida, 12–13, 26, 40, 320, 355, 356–357,
    365
Onondaga, 12–13, 39–40
Opechancanough, 5, 6, 11
Opothleyaholo, Chief, 78, 109, 149
Oraibi, 238
oral culture, attribution problem and, vii–viii
Oregon, 114, 128, 329–330, 331, 369
    reservations in, 206, 214, 372
    termination policy in, 287, 290–291
Oregon Donation Land Law (1850), 139
Oregon Environmental Quality Commission,
    373
Oregon Territory, 134–135, 138–140, 142
Ortega, Marina, 362
Osage, 36, 55–58, 66–67, 89, 99, 111, 112,
    225, 311
    allotment and, 229, 242
    burials of, 247
    leasing and, 259, 263–264
    oil rights of, 242, 244, 263–264, 314
    removal of, 157–160
    termination policy and, 288
Osage Nation Organization, 311
Osceola, 85
Oto, 88, 112, 147, 246–247, 286
Ottawa, 23, 30, 45–46, 88, 119, 122, 159,
    288
Ouray, 143
Owen, Amos, 279
Owhi, 140–141

Page, John, 93
Paiute, ix, 128, 143, 163–168, 170, 171, 176,
    227, 245
    Depression and, 270–271
    fishing of, 264–265

northern, 112, 142
reservations of, 163–168, 216, 224, 247,
    259, 264–265, 270–271, 277, 278,
    283, 309, 372
southern, 112, 287
Paiute War (Pyramid Lake War) (1860),
    143
Palouse, 112, 128, 142
Pamunkey, 5, 115–116
pan-Indianism, 47–49, 64, 127, 298, 339–
    340
Papago (Tohono O'odham; Desert People),
    xvii, 112, 128, 209, 227, 266, 267,
    353
    Sand (Hia-Ced O'odham), 355
Papago Indian League, 267
Paris, Treaty of (1763), 20, 32, 38
Parker, Ely, 158, 219
Parker, Quanah, 190
Park Service, U.S., 358
Pasqual, 134
Passamaquoddy, xxviii, 346
paternalism, 170–171, 204, 238, 280, 309,
    333–334, 338, 379
Patterson, Bradley, 320
Pawnee, xx, 57, 66, 88, 112, 120, 129, 157,
    160
Pawtuxet, 8
Peace Policy, 158, 162, 203
Peltier, Leonard, 337
Pend d'Oreille, 141
Pennacook, xxviii
Pennsylvania, 39, 42, 202, 213
    colonial period in, 21, 24, 28–29, 34, 38
    dam projects in, 299–300
Penobscot, xx, xxviii, 6, 346
Peopeomoxmox, 140–141
Peoria, xxviii, 119, 229, 288
Pequot, xxviii, 10–11, 21, 48, 357, 364
Pequot War (1636–1637), 10–11
Permanent Indian Territory, see Indian
    Territory
Pettigrew, Richard F., 220
peyotism, 247
Piankashaw, xxviii, 39, 46, 88, 119
Pickens, Israel, 78
Pick-Sloan Plan, 300, 325
Piegan, 112
Pierce, Franklin, viii
Pierre, George, 284
Pike, Albert, 149
Pilgrims, 8
Pima, 112, 128, 261–262
Pine Ridge agency, 216, 222, 223, 227, 260–
    261, 276, 279, 301, 310–311, 312,
    314, 335–337
Pit River Indians, 327
Pitt, Louie, 370
Plains Indians, xx, 55–58, 114, 130–131,
    154, 164, 312
    horse culture of, 55, 129, 144
    resistance of, 183–196

see also Comanche; Kansa; Kiowa; Omaha Indians; Osage; Pawnee; Ponca; Quapaw; Sioux; Wichita Indians
Platte River, 111, 183, 188, 192
Plenty-Coups, 190
pneumonia, 125, 150, 292, 341
Pocahontas, 5
poisonings, 46, 174, 177
Pokanoket, 10, 48
police, Indian, 126, 222–223, 238, 265
Pomo, *112*, 128, 357, 366, 374
Ponca, 55, *88, 112,* 146–147, 160–163, 172, 297
Pontiac, 30
Pontiac's Rebellion (1763), 30
Pope, John, 205
population:
   animal, xx, 18–19
   Indian, xvii–xviii, 7–8, 23, 114, 123, 124, 129–130, 138, 218, 231
   of non-Indians, 31, 35, 59–60, 114, 218
Porter, N. S., 226
Porter, Pleasant, 238
Potawatomi, xx, *xxviii,* 23, 37, 45–46, 48, 63–66, *88,* 119, 121, 159, 228, 286, 288
Powder River, 188, 189, 194–195, 208
Powhatan (Wahunsonacock), 4–6
Powhatan Confederacy, *xxviii,* 4–7, 11, 55
powwow circuit, 298, 312, 375
Pratt, Richard, 202, 221
"praying towns," 15–16, 115, 170
Presbyterians, 120, 138
Presidential Commission on Indian Reservation Economics, 352
prior-appropriation laws, 237, 238
Proclamation of 1763, 32, *34,* 35, 37
Prophetstown, 48
Provost, Cecil, 281
Prucha, Francis Paul, 379
Public Law 280, 287
Pueblo cultures, xvi, xviii, *112,* 128, 253, 272
   see also Hopi; Zuni
Pueblo Lands Act, 268–269
Pueblo Lands Board, 268–269
Pueblo Revolt (1680), 31, 98
Puritans, 8, 9, 15, 16
Puts-on-His-Shoes, 244
Puyallup, *112,* 128, 329, 330, 331
Pyramid Lake, 164–168, 237
Pyramid Lake reservation, 163–168, 216, 224, 247, 259, 264–265, 270–271, 277, 278, 283, 372
Pyramid Lake War (Paiute War) (1860), 143

Quakers, 30, 159, 160, 190, 206–208
Quapaw, xvi, 55, 56, *88, 112,* 285
Quash-qua-me, 60, 61
Quinault, *112,* 265
Quinnipiac, 14, 15, 17

racial mixing, mixed-blood Indians, 3, 5, 6, 50, 69–70, 107, 116, 149, 155, 219, 226, 281, 287, 297, 378
railroad, 122, 141, 156, 157, 165, 181, 294
Ramona (Jackson), 318*n*
Reagan, Ronald, 351, 352, 353
Red Cloud, 173, 184, 185, 188–189, 192, 207, 214
Red Cloud, James, 260
Red Dog, 146
Red Jacket, 41
Red River, 63, 67, 101, 125, 126
Red River War (1874–1875), 190–191
Red Sticks, 54, 83
Red Tomahawk, 223
Reid, John, 271
Reifel, Ben, 275, 282
religion:
   native, 7, 16, 215, 216, 220, 222–224, 247, 312, 321, 323, 375
   see also Christianity; missionaries
relocation, 293–299, 301, 304–307, 312, 313
removal agents, 71, 73, 75, 91–97
Reno, Marcus, 195
reservations, xv–xviii, xxiii, 41, 52, 172–173
   allotment and, 215, 216–221, 225–232
   Anglicization on, 174–175, 201–203, 217, 244–248
   in colonial period, 14–15, 17, 20, 21, 28, 29, 132
   government appropriation of, 260, 265–266, 268, 299–307
   map of, *214*
   in nineteenth century, 100–101, 115–117, 119–122, 124–125, 133–140, 142, 147–148, 154–161, 163–171, 174–182, 188–190, 192–198, 200–206, 208–213
   paternalism and, 170–171, 204
   presidential mandate (executive order), 156, 165, 224, 263, 267, 268
   in twentieth century, 255–271, 273–282, 284–295, 298–317, 322–325, 335–338, 340–347, 350–357, 360–373
   see also specific states and reservations
resettlers, use of term, x
Rhode Island, 29, *34,* 116, 159
"Richland Man," x*n*
Richter, Daniel, viii
Rickard, Clinton, 283
Ridge, John, 71–72, 106–107
Ridge, Major, 73–74, 106–107
Rio Grande, 55, 128, 175, 187
riparian rights, 237
Robertson, Paul, 256
Robertson, Sam, 249, 251
Rockefeller family, 254
Rock Island, 59–62
Rock River, 59, 64
Rocky Mountain News, 255
Rocky Mountains, 32, 52, 183
Rogue River Indians, 139–140

Rogue River War (1853–1855), 139
Rolfe, John, 5
Roosevelt, Franklin Delano, 272
Roosevelt, Theodore, 229, 242, 265–266
Rosebud reservation, 222, 240, 276, 277,
    297, 301, 313, 334, 368
Ross, John, 59, 69–70, 72, 73, 75, 96, 106,
    107, 123, 127
  Civil War and, 148–149, 151
Ross, Mrs. John, 73
Roubideaux, Antoine, 274, 279
Roubideaux, Ramon, 274, 280
Rough Rock Demonstration School, 341
Round Valley reservation, 164, 170
Royer, Daniel F., 222
Runnels, Hardin, 125
Rushmore, Mount, occupation of, 317, 333

Sac, xxviii, 59–60, 88, 162–163, 230, 288
  in Indian Territory, 119, 120, 121, 162,
    229
sacred land, xvii, xxi–xxii, 268, 269, 358–
    359, 373
St. Augustine, Fla., 3
St. Clair, Arthur, 44
Salamanca, N.Y., 350–351
Salt Creek Massacre (1871), 190
Samish tribe, 355
San Carlos reservation, 209–212, 266, 277,
    312–313, 342
Sand Creek, 183–184
Sandoz, Mari, 318n
San Miguel de Gualdape, 3
Santa Anna, Antonio López de, 100
Santa Clara Pueblo, 378
Santa Fe, N.M., 129
Santa Fe Trail, 129
Saponi, xxviii, 20, 21
Satank, xxiii
Satanta, xxiii, 187, 189, 190, 191
Sauk, 23 30, 46, 48
Saukenuk, 59–62, 64, 66
Saylor, John P., 300
Scarooyady, 27
Schaghticoke, 20–21, 27
Schurz, Carl, 161, 171
Scott, Hugh, 246, 255
Scott, Winfield, 92, 96
Seattle, Chief, viii, 140
Second Seminole War (1835–1843), 85–87,
    118
self-sufficiency, 217, 218, 256–257, 284,
    289, 306, 309, 351
Sells, Cato, 249–251, 253, 261
Seminole, xxviii, 55, 68, 82–87, 88, 118–
    119, 318, 339, 363, 375
  allotment and, 229, 230
  in Indian Territory, 102, 103, 104, 108,
    111, 118–119, 124, 149–152, 225,
    229, 230
  removal of, 90, 91, 92, 94, 95, 97, 98

Senate, U.S., 78, 97, 134, 135, 141, 239,
    254, 268, 296
  Committee on the Public Lands of, 58
  termination policy and, 280, 281
Seneca, 6, 12–13, 23, 46, 88, 115, 158, 350–
    351, 362, 365
  in American Revolution, 39–40
  dam projects and, 298–301, 323, 350
Seneca Oil Company, 350
Sequoyah, 68
Sequoyah, Lloyd, 323
Sequoyah (proposed Indian state), 239
Serrano, 128
settlers, use of term, ix–x
Seventh Cavalry, 195, 223–224
Seven Years' War (1756–1763), 29, 32
Shasta, 112
Shawnee, xxviii, 24, 30, 32, 33, 35, 37–40,
    44–49, 63, 88, 235
  in American Revolution, 39, 40
  business council of, 241
  Creek merger with, 109
  in Indian Territory, 109, 111, 119, 121,
    122, 149, 150, 152, 153
  Iroquois ceding of land of, 37, 38
  raids of, 56–57
  in Texas, 99, 101
Shawnee Wolves, 234–235
Shebala, Rudy, 371
sheep, 36, 51, 53, 116, 177, 181, 267, 270
Shelton, 246
Sheridan, Phil, 189
Sherman, William Tecumseh, 158, 180–181
Shipe, H. W., 266
Shiprock Agency, 246
Shirley, Jim, 276
Shoshone, 112, 128, 360
  allotment and, 226–227
  of Wind River reservation, 164, 170, 171,
    314
Siletz, 112, 128, 249, 345
silver, 143, 172
Simmons, Hoxie, 249
Sinkyone Indians, 265
Sinkyone Wilderness State Park, 358
Sioux, xv, xxiv, 13, 64, 120, 129, 157, 215,
    247–252, 268
  activism of, 335–337
  Black Hills claim of, 242, 268, 301, 308,
    333
  Brule, 146, 161, 274, 295, 297
  business council of, 241–242, 252
  citizenship ceremony of, 248
  Crook's proposal and, 221–222
  dam projects and, 301–307
  Dawes Act opposed by, 220–221
  factionalization of, 303–304
  Ghost Dance and, 222–224
  Hunkpapa, 188, 304
  Indian Reorganization Act and, 274–279
  Lakota, xx, xxv, 130, 245, 358, 375
  leasing and, 260–261

Oglala, 146, 184, 185, 188–189, 194, 242, 245, 310–311, 326, 333, 336, 339
relocation and, 293–294, 295
reservations of, 188, 189, 192–196, 205, 208, 217–218, 220–226, 240–242, 244, 245, 250, 251–252, 256, 257, 264, 275, 277, 279, 297, 301–302, 310–311, 340, 342, 354
resistance of, 184–186, 192–196, 222–224
Santee (eastern), xviii, *112*, 119, 168–169, 184, 256
Sisseton, 225–226, 249, 275, 295, 311, 360
Sun Dance of, xxi, 202, 245, 274, 277
Teton, *112*, 304
Wahpeton, 225–226, 360
at Wounded Knee, 223–224
Yankton, *112*, 183, 248, 250, 274, 301, 318, 362
Yanktonai, *112*, 304
Sioux Manufacturing Corporation, 371
Sitting Bull, 173, 192, 195, 196, 199, 204–205, 208, 354
arrest and death of, 222–223
slaves, slavery:
Indian, 3, 8, 11, 25, 209
runaway, 83, 84
Sloan, Thomas, 232
Small Business Administration, 320, 343
smallpox, 7, 8, 9, 24–25, 66, 98, 116, 130, 150
Smiley, Albert K., 232
Smisken, Harry, 373
Smith, Edward P., 246–247
Smith, Finis, 321
Smith, John, 5
Smithsonian Institution, 348
Smohalla, 198
Snake, Reuben, 311–312, 313, 316, 328, 341, 347
"Snake Indian" resistance, 230, 238–239
Society of American Indians, 232, 244
South Carolina, 25, *34*, 39, 40, 41, 49, 116–117, 288
see also Carolina colony
South Dakota, 52, 55, 169, 188, 207, 249, 279
reservations in, *214*, 225–226, 244, 248, 354, 367–368
South Plains war, xxiv
sovereignty, problems of, 370, 377–380
Spanish, Spain, 8
colonialism of, 2, 3–4, 9, 12, 13, 15, 24, 25, 26, 29, 31–32, *34*, 52, 54, 55, 56, 83, 98, 99, 129, 131, 133
Speckled Snake, 59
Spokane Indians, *112*, 141–142
Spokane War (Coeur d'Alene War) (1858), 142
"Spokan Garry," 141–142
Spoon, Decorah, 63
Spotted Tail, 203

Squanto (Tisquantum), 8
squatters, 18, 28, 31, 35, 131, 256, 258, 277, 278, 309
Stand By, 246
Standing Bear, 147, 160–161, 172
Standing Bear, Luther, xxi, 192–193, 204
Standing Rock reservation, 222–223, 301, 303–307, 327, 344, 354
unemployment on, 312, 313
Stands-in-Timber, John, 184, 195, 207
Starr, James, 329
Starr, Louis, Jr., 329
starvation, 66, 67, 84, 93, 144, 169, 196, 204–205, 222
Steiner, Stan, 338
Sterling, Snake, 247
Stevens, Isaac, 140, 141–142, 197, 330
Stockbridge Indians, 40
Stokes, Montfort, 66–67, 110
Stricker, John, 362
Strike Axe, 225
suicide, xxiii, 78, 191
Sun Dance, xxi, 202, 245, 274, 277, 312, 340
Supreme Court, U.S., 70, 156, 203, 268, 298–299, 311, 321, 328, 331, 357, 378
Lone Wolf v. *Hitchcock* and, 240
Williams v. *Lee* and, 361
Winters v. *United States* and, 237–238
Worcester v. *Georgia* and, 71–72, 361
Suquamish, 140, 361
"surplus" land, 218, 224–227, 230, 231, 233, 237, 240, 251–252, 258, 272, 277
Susquehannock, *xxviii*, 23
Sutter, John, 133

Tahkeal, Clarence, 330
Talequah, 111, 123
Taos Pueblo, 268–269, 308, 321, 322–323, 327
Tappan, Samuel, 180–181
Tarshar, 67
Tawakoni, *88*
taxes, 253, 267, 271, 283, 288, 289–290, 297, 310–311, 369, 370, 372
Tecumseh, xxii, 33, 47–49, 60
Tejon reservation, 136
Teller, Henry, 219, 234
Tellico Dam project, 323
Ten Bears, 187
Tennessee, xv, 49, 52–55, 87, 90
Tennessee Valley Authority, 323
Tenskawatawa, 47–48, 53, 214
termination policy, 280–291, 296–297, 309, 328, 345, 354
congressional hearings on, 285–286
Texas, xvi, xxiii, 54, 56, 68, 98–101, 114, 150–151, 190–191, *214*, 287
Cherokee in, 99–101, 106, 268, 308
East, 99, 100, 127, 191
Indian removal in, 100–101, 125, 127

Texas, Republic of, 100
Texas Rangers, 124
Thackery, Frank, 234, 235
theft, 124, 154, 155, 157–159, 176, 254
Thom, Mel, 341, 342
Thomas, Robert, 323–324
Thomas, William Holland, 72
Thornton, Russell, 129–130
Tidewater Indians, 4–8, 11
Tigua Indians, 365
Tillamoor, *112*
Tilokaikt, 139
timber and forest resources, 19, 48, 265–266,
    268, 279, 286, 290–291, 297, 357–
    358, 371, 373
Timucuan, 25
Tisquantum (Squanto), 8
Tocobaga, 25
Tohono O'odham, *see* Papago
Tongue River, 207, 208
Tonkawa, *88, 112,* 374
Toohoolhoolzote, xxii, xxiii, 197–198, 199
tourism, 342, 344–345, 358, 371
toxic waste dumps, 368–369, 370, 373
trade, xx, 39, 98, 115, 118, 129, 293
    in alcohol, 24, 36–37, 46, 126, 212, 263–
        264
    in colonial period, 2–6, 9, 12–13, 18–19,
        22, 23, 24, 27, 30, 31–32
    devastation due to, 12–13, 24, 56
    fur, 2, 3, 12, 13, 19, 56, 129
    of Plains Indians, 55–58
Trail of Broken Treaties, 334
Trail of Tears, 75, 88, 90, 111
Treasury, U.S., 160, 308, 344
treaties and agreements, 62, 73–79, 156, 192,
    240, 300, 329
    Cherokee and, 49, 50, 51, 74–75, 106, 107
    Creek and, 76–79
    eighteenth-century, 20, 27, 28, 37, 38, 40,
        45–46, 48, 50, 51, 54, 298–299
    1800–1819, 46, 55, 57, 59, 60, 63, 98,
        109
    of 1820s, 63, 73, 76, 77, 78, 83, 84
    of 1830s, 65, 74–75, 84, 100, 106, 107
    of 1850s, 115, 144–145
    of 1860s, 146, 185, 188, 189, 193, 196,
        197
    of 1870s, 195–196
    Seminoles and, 83, 84, 124
    seventeenth-century, 6, 9, 18
    in West, 131–132, 139–143, 336
treaty chiefs, 44–47, 51
Treaty Party, Cherokee, 73–74, 102, 106–
    107
Tribal Land Enterprise, 277
tribe:
    in colonial period, 4, 23
    use of term, vii–ix, 22
Tribolett, Bob, 212
Truckee John, 166
Truckee River, 166, 167, 237

Truman, Harry S., 283
Tse-ne-gat, 254–255
Tucson "Committee of Public Safety," 209
Tucson Ring, 212
Tulalip, 142
Tularosa reservation, 182
Tuscarora, *xxviii,* 22, 25, 40, 298–299
Tuskeneah, 79
Tutelo, *xxviii,* 20
Two Strike, 222

Udall, Stewart, 309
Uintah-Ouray reservation, 287, 297
Umatilla, 141, 251, 329, 331
unemployment, 290, 312, 313, 343, 351,
    365, 366, 368–369
Union, the, 149–151, 183
United Southeastern Tribes, 322, 326
University of Chicago Conference (1961),
    327
Upper Towns:
    Cherokee, 51, 52
    Creek, 54, 107–108, 109
urban Indians, 293–295, 298, 317, 325, 327,
    346
Utah, xvi–xvii, 98, 128, 142–143, 254–255,
    287
    reservations in, *214,* 355
Utah International, Inc., 324
Utah Territory, 142–143
Ute, *112,* 128, 131–132, 170, 176, 287, 297,
    308, 355, 372
    uprising of, 254–255
Utley, Robert, ix, 224

Vanandra, Cato, 297
Van Buren, Martin, 65, 75
Verde reservation, 209–210
Vermont, xxi, 26, 41, 359–360
Vermont Supreme Court, 360
Veterans Affairs Department, U.S., 375
Vicksburg, Miss., 91, 93
Victorio, 210, 211
Victorio War (1879), 211
Vinje, David, 343–344, 370
Virginia, xxi, 39, 42–43, 49, 115–116, 355
    colonial period in, 2, 4–7, 11, 12, 18, 20,
        21, 23, 26, 27, 31, *34,* 38
    visions and prophecies, xxiv, xxv, 30, 53,
        195, 215, 216, 247

Wabash, 39
Waco, *88, 112*
Wadena, Darrell (Chip), 363
Wahquahboshkuk, 228
Wahunsonacock (Powhatan), 4–6
Wahwassuck, John, 286
Walker, Neola, 245
Walker, Robert J., 127
Walker River reservation, 164, 224, 258
Walla Walla, *112,* 128, 140–141
Wallowa Valley, 197, 199, 200

Wampanoag, *xxviii,* 9, 17, 55, 159
wampum, 9, 12, 20
Wanapum, 198
Waowowanoonk (Peter Wilson), 350
War Department, U.S., 62, 154, 203
War of 1812, 49, 54, 57–58, 63
War on Poverty, 319–320, 334, 335, 341
Warren, Earl, 298
Washakie, 192
Washington, George, 39, 357
Washington, D.C., 79, 189, 193, 228, 240,
     250, 252, 268, 285–286, 303, 334,
     338
  Cherokee leaders in, 72, 73–74, 79
  humanitarian reformers in, 186–187
Washington, Treaty of (1821), 76
Washington State, x*n,* 114, 128, 329–333,
     355, 359
  reservations in, 201, *214,* 224, 260
Washington Supreme Court, 329
Washington Territory, 140–142
water rights, 237–238, 253, 257–258, 324–
     325, 371, 372–374
Watie, Stand, 71, 74, 106–107, 149, 150,
     151
Watkins, Arthur, 284–287, 289
Watt, James, 352
Wayne, Anthony "Mad Anthony," 45
Wayne, Leonard, 329
Wea, *xxviii,* 39, 46, 63, *88,* 119
weapons, 6, 7, 13, 23, 24, 25, 46, 54–57, 68,
     223–224
  of Plains Indians, 55, 56, 57, 63
Weber, David, x, 16–17
West, Elliott, 130
West, Westward expansion, 113–115, 120,
     131–143, 157–212, 215–269
  diversity of, 128–129
  political power of, 249
  *see also specific territories, states and
     Indian tribes*
Western Indian Gaming Conference, 366
Western Shoshone National Council, 360
West India Company, 14
Wheeler-Howard Act (Indian Reorganization
     Act; IRA) (1934), 272–281, 335
White, Noah, 279
White, Richard, 5, 41
White-Buffalo-in-the-Distance, 113, 114
White Calf, 204
White Cloud, 60
White Earth Land Recovery Project, 374
White Mountain reservation, 277, 345
White Mountains, 209, 210
whites, use of term, ix
White Sticks, 54, 83
White Warrior (William McIntosh), 76–77,
     108
Whitman, Marcus, 138
Whitman, Narcissa, 138
Wichita Indians, xvi, 66, *88,* 111, *112,* 188,
     191

Wild Cat (Coacoochee), 118–119, 124
Wild Hog, 195, 207
Wilhautyah, 197
Wilkinson, Wilbur, 362–363
Willamette Valley, 111, 138, 139
Williams, Roger, xix, 14
Williams v. *Lee,* 361
Wilson, Peter (Waowowanoonk), 350
Wilson, Richard, 335–336, 337, 342
Wilson, Woodrow, 248, 249, 259, 267
Wind River reservation, 164, 170, 171, 314,
     325
Winnebago, *xxviii,* 23, 48, 60, 63, 64–65,
     245, 247, 311–312, 341, 365
  activism of, 316–317, 322, 328
  reservations of, 119, 169, 216, 232–233,
     279, 316–317, 347
Winnemucca, Chief, 142
Winnemucca, Sarah, 143, 167, 168
Winters Doctrine, 237–238, 257
Winters v. *United States,* 237–238
Wintu, xxv
Wisconsin, 37, 65, 311–312, 355, 356–357
  termination policy in, 287, 289–290, 296–
     297, 328
Wiyot, *112,* 135
Wolf Chief, 250
Wooden Legs, John, 228, 292, 309, 310
Woodward, George, 295–296
Wool, Ellis, 74
Worcester v. *Georgia,* 71–72, 361
World War I, 244, 251, 257, 260–261, 262,
     266
World War II, 279–280, 282
Wounded Knee:
  Battle of (1890), 223–224, 318
  second Battle of (1973), 317, 335–337,
     339
Wovoka, 215, 216
Wyandot, *88,* 122, 285, 288
Wynkoop, Edward, 186
Wyoming, 52, 128, 130, 169, 172, 188, 226–
     227, 358
  reservations in, *214,* 300, 314, 325

Yakima, *112,* 128, 139–142, 251, 329, 373
Yakima War (1855–1856), 141–142
Yamasee, *xxviii,* 22, 25, 83
Yavapia, *113,* 128
Yellow Hair, 220
Yellowstone National Park, 199
Yellow Wolf, 200
Yokeoma, 238
Yokut, *112,* 128, 138
Yuchi, 83
Yuki, 357
Yuma, *112,* 228, 230, 262
Yurok, *112,* 128, 137

Zimmerman, William, 282
Zimmerman Plan, 282
Zuni, *112,* 131, 342